ANALYSIS OF DERIVATIVES FOR THE CFA® PROGRAM

Don M. Chance, Ph.D., CFA
Louisiana State University

ASSOCIATION FOR INVESTMENT MANAGEMENT AND RESEARCH®

To obtain the AIMR *Product Catalog,* contact:
AIMR, P.O. Box 3668, Charlottesville, Virginia 22903, USA
Phone (001) 434-951-5499 or 800-247-8132; Fax (001) 434-951-5262;
E-mail Info@aimr.org
or visit AIMR's World Wide Web site at
www.aimr.org
to view the AIMR publications list.

This publication is designed to provide accurate and authoritative information in regard to the subject matter covered. It is sold with the understanding that the publisher is not engaged in rendering legal, accounting, or other professional service. If legal advice or other expert assistance is required, the services of a competent professional should be sought.

ISBN 0-935015-93-0

Cover design by Lisa Smith

Printed in the United States of America
by United Book Press, Inc., Baltimore, MD
August 2003

PREFACE

Analysis of Derivatives for the CFA® Program represents the fourth step in an ongoing effort by the Association for Investment Management and Research® (AIMR®) to produce a set of coordinated, comprehensive, and practitioner-oriented textbook readings specifically designed for the three levels of the Chartered Financial Analyst® Program. The first step was the June 2000 publication of two volumes on fixed income analysis and portfolio management: *Fixed Income Analysis for the Chartered Financial Analyst Program* and *Fixed Income Readings for the Chartered Financial Analyst Program*. The second step was the August 2001 publication of *Quantitative Methods for Investment Analysis*. The third step was the August 2002 publication of *Analysis of Equity Investments: Valuation*. Given the favorable reception of these books and the expected favorable reception of the current book, similar textbooks in other topic areas are planned for the future.

This book uses a blend of theory and practice to deliver the derivatives analysis portion of the CFA Candidate Body of Knowledge (CBOK™) curriculum. The CBOK is the result of an extensive job analysis conducted periodically, most recently during 2000–01. Regional job analysis panels of CFA practitioners convened in 10 cities around the world: Boston, Chicago, Hong Kong, London, Los Angeles, New York, Toronto, Seattle, Tokyo, and Zurich. These and other practitioner panels specified the Global Body of Knowledge—what the investment expert needs to know. From this, they derived the CBOK to encompass what the investment generalist needs to know to be effective on the job. *Analysis of Derivatives for the CFA Program* is a book reflecting the work of these expert panels. The reader can thus be assured that the book captures current practice and reflects what the general investment practitioner needs to know about derivatives.

In producing this book, AIMR drew on input from numerous CFA charterholder reviewers, derivatives consultants, and AIMR professional staff members. The chapters were designed to include detailed learning outcome statements at the outset, illustrative in-chapter problems with solutions, and extensive end-of-chapter questions and problems with complete solutions, all prepared with CFA candidate distance learning in mind. In addition, the examples and problems reflect the global investment community. Starting from a U.S.-based program of approximately 2,000 examinees each year during the 1960s and 1970s, the CFA Program has evolved into a pervasive global certification program that currently involves more than 100,000 candidates annually from more than 150 countries. Through curriculum improvements such as this book, the CFA Program should continue to appeal to new candidates around the globe in future years.

The treatment in this volume is intended to communicate a practical risk management approach to derivatives for the investment generalist. Advanced concepts are included if needed by the generalist, but specialist topics are intentionally excluded. The book provides a base for further specialist work if desired. Unlike many alternative works, the book does not simply deliver an explanation of various derivatives instruments and positions but provides motivation for every derivatives position by explaining what the manager wants to accomplish prior to addressing the details of the position. I believe CFA candidates will find this text superior to other derivatives texts for use in a distance-learning framework. The text presents difficult concepts efficiently and with a minimum of mathematical notation. The presentation is academically rigorous yet based on practice and intuition. Finally, in keeping with the tradition of the CFA Program, the text proceeds from tools to analysis to synthesis, with the last four chapters focusing on risk management. Although designed with the CFA candidate in mind, the book should have broad appeal in the practitioner and other marketplaces.

AIMR Vice President Dennis McLeavey, CFA, spearheaded the effort to develop this book and the other CFA Program book projects. Having someone involved in the editorial role of all the projects results in more consistent pedagogy and more even coverage across these various works than would be possible otherwise. All of the authors who have worked with Dennis remark on his thoroughness, attention to detail, and commitment to the projects. Dennis has a long and distinguished history of involvement with the CFA Program. Before joining AIMR full time, he served on various AIMR committees.

On many levels, Don Chance, CFA, was the perfect individual to author this work. First, Don is a CFA charterholder and is committed to the mission of the CFA Program. Second, he is one of the leading derivatives experts in the world and is often quoted on derivatives topics in the media. Third, and extremely valuable for this project, Don has many years of experience in preparing candidates for the CFA examinations and has first-hand insight into the unique problems encountered by candidates in a distance-learning environment. Fourth, and most important, he is an experienced author, having written numerous journal articles and textbooks.

The strong support of two groups should be acknowledged. Peter Mackey, CFA, Chair of the Candidate Curriculum Committee, and the other members of the Executive Advisory Board of the Candidate Curriculum Committee (Alan Meder, CFA, James Bronson, CFA, and Matt Scanlan, CFA) identified the area of derivatives as one worthy of priority attention. Finally, without the encouragement and support of AIMR CEO Tom Bowman and the AIMR Board of Governors, this project, intended to materially enhance the CFA Program, would not have been possible.

Robert R. Johnson, Ph.D., CFA
Senior Vice President
Association for Investment Management and Research

July 2003

FOREWORD

When Dennis McLeavey and Bob Johnson approached me about writing a derivatives book for use in the CFA® Program, I was honored and excited. Having been involved in the CFA Program for about 15 years, I would now have the chance to be directly involved in determining what CFA charterholders should know about derivatives and how they should go about learning the material.

Being the risk management type, however, my first inclination is to see the downside, so I approached the project with some trepidation. Having written other books and numerous (sometimes) highly technical articles on derivatives, I wondered if an introductory-level book on derivatives geared not toward the derivatives specialist but toward financial analysts—primarily those studying for the CFA examination—would be well received by fellow derivatives specialists. Visions of book reviews by derivatives professionals asserting that the book is too basic and would not serve the needs of a trader or quant worried me. But their observations would be correct. The CFA examination is designed to train financial analysts, not traders or quants. What CFA charterholders need to know about derivatives is not the same as what derivatives specialists need to know. And when these groups do need to know the same material, the approach to learning it is necessarily different. Also, CFA charterholders come from different backgrounds, have different technical skills, and think differently about financial problems than do traders and quants. A different approach is therefore needed.

This book is part of a formal integrated package of materials that prepares the CFA candidate for the examination. This consideration is the driving force behind how the material is presented. Derivatives is only one part of the curriculum, but an important part. My experience with CFA candidates over the years tells me that this is an area they find among the most challenging hurdles in passing the examination. Accordingly, we have gone to great lengths to elevate the quality and pedagogical features of this book.

As any CFA candidate knows, the Learning Outcome Statements (LOSs) identify in a concise manner the concepts that the candidate must learn. Each LOS is then covered within the chapter. The chapter ends with a set of items called "Key Points." There is a one-to-one correspondence between each LOS and each Key Point. Although the candidate should not rely exclusively on the Key Points, they should be very useful as a concise review of the important concepts.

When it comes to learning derivatives, there is no substitute for working problems. Accordingly, the material is liberally supported with numerical examples. Each concept is illustrated not only with a numerical example but also by a subsequent detailed practice problem. At the end of the chapter are approximately 20 more study problems with complete solutions. It would be virtually impossible for the candidate to say "I need more problems to work."

The organizational structure of the book is also conducive to finding one's way around easily. Each section of the book is numbered. For example, consider the material in Chapter 3 on futures markets. Section 6 is called Types of Futures Contracts. Within

Section 6 are subsections called 6.1: Short-Term Interest Rate Futures Contracts, 6.2: Intermediate- and Long-Term Interest Rate Futures Contracts, 6.3: Stock Index Futures Contracts, and 6.4: Currency Futures Contracts. Numbering sections provides a definitive linkage among subtopics and between subtopics and the master topic.

The book contains bolded terms, which are defined in a glossary at the end of the book. Key equations are numbered, and a list of these equations also appears at the end of the book.

Although the author gets most of the credit, many people participated in this project: Richard Applebach, CFA; Carl Bang, CFA; Pierre Bouvier, CFA; Robert Ernst, CFA; Darlene Halwas, CFA; Walter Haslett, CFA; Stanley Jacobs, CFA; Sandra Krueger, CFA; Robert Lamy, CFA; Erin Lorenzen, CFA; Barbara MacLeod, CFA; John Piccione, CFA; Jerald Pinto, CFA; Craig Ruff, CFA; and David Smith, CFA, provided reviews of the individual chapters. Murli Rajan, CFA, and Sanjiv Sabherwal created the end-of-chapter problems and solutions, and both Louis James, CFA, and Greg Noronha, CFA performed detailed proofreading.

A special note of thanks goes to Fiona Russell and Jerry Pinto. Fiona did the copyediting. This has been the first time I have ever had a copyeditor who understood the subject, and it was a refreshing experience. Jerry Pinto went over the book with a fine-toothed comb, catching items that would have required a microscope for most people. I cannot imagine the quality of the book coming close to our objectives without their input.

Dennis McLeavey of AIMR served as the senior editor and worked closely enough with me to deserve his name on the book, but he modestly let me take all of the credit. Dennis read every word many times and shaped the book into the CFA framework, making sure that the concepts discussed in this book were consistent with treatments elsewhere in the curriculum.

If I listed everything Wanda Lauziere did on this book, I would quickly run out of space. Let's just say she did everything else not covered in the above paragraphs. If you ever write a book, you will know the enormous amount of work that must get done but is never obvious to the reader. Wanda got things done and kept us all on schedule, while injecting enough humor to remind me that we could all do this project and have fun at the same time. I jokingly tell Wanda that she could now probably pass the derivatives part of the exam.

Because I am now affiliated with Louisiana State University, the name of my former employer, Virginia Polytechnic Institute, does not appear formally in connection with this book. The entire book was written during my time at Virginia Tech, so I want to especially thank the Pamplin College of Business of Virginia Tech for its support and encouragement of my efforts to learn more and teach more about derivatives.

Finally, I would like to thank my family. My wife, Jan, and my daughters Kim and Ashley have always been there with great love and humor. While they cannot imagine I could possibly know enough about a subject to write this much, they know I enjoy trying to convince people that I do.

Don M. Chance
July 2003

ABOUT THE AUTHOR

Don M. Chance, CFA, holds the William H. Wright, Jr. Endowed Chair for Financial Services at Louisiana State University. He earned his CFA charter in 1986. He has extensive experience as a consultant and is widely quoted in the local, regional, and national media on matters related to derivatives, risk management, and financial markets in general. Dr. Chance has served as an instructor in professional training programs. He is a consultant and advisor to AIMR in many capacities, including authorship of monographs on managed futures and real options, and he has spoken at many conferences of AIMR and other organizations. He is the author of the university text *An Introduction to Derivatives and Risk Management,* 6th edition (forthcoming 2004), *Essays in Derivatives* (1998), and many academic and practitioner articles. Dr. Chance was formerly First Union Professor of Financial Risk Management at Virginia Polytechnic Institute, where he founded its student-managed investment fund. He holds a Ph.D. in finance from Louisiana State University.

CONTENTS

DERIVATIVE MARKETS AND INSTRUMENTS

LEARNING OUTCOMES

After completing this chapter, you will be able to do the following:

- Define the concept of a derivative.
- Describe the differences between exchange-traded and over-the-counter derivatives.
- Define a forward commitment and identify the different types of forward commitments.
- Describe the basic characteristics of forward contracts, futures contracts, and swaps.
- Define a contingent claim and identify the different types of contingent claims.
- Describe the basic characteristics of options and distinguish between an option to buy and an option to sell.
- Discuss the different ways to measure the size of the global derivatives market.
- Identify the purposes and criticisms of derivative markets.
- Explain the concept of arbitrage and the role it plays in determining prices and in promoting market efficiency.

---

1 INTRODUCTION

The concept of risk is at the heart of investment management. Financial analysts and portfolio managers continually identify, measure, and manage risk. In a simple world where only stocks and bonds exist, the only risks are the fluctuations associated with market values and the potential for a creditor to default. Measuring risk often takes the form of standard deviations, betas, and probabilities of default. In the above simple setting, managing risk is limited to engaging in stock and bond transactions that reduce or increase risk. For example, a portfolio manager may hold a combination of a risky stock portfolio and a risk-free bond, with the relative allocations determined by the investor's tolerance for risk. If for some reason the manager desires a lower level of risk, the only transactions available to adjust the risk downward are to reduce the allocation to the risky stock portfolio and increase the allocation to the risk-free bond.

But we do not live in a simple world of only stocks and bonds, and in fact investors can adjust the level of risk in a variety of ways. For example, one way to reduce risk is to use insurance, which can be described as the act of paying someone to assume a risk for you. The financial markets have created their own way of offering insurance against financial loss in the form of contracts called **derivatives**. *A derivative is a financial instrument that offers a return based on the return of some other underlying asset.* In this sense, its return is *derived* from another instrument—hence, the name.

As the definition states, a derivative's performance is based on the performance of an underlying asset. This underlying asset is often referred to simply as the **underlying**.[1] It trades in a market in which buyers and sellers meet and decide on a price; the seller then delivers the asset to the buyer and receives payment. The price for immediate purchase of the underlying asset is called the **cash price** or **spot price** (in this book, we will use the latter term). A derivative also has a defined and limited life: A derivative contract initiates on a certain date and terminates on a later date. Often the derivative's payoff is determined and/or made on the expiration date, although that is not always the case. In accordance with the usual rules of law, a derivative contract is an agreement between two parties in which each does something for the other. In some cases, as in the simple insurance analogy, a derivative contract involves one party paying the other some money and receiving coverage against potential losses. In other cases, the parties simply agree that each will do something for the other at a later date. In other words, no money need change hands up front.

We have alluded to several general characteristics of derivative contracts. Let us now turn to the specific types of derivatives that we will cover in this book.

2   TYPES OF DERIVATIVES

In this section, we take a brief look at the different types of derivative contracts. This brief treatment serves only as a short introduction to familiarize you with the general ideas behind the contracts. We shall examine these derivatives in considerable detail in later chapters.

Let us start by noting that derivative contracts are created on and traded in two distinct but related types of markets: exchange traded and over the counter. Exchange-traded contracts have standard terms and features and are traded on an organized derivatives trading facility, usually referred to as a futures exchange or an options exchange. Over-the-counter contracts are any transactions created by two parties anywhere else. We shall examine the other distinctive features of these two types of contracts as we proceed.

Derivative contracts can be classified into two general categories: forward commitments and contingent claims. In the following section, we examine forward commitments, which are contracts in which the two parties enter into an agreement to engage in a transaction at a later date at a price established at the start. Within the category of forward commitments, two major classifications exist: exchanged-traded contracts, specifically futures, and over-the-counter contracts, which consist of forward contracts and swaps.

2.1 FORWARD COMMITMENTS

The **forward contract** is an agreement between two parties in which one party, the buyer, agrees to buy from the other party, the seller, an underlying asset at a future date at a price established at the start. The parties to the transaction specify the forward contract's terms and conditions, such as when and where delivery will take place and the precise identity of the underlying. In this sense, the contract is said to be *customized*. Each party is subject to the possibility that the other party will default.

---

[1] On behalf of the financial world, we apologize to all English teachers. "Underlying" is not a noun, but in the world of derivatives it is commonly used as such. To be consistent with that terminology, we use it in that manner here.

Many simple, everyday transactions are forms of forward commitments. For example, when you order a pizza for delivery to your home, you are entering into an agreement for a transaction to take place later ("30 minutes or less," as some advertise) at a price agreed on at the outset. Although default is not likely, it could occur—for instance, if the party ordering the pizza decided to go out to eat, leaving the delivery person wondering where the customer went. Or perhaps the delivery person had a wreck on the way to delivery and the pizza was destroyed. But such events are extremely rare.

Forward contracts in the financial world take place in a large and private market consisting of banks, investment banking firms, governments, and corporations. These contracts call for the purchase and sale of an underlying asset at a later date. The underlying asset could be a security (i.e., a stock or bond), a foreign currency, a commodity, or combinations thereof, or sometimes an interest rate. In the case of an interest rate, the contract is not on a bond from which the interest rate is derived but rather on the interest rate itself. Such a contract calls for the exchange of a single interest payment for another at a later date, where at least one of the payments is determined at the later date.[2]

As an example of someone who might use a forward contract in the financial world, consider a pension fund manager. The manager, anticipating a future inflow of cash, could engage in a forward contract to purchase a portfolio equivalent to the S&P 500 at a future date—timed to coincide with the future cash inflow date—at a price agreed on at the start. When that date arrives, the cash is received and used to settle the obligation on the forward contract.[3] In this manner, the pension fund manager commits to the position in the S&P 500 without having to worry about the risk that the market will rise during that period. Other common forward contracts include commitments to buy and sell a foreign currency or a commodity at a future date, locking in the exchange rate or commodity price at the start.

The forward market is a private and largely unregulated market. Any transaction involving a commitment between two parties for the future purchase/sale of an asset is a forward contract. Although pizza deliveries are generally not considered forward contracts, similar transactions occur commonly in the financial world. Yet we cannot simply pick up *The Wall Street Journal* or *The Financial Times* and read about them or determine how many contracts were created the previous day.[4] They are private transactions for a reason: The parties want to keep them private and want little government interference. This need for privacy and the absence of regulation does not imply anything illegal or corrupt but simply reflects a desire to maintain a prudent level of business secrecy.

Recall that we described a forward contract as an agreement between two parties in which one party, the buyer, agrees to buy from the other party, the seller, an underlying asset at a future date at a price agreed upon at the start. A **futures contract** is a variation of a forward contract that has essentially the same basic definition but some additional features that clearly distinguish it from a forward contract. For one, a futures contract is not a private and customized transaction. Instead, it is a public, standardized transaction that takes place on a futures exchange. A futures exchange, like a stock exchange, is an organization that provides a facility for engaging in futures transactions and establishes a mech-

---

[2] These instruments are called forward rate agreements and will be studied in detail in Chapter 2.

[3] The settling of the forward contract can occur through delivery, in which case the buyer pays the agreed-upon price and receives the asset from the seller, or through an equivalent cash settlement. In the latter case, the seller pays the buyer the difference between the market price and the agreed-upon price if the market price is higher. The buyer pays the seller the difference between the agreed-upon price and the market price if the agreed-upon price is higher.

[4] In Section 4 of this chapter, we will look at some ways to measure the amount of this type of trading.

anism through which parties can buy and sell these contracts. The contracts are standard-ized, which means that the exchange determines the expiration dates, the underlying, how many units of the underlying are included in one contract, and various other terms and conditions.

Probably the most important distinction between a futures contract and a forward contract, however, lies in the default risk associated with the contracts. As noted above, in a forward contract, the risk of default is a concern. Specifically, the party with a loss on the contract could default. Although the legal consequences of default are severe, parties nonetheless sometimes fall into financial trouble and are forced to default. For that reason, only solid, creditworthy parties can generally engage in forward contracts. In a futures contract, however, the futures exchange guarantees to each party that if the other fails to pay, the exchange will pay. In fact, the exchange actually writes itself into the middle of the contract so that each party effectively has a contract with the exchange and not with the other party. The exchange collects payment from one party and disburses payment to the other.

The futures exchange implements this performance guarantee through an organiza-tion called the clearinghouse. For some futures exchanges, the clearinghouse is a separate corporate entity. For others, it is a division or subsidiary of the exchange. In either case, however, the clearinghouse protects itself by requiring that the parties settle their gains and losses to the exchange on a daily basis. This process, referred to as the daily settlement or marking to market, is a critical distinction between futures and forward contracts. With futures contracts, profits and losses are charged and credited to participants' accounts each day. This practice prevents losses from accumulating without being collected. For forward contracts, losses accumulate until the end of the contract.[5]

One should not get the impression that forward contracts are rife with credit losses and futures contracts never involve default. Credit losses on forward contracts are ex-tremely rare, owing to the excellent risk management practices of participants. In the case of futures contracts, parties do default on occasion. In fact, it is likely that there are more defaults on futures contracts than on forward contracts.[6] Nonetheless, the exchange guar-antee has never failed for the party on the other side of the transaction. Although the pos-sibility of the clearinghouse defaulting does exist, the probability of such a default happening is extremely small. Thus, we can generally assume that futures contracts are default-free. In contrast, the possibility of default, although relatively small, exists for forward contracts.

Another important distinction between forward contracts and futures contracts lies in the ability to engage in offsetting transactions. Forward contracts are generally designed to be held until expiration. It is possible, however, for a party to engage in the opposite transaction prior to expiration. For example, a party might commit to purchase one million euros at a future date at an exchange rate of $0.85/€. Suppose that later the euro has a for-

---

[5] Although this process of losses accumulating on forward contracts until the expiration day is the standard format for a contract, modern risk management procedures include the possibility of forcing a party in debt to periodically pay losses accrued prior to expiration. In addition, a variety of risk-reducing techniques, such as the use of collateral, are used to mitigate the risk of loss. We discuss these points in more detail in Chapters 2 and 9.

[6] Defaults are more likely for futures contracts than for forward contracts because participants in the forward markets must meet higher creditworthiness standards than those in the futures markets. Indeed, many individuals participate in the futures markets; forward market participants are usually large, creditworthy companies. But the forward markets have no guarantor of performance, while the futures markets do. Therefore, participants in the forward markets have incurred credit losses in the past, while participants in the futures markets have not.

ward price of $0.90/€. The party might then choose to engage in a new forward contract to sell the euro at the new price of $0.90/€. The party then has a commitment to buy the euro at $0.85 and sell it at $0.90. The risk associated with changes in exchange rates is eliminated, but both transactions remain in place and are subject to default.[7]

In futures markets, the contracts have standardized terms and trade in a market that provides sufficient liquidity to permit the parties to enter the market and offset transactions previously created. The use of contracts with standardized terms results in relatively widespread acceptance of these terms as homogeneous agreed-upon standards for trading these contracts. For example, a U.S. Treasury bond futures contract covering $100,000 face value of Treasury bonds, with an expiration date in March, June, September, or December, is a standard contract. In contrast, if a party wanted a contract covering $120,000 of Treasury bonds, he would not find any such instrument in the futures markets and would have to create a nonstandard instrument in the forward market. The acceptance of standardized terms makes parties more willing to trade futures contracts. Consequently, futures markets offer the parties liquidity, which gives them a means of buying and selling the contracts. Because of this liquidity, a party can enter into a contract and later, before the contract expires, enter into the opposite transaction and offset the position, much the same way one might buy or sell a stock or bond and then reverse the transaction later. This reversal of a futures position completely eliminates any further financial consequences of the original transaction.[8]

A **swap** is a variation of a forward contract that is essentially equivalent to a series of forward contracts. Specifically, a swap is an agreement between two parties to exchange a series of future cash flows. Typically at least one of the two series of cash flows is determined by a later outcome. In other words, one party agrees to pay the other a series of cash flows whose value will be determined by the unknown future course of some underlying factor, such as an interest rate, exchange rate, stock price, or commodity price. The other party promises to make a series of payments that could also be determined by a second unknown factor or, alternatively, could be preset. We commonly refer to swap payments as being "fixed" or "floating" (sometimes "variable").

We noted that a forward contract is an agreement to buy or sell an underlying asset at a future date at a price agreed on today. A swap in which one party makes a single fixed payment and the other makes a single floating payment amounts to a forward contract. One party agrees to make known payments to the other and receive something unknown in return. This type of contract is like an agreement to buy at a future date, paying a fixed amount and receiving something of unknown future value. That the swap is a *series* of such payments distinguishes it from a forward contract, which is only a single payment.[9]

Swaps, like forward contracts, are private transactions and thus not subject to direct regulation.[10] Swaps are arguably the most successful of all derivative transactions. Probably the most common use of a swap is a situation in which a corporation, currently

---

[7] It is possible for the party engaging in the first transaction to engage in the second transaction with the same party. The two parties agree to cancel their transactions, settling the difference in value in cash and thereby eliminating the risk associated with exchange rates as well as the possibility of default.

[8] A common misconception is that, as a result of their standardized terms, futures contracts are liquid but nonstandardized forward contracts are illiquid. This is not always the case; many futures contracts have low liquidity and many forward contracts have high liquidity.

[9] A few other distinctions exist between swaps and forward contracts, such as the fact that swaps can involve both parties paying a variable amount.

[10] Like all over-the-counter derivatives transactions, swaps are subject to indirect regulatory oversight in that the companies using them could be regulated by securities or banking authorities. In addition, swaps, like all contracts, are subject to normal contract and civil law.

borrowing at a floating rate, enters into a swap that commits it to making a series of inter-est payments to the swap counterparty at a fixed rate, while receiving payments from the swap counterparty at a rate related to the floating rate at which it is making its loan pay-ments. The floating components cancel, resulting in the effective conversion of the origi-nal floating-rate loan to a fixed-rate loan.

Forward commitments (whether forwards, futures, or swaps) are firm and binding agreements to engage in a transaction at a future date. They obligate each party to com-plete the transaction, or alternatively, to offset the transaction by engaging in another trans-action that settles each party's financial obligation to the other. Contingent claims, on the other hand, allow one party the flexibility to not engage in the future transaction, depend-ing on market conditions.

2.2 CONTINGENT CLAIMS

Contingent claims are derivatives in which the payoffs occur if a specific event happens. We generally refer to these types of derivatives as options. Specifically, an **option** is a financial instrument that gives one party the right, but not the obligation, to buy or sell an underlying asset from or to another party at a fixed price over a specific period of time. An option that gives the right to buy is referred to as a call; an option that gives the right to sell is referred to as a put. The fixed price at which the underlying can be bought or sold is called the exercise price, strike price, striking price, or strike, and is determined at the outset of the transaction. In this book, we refer to it as the exercise price, and the action of buying or selling the underlying at the exercise price is called exercising the option. The holder of the option has the right to exercise it and will do so if conditions are advantageous; otherwise, the option will expire unexercised. Thus, the payoff of the option is contingent on an event taking place, so options are sometimes referred to as contingent claims.

In contrast to participating in a forward or futures contract, which represents a *com-mitment* to buy or sell, owning an option represents the *right* to buy or sell. To acquire this right, the buyer of the option must pay a price at the start to the option seller. This price is called the option premium or sometimes just the option price. In this book, we usually refer to it as the option price.

Because the option buyer has the right to buy or sell an asset, the seller of the option has the potential commitment to sell or buy this asset. If the option buyer has the right to buy, the option seller may be obligated to sell. If the option buyer has the right to sell, the option seller may be obligated to buy. As noted above, the option seller receives the amount of the option price from the option buyer for his willingness to bear this risk.

An important distinction we made between forward and futures contracts was that the former are customized private transactions between two parties without a guarantee against losses from default. The latter are standardized contracts that take place on futures exchanges and are guaranteed by the exchange against losses from default. For options, both types of contracts—over-the-counter customized and exchange-listed standardized—exist. In other words, the buyer and seller of an option can arrange their own terms and cre-ate an option contract. Alternatively, the buyer and seller can meet directly, or through their brokers, on an options exchange and trade standardized options. In the case of customized options, the buyer is subject to the possibility of the seller defaulting when and if the buyer decides to exercise the option. Because the option buyer is not obligated to do anything be-yond paying the original price, the seller of any type of option is not subject to the buyer defaulting. In the case of a standardized option, the buyer does not face the risk of the seller defaulting. The exchange, through its clearinghouse, guarantees the seller's perform-ance to the buyer.

A variety of other instruments contain options and thus are forms of contingent claims. For instance, many corporations issue convertible bonds offering the holder an optionlike feature that enables the holder to participate in gains on the market price of the corporation's stock without having to participate in losses on the stock. Callable bonds are another example of a common financial instrument that contains an option, in this case the option of the issuer to pay off the bond before its maturity. Options themselves are often characterized in terms of standard or fairly basic options and more advanced options, often referred to as exotic options. There are also options that are not even based on assets but rather on futures contracts or other derivatives. A very widely used group of options is based on interest rates.

Another common type of option is contained in asset-backed securities. An asset-backed security is a claim on a pool of securities. The pool, which might be mortgages, loans, or bonds, is a portfolio assembled by a financial institution that then sells claims on the portfolio. Often, the borrowers who issued the mortgages, loans, or bonds have the right to pay off their debts early, and many choose to do so when interest rates fall significantly. They then refinance their loans by taking out a new loan at a lower interest rate. This right, called a prepayment feature, is a valuable option owned by the borrower. Holders of asset-backed securities bear the risk associated with prepayment options and hence are sellers of those options. The holders, or option sellers, receive a higher promised yield on their bond investment than they would have received on an otherwise equivalent bond without the option.

With an understanding of derivatives, there are no limits to the types of financial instruments that can be constructed, analyzed, and applied to achieve investment objectives. What you learn from this book and the CFA Program will help you recognize and understand the variety of derivatives that appear in many forms in the financial world.

Exhibit 1-1 presents a classification of the types of derivative contracts as we have described them. Note that we have partitioned derivatives into those that are exchange-traded and those that trade in the over-the-counter market. The exhibit also notes some other categories not specifically mentioned above. These instruments are included for completeness, but they are relatively advanced and not covered in this first chapter.

EXHIBIT 1-1   A Classification of Derivatives

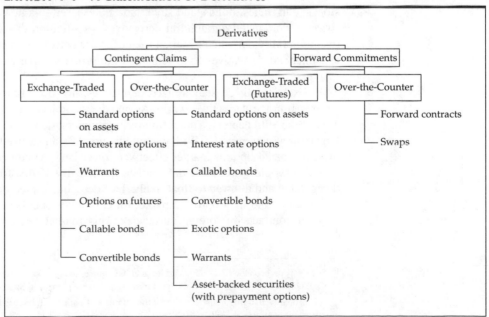

We have now looked at the basic characteristics of derivative contracts. In order to better understand and appreciate derivatives, we should take a quick look at where they came from and where they are now. Accordingly, we take a brief look at the history and current state of derivative markets.

3   DERIVATIVE MARKETS: PAST AND PRESENT

Derivative markets have an exciting and colorful history. Examining that history gives insights that help us understand the structure of these markets as they exist today.

The basic characteristics of derivative contracts can be found throughout the history of humankind. Agreements to engage in a commercial transaction as well as agreements that provide the right to engage in a commercial transaction date back hundreds of years. In medieval times, contracts for the future delivery of an asset with the price fixed at the time of the contract initiation were frequent. Early indications of futures markets were seen in Japan many hundreds of years ago. The futures markets generally trace their roots, however, to the 1848 creation of the Chicago Board of Trade, the first organized futures market. Its origins resulted from the burgeoning grain markets in Chicago, which created a need for a farmer to secure a price at one point in time, store the grain, and deliver it at a later point in time. At around the same time, customized option transactions were being offered, including some by the well known financier Russell Sage, who found a clever way to offer combinations of customized options that replicated a loan at a rate that exceeded the maximum allowable rate under the then-existing usury laws.[11]

In the century that followed, the futures industry grew rapidly. Institutions such as the Chicago Board of Trade, the Chicago Mercantile Exchange, and later, the New York Mercantile Exchange and the Chicago Board Options Exchange became the primary forces in the global derivatives industry. These exchanges created and successfully marketed many innovative derivative contracts.[12] Although the first 100 years of futures exchanges were dominated by trading in futures on agricultural commodities, the 1970s saw the introduction of futures on financial instruments such as currencies, bonds, and stock indices. These "financial futures," as well as newly introduced options on individual stocks, currencies, bonds, and stock indices, ushered in a new era in which financial derivatives dominated agricultural derivatives—a situation that continues today. Although the commodity derivatives market includes very active contracts in oil and precious metals, financial derivatives have remained the primary force in the worldwide derivatives market.

Exchange-listed standardized derivatives, however, have hardly been the only instruments in the derivatives world. As noted, customized options have been around since at least the 19th century. The customized-options market flourished until the early 1970s, largely as a retail product. With the introduction of standardized options in 1973, however, the customized options market effectively died. But something else was going on at the time that would later revive this market. In the early 1970s, foreign exchange rates were deregulated and allowed to float freely. This deregulation led not only to the development of a futures, and later options, market for currencies but also to a market for customized forward contracts in foreign currencies. This market became known as the interbank

---

[11] Sage was perhaps the first options arbitrageur. Of course, usury laws are rare these days and most investors understand put–call parity, so do not expect to make any money copying Sage's scheme.

[12] It is probably also important to note that the futures and options exchanges have introduced many unsuccessful contracts as well.

EXHIBIT 1-2   Global Derivatives Exchanges

North America
American Stock Exchange
Bourse de Montreal
BrokerTec Futures Exchange
Chicago Board Options Exchange
Chicago Board of Trade
Chicago Mercantile Exchange
International Securities Exchange (New York)
Kansas City Board of Trade
Minneapolis Grain Exchange
New York Board of Trade
New York Mercantile Exchange
Pacific Exchange (San Francisco)
Philadelphia Stock Exchange
Winnipeg Commodity Exchange

Asia
Central Japan Commodity Exchange
Dalian Commodity Exchange
Hong Kong Exchanges & Clearing
Kansai Commodities Exchange (Osaka)
Korea Futures Exchange
Korea Stock Exchange
Malaysia Derivatives Exchange
New Zealand Futures & Options Exchange
Osaka Mercantile Exchange
Shanghai Futures Exchange
Singapore Commodity Exchange
Singapore Exchange
Tokyo Commodity Exchange
Tokyo Grain Exchange
Tokyo International Financial Futures
   Exchange
Tokyo Stock Exchange
Zhengzhou Commodity Exchange

Europe
Bolsa de Valores de Lisboa e Porto
Borsa Italiana
Budapest Commodity Exchange
Eurex Frankfurt
Eurex Zurich
Euronext Amsterdam
Euronext Brussels
Euronext Paris
FUTOP Market (Copenhagen)
Helsinki Exchanges Group
International Petroleum Exchange of London
London International Financial Futures and
   Options Exchange
London Metal Exchange
MEFF Renta Fija (Barcelona)
MEFF Renta Variable (Madrid)
OM London Exchange
OM Stockholm Exchange
Romanian Commodity Exchange
Sibiu Monetary–Financial and Commodities
   Exchange (Romania)
Tel Aviv Stock Exchange
Wiener Borse AG (Vienna)

South America
Bolsa de Mercadorias & Futuros (Sao Paulo)
Mercado a Termino de Buenos Aires
Santiago Stock Exchange

Africa
South African Futures Exchange

Australia
Australian Stock Exchange
Sydney Futures Exchange

Source: Futures [magazine] *2002 Sourcebook.*

market because it was largely operated within the global banking community, and it grew rapidly. Most importantly, it set the stage for the banking industry to engage in other customized derivative transactions.

Spurred by deregulation of their permitted activities during the 1980s, banks discovered that they could create derivatives of all forms and sell them to corporations and institutions that had risks that could best be managed with products specifically tailored for a given situation. These banks make markets in derivative products by assuming the risks

that the corporations want to eliminate. But banks are not in the business of assuming un-
wanted risks. They use their vast resources and global networks to transfer or lay off the
risk elsewhere, often in the futures markets. If they successfully lay off these risks, they
can profit by buying and selling the derivatives at a suitable bid–ask spread. In addition to
banks, investment banking firms also engage in derivatives transactions of this sort. The
commercial and investment banks that make markets in derivatives are called **derivatives
dealers**. Buying and selling derivatives is a natural extension of the activity these banks
normally undertake in financial markets. This market for customized derivatives is what
we refer to as the over-the-counter derivatives market.

By the end of the 20th century, the derivatives market reached a mature stage, growing at only a slow pace but providing a steady offering of existing products and a continuing slate of new products. Derivatives exchanges underwent numerous changes, often
spurred by growing competition from the over-the-counter market. Some merged; others
that were formerly nonprofit corporations have since become profit making. Some derivatives exchanges have even experimented with offering somewhat customized transactions.
Nearly all have lobbied heavily for a reduction in the level or structure of the regulations
imposed on them. Some derivatives exchanges have altered the manner in which trading
takes place, from the old system of face-to-face on a trading floor (in sections called pits)
to off-floor electronic trading in which participants communicate through computer
screens. This type of transacting, called electronic trading, has even been extended to the
Internet and, not surprisingly, is called e-trading. Pit trading is still the primary format for
derivatives exchanges in the United States, but electronic trading is clearly the wave of the
future. As the dominant form of trading outside the United States, it will likely replace pit
trading in the United States in coming years.

Exhibit 1-2 (on page 9) lists all global derivatives exchanges as of January 2002.
Note that almost every country with a reasonably advanced financial market system has a
derivatives exchange.

We cannot technically identify where over-the-counter derivatives markets exist.
These types of transactions can conceivably occur anywhere two parties can agree to engage in a transaction. It is generally conceded, however, that London and New York are the
primary markets for over-the-counter derivatives; considerable activity also takes place in
Tokyo, Paris, Frankfurt, Chicago, Amsterdam, and many other major world cities.

Now we know where the derivative markets are, but are they big enough for us to
care about? We examine this question in Section 4.

4   HOW BIG IS THE DERIVATIVES MARKET?

Good question. And the answer is: We really do not know. Because trading in exchange-
listed contracts, such as futures and some options, is recorded, volume figures for those
types of contracts are available. Exhibit 1-3 presents summary statistics for contract
volume of global futures and options for 2000 and 2001. Note that in 2001, the largest
category is equity indices. In 2000, the largest category was individual equities, followed
by interest rates. In prior years, the largest category had been interest rates.

Currently, the United States accounts for approximately 35 percent of global futures
and options volume. The largest exchange in the world, however, is the Korea Stock
Exchange, which trades an exceptionally large volume of options on a Korean stock index.
The second-largest exchange (and the largest exchange in terms of futures volume only) is
the combined German–Swiss exchange called Eurex. The other largest exchanges (in order of 2001 volume) are the Chicago Mercantile Exchange, the Chicago Board of Trade,
the London International Financial Futures and Options Exchange, the Paris Bourse, the

EXHIBIT 1-3   Global Exchange-Traded Futures and Options Contract Volume
(in millions of contracts)

Contract Type	2000	2001
Equity indices	674.8	1,470.3
Interest rates	844.3	1,216.1
Individual equities	969.7	1,112.7
Energy	154.8	166.9
Agricultural	185.7	156.5
Nonprecious metals	75.7	70.2
Currencies	47.0	49.2
Precious metals	36.2	39.1
Other	1.3	0.8
Overall Total	2,989.5	4,281.8

Source: Futures Industry (January/February 2002).

New York Mercantile Exchange, the Bolsa de Mercadorias & Futuros of Brazil, and the Chicago Board Options Exchange. All of these exchanges traded at least 70 million contracts in 2001.[13]

One important factor that must be considered, however, in looking at trading volume as a measure of activity is that the futures and options exchanges influence their own volume by designating a contract's size. For example, a standard option in the United States covers 100 shares of the underlying stock. If an investor takes a position in options on 1,000 shares of stock, the investor would trade 10 options. If the options exchange had designated that the contract size be 200 options, then the investor would trade only five contracts. Although there are often good reasons for setting a contract size at a certain level, volume comparisons must be taken with a degree of skepticism.[14]

The over-the-counter derivatives market is much more difficult to measure. Because the transactions are private, unregulated, and can take place virtually anywhere two parties can enter into an agreement, no official tabulation exists that allows us to identify the size of the market. Information is available, however, from semiannual surveys conducted by the Bank for International Settlements (BIS) of Basel, Switzerland, an international organization of central banks. The BIS publishes this data in its semiannual report "Regular OTC Derivatives Market Statistics," available on its Web site at www.bis.org/publ/regpubl.htm.

Exhibit 1-4 presents two charts constructed from the 30 June 2001 BIS survey and shows figures for foreign exchange, interest rate, equity, and commodity derivatives

---

[13] *Futures Industry* (January/February 2002).

[14] For example, in 1999 the volume of Treasury bond futures on the Chicago Board of Trade was about 90 million contracts while the volume of Eurodollar futures on the Chicago Mercantile Exchange was about 93 million contracts. Consequently, at that time these two contracts appeared to have about the same amount of activity. But the Treasury bond contract covers Treasury bonds with a face value of $100,000 while the Eurodollar contract covers Eurodollars with a face value of $1,000,000. Thus, the Eurodollar futures market was arguably 10 times the size of the Treasury bond futures market. In 2002, about three Eurodollar futures contracts were traded for every Treasury bond futures contract traded.

EXHIBIT 1-4A   Outstanding Notional Principal of Global Over-the-Counter Derivatives, 30 June 2001 (billions)

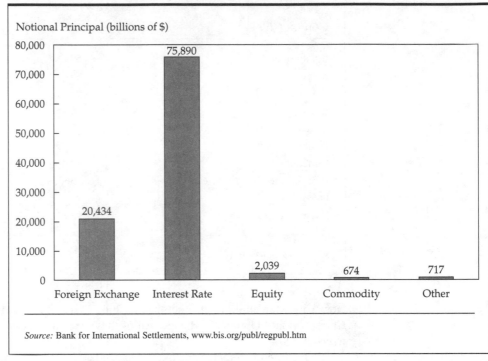

Source: Bank for International Settlements, www.bis.org/publ/regpubl.htm

transactions. The "other" category, however, does include transactions of these types and reflects the BIS's estimates of positions taken by parties that do not report in this survey. It is used primarily to obtain an estimate for the overall size of the market and is not broken down by category.

For over-the-counter derivatives, notional principal is the most widely used measure of market size. Notional principal measures the amount of the underlying asset covered by a derivative contract. For example, a swap involving interest payments on ¥500 million has a notional principal of ¥500 million. The actual payments made in the swap, however, are merely interest payments on ¥500 million and do not come close to ¥500 million.[15] Thus, although notional principal is a commonly used measure of the size of the market, it can give a misleading impression by suggesting that it reflects the amount of money involved.[16]

Nonetheless, we would be remiss if we failed to note the market size as measured by notional principal. Based on Exhibit 1-4A, the total notional principal summing over these

---

[15] In fact, the payments on a swap are even smaller than the interest payments on the notional principal. Swap interest payments usually equal only the difference between the interest payments owed by the two parties.

[16] The over-the-counter derivatives industry originally began the practice of measuring its size by notional principal. This was a deliberate tactic designed to make the industry look larger so it would be more noticed and viewed as a significant and legitimate force. As it turns out, this tactic backfired, resulting in fears that more money was involved and at risk of loss than really was. Calls for increased scrutiny of the industry by government authorities resulted in the industry backpedaling on its use of notional principal and focusing more on market value as a measure of its size. Nonetheless, notional principal continues to be used as one, if not the primary, measure of the industry's size.

EXHIBIT 1-4B Outstanding Market Value of Global Over-the-Counter Derivatives, 30 June 2001 (billions)

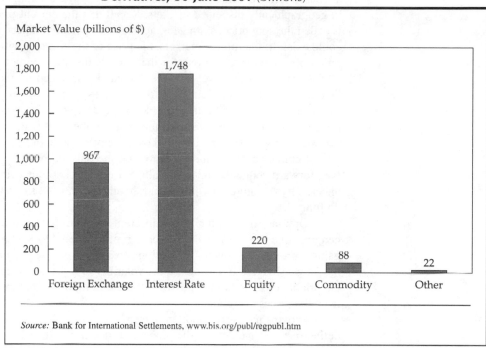

Source: Bank for International Settlements, www.bis.org/publ/regpubl.htm

five categories is almost $100 trillion. Also note that interest rate derivatives are the most widely used category by far.

Exhibit 1-4B gives another picture of the size of the market by indicating the market value of over-the-counter derivatives. Market value indicates the economic worth of a derivative contract and represents the amount of money that would change hands if these transactions were terminated at the time of the report. The total market value for all categories is about $3 trillion. Market value is a better indication of the size of the market because it more accurately represents the actual money involved. Nonetheless, market value is subject to greater errors in estimation and thus is a less reliable measure than notional principal.

Although it is impossible to determine where these contracts originate, dollar-denominated derivatives represented about 34 percent of the global interest rate derivatives market in 2001, with euro-denominated derivatives accounting for about 27 percent and yen-denominated derivatives representing 17 percent.

Whether notional principal or market value is used, it is clear that the derivatives industry is large by any standard. Derivatives are widely available in global asset markets, and consequently, understanding derivatives is essential to operating in these markets, whether one chooses to use them or not.

Because derivative markets have been created around the world, there must be a reason for their continued existence. Let us now look at why derivative markets exist.

5 THE PURPOSES OF DERIVATIVE MARKETS

Derivative markets serve a variety of purposes in global social and economic systems. One of the primary functions of futures markets is **price discovery**. Futures markets provide valuable information about the prices of the underlying assets on which futures contracts are based. They provide this information in two ways. First, many of these assets are traded in geographically dispersed markets. Recall that the current price of the underlying asset is called the spot price. With geographically dispersed markets, many different spot prices could exist. In the futures markets, the price of the contract with the shortest time to expiration often serves as a proxy for the price of the underlying asset. Second, the prices of all futures contracts serve as prices that can be accepted by those who trade contracts in lieu of facing the risk of uncertain future prices. For example, a company that mines gold can hedge by selling a futures contract on gold expiring in two months, which locks in the price of gold two months later. In this manner, the two-month futures price substitutes for the uncertainty of the price of gold over the next two months.[17]

Futures contracts are not, however, the only derivatives that serve this purpose. In fact, forward contracts and swaps allow users to substitute a single locked-in price for the uncertainty of future spot prices and thereby permit the same form of price discovery as do futures.

Options work in a slightly different manner. They are used in a different form of hedging, one that permits the holder to protect against loss while allowing participation in gains if prices move favorably. Options do not so much reveal *prices* as they reveal *volatility*. As we shall see in Chapter 4, the volatility of the underlying asset is a critical factor in the pricing of options. It is possible, therefore, to infer what investors feel about volatility from the prices of options.

Perhaps the most important purpose of derivative markets is **risk management**. We define risk management as the process of identifying the desired level of risk, identifying the actual level of risk, and altering the latter to equal the former. Often this process is described as hedging, which generally refers to the reduction, and in some cases the elimination, of risk. On the other side is the process called speculation. Traditional discussions of derivatives refer to hedging and speculation as complementary activities. In general, hedgers seek to eliminate risk and need speculators to assume risk, but such is not always the case. Hedgers often trade with other hedgers, and speculators often trade with other speculators. All one needs to hedge or speculate is a party with opposite beliefs or opposite risk exposure. For example, a corporation that mines gold could hedge the future sale of gold by entering into a derivative transaction with a company that manufactures jewelry. Both of these companies are hedgers, seeking to avoid the uncertainty of future gold prices by locking in a price for a future transaction. The mining corporation has concerns about a price decrease, and the jewelry manufacturer is worried about a price increase.

An unfortunate consequence of the use of the terms "hedging" and "speculating" is that hedgers are somehow seen as on the high moral ground and speculators are sometimes seen as evil—a distortion of the role of speculators. In fact, there need be very little difference between hedgers and speculators. To restate an example we used when discussing swaps, consider a corporation that currently borrows at a floating rate. A common response to a fear of rising interest rates is for the corporation to use an interest rate swap in which it will make payments at a fixed rate and receive payments at a floating rate. The floating-rate payments it receives from the swap offset the floating-rate payments on the loan, thereby effectively converting the loan to a fixed-rate loan. The company is now borrowing at a fixed rate and, in the eyes of many, hedging.

---

[17] Some people view futures prices as revealing expectations of future spot prices of the underlying asset, and in that sense, leading to price discovery. This view, however, is incorrect. Futures prices are not necessarily expectations of future spot prices. As we discussed above, they allow a substitution of the futures price for the uncertainty of future spot prices of the asset. In that sense they permit the acceptance of a sure price and the avoidance of risk.

But is the company really hedging? Or is it simply making a bet that interest rates will increase? If interest rates decrease, the company will be losing money in the sense of the lost opportunity to borrow at a lower rate. From a budgeting and cash flow standpoint, however, its fixed interest payments are set in stone. Moreover, the market value of a fixed-rate loan is considerably more volatile than that of a floating-rate loan. Thus, our "hedging" corporation can be viewed as taking more risk than it originally had.

The more modern view of the reason for using derivatives does not refer to hedging or speculation. Although we shall sometimes use those terms, we shall use them carefully and make our intentions clear. In the grander scheme of things, derivatives are tools that enable companies to more easily practice risk management. In the context of our corporation borrowing at the floating rate, it made a conscious decision to borrow at a fixed rate. Engaging in the swap is simply an activity designed to align its risk with the risk it wants, given its outlook for interest rates. Whether one calls this activity hedging or speculation is not even very important. The company is simply managing risk.

Derivative markets serve several other useful purposes. As we show later when exploring the pricing of derivative contracts, they improve market efficiency for the underlying assets. Efficient markets are fair and competitive and do not allow one party to easily take money from another. As a simple example, we shall learn in Chapter 3 that buying a stock index fund can be replicated by buying a futures on the fund and investing in risk-free bonds the money that otherwise would have been spent on the fund. In other words, the fund and the combination of the futures and risk-free bond will have the same performance. But if the fund costs more than the combination of the futures and risk-free bond, investors have the opportunity to avoid the overpriced fund and take the combination.[18] This decreased demand for the fund will lower its price. The benefits to investors who do not even use derivatives should be clear: They can now invest in the fund at a more attractive price, because the derivatives market forced the price back to its appropriate level.

Derivative markets are also characterized by relatively low transaction costs. For example, the cost of investing in a stock index portfolio is as much as 20 times the cost of buying a futures contract on the index and a risk-free bond as described above. One might reasonably ask why derivatives are so much less expensive in terms of transaction costs. The answer is that derivatives are designed to provide a means of managing risk. As we have previously described, they serve as a form of insurance. Insurance cannot be a viable product if its cost is too high relative to the value of the insured asset. In other words, derivatives must have low transaction costs; otherwise, they would not exist.

It would be remiss to overlook the fact that derivative markets have been subject to many criticisms. We next present some of these complaints and the reasons behind them.

6 CRITICISMS OF DERIVATIVE MARKETS

Derivatives have been highly controversial for a number of reasons. For one, they are very complex. Much of the criticism has stemmed from a failure to understand derivatives. When derivatives fail to do their job, it is often the derivatives themselves, rather than the users of derivatives, that take the blame. Yet, in many cases, the critics of derivatives simply do not understand them well enough. As described in Section 2, when homeowners take out mortgages, they usually receive a valuable option: the right to prepay their

---

[18] Some investors, called arbitrageurs, will even find ways to sell the fund short to eliminate the risk of holding the futures and the bond, earning a profit from any discrepancy in their prices. We shall cover this type of transaction later in this chapter.

mortgages. When interest rates fall, homeowners often pay off their mortgages, refinancing them at lower rates. The holders of these mortgages usually sell them to other parties, which can include small organizations and individuals. Thus, we often find unsophisticated investors holding securities based on the payments from mortgages. When homeowners refinance, they capture huge interest savings. Where does this money come from? It comes from the pockets of the holders of mortgage securities. When these unsophisticated investors lose a lot of money, derivatives usually get the blame. Yet these losses went into the pockets of homeowners in the form of interest savings. Who is to blame? Probably the brokers, who sold the securities to investors who did not know what they were buying—which leads us to the next common criticism of derivatives.

The complexity of derivatives means that sometimes the parties that use them do not understand them well. As a result, they are often used improperly, leading to potentially large losses. Such an argument can, however, be used to describe fire, electricity, and chemicals. Used improperly, perhaps in the hands of a child or someone who does not know how to use them, all of these can be extremely dangerous. Yet, we know that sufficient knowledge of fire, electricity, and chemicals to use them properly is not very difficult to obtain. The same is true for derivatives; treat them with respect and healthy doses of knowledge.

Derivatives are also mistakenly characterized as a form of legalized gambling. Although gambling is certainly legal in many parts of the world, derivatives are often viewed as a government's sanction of gambling via the financial markets. But there is an important distinction between gambling and derivatives: The benefits of derivatives extend much further across society. By providing a means of managing risk along with the other benefits discussed above, derivatives make financial markets work better. The organized gambling industry affects the participants, the owners of casinos, and perhaps some citizens who benefit from state lotteries. Organized gambling does not, however, make society function better, and it arguably incurs social costs.

We have taken a look at what derivatives are, where they come from, where they are now, why we have them, and what people think of them. Understanding derivatives, however, requires a basic understanding of the market forces that govern derivative prices. Although we shall cover derivative pricing in more detail in later chapters, here we take a brief look at the process of pricing derivatives by examining some important fundamental principles.

7   ELEMENTARY PRINCIPLES OF DERIVATIVE PRICING

In this section, we take a preliminary glance at how derivative contracts are priced. First, we introduce the concept of **arbitrage**. Arbitrage occurs when equivalent assets or combinations of assets sell for two different prices. This situation creates an opportunity to profit at no risk with no commitment of money. Let us start with the simplest (and least likely) opportunity for arbitrage: the case of a stock selling for more than one price at a given time. Assume that a stock is trading in two markets simultaneously. Suppose the stock is trading at $100 in one market and $98 in the other market. We simply buy a share for $98 in one market and immediately sell it for $100 in the other. We have no net position in the stock, so it does not matter what price the stock moves to. We make an easy $2 at no risk and we did not have to put up any funds of our own. The sale of the stock at $100 was more than adequate to finance the purchase of the stock at $98. Naturally, many market participants would do this, which would create downward pressure on the price of the stock in the market where it trades for $100 and upward pressure on the price of the stock in the market where it trades for $98. Eventually the two prices must come together so that there is but a single price for the stock. Accordingly, the principle that no arbitrage opportunities should be available is often referred to as the **law of one price**.

Recall that we mentioned in Section 5 that an asset can potentially trade in different geographic markets and, therefore, have several spot prices. This potential would appear to violate the law of one price, but in reality, the law is still upheld. A given asset selling in two different locations is not necessarily the same asset. If a buyer in one location discovered that it is possible to buy the asset more cheaply in another location, the buyer would still have to incur the cost of moving the asset to the buyer's location. Transportation costs could offset any such price differences.[19]

Now suppose we face the situation illustrated in Exhibit 1-5 on page 18. In Exhibit 1-5A, observe that we have one stock, AXE Electronics, which today is worth $50 and which, one period later, will be worth either $75 or $40. We shall denote these prices as AXE = 50, AXE^+ = 75, and AXE^- = 40. Another stock, BYF Technology, is today worth $38 and one period later will be worth $60 or $32. Thus, BYF = 38, BYF^+ = 60, and BYF^- = 32. Let us assume the risk-free borrowing and lending rate is 4 percent. We assume no dividends on either stock during the period covered by this example.

The opportunity exists to make a profit at no risk without committing any of our funds, as demonstrated in Exhibit 1-5B. Suppose we borrow 100 shares of stock AXE, which is selling for $50, and sell short, thereby receiving $5,000. We take $4,750 and purchase 125 shares of stock BYF. We invest the remaining $250 in risk-free bonds at 4 percent. This transaction will not require us to put up any funds of our own: The short sale will be sufficient to fund the investment in BYF and leave money to invest in risk-free bonds.

If the top outcome in Exhibit 1-5 occurs, we sell the 125 shares of BYF for 125 × $60 = $7,500. This amount is sufficient to buy back the 100 shares of AXE, which is selling for $75. But we will also have the bonds, which are worth $250 × 1.04 = $260. If the bottom outcome occurs, we sell the 125 shares of BYF for 125 × $32 = $4,000—enough money to buy back the 100 shares of AXE, which is selling for $40. Again, we will have the risk-free bonds, worth $260. Regardless of the outcome, we end up with $260.

Recall that we put up no money of our own and ended up with a sure $260. It should be apparent that this is an extremely attractive transaction, so everyone would do it. The combined actions of multiple investors would drive down the price of AXE and/or drive up the price of BYF until an equilibrium was reached at which this transaction would not be profitable. Assuming stock BYF's price remained constant, stock AXE would fall to $47.50. Or assuming stock AXE's price remained constant, stock BYF would rise to $40.

Of course, this example is extremely simplified. Clearly a stock price can change to more than two other prices. Also, if a given stock is at one price, another stock may be at any other price. We have created a simple case here to illustrate a point. But as you will learn in Chapter 4, when derivatives are involved, the simplification here is relatively safe. In fact, it is quite appropriate.

Now we look at another type of arbitrage opportunity, which involves a forward contract and will establish an appropriate price for the forward contract. Let stock AXE sell for $50. We borrow $50 at 4 percent interest by issuing a risk-free bond, use the money to buy one share of stock AXE, and simultaneously enter into a forward contract to sell this share at a price of $54 one period later. The stock will then move to either $75 or $40 in

---

[19] One might reasonably wonder if finding a consumer article selling in Wal-Mart at a lower price than in Target is not a violation of the law of one price. It certainly is, but we make no claim that the market for consumer products is efficient. Our focus is on the financial markets where, for example, Goldman Sachs can hardly offer shares of IBM at one price while Merrill Lynch offers them at another.

EXHIBIT 1-5A   Arbitrage Opportunity with Stock AXE, Stock BYF, and a Risk-Free Bond

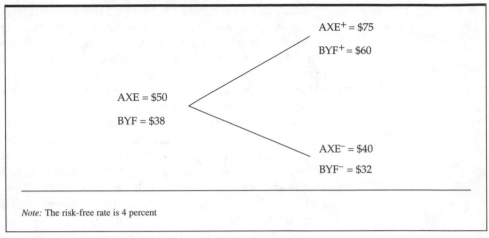

Note: The risk-free rate is 4 percent

EXHIBIT 1-5B   Execution of Arbitrage Transaction with Stock AXE, Stock BYF, and a Risk-Free Bond

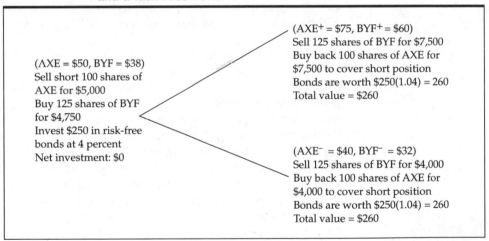

the next period; the forward contract will require that we deliver the stock and accept $54 for it; and we shall owe $50 × 1.04 = $52 on the loan.

Let us look at the two outcomes. Suppose stock AXE goes to $75. We deliver the stock to settle the obligation on the forward contract and receive $54 for it. We use $52 of the $54 to pay back the loan, leaving a gain of $2. Now suppose AXE goes to $40. We deliver the stock, fulfilling the obligation of the forward contract, and receive $54. Again, we use $52 of the $54 to pay back the loan, leaving a gain of $2.

In either case we made $2, free and clear. In fact, we can even accommodate the possibility of more than two future prices for AXE. The key point is that we faced no risk and did not have to put up any of our own money, but we ended up with $2—clearly a good deal. In fact, this is what we would call an arbitrage profit. But from where did it originate?

It turns out that the forward price we received, $54, was an inappropriate price given current market conditions. In fact, it was just an arbitrary price, made up to illustrate the point. To eliminate the opportunity to earn the $2 profit, the forward price should be $52—equal, not coincidentally, to the amount owed on the loan. It is also no coincidence that $52 is the price of the asset increased by the rate of interest. We will discuss this point further in Chapter 2.

In this example, many market participants would do this transaction as long it generates an arbitrage profit. These forces of arbitrage would either force the forward price down or force the price of the stock up until an equilibrium is reached that eliminates the opportunity to profit at no risk with no commitment of one's own funds.

We have just had a taste of not only the powerful forces of arbitrage but also a pricing model for one derivative, the forward contract. In this simple example, according to the pricing model, the forward price should be the spot price increased by the interest rate. Although there is a lot more to derivative pricing than shown here, the basic principle remains the same regardless of the type of instrument or the complexity of the setting: *Prices are set to eliminate the opportunity to profit at no risk with no commitment of one's own funds.* There are no opportunities for arbitrage profits.

Lest we be too naive, however, we must acknowledge that there is a large industry of arbitrageurs. So how can such an industry exist if there are no opportunities for riskless profit? One explanation is that most of the arbitrage transactions are more complex than this simple example and involve estimating information, which can result in differing opinions. Arbitrage involving options, for example, usually requires estimates of a stock's volatility. Different participants have different opinions about this volatility. It is quite possible that two counterparties trading with each other can believe that each is arbitraging against the other.

But more importantly, the absence of arbitrage opportunities is upheld, ironically, only if participants believe that arbitrage opportunities *do* exist. If market traders believe that no opportunities exist to earn arbitrage profits, then they will not follow market prices and compare these prices with what they ought to be, as in the forward contract example given above. Without participants watching closely, prices would surely get out of line and offer arbitrage opportunities. Thus, eliminating arbitrage opportunities requires that participants be vigilant to arbitrage opportunities. In other words, strange as it may sound, disbelief and skepticism concerning the absence of arbitrage opportunities are required in order that it hold as a legitimate principle.

Markets in which arbitrage opportunities are either nonexistent or are quickly eliminated are relatively efficient markets. Recall from your study of portfolio theory and investment analysis that efficient markets are those in which it is not possible, except by chance, to earn returns in excess of those that would be fair compensation for the risk assumed. Although abnormal returns can be earned in a variety of ways, arbitrage profits are definitely examples of abnormal returns, relatively obvious to identify and easy to capture. Thus, they are the most egregious violations of the principle of market efficiency. A market in which arbitrage profits do not exist is one in which the most obvious violations of market efficiency have been eliminated.

Throughout this book, we shall study derivatives by using the principle of arbitrage as a guide. We will assume that arbitrage opportunities cannot exist for any significant length of time. Thus, prices must conform to models that assume no arbitrage. On the other hand, we do not want to take the absence of arbitrage opportunities so seriously that we give up and believe that arbitrage opportunities never exist. Otherwise, they will arise, and someone else will take them from us.

We have now completed this introductory chapter, which has touched only lightly on the world of derivatives. The remainder of the book is organized as follows: Chapter 2 on forwards, Chapter 3 on futures, Chapter 4 on options, and Chapter 5 on swaps provide details describing the types of instruments and how they are priced. Chapter 6 on forwards and futures, Chapter 7 on options, and Chapter 8 on swaps discuss strategies using these instruments. Chapter 9 covers the integrative topic of risk management, introducing concepts and issues related to the management of risk and some tools and techniques for managing risk. We now proceed to Chapter 2, which looks at forward markets and contracts.

KEY POINTS

- A derivative contract is a financial instrument with a return that is obtained from or "derived" from the return of another underlying financial instrument.

- Exchange-traded derivatives are created, authorized, and traded on a derivatives exchange, an organized facility for trading derivatives. Exchange-traded derivatives are standardized instruments with respect to certain terms and conditions of the contract. They trade in accordance with rules and specifications prescribed by the derivatives exchange and are usually subject to governmental regulation. Exchange-traded derivatives are guaranteed by the exchange against loss resulting from the default of one of the parties. Over-the-counter derivatives are transactions created by any two parties off of a derivatives exchange. The parties set all of their own terms and conditions, and each assumes the credit risk of the other party.

- A forward commitment is an agreement between two parties in which one party agrees to buy and the other agrees to sell an asset at a future date at a price agreed on today. The three types of forward commitments are forward contracts, futures contracts, and swaps.

- A forward contract is a forward commitment created in the over-the-counter market. A futures contract is a forward commitment created and traded on a futures exchange. A swap is an over-the-counter transaction consisting of a series of forward commitments.

- A contingent claim is a derivative contract with a payoff dependent on the occurrence of a future event. The primary types of contingent claims are options, but other types involve variations of options, often combined with other financial instruments or derivatives.

- An option is a derivative contract giving one party the right to buy or sell an underlying asset at a fixed price over a period of time or at a specific point in time. The party obtaining the right pays a premium (the option price) at the start and receives the right to buy or sell, as prescribed by the contract. The two types of options are a call (the right to buy) and a put (the right to sell).

- The size of the global derivatives market can be measured by notional principal, which is the amount of the underlying on which a derivative is based, and by market value, which is the economic worth of the derivative.

- Derivative markets serve many useful purposes such as providing price discovery, facilitating risk management, making markets more efficient, and lowering transaction costs. Derivatives are often criticized as being excessively dangerous for unknowledgeable investors and have been inappropriately likened to gambling.

- Arbitrage is a process through which an investor can buy an asset or combination of assets at one price and concurrently sell at a higher price, thereby earning a profit without investing any money or being exposed to any risk. The combined actions of many investors engaging in arbitrage results in rapid price adjustments that eliminate these opportunities, thereby bringing prices back in line and making markets more efficient.

PROBLEMS

1. For all parties involved, which of the following financial instruments is NOT an example of a forward commitment?
   A. Swap
   B. Call option
   C. Futures contract
   D. Forward contract

2. The main risk faced by an individual who enters into a forward contract to buy the S&P 500 Index is that
   A. the market may rise.
   B. the market may fall.
   C. market volatility may rise.
   D. market volatility may fall.

3. Which of the following statements is *most* accurate?
   A. Futures contracts are private transactions.
   B. Forward contracts are marked to market daily.
   C. Futures contracts have more default risk than forward contracts.
   D. Forward contracts require that both parties to the transaction have a high degree of creditworthiness.

4. Which of the following statements is *least* accurate?
   A. Futures contracts are easier to offset than forward contracts.
   B. Forward contracts are generally more liquid than futures contracts.
   C. Forward contracts are easier to tailor to specific needs than futures contracts.
   D. Futures contracts are characterized by having a clearinghouse as an intermediary.

5. A swap is *best* characterized as a
   A. series of forward contracts.
   B. derivative contract that has not gained widespread popularity.
   C. single fixed payment in exchange for a single floating payment.
   D. contract that is binding on only one of the parties to the transaction.

6. Which of the following is *most* representative of forward contracts and contingent claims?

	Forward Contracts	Contingent Claims
A.	Premium paid at inception	Premium paid at inception
B.	Premium paid at inception	No premium paid at inception
C.	No premium paid at inception	Premium paid at inception
D.	No premium paid at inception	No premium paid at inception

7. For the long position, the *most likely* advantage of contingent claims over forward commitments is that contingent claims
   A. are easier to offset than forward commitments.
   B. have lower default risk than forward commitments.
   C. permit gains while protecting against losses.
   D. are typically cheaper to initiate than forward commitments.

8. For derivative contracts, the notional principal is *best* described as
   A. the amount of the underlying asset covered by the contract.
   B. a measure of the actual payments made and received in the contract.
   C. tending to underestimate the actual payments made and received in the contract.
   D. being, conceptually and in aggregate, the best available measure of the size of the market.

9. By volume, the most widely used group of derivatives is the one with contracts written on which of the following types of underlying assets?
   A. Financial
   B. Commodities
   C. Energy-related
   D. Precious metals

10. Which of the following is *least* likely to be a purpose served by derivative markets?
    A. Arbitrage
    B. Price discovery
    C. Risk management
    D. Hedging and speculation

11. The *most likely* reason derivative markets have flourished is that
    A. derivatives are easy to understand and use.
    B. derivatives have relatively low transaction costs.
    C. the pricing of derivatives is relatively straightforward.
    D. strong regulation ensures that transacting parties are protected from fraud.

12. If the risk-free rate of interest is 5 percent and an investor enters into a transaction that has no risk, the rate of return the investor should earn in the absence of arbitrage opportunities is
    A. 0%.
    B. between 0% and 5%.
    C. 5%.
    D. more than 5%.

13. If the spot price of gold is $250 per ounce and the risk-free rate of interest is 10 percent per annum, the six-month forward price per ounce of gold, in equilibrium, should be *closest* to
    A. $250.00.
    B. $256.25.
    C. $262.50.
    D. $275.00.

14. Concerning efficient financial (including derivative) markets, the *most appropriate* description is that
    A. it is often possible to earn abnormal returns.
    B. the law of one price holds only in the academic literature.
    C. arbitrage opportunities rarely exist and are quickly eliminated.
    D. arbitrage opportunities often exist and can be exploited for profit.

15. Stock A costs $10.00 today and its price will be either $7.50 or $12.50 next period. Stock B's price will be either $18.00 or $30.00 next period. If risk-free borrowing and lending are possible at 8 percent per period, neither stock pays dividends, and it is possible to buy and sell fractional shares, Stock B's equilibrium price today should be *closest* to
    A. $19.00.
    B. $21.00.
    C. $24.00.
    D. $26.00.

SOLUTIONS

1. B A call option is not binding on *both* parties in the same sense that the other financial instruments are. The call option gives the holder a right but does not impose an obligation.

2. B If the market falls, the buyer of a forward contract could pay more for the index, as determined by the price that was contracted for at the inception of the contract, than the index is worth when the contract matures. Although it is possible that a rise in interest rates could cause the market to fall, this might not always happen and thus is a secondary consideration.

3. D Forward contracts are usually private transactions that do not have an intermediary such as a clearinghouse to guarantee performance by both parties. This type of transaction requires a high degree of creditworthiness for both parties.

4. B Forward contracts are usually less liquid than futures contracts because they are typically private transactions tailored to suit both parties, unlike futures contracts, which are usually for standardized amounts and are exchange traded.

5. A A swap is most like a series of forward contracts. An example is a swap in which one party makes a set of fixed-rate payments over time in exchange for a set of floating-rate payments based on some notional amount.

6. C Unlike a contingent claim, a forward commitment typically requires no premium to be paid up front. An intuitive way to look at this is to realize that a forward commitment is binding on both parties, so any up-front fees would cancel, while a contingent claim is binding only on the party in the short position. For this, the party in the short position demands (and receives) compensation.

7. C Because the holder of a contingent claim (the party in the long position) has a right but not an obligation, she will only exercise when it is in her best interest to do so and not otherwise. This will happen only when she stands to gain and never when she stands to lose.

8. A The notional principal is the amount of the underlying asset covered by the derivative contract.

9. A The most widely used derivative contracts are written on underlying assets that are financial, such as Treasury instruments and stock indices.

10. A Arbitrage, or the absence of it, is the basis for pricing most derivative contracts. Consequently, it is relatively unusual, although certainly not impossible, for derivative markets to be used to generate arbitrage profits.

11. B One reason derivative markets have flourished is that they have relatively low transaction costs. For example, buying a risk-free Treasury security and a futures contract on the S&P 500 Index to replicate payoffs to the index is cheaper than buying the 500 stocks in the index in their proper proportions to get the same payoff.

12. C In the absence of arbitrage opportunities, an investor bearing no risk should expect to earn the risk-free rate.

13. C The six-month forward price of gold should be $250 \times [1 + (0.10/2)] = 250 \times (1.05) = \$262.50$.

14. C Efficient markets are characterized by the absence, or the rapid elimination, of arbitrage opportunities.

15. C Stock B should be priced at $24.00 today. To see this, imagine selling 2.4 shares of A short for $24.00, and buying one share of B. Now, in the next period, suppose B is worth $30.00. Then selling B permits you to buy 2.4 shares of A (at $12.50 per share) to return the shares sold short. Alternatively, if B is worth $18.00, selling B permits you to still buy 2.4 shares of A (at $7.50) to return them. The same no-profit situation holds if you sell one share of B and buy 2.4 shares of A. An alternative explanation lies in the fact that in each of the two outcomes, the price of B is 2.4 times the price of A. Thus, the price of B today must be 2.4 times the price of A.

2

FORWARD MARKETS AND CONTRACTS

LEARNING OUTCOMES

After completing this chapter, you will be able to do the following:

- Discuss the differences between the positions held by the long and short parties to a forward contract.
- Describe the procedures for settling a forward contract at expiration.
- Discuss how a party to a forward contract can terminate a position prior to expiration and how credit risk is affected by the way in which a position is terminated.
- Explain the difference between a dealer and an end user of a forward contract.
- Describe the essential characteristics of equity forward contracts.
- Describe the essential characteristics of forward contracts on zero-coupon and coupon bonds.
- Explain the characteristics of the Eurodollar time deposit market.
- Define LIBOR and Euribor.
- Describe the essential characteristics of forward rate agreements (FRAs).
- Calculate the payment at expiration of an FRA and explain each of the component terms.
- Describe the essential characteristics of currency forward contracts.
- Explain how the price of a forward contract is determined.
- Explain how the value of a forward contract is determined at initiation, during the life of the contract, and at expiration.
- Explain why valuation of a forward contract is important.
- Define an off-market forward contract and explain how it differs from the more standard type of forward contract.
- Explain how an equity forward contract is priced and valued, given the different possible patterns of dividend payments, and calculate its price and value.
- Explain how a forward contract on a fixed-income security is priced and valued, and calculate its price and value.
- Explain how an FRA is priced and valued, and calculate its price and value.
- Explain how a forward contract on a currency is priced and valued, and be able to calculate its price and value.
- Explain how credit risk arises in a forward contract and how market value is a measure of the credit risk to a party in a forward contract.

1 INTRODUCTION

In Chapter 1, we gave a general overview of global derivative markets. We identified those markets as forward markets, futures markets, options markets, and swap markets. The following series of chapters focuses individually on those markets. We begin with forward markets.

First recall our definition of a forward contract: *A forward contract is an agreement between two parties in which one party, the buyer, agrees to buy from the other party, the seller, an underlying asset or other derivative, at a future date at a price established at the start of the contract.* Therefore, it is a commitment by two parties to engage in a transaction at a later date with the price set in advance. The buyer is often called the **long** and the seller is often called the **short**.[1] Although any two parties can agree on such a contract, in this book we are interested only in forward contracts that involve large corporations, financial institutions, nonprofit organizations, or governments.

Recalling an example from Chapter 1, a pension fund manager, anticipating the receipt of cash at a future date, might enter into a commitment to purchase a stock portfolio at a later date at a price agreed on today. By doing so, the manager's position is unaffected by any changes in the value of the stock portfolio between today and the date of the actual investment in the stock portfolio. In this sense, the manager is hedged against an increase in stock prices until the cash is received and invested. The disadvantage of such a transaction is that the manager is also hedged against any decreases in stock prices. If stock prices fall between the time the commitment is established and the time the cash is received, the manager will regret having entered into the forward contract because the stock could have been acquired at a lower price. But that is the nature of a forward contract hedge: It locks in a price.

An important feature of a forward contract is that neither party pays any money at the start. In Chapter 9, we shall look at how the parties might require some collateral to minimize the risk of default, but for most of this book, we shall ignore this point. So keep in mind this very important aspect of forward contracts: *No money changes hands at the start.*

1.1 DELIVERY AND SETTLEMENT OF A FORWARD CONTRACT

When a forward contract expires, there are two possible arrangements that can be used to settle the obligations of the parties. A deliverable forward contract stipulates that the long will pay the agreed-upon price to the short, who in turn will deliver the underlying asset to the long, a process called **delivery**. An alternative procedure, called **cash settlement**, permits the long and short to pay the net cash value of the position on the delivery date. For example, suppose two parties agree to a forward contract to deliver a zero-coupon bond at a price of $98 per $100 par. At the contract's expiration, suppose the underlying zero-coupon bond is selling at a price of $98.25. The long is due to receive from the short an asset worth $98.25, for which a payment to the short of $98.00 is required. In a cash-settled forward contract, the short simply pays the long $0.25. If the zero-coupon bond were selling for $97.50, the long would pay the short $0.50. Delivery of a zero-coupon bond is not a difficult thing to do, however, and cash-settled contracts are more commonly used in situations where delivery is impractical.[2] For example, if the underlying is the

---

[1] As pointed out in Chapter 1 with respect to the word *underlying*, the derivatives industry often uses nouns, verbs, adjectives, and adverbs as parts of speech other than what they are. Hence, words like *long* and *short* are used not as adjectives but as nouns.

[2] Be aware, however, that the choice of delivery or cash settlement is not an option available at expiration. It is negotiated between the parties at the start.

Russell 3000 Index, the short would have to deliver to the long a portfolio containing each of the Russell 3000 stocks proportionate to its weighting in the index. Consequently, cash settlement is much more practical. Cash-settled forward contracts are sometimes called **NDFs**, for **nondeliverable forwards**, although this term is used predominately with respect to foreign exchange forwards.

1.2 DEFAULT RISK AND FORWARD CONTRACTS

An important characteristic of forward contracts is that they are subject to default. Regardless of whether the contract is for delivery or cash settlement, the potential exists for a party to default. In the zero-coupon bond example above, the long might be unable to pay the $98 or the short might be unable to buy the zero-coupon bond and make delivery of the bond to the long. Generally speaking, however, forward contracts are structured so that only the party owing the greater amount can default. In other words, if the short is obligated to deliver a zero-coupon bond selling for more than $98, then the long would not be obligated to make payment unless the short makes delivery. Likewise, in a cash settled contract, only one party—the one owing the greater amount—can default. We discuss the nature of this credit risk in the following section and in Section 5 after we have determined how to value forward contracts. We also address the topic of credit risk in derivative contracts in Chapter 9.

1.3 TERMINATION OF A FORWARD CONTRACT

Let us note that a forward contract is nearly always constructed with the idea that the participants will hold on to their positions until the contract expires and either engage in delivery of the asset or settle the cash equivalent, as required in the specific contract. The possibility exists, however, that at least one of the participants might wish to terminate the position prior to expiration. For example, suppose a party goes long, meaning that she agrees to buy the asset at the expiration date at the price agreed on at the start, but she subsequently decides to terminate the contract before expiration. We shall assume that the contract calls for delivery rather than cash settlement at expiration.

To see the details of the contract termination, suppose it is part of the way through the life of the contract, and the long decides that she no longer wishes to buy the asset at expiration. She can then re-enter the market and create a new forward contract expiring at the same time as the original forward contract, taking the position of the seller instead. Because of price changes in the market during the period since the original contract was created, this new contract would likely have a different price at which she would have to commit to sell. She would then be long a contract to buy the asset at expiration at one price and short a contract to sell the asset at expiration at a different price. It should be apparent that she has no further exposure to the price of the asset.

For example, suppose she is long to buy at $40 and short to deliver at $42. Depending on the characteristics of the contract, one of several possibilities could occur at expiration. Everything could go as planned—the party holding the short position of the contract on which she is long at $40 delivers the asset to her, and she pays him $40. She then delivers the asset to the party who is long the contract on which she is short at $42. That party pays her $42. She nets $2. The transaction is over.

There is always a possibility that her counterparty on the long contract could default. She is still obligated to deliver the asset on the short contract, for which she will receive $42. But if her counterparty on the long contract defaults, she has to buy the asset in the market and could suffer a significant loss. There is also a possibility that the counterparty on her short contract could fail to pay her the $42. Of course, she would then not deliver the asset but would be exposed to the risk of changes in the asset's price. This type of problem illustrates the credit risk in a forward contract. We shall cover credit risk in more detail in Section 5 of this chapter and in Chapter 9.

To avoid the credit risk, when she re-enters the market to go short the forward contract, she could contact the same counterparty with whom she engaged in the long forward contract. They could agree to cancel both contracts. Because she would be owed $2 at expiration, cancellation of the contract would result in the counterparty paying her the present value of $2. This termination or offset of the original forward position is clearly desirable for both counterparties because it eliminates the credit risk.[3] It is always possible, however, that she might receive a better price from another counterparty. If that price is sufficiently attractive and she does not perceive the credit risk to be too high, she may choose to deal with the other counterparty and leave the credit risk in the picture.

2 THE STRUCTURE OF GLOBAL FORWARD MARKETS

The global market for forward contracts is part of a vast network of financial institutions that make markets in these instruments as well as in other related derivatives, such as swaps and options. Some dealers specialize in certain markets and contracts, such as forward contracts on the euro or forward contracts on Japanese equity products. These dealers are mainly large global banking institutions, but many large non-banking institutions, such as Goldman Sachs and Merrill Lynch, are also big players in this market.

Dealers engage in transactions with two types of parties: end users and other dealers. An end user is typically a corporation, nonprofit organization, or government.[4] An end user is generally a party with a risk management problem that is searching for a dealer to provide it with a financial transaction to solve that problem. Although the problem could simply be that the party wants to take a position in anticipation of a market move, more commonly the end user has a risk it wants to reduce or eliminate.

As an example, Hoffman-LaRoche, the large Swiss pharmaceutical company, sells its products globally. Anticipating the receipt of a large amount of cash in U.S. dollars and worried about a decrease in the value of the dollar relative to the Swiss franc, it could buy a forward contract to sell the dollar and buy Swiss francs. It might seek out a dealer such as UBS Warburg, the investment firm affiliated with the large Swiss bank UBS, or it might approach any of the other large multinational banks with which it does business. Or it might end up dealing with a non-bank entity, like Merrill Lynch. Assume that Hoffman-LaRoche enters into this contract with UBS Warburg. Hoffman-LaRoche is the end user; UBS Warburg is the dealer.

Transactions in forward contracts typically are conducted over the phone. Each dealer has a quote desk, whose phone number is well known to the major participants in the market. If a party wishes to conduct a transaction, it simply phones the dealer for a quote. The dealer stands ready to take either side of the transaction, quoting a bid and an ask price or rate. The bid is the price at which the dealer is willing to pay for the future purchase of the asset, and the ask is the price at which the dealer is willing to sell. When a dealer engages in a forward transaction, it has then taken on risk from the other party. For example, in the aforementioned transaction of Hoffman-LaRoche and UBS Warburg, by entering into the contract, UBS Warburg takes on a risk that Hoffman-LaRoche has eliminated. Specifically, UBS Warburg has now committed to buying dollars and selling Swiss francs at a future date. Thus, UBS Warburg is effectively long the dollar and stands

---

[3] This statement is made under the assumption that the parties do not want the credit risk. Credit risk, like other risks, however, can be a risk that some parties want because of the potential for earning attractive returns by using their expertise in measuring the actual credit risk relative to the credit risk as perceived by the market. In addition, credit risk offers diversification benefits. We will discuss these points more fully in Chapter 9.

[4] The U.S. government does not transact in forward contracts or other derivatives, but some foreign governments and central banks do. Within the United States, however, some state and local governments do engage in forward contracts and other derivatives.

to gain from a strengthening dollar/weakening Swiss franc. Typically dealers do not want to hold this exposure. Rather, they find another party to offset the exposure with another derivative or spot transaction. Thus, UBS Warburg is a wholesaler of risk—buying it, selling it, and trying to earn a profit off the spread between its buying price and selling price.

One might reasonably wonder why Hoffman-LaRoche could not avoid the cost of dealing with UBS Warburg. In some cases, it might be able to. It might be aware of another party with the exact opposite needs, but such a situation is rare. The market for financial products such as forward contracts is made up of wholesalers of risk management products who use their technical expertise, their vast network of contacts, and their access to critical financial market information to provide a more efficient means for end users to engage in such risk management transactions.

Dealers such as UBS Warburg lay off the risk they do not wish to assume by transacting with other dealers and potentially other end users. If they do this carefully, quickly, and at accurate prices, they can earn a profit from this market-making activity. One should not get the impression, however, that market making is a highly profitable activity. The competition is fierce, which keeps bid–ask spreads very low and makes it difficult to earn much money on a given transaction. Indeed, many market makers do not make much money on individual transactions—they typically make a small amount of money on each transaction and do a large number of transactions. They may even lose money on some standard transactions, hoping to make up losses on more-complicated, nonstandard transactions, which occur less frequently but have higher bid–ask spreads.

Risk magazine conducts annual surveys to identify the top dealers in various derivative products. Exhibit 2-1 presents the results of those surveys for two of the forward products we cover here, currency and interest rate forwards. Interest rate forwards are called forward rate agreements (FRAs). In the next section, we shall study the different types of forward contracts and note that there are some others not covered in the *Risk* surveys.

One of these surveys was sent to banks and investment banks that are active dealers in over-the-counter derivatives. The other survey was sent to end users. The tabulations are based on respondents' simple rankings of who they think are the best dealers. Although the identities of the specific dealer firms are not critical, it is interesting and helpful to be aware of the major players in these types of contracts. Most of the world's leading global financial institutions are listed, but many other big names are not. It is also interesting to observe that the perceptions of the users of these dealer firms' services differ somewhat from the dealers' self-perceptions. Be aware, however, that the rankings change, sometimes drastically, each year.

EXHIBIT 2-1   *Risk* **Magazine Surveys of Banks, Investment Banks, and Corporate End Users to Determine the Top Three Dealers in Currency and Interest Rate Forwards**

Currencies	Respondents	
	Banks and Investment Banks	Corporate End Users
Currency Forwards		
$/€	UBS Warburg	Citigroup
	Deutsche Bank	Royal Bank of Scotland
	JP Morgan Chase	JP Morgan Chase/Bank of America
$/¥	UBS Warburg	Citigroup
	Citigroup	Bank of America
	JP Morgan Chase	JP Morgan Chase/UBS Warburg

$/£	UBS Warburg	Royal Bank of Scotland
	Royal Bank of Scotland	Citigroup
	Hong Kong Shanghai Banking Corporation	UBS Warburg
$/SF	UBS Warburg	UBS Warburg
	Credit Suisse First Boston	Citigroup
	BNP Paribas	Credit Suisse First Boston

Interest Rate Forwards (FRAs)

$	JP Morgan Chase	JP Morgan Chase
	Bank of America	Royal Bank of Scotland
	Deutsche Bank	Bank of America
€	Deutsche Bank	Royal Bank of Scotland
	Intesa BCI	JP Morgan Chase
	Royal Bank of Scotland	Deutsche Bank
¥	Mizuho Securities	Citigroup
	JP Morgan Chase	Merrill Lynch
	BNP Paribas	Hong Kong Shanghai Banking Corporation
£	Royal Bank of Scotland	Royal Bank of Scotland
	Commerzbank	Bank of America/ING Barings
	Deutsche Bank	
SF	Credit Suisse First Boston	UBS Warburg
	UBS Warburg	Credit Suisse First Boston
	Deutsche Bank	Citigroup/ING Barings

Note: $ = US dollar, € = euro, ¥ = Japanese yen, £ = U.K. pound sterling, SF = Swiss franc.

Source: Risk, September 2002, pp. 30–67 for banks and investment banking dealer respondents, and June 2002, pp. 24–34 for end user respondents. The end user survey provides responses from corporations and asset managers. The above results are for corporate respondents only.

3   TYPES OF FORWARD CONTRACTS

In this section, we examine the types of forward contracts that fall within the scope of this book. By the word "types," we mean the underlying asset groups on which these forward contracts are created. Because the CFA Program focuses on the asset management industry, our primary interest is in equity, interest rate and fixed-income, and currency forwards.

3.1 EQUITY FORWARDS

An **equity forward** is a contract calling for the purchase of an individual stock, a stock portfolio, or a stock index at a later date. For the most part, the differences in types of equity forward contracts are only slight, depending on whether the contract is on an individual stock, a portfolio of stocks, or a stock index.

3.1.1 FORWARD CONTRACTS ON INDIVIDUAL STOCKS

Consider an asset manager responsible for the portfolio of a high-net-worth individual. As is sometimes the case, such portfolios may be concentrated in a small number of stocks, sometimes stocks that have been in the family for years. In many cases, the individual may be part of the founding family of a particular company. Let us say that the stock is called Gregorian Industries, Inc., or GII, and the client is so heavily invested in this stock that her portfolio is not diversified. The client notifies the portfolio manager of her need for $2 million in cash in six months. This cash can be raised by selling 16,000 shares at the current price of $125 per share. Thus, the risk exposure concerns the market value of $2 million of stock. For whatever reason, it is considered best not to sell the stock any earlier than necessary. The portfolio manager realizes that a forward contract to sell GII in six months will accomplish the client's desired objective. The manager contacts a forward contract dealer and obtains a quote of $128.13 as the price at which a forward contract to sell the stock in six months could be constructed.[5] In other words, the portfolio manager could enter into a contract to sell the stock to the dealer in six months at $128.13. We assume that this contract is deliverable, meaning that when the sale is actually made, the shares will be delivered to the dealer. Assuming that the client has some flexibility in the amount of money needed, let us say that the contract is signed for the sale of 15,600 shares at $128.13, which will raise $1,998,828. Of course when the contract expires, the stock could be selling for any price. The client can gain or lose on the transaction. If the stock rises to a price above $128.13 during the six-month period, the client will still have to deliver the stock for $128.13. But if the price falls, the client will still get $128.13 per share for the stock.

3.1.2 FORWARD CONTRACTS ON STOCK PORTFOLIOS

Because modern portfolio theory and good common sense dictate that investors should hold diversified portfolios, it is reasonable to assume that forward contracts on specific stock portfolios would be useful. Suppose a pension fund manager knows that in three months he will need to sell about $20 million of stock to make payments to retirees. The manager has analyzed the portfolio and determined the precise identities of the stocks he wants to sell and the number of shares of each that he would like to sell. Thus the manager has designated a specific subportfolio to be sold. The problem is that the prices of these stocks in three months are uncertain. The manager can, however, lock in the sale prices by entering into a forward contract to sell the portfolio. This can be done one of two ways.

The manager can enter into a forward contract on each stock that he wants to sell. Alternatively, he can enter into a forward contract on the overall portfolio. The first way would be more costly, as each contract would incur administrative costs, whereas the second way would incur only one set of costs.[6] Assume that the manager chooses the second method. He provides a list of the stocks and number of shares of each he wishes to sell to the dealer and obtains a quote. The dealer gives him a quote of $20,200,000. So, in three months, the manager will sell the stock to the dealer and receive $20,200,000. The transaction can be structured to call for either actual delivery or cash settlement, but in either case, the client will effectively receive $20,200,000 for the stock.[7]

---

[5] In Section 4, we shall learn how to calculate forward prices such as this one.

[6] Ignoring those costs, there would be no difference in doing forward contracts on individual stocks or a single forward contract on a portfolio. Because of the non-linearity of their payoffs, this is not true for options. A portfolio of options is not the same as an option on a portfolio, but a portfolio of forward contracts is the same as a forward contract on a portfolio, ignoring the aforementioned costs.

[7] If, for example, the stock is worth $20,500,000 and the transaction calls for delivery, the manager will transfer the stocks to the dealer and receive $20,200,000. The client effectively takes an opportunity loss of $300,000. If the transaction is structured as a cash settlement, the client will pay the dealer $300,000. The client would then sell the stock in the market, receiving $20,500,000 and netting $20,200,000 after settling the forward contract with the dealer. Similarly, if the stock is selling for less than the amount guaranteed by the forward contract, the client will deliver the stock and receive $20,200,000 or, if the transaction is cash settled, the client will sell the stock in the market and receive a cash payment from the dealer, making the effective sale price still $20,200,000.

3.1.3 FORWARD CONTRACTS ON STOCK INDICES

Many equity forward contracts are based on a stock index. For example, consider a U.K. asset manager who wants to protect the value of her portfolio that is a Financial Times Stock Exchange 100 index fund, or who wants to eliminate a risk for which the FTSE 100 Index is a sufficiently accurate representation of the risk she wishes to eliminate. For example, the manager may be anticipating the sale of a number of U.K. blue chip shares at a future date. The manager could, as in our stock portfolio example, take a specific portfolio of stocks to a forward contract dealer and obtain a forward contract on that portfolio. She realizes, however, that a forward contract on a widely accepted benchmark would result in a better price quote, because the dealer can more easily hedge the risk with other transactions. Moreover, the manager is not even sure which stocks she will still be holding at the later date. She simply knows that she will sell a certain amount of stock at a later date and believes that the FTSE 100 is representative of the stock that she will sell. The manager is concerned with the systematic risk associated with the U.K. stock market, and accordingly, she decides that selling a forward contract on the FTSE 100 would be a good way to manage the risk.

Assume that the portfolio manager decides to protect £15,000,000 of stock. The dealer quotes a price of £6,000 on a forward contract covering £15,000,000. We assume that the contract will be cash settled because such index contracts are nearly always done that way. When the contract expiration date arrives, let us say that the index is at £5,925—a decrease of 1.25 percent from the forward price. Because the manager is short the contract and its price went down, the transaction makes money. But how much did it make on a notional principal of £15,000,000?

The index declined by 1.25 percent. Thus, the transaction should make $0.0125 \times$ £15,000,000 = £187,500. In other words, the dealer would have to pay £187,500 in cash. If the portfolio were a FTSE 100 index fund, then it would be viewed as a portfolio initially worth £15,000,000 that declined by 1.25 percent, a loss of £187,500. The forward contract offsets this loss. Of course, in reality, the portfolio is not an index fund and such a hedge is not perfect, but as noted above, there are sometimes reasons for preferring that the forward contract be based on an index.

3.1.4 THE EFFECT OF DIVIDENDS

It is important to note the effect of dividends in equity forward contracts. Any equity portfolio nearly always has at least a few stocks that pay dividends, and it is inconceivable that any well-known equity index would not have some component stocks that pay dividends. Equity forward contracts typically have payoffs based only on the price of the equity, value of the portfolio, or level of the index. They do not ordinarily pay off any dividends paid by the component stocks. An exception, however, is that some equity forwards on stock indices are based on total return indices. For example, there are two versions of the well-known S&P 500 Index. One represents only the market value of the stocks. The other, called the S&P 500 Total Return Index, is structured so that daily dividends paid by the stocks are reinvested in additional units of the index, as though it were a portfolio. In this manner, the rate of return on the index, and the payoff of any forward contract based on it, reflects the payment and reinvestment of dividends into the underlying index. Although this feature might appear attractive, it is not necessarily of much importance in risk management problems. The variability of prices is so much greater than the variability of dividends that managing price risk is considered much more important than worrying about the uncertainty of dividends.

In summary, equity forwards can be based on individual stocks, specific stock portfolios, or stock indices. Moreover, these underlying equities often pay dividends, which can affect forward contracts on equities. Let us now look at bond and interest rate forward contracts.

3.2 BOND AND INTEREST RATE FORWARD CONTRACTS

Forward contracts on bonds are similar to forward contracts on interest rates, but the two are different instruments. Forward contracts on bonds, in fact, are no more difficult to understand than those on equities. Drawing on our experience of Section 3.1, we simply extend the notion of a forward contract on an individual stock, a specific stock portfolio, or a stock index to that of a forward contract on an individual bond, a specific bond portfolio, or a bond index.[8]

3.2.1 FORWARD CONTRACTS ON INDIVIDUAL BONDS AND BOND PORTFOLIOS

Although a forward contract on a bond and one on a stock are similar, some basic differences nonetheless exist between the two. For example, the bond may pay a coupon, which corresponds somewhat to the dividend that a stock might pay. But unlike a stock, a bond matures, and a forward contract on a bond must expire prior to the bond's maturity date. In addition, bonds often have many special features such as calls and convertibility. Finally, we should note that unlike a stock, a bond carries the risk of default. A forward contract written on a bond must contain a provision to recognize how default is defined, what it means for the bond to default, and how default would affect the parties to the contract.

In addition to forward contracts on individual bonds, there are also forward contracts on portfolios of bonds as well as on bond indices. The technical distinctions between forward contracts on individual bonds and collections of bonds, however, are relatively minor.

The primary bonds for which we shall consider forward contracts are default-free zero-coupon bonds, typically called Treasury bills or T-bills in the United States, which serve as a proxy for the risk-free rate.[9] In a forward contract on a T-bill, one party agrees to buy the T-bill at a later date, prior to the bill's maturity, at a price agreed on today. T-bills are typically sold at a discount from par value and the price is quoted in terms of the discount rate. Thus, if a 180-day T-bill is selling at a discount of 4 percent, its price per $1 par will be $1 - 0.04(180/360) = \$0.98$. The use of 360 days is the convention in calculating the discount. So the bill will sell for $0.98. If purchased and held to maturity, it will pay off $1. This procedure means that the interest is deducted from the face value in advance, which is called **discount interest**.

The T-bill is usually traded by quoting the discount rate, not the price. It is understood that the discount rate can be easily converted to the price by the above procedure. A forward contract might be constructed that would call for delivery of a 90-day T-bill in 60 days. Such a contract might sell for $0.9895, which would imply a discount rate of 4.2 percent because $1 - 0.042(90/360) = \$0.9895$. Later in this chapter, we shall see how forward prices of T-bills are derived.

In addition to forward contracts on zero-coupon bonds/T-bills, we shall consider forward contracts on default-free coupon-bearing bonds, also called Treasury bonds in the United States. These instruments pay interest, typically in semiannual installments, and can sell for more (less) than par value if the yield is lower (higher) than the coupon rate. Prices are typically quoted without the interest that has accrued since the last coupon date, but with a few exceptions, we shall always work with the full price—that is, the price including accrued interest. Prices are often quoted by stating the yield. Forward contracts

---

[8] It may be useful to review Chapters 1 and 3 of *Fixed Income Analysis for the Chartered Financial Analyst Program* by Frank J. Fabozzi, New Hope, PA: Frank J. Fabozzi Associates (2000).

[9] A government-issued zero-coupon bond is typically used as a proxy for a risk-free asset because it is assumed to be free of default risk. It can be purchased and held to maturity, thereby eliminating any market value risk, and it has no reinvestment risk because it has no coupons. If the bond is liquidated before maturity, however, some market value risk exists in addition to the risk associated with reinvesting the market price.

call for delivery of such a bond at a date prior to the bond's maturity, for which the short pays the long the agreed-upon price.

3.2.2   FORWARD CONTRACTS ON INTEREST RATES: FORWARD RATE AGREEMENTS

So far in Section 3.2 we have discussed forward contracts on actual fixed-income securities. Fixed-income security prices are driven by interest rates. A more common type of forward contract is the interest rate forward contract, more commonly called a **forward rate agreement** or **FRA**. Before we can begin to understand FRAs, however, we must examine the instruments on which they are based.

There is a large global market for time deposits in various currencies issued by large creditworthy banks. This market is primarily centered in London but also exists elsewhere, though not in the United States. The primary time deposit instrument is called the **Eurodollar**, which is a dollar deposited outside the Unites States. Banks borrow dollars from other banks by issuing Eurodollar time deposits, which are essentially short-term unsecured loans. In London, the rate on such dollar loans is called the London Interbank Rate. Although there are rates for both borrowing and lending, in the financial markets the lending rate, called the **London Interbank Offer Rate** or **LIBOR**, is more commonly used in derivative contracts. LIBOR is the rate at which London banks lend dollars to other London banks. Even though it represents a loan outside of the United States, LIBOR is considered to be the best representative rate on a dollar borrowed by a private, i.e., nongovernmental, high-quality borrower. It should be noted, however, that the London market includes many branches of banks from outside the United Kingdom, and these banks are also active participants in the Eurodollar market.

A Eurodollar time deposit is structured as follows. Let us say a London bank such as NatWest needs to borrow $10 million for 30 days. It obtains a quote from the Royal Bank of Scotland for a rate of 5.25 percent. Thus, 30-day LIBOR is 5.25 percent. If NatWest takes the deal, it will owe $10,000,000 \times [1 + 0.0525(30/360)] = $10,043,750 in 30 days. Note that, like the Treasury bill market, the convention in the Eurodollar market is to prorate the quoted interest rate over 360 days. In contrast to the Treasury bill market, the interest is not deducted from the principal. Rather, it is added on to the face value, a procedure appropriately called **add-on interest**. The market for Eurodollar time deposits is quite large, and the rates on these instruments are assembled by a central organization and quoted in financial newspapers. The British Bankers Association publishes a semi-official Eurodollar rate, compiled from an average of the quotes of London banks.

The U.S. dollar is not the only instrument for which such time deposits exist. Eurosterling, for example, trades in Tokyo, and Euroyen trades in London. You may be wondering about Euroeuro. Actually, there is no such entity as Euroeuro, at least not by that name. The Eurodollar instrument described here has nothing to do with the European currency known as the euro. Eurodollars, Euroyen, Eurosterling, etc. have been around longer than the euro currency and, despite the confusion, have retained their nomenclature. An analogous instrument does exist, however—a euro-denominated loan in which one bank borrows euros from another. Trading in euros and euro deposits occurs in most major world cities, and two similar rates on such euro deposits are commonly quoted. One, called EuroLIBOR, is compiled in London by the British Bankers Association, and the other, called Euribor, is compiled in Frankfurt and published by the European Central Bank. Euribor is more widely used and is the rate we shall refer to in this book.

Now let us return to the world of FRAs. FRAs are contracts in which the underlying is neither a bond nor a Eurodollar or Euribor deposit but simply an interest payment made in dollars, Euribor, or any other currency at a rate appropriate for that currency. Our primary focus will be on dollar LIBOR and Euribor, so we shall henceforth adopt the terminology LIBOR to represent dollar LIBOR and Euribor to represent the euro deposit rate.

Because the mechanics of FRAs are the same for all currencies, for illustrative purposes we shall use LIBOR. Consider an FRA expiring in 90 days for which the underlying is 180-day LIBOR. Suppose the dealer quotes this instrument at a rate of 5.5 percent. Suppose the end user goes long and the dealer goes short. The end user is essentially long the rate and will benefit if rates increase. The dealer is essentially short the rate and will benefit if rates decrease. The contract covers a given notional principal, which we shall assume is $10 million.

The contract stipulates that at expiration, the parties identify the rate on new 180-day LIBOR time deposits. This rate is called 180-day LIBOR. It is, thus, the underlying rate on which the contract is based. Suppose that at expiration in 90 days, the rate on 180-day LIBOR is 6 percent. That 6 percent interest will be paid 180 days later. Therefore, the present value of a Eurodollar time deposit at that point in time would be

$$\frac{\$10,000,000}{1 + 0.06\left(\dfrac{180}{360}\right)}$$

At expiration, then, the end user, the party going long the FRA in our example, receives the following payment from the dealer, which is the party going short:

$$\$10,000,000 \left[\frac{(0.06 - 0.055)\left(\dfrac{180}{360}\right)}{1 + 0.06\left(\dfrac{180}{360}\right)} \right] = \$24,272$$

If the underlying rate is less than 5.5 percent, the payment is calculated based on the difference between the 5.5 percent rate and the underlying rate and is paid by the long to the short. It is important to note that even though the contract expires in 90 days, the rate is on a 180-day LIBOR instrument; therefore, the rate calculation adjusts by the factor 180/360. The fact that 90 days have elapsed at expiration is not relevant to the calculation of the payoff.

Before presenting the general formula, let us review the calculations in the numerator and denominator. In the numerator, we see that the contract is obviously paying the difference between the actual rate that exists in the market on the contract expiration date and the agreed-upon rate, adjusted for the fact that the rate applies to a 180-day instrument, multiplied by the notional principal. The divisor appears because when Eurodollar rates are quoted in the market, they are based on the assumption that the rate applies to an instrument that accrues interest at that rate with the interest paid a certain number of days (here 180) later. When participants determine this rate in the London Eurodollar market, it is understood to apply to a Eurodollar time deposit that begins now and matures 180 days later. So the interest on an actual Eurodollar deposit would not be paid until 180 days later. Thus, it is necessary to adjust the FRA payoff to reflect the fact that the rate implies a payment that would occur 180 days later on a standard Eurodollar deposit. This adjustment is easily done by simply discounting the payment at the current LIBOR, which here is 6 percent, prorated over 180 days. These conventions are also followed in the market for FRAs with other underlying rates.

In general, the FRA payoff formula (from the perspective of the party going long) is

$$\text{Notional principal} \left[\frac{(\text{Underlying rate at expiration} - \text{Forward contract rate})\left(\dfrac{\text{Days in underlying rate}}{360}\right)}{1 + \text{Underlying rate at expiration}\left(\dfrac{\text{Days in underlying rate}}{360}\right)} \right]$$

where *forward contract rate* represents the rate the two parties agree will be paid and *days in underlying rate* refers to the number of days to maturity of the instrument on which the underlying rate is based.

One somewhat confusing feature of FRAs is the fact that they mature in a certain number of days and are based on a rate that applies to an instrument maturing in a certain number of days measured from the maturity of the FRA. Thus, there are two day figures associated with each contract. Our example was a 90-day contract on 180-day LIBOR. To avoid confusion, the FRA markets use a special type of terminology that converts the number of days to months. Specifically, our example FRA is referred to as a 3 × 9, reflecting the fact that the contract expires in three months and that six months later, or nine months from the contract initiation date, the interest is paid on the underlying Eurodollar time deposit on whose rate the contract is based.[10]

FRAs are available in the market for a variety of maturities that are considered somewhat standard. Exhibit 2-2 presents the most common maturities. Most dealers follow the convention that contracts should expire in a given number of exact months and should be on the most commonly traded Eurodollar rates such as 30-day LIBOR, 60-day LIBOR, 90-day LIBOR, 180-day LIBOR, and so on. If a party wants a contract expiring in 37 days on 122-day LIBOR, it would be considered an exception to the standard, but most dealers would be willing to make a market in such an instrument. Such nonstandard instruments are called *off the run*. Of course, FRAs are available in all of the leading currencies.

EXHIBIT 2-2   FRA Descriptive Notation and Interpretation

Notation	Contract Expires in	Underlying Rate
1 × 3	1 month	60-day LIBOR
1 × 4	1 month	90-day LIBOR
1 × 7	1 month	180-day LIBOR
3 × 6	3 months	90-day LIBOR
3 × 9	3 months	180-day LIBOR
6 × 12	6 months	180-day LIBOR
12 × 18	12 months	180-day LIBOR

Note: This list is not exhaustive and represents only the most commonly traded FRAs.

The FRA market is large, but not as large as the swaps market. It is important, however, to understand FRAs before trying to understand swaps. As we will show in Chapter 5, a swap is a special combination of FRAs. But let us now turn to another large forward market, the market for currency forwards.

3.3   CURRENCY FORWARD CONTRACTS

Spurred by the relaxation of government controls over the exchange rates of most major currencies in the early 1970s, a currency forward market developed and grew extremely large. Currency forwards are widely used by banks and corporations to manage foreign exchange risk. For example, suppose Microsoft has a European subsidiary that expects to send it €12 million in three months. When Microsoft receives the euros, it will then con-

---

[10] The notation "3 × 9" is pronounced "three by nine."

vert them to dollars. Thus, Microsoft is essentially long euros because it will have to sell euros, or equivalently, it is short dollars because it will have to buy dollars. A currency forward contract is especially useful in this situation, because it enables Microsoft to lock in the rate at which it will sell euros and buy dollars in three months. It can do this by going short the forward contract, meaning that it goes short the euro and long the dollar. This arrangement serves to offset its otherwise long-euro, short-dollar position. In other words, it needs a forward contract to sell euros and buy dollars.

For example, say Microsoft goes to JP Morgan Chase and asks for a quote on a currency forward for €12 million in three months. JP Morgan Chase quotes a rate of $0.925, which would enable Microsoft to sell euros and buy dollars at a rate of $0.925 in three months. Under this contract, Microsoft would know it could convert its €12 million to 12,000,000 × $0.925 = $11,100,000. The contract would also stipulate whether it will settle in cash or will call for Microsoft to actually deliver the euros to the dealer and be paid $11,100,000. This simplified example is a currency forward hedge, a transaction we explore more thoroughly in Chapter 6.

Now let us say that three months later, the spot rate for euros is $0.920. Microsoft is quite pleased that it locked in a rate of $0.925. It simply delivers the euros and receives $11,100,000 at an exchange rate of $0.925.[11] Had rates risen, however, Microsoft would still have had to deliver the euros and accept a rate of $0.925.

A few variations of currency forward contracts exist, but most of them are somewhat specialized and beyond the objectives of this book. Let us now take a very brief look at a few other types of forward contracts.

3.4 Other Types of Forward Contracts

Although this book focuses primarily on the financial derivatives used by asset managers, we should mention here some of the other types. Commodity forwards—in which the underlying asset is oil, a precious metal, or some other commodity—are widely used. In addition, the derivatives industry has created forward contracts and other derivatives on various sources of energy (electricity, gas, etc.) and even weather, in which the underlying is a measure of the temperature or the amount of disaster damage from hurricanes, earthquakes, or tornados.

Many of these instruments are particularly difficult to understand, price, and trade. Nonetheless, through the use of derivatives and indirect investments, such as hedge funds, they can be useful for managing risk and investing in general. They are not, however, the focus of this book.

In the examples and illustrations used above, we have made reference to certain prices. Determining appropriate prices and fair values of financial instruments is a central objective of much of the process of asset management. Accordingly, pricing and valuation occupies a major portion of the CFA Program. As such, we turn our attention to the pricing and valuation of forward contracts.

4 PRICING AND VALUATION OF FORWARD CONTRACTS

Before getting into the actual mechanics of pricing and valuation, the astute reader might wonder whether we are being a bit redundant. Are pricing and valuation not the same thing?

---

[11] Had the contract been structured to settle in cash, the dealer would have paid Microsoft 12,000,000 × ($0.925 − $0.920) = $60,000. Microsoft would have converted the euros to dollars at the current spot exchange rate of $0.920, receiving 12,000,000 × $0.920 = $11,040,000. Adding the $60,000 payment from the dealer, Microsoft would have received $11,100,000, an effective rate of $0.925.

An equity analyst often finds that a stock is priced at more or less than its fair market value and uses this conclusion as the basis for a buy or sell recommendation.[12] In an efficient market, the price of a stock would always equal its value or the price would quickly converge to the value. Thus, for all practical purposes, pricing and valuation would be the same thing. In general, when we speak of the value and price of an *asset*, we are referring to what that asset is worth and what it sells for. With respect to certain *derivatives*, however, value and price take on slightly different meanings.

So let us begin by defining value: *Value is what you can sell something for or what you must pay to acquire something.* This applies to stocks, bonds, derivatives, and used cars.[13] Accordingly, *valuation is the process of determining the value of an asset or service.* Pricing is a related but different concept; let us explore what we mean by pricing a forward contract.

A forward contract price is the fixed price or rate at which the transaction scheduled to occur at expiration will take place. This price is agreed to on the contract initiation date and is commonly called the **forward price** or **forward rate**. Pricing means to determine the forward price or forward rate. Valuation, however, means to determine the amount of money that one would need to pay or would expect to receive to engage in the transaction. Alternatively, if one already held a position, valuation would mean to determine the amount of money one would either have to pay or expect to receive in order to get out of the position. Let us look at a generic example.

4.1 GENERIC PRICING AND VALUATION OF A FORWARD CONTRACT

Because derivative contracts have finite lives, it is important to carefully specify the time frame in which we are operating. We denote time in the following manner: Today is identified as time 0. The expiration date is time T. Time t is an arbitrary time between today and the expiration. Usually when we refer to "today," we are referring to the date on which the contract is created. Later we shall move forward to time t and time T, which will then be "today."

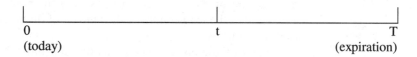

$$
\begin{array}{lll}
0 & t & T \\
\text{(today)} & & \text{(expiration)}
\end{array}
$$

The price of the underlying asset in the spot market is denoted as S_0 at time 0, S_t at time t, and S_T at time T. The forward contract price, established when the contract is initiated at time 0, is $F(0,T)$. This notation indicates that $F(0,T)$ is the price of a forward contract initiated at time 0 and expiring at time T. The value of the forward contract is $V_0(0,T)$. This notation indicates that $V_0(0,T)$ is the value at time 0 of a forward contract initiated at time 0 and expiring at time T. In this book, subscripts always indicate that we are at a specific point in time.

We have several objectives in this analysis. First, we want to determine the forward price $F(0,T)$. We also want to determine the forward contract value today, denoted $V_0(0,T)$, the value at a point during the life of the contract such as time t, denoted $V_t(0,T)$, and the value at expiration, denoted $V_T(0,T)$. Valuation is somewhat easier to grasp from the perspective of the party holding the long position, so we shall take that point of view in this example. Once that value is determined, the value to the short is obtained by simply changing the sign.

---

[12] From your study of equity analysis, you should recall that we often use the discounted cash flow model, sometimes combined with the capital asset pricing model, to determine the fair market value of a stock.

[13] Be careful. You may think the "value" of a certain used car is $5,000, but if no one will give you that price, it can hardly be called the value.

If we are at expiration, we would observe the spot price as S_T. The long holds a position to buy the asset at the already agreed-upon price of $F(0,T)$. Thus, the value of the forward contract at expiration should be obvious: $S_T - F(0,T)$. If the value at expiration does not equal this amount, then an arbitrage profit can be easily made. For example, suppose the forward price established at the initiation of the contract, $F(0,T)$, is $20. Now at expiration, the spot price, S_T, is $23. The contract value must be $3. If it were more than $3, then the long would be able to sell the contract to someone for more than $3—someone would be paying the long more than $3 to obtain the obligation of buying a $23 asset for $20. Obviously, no one would do that. If the value were less than $3, the long would have to be willing to sell for less than $3 the obligation of buying a $23 asset for $20. Obviously, the long would not do that. Thus, we state that the value at expiration of a forward contract established at time 0 is

$$V_T(0,T) = S_T - F(0,T) \tag{2-1}$$

Note that the value of a forward contract can also be interpreted as its profit, the difference between what the long pays for the underlying asset, $F(0,T)$, and what the long receives, the asset price S_T. Of course, we have still not explained how $F(0,T)$ is determined, but the above equation gives the value of the contract at expiration, at which time $F(0,T)$ would certainly be known because it was agreed on at the initiation date of the contract.

Now let us back up to the time when the contract was originated. Consider a contract that expires in one year. Suppose that the underlying asset is worth $100 and that the forward price is $108. We do not know if $108 is the correct forward price; we will simply try it and see.

Suppose we buy the asset for $100 and sell the forward contract for $108. We hold the position until expiration. We assume that there are no direct costs associated with buying or holding the asset, but we must recognize that we lose interest on the $100 tied up in the asset. Assume that the interest rate is 5 percent.

Recall that no money changes hands at the start with a forward contract. Consequently, the $100 invested in the asset is the full outlay. At the end of the year, the forward contract expires and we deliver the asset, receiving $108 for it—not bad at all. At a 5 percent interest rate, we lose only $5 in interest on the $100 tied up in the asset. We receive $108 for the asset regardless of its price at expiration. We can view $108 − $105 = $3 as a risk-free profit, which more than covered the cost. In fact, if we had also borrowed the $100 at 5 percent, we could have done this transaction without putting up any money of our own. We would have more than covered the interest on the borrowed funds and netted a $3 risk-free profit. This profit is essentially free money—there is no cost and no risk. Thus, it is an arbitrage profit, a concept we introduced in Chapter 1 and a dominant theme throughout this book. We would certainly want to execute any transaction that would generate an arbitrage profit.

In the market, the forces of arbitrage would then prevail. Other market participants would execute this transaction as well. Although it is possible that the spot price would bear some of the adjustment, in this book we shall always let the derivative price make the full adjustment. Consequently, the derivative price would have to come down to $105.

If the forward price were below $105, we could also earn an arbitrage profit, although it would be a little more difficult because the asset would have to be sold short. Suppose the forward price is $103. If the asset were a financial asset, we could borrow it and sell it short. We would receive $100 for it and invest that $100 at the 5 percent rate. We would simultaneously buy a forward contract. At expiration, we would take delivery of the asset paying $103 and then deliver it to the party from whom we borrowed it. The short position is now covered, and we still have the $100 invested plus 5 percent interest on it. This transaction offers a clear arbitrage profit of $2. Again, the forces of arbitrage would cause other market participants to undertake the transaction, which would push the forward price up to $105.

If short selling is not permitted, too difficult, or too costly, a market participant who already owns the asset could sell it, invest the $100 at 5 percent, and buy a forward contract. At expiration, he would pay $103 and take delivery on the forward contract, which would return him to his original position of owning the asset. He would now, however, receive not only the stock but also 5 percent interest on $100. Again, the forces of arbitrage would make this transaction attractive to other parties who held the asset, provided they could afford to part with it for the necessary period of time.[14]

Going back to the situation in which the forward contract price was $103, an arbitrage profit could, however, be eliminated if the party going long the forward contract were required to pay some money up front. For example, suppose the party going long the forward contract paid the party going short $1.9048. Then the party going long would lose $1.9048 plus interest on this amount. Notice that $1.9048 compounded at 5 percent interest equals precisely $2, which not surprisingly is the amount of the arbitrage profit.

Thus, if the forward price were $103, the value of the contract would be $1.9048. With $T = 1$, this value equals

$$V_0(0,T) = V_0(0,1) = \$100 - \$103/1.05 = \$1.9048$$

Therefore, to enter into this contract at this forward price, one party must pay another. Because the value is positive, it must be paid by the party going long the forward contract to the party going short. Parties going long must pay positive values; parties going short pay negative values.[15]

If the forward price were $108, the value would be

$$V_0(0,T) = \$100 - \$108/1.05 = -\$2.8571$$

In this case, the value is negative and would have to be paid from the short to the long. Doing so would eliminate the arbitrage profit that the short would have otherwise been able to make, given the forward price of $108.

Arbitrage profits can be eliminated with an up-front payment from long to short or vice versa that is consistent with the forward price the parties select. The parties could simply negotiate a forward price, and any resulting market value could be paid from one party to the other. *It is customary, however, in the forward market for the initial value to be set to zero.* This convention eliminates the necessity of either party making a payment to the other and results in a direct and simple determination of the forward price. Specifically, setting $V_0(0,T) = 0$ and letting r represent the interest rate,

$$V_0(0,T) = S_0 - F(0,T)/(1 + r) = 0$$

which means that $F(0,T) = S_0(1 + r)$. In our example, $F(0,T) = \$100(1.05) = \$105$, which is the forward price that eliminates the arbitrage profit.

---

[14] In other words, a party holding the asset must be willing to part with it for the length of time it would take for the forces of arbitrage to bring the price back in line, thereby allowing the party to capture the risk-free profit and return the party to its original state of holding the asset. The period of time required for the price to adjust should be very short if the market is relatively efficient.

[15] For example, when a stock is purchased, its value, which is always positive, is paid from the long to the short. This is true for any asset.

Our forward price formula can be interpreted as saying that the forward price is the spot price compounded at the risk-free interest rate. In our example, we had an annual interest rate of r and one year to expiration. With today being time 0 and expiration being time T, the time $T - 0 = T$ is the number of years to expiration of the forward contract. Then we more generally write the forward price as

$$F(0,T) = S_0(1 + r)^T \qquad\qquad (2\text{-}2)$$

Again, this result is consistent with the custom that no money changes hands at the start of a forward contract, meaning that the value of a forward contract at its start is zero.

Exhibit 2-3 summarizes the process of pricing a forward contract. At time 0, we buy the asset and sell a forward contract for a total outlay of the spot price of the asset.[16] Over the life of the contract, we hold the asset and forgo interest on the money. At expiration, we deliver the asset and receive the forward price for a payoff of $F(0,T)$. The overall transaction is risk free and equivalent to investing the spot price of the asset in a risk-free bond that pays $F(0,T)$ at time T. Therefore, the payoff at T must be the future value of the spot price invested at the risk-free rate. This equality can be true only if the forward price is the spot price compounded at the risk-free rate over the life of the asset.

EXHIBIT 2-3   Pricing a Forward Contract

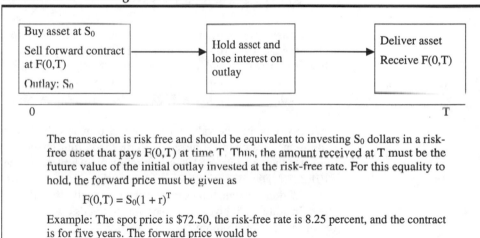

The transaction is risk free and should be equivalent to investing S_0 dollars in a risk-free asset that pays $F(0,T)$ at time T. Thus, the amount received at T must be the future value of the initial outlay invested at the risk-free rate. For this equality to hold, the forward price must be given as

$$F(0,T) = S_0(1 + r)^T$$

Example: The spot price is $72.50, the risk-free rate is 8.25 percent, and the contract is for five years. The forward price would be

$$F(0,T) = F(0,5) = 72.50(1.0825)^5 = 107.76$$

A contract in which the initial value is intentionally set at a nonzero value is called an **off-market FRA**. In such a contract, the forward price is set arbitrarily in the process of negotiation between the two parties. Given the chosen forward price, the contract will have a nonzero value. As noted above, if the value is positive, the long pays that amount up front to the short. If it is negative, the short pays that amount up front to the long. Although off-market FRAs are not common, we shall use them in Chapter 5 when studying swaps.

Now suppose we are at a time t, which is a point during the life of the contract. We may want to know the value of the forward contract for several reasons. For one, it makes good

---

[16] Remember that in a forward contract, neither party pays anything for the forward contract at the start.

business sense to know the monetary value of an obligation to do something at a later date. Also, accounting rules require that a company mark its derivatives to their current market values and report the effects of those values in income statements and balance sheets. In addition, the market value can be used as a gauge of the credit exposure. Finally, the market value can be used to determine how much money one party can pay the other to terminate the contract.

Let us start by assuming that we established a long forward contract at time 0 at the price F(0,T). Of course, its value at time 0 was zero. But now it is time t, and we want to know its new value, $V_t(0,T)$. Let us consider what it means to hold the position of being long at time t a forward contract established at time 0 at the price F(0,T) and expiring at time T:

We will have to pay F(0,T) dollars at T.

We will receive the underlying asset, which will be worth S_T, at T.

At least part of the value will clearly be the present value of a payment of F(0,T), or in other words, $-F(0,T)/(1 + r)^{T-t}$. The other part of the contract value comes from the fact that we have a claim on the asset's value at T. We do not know what S_T (the asset value at T) will be, but we do know that the market tells us its present value is S_t, the current asset price. *By definition, an asset's value today is the present value of its future value.*[17] Thus we can easily value our forward contract at time t during the life of the contract:

$$V_t(0,T) = S_t - F(0,T)/(1 + r)^{(T-t)} \qquad \textbf{(2-3)}$$

Consider our earlier example in which we entered into a one-year forward contract to buy the asset at $105. Now assume it is three months later and the price of the asset is $102. With t = 0.25 and T = 1, the value of the contract would be

$$V_t(0,T) = V_{0.25}(0,1) = \$102 - \$105/(1.05)^{0.75} = \$0.7728$$

Again, why is this the value? The contract provides the long with a claim on the asset at expiration. That claim is currently worth the current asset value of $102. That claim also obligates the long to pay $105 at expiration, which has a present value of $105/(1.05)^{0.75} = $101.2272. Thus, the long position has a value of $102 − $101.2272 = $0.7728.

As noted above, this market value may well affect the income statement and balance sheet. In addition, it gives an idea of the contract's credit exposure, a topic we have touched on and will cover in more detail in Section 5 and in Chapter 9. Finally, we noted earlier that a party could re-enter the market and offset the contract by paying the counterparty or having the counterparty pay him a cash amount. This cash amount is the market value as calculated here.[18]

Exhibit 2-4 summarizes how we value a forward contract. If we went long a forward contract at time 0 and we are now at time t prior to expiration, we hold a claim on the asset at expiration and are obligated to pay the forward price at expiration. The claim on the asset is worth its current price; the obligation to pay the forward price at expiration is worth the negative of its present value. Thus, the value of the forward contract is the current spot price minus the forward price discounted from expiration back to the present.

---

[17] This statement is true for any type of asset or financial instrument. It always holds by definition.

[18] If the market value is positive, the value of the asset exceeds the present value of what the long promises to pay. Thus, it makes sense that the short must pay the long. If the market value is negative, then the present value of what the long promises to pay exceeds the value of the asset. Then, it makes sense that the long must pay the short.

EXHIBIT 2-4   Valuing a Forward Contract

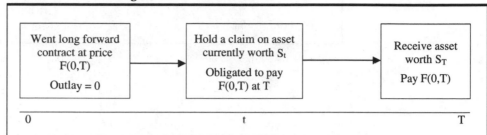

The value of the forward contract at t must be the value of what it will produce at T:

$$V_t(0,T) = S_t - F(0,T)/(1 + r)^{(T-t)}$$

Example: A two-year forward contract was established with a price of $62.25. Now, a year and a half later (t = 1.5), the spot price is $71.19 and the risk-free rate is 7 percent. The value of the forward contract is

$$V_t(0,T) = V_{1.5}(0,2) = 71.19 - 62.25/(1.07)^{0.5} = 11.01$$

Therefore, we have seen that the forward contract value is zero today: the asset price minus the present value of the forward price at a time prior to expiration, and the asset price minus the forward price at expiration. It may be helpful to note that in general, we can always say that *the forward contract value is the asset price minus the present value of the exercise price,* because given $V_t(0,T) = S_t - F(0,T)/(1 + r)^{(T-t)}$:

If t = 0, $V_t(0,T) = V_0(0,T) = S_0 - F(0,T)/(1 + r)^T = 0$
     because $F(0,T) = S_0(1 + r)^T$

If t = T, $V_t(0,T) = V_T(0,T) = S_T - F(0,T)/(1 + r)^0 = S_T - F(0,T)$

The formulas for pricing and valuation of a forward contract are summarized in Exhibit 2-5.

EXHIBIT 2-5   Pricing and Valuation Formulas for a Forward Contract

Today = time 0
Arbitrary point during the contract's life = time t
Expiration = time T

Value of a forward contract at any time t:

$$V_t(0,T) = S_t - F(0,T)/(1 + r)^{(T-t)}$$

Value of a forward contract at expiration (t = T):

$$V_T(0,T) = S_T - F(0,T)$$

Value of a forward contract at initiation (t = 0):

$$V_0(0,T) = S_0 - F(0,T)/(1 + r)^T$$

Customarily, no money changes hands at initiation so $V_0(0,T)$ is set equal to zero. Thus,

$$F(0,T) = S_0(1 + r)^T$$

PRACTICE PROBLEM 1

An investor holds title to an asset worth €125.72. To raise money for an unrelated purpose, the investor plans to sell the asset in nine months. The investor is concerned about uncertainty in the price of the asset at that time. The investor learns about the advantages of using forward contracts to manage this risk and enters into such a contract to sell the asset in nine months. The risk-free interest rate is 5.625 percent.

A. Determine the appropriate price the investor could receive in nine months by means of the forward contract.

B. Suppose the counterparty to the forward contract is willing to engage in such a contract at a forward price of €140. Explain what type of transaction the investor could execute to take advantage of the situation. Calculate the rate of return (annualized), and explain why the transaction is attractive.

C. Suppose the forward contract is entered into at the price you computed in Part A. Two months later, the price of the asset is €118.875. The investor would like to evaluate her position with respect to any gain or loss accrued on the forward contract. Determine the market value of the forward contract at this point in time from the perspective of the investor in Part A.

D. Determine the value of the forward contract at expiration assuming the contract is entered into at the price you computed in Part A and the price of the underlying asset is €123.50 at expiration. Explain how the investor did on the overall position of both the asset and the forward contract in terms of the rate of return.

SOLUTIONS

A. $T = 9/12 = 0.75$
  $S_0 = 125.72$
   $r = 0.05625$

  $$F(0,T) = 125.72(1.05625)^{0.75} = 130.99$$

B. As found in Part A, the forward contract should be selling at €130.99, but it is selling for €140. Consequently, it is overpriced—and an overpriced contract should be sold. Because the investor holds the asset, she will be hedged by selling the forward contract. Consequently, her asset, worth €125.72 when the forward contract is sold, will be delivered in nine months and she will receive €140 for it. The rate of return will be

  $$\left(\frac{140}{125.72}\right) - 1 = 0.1136$$

This risk-free return of 11.36 percent for nine months is clearly in excess of the 5.625 percent annual rate. In fact, a rate of 11.36 percent for nine months annualizes to

$$(1.1136)^{12/9} - 1 = 0.1543$$

An annual risk-free rate of 15.43 percent is clearly preferred over the actual risk-free rate of 5.625 percent. The position is not only hedged but also earns an arbitrage profit.

C. $t = 2/12$
$T - t = 9/12 - 2/12 = 7/12$
$S_t - 118.875$
$F(0,T) = 130.99$

$$V_t(0,T) = V_{2/12}(0,9/12) = 118.875 \quad 130.99/(1.05625)^{7/12} = -8.0$$

The contract has a negative value. Note, however, that in this form, the answer applies to the holder of the long position. This investor is short. Thus, the value to the investor in this problem is positive 8.0.

D. $S_T = 123.50$

$$V_T(0,T) = V_{9/12}(0,9/12) = 123.50 - 130.99 = -7.49$$

This amount is the value to the long. This investor is short, so the value is a positive 7.49. The investor incurred a loss on the asset of $125.72 - 123.50 = 2.22$. Combined with the gain on the forward contract, the net gain is $7.49 - 2.22 = 5.27$. A gain of 5.27 on an asset worth 125.72 when the transaction was initiated represents a return of $5.27/125.72 = 4.19$ percent. When annualized, the rate of return equals

$$(1.0419)^{12/9} - 1 = 0.05625$$

It should come as no surprise that this number is the annual risk-free rate. The transaction was executed at the no-arbitrage forward price of €130.99. Thus, it would be impossible to earn a return higher or lower than the risk-free rate.

In our examples, there were no costs or cash flows associated with holding the underlying assets. In the specific examples below for equity derivatives, fixed-income and interest rate derivatives, and currency derivatives, we present cases in which cash flows on the underlying asset will slightly alter our results. We shall ignore any costs of holding assets. Such costs are primarily associated with commodities, an asset class we do not address in this book.

4.2 PRICING AND VALUATION OF EQUITY FORWARD CONTRACTS

Equity forward contracts are priced and valued much like the generic contract described above, with one important additional feature. Many stocks pay dividends, and the effects of these dividends must be incorporated into the pricing and valuation process. Our concern is with the dividends that occur over the life of the forward contract, but not with those that may come after the contract ends. Following standard procedure, we assume that these dividends are known or are a constant percentage of the stock price.

We begin with the idea of a forward contract on either a single stock, a portfolio of stocks, or an index in which dividends are to be paid during the life of the contract. Using the time notation that today is time 0, expiration is time T, and there is an arbitrary time t during its life when we need to value the contract, assume that dividends can be paid at various times during the life of the contract between t and T.[19]

In the examples that follow, we shall calculate present and future values of this stream of dividends over the life of the forward contract. Given a series of these dividends of D_1, D_2, . . . D_n, whose values are known, that occur at times t_1, t_2, . . . t_n, the present value will be defined as PV(D,0,T) and computed as

$$PV(D,0,T) = \sum_{i=1}^{n} \frac{D_i}{(1 + r)^{t_i}}$$

The future value will be defined as FV(D,0,T) and computed as

$$FV(D,0,T) = \sum_{i=1}^{n} D_i(1 + r)^{T-t_i}$$

Recall that the forward price is established by eliminating any opportunity to arbitrage from establishing a forward contract without making any cash outlay today, as is customary with forward contracts. We found that the forward price is the spot price compounded at the risk-free interest rate. To include dividends, we adjust our formula slightly to

$$F(0,T) = [S_0 - PV(D,0,T)](1 + r)^T \qquad \textbf{(2-4)}$$

In other words, we simply subtract the present value of the dividends from the stock price. Note that the dividends reduce the forward price, a reflection of the fact that holders of long positions in forward contracts do not benefit from dividends in comparison to holders of long positions in the underlying stock.

For example, consider a stock priced at $40, which pays a dividend of $3 in 50 days. The risk-free rate is 6 percent. A forward contract expiring in six months (T = 0.5) would have a price of

$$F(0,T) = F(0,0.5) = [\$40 - \$3/(1.06)^{50/365}](1.06)^{0.5} = \$38.12$$

If the stock had more than one dividend, we would simply subtract the present value of all dividends over the life of the contract from the stock price, as in the following example.

The risk-free rate is 4 percent. The forward contract expires in 300 days and is on a stock currently priced at $35, which pays quarterly dividends according to the following schedule:

Days to Ex-Dividend Date	Dividend
10	$0.45
102	$0.45
193	$0.45
283	$0.45

---

[19] Given the way dividends are typically paid, the right to the dividend leaves the stock on the ex-dividend date, which is prior to the payment date. To precisely incorporate this feature, either the dividend payment date should be the ex-dividend date or the dividend should be the present value at the ex-dividend date of the dividend to be paid at a later date. We shall ignore this point here and assume that it would be taken care of in practice.

The present value of the dividends is found as follows:

$$PV(D,0,T) = \$0.45/(1.04)^{10/365} + \$0.45/(1.04)^{102/365}$$
$$+ \$0.45/(1.04)^{193/365} + \$0.45/(1.04)^{283/365} = \$1.77$$

The time to expiration is $T = 300/365$. Therefore, the forward price equals

$$F(0,T) = F(0,300/365) = (\$35 - \$1.77)(1.04)^{300/365} = \$34.32$$

Another approach to incorporating the dividends is to use the future value of the dividends. With this forward contract expiring in 300 days, the first dividend is reinvested for 290 days, the second for 198 days, the third for 107 days, and the fourth for 17 days. Thus,

$$FV(D,0,T) = \$0.45(1.04)^{290/365} + \$0.45(1.04)^{198/365}$$
$$+ \$0.45(1.04)^{107/365} + \$0.45(1.04)^{17/365} = \$1.83$$

To obtain the forward price, we compound the stock value to expiration and subtract the future value of the dividends. Thus, the forward price would be

$$F(0,T) = S_0(1 + r)^T - FV(D,0,T) \tag{2-5}$$

This formula will give the same answer as the one using the present value of the dividends, as shown below:

$$F(0,300/365) = \$35(1.04)^{300/365} - \$1.83 = \$34.32$$

An alternative way to incorporate dividends is to express them as a fixed percentage of the stock price. The more common version of this formulation is to assume that the stock, portfolio, or index pays dividends continuously at a rate of δ^c. By specifying the dividends in this manner, we are allowing the dividends to be uncertain and completely determined by the stock price at the time the dividends are being paid. In this case, the stock is constantly paying a dividend at the rate δ^c. In Chapter 3, we will again discuss how to incorporate dividends.

Because we pay dividends continuously, for consistency we must also compound the interest continuously. The continuously compounded equivalent of the discrete risk-free rate r will be denoted r^c and is found as $r^c = \ln(1 + r)$.[20] The future value of \$1 at time T is $\exp(r^c T)$. Then the forward price is given as

$$F(0,T) = (S_0 e^{-\delta^c T})e^{r^c T} \tag{2-6}$$

The term in parentheses, the stock price discounted at the dividend yield rate, is equivalent to the stock price minus the present value of the dividends. This value is then compounded at the risk-free rate over the life of the contract, just as we have done in the other versions.

---

[20] The notation "ln" stands for natural logarithm. A logarithm is the power to which its base must be raised to equal a given number. The base of the natural logarithm system is e, approximately 2.71828. With an interest rate of $r = 0.06$, we would have $r^c = \ln(1.06) = 0.058$. Then $e^{0.058} = 1.06$ is called the exponential function and often written as $\exp(0.058) = 1.06$. The future value factor is thus $\exp(r^c)$. The present value factor is $1/\exp(r^c)$ or $\exp(-r^c)$. If the period is more or less than one year, we also multiply the rate by the number of years or fraction of a year—that is, $\exp(-r^c T)$ or $\exp(r^c T)$.

Some people attach significance to whether the forward price is higher than the spot price. It is important to note that the forward price should not be interpreted as a forecast of the future price of the underlying. This misperception is common. If the forward price is higher than the spot price, it merely indicates that the effect of the risk-free rate is greater than the effect of the dividends. In fact, such is usually the case with equity forwards. Interest rates are usually greater than dividend yields.

As an example, consider a forward contract on France's CAC 40 Index. The index is at 5475, the continuously compounded dividend yield is 1.5 percent, and the continuously compounded risk-free interest rate is 4.625 percent. The contract life is two years. With T = 2, the contract price is, therefore,

$$F(0,T) = F(0,2) = (5475 \times e^{-0.015(2)})e^{0.04625(2)} = 5828.11$$

This specification involving a continuous dividend yield is commonly used when the underlying is a portfolio or stock index. If a single stock in the portfolio pays a dividend, then the portfolio or index can be viewed as paying a dividend. Given the diversity of dividend policies and ex-dividend dates, such an assumption is usually considered a reasonable approximation for stock portfolios or stock indices, but the assumption is not as appropriate for individual stocks. No general agreement exists on the most appropriate approach, and you must become comfortable with all of them. To obtain the appropriate forward price, the most important point to remember is that one way or another, the analysis must incorporate the dividend component of the stock price, portfolio value, or index level. If the contract is not trading at the correct price, then it is mispriced and arbitrage, as described in the generic forward contract pricing section, will force an alignment between the market forward price and the theoretical forward price.

Recall that the value of a forward contract is the asset price minus the forward price discounted back from the expiration date. Regardless of how the dividend is specified or even whether the underlying stock, portfolio, or index pays dividends, the valuation formulas for a forward contract on a stock differ only in that the stock price is adjusted by removing the present value of the remaining dividends:

$$V_t(0,T) = S_t - PV(D,t,T) - F(0,T)/(1 + r)^{(T-t)} \qquad (2\text{-}7)$$

where we now note that the dividends are only those paid after time t. If we are using continuous compounding,

$$V_t(0,T) = S_t e^{-\delta^c(T-1)} - F(0,T)e^{-r^c(T-t)} \qquad (2\text{-}8)$$

At the contract initiation date, t = 0 and $V_0(0,T)$ is set to zero because no cash changes hands. At expiration, t = T and no dividends remain, so the valuation formula reduces to $S_T - F(0,T)$.

The formulas for pricing and valuation of equity forward contracts are summarized in Exhibit 2-6.

EXHIBIT 2-6   Pricing and Valuation Formulas for Equity Forward Contracts

Forward price = (Stock price − Present value of dividends over life of contract) × $(1 + r)^T$

or (Stock price) × $(1 + r)^T$ minus Future value of dividends over life of contract

Discrete dividends over the life of the contract:

$$F(0,T) = [S_0 - PV(D,0,T)](1 + r)^T \text{ or } S_0(1 + r)^T - FV(D,0,T)$$

Continuous dividends at the rate δ^c:

$$F(0,T) = (S_0 e^{-\delta^c T}) e^{r^c T}$$

Value of forward contract:

$$V_t(0,T) = S_t - PV(D,t,T) - F(0,T)/(1 + r)^{(T-t)}$$

or

$$V_t(0,T) = S_t e^{-\delta^c(T-t)} - F(0,T) e^{-r^c(T-t)}$$

PRACTICE PROBLEM 2

An asset manager anticipates the receipt of funds in 200 days, which he will use to purchase a particular stock. The stock he has in mind is currently selling for $62.50 and will pay a $0.75 dividend in 50 days and another $0.75 dividend in 140 days. The risk-free rate is 4.2 percent. The manager decides to commit to a future purchase of the stock by going long a forward contract on the stock.

A. At what price would the manager commit to purchase the stock in 200 days through a forward contract?

B. Suppose the manager enters into the contract at the price you found in Part A. Now, 75 days later, the stock price is $55.75. Determine the value of the forward contract at this point.

C. It is now the expiration day, and the stock price is $58.50. Determine the value of the forward contract at this time.

SOLUTIONS

$S_0 = \$62.50$
$T = 200/365$
$D_1 = \$0.75, t_1 = 50/365$
$D_2 = \$0.75, t_2 = 140/365$
$r = 0.042$

A. First find the present value of the dividends:

$$\$0.75/(1.042)^{50/365} + \$0.75/(1.042)^{140/365} = \$1.48$$

Then find the forward price:

$$F(0,T) = F(0,200/365) = (\$62.50 - \$1.48)(1.042)^{200/365} = \$62.41$$

B. We must now find the present value of the dividends 75 days after the contract begins. The first dividend has already been paid, so it is not relevant. Because only one remains, the second dividend is now the "first" dividend. It will be paid in

65 days. Thus, $t_1 - t = 65/365$. The present value of this dividend is $\$0.75/(1.042)^{65/365} = \$0.74$. The other information is

$$t = 75/365$$
$$T - t = (200 - 75)/365 = 125/365$$
$$S_t = \$55.75$$

The value of the contract is, therefore,

$$V_t(0,T) = V_{75/365}(0,200/365) = (\$55.75 - \$0.74) - \$62.41/(1.042)^{125/365}$$
$$= -\$6.53$$

Thus, the contract has a negative value.

C. $S_T = \$58.50$

The value of the contract is

$$V_{200/365}(0,200/365) = V_T(0,T) = \$58.50 - \$62.41 = -\$3.91$$

Thus, the contract expires with a value of negative $\$3.91$.

4.3 PRICING AND VALUATION OF FIXED-INCOME AND INTEREST RATE FORWARD CONTRACTS

Forward contracts on fixed-income securities are priced and valued in a virtually identical manner to their equity counterparts. We can use the above formulas if S_t represents the bond price at time t and D_i represents a coupon paid at time t_i. We denote B^c as a coupon bond and then use notation to draw attention to those coupons that must be included in the forward contract pricing calculations. We will let $B_t^c(T + Y)$ represent the bond price at time t, T is the expiration date of the forward contract, Y is the remaining maturity of the bond on the forward contract expiration, and $(T + Y)$ is the time to maturity of the bond at the time the forward contract is initiated. Consider a bond with n coupons to occur before its maturity date. Converting our formula for a forward contract on a stock into that for a forward contract on a bond and letting CI be the coupon interest over a specified period of time, we have a forward price of

$$F(0,T) = [B_0^c(T + Y) - PV(CI,0,T)](1 + r)^T \tag{2-9}$$

where $PV(CI,0,T)$ is the present value of the coupon interest over the life of the forward contract. Alternatively, the forward price can be obtained as

$$F(0,T) = [B_0^c(T + Y)](1 + r)^T - FV(CI,0,T) \tag{2-10}$$

where $FV(CI,0,T)$ is the future value of the coupon interest over the life of the forward contract.

The value of the forward contract at time t would be

$$V_t(0,T) = B_t^c(T + Y) - PV(CI,t,T) - F(0,T)/(1 + r)^{(T-t)} \tag{2-11}$$

at time t; note that the relevant coupons are only those remaining as of time t until expiration of the forward contract. As in the case for stock, this formula will reduce to the appropriate values at time 0 and at expiration. For example, at expiration, no coupons would remain, t = T, and $V_T(0,T) = B_T^c(T + Y) - F(0,T)$. At time t = 0, the contract is being initiated and has a zero value, which leads to the formula for F(0,T) above.

Consider a bond with semiannual coupons. The bond has a current maturity of 583 days and pays four coupons, each six months apart. The next coupon occurs in 37 days, followed by coupons in 219 days, 401 days, and 583 days, at which time the principal is repaid. Suppose that the bond price, which includes accrued interest, is \$984.45 for a \$1,000 par, 4 percent coupon bond. The coupon rate implies that each coupon is \$20. The risk-free interest rate is 5.75 percent. Assume that the forward contract expires in 310 days. Thus, T = 310, T + Y = 583, and Y = 273, meaning that the bond has 273 days remaining after the forward contract expires. Note that only the first two coupons occur during the life of the forward contract.

The present value of the coupons is

$$\$20/(1.0575)^{37/365} + \$20/(1.0575)^{219/365} = \$39.23$$

The forward price if the contract is initiated now is

$$F(0,T) = (\$984.45 - \$39.23)(1.0575)^{310/365} = \$991.18$$

Thus, we assume that we shall be able to enter into this contract to buy the bond in 310 days at the price of \$991.18.

Now assume it is 15 days later and the new bond price is \$973.14. Let the risk-free interest rate now be 6.75 percent. The present value of the remaining coupons is

$$\$20/(1.0675)^{22/365} + \$20/(1.0675)^{204/365} = \$39.20$$

The value of the forward contract is thus

$$\$973.14 - \$39.20 - \$991.19/(1.0675)^{295/365} = -\$6.28$$

The contract has gone from a zero value at the start to a negative value, primarily as a result of the decrease in the price of the underlying bond.

If the bond is a zero-coupon bond/T-bill, we can perform the same analysis as above, but we simply let the coupons equal zero.

Exhibit 2-7 summarizes the formulas for the pricing and valuation of forward contracts on fixed-income securities.

EXHIBIT 2-7   Pricing and Valuation Formulas for Fixed Income Forward Contracts

Forward price = (Bond price − Present value of coupons over life of contract)$(1 + r)^T$ or
(Bond price)$(1 + r)^T$ − Future value of coupons over life of contract

Price of forward contract on bond with coupons CI:

$$F(0,T) = [B_0^c(T + Y) - PV(CI,0,T)](1 + r)^T$$

$$\text{or } [B_0^c(T + Y)](1 + r)^T - FV(CI,0,T)$$

Value of forward contract on bond with coupons CI:

$$V_t(0,T) = B_t^c(T + Y) - PV(CI,t,T) - F(0,T)/(1 + r)^{(T-t)}$$

PRACTICE PROBLEM 3

An investor purchased a bond when it was originally issued with a maturity of five years. The bond pays semiannual coupons of $50. It is now 150 days into the life of the bond. The investor wants to sell the bond the day after its fourth coupon. The first coupon occurs 181 days after issue, the second 365 days, the third 547 days, and the fourth 730 days. At this point (150 days into the life of the bond), the price is $1,010.25. The bond prices quoted here include accrued interest.

A. At what price could the owner enter into a forward contract to sell the bond on the day after its fourth coupon? Note that the owner would receive that fourth coupon. The risk-free rate is currently 8 percent.

B. Now move forward 365 days. The new risk-free interest rate is 7 percent and the new price of the bond is $1,025.375. The counterparty to the forward contract believes that it has received a gain on the position. Determine the value of the forward contract and the gain or loss to the counterparty at this time. Note that we have now introduced a new risk-free rate, because interest rates can obviously change over the life of the bond and any calculations of the forward contract value must reflect this fact. The new risk-free rate is used instead of the old rate in the valuation formula.

SOLUTIONS

A. First we must find the present value of the four coupons over the life of the forward contract. At the 150th day of the life of the bond, the coupons occur 31 days from now, 215 days from now, 397 days from now, and 580 days from now. Keep in mind that we need consider only the first four coupons because the owner will sell the bond on the day after the fourth coupon. The present value of the coupons is

$$\$50/(1.08)^{31/365} + \$50/(1.08)^{215/365} + \$50/(1.08)^{397/365} + \$50/(1.08)^{580/365} = \$187.69$$

Because we want the forward contract to expire one day after the fourth coupon, it expires in $731 - 150 = 581$ days. Thus, $T = 581/365$.

$$F(0,T) = F(0,581/365) = (\$1,010.25 - \$187.69)(1.08)^{581/365} = \$929.76$$

B. It is now 365 days later—the 515th day of the bond's life. There are two coupons to go, one occurring in $547 - 515 = 32$ days and the other in $730 - 515 = 215$ days. The present value of the coupons is now

$$\$50/(1.07)^{32/365} + \$50/(1.07)^{215/365} = \$97.75$$

To address the value of the forward contract and the gain or loss to the counterparty, note that $731 - 515 = 216$ days now remain until the contract's expiration. Because the bondholder would sell the forward contract to hedge the future sale price of the bond, the bondholder's counterparty to the forward contract would hold a long position. The value of the forward contract is the current spot price minus the present value of the coupons minus the present value of the forward price:

$$\$1,025.375 - \$97.75 - \$929.76/(1.07)^{216/365} = \$34.36$$

Because the contract was initiated with a zero value at the start and the counterparty is long the contract, the value of $34.36 represents a gain to the counterparty.

Now let us look at the pricing and valuation of FRAs. Previously we used the notations t and T to represent the time to a given date. The expressions t or T were, respectively, the number of days to time point t or T, each divided by 365. In the FRA market, contracts are created with specific day counts. We will use the letter h to refer to the day on which the FRA expires and the letter g to refer to an arbitrary day prior to expiration. Consider the time line shown below. We shall initiate an FRA on day 0. The FRA expires on day h. The rate underlying the FRA is the rate on an m-day Eurodollar deposit. Thus, there are h days from today until the FRA expiration and h + m days until the maturity date of the Eurodollar instrument on which the FRA rate is based. The date indicated by g will simply be a date during the life of the FRA at which we want to determine a value for the FRA.

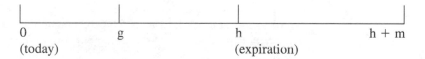

0 (today) g h (expiration) h + m

Now let us specify some notation. We let $L_i(j)$ represent the rate on a j-day LIBOR deposit on an arbitrary day i, which falls somewhere in the above period from 0 to h, inclusive. Remember that this instrument is a j-day loan from one bank to another. For example, the bank borrowing \$1 on day i for j days will pay back the amount

$$\$1\left[1 + L_i(j)\left(\frac{j}{360}\right)\right]$$

in j days.

The rate for m-day LIBOR on day h, $L_h(m)$, will determine the payoff of the FRA. We denote the fixed rate on the FRA as FRA(0,h,m), which stands for the rate on an FRA established on day 0, expiring on day h, and based on m-day LIBOR. We shall use a \$1 notional principal for the FRA, which means that at expiration its payoff is

$$\frac{[L_h(m) - FRA(0,h,m)]\left(\frac{m}{360}\right)}{1 + L_h(m)\left(\frac{m}{360}\right)} \tag{2-12}$$

The numerator is the difference between the underlying LIBOR on the expiration day and the rate agreed on when the contract was initiated, multiplied by the adjustment factor m/360. Both of these rates are annual rates applied to a Eurodollar deposit of m days; hence, multiplying by m/360 is necessary. The denominator discounts the payoff by the m-day LIBOR in effect at the time of the payoff. As noted earlier, this adjustment is necessary because the rates in the numerator apply to Eurodollar deposits created on day h and paying off m days later. If the notional principal is anything other than \$1, we also must multiply the above payoff by the notional principal to determine the actual payoff.

To derive the formula for pricing an FRA, a specific arbitrage transaction involving Eurodollars and FRAs is required. We omit the details of this somewhat complex transaction, but the end result is that the FRA rate is given by the following formula:

$$FRA(0,h,m) = \left[\frac{1 + L_0(h+m)\left(\frac{h+m}{360}\right)}{1 + L_0(h)\left(\frac{h}{360}\right)} - 1\right]\left(\frac{360}{m}\right) \tag{2-13}$$

This somewhat awkward-looking formula is actually just the formula for a LIBOR forward rate, given the interest payment conventions in the FRA market. The numerator is the future value of a Eurodollar deposit of h + m days. The denominator is the future value of a shorter-term Eurodollar deposit of h days. This ratio is 1 plus a rate; subtracting 1 and multiplying by 360/m annualizes the rate.[21]

Consider a 3 × 9 FRA. This instrument expires in 90 days and is based on 180-day LIBOR. Thus, the Eurodollar deposit on which the underlying rate is based begins in 90 days and matures in 270 days. Because we are on day 0, h = 90, m = 180, and h + m = 270. Let the current rates be

$$L_0(h) = L_0(90) = 0.056$$

$$L_0(h + m) = L_0(270) = 0.06$$

In other words, the 90-day rate is 5.6 percent, and the 270-day rate is 6 percent.

With h = 90 and m = 180, using our formula for the FRA rate, we obtain

$$FRA(0,h,m) = FRA(0,90,180) = \left[\frac{1 + 0.06\left(\frac{270}{360}\right)}{1 + 0.056\left(\frac{90}{360}\right)} - 1 \right] \left(\frac{360}{180}\right) = 0.0611$$

So to enter into an FRA on day 0, the rate would be 6.11 percent.[22]

As noted, the initial outlay for entering the forward contract is zero. Thus, the initial value is zero. Later during the life of the contract, its value will rise above or fall below zero. Now let us determine the value of an FRA during its life. Specifically, we use the notation $V_g(0,h,m)$ to represent the value of an FRA on day g, prior to expiration, which was established on day 0, expires on day h, and is based on m-day LIBOR. Omitting the derivation, the value of the FRA will be

$$V_g(0,h,m) = \frac{1}{1 + L_g(h - g)\left(\frac{h - g}{360}\right)} - \frac{1 + FRA(0,h,m)\left(\frac{m}{360}\right)}{1 + L_g(h + m - g)\left(\frac{h + m - g}{360}\right)} \quad \textbf{(2-14)}$$

This formula looks complicated, but the ideas behind it are actually quite simple. Recall that we are at day g. The first term on the right-hand side is the present value of $1 received at day h. The second term is the present value of 1 plus the FRA rate to be received on day h + m, the maturity date of the underlying Eurodollar time deposit.

Assume that we go long the FRA, and it is 25 days later. We need to assign a value to the FRA. First note that g = 25, h − g = 90 − 25 = 65, and h + m − g = 90 + 180 − 25 = 245. In other words, we are 25 days into the contract, 65 days remain until expiration, and 245 days remain until the maturity of the Eurodollar deposit on which the underlying LIBOR is based. First we need information about the new term structure. Let

$$L_g(h - g) = L_{25}(65) = 0.059$$

$$L_g(h + m - g) = L_{25}(245) = 0.065$$

---

[21] To compare with the traditional method of calculating a forward rate, consider a two-year rate of 10 percent and a one-year rate of 9 percent. The forward rate is $[(1.10)^2/(1.09)] - 1 = 0.1101$. The numerator is the future value of the longer-term bond, and the denominator is the future value of the shorter-term bond. The ratio is 1 plus the rate. We do not need to annualize in this example, because the forward rate is on a one-year bond.

[22] It is worthwhile to point out again that this rate is the forward rate in the LIBOR term structure.

We now use the formula for the value of the FRA to obtain

$$V_g(0,h,m) = V_{25}(0,90,180) = \frac{1}{1 + 0.059\left(\frac{65}{360}\right)} - \frac{1 + 0.0611\left(\frac{180}{360}\right)}{1 + 0.065\left(\frac{245}{360}\right)} = 0.0026$$

Thus, we went long this FRA on day 0. Then 25 days later, the term structure changes to the rates used here and the FRA has a value of $0.0026 per $1 notional principal. If the notional principal is any amount other than $1, we multiply the notional principal by $0.0026 to obtain the full market value of the FRA.

We summarize the FRA formulas in Exhibit 2-8. We have now looked at the pricing and valuation of equity, fixed-income, and interest rate forward contracts. One of the most widely used types of forward contracts is the currency forward. The pricing and valuation of currency forwards is remarkably similar to that of equity forwards.

EXHIBIT 2-8   Pricing and Valuation Formulas for Interest Rate Forward Contracts (FRAs)

Forward price (rate):

$$FRA(0,h,m) = \left[\frac{1 + L_0(h + m)\left(\frac{h + m}{360}\right)}{1 + L_0(h)\left(\frac{h}{360}\right)} - 1\right]\left(\frac{360}{m}\right)$$

Value of FRA on day g:

$$V_g(0,h,m) = \frac{1}{1 + L_g(h - g)\left(\frac{h - g}{360}\right)} - \frac{1 + FRA(0,h,m)\left(\frac{m}{360}\right)}{1 + L_g(h + m - g)\left(\frac{h + m - g}{360}\right)}$$

PRACTICE PROBLEM 4

A corporate treasurer needs to hedge the risk of the interest rate on a future transaction. The risk is associated with the rate on 180-day Euribor in 30 days. The relevant term structure of Euribor is given as follows:

30-day Euribor	5.75%
210-day Euribor	6.15%

A. State the terminology used to identify the FRA in which the manager is interested.

B. Determine the rate that the company would get on an FRA expiring in 30 days on 180-day Euribor.

C. Suppose the manager went long this FRA. Now, 20 days later, interest rates have moved significantly downward to the following:

10-day Euribor	5.45%
190-day Euribor	5.95%

The manager would like to know where the company stands on this FRA transaction. Determine the market value of the FRA for a €20 million notional principal.

D. On the expiration day, 180-day Euribor is 5.72 percent. Determine the payment made to or by the company to settle the FRA contract.

SOLUTIONS

A. This transaction would be identified as a 1×7 FRA.

B. Here the notation would be h = 30, m = 180, h + m = 210. Then

$$\text{FRA}(0,h,m) = \text{FRA}(0,30,180) = \left[\frac{1 + 0.0615\left(\frac{210}{360}\right)}{1 + 0.0575\left(\frac{30}{360}\right)} - 1 \right]\left(\frac{360}{180}\right) = 0.0619$$

C. Here g = 20, h − g = 30 − 20 = 10, h + m − g = 30 + 180 − 20 = 190. The value of the FRA for a €1 notional principal would be

$$V_g(0,h,m) = V_{20}(0,30,180) = \frac{1}{1 + 0.0545\left(\frac{10}{360}\right)} - \frac{1 + 0.0619\left(\frac{180}{360}\right)}{1 + 0.0595\left(\frac{190}{360}\right)} = -0.0011$$

Thus, for a notional principal of €20 million, the value would be €20,000,000(−0.0011) = −€22,000.

D. At expiration, the payoff is

$$\frac{[L_h(m) - \text{FRA}(0,h,m)]\left(\frac{m}{360}\right)}{1 + L_h(m)\left(\frac{m}{360}\right)} = \frac{(0.0572 - 0.0619)\left(\frac{180}{360}\right)}{1 + 0.0572\left(\frac{180}{360}\right)} = -0.0023$$

For a notional principal of €20 million, the payoff would then be €20,000,000(−0.0023) = −€46,000. Thus, €46,000 would be paid by the company, because it is long and the final rate was lower than the FRA rate.

4.4 PRICING AND VALUATION OF CURRENCY FORWARD CONTRACTS

Foreign currency derivative transactions as well as spot transactions must be handled with care. The exchange rate can be quoted in terms of units of the domestic currency per unit of foreign currency, or units of the foreign currency per unit of the domestic currency. In this book, we shall always quote exchange rates in terms of units of the domestic currency per unit of the foreign currency, which is also called a direct quote. This approach is in keeping with the way in which other underlying assets are quoted. For example, from the perspective of a U.S. investor, a stock that sells for $50 is quoted in units of the domestic currency per unit (share) of stock. Likewise, if the euro exchange rate is quoted as $0.90, then the euro sells for $0.90 per unit, which is one euro. Alternatively, we could quote that $1 sells for 1/$0.90 = €1.1111—that is, €1.1111 per $1; in this case, units of foreign currency per one unit of domestic currency from the perspective of a U.S. investor. In fact, this type of quote is commonly used and is called an indirect quote. Taking that approach, however, we would quote the stock price as 1/$50 = 0.02 shares per $1, a very unusual and awkward way to quote a stock price.

By taking the approach of quoting prices in terms of units of the domestic currency per unit of foreign currency, we facilitate a comparison of currencies and their derivatives with equities and their derivatives—a topic we have already covered. For example, we have previously discussed the case of a stock selling for S_0, which represents units of the domestic currency per share of stock. Likewise, we shall treat the currency as having an exchange rate of S_0, meaning that it is selling for S_0. We also need the foreign interest rate, denoted as r^f, and the domestic interest rate, denoted as r.[23]

Consider the following transactions executed today (time 0), assuming a contract expiration date of T:

Take $S_0/(1 + r^f)^T$ units of the domestic currency and convert it to $1/(1 + r^f)^T$ units of the foreign currency.[24]

Sell a forward contract to deliver one unit of the foreign currency at the rate F(0,T) expiring at time T.

Hold the position until time T. The $(1 + r^f)^T$ units of foreign currency will accrue interest at the rate r^f and grow to one unit of the currency at T as follows:

$$\left(\frac{1}{1 + r^f}\right)^T (1 + r^f)^T = 1$$

Thus, at expiration we shall have one unit of the foreign currency, which is then delivered to the holder of the long forward contract, who pays the amount F(0,T). This amount was known at the start of the transaction. Because the risk has been hedged away, the exchange rate at expiration is irrelevant. Hence, this transaction is risk-free. Accordingly, the present value of F(0,T), found by discounting at the domestic risk-free interest rate, must equal the initial outlay of $S_0/(1 + r^f)^T$. Setting these amounts equal and solving for F(0,T) gives

$$F(0,T) = \left[\frac{S_0}{(1 + r^f)^T}\right](1 + r)^T \qquad (2\text{-}15)$$

The term in brackets is the spot exchange rate discounted by the foreign interest rate. This term is then compounded at the domestic interest rate to the expiration day.[25]

Recall that in pricing equity forwards, we always reduced the stock price by the present value of the dividends and then compounded the resulting value to the expiration date. We can view currencies in the same way. The stock makes cash payments that happen to

---

[23] We do not use a superscript "d" for the domestic rate, because in all previous examples we have used r to denote the interest rate in the home country of the investor.

[24] In other words, if one unit of the foreign currency costs S_0, then $S_0/(1 + r^f)^T$ units of the domestic currency would, therefore, buy $1/(1 + r^f)^T$ units of the foreign currency.

[25] It is also common to see the above Equation 2-15 written inversely, with the spot rate divided by the domestic interest factor and compounded by the foreign interest factor. This variation would be appropriate if the spot and forward rates were quoted in terms of units of the foreign currency per unit of domestic currency (indirect quotes). As we mentioned earlier, however, it is easier to think of a currency as just another asset, which naturally should have its price quoted in units of the domestic currency per unit of the asset or foreign currency.

be called dividends; the currency makes cash payments that happen to be called interest. Although the time pattern of how a stock pays dividends is quite different from the time pattern of how interest accrues, the general idea is the same. After reducing the spot price or rate by any cash flows over the life of the contract, the resulting value is then compounded at the risk-free rate to the expiration day.

The formula we have obtained here is simply a variation of the formula used for other types of forward contracts. In international financial markets, however, this formula has acquired its own name: **interest rate parity** (sometimes called covered interest rate parity). It expresses the equivalence, or parity, of spot and forward exchange rates, after adjusting for differences in the interest rates in the two countries. One implication of interest rate parity is that the forward rate will exceed (be less than) the spot rate if the domestic interest rate exceeds (is less than) the foreign interest rate. With a direct quote, if the forward rate exceeds (is less than) the spot rate, the foreign currency is said to be selling at a premium (discount). One should not, on the basis of this information, conclude that a currency selling at a premium is expected to increase or one selling at a discount is expected to decrease. A forward premium or discount is merely an implication of the relationship between interest rates in the two countries. More information would be required to make any assumptions about the outlook for the exchange rate.

If the forward rate in the market does not equal the forward rate given by interest rate parity, then an arbitrage transaction can be executed. Indeed, a similar relationship is true for any of the forward rates we have studied. In the foreign exchange markets, however, this arbitrage transaction has its own name: **covered interest arbitrage**. If the forward rate in the market is higher than the rate given by interest rate parity, then the forward rate is too high. When the price of an asset or derivative is too high, it should be sold. Thus, a trader would 1) sell the forward contract at the market rate, 2) buy $1/(1 + r^f)^T$ units of the foreign currency, 3) hold the position, earning interest on the currency, and 4) at maturity of the forward contract deliver the currency and be paid the forward rate. This arbitrage transaction would earn a return in excess of the domestic risk-free rate without any risk. If the forward rate is less than the rate given by the formula, the trader does the opposite, selling the foreign currency and buying a forward contract, in a similar manner. The combined actions of many traders undertaking this transaction will bring the forward price in the market in line with the forward price given by the model.

In Equation 2-15, both interest rates were annual rates with discrete compounding. In dealing with equities, we sometimes assume that the dividend payments are made continuously. Similarly, we could also assume that interest is compounded continuously. If that is the case, let r^{fc} be the continuously compounded foreign interest rate, defined as $r^{fc} = \ln(1 + r^f)$, and as before, let r^c be the continuously compounded domestic interest rate. Then the forward price is given by the same formula, with appropriately adjusted symbols, as we obtained when working with equity derivatives:

$$F(0,T) = (S_0 e^{-r^{fc}T}) e^{r^c T} \qquad\qquad\qquad\qquad (2\text{-}16)$$

Now consider how we might value a foreign currency forward contract at some point in time during its life. In fact, we already know how: We simply apply to foreign currency forward contracts what we know about the valuation of equity forwards during the contract's life. Recall that the value of an equity forward is the stock price minus the present value of the dividends over the remaining life of the contract minus the present value of the forward price over the remaining life of the contract. An analogous formula for a currency forward gives us

$$V_t(0,T) = \frac{S_t}{(1 + r^f)^{(T-t)}} - \frac{F(0,T)}{(1 + r)^{(T-t)}} \qquad\qquad\qquad (2\text{-}17)$$

In other words, we take the current exchange rate at time t, S_t, discount it by the foreign interest rate over the remaining life of the contract, and subtract the forward price discounted by the domestic interest rate over the remaining life of the contract. Under the assumption that we are using continuous compounding and discounting, the formula would be

$$V_t(0,T) = (S_t e^{-r^{fc}(T-t)}) - F(0,T)e^{-r^c(T-t)} \qquad \text{(2-18)}$$

For example, suppose the domestic currency is the U.S. dollar and the foreign currency is the Swiss franc. Let the spot exchange rate be \$0.5987, the U.S. interest rate be 5.5 percent, and the Swiss interest rate be 4.75 percent. We assume these interest rates are fixed and will not change over the life of the forward contract. We also assume that these rates are based on annual compounding and are not quoted as LIBOR-type rates. Thus, we compound using formulas like $(1 + r)^T$, where T is the number of years and r is the annual rate.[26]

Assuming the forward contract has a maturity of 180 days, we have T = 180/365. Using the above formula for the forward rate, we find that the forward price should be

$$F(0,T) = F(0,180/365) = \left[\frac{\$0.5987}{(1.0475)^{180/365}}\right](1.055)^{180/365} = \$0.6008$$

Thus, if we entered into a forward contract, it would call for us to purchase (if long) or sell (if short) one Swiss franc in 180 days at a price of \$0.6008.

Suppose we go long this forward contract. It is now 40 days later, or 140 days until expiration. The spot rate is now \$0.65. As assumed above, the interest rates are fixed. With t = 40/365 and T − t = 140/365, the value of our long position is

$$V_t(0,T) = V_{40/365}(0,180/365) = \frac{\$0.6500}{(1.0475)^{140/365}} - \frac{\$0.6008}{(1.055)^{140/365}} = \$0.0499$$

So the contract value is \$0.0499 per Swiss franc. If the notional principal were more than one Swiss franc, we would simply multiply the notional principal by \$0.0499.

If we were working with continuously compounded rates, we would have $r^c = \ln(1.055) = 0.0535$ and $r^{fc} = \ln(1.0475) = 0.0464$. Then the forward price would be $F(0,T) = F(0,180/365) = (0.5987e^{-0.0464(180/365)})e^{0.0535(180/365)} = 0.6008$, and the value 40 days later would be $V_{40/365}(0,180/365) = 0.65e^{-0.0464(140/365)} - 0.6008e^{-0.0535(140/365)} = 0.0499$. These are the same results we obtained working with discrete rates.

Exhibit 2-9 summarizes the formulas for pricing and valuation of currency forward contracts.

EXHIBIT 2-9   Pricing and Valuation Formulas for Currency Forward Contracts

Forward price (rate) = (Spot price discounted by foreign interest rate) compounded at domestic interest rate:

Discrete interest: $F(0,T) = \left[\dfrac{S_0}{(1 + r^f)^T}\right](1 + r)^T$

Continuous interest: $F(0,T) = (S_0 e^{-r^{fc}T})e^{r^c T}$

---

[26]If these were LIBOR-style rates, the interest would be calculated using the factor 1 + [Rate(Days/360)].

Value of forward contract:

$$\text{Discrete interest: } V_t(0,T) = \left[\frac{S_t}{(1 + r^f)^{(T-t)}}\right] - \frac{F(0,T)}{(1 + r)^{(T-t)}}$$

$$\text{Continuous interest: } V_t(0,T) = [S_t e^{-r^{fc}(T-t)}] - F(0,T)e^{-r^c(T-t)}$$

Note: The exchange rate is quoted in units of domestic currency per unit of foreign currency.

PRACTICE PROBLEM 5

The spot rate for British pounds is $1.76. The U.S. risk-free rate is 5.1 percent, and the U.K. risk-free rate is 6.2 percent; both are compounded annually. One-year forward contracts are currently quoted at a rate of $1.75.

A. Identify a strategy with which a trader can earn a profit at no risk by engaging in a forward contract, regardless of her view of the pound's likely movements. Carefully describe the transactions the trader would make. Show the rate of return that would be earned from this transaction. Assume the trader's domestic currency is U.S. dollars.

B. Suppose the trader simply shorts the forward contract. It is now one month later. Assume interest rates are the same, but the spot rate is now $1.72. What is the gain or loss to the counterparty on the trade?

C. At expiration, the pound is at $1.69. What is the value of the forward contract to the short at expiration?

SOLUTIONS

A. The following information is given:

$$S_0 = \$1.76$$
$$r = 0.051$$
$$r^f = 0.062$$
$$T = 1.0$$

The forward price should be

$$F(0,T) = \left(\frac{\$1.76}{1.062}\right)(1.051) = \$1.7418$$

With the forward contract selling at $1.75, it is slightly overpriced. Thus, the trader should be able to buy the currency and sell a forward contract to earn a return in excess of the risk-free rate at no risk. The specific transactions are as follows:

• Take $1.76/(1.062) = $1.6573. Use it to buy 1/1.062 = £0.9416.
• Sell a forward contract to deliver £1.00 in one year at the price of $1.75.
• Hold the position for one year, collecting interest at the U.K. risk-free rate of 6.2 percent. The £0.9416 will grow to (0.9416)(1.062) = £1.00.
• At expiration, deliver the pound and receive $1.75. This is a return of

$$\frac{1.75}{1.6573} - 1 = 0.0559$$

A risk-free return of 5.59 percent is better than the U.S. risk-free rate of 5.1 percent, a result of the fact that the forward contract is overpriced.

B. We now need the value of the forward contract to the counterparty, who went long at $1.75. The inputs are

$$t = 1/12$$
$$S_t = \$1.72$$
$$T - t = 11/12$$
$$F(0,T) = \$1.75$$

The value of the forward contract to the long is

$$V_t(0,T) = \frac{1.72}{(1.062)^{11/12}} - \frac{1.75}{(1.051)^{11/12}} - -0.0443$$

which is a loss of $0.0443 to the long and a gain of $0.0443 to the short.

C. The pound is worth $1.69 at expiration. Thus, the value to the long is

$$V_T(0,T) = 1.69 - 1.75 = -0.06$$

and the value to the short is +$0.06. Note the minus sign in the equation $V_T(0,T) = -0.06$. The value to the long is always the spot value at expiration minus the original forward price. The short will be required to deliver the foreign currency and receive $1.75, which is $0.06 more than market value of the pound. The contract's value to the short is thus $0.06, which is the negative of its value to the long.

We have now seen how to determine the price and value of equity, fixed-income and interest rate, and currency forward contracts. We observed that the price is determined such that no arbitrage opportunities exist for either the long or the short. We have found that the value of a forward contract is the amount we would pay or receive to enter or exit the contract. Because no money changes hands up front, the value of a forward contract when initiated is zero. The value at expiration is determined by the difference between the spot price or rate at expiration and the forward contract price or rate. The value prior to expiration can also be determined and is the present value of the claim at expiration.

Determining the value of a forward contract is important for several reasons. One, however, is particularly important: Forward contracts contain the very real possibility that one of the parties might default. By knowing the market value, one can determine the amount of money at risk if a counterparty defaults. Let us now look at how credit risk enters into a forward contract.

5 CREDIT RISK AND FORWARD CONTRACTS

To illustrate how credit risk affects a forward contract, consider the currency forward contract example we just finished in the previous section. It concerns a contract that expires in 180 days in which the long will pay a forward rate of $0.6008 for each Swiss franc to be received at expiration. Assume that the contract covers 10 million Swiss francs. Let us look at the problem from the point of view of the holder of the long position and the credit risk faced by this party.

Assume it is the contract expiration day and the spot rate for Swiss francs is $0.62. The long is due to receive 10 million Swiss francs and pay $0.6008 per Swiss franc, or

$6,008,000 in total. Now suppose that perhaps because of bankruptcy or insolvency, the short cannot come up with the $6,200,000 that it would take to purchase the Swiss francs on the open market at the prevailing spot rate.[27] In order to obtain the Swiss francs, the long would have to buy them in the open market. Doing so would incur an additional cost of $6,200,000 − $6,008,000 = $192,000, which can be viewed as the credit risk at the point of expiration when the spot rate is $0.62. Not surprisingly, this amount is also the market value of the contract at this point.

This risk is an immediate risk faced at expiration. Prior to expiration, the long faces a potential risk that the short will default. If the long wanted to gauge the potential exposure, he would calculate the current market value. In the example we used in which the long is now 40 days into the life of the contract, the market value to the long is $0.0499 per Swiss franc. Hence, the long's exposure would be 10,000,000($0.0499) = $499,000. Although no payments are due at this point, $499,000 is the market value of the claim on the payment at expiration. Using an estimate of the probability that the short would default, the long can gauge the expected credit loss from the transaction by multiplying that probability by $499,000.

The market value of a forward contract reflects the current value of the claim at expiration, given existing market conditions. If the Swiss franc rises significantly, the market value will increase along with it, thereby exposing the long to the potential for even greater losses. Many participants in derivatives markets estimate this potential loss by running simulations that attempt to reflect the potential market value of the contract along with the probability of the counterparty defaulting.

We have viewed credit risk from the viewpoint of the long, but what about the short's perspective? In the case in which we went to expiration and the short owed the long the greater amount, the short faces no credit risk. In the case prior to expiration in which the contract's market value was positive, the value of the future claim was greater to the long than to the short. Hence, the short still did not face any credit risk.

The short would face credit risk, however, if circumstances were such that the value of the transaction were negative to the long, which would make the value to the short positive. In that case, the scenario discussed previously in this section would apply from the short's perspective.

In Chapter 9, we shall discuss methods of managing the credit risk of various types of derivatives transactions. At this point, however, it will be helpful to specifically examine one particular method. Let us go back to the long currency forward contract that had a market value of $499,000. As it stands at this time, the holder of the long position has a claim on the holder of the short position that is worth $499,000. Suppose the two parties had agreed when they entered into the transaction that in 40 days, the party owing the greater amount to the other would pay the amount owed and the contract would be repriced at the new forward rate. Now on the 40th day, the short would pay the long $499,000. Recalling that the U.S. interest rate was 5.5 percent and the Swiss interest rate was 4.75 percent, the contract, which now has 140 days to go (T = 140/365), would then be repriced to the rate

$$F(0,T) = F(0,140/365) = \left[\frac{\$0.65}{(1.0475)^{140/365}} \right] (1.055)^{140/365} = \$0.6518$$

---

[27]Even if the short already holds the Swiss franc, she might be declaring bankruptcy or otherwise unable to pay debts such that the forward contract claim is combined with the claims of all of the short's other creditors.

In other words, from this point, the contract has a new rate of $0.6518. The long now agrees to pay $0.6518 for the currency from the short in 140 days.

What the two parties have done is called **marking to market**. They have settled up the amount owed and marked the contract to its current market rate. If the parties agree in advance, a forward contract can be marked to market at whatever dates the parties feel are appropriate. Marking to market keeps one party from becoming too deeply indebted to the other without paying up. At the dates when the contract is marked to market, the parties restructure the contract so that it remains in force but with an updated price.

Forward contracts and swaps are sometimes marked to market to mitigate credit risk. In Chapter 3, we shall examine futures contracts. A distinguishing characteristic of futures contracts is that they are marked to market every day. In essence, they are forward contracts that are marked to market and repriced daily to reduce the credit risk.

6   THE ROLE OF FORWARD MARKETS

In this chapter we have discussed many aspects of forward contracts and forward markets. We will conclude the chapter (and each of the following chapters, which cover futures, options, and swaps) with a brief discussion of the role that these markets play in our financial system. Although forward, futures, options, and swap markets serve similar purposes in our society, each market is unique. Otherwise, these markets would consolidate.

Forward markets may well be the least understood of the various derivative markets. In contrast to their cousins, futures contracts, forward contracts are a far less visible segment of the financial markets. Both forwards and futures serve a similar purpose: They provide a means in which a party can commit to the future purchase or sale of an asset at an agreed-upon price, without the necessity of paying any cash until the asset is actually purchased or sold. In contrast to futures contracts, forward contracts are private transactions, permitting the ultimate in customization. As long as a counterparty can be found, a party can structure the contract completely to its liking. Futures contracts are standardized and may not have the exact terms required by the party. In addition, futures contracts, with their daily marking to market, produce interim cash flows that can lead to imperfections in a hedge transaction designed not to hedge interim events but to hedge a specific event at a target horizon date. Forward markets also provide secrecy and have only a light degree of regulation. In general, forward markets serve a specialized clientele, specifically large corporations and institutions with specific target dates, underlying assets, and risks that they wish to take or reduce by committing to a transaction without paying cash at the start.

As Chapter 5 will make clear, however, forward contracts are just miniature versions of swaps. A swap can be viewed as a series of forward contracts. Swaps are much more widely used than forward contracts, suggesting that parties that have specific risk management needs typically require the equivalent of a series of forward contracts. A swap contract consolidates a series of forward contracts into a single instrument at lower cost.

Forward contracts are the building blocks for constructing and understanding both swaps and futures. Swaps and futures are more widely used and better known, but forward contracts play a valuable role in helping us understand swaps and futures. Moreover, as noted, for some parties, forward contracts serve specific needs not met by other derivatives.

In Chapter 3 we shall look at futures contracts. We shall demonstrate how similar they are to forward contracts, but the differences are important, and some of their benefits to society are slightly different and less obvious than those of forwards.

KEY POINTS

- The holder of a long forward contract (the "long") is obligated to take delivery of the underlying asset and pay the forward price at expiration. The holder of a short forward contract (the "short") is obligated to deliver the underlying asset and accept payment of the forward price at expiration.

- At expiration, a forward contract can be terminated by having the short make delivery of the underlying asset to the long or having the long and short exchange the equivalent cash value. If the asset is worth more (less) than the forward price, the short (long) pays the long (short) the cash difference between the market price or rate and the price or rate agreed on in the contract.

- A party can terminate a forward contract prior to expiration by entering into an opposite transaction with the same or a different counterparty. It is possible to leave both the original and new transactions in place, thereby leaving both transactions subject to credit risk, or to have the two transactions cancel each other. In the latter case, the party owing the greater amount pays the market value to the other party, resulting in the elimination of the remaining credit risk. This elimination can be achieved, however, only if the counterparty to the second transaction is the same counterparty as in the first.

- A dealer is a financial institution that makes a market in forward contracts and other derivatives. A dealer stands ready to take either side of a transaction. An end user is a party that comes to a dealer needing a transaction, usually for the purpose of managing a particular risk.

- Equity forward contracts can be written on individual stocks, specific stock portfolios, or stock indices. Equity forward contract prices and values must take into account the fact that the underlying stock, portfolio, or index could pay dividends.

- Forward contracts on bonds can be based on zero-coupon bonds or on coupon bonds, as well as portfolios or indices based on zero-coupon bonds or coupon bonds. Zero-coupon bonds pay their return by discounting the face value, often using a 360-day year assumption. Forward contracts on bonds must expire before the bond's maturity. In addition, a forward contract on a bond can be affected by special features of bonds, such as callability and convertibility.

- Eurodollar time deposits are dollar loans made by one bank to another. Although the term "Eurodollars" refers to dollar-denominated loans, similar loans exist in other currencies. Eurodollar deposits accrue interest by adding it on to the principal, using a 360-day year assumption. The primary Eurodollar rate is called LIBOR.

- LIBOR stands for London Interbank Offer Rate, the rate at which London banks are willing to lend to other London banks. Euribor is the rate on a euro time deposit, a loan made by banks to other banks in Frankfurt in which the currency is the euro.

- An FRA is a forward contract in which one party, the long, agrees to pay a fixed interest payment at a future date and receive an interest payment at a rate to be determined at expiration. FRAs are described by a special notation. For example, a 3×6 FRA expires in three months; the underlying is a Eurodollar deposit that begins in three months and ends three months later, or six months from now.

- The payment of an FRA at expiration is based on the net difference between the underlying rate and the agreed-upon rate, adjusted by the notional principal and the number of days in the instrument on which the underlying rate is based. The payoff is also discounted, however, to reflect the fact that the underlying rate on which the instrument is based assumes that payment will occur at a later date.

- A currency forward contract is a commitment for one party, the long, to buy a currency at a fixed price from the other party, the short, at a specific date. The contract can be settled by actual delivery, or the two parties can choose to settle in cash on the expiration day.

- A forward contract is priced by assuming that the underlying asset is purchased, a forward contract is sold, and the position is held to expiration. Because the sale price of the asset is locked in as the forward price, the transaction is risk free and should earn the risk-free rate. The forward price is then obtained as the price that guarantees a return of the risk-free rate. If the forward price is too high or too low, an arbitrage profit in the form of a return in excess of the risk-free rate can be earned. The combined effects of all investors executing arbitrage transactions will force the forward price to converge to its arbitrage-free level.

- The value of a forward contract is determined by the fact that a long forward contract is a claim on the underlying asset and a commitment to pay the forward price at expiration. The value of a forward contract is, therefore, the current price of the asset less the present value of the forward price at expiration. Because no money changes hands at the start, the value of the forward contract today is zero. The value of a forward contract at expiration is the price of the underlying asset minus the forward price.

- Valuation of a forward contract is important because 1) it makes good business sense to know the values of future commitments, 2) accounting rules require that forward contracts be accounted for in income statements and balance sheets, 3) the value gives a good measure of the credit exposure, and 4) the value can be used to determine the amount of money one party would have to pay another party to terminate a position.

- An off-market forward contract is established with a nonzero value at the start. The contract will, therefore, have a positive or negative value and require a cash payment at the start. A positive value is paid by the long to the short; a negative value is paid by the short to the long. In an off-market forward contract, the forward price will not equal the price of the underlying asset compounded at the risk-free rate but rather will be set in the process of negotiation between the two parties.

- An equity forward contract is priced by taking the stock price, subtracting the present value of the dividends over the life of the contract, and then compounding this amount at the risk-free rate to the expiration date of the contract. The present value of the dividends can be found by assuming the dividends are risk-free and calculating their present value using the risk-free rate of interest. Or one can assume that dividends are paid at a constant continuously compounded rate and then discount the stock price by the exponential function using the continuously compounded dividend rate. Alternatively, an equity forward can be priced by compounding the stock price to the expiration date and then subtracting the future value of the dividends at the expiration date. The value of an equity forward contract is the stock price minus the present value of the dividends minus the present value of the forward price that will be paid at expiration.

- To price a fixed-income forward contract, take the bond price, subtract the present value of the coupons over the life of the contract, and compound this amount at the risk-free rate to the expiration date of the contract. The value of a fixed-income forward contract is the bond price minus the present value of the coupons minus the present value of the forward price that will be paid at expiration.

- The price of an FRA, which is actually a rate, is simply the forward rate embedded in the term structure of the FRA's underlying rate. The value of an FRA based on a Eurodollar deposit is the present value of $1 to be received at expiration minus the present value of $1 plus the FRA rate to be received at the maturity date of the Eurodollar deposit on which the FRA is based, with appropriate (days/360) adjustments.

• The price, which is actually an exchange rate, of a forward contract on a currency is the spot rate discounted at the foreign interest rate over the life of the contract and then compounded at the domestic interest rate to the expiration date of the contract. The value of a currency forward contract is the spot rate discounted at the foreign interest rate over the life of the contract minus the present value of the forward rate at expiration.

• Credit risk in a forward contract arises when the counterparty that owes the greater amount is unable to pay at expiration or declares bankruptcy prior to expiration. The market value of a forward contract is a measure of the net amount one party owes the other. Only one party, the one owing the lesser amount, faces credit risk at any given time. Because the market value can change from positive to negative, however, the other party has the potential for facing credit risk at a later date. Counterparties occasionally mark forward contracts to market, with one party paying the other the current market value; they then reprice the contract to the current market price or rate.

• Forward markets play an important role in society, providing a means by which a select clientele of parties can engage in customized, private, unregulated transactions that commit them to buying or selling an asset at a later date at an agreed-upon price without paying any cash at the start. Forward contracts also are a simplified version of both futures and swaps and, therefore, form a basis for understanding these other derivatives.

PROBLEMS

1. **A.** Calculate the price for a T-bill with a face value of $10,000, 153 days to maturity, and a discount yield of 1.74 percent.
   B. Calculate the asked discount yield for a T-bill that has 69 days to maturity, a face value of $10,000, and a price of $9,950.

2. Assume that 60-day LIBOR is 4.35 percent. You are based in London and need to borrow $20,000,000 for 60 days. What is the total amount you will owe in 60 days?

3. The treasurer of Company A expects to receive a cash inflow of $15,000,000 in 90 days. The treasurer expects short-term interest rates to fall during the next 90 days. In order to hedge against this risk, the treasurer decides to use an FRA that expires in 90 days and is based on 90-day LIBOR. The FRA is quoted at 5 percent. At expiration, LIBOR is 4.5 percent. Assume that the notional principal on the contract is $15,000,000.
   A. Indicate whether the treasurer should take a long or short position to hedge interest rate risk.
   B. Using the appropriate terminology, identify the type of FRA used here.
   C. Calculate the gain or loss to Company A as a consequence of entering the FRA.

4. Suppose that a party wanted to enter into a FRA that expires in 42 days and is based on 137-day LIBOR. The dealer quotes a rate of 4.75 percent on this FRA. Assume that at expiration, the 137-day LIBOR is 4 percent and the notional principal is $20,000,000.
   A. What is the term used to describe such nonstandard instruments?
   B. Calculate the FRA payoff on a long position.

5. Assume Sun Microsystems expects to receive €20,000,000 in 90 days. A dealer provides a quote of $0.875 for a currency forward contract to expire in 90 days. Suppose that at the end of 90 days, the rate is $0.90. Assume that settlement is in cash. Calculate the cash flow at expiration if Sun Microsystems enters into a forward contract expiring in 90 days to buy dollars at $0.875.

6. Consider a security that sells for $1,000 today. A forward contract on this security that expires in one year is currently priced at $1,100. The annual rate of interest is 6.75 percent. Assume that this is an off-market forward contract.
   A. Calculate the value of the forward contract today, $V_0(0,T)$.
   B. Indicate whether payment is made by the long to the short or vice versa.

7. Assume that you own a security currently worth $500. You plan to sell it in two months. To hedge against a possible decline in price during the next two months, you enter into a forward contract to sell the security in two months. The risk-free rate is 3.5 percent.
   A. Calculate the forward price on this contract.
   B. Suppose the dealer offers to enter into a forward contract at $498. Indicate how you could earn an arbitrage profit.
   C. After one month, the security sells for $490. Calculate the gain or loss to your position.

8. Consider an asset currently worth $100. An investor plans to sell it in one year and is concerned that the price may have fallen significantly by then. To hedge this risk, the investor enters into a forward contract to sell the asset in one year. Assume that the risk-free rate is 5 percent.
   A. Calculate the appropriate price at which this investor can contract to sell the asset in one year.

B. Three months into the contract, the price of the asset is $90. Calculate the gain or loss that has accrued to the forward contract.

C. Assume that five months into the contract, the price of the asset is $107. Calculate the gain or loss on the forward contract.

D. Suppose that at expiration, the price of the asset is $98. Calculate the value of the forward contract at expiration. Also indicate the overall gain or loss to the investor on the whole transaction.

E. Now calculate the value of the forward contract at expiration assuming that at expiration, the price of the asset is $110. Indicate the overall gain or loss to the investor on the whole transaction. Is this amount more or less than the overall gain or loss from Part D?

9. A security is currently worth $225. An investor plans to purchase this asset in one year and is concerned that the price may have risen by then. To hedge this risk, the investor enters into a forward contract to buy the asset in one year. Assume that the risk-free rate is 4.75 percent.

A. Calculate the appropriate price at which this investor can contract to buy the asset in one year.

B. Four months into the contract, the price of the asset is $250. Calculate the gain or loss that has accrued to the forward contract.

C. Assume that eight months into the contract, the price of the asset is $200. Calculate the gain or loss on the forward contract.

D. Suppose that at expiration, the price of the asset is $190. Calculate the value of the forward contract at expiration. Also indicate the overall gain or loss to the investor on the whole transaction.

E. Now calculate the value of the forward contract at expiration assuming that at expiration, the price of the asset is $240. Indicate the overall gain or loss to the investor on the whole transaction. Is this amount more or less than the overall gain or loss from Part D?

10. Assume that a security is currently priced at $200. The risk-free rate is 5 percent.

A. A dealer offers you a contract in which the forward price of the security with delivery in three months is $205. Explain the transactions you would undertake to take advantage of the situation.

B. Suppose the dealer were to offer you a contract in which the forward price of the security with delivery in three months is $198. How would you take advantage of the situation?

11. Assume that you own a dividend-paying stock currently worth $150. You plan to sell the stock in 250 days. In order to hedge against a possible price decline, you wish to take a short position in a forward contract that expires in 250 days. The risk-free rate is 5.25 percent. Over the next 250 days, the stock will pay dividends according to the following schedule:

Days to Next Dividend	Dividends per Share
30	$1.25
120	$1.25
210	$1.25

A. Calculate the forward price of a contract established today and expiring in 250 days.

B. It is now 100 days since you entered the forward contract. The stock price is $115. Calculate the value of the forward contract at this point.

C. At expiration, the price of the stock is $130. Calculate the value of the forward contract at expiration.

12. A portfolio manager expects to purchase a portfolio of stocks in 90 days. In order to hedge against a potential price increase over the next 90 days, she decides to take a long position on a 90-day forward contract on the S&P 500 stock index. The index is currently at 1145. The continuously compounded dividend yield is 1.75 percent. The discrete risk-free rate is 4.25 percent.

A. Calculate the no-arbitrage forward price on this contract.

B. It is now 28 days since the portfolio manager entered the forward contract. The index value is at 1225. Calculate the value of the forward contract 28 days into the contract.

C. At expiration, the index value is 1235. Calculate the value of the forward contract.

13. An investor purchased a newly issued bond with a maturity of 10 years 200 days ago. The bond carries a coupon rate of 8 percent paid semiannually and has a face value of $1,000. The price of the bond with accrued interest is currently $1,146.92. The investor plans to sell the bond 365 days from now. The schedule of coupon payments over the first two years, from the date of purchase, is as follows:

Coupon	Days after Purchase	Amount
First	181	$40
Second	365	$40
Third	547	$40
Fourth	730	$40

A. Should the investor enter into a long or short forward contract to hedge his risk exposure? Calculate the no-arbitrage price at which the investor should enter the forward contract. Assume that the risk-free rate is 6 percent.

B. The forward contract is now 180 days old. Interest rates have fallen sharply, and the risk-free rate is 4 percent. The price of the bond with accrued interest is now $1,302.26. Determine the value of the forward contract now and indicate whether the investor has accrued a gain or loss on his position.

14. A corporate treasurer wishes to hedge against an increase in future borrowing costs due to a possible rise in short-term interest rates. She proposes to hedge against this risk by entering into a long 6 × 12 FRA. The current term structure for LIBOR is as follows:

Term	Interest Rate
30 day	5.10%
90 day	5.25%
180 day	5.70%
360 day	5.95%

A. Indicate when this 6 × 12 FRA expires and identify which term of the LIBOR this FRA is based on.

B. Calculate the rate the treasurer would receive on a 6 × 12 FRA.

Suppose the treasurer went long this FRA. Now, 45 days later, interest rates have risen and the LIBOR term structure is as follows:

Term	Interest Rate
135 day	5.90%
315 day	6.15%

   C. Calculate the market value of this FRA based on a notional principal of $10,000,000.

   D. At expiration, the 180-day LIBOR is 6.25 percent. Calculate the payoff on the FRA. Does the treasurer receive a payment or make a payment to the dealer?

15. A financial manager needs to hedge against a possible decrease in short term interest rates. He decides to hedge his risk exposure by going short on an FRA that expires in 90 days and is based on 90-day LIBOR. The current term structure for LIBOR is as follows:

Term	Interest Rate
30 day	5.83%
90 day	6.00%
180 day	6.14%
360 day	6.51%

   A. Identify the type of FRA used by the financial manager using the appropriate terminology.

   B. Calculate the rate the manager would receive on this FRA.

It is now 30 days since the manager took a short position in the FRA. Interest rates have shifted down, and the new term structure for LIBOR is as follows:

Term	Interest Rate
60 day	5.50%
150 day	5.62%

   C. Calculate the market value of this FRA based on a notional principal of $15,000,000.

16. Consider a U.S.-based company that exports goods to Switzerland. The U.S. company expects to receive payment on a shipment of goods in three months. Because the payment will be in Swiss francs, the U.S. company wants to hedge against a decline in the value of the Swiss franc over the next three months. The U.S. risk-free rate is 2 percent, and the Swiss risk-free rate is 5 percent. Assume that interest rates are expected to remain fixed over the next six months. The current spot rate is $0.5974.

   A. Indicate whether the U.S. company should use a long or short forward contract to hedge currency risk.

   B. Calculate the no-arbitrage price at which the U.S. company could enter into a forward contract that expires in three months.

   C. It is now 30 days since the U.S. company entered into the forward contract. The spot rate is $0.55. Interest rates are the same as before. Calculate the value of the U.S. company's forward position.

17. The euro currently trades at $1.0231. The dollar risk-free rate is 4 percent, and the euro risk-free rate is 5 percent. Six-month forward contracts are quoted at a rate of $1.0225. Indicate how you might earn a risk-free profit by engaging in a forward contract. Clearly outline the steps you undertake to earn this risk-free profit.

18. Suppose that you are a U.S.-based importer of goods from the United Kingdom. You expect the value of the pound to increase against the U.S. dollar over the next 30 days. You will be making payment on a shipment of imported goods in 30 days and want to hedge your currency exposure. The U.S. risk-free rate is 5.5 percent, and the U.K. risk-free rate is 4.5 percent. These rates are expected to remain unchanged over the next month. The current spot rate is $1.50.
    A. Indicate whether you should use a long or short forward contract to hedge the currency risk.
    B. Calculate the no-arbitrage price at which you could enter into a forward contract that expires in 30 days.
    C. Move forward 10 days. The spot rate is $1.53. Interest rates are unchanged. Calculate the value of your forward position.

19. Consider the following: The U.S. risk-free rate is 6 percent, the Swiss risk-free rate is 4 percent, and the spot exchange rate between the United States and Switzerland is $0.6667.
    A. Calculate the continuously compounded U.S. and Swiss risk-free rates.
    B. Calculate the price at which you could enter into a forward contract that expires in 90 days.
    C. Calculate the value of the forward position 25 days into the contract. Assume that the spot rate is $0.65.

20. The Japanese yen currently trades at $0.00812. The U.S. risk-free rate is 4.5 percent, and the Japanese risk-free rate is 2.0 percent. Three-month forward contracts on the yen are quoted at $0.00813. Indicate how you might earn a risk-free profit by engaging in a forward contract. Outline your transactions.

SOLUTIONS   1. **A.** Discount yield $= 0.0174 = \left(\dfrac{10{,}000 - \text{Price}}{10{,}000}\right)\left(\dfrac{360}{153}\right)$

Price $= \$9{,}926.05$

B. Discount yield $= \left(\dfrac{10{,}000 - 9{,}950}{10{,}000}\right)\left(\dfrac{360}{69}\right) = 0.0261$

2. $\$20{,}000{,}000\,[1 + 0.0435(60/360)] = \$20{,}145{,}000$

3. **A.** Taking a short position will hedge the interest rate risk for Company A. The gain on the contract will offset the reduced interest rate that can be earned when rates fall.

B. This is a 3 × 6 FRA.

C. $\$15{,}000{,}000\left[\dfrac{(0.045 - 0.05)(90/360)}{1 + 0.045(90/360)}\right] = -\$18{,}541.41$

The negative sign indicates a gain to the short position, which Company A holds.

4. **A.** These instruments are called off-the-run FRAs.

B. $\$20{,}000{,}000\left[\dfrac{(0.04 - 0.0475)(137/360)}{1 + 0.04(137/360)}\right] = -\$56{,}227.43$

Because the party is long, this amount represents a loss.

5. The contract is settled in cash, so the settlement would be €20,000,000(0.875 − 0.90) = −\$500,000. This amount would be paid by Sun Microsystems to the dealer. Sun would convert euros to dollars at the spot rate of \$0.90, receiving €20,000,000 × (0.90) = \$18,000,000. The net cash receipt is \$17,500,000, which results in an effective rate of \$0.875.

6. **A.** $S_0 = \$1{,}000$
$F(0,T) = \$1{,}100$
$T = 1$
$V_0(0,T) = \$1{,}000 - \$1{,}100/(1.0675) = -\$30.44$

B. Because the value is negative, the payment is made by the short to the long.

7. **A.** $S_0 = \$500$
$T = 2/12 = 0.1667$
$r = 0.035$
$F(0,T) = \$500 \times (1.035)^{0.1667} = \$502.88$

B. Sell the security for \$500 and invest at 3.5 percent for two months. At the end of two months, you will have \$502.88. Enter into a forward contract now to buy the security at \$498 in two months.
Arbitrage profit $= \$502.88 - \$498 = \$4.88$

C. $S_t = \$490$
$t = 1/12 = 0.0833$
$T = 2/12 = 0.1667$
$T - t = 0.0834$
$r = 0.035$
$V_t(0,T) = \$490.00 - \$502.88/(1.035)^{0.0834} = -\$11.44.$ This represents a gain to the short position.

8. **A.** $S_0 = \$100$
$T = 1$
$r = 0.05$
$F(0,T) = \$100(1.05) = \$105$

B. $S_t = \$90$
$t = 3/12 = 0.25$
$T = 1$
$T - t = 0.75$
$r = 0.05$
$V_t(0,T) = \$90 - \$105/(1.05)^{0.75} = -\$11.23$
The investor is short so this represents a gain.

C. $S_t = \$107$
$t = 5/12 = 0.4167$
$T = 1$
$T - t = 0.5834$
$r = 0.05$
$V_t(0,T) = \$107 - \$105/(1.05)^{0.5834} = \$4.95$
The investor is short, so this represents a loss to the short position.

D. $S_t = \$98$
$F(0,T) = \$105$
$V_T(0,T) = \$98 - \$105 = -\$7$
Gain to short position $= \$7$
Loss on asset $= -\$2$ (based on $\$100 - \$98$)
Net gain $= \$5$
This represents a return of 5 percent on an asset worth $100, the same as the risk-free rate.

E. $S_t = \$110$
$F(0,T) = \$105$
$V_T(0,T) = 110 - 105 = \$5$
Loss to short position $= -\$5$
Gain on asset $= \$10$ (based on $\$110 - \$100$)
Net gain $= \$5$
This represents a return of 5 percent on an asset worth $100, the same as the risk-free rate. The overall gain on the transaction is the same as in Part D because the forward contract was executed at the no arbitrage price of $105.

9. A. $S_0 = \$225$
$T = 1$
$r = 0.0475$
$F(0,T) = \$225(1.0475) = \$235.69$

B. $S_t = \$250$
$t = 4/12 = 0.3333$
$T = 1$
$T - t = 0.6667$
$r = 0.0475$
$V_t(0,T) = \$250.00 - \$235.69/(1.0475)^{0.6667} = \$21.49$
The investor is long, so a positive value represents a gain.

C. $S_t = \$200$
$t = 8/12 = 0.6667$
$T = 1$
$T - t = 0.3333$
$r = 0.0475$
$V_t(0,T) = \$200.00 - \$235.69/(1.0475)^{0.3333} = -\$32.07$
The investor is long, so this represents a loss to the long position.

D. $S_t = \$190$
$F(0,T) = \$235.69$

$V_T(0,T) = \$190.00 - \$235.69 = -\$45.69$
Loss to long position $= -\$45.69$
Gain on asset $\quad\quad = \$35.00$ (based on $\$225 - \$190$)
Net loss $\quad\quad\quad\quad = -\$10.69$

E. $S_t = \$240$
$F(0,T) = \$235.69$
$V_T(0,T) = \$240.00 - \$235.69 = \$4.31$
Gain to long position $= \$4.31$
Loss on asset $\quad\quad = -\$15.00$ (based on $\$240 - \$225$)
Net loss $\quad\quad\quad\quad = -\$10.69$

This loss is the same as the loss in Part D. In fact, the loss would be the same for any other price as well, because the forward contract was executed at the no-arbitrage price of $\$235.69$. The loss of $\$10.69$ is the risk-free rate of 4.75 percent applied to the initial asset price of $\$225$.

10. A. The no-arbitrage forward price is $F(0,T) = \$200(1.05)3/12 = \$202.45$.

Because the forward contract offered by the dealer is overpriced, sell the forward contract and buy the security now. Doing so will yield an arbitrage profit of $\$2.55$.

Borrow $\$200$ and buy security. At the end of three months, repay $\quad$ $\$202.45$
At the end of three months, deliver the security for $\quad\quad\quad\quad$ $\$205.00$
Arbitrage profit $\quad\quad\quad\quad\quad\quad\quad\quad\quad\quad\quad\quad\quad\quad\quad\quad\quad\quad$ $\$2.55$

B. At a price of $\$198.00$, the contract offered by the dealer is underpriced relative to the no-arbitrage forward price of $\$202.45$. Enter into a forward contract to buy in three months at $\$198.00$. Short the stock now, and invest the proceeds. Doing so will yield an arbitrage profit of $\$4.45$.

Short security for $\$200$ and invest proceeds for three months $\quad$ $\$202.45$
At the end of three months, buy the security for $\quad\quad\quad\quad\quad$ $\$198.00$
Arbitrage profit $\quad\quad\quad\quad\quad\quad\quad\quad\quad\quad\quad\quad\quad\quad\quad\quad\quad\quad$ $\$4.45$

11. A. $S_0 = \$150$
$T = 250/365$
$r = 0.0525$
$PV(D,0,T) = \$1.25/(1.0525)^{30/365} + \$1.25/(1.0525)^{120/365} + \$1.25/(1.0525)^{210/365}$
$\quad\quad\quad\quad = \$3.69$
$F(0,T) = (\$150.00 - \$3.69)(1.0525)^{250/365} = \$151.53$

B. $S_t = \$115$
$F(0,T) = \$151.53$
$t = 100/365$
$T = 250/365$
$T - t = 150/365$
$r = 0.0525$
After 100 days, two dividends remain: the first one in 20 days, and the second one in 110 days.
$PV(D,t,T) = \$1.25/(1.0525)^{20/365} + \$1.25/(1.0525)^{110/365} = \$2.48$
$V_t(0,T) = \$115.00 - \$2.48 - \$151.53/(1.0525)^{150/365} = -\$35.86$
A negative value is a gain to the short.

C. $S_T = \$130$
$F(0,T) = \$151.53$
$V_T(0,T) = \$130.00 - \$151.53 = -\$21.53$
The contract expires with a value of negative $\$21.53$, a gain to the short.

12. A. $S_0 = \$1,145$
$T = 90/365 = 0.2466$

$r = 0.0425$

$r^c = \ln(1 + 0.0425) = 0.0416$

$\delta^c = 0.0175$

$F(0,T) = (\$1,145 \times e^{-0.0175(0.2466)})(e^{0.0416(0.2466)}) = \$1,151.83$

B. $S_t = \$1,225$

$T = 90/365 = 0.2466$

$t = 28/365 = 0.0767$

$T - t = 0.1699$

$r = 0.0425$

$r^c = \ln(1 + 0.0425) = 0.0416$

$\delta^c = 0.0175$

$V_t(0,T) = (\$1,225 \times e^{-0.0175(0.1699)}) - (1151.83e^{-0.0416(0.1699)}) = \$61.36$

This is a gain to the long position.

C. $S_T = \$1,235$

$F(0,T) = \$1,151.83$

$V_T(0,T) = \$1,235.00 - \$1,151.83 = \$83.17$

The contract expires with a value of \$83.17, a gain to the long.

13. A. The investor should enter into a short forward contract, locking in the price at which he can sell the bond in 365 days.

$B_0^c(T + Y) = \$1,146.92$

$T = 365/365 = 1$

$r = 0.06$

Between now (i.e., 200 days since the original purchase) and the next 365 days, the investor will receive two coupons, the first 165 days from now and the second 347 days from now.

$PV(CI,0,T) = \$40/(1.06)^{165/365} + \$40/(1.06)^{347/365} = \$76.80$

$F(0,T) = (\$1,146.92 - \$76.81)(1.06)^{365/365} = \$1,134.32$

B. $B_t^c(T + Y) = \$1,302.26$

$F(0,T) = \$1,134.32$

$t = 180/365$

$T = 365/365$

$T - t = 185/365$

$r = 0.04$

We are now on the 380th day of the bond's life. One more coupon payment remains until the expiration of the forward contract. The coupon payment is in $547 - 380 = 167$ days.

$PV(CI,0,T) = \$40/(1.04)^{167/365} = \$39.29$

$V_t(0,T) = \$1,302.26 - \$39.29 - \$1,134.32/(1.04)^{185/365} = \$150.98$

A positive value is a loss to the short position.

14. A. A 6×12 FRA expires in 180 days and is based on 180-day LIBOR.

B. $h = 180$

$m = 180$

$h + m = 360$

$L_0(h + m) = 0.0595$

$L_0(h) = 0.057$

$$FRA(0,h,m) = \left[\frac{1 + 0.0595\left(\dfrac{360}{360}\right)}{1 + 0.0570\left(\dfrac{180}{360}\right)} - 1\right]\left(\frac{360}{180}\right) = 0.0603$$

C. $h = 180$
$m = 180$
$g = 45$
$h - g = 135$
$h + m - g = 315$
$L_{45}(h - g) = 0.0590$
$L_{45}(h + m - g) = 0.0615$

$$V_t(0,h,m) = \frac{1}{1 + 0.0590\left(\frac{135}{360}\right)} - \frac{1 + 0.0603\left(\frac{180}{360}\right)}{1 + 0.0615\left(\frac{315}{360}\right)} = 0.0081$$

For \$10,000,000 notional principal, the value of the FRA would be $= 0.0081 \times 10,000,000 = \$8,100$.

D. $h = 180$
$m = 180$
$L_{180}(h + m) = 0.0625$

At expiration, the payoff is $\dfrac{(0.0625 - 0.0603)\left(\frac{180}{360}\right)}{1 + 0.0625\left(\frac{180}{360}\right)} = 0.001067$

Based on a notional principal of \$10,000,000, the corporation, which is long, will receive $\$10,000,000 \times 0.001067 = \$10,670$ from the dealer.

15. A. A 3×6 FRA expires in 90 days and is based on 90-day LIBOR.

B. $h = 90$
$m = 90$
$h + m = 180$
$L_0(h) = 0.06$
$L_0(h + m) = 0.0614$

$$FRA(0,h,m) = \left[\frac{1 + 0.0614\left(\frac{180}{360}\right)}{1 + 0.06\left(\frac{90}{360}\right)} - 1\right]\left(\frac{360}{90}\right) = 0.0619$$

C. $h = 90$
$m = 90$
$g = 30$
$h - g = 60$
$h + m - g = 150$
$L_{30}(h - g) = 0.055$
$L_{30}(h + m - g) = 0.0562$

$$V_t(0,h,m) = \frac{1}{1 + 0.055\left(\frac{60}{360}\right)} - \frac{1 + 0.0619\left(\frac{90}{360}\right)}{1 + 0.0562\left(\frac{150}{360}\right)}$$

$$= -0.001323$$

For \$15,000,000 notional principal, the value of the FRA would be $= -0.001323 \times 15,000,000 = -\$19,845$. Because the manager is short, this represents a gain to his company.

16. A. The risk to the U.S. company is that the value of the Swiss franc will decline and it will receive fewer U.S. dollars on conversion. To hedge this risk, the company should enter into a contract to sell Swiss francs forward.

    B. $S_0 = \$0.5974$
$T = 90/365$
$r = 0.02$
$r^f = 0.05$

$$F(0,T) = \left[\frac{0.5974}{(1.05)^{90/365}}\right](1.02)^{90/365} = \$0.5931$$

    C. $S_t = \$0.55$
$T = 90/365$
$t = 30/365$
$T - t = 60/365$
$r = 0.02$
$r^f = 0.05$

$$V_t(0,T) = \frac{\$0.55}{(1.05)^{60/365}} - \frac{\$0.5931}{(1.02)^{60/365}} = -\$0.0456$$

This represents a gain to the short position of \$0.0456 per Swiss franc. In this problem, the U.S. company holds the short forward position.

17. First calculate the fair value or arbitrage-free price of the forward contract:
$S_0 = \$1.0231$
$T = 180/365$
$r = 0.04$
$r^f = 0.05$

$$F(0,T) = \left[\frac{1.0231}{(1.05)^{180/365}}\right](1.04)^{180/365} = \$1.0183$$

The dealer quote for the forward contract is \$1.0225; thus, the forward contract is overpriced. To earn a risk-free profit, you should enter into a forward contract to sell euros forward in six months at \$1.0225. At the same time, buy euros now.

    i. Take $\dfrac{\$1.0231}{(1.05)^{180/365}} = \$0.9988$. Use it to buy $\dfrac{1}{(1.05)^{180/365}} = 0.9762$ euros.

    ii. Enter a forward contract to deliver €1.00 at \$1.0225 in six months.

    iii. Invest €0.9762 for six months at 4.5 percent per year and receive €0.9762 × $1.05^{180/365} = $ €1.00 at the end of six months.

    iv. At expiration, deliver the euro and receive \$1.0225. Return over six months is
$\dfrac{\$1.0225}{\$0.9988} - 1 = 0.0237$, or 4.74 percent a year.

This risk-free annual return of 4.74 percent exceeds the U.S. risk-free rate of 4 percent.

18. A. The risk to you is that the value of the British pound will rise over the next 30 days and it will require more U.S. dollars to buy the necessary pounds to make payment. To hedge this risk you should enter a forward contract to buy British pounds.

    B. $S_0 = \$1.50$
$T = 30/365$
$r = 0.055$

$r^f = 0.045$

$$F(0,T) = \left[\frac{\$1.50}{(1.04)^{30/365}} \right)(1.055)^{30/365} = \$1.5018$$

C. $S_t = \$1.53$
   $T = 30/365$
   $t = 10/365$
   $T - t = 20/365$
   $r = 0.055$
   $r^f = 0.045$

$$V_t(0,T) = \frac{\$1.53}{1.045^{20/365}} - \frac{\$1.5012}{1.055^{20/365}} = \$0.0295$$

Because you are long, this is a gain of $0.0295 per British pound.

19. A. $r^{fc} = \ln(1.04) = 0.0392$
   $r^c = \ln(1.06) = 0.0583$

B. $S_0 = \$0.6667$
   $T = 90/365$
   $r^{fc} = 0.0392$
   $r^c = 0.0583$
   $F(0,T) = (\$0.6667 \times e^{-0.0392(90/365)})(e^{0.0583(90/365)}) = \$0.6698$

C. $S_t = \$0.65$
   $T = 90/365$
   $t = 25/365$
   $T - t = 65/365$
   $r^{fc} = 0.0392$
   $r^c = 0.0583$
   $V_t(0,T) = (\$0.65 \times e^{-0.0392(65/365)}) - (\$0.6698 \times e^{-0.0583(65/365)}) = -\$0.0174$
   The value of the contract is $-$0.0174 per Swiss franc.

20. First, calculate the fair value or arbitrage free price of the forward contract:
   $S_0 = \$0.00812$ per yen
   $T = 90/365$
   $r = 0.045$
   $r^f = 0.02$

$$F(0,T) = \left[\frac{\$0.00812}{(1.02)^{90/365}} \right](1.045)^{90/365} = \$0.00817$$

The dealer quote for the forward contract is $0.00813. Therefore, the forward contract is underpriced. To earn a risk-free profit, you should enter into a forward contract to buy yen in three months at $0.00813. At the same time, sell yen now.

i. The spot rate of $0.00812 per yen is equivalent to ¥123.15 per U.S. dollar. Take
$\frac{¥123.15}{(1.045)^{90/365}} = ¥121.82$. Use it to buy $\frac{1}{(1.045)^{90/365}} = 0.9892$ U.S. dollars.

ii. Enter a forward contract to buy yen at $0.00813 in three months. One U.S.
dollar will buy $\frac{1}{\$0.00813} = ¥123.00$

iii. Invest $0.9892 for three months at 4.5 percent a year and receive $0.9892 \times 1.045^{90/365} = \$1.00$ at the end of three months.

iv. At expiration, deliver the dollar and receive ¥123. The return over three months is $\dfrac{¥123.00}{¥121.82} - 1 = 0.00969$, or 3.88 percent a year.

Because we began our transactions in yen, the relevant comparison for the return from our transactions is the Japanese risk-free rate. The 3.88 percent return above exceeds the Japanese risk-free rate of 2 percent. Therefore, we could borrow yen at 2 percent and engage in the above transactions to earn a risk-free return of 3.88 percent that exceeds the rate of borrowing.

CHAPTER 3

FUTURES MARKETS AND CONTRACTS

LEARNING OUTCOMES

After completing this chapter, you will be able to do the following:

- Identify the institutional features that distinguish futures contracts from forward contracts.
- Understand the origins of modern futures markets.
- List the primary characteristics of futures contracts.
- Explain the difference between margin in the securities markets and margin in the futures markets.
- Describe how a futures trade takes place.
- Describe how a futures position may be closed out prior to expiration.
- Define initial margin, maintenance margin, variation margin, and settlement price.
- Describe the process of marking to market.
- Compute the margin balance given the previous day's balance and the new futures price.
- Explain price limits, limit move, limit up, limit down, and locked limit.
- Describe how a futures contract can be terminated by either a closeout at expiration, delivery, an equivalent cash settlement, or an exchange for physicals.
- Explain delivery options in futures contracts.
- Distinguish among scalpers, day traders, and position traders.
- Describe the primary characteristics of the following types of futures contracts: Treasury bill, Eurodollar, Treasury bond, stock index, and currency.
- Explain why the futures price must converge to the spot price at expiration.
- Explain how to determine the value of a futures contract.
- Explain how forward and futures prices differ.
- Describe how an arbitrage transaction is constructed to derive the futures price.
- Identify the different types of monetary and nonmonetary benefits and costs associated with holding the underlying asset, and explain how they affect the futures price.
- Define backwardation and contango.
- Discuss whether futures prices equal expected spot prices.

- Describe and illustrate how to price Treasury bill futures.
- Explain the concept of an implied repo rate.
- Describe and illustrate the difficulties in determining the price of Eurodollar futures.
- Describe and illustrate how to price Treasury bond futures.
- Describe and illustrate how to price stock index futures.
- Describe and illustrate how to price currency futures.
- Discuss the role of futures markets and exchanges in financial systems and in society.

1   INTRODUCTION

In Chapter 1, we undertook a general overview of derivative markets. In Chapter 2, we focused on forward markets. Now we explore futures markets in a similar fashion. Although we shall see a clear similarity between forward and futures contracts, critical distinctions nonetheless exist between the two.

In Chapter 1 we learned that, like a forward contract, *a futures contract is an agreement between two parties in which one party, the buyer, agrees to buy from the other party, the seller, an underlying asset or other derivative, at a future date at a price agreed on today.* Unlike a forward contract, however, a futures contract is not a private and customized transaction but rather a public transaction that takes place on an organized futures exchange. In addition, a futures contract is standardized—the exchange, rather than the individual parties, sets the terms and conditions, with the exception of price. As a result, futures contracts have a secondary market, meaning that previously created contracts can be traded. Also, parties to futures contracts are guaranteed against credit losses resulting from the counterparty's inability to pay. A clearinghouse provides this guarantee via a procedure in which it converts gains and losses that accrue on a daily basis into actual cash gains and losses. Futures contracts are regulated at the federal government level; as we noted in Chapter 2, forward contracts are essentially unregulated. Futures contracts are created on organized trading facilities referred to as futures exchanges, whereas forward contracts are not created in any specific location but rather initiated between any two parties who wish to enter into such a contract. Finally, each futures exchange has a division or subsidiary called a clearinghouse that performs the specific responsibilities of paying and collecting daily gains and losses as well as guaranteeing to each party the performance of the other.

In a futures transaction, one party, the long, is the buyer and the other party, the short, is the seller. The buyer agrees to buy the underlying at a later date, the expiration, at a price agreed on at the start of the contract. The seller agrees to sell the underlying to the buyer at the expiration, at the price agreed on at the start of the contract. Every day, the futures contract trades in the market and its price changes in response to new information. Buyers benefit from price increases, and sellers benefit from price decreases. On the expiration day, the contract terminates and no further trading takes place. Then, either the buyer takes delivery of the underlying from the seller, or the two parties make an equivalent cash settlement. We shall explore each of these characteristics of futures contracts in more detail. First, however, it is important to take a brief look at how futures markets came into being.

1.1 A Brief History of Futures Markets

Although vestiges of futures markets appear in the Japanese rice markets of the 18th century and perhaps even earlier, the mid-1800s marked the first clear origins of modern futures markets. For example, in the United States in the 1840s, Chicago was becoming a major transportation and distribution center for agricultural commodities. Its central location and access to the Great Lakes gave Chicago a competitive advantage over other U.S. cities. Farmers from the Midwest would harvest their grain and take it to Chicago for sale. Grain production, however, is seasonal. As a result, grain prices would rise sharply just prior to the harvest but then plunge when the grain was brought to the market. Too much grain at one time and too little at another resulted in severe problems. Grain storage facilities in Chicago were inadequate to accommodate the oversupply. Some farmers even dumped their grain in the Chicago River because prices were so low that they could not afford to take their grain to another city to sell.

To address this problem, in 1848 a group of businessmen formed an organization later named the Chicago Board of Trade (CBOT) and created an arrangement called a "to-arrive" contract. These contracts permitted farmers to sell their grain before delivering it. In other words, farmers could harvest the grain and enter into a contract to deliver it at a much later date at a price already agreed on. This transaction allowed the farmer to hold the grain in storage at some other location besides Chicago. On the other side of these contracts were the businessmen who had formed the Chicago Board of Trade.

It soon became apparent that trading in these to-arrive contracts was more important and useful than trading in the grain itself. Soon the contracts began trading in a type of secondary market, which allowed buyers and sellers to discharge their obligations by passing them on, for a price, to other parties. With the addition of the clearinghouse in the 1920s, which provided a guarantee against default, modern futures markets firmly established their place in the financial world. It was left to other exchanges, such as today's Chicago Mercantile Exchange, the New York Mercantile Exchange, Eurex, and the London International Financial Futures Exchange, to develop and become, along with the Chicago Board of Trade, the global leaders in futures markets.

We shall now explore the important features of futures contracts in more detail.

1.2 Public Standardized Transactions

A private transaction is not generally reported in the news or to any price reporting service. Forward contracts are private contracts. Just as in most legal contracts, the parties do not publicly report that they have engaged in a contract. In contrast, a futures transaction is reported to the futures exchange, the clearinghouse, and at least one regulatory agency. The price is recorded and available from price reporting services and even on the Internet.[1]

We noted that a futures transaction is not customized. Recall from Chapter 2 that in a forward contract, the two parties establish all of the terms of the contract, including the identity of the underlying, the expiration date, and the manner in which the contract is settled (cash or actual delivery) as well as the price. The terms are customized to meet the needs of both parties. In a futures contract, the price is the only term established by the two parties; the exchange establishes all other terms. Moreover, the terms that are established by the exchange are standardized, meaning that the exchange selects a number of choices for underlyings, expiration dates, and a variety of other contract-specific items. These standardized terms are well known to all parties. If a party wishes to trade a futures contract, it must accept these terms. The only alternative would be to create a similar but customized contract on the forward market.

---

[1] The information reported to the general public does not disclose the identity of the parties to transactions but only that a transaction took place at a particular price.

With respect to the underlying, for example, a given asset has a variety of specifications and grades. Consider a futures contract on U.S. Treasury bonds. There are many different Treasury bonds with a variety of characteristics. The futures exchange must decide which Treasury bond or group of bonds the contract covers. One of the most actively traded commodity futures contracts is oil, but there are many different types of oil.[2] To which type of oil does the contract apply? The exchange decides at the time it designs the contract.

The parties to a forward contract set its expiration at whatever date they want. For a futures contract, the exchange establishes a set of expiration dates. The first specification of the expiration is the month. An exchange might establish that a given futures contract expires only in the months of March, June, September, and December. The second specification determines how far the expirations go out into the future. For example, in January of a given year, there may be expirations of March, June, September, and December. Expirations might also be available for March, June, September, and December of the following year, and perhaps some months of the year after that. The exchange decides which expiration months are appropriate for trading, based on which expirations they believe would be actively traded. Treasury bond futures have expirations going out only about a year. Eurodollar futures, however, have expirations that go out about 10 years.[3] The third specification of the expiration is the specific day of expiration. Many, but not all, contracts expire some time during the third week of the expiration month.

The exchange determines a number of other contract characteristics, including the contract size. For example, one Eurodollar futures contract covers $1 million of a Eurodollar time deposit. One U.S. Treasury bond futures contract covers $100,000 face value of Treasury bonds. One futures contract on crude oil covers 1,000 barrels. The exchange also decides on the price quotation unit. For example, Treasury bond futures are quoted in points and 32nds of par of 100. Hence, you will see a price like 104 21/32, which means 104.65625. With a contract size of $100,000, the actual price is $104,656.25.

The exchange also determines what hours of the day trading takes place and at what physical location on the exchange the contract will be traded. Many futures exchanges have a trading floor, which contains octagonal-shaped pits. A contract is assigned to a certain pit. Traders enter the pits and express their willingness to buy and sell by calling out and/or indicating by hand signals their bids and offers. Some exchanges have electronic trading, which means that trading takes place on computer terminals, generally located in companies' offices. Some exchanges have both floor trading and electronic trading; some have only one or the other.

1.3 HOMOGENIZATION AND LIQUIDITY

By creating contracts with generally accepted terms, the exchange standardizes the instrument. In contrast, forward contracts are quite heterogeneous because they are customized. Standardizing the instrument makes it more acceptable to a broader group of participants, with the advantage being that the instrument can then more easily trade in a type of secondary market. Indeed, the ability to sell a previously purchased contract or purchase a previously sold contract is one of the important features of futures contracts. A futures contract is therefore said to have liquidity in contrast to a forward contract, which does not generally trade after it has been created.[4] This ability to trade a previously opened contract

---

[2] Some of the main types are Saudi Arabian light crude, Brent crude, and West Texas intermediate crude.

[3] You may be wondering why some Eurodollar futures contracts have such long expirations. Dealers in swaps and forward rate agreements use Eurodollar futures to hedge their positions. Many of those over-the-counter contracts have very long expirations.

[4] The notion of liquidity here is only that a market exists for futures contracts, but this does not imply a high degree of liquidity. There may be little trading in a given contract, and the bid–ask spread can be high. In contrast, some forward markets can be very liquid, allowing forward contracts to be offset, as described in Chapter 2.

allows participants in this market to offset the position before expiration, thereby obtaining exposure to price movements in the underlying without the actual requirement of holding the position to expiration. We shall discuss this characteristic further when we describe futures trading in Section 2.

1.4 THE CLEARINGHOUSE, DAILY SETTLEMENT, AND PERFORMANCE GUARANTEE

Another important distinction between futures and forwards is that the futures exchange guarantees to each party the performance of the other party, through a mechanism known as the clearinghouse. This guarantee means that if one party makes money on the transaction, it does not have to worry about whether it will collect the money from the other party because the clearinghouse ensures it will be paid. In contrast, each party to a forward contract assumes the risk that the other party will default.

An important and distinguishing feature of futures contracts is that the gains and losses on each party's position are credited and charged on a daily basis. This procedure, called **daily settlement** or **marking to market**, essentially results in paper gains and losses being converted to cash gains and losses each day. It is also equivalent to terminating a contract at the end of each day and reopening it the next day at that settlement price. In some sense, a futures contract is like a strategy of opening up a forward contract, closing it one day later, opening up a new contract, closing it one day later, and continuing in that manner until expiration. The exact manner in which the daily settlement works will be covered in more detail later in Section 3.

1.5 REGULATION

In most countries, futures contracts are regulated at the federal government level. State and regional laws may also apply. In the United States, the Commodity Futures Trading Commission regulates the futures market. In the United Kingdom, the Securities and Futures Authority regulates both the securities and futures markets.

Federal regulation of futures markets generally arises out of a concern to protect the general public and other futures market participants, as well as through a recognition that futures markets affect all financial markets and the economy. Regulations cover such matters as ensuring that prices are reported accurately and in a timely manner, that markets are not manipulated, that professionals who offer their services to the public are qualified and honest, and that disputes are resolved. In the United States, the government has delegated some of these responsibilities to an organization called the National Futures Association (NFA). An industry self-regulatory body, the NFA was created with the objective of having the industry regulate itself and reduce the federal government's burden.

2 FUTURES TRADING

In this section, we look more closely at how futures contracts are traded. As noted above, futures contracts trade on a futures exchange either in a pit or on a screen or electronic terminal.

We briefly mentioned pit trading, also known as floor-based trading, in Section 1.2. Pit trading is a very physical activity. Traders stand in the pit and shout out their orders in the form of prices they are willing to pay or accept. They also use hand signals to indicate their bids and offers.[5] They engage in transactions with other traders in the pits by simply agreeing on a price and number of contracts to trade. The activity is fast, furious, exciting, and stressful. The average pit trader is quite young, owing to the physical demands of the job and the toll it takes on body and mind. In recent years, more trading has come off of the exchange floor to electronic screens or terminals. In electronic or screen-based trading,

---

[5] Hand signals facilitate trading with someone who is too far away in the pit for verbal communication.

exchange members enter their bids and offers into a computer system, which then displays this information and allows a trader to consummate a trade electronically. In the United States, pit trading is dominant, owing to its long history and tradition. Exchange members who trade on the floor enjoy pit trading and have resisted heavily the advent of electronic trading. Nonetheless, the exchanges have had to respond to market demands to offer electronic trading. In the United States, both pit trading and electronic trading are used, but in other countries, electronic trading is beginning to drive pit trading out of business.[6]

A person who enters into a futures contract establishes either a long position or a short position. Similar to forward contracts, long positions are agreements to buy the underlying at the expiration at a price agreed on at the start. Short positions are agreements to sell the underlying at a future date at a price agreed on at the start. When the position is established, each party deposits a small amount of money, typically called the margin, with the clearinghouse. Then, as briefly described in Section 1.4, the contract is marked to market, whereby the gains are distributed to and the losses collected from each party. We cover this marking-to-market process in more detail in the next section. For now, however, we focus only on the opening and closing of the position.

A party that has opened a long position collects profits or incurs losses on a daily basis. At some point in the life of the contract prior to expiration, that party may wish to re-enter the market and close out the position. This process, called **offsetting**, is the same as selling a previously purchased stock or buying back a stock to close a short position. The holder of a long futures position simply goes back into the market and offers the identical contract for sale. The holder of a short position goes back into the market and offers to buy the identical contract. It should be noted that when a party offsets a position, it does not necessary do so with the same counterparty to the original contract. In fact, rarely would a contract be offset with the same counterparty. Because of the ability to offset, futures contracts are said to be fungible, which means that any futures contract with any counterparty can be offset by an equivalent futures contract with another counterparty. Fungibility is assured by the fact that the clearinghouse inserts itself in the middle of each contract and, therefore, becomes the counterparty to each party.

For example, suppose in early January a futures trader purchases an S&P 500 stock index futures contract expiring in March. Through 15 February, the trader has incurred some gains and losses from the daily settlement and decides that she wants to close the position out. She then goes back into the market and offers for sale the March S&P 500 futures. Once she finds a buyer to take the position, she has a long and short position in the same contract. The clearinghouse considers that she no longer has a position in that contract and has no remaining exposure, nor any obligation to make or take delivery at expiration. Had she initially gone short the March futures, she might re-enter the market in February offering to buy it. Once she finds a seller to take the opposite position, she becomes long and short the same contract and is considered to have offset the contract and therefore have no net position.

3 THE CLEARINGHOUSE, MARGINS, AND PRICE LIMITS

As briefly noted in the previous section, when a trader takes a long or short position in a futures, he must first deposit sufficient funds in a margin account. This amount of money is traditionally called the margin, a term derived from the stock market practice in which an investor borrows a portion of the money required to purchase a certain amount of stock.

---

[6] For example, in France electronic trading was introduced while pit trading continued. Within two weeks, all of the volume had migrated to electronic trading and pit trading was terminated.

Margin in the stock market is quite different from margin in the futures market. In the stock market, "margin" means that a loan is made. The loan enables the investor to reduce the amount of his own money required to purchase the securities, thereby generating leverage or gearing, as it is sometimes known. If the stock goes up, the percentage gain to the investor is amplified. If the stock goes down, however, the percentage loss is also amplified. The borrowed money must eventually be repaid with interest. The margin percentage equals the market value of the stock minus the market value of the debt divided by the market value of the stock—in other words, the investor's own equity as a percentage of the value of the stock. For example, in the United States, regulations permit an investor to borrow up to 50 percent of the initial value of the stock. This percentage is called the initial margin requirement. On any day thereafter, the equity or percentage ownership in the account, measured as the market value of the securities minus the amount borrowed, can be less than 50 percent but must be at least a percentage known as the maintenance margin requirement. A typical maintenance margin requirement is 25 to 30 percent.

In the futures market, by contrast, the word **margin** is commonly used to describe the amount of money that must be put into an account by a party opening up a futures position, but the term is misleading. When a transaction is initiated, a futures trader puts up a certain amount of money to meet the **initial margin requirement**; however, the remaining money is not borrowed. The amount of money deposited is more like a down payment for the commitment to purchase the underlying at a later date. Alternatively, one can view this deposit as a form of good faith money, collateral, or a performance bond: The money helps ensure that the party fulfills his or her obligation.[7] Moreover, both the buyer and the seller of a futures contract must deposit margin.

In securities markets, margin requirements are normally set by federal regulators. In the United States, maintenance margin requirements are set by the securities exchanges and the NASD. In futures markets, margin requirements are set by the clearinghouses. In further contrast to margin practices in securities markets, futures margins are traditionally expressed in dollar terms and not as a percentage of the futures price. For ease of comparison, however, we often speak of the futures margin in terms of its relationship to the futures price. In futures markets, the initial margin requirement is typically much lower than the initial margin requirement in the stock market. In fact, futures margins are usually less than 10 percent of the futures price.[8] Futures clearinghouses set their margin requirements by studying historical price movements. They then establish minimum margin levels by taking into account normal price movements and the fact that accounts are marked to market daily. The clearinghouses thus collect and disburse margin money every day. Moreover, they are permitted to do so more often than daily, and on some occasions they have used that privilege. By carefully setting margin requirements and collecting margin money every day, clearinghouses are able to control the risk of default.

In spite of the differences in margin practices for futures and securities markets, the effect of leverage is similar for both. By putting up a small amount of money, the trader's gains and losses are magnified. Given the tremendously low margin requirements of futures markets, however, the magnitude of the leverage effect is much greater in futures markets. We shall see how this works as we examine the process of the daily settlement.

---

[7] In fact, the Chicago Mercantile Exchange uses the term "performance bond" instead of "margin." Most other exchanges use the term "margin."

[8] For example, the margin requirement of the Eurodollar futures contract at the Chicago Mercantile Exchange has been less than one-tenth of one percent of the futures price. An exception to this requirement, however, is individual stock futures, which in the United States have margin requirements comparable to those of the stock market.

As previously noted, each day the clearinghouse conducts an activity known as the daily settlement, also called marking to market. This practice results in the conversion of gains and losses on paper into actual gains and losses. As margin account balances change, holders of futures positions must maintain balances above a level called the **maintenance margin requirement**. The maintenance margin requirement is lower than the initial margin requirement. On any day in which the amount of money in the margin account at the end of the day falls below the maintenance margin requirement, the trader must deposit sufficient funds to bring the balance back up to the initial margin requirement. Alternatively, the trader can simply close out the position but is responsible for any further losses incurred if the price changes before a closing transaction can be made.

To provide a fair mark-to-market process, the clearinghouse must designate the official price for determining daily gains and losses. This price is called the **settlement price** and represents an average of the final few trades of the day. It would appear that the closing price of the day would serve as the settlement price, but the closing price is a single value that can potentially be biased high or low or perhaps even manipulated by an unscrupulous trader. Hence, the clearinghouse takes an average of all trades during the closing period (as defined by each exchange).

Exhibit 3-1 provides an example of the marking-to-market process that occurs over a period of six trading days. We start with the assumption that the futures price is $100 when the transaction opens, the initial margin requirement is $5, and the maintenance margin requirement is $3. In Panel A, the trader takes a long position of 10 contracts on Day 0, depositing $50 ($5 times 10 contracts) as indicated in Column 3. At the end of the day, his ending balance is $50.[9] Although the trader can withdraw any funds in excess of the initial margin requirement, we shall assume that he does not do so.[10]

EXHIBIT 3-1   Mark-to-Market Example

Initial futures price = $100, Initial margin requirement = $5, Maintenance margin requirement = $3

A. *Holder of Long Position of 10 Contracts*

Day (1)	Beginning Balance (2)	Funds Deposited (3)	Settlement Price (4)	Futures Price Change (5)	Gain/ Loss (6)	Ending Balance (7)
0	0	50	100.00			50
1	50	0	99.20	−0.80	−8	42
2	42	0	96.00	−3.20	−32	10
3	10	40	101.00	5.00	50	100
4	100	0	103.50	2.50	25	125
5	125	0	103.00	−0.50	−5	120
6	120	0	104.00	1.00	10	130

---

[9] Technically, we are assuming that the position was opened at the settlement price on Day 0. If the position is opened earlier during the day, it would be marked to the settlement price at the end of the day.

[10] Virtually all professional traders are able to deposit interest-earning assets, although many other account holders are required to deposit cash. If the deposit earns interest, there is no opportunity cost and no obvious necessity to withdraw the money to invest elsewhere.

B. *Holder of Short Position of 10 Contracts*

Day (1)	Beginning Balance (2)	Funds Deposited (3)	Settlement Price (4)	Futures Price Change (5)	Gain/ Loss (6)	Ending Balance (7)
0	0	50	100.00			50
1	50	0	99.20	−0.80	8	58
2	58	0	96.00	−3.20	32	90
3	90	0	101.00	5.00	−50	40
4	40	0	103.50	2.50	−25	15
5	15	35	103.00	−0.50	5	55
6	55	0	104.00	1.00	−10	45

The ending balance on Day 0 is then carried forward to the beginning balance on Day 1. On Day 1, the futures price moves down to 99.20, as indicated in Column 4 of Panel A. The futures price change, Column 5, is −0.80 (99.20 − 100). This amount is then multiplied by the number of contracts to obtain the number in Column 6 of −0.80 × 10 = −$8. The ending balance, Column 7, is the beginning balance plus the gain or loss. The ending balance on Day 1 of $42 is above the maintenance margin requirement of $30, so no funds need to be deposited on Day 2.

On Day 2 the settlement price goes down to $96. Based on a price decrease of $3.20 per contract and 10 contracts, the loss is $32, lowering the ending balance to $10. This amount is $20 below the maintenance margin requirement. Thus, the trader will get a margin call the following morning and must deposit $40 to bring the balance up to the initial margin level of $50. This deposit is shown in Column 3 on Day 3.

Here, we must emphasize two important points. First, additional margin that must be deposited is the amount sufficient to bring the ending balance up to the initial margin requirement, not the maintenance margin requirement.[11] This additional margin is called the **variation margin**. In addition, the amount that must be deposited the following day is determined regardless of the price change the following day, which might bring the ending balance well above the initial margin requirement, as it does here, or even well below the maintenance margin requirement. Thus, another margin call could occur. Also note that when the trader closes the position, the account is marked to market to the final price at which the transaction occurs, not the settlement price that day.

Over the six-day period, the trader in this example deposited $90. The account balance at the end of the sixth day is $130—nearly a 50 percent return over six days; not bad. But look at Panel B, which shows the position of a holder of 10 short contracts over that same period. Note that the short gains when prices decrease and loses when prices increase. Here the ending balance falls below the maintenance margin requirement on Day 4, and the short must deposit $35 on Day 5. At the end of Day 6, the short has deposited $85 and the balance is $45, a loss of $40 or nearly 50 percent, which is the same $40 the long made. Both cases illustrate the leverage effect that magnifies gains and losses.

When establishing a futures position, it is important to know the price level that would trigger a margin call. In this case, it does not matter how many contracts one has. The price change would need to fall for a long position (or rise for a short position) by the difference between the initial and maintenance margin requirements. In this example, the

---

[11] In the stock market, one must deposit only the amount necessary to bring the balance up to the maintenance margin requirement.

difference between the initial and maintenance margin requirements is $5 − $3 = $2. Thus, the price would need to fall from $100 to $98 for a long position (or rise from $100 to $102 for a short position) to trigger a margin call.

As described here, when a trader receives a margin call, he is required to deposit funds sufficient to bring the account balance back up to the initial margin level. Alternatively, the trader can choose to simply close out the position as soon as possible. For example, consider the position of the long at the end of the second day when the margin balance is $10. This amount is $20 below the maintenance level, and he is required to deposit $40 to bring the balance up to the initial margin level. If he would prefer not to deposit the additional funds, he can close out the position as soon as possible the following day. Suppose, however, that the price is moving quickly at the opening on Day 3. If the price falls from $96 to $95, he has lost $10 more, wiping out the margin account balance. In fact, if it fell any further, he would have a negative margin account balance. He is still responsible for these losses. Thus, the trader could lose more than the amount of money he has placed in the margin account. The total amount of money he could lose is limited to the price per contract at which he bought, $100, times the number of contracts, 10, or $1,000. Such a loss would occur if the price fell to zero, although this is not likely. This potential loss may not seem like a lot, but it is certainly large relative to the initial margin requirement of $50. For the holder of the short position, there is no upper limit on the price and the potential loss is theoretically infinite.

PRACTICE PROBLEM 1

Consider a futures contract in which the current futures price is $82. The initial margin requirement is $5, and the maintenance margin requirement is $2. You go long 20 contracts and meet all margin calls but do not withdraw any excess margin. Assume that on the first day, the contract is established at the settlement price, so there is no mark-to-market gain or loss on that day.

A. Complete the table below and provide an explanation of any funds deposited.

Day	Beginning Balance	Funds Deposited	Futures Price	Price Change	Gain/Loss	Ending Balance
0			82			
1			84			
2			78			
3			73			
4			79			
5			82			
6			84			

B. Determine the price level that would trigger a margin call.

SOLUTIONS

A.

Day	Beginning Balance	Funds Deposited	Futures Price	Price Change	Gain/Loss	Ending Balance
0	0	100	82			100
1	100	0	84	2	40	140

2	140	0	78	−6	−120	20
3	20	80	73	−5	−100	0
4	0	100	79	6	120	220
5	220	0	82	3	60	280
6	280	0	84	2	40	320

On Day 0, you deposit $100 because the initial margin requirement is $5 per contract and you go long 20 contracts. At the end of Day 2, the balance is down to $20, which is $20 below the $40 maintenance margin requirement ($2 per contract times 20 contracts). You must deposit enough money to bring the balance up to the initial margin requirement of $100 ($5 per contract times 20 contracts). So on Day 3, you deposit $80. The price change on Day 3 causes a gain/loss of −$100, leaving you with a balance of $0 at the end of Day 3. On Day 4, you must deposit $100 to return the balance to the initial margin level.

B. A price decrease to $79 would trigger a margin call. This calculation is based on the fact that the difference between the initial margin requirement and the maintenance margin requirement is $3. If the futures price starts at $82, it can fall by $3 to $79 before it triggers a margin call.

Some futures contracts impose limits on the price change that can occur from one day to the next. Appropriately, these are called **price limits**. These limits are usually set as an absolute change over the previous day. Using the example above, suppose the price limit was $4. This would mean that each day, no transaction could take place higher than the previous settlement price plus $4 or lower than the previous settlement price minus $4. So the next day's settlement price cannot go beyond the price limit and thus no transaction can take place beyond the limits.

If the price at which a transaction would be made exceeds the limits, then price essentially freezes at one of the limits, which is called a **limit move**. If the price is stuck at the upper limit, it is called **limit up**; if stuck at the lower limit, it is called **limit down**. If a transaction cannot take place because the price would be beyond the limits, this situation is called **locked limit**. By the end of the day, unless the price has moved back within the limits, the settlement price will then be at one of the limits. The following day, the new range of acceptable prices is based on the settlement price plus or minus limits. The exchanges have different rules that provide for expansion or contraction of price limits under some circumstances. In addition, not all contracts have price limits.

Finally, we note that the exchanges have the power to mark contracts to market whenever they deem it necessary. Thus, they can do so during the trading day rather than wait until the end of the day. They sometimes do so when abnormally large market moves occur.

The daily settlement procedure is designed to collect losses and distribute gains in such a manner that losses are paid before becoming large enough to impose a serious risk of default. Recall that the clearinghouse guarantees to each party that it need not worry about collecting from the counterparty. The clearinghouse essentially positions itself in the middle of each contract, becoming the short counterparty to the long and the long counterparty to the short. The clearinghouse collects funds from the parties incurring losses in this daily settlement procedure and distributes them to the parties incurring gains. By doing so each day, the clearinghouse ensures that losses cannot build up. Of course, this process offers no guarantee that counterparties will not default. Some defaults do occur, but the counterparty is defaulting to the clearinghouse, which has never failed to pay off the opposite party. In the unlikely event that the clearinghouse were unable to pay, it would turn to a reserve fund or to the exchange, or it would levy a tax on exchange members to cover losses.

4   DELIVERY AND CASH SETTLEMENT

As previously described, a futures trader can close out a position before expiration. If the trader holds a long position, she can simply enter into a position to go short the same futures contract. From the clearinghouse's perspective, the trader holds both a long and short position in the same contract. These positions are considered to offset and, therefore, there is no open position in place. Most futures contracts are offset before expiration. Those that remain in place are subject to either delivery or a final cash settlement. Here we explore this process, which determines how a futures contract terminates at expiration.

When the exchange designs a futures contract, it specifies whether the contract will terminate with delivery or cash settlement. If the contract terminates in delivery, the clearinghouse selects a counterparty, usually the holder of the oldest long contract, to accept delivery. The holder of the short position then delivers the underlying to the holder of the long position, who pays the short the necessary cash for the underlying. Suppose, for example, that two days before expiration, a party goes long one futures contract at a price of $50. The following day (the day before expiration), the settlement price is $52. The trader's margin account is then marked to market by crediting it with a gain of $2. Then suppose that the next day the contract expires with the settlement price at $53. As the end of the trading day draws near, the trader has two choices. She can attempt to close out the position by selling the futures contract. The margin account would then be marked to market at the price at which she sells. If she sells close enough to the expiration, the price she sold at would be very close to the final settlement price of $53. Doing so would add $1 to her margin account balance.

The other choice is to leave the position open at the end of the trading day. Then she would have to take delivery. If that occurred, she would be required to take possession of the asset and pay the short the settlement price of the previous day. Doing so would be equivalent to paying $52 and receiving the asset. She could then sell the asset for its price of $53, netting a $1 gain, which is equivalent to the final $1 credited to her margin account if she had terminated the position at the settlement price of $53, as described above.[12]

An alternative settlement procedure, which we described in Chapter 2 on forward contracts, is cash settlement. The exchange designates certain futures contracts as cash-settled contracts. If the contract used in this example were cash settled, then the trader would not need to close out the position close to the end of the expiration day. She could simply leave the position open. When the contract expires, her margin account would be marked to market for a gain on the final day of $1. Cash settlement contracts have some advantages over delivery contracts, particularly with respect to significant savings in transaction costs.[13]

---

[12] The reason she pays the settlement price of the previous day is because on the previous day when her account was marked to market, she essentially created a new futures position at a price of $52. Thus, she committed to purchase the asset at expiration, just one day later, at a price of $52. The next day when the contract expires, it is then appropriate that she buy the underlying for $52.

[13] Nonetheless, cash settlement has been somewhat controversial in the United States. If a contract is designated as cash settlement, it implies that the buyer of the contract never intended to actually take possession of the underlying asset. Some legislators and regulators feel that this design is against the spirit of the law, which views a futures contract as a commitment to buy the asset at a later date. Even though parties often offset futures contracts prior to expiration, the possibility of actual delivery is still present in contracts other than those settled by cash. This controversy, however, is relatively minor and has caused no serious problems or debates in recent years.

Exhibit 3-2 illustrates the equivalence of these three forms of delivery. Note, however, that because of the transaction costs of delivery, parties clearly prefer a closeout or cash settlement over physical delivery, particularly when the underlying asset is a physical commodity.

EXHIBIT 3-2   Closeout versus Physical Delivery versus Cash Settlement

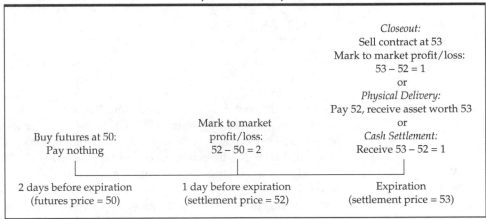

Contracts designated for delivery have a variety of features that can complicate delivery. In most cases, delivery does not occur immediately after expiration but takes place over several days. In addition, many contracts permit the short to choose when delivery takes place. For many contracts, delivery can be made any business day of the month. The delivery period usually includes the days following the last trading day of the month, which is usually in the third week of the month.

In addition, the short often has other choices regarding delivery, a major one being exactly which underlying asset is delivered. For example, a futures contract on U.S. Treasury bonds trading at the Chicago Board of Trade permits the short to deliver any of a number of U.S. Treasury bonds.[14] The wheat futures contract at the Chicago Board of Trade permits delivery of any of several types of wheat. Futures contracts calling for physical delivery of commodities often permit delivery at different locations. A given commodity delivered to one location is not the same as that commodity delivered to another because of the costs involved in transporting the commodity. The short holds the sole right to make decisions about what, when, and where to deliver, and the right to make these decisions can be extremely valuable. The right to make a decision concerning these aspects of delivery is called a **delivery option**.

Some futures contracts that call for delivery require delivery of the actual asset, and some use only a book entry. For example, in this day and age, no one physically handles U.S. Treasury bonds in the form of pieces of paper. Bonds are transferred electronically over the Federal Reserve's wire system. Other contracts, such as oil or wheat, do actually involve the physical transfer of the asset. Physical delivery is more common when the underlying is a physical commodity, whereas book entry is more common when the underlying is a financial asset.

Futures market participants use one additional delivery procedure, which is called **exchange for physicals (EFP)**. In an EFP transaction, the long and short arrange an alternative delivery procedure. For example, the Chicago Board of Trade's wheat futures

---

[14] We shall cover this feature in more detail in Sections 6.2 and 7.2.3.

contracts require delivery on certain dates at certain locations either in Chicago or in a few other specified locations in the Midwest. If the long and short agree, they could effect delivery by having the short deliver the wheat to the long in, for example, Omaha. The two parties would then report to the Chicago Board of Trade that they had settled their contract outside of the exchange's normal delivery procedures, which would be satisfactory to the exchange.

5   FUTURES EXCHANGES

A futures exchange is a legal corporate entity whose shareholders are its members. The members own memberships, more commonly called **seats**. Exchange members have the privilege of executing transactions on the exchange. Each member acts as either a **floor trader** or a **broker**. Floor traders are typically called **locals**; brokers are typically called **futures commission merchants (FCMs)**. Locals are market makers, standing ready to buy and sell by quoting a bid and an ask price. They are the primary providers of liquidity to the market. FCMs execute transactions for other parties off the exchange.

The locals on the exchange floor typically trade according to one of several distinct styles. The most common is called scalping. A **scalper** offers to buy or sell futures contracts, holding the position for only a brief period of time, perhaps just seconds. Scalpers attempt to profit by buying at the bid price and selling at the higher ask price. A **day trader** holds a position open somewhat longer but closes all positions at the end of the day.[15] A **position trader** holds positions open overnight. Day traders and position traders are quite distinct from scalpers in that they attempt to profit from the anticipated direction of the market; scalpers are trying simply to buy at the bid and sell at the ask.

Recall that futures exchanges have trading either on the floor or off the floor on electronic terminals, or in some cases, both. As previously described, floor trading in the United States takes place in pits, which are octagonal, multi-tiered areas where floor traders stand and conduct transactions. Traders wear jackets of specific colors and badges to indicate such information as what type of trader (FCM or local) they are and whom they represent.[16] As noted, to indicate a willingness to trade, a trader shouts and uses a set of standard hand signals. A trade is consummated by two traders agreeing on a price and a number of contracts. These traders might not actually say anything to each other; they may simply use a combination of hand signals and/or eye contact to agree on a transaction. When a transaction is agreed on, the traders fill out small paper forms and turn them over to clerks, who then see that the transactions are entered into the system and reported.

Each trader is required to have an account at a clearing firm. The clearing firms are the actual members of the clearinghouse. The clearinghouse deals only with the clearing firms, which then deal with their individual and institutional customers.

In electronic trading, the principles remain essentially the same but the traders do not stand in the pits. In fact, they do not see each other at all. They sit at computer terminals, which enable them to see the bids and offers of other traders. Transactions are executed by the click of a computer mouse or an entry from a keyboard.

Exhibit 3-3 lists the world's 20 leading futures exchanges in 2001, ranked by trading volume. Recall from Chapter 1 that trading volume can be a misleading measure of the

---

[15] The term "day trader" has been around the futures market for a long time but has recently acquired a new meaning in the broader financial markets. The term is now used to describe individual investors who trade stocks, often over the Internet, during the day for a living or as a hobby. In fact, the term has even been used in a somewhat pejorative manner, in that day traders are often thought of as naïve investors speculating wildly with money they can ill afford to lose.

[16] For example, an FCM or local could be trading for himself or could represent a company.

size of a futures markets; nonetheless, it is the measure primarily used. The structure of global futures exchanges has changed considerably in recent years. Exchanges in the United States, primarily the Chicago Board of Trade and the Chicago Mercantile Exchange, were clearly the world leaders in the past. Note that the volume leader now, however, is Eurex, the combined German–Swiss exchange. Eurex has been so successful partly because of its decision to be an all-electronic futures exchange, whereas the Chicago exchanges are still primarily pit-trading exchanges. Note the popularity of futures trading in Japan; four of the 20 leading exchanges are Japanese.

EXHIBIT 3-3   The World's 20 Leading Futures Exchanges

Exchange and Location	Volume in 2001 (Number of Contracts)
Eurex (Germany and Switzerland)	435,141,707
Chicago Mercantile Exchange (United States)	315,971,885
Chicago Board of Trade (United States)	209,988,002
London International Financial Futures and Options Exchange (United Kingdom)	161,522,775
Bolsa de Mercadorias & Futuros (Brazil)	94,174,452
New York Mercantile Exchange (United States)	85,039,984
Tokyo Commodity Exchange (Japan)	56,538,245
London Metal Exchange (United Kingdom)	56,224,495
Paris Bourse SA (France)	42,042,673
Sydney Futures Exchange (Australia)	34,075,508
Korea Stock Exchange (Korea)	31,502,184
Singapore Exchange (Singapore)	30,606,546
Central Japan Commodity Exchange (Japan)	27,846,712
International Petroleum Exchange (United Kingdom)	26,098,207
OM Stockholm Exchange (Sweden)	23,408,198
Tokyo Grain Exchange (Japan)	22,707,808
New York Board of Trade (United States)	14,034,168
MEFF Renta Variable (Spain)	13,108,293
Tokyo Stock Exchange (Japan)	12,465,433
South African Futures Exchange (South Africa)	11,868,242

Source: Futures Industry, January/February 2002

6 TYPES OF FUTURES CONTRACTS

The different types of futures contracts are generally divided into two main groups: commodity futures and financial futures. Commodity futures cover traditional agricultural, metal, and petroleum products. Financial futures include stocks, bonds, and currencies. Exhibit 3-4 gives a broad overview of the most active types of futures contracts traded on global futures exchanges. These contracts are those covered by the *Wall Street Journal* on the date indicated.

EXHIBIT 3-4   Most-Active Global Futures Contracts as Covered by the *Wall Street Journal*, 18 June 2002

Commodity Futures		Financial Futures
Corn (CBOT)	Treasury Bonds (CBOT)	Euro (CME)
Oats (CBOT)	Treasury Notes (CBOT)	Euro–Sterling (NYBOT)
Soybeans (CBOT)	10-Year Agency Notes (CBOT)	Euro–U.S. Dollar (NYBOT)
Soybean Meal (CBOT)	10-Year Interest Rate Swaps (CBOT)	Euro–Yen (NYBOT)
Soybean Oil (CBOT)	2-Year Agency Notes (CBOT)	Dow Jones Industrial Average (CBOT)
Wheat (CBOT, KCBT, MGE)	5-Year Treasury Notes (CBOT)	Mini Dow Jones Industrial Average (CBOT)
Canola (WPG)	2-Year Treasury Notes (CBOT)	S&P 500 Index (CME)
Barley (WPG)	Federal Funds (CBOT)	Mini S&P 500 Index (CME)
Feeder Cattle (CME)	Municipal Bond Index (CBOT)	S&P Midcap 400 Index (CME)
Live Cattle (CME)	Treasury Bills (CME)	Nikkei 225 (CME)
Lean Hogs (CME)	1-Month LIBOR (CME)	Nasdaq 100 Index (CME)
Pork Bellies (CME)	Eurodollar (CME)	Mini Nasdaq Index (CME)
Milk (CME)	Euroyen (CME, SGX)	Goldman Sachs Commodity Index (CME)
Lumber (CME)	Short Sterling (LIFFE)	Russell 1000 Index (CME)
Cocoa (NYBOT)	Long Gilt (LIFFE)	Russell 2000 Index (CME)
Coffee (NYBOT)	3-Month Euribor (LIFFE)	NYSE Composite Index (NYBOT)
World Sugar (NYBOT)	3-Month Euroswiss (LIFFE)	U.S. Dollar Index (NYBOT)
Domestic Sugar (NYBOT)	Canadian Bankers Acceptance (ME)	Share Price Index (SFE)
Cotton (NYBOT)	10-Year Canadian Government Bond (ME)	CAC 40 Stock Index (MATIF)
Orange Juice (NYBOT)	10-Year Euro Notional Bond (MATIF)	Xetra Dax (EUREX)
Copper (NYMEX)	3-Month Euribor (MATIF)	FTSE 200 Index (LIFFE)
Gold (NYMEX)	3-Year Commonwealth T-Bonds (SFE)	Dow Jones Euro Stoxx 50 Index (EUREX)
Platinum (NYMEX)	5-Year German Euro Government Bond (EUREX)	Dow Jones Stoxx 50 Index (EUREX)
Palladium (NYMEX)	10-Year German Euro Government Bond (EUREX)	
Silver (NYMEX)	2-Year German Euro Government Bond (EUREX)	
Crude Oil (NYMEX)	Japanese Yen (CME)	
No. 2 Heating Oil (NYMEX)	Canadian Dollar (CME)	
Unleaded Gasoline (NYMEX)	British Pound (CME)	
Natural Gas (NYMEX)	Swiss Franc (CME)	
Brent Crude Oil (IPEX)	Australian Dollar (CME)	
Gas Oil (IPEX)	Mexican Peso (CME)	

Exchange codes: CBOT (Chicago Board of Trade), CME (Chicago Mercantile Exchange), LIFFE (London International Financial Futures Exchange), WPG (Winnipeg Grain Exchange), EUREX (Eurex), NYBOT (New York Board of Trade), IPEX (International Petroleum Exchange), MATIF (Marché a Terme International de France), ME (Montreal Exchange), MGE (Minneapolis Grain Exchange), SFE (Sydney Futures Exchange), SGX (Singapore Exchange), KCBT (Kansas City Board of Trade), NYMEX (New York Mercantile Exchange)

Note: These are not the only global futures contracts but are those covered in the *Wall Street Journal* on the date given and represent the most active contracts at that time.

Our primary focus in this book is on financial and currency futures contracts. Within the financials group, our main interest is on interest rate and bond futures, stock index futures, and currency futures. We may occasionally make reference to a commodity futures contract, but that will primarily be for illustrative purposes. In the following subsections, we introduce the primary contracts we shall focus on. These are U.S. contracts, but they resemble most types of futures contracts found on exchanges throughout the world. Full contract specifications for these and other contracts are available on the Web sites of the futures exchanges, which are easy to locate with most Internet search engines.

6.1 SHORT-TERM INTEREST RATE FUTURES CONTRACTS

The primary short-term interest rate futures contracts are those on U.S. Treasury bills and Eurodollars on the Chicago Mercantile Exchange.

6.1.1 TREASURY BILL FUTURES

The Treasury bill contract, launched in 1976, was the first interest rate futures contract. It is based on a 90-day U.S. Treasury bill, one of the most important U.S. government debt instruments (described in Chapter 2, Section 3.2.1). The Treasury bill, or T-bill, is a discount instrument, meaning that its price equals the face value minus a discount representing interest. The discount equals the face value multiplied by the quoted rate times the days to maturity divided by 360. Thus, using the example from Chapter 2, if a 180-day T-bill is selling at a discount of 4 percent, its price per $1 par is $1 - 0.04(180/360) = 0.98$. An investor who buys the bill and holds it to maturity would receive $1 at maturity, netting a gain of $0.02.

The futures contract is based on a 90-day $1,000,000 U.S. Treasury bill. Thus, on any given day, the contract trades with the understanding that a 90-day T-bill will be delivered at expiration. While the contract is trading, its price is quoted as 100 minus the rate quoted as a percent priced into the contract by the futures market. This value, 100 − Rate, is known as the IMM Index; IMM stands for International Monetary Market, a division of the Chicago Mercantile Exchange. The IMM Index is a reported and publicly available price; however, it is not the actual futures price, which is

$$100 - (Rate/100)(90/360)$$

For example, suppose on a given day the rate priced into the contract is 6.25 percent. Then the quoted price will be $100 - 6.25 = 93.75$. The actual futures price would be

$$\$1,000,000[1 - 0.0625(90/360)] = \$984,375$$

Recall, however, that except for the small margin deposit, a futures transaction does not require any cash to be paid up front. As trading takes place, the rate fluctuates with market interest rates and the associated IMM Index price changes accordingly. The actual futures price, as calculated above, also fluctuates according to the above formula, but interestingly, that price is not very important. The same information can be captured more easily by referencing the IMM Index than by calculating the actual price.

Suppose, for example, that a trader had his account marked to market to the above price, 6.25 in terms of the rate, 93.75 in terms of the IMM Index, and $984,375 in terms of the actual futures price. Now suppose the rate goes to 6.50, an increase of 0.25 or 25 basis points. The IMM Index declines to 93.50, and the actual futures price drops to

$$\$1,000,000[1 - 0.065(90/360)] = \$983,750$$

Thus, the actual futures price decreased by \$984,375 − \$983,750 = \$625. A trader who is long would have a loss of \$625; a trader who is short would have a gain of \$625.

This \$625 gain or loss can be arrived at more directly, however, by simply noting that each basis point move is equivalent to \$25.[17] This special design of the contract makes it easy for floor traders to do the necessary arithmetic in their heads. For example, if floor traders observe the IMM Index move from 93.75 to 93.50, they immediately know that it has moved down 25 basis points and that 25 basis points times \$25 per basis point is a loss of \$625. The minimum tick size is one-half basis point or \$12.50.

T-bill futures contracts have expirations of the current month, the next month, and the next four months of March, June, September, and December. Because of the small trading volume, however, only the closest expiration has much trading volume, and even that one is only lightly traded. T-bill futures expire specifically on the Monday of the week of the third Wednesday each month and settle in cash rather than physical delivery of the T-bill, as described in Section 4.

As important as Treasury bills are in U.S. financial markets, however, today this futures contract is barely active. The Eurodollar contract is considered much more important because it reflects the interest rate on a dollar borrowed by a high-quality private borrower. The rates on T-bills are considered too heavily influenced by U.S. government policies, budget deficits, government funding plans, politics, and Federal Reserve monetary policy. Although unquestionably Eurodollar rates are affected by those factors, market participants consider them much less directly influenced. But in spite of this relative inactivity, T-bill futures are useful instruments for illustrating certain principles of futures market pricing and trading. Accordingly, we shall use them on some occasions. For now, however, we turn to the Eurodollar futures contract.

6.1.2 EURODOLLAR FUTURES

Recall that in Chapter 2, we devoted a good bit of effort to understanding Eurodollar forward contracts, known as FRAs. These contracts pay off based on LIBOR on a given day. The Eurodollar futures contract of the Chicago Mercantile Exchange is based on \$1 million notional principal of 90-day Eurodollars. Specifically, the underlying is the rate on a 90-day dollar-denominated time deposit issued by a bank in London. As we described in Chapter 2, this deposit is called a Eurodollar time deposit, and the rate is referred to as LIBOR (London Interbank Offer Rate). On a given day, the futures contract trades based on the understanding that at expiration, the official Eurodollar rate, as compiled by the British Bankers Association (BBA), will be the rate at which the final settlement of the contract is made. While the contract is trading, its price is quoted as 100 minus the rate priced into the contract by futures traders. Like its counterpart in the T-bill futures market, this value, 100 − Rate, is also known as the IMM Index.

As in the T-bill futures market, on a given day, if the rate priced into the contract is 5.25 percent, the quoted price will be 100 − 5.25 = 94.75. With each contract based on \$1 million notional principal of Eurodollars, the actual futures price is

$$\$1,000,000[1 - 0.0525(90/360)] = \$986,875$$

Like the T-bill contract, the actual futures price moves \$25 for every basis point move in the rate or IMM Index price.

---

[17] Expressed mathematically, \$1,000,000[0.0001(90/360)] = \$25. In other words, any move in the last digit of the rate (a basis point) affects the actual futures price by \$25.

As with all futures contracts, the price fluctuates on a daily basis and margin accounts are marked to market according to the exchange's official settlement price. At expiration, the final settlement price is the official rate quoted on a 90-day Eurodollar time deposit by the BBA. That rate determines the final settlement. Eurodollar futures contracts do not permit actual delivery of a Eurodollar time deposit; rather, they settle in cash, as described in Section 4.

The Eurodollar futures contract is one of the most active in the world. Because its rate is based on LIBOR, it is widely used by dealers in swaps, FRAs, and interest rate options to hedge their positions taken in dollar-denominated over-the-counter interest rate derivatives. Such derivatives usually use LIBOR as the underlying rate.

It is important to note, however, that there is a critical distinction between the manner in which the interest calculation is built into the Eurodollar futures contract and the manner in which interest is imputed on actual Eurodollar time deposits. Recall from Chapter 2 that when a bank borrows $1 million at a rate of 5 percent for 90 days, the amount it will owe in 90 days is

$$\$1,000,000[1 + 0.05(90/360)] = \$1,012,500$$

Interest on Eurodollar time deposits is computed on an add-on basis to the principal. As described in this section, however, it appears that in computing the futures price, interest is deducted from the principal so that a bank borrowing $1,000,000 at a rate of 5 percent would receive

$$\$1,000,000[1 - 0.05(90/360)] = \$987,500$$

and would pay back $1,000,000. This procedure is referred to as discount interest and is used in the T-bill market.

The discount interest computation associated with Eurodollar futures is merely a convenience contrived by the futures exchange to facilitate quoting prices in a manner already familiar to its traders, who were previously trading T-bill futures. This inconsistency between the ways in which Eurodollar futures and Eurodollar spot transactions are constructed causes some pricing problems, as we shall see in Section 7.2.2.

The minimum tick size for Eurodollar futures is 1 basis point or $25. The available expirations are the next two months plus March, June, September, and December. The expirations go out about 10 years, a reflection of their use by over-the-counter derivatives dealers to hedge their positions in long-term interest rate derivatives. Eurodollar futures expire on the second business day on which London banks are open before the third Wednesday of the month and terminate with a cash settlement.

6.2 INTERMEDIATE- AND LONG-TERM INTEREST RATE FUTURES CONTRACTS

In U.S. markets, the primary interest-rate-related instruments of intermediate and long maturities are U.S. Treasury notes and bonds. The U.S. government issues both instruments: Treasury notes have an original maturity of 2 to 10 years, and Treasury bonds have an original maturity of more than 10 years. Futures contracts on these instruments are very actively traded on the Chicago Board of Trade. For the most part, there are no real differences in the contract characteristics for Treasury note and Treasury bond futures; the underlying bonds differ slightly, but the futures contracts are qualitatively the same. We shall focus here on one of the most active instruments, the U.S. Treasury bond futures contract.

The contract is based on the delivery of a U.S. Treasury bond with any coupon but with a maturity of at least 15 years. If the deliverable bond is callable, it cannot be callable for at least 15 years from the delivery date.[18] These specifications mean that there are potentially a large number of deliverable bonds, which is exactly the way the Chicago Board of Trade, the Federal Reserve, and the U.S. Treasury want it. They do not want a potential run on a single issue that might distort prices. By having multiple deliverable issues, however, the contract must be structured with some fairly complicated procedures to adjust for the fact that the short can deliver whatever bond he chooses from among the eligible bonds. This choice gives the short a potentially valuable option and puts the long at a disadvantage. Moreover, it complicates pricing the contract, because the identity of the underlying bond is not clear. Although when referring to a futures contract on a 90-day Eurodollar time deposit we are relatively clear about the underlying instrument, a futures contract on a long-term Treasury bond does not allow us the same clarity.

To reduce the confusion, the exchange declares a standard or hypothetical version of the deliverable bond. This hypothetical deliverable bond has a 6 percent coupon. When a trader holding a short position at expiration delivers a bond with a coupon greater (less) than 6 percent, she receives an upward (a downward) adjustment to the price paid for the bond by the long. The adjustment is done by means of a device called the **conversion factor**. In brief, the conversion factor is the price of a $1.00 par bond with a coupon and maturity equal to those of the deliverable bond and a yield of 6 percent. Thus, if the short delivers a bond with a coupon greater (less) than 6 percent, the conversion factor exceeds (is less than) 1.0.[19] The amount the long pays the short is the futures price at expiration multiplied by the conversion factor. Thus, delivery of a bond with coupon greater (less) than the standard amount, 6 percent, results in the short receiving an upward (a downward) adjustment to the amount received. A number of other technical considerations are also involved in determining the delivery price.[20]

The conversion factor system is designed to put all bonds on equal footing. Ideally, application of the conversion factor would result in the short finding no preference for delivery of any one bond over any other. That is not the case, however, because the complex relationships between bond prices cannot be reduced to a simple linear adjustment, such as the conversion factor method. As a result, some bonds are cheaper to deliver than others. When making the delivery decision, the short compares the cost of buying a given bond on the open market with the amount she would receive upon delivery of that bond. The former will always exceed the latter; otherwise, a clear arbitrage opportunity would be available. The most attractive bond for delivery would be the one in which the amount received for delivering the bond is largest relative to the amount paid on the open market for the bond. The bond that minimizes this loss is referred to as the **cheapest-to-deliver** bond.

At any time during the life of a Treasury bond futures contract, traders can identify the cheapest-to-deliver bond. Determining the amount received at delivery is straightforward; it equals the current futures price times the conversion factor for a given bond. To determine the amount the bond would cost at expiration, one calculates the forward price of the bond, positioned at the delivery date. Of course, this is just a forward computation; circumstances could change by the expiration date. But this forward calculation gives a picture of circumstances as they currently stand and identifies which bond is currently the cheapest to deliver. That bond is then considered the bond most likely to be delivered.

---

[18] The U.S. government no longer issues callable bonds but has done so in the past.

[19] This statement is true regardless of the maturity of the deliverable bond. Any bond with a coupon in excess of its yield is worth more than its par value.

[20] For example, the actual procedure for delivery of U.S. Treasury bonds is a three-day process starting with the short notifying the exchange of intention to make delivery. Delivery actually occurs several days later. In addition, as is the custom in U.S. bond markets, the quoted price does not include the accrued interest. Accordingly, an adjustment must be made.

Recall that one problem with this futures contract is that the identity of the underlying bond is unclear. Traders traditionally treat the cheapest to deliver as the bond that underlies the contract. As time passes and interest rates change, however, the cheapest-to-deliver bond can change. Thus, the bond underlying the futures contract can change, adding an element of uncertainty to the pricing and trading of this contract.

With this complexity associated with the U.S. Treasury bond futures contract, one might suspect that it is less actively traded. In fact, the opposite is true: Complexity creates extraordinary opportunities for gain for those who understand what is going on and can identify the cheapest bond to deliver.

The Chicago Board of Trade's U.S. Treasury bond futures contract covers $100,000 par value of U.S. Treasury bonds. The expiration months are March, June, September, and December. They expire on the seventh business day preceding the last business day of the month and call for actual delivery, through the Federal Reserve's wire system, of the Treasury bond. Prices are quoted in points and 32nds, meaning that you will see prices like 98 18/32, which equals 98.5625. For a contract covering $100,000 par value, for example, the price is $98,562.50. The minimum tick size is 1/32, which is $31.25.

In addition to the futures contract on the long-term government bond, there are also very similar futures contracts on intermediate-term government bonds. The Chicago Board of Trade's contracts on 2-, 5-, and 10-year Treasury notes are very actively traded and are almost identical to its long-term bond contract, except for the exact specification of the underlying instrument. Intermediate and long-term government bonds are important instruments in every country's financial markets. They give the best indication of the long-term default-free interest rate and are often viewed as a benchmark bond for various comparisons in financial markets.[21] Accordingly, futures contracts on such bonds play an important role in a country's financial markets and are almost always among the most actively traded contracts in futures markets around the world.

If the underlying instrument is not widely available and not actively traded, the viability of a futures contract on it becomes questionable. The reduction seen in U.S. government debt in the late 1990s has led to a reduction in the supply of intermediate and long-term government bonds, and some concern has arisen over this fact. In the United States, some efforts have been made to promote the long-term debt of Fannie Mae and Freddie Mac as substitute benchmark bonds.[22] It remains to be seen whether such efforts will be necessary and, if so, whether they will succeed.

6.3 STOCK INDEX FUTURES CONTRACTS

One of the most successful types of futures contracts of all time is the class of futures on stock indices. Probably the most successful has been the Chicago Mercantile Exchange's contract on the Standard and Poor's 500 Stock Index. Called the S&P 500 Stock Index futures, this contract premiered in 1982 and has benefited from the widespread acceptance of the S&P 500 Index as a stock market benchmark. The contract is quoted in terms of a

---

[21] For example, the default risk of a corporate bond is often measured as the difference between the corporate bond yield and the yield on a Treasury bond or note of comparable maturity. Fixed rates on interest rate swaps are usually quoted as a spread over the rate on a Treasury bond or note of comparable maturity.

[22] Fannie Mae is the Federal National Mortgage Association, and Freddie Mac is the Federal Home Loan Mortgage Corporation. These institutions were formerly U.S. government agencies that issued debt to raise funds to buy and sell mortgages and mortgage-backed securities. These institutions are now publicly traded corporations but are considered to have extremely low default risk because of their critical importance in U.S. mortgage markets. It is believed that an implicit Federal government guarantee is associated with their debt. Nonetheless, it seems unlikely that the debt of these institutions could take over that of the U.S. government as a benchmark. The Chicago Board of Trade has offered futures contracts on the bonds of these organizations, but the contracts have not traded actively.

price on the same order of magnitude as the S&P 500 itself. For example, if the S&P 500 Index is at 1183, a two-month futures contract might be quoted at a price of, say, 1187. We shall explain how to determine a stock index futures price in Section 7.3.

The contract implicitly contains a multiplier, which is (appropriately) multiplied by the quoted futures price to produce the actual futures price. The multiplier for the S&P 500 futures is $250. Thus, when you hear of a futures price of 1187, the actual price is 1187($250) = $296,750.

S&P 500 futures expirations are March, June, September, and December and go out about two years, although trading is active only in the nearest two to three expirations. With occasional exceptions, the contracts expire on the Thursday preceding the third Friday of the month. Given the impracticality of delivering a portfolio of the 500 stocks in the index combined according to their relative weights in the index, the contract is structured to provide for cash settlement at expiration.

The S&P 500 is not the only active stock index futures contract. In fact, the Chicago Mercantile Exchange has a smaller version of the S&P 500 contract, called the Mini S&P 500, which has a multiplier of $50 and trades only electronically. Other widely traded contracts in the United States are on the Dow Jones Industrials, the S&P Midcap 400, and the Nasdaq 100. Virtually every developed country has a stock index futures contract based on the leading equities of that country. Well-known stock index futures contracts around the world include the United Kingdom's FTSE 100 (pronounced "Footsie 100"), Japan's Nikkei 225, France's CAC 40, and Germany's DAX 30.

6.4 CURRENCY FUTURES CONTRACTS

In Chapter 2 we described forward contracts on foreign currencies. There are also futures contracts on foreign currencies. Although the forward market for foreign currencies is much more widely used, the futures market is still quite active. In fact, currency futures were the first futures contracts not based on physical commodities. Thus, they are sometimes referred to as the first financial futures contracts, and their initial success paved the way for the later introduction of interest rate and stock index futures.

Compared with forward contracts on currencies, currency futures contracts are much smaller in size. In the United States, these contracts trade at the Chicago Mercantile Exchange with a small amount of trading at the New York Board of Trade. In addition there is some trading on exchanges outside the United States. The characteristics we describe below refer to the Chicago Mercantile Exchange's contract.

In the United States, the primary currencies on which trading occurs are the euro, Canadian dollar, Swiss franc, Japanese yen, British pound, Mexican peso, and Australian dollar. Each contract has a designated size and a quotation unit. For example, the euro contract covers €125,000 and is quoted in dollars per euro. A futures price such as $0.8555 is stated in dollars and converts to a contract price of

$$125,000(\$0.8555) = \$106,937.50$$

The Japanese yen futures price is structured somewhat differently. Because of the large number of yen per dollar, the contract covers ¥12,500,000 and is quoted without two zeroes that ordinarily precede the price. For example, a price might be stated as 0.8205, but this actually represents a price of 0.008205, which converts to a contract price of

$$12,500,000(0.008205) = \$102,562.50$$

Alternatively, a quoted price of 0.8205 can be viewed as 1/0.008205 = ¥121.88 per dollar.

Currency futures contracts expire in the months of March, June, September, and December. The specific expiration is the second business day before the third Wednesday of the month. Currency futures contracts call for actual delivery, through book entry, of the underlying currency.

We have briefly examined the different types of futures contracts of interest to us. Of course there are a variety of similar instruments trading on futures exchanges around the world. The purpose of this book, however, is not to provide institutional details, which can be obtained at the Web sites of the world's futures exchanges, but rather to enhance your understanding of the important principles necessary to function in the world of derivatives.

Until now we have made reference to prices of futures contracts. Accordingly, let us move forward and examine the pricing of futures contracts.

7 PRICING AND VALUATION OF FUTURES CONTRACTS

In Chapter 2, we devoted considerable effort to understanding the pricing and valuation of forward contracts. We first discussed the notion of what it means to *price* a forward contract in contrast to what it means to *value* a forward contract. Recall that pricing means to assign a fixed price or rate at which the underlying will be bought by the long and sold by the short at expiration. In assigning a forward price, we set the price such that the value of the contract is zero at the start. A zero-value contract means that the present value of the payments promised by each party to the other is the same, a result in keeping with the fact that neither party pays the other any money at the start. The value of the contract to the long is the present value of the payments promised by the short to the long minus the present value of the payments promised by the long to the short. Although the value is zero at the start, during the life of the contract, the value will fluctuate as market conditions change; the original forward contract price, however, stays the same.

In Chapter 2, we presented numerous examples of how to apply the concept of pricing and valuation when dealing with forward contracts on stocks, bonds, currencies, and interest rates. To illustrate the concepts of pricing and valuation, we started with a generic forward contract. Accordingly, we do so here in the futures chapter. We assume no transaction costs.

7.1 GENERIC PRICING AND VALUATION OF A FUTURES CONTRACT

As we did with forward contracts, we start by illustrating the time frame within which we are working:

	t − 1		t	T
0				
(today)				(expiration)

Today is time 0. The expiration date of the futures contract is time T. Times $t - 1$ and t are arbitrary times between today and the expiration and are the points at which the contract will be marked to market. Thus, we can think of the three periods depicted above, 0 to $t - 1$, $t - 1$ to t, and t to T, as three distinct trading days with times $t - 1$, t, and T being the end of each of the three days.

The price of the underlying asset in the spot market is denoted as S_0 at time 0, S_{t-1} at time $t - 1$, S_t at time t, and S_T at time T. We denote the futures contract price at time 0 as $f_0(T)$. This notation indicates that $f_0(T)$ is the price of a futures contract at time 0 that expires at time T. Unlike forward contract prices, however, futures prices fluctuate in an open and competitive market. The marking-to-market process results in each futures contract being terminated every day and reinitiated. Thus, we not only have a futures price set at time 0 but we also have a new one at time t − 1, at time t, and at time T. In other words,

$f_0(T)$ = price of a futures contract at time 0 that expires at time T

$f_{t-1}(T)$ = price of a futures contract at time t − 1 that expires at time T

$f_t(T)$ = price of a futures contract at time t that expires at time T

$f_T(T)$ = price of a futures contract at time T that expires at time T

Note, however, that $f_{t-1}(T)$ and $f_t(T)$ are also the prices of contracts newly established at times t − 1 and t for delivery at time T. Futures contracts are homogeneous and fungible. Any contract for delivery of the underlying at T is equivalent to any other contract, regardless of when the contracts were created.[23]

The value of the futures contract is denoted as $v_0(T)$. This notation indicates that $v_0(T)$ is the value at time 0 of a futures contract expiring at time T. We are also interested in the values of the contract prior to expiration, such as at time t, denoted as $v_t(T)$, as well as the value of the contract at expiration, denoted as $v_T(T)$.[24]

7.1.1   THE FUTURES PRICE AT EXPIRATION

Now suppose we are at time T. The spot price is S_T and the futures price is $f_T(T)$. To avoid an arbitrage opportunity, *the futures price must converge to the spot price at expiration*:

$$f_T(T) = S_T \tag{3-1}$$

Consider what would happen if this were not the case. If $f_T(T) < S_T$, a trader could buy the futures contract, let it immediately expire, pay $f_T(T)$ to take delivery of the underlying, and receive an asset worth S_T. The trader would have paid $f_T(T)$ and received an asset worth S_T, which is greater, at no risk. If $f_T(T) > S_T$, the trader would go short the futures, buy the asset for S_T, make delivery, and receive $f_T(T)$ for the asset, for which he paid a lesser amount. Only if $f_T(T) = S_T$ does this arbitrage opportunity go away. Thus, the futures price must equal the spot price at expiration.

Another way to understand this point is to recall that by definition, a futures contract calls for the delivery of an asset at expiration at a price determined when the transaction is initiated. If expiration is right now, a futures transaction is equivalent to a spot transaction, so the futures price must equal the spot price.

---

[23] As an analogy from the bond markets, consider a 9 percent coupon bond, originally issued with 10 years remaining. Three years later, that bond is a 9 percent seven-year bond. Consider a newly issued 9 percent coupon bond with seven years maturity and the same issuer. As long as the coupon dates are the same and all other terms are the same, these two bonds are fungible and are perfect substitutes for each other.

[24] It is important at this point to make some comments about notation. First, note that in Chapter 2 we use an uppercase F and V for forward contracts; here we use lowercase f and v for futures contracts. Also, we follow the pattern of using subscripts to indicate a price or value at a particular point in time. The arguments in parentheses refer to characteristics of a contract. Thus, in Chapter 2 we described the price of a forward contract as F(0,T) meaning the price of a forward contract initiated at time 0 and expiring at time T. This price does not fluctuate during the life of the contract. A futures contract, however, reprices on a daily basis. Its original time of initiation does not matter—it is reinitiated every day. Hence, futures prices are indicated by notation such as $f_0(T)$ and $f_t(T)$. We follow a similar pattern for value, using $V_0(0,T)$, $V_t(0,T)$, and $V_T(0,T)$ for forwards and $v_0(T)$, $v_t(T)$, and $v_T(T)$ for futures.

7.1.2 VALUATION OF A FUTURES

Let us consider how to determine the value of a futures contract. We already agreed that because no money changes hands, the value of a forward contract at the initiation date is zero. For the same reason, *the value of a futures contract at the initiation date is zero.* Thus,

$$v_0(T) = 0 \qquad\qquad (3\text{-}2)$$

Now let us determine the value of the contract during its life. Suppose we are at the end of the second day, at time t. In our diagram above, this point would be essentially at time t, but perhaps just an instant before it. So let us call it time t−. An instant later, we call the time point t+. In both cases, the futures price is $f_t(T)$. The contract was previously marked to market at the end of day t − 1 to a price of $f_{t-1}(T)$. An instant later when the futures account is marked to market, the trader will receive a gain of $f_t(T) - f_{t-1}(T)$. We can reasonably ignore the present value difference of receiving this money an instant later. Let us now state more formally that the value of a futures contract is

$$v_{t+}(T) = f_t(T) - f_{t-1}(T) \; \textit{an instant before the account is marked to market} \quad (3\text{-}3)$$

$$v_{t-}(T) = 0 \; \textit{as soon as the account is marked to market}$$

Suppose, however, that the trader is at a time j during the second trading day, between t − 1 and t. The accumulated gain or loss since the account was last marked to market is $f_j(T) - f_{t-1}(T)$. If the trader closes the position out, he would receive or be charged this amount at the end of the day. So the value at time j would be $f_j(T) - f_{t-1}(T)$ discounted back from the end of the day at time t until time j—that is, a fraction of a day. It is fairly routine to ignore this intraday interest. Thus, in general we say that *the value of a futures contract before it has been marked to market is the gain or loss accumulated since the account was last marked to market.*

So to recap, the value of a futures contract is the accumulated gain or loss since the last mark to market. The holder of a futures contract has a claim or liability on this amount. Once that claim is captured or the liability paid through the mark-to-market process, the contract is repriced to its current market price and the claim or liability goes back to a value of zero. Using these results, determining the value of a futures contract at expiration is easy. An instant before expiration, it is simply the accumulated profit since the last mark to market. At expiration, the value goes back to zero. With respect to the value of the futures, expiration is no different from any other day. Exhibit 3-5 summarizes the principles of valuation.

EXHIBIT 3-5 The Value of a Futures Contract Before and After Marking to Market

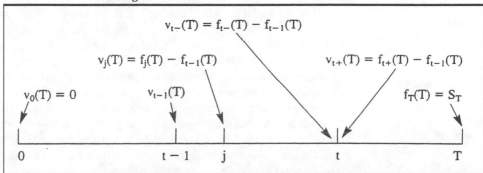

In Chapter 2, we devoted considerable effort toward understanding how forward contracts are valued. When holding positions in forward contracts, we are forced to assign values to instruments that do not trade in an open market with widely disseminated prices. Thus, it is important that we understand how forward contracts are valued. When dealing with futures contracts, the process is considerably simplified. Because futures contracts are generally quite actively traded, there is a market with reliable prices that provides all of the information we need. For futures contracts, we see that the value is simply the observable price change since the last mark to market.

7.1.3 FORWARD AND FUTURES PRICES

For all financial instruments, it is important to be able to determine whether the price available in the market is an appropriate one. Hence, we engage in the process of "pricing" the financial instrument. A major objective of this chapter is to determine the appropriate price of a futures contract. Given the similarity between futures and forward prices, however, we can benefit from studying forward contract pricing, which was covered in Chapter 2. But first, we must look at the similarities and differences between forward and futures contracts.

Recall that futures contracts settle daily and are essentially free of default risk. Forward contracts settle only at expiration and are subject to default risk. Yet both types of contracts allow the party to purchase or sell the underlying asset at a price agreed on in advance. It seems intuitive that futures prices and forward prices would be relatively close to each other.

The issues involved in demonstrating the relationship between futures and forward prices are relatively technical and beyond the scope of this book. We can, however, take a brief and fairly nontechnical look at the question. First let us ignore the credit risk issue. We shall assume that the forward contract participants are prime credit risks. We focus only on the technical distinction caused by the daily marking to market.

The day before expiration, both the futures contract and the forward contract have one day to go. At expiration, they will both settle. These contracts are therefore the same. At any other time prior to expiration, futures and forward prices can be the same or different. If interest rates are constant or at least known, any effect of the addition or subtraction of funds from the marking-to-market process can be shown to be neutral. If interest rates are positively correlated with futures prices, traders with long positions will prefer futures over forwards, because they will generate gains when interest rates are going up, and traders can invest those gains for higher returns. Also, traders will incur losses when interest rates are going down and can borrow to cover those losses at lower rates. Because traders holding long positions prefer the marking to market of futures over forwards when futures prices are positively correlated with interest rates, futures will carry higher prices than forwards. Conversely, when futures prices are negatively correlated with interest rates, traders will prefer not to mark to market, so forward contracts will carry higher prices.

Because interest rates and fixed-income security prices move in opposite directions, interest rate futures are good examples of cases in which forward and futures prices should be inversely related. Alternatively, when inflation is high, interest rates are high and investors oftentimes put their money in such assets as gold. Thus, gold futures prices and interest rates would tend to be positively correlated. It would be difficult to identify a situation in which futures prices are not correlated with interest rates. Zero correlation is rare in the financial world, but we can say that when the correlation is low or close to zero, the difference between forward and futures prices would be very small.

At this introductory level of treatment, we shall make the simplifying assumption that futures prices and forward prices are the same. We do so by ignoring the effects of marking a futures contract to market. In practice, some significant issues arise related to the marking-to-market process, but they detract from our ability to understand the important concepts in pricing and trading futures and forwards.

Therefore, based on the equivalence we are assuming between futures and forwards, we can assume that the value of a futures contract at expiration, before marking to market, is

$$v_T(T) = f_T(T) - f_0(T) = S_T - f_0(T)$$

with the spot price substituted for the futures price at T, given what we know about their convergence.

7.1.4 PRICING FUTURES CONTRACTS

Now let us proceed to the pricing of futures contracts. As we did with forward contracts, we consider the case of a generic underlying asset priced at $100. A futures contract calls for delivery of the underlying asset in one year at a price of $108. Let us see if $108 is the appropriate price for this futures contract.

Suppose we buy the asset for $100 and sell the futures contract. We hold the position until expiration. For right now, we assume no costs are involved in holding the asset. We do, however, lose interest on the $100 tied up in the asset for one year. We assume that this opportunity cost is at the risk-free interest rate of 5 percent.

Recall that no money changes hands at the start of a futures contract. Moreover, we can reasonably ignore the rather small margin deposit that would be required. In addition, margin deposits can generally be met by putting up interest-earning securities, so there is really no opportunity cost. As discussed in the previous section, we also will assume away the daily settlement procedure; in other words, the value of the futures contract paid out at expiration is the final futures price minus the original futures price. Because the final futures price converges to the spot price, the final payout is the spot price minus the original futures price.

So at the contract expiration, we are short the futures and must deliver the asset, which we own. We do so and receive the original futures price for it. So we receive $108 for an asset purchased a year ago at $100. At a 5 percent interest rate, we lose only $5 in interest, so our return in excess of the opportunity cost is 3 percent risk free. This risk-free return in excess of the risk-free rate is clearly attractive and would induce traders to buy the asset and sell the futures. This arbitrage activity would drive the futures price down until it reaches $105.

If the futures price falls below $105, say to $102, the opposite arbitrage would occur. The arbitrageur would buy the futures, but either we would need to be able to borrow the asset and sell it short, or investors who own the asset would have to be willing to sell it and buy the futures. They would receive the asset price of $100 and invest it at 5 percent interest. Then at expiration, those investors would get the asset back upon taking delivery, paying $102. This transaction would net a clear and risk-free profit of $3, consisting of interest of $5 minus a $2 loss from selling the asset at $100 and buying it back at $102. Again, through the buying of the futures and shorting of the asset, the forces of arbitrage would cause prices to realign to $105.

Some difficulties occur with selling short certain assets. Although the financial markets make short selling relatively easy, some commodities are not easy to sell short. In such a case, it is still possible for arbitrage to occur. If investors who already own the asset sell it and buy the futures, they can reap similar gains at no risk. Because our interest is in financial instruments, we shall ignore these commodity market issues and assume that short selling can be easily executed.[25]

---

[25] Keep in mind that there are some restrictions on the short selling of financial instruments, such as uptick rules and margin requirements, but we will not concern ourselves with these impediments here.

If the market price is not equal to the price given by the model, it is important to note that regardless of the asset price at expiration, the above arbitrage guarantees a risk-free profit. That profit is known at the time the parties enter the transaction. Exhibit 3-6 summarizes and illustrates this point.

EXHIBIT 3-6   The Risk-Free Nature of Long and Short Futures Arbitrage

Asset is priced at $100, futures is priced at $f_0(T)$ and expires in one year. Interest rate over the life of the futures is 5 percent.

Time	Long Asset, Short Futures Arbitrage	Short Asset, Long Futures Arbitrage
Today (time 0)	Buy asset at $100 Sell futures at $f_0(T)$	Sell short asset for $100 Buy futures for $f_0(T)$
Expiration (time T)	Asset price is S_T Futures price converges to asset price Deliver asset Profit on asset after accounting for the 5 percent ($5) interest lost from $100 tied up in the investment in the asset: $S_T - 100 - 5$ Profit on futures: $f_0(T) - S_T$ Total profit: $f_0(T) - 100 - 5$	Asset price is S_T Futures price converges to asset price Take delivery of asset Profit on asset after accounting for the 5 percent ($5) interest earned on the $100 received from the short sale of the asset: $100 + 5 - S_T$ Profit on futures: $S_T - f_0(T)$ Total profit: $100 + 5 - f_0(T)$

Conclusion: The asset price at expiration has no effect on the profit captured at expiration for either transaction. The profit is known today. To eliminate arbitrage, the futures price today, $f_0(T)$, must equal $100 + 5 = \$105$.

The transactions we have described are identical to those using forward contracts. We did note with forward contracts, however, that one can enter into an off-market forward contract, having one party pay cash to another to settle any difference resulting from the contract not trading at its arbitrage-free value up front. In the futures market, this type of arrangement is not permitted; all contracts are entered into without any cash payments up front.

So in general, through the forces of arbitrage, we say that *the futures price is the spot price compounded at the risk-free rate*:

$$f_0(T) = S_0(1 + r)$$

It is important, however, to write this result in a form we are more likely to use. In the above form, we specify r as the interest rate over the life of the futures contract. In financial markets, however, interest rates are nearly always specified as annual rates. Therefore, to compound the asset price over the life of the futures, we let r equal an annual rate and specify the life of the futures as T years. Then the futures price is found as

$$f_0(T) = S_0(1 + r)^T \tag{3-4}$$

The futures price is the spot price compounded over the life of the contract, T years, at the annual risk-free rate, r. From this point on, we shall use this more general specification.

As an example, consider a futures contract that has a life of 182 days; the annual interest rate is 5 percent. Then $T = 182/365$ and $r = 0.05$. If the spot price is $100, the futures price would then be

$$f_0(T) = S_0(1 + r)^T$$

$$f_0(182/365) = 100(1.05)^{182/365}$$

$$= 102.46$$

If the futures is selling for more than $102.46, an arbitrageur can buy the asset for $100 and sell the futures for whatever its price is, hold the asset (losing interest on $100 at an annual rate of 5 percent) and deliver it to receive the futures price. The overall strategy will net a return in excess of 5 percent a year at no risk. If the futures is selling for less than $102.46, the arbitrageur can borrow the asset, sell it short, and buy the futures. She will earn interest on the funds obtained from the short sale and take delivery of the asset at the futures expiration, paying the original futures price. The overall transaction results in receiving $100 up front and paying back an amount less than the 5 percent risk-free rate, making the transaction like a loan that is paid back at less than the risk-free rate. If one could create such a loan, one could use it to raise funds and invest the funds at the risk-free rate to earn unlimited gains.

7.1.5 PRICING FUTURES CONTRACTS WHEN THERE ARE STORAGE COSTS

Except for opportunity costs, we have until now ignored any costs associated with holding the asset. In many asset markets, there are significant costs, other than the opportunity cost, to holding an asset. These costs are referred to as **storage costs** or **carrying costs** and are generally a function of the physical characteristics of the underlying asset. Some assets are easy to store; some are difficult. For example, assume the underlying is oil, which has significant storage costs but a very long storage life.[26] One would not expect to incur costs associated with a decrease in quality of the oil. Significant risks do exist, however, such as spillage, fire, or explosion. Some assets on which futures are based are at risk for damage. For example, cattle and pigs can become ill and die during storage. Grains are subject to pest damage and fire. All of these factors have the potential to produce significant storage costs, and protection such as insurance leads to higher storage costs for these assets. On the other hand, financial assets have virtually no storage costs. Of course, all assets have one significant storage cost, which is the opportunity cost of money tied up in the asset, but this effect is covered in the present value calculation.

It is reasonable to assume that the storage costs on an asset are a function of the quantity of the asset to be stored and the length of time in storage. Let us specify this cost with the variable FV(SC,0,T), which denotes the value at time T (expiration) of the storage costs (excluding opportunity costs) associated with holding the asset over the period 0 to T. By specifying these costs as of time T, we are accumulating the costs and compounding the interest thereon until the end of the storage period. We can reasonably assume that when storage is initiated, these costs are known.[27]

Revisiting the example we used previously, we would buy the asset at S_0, sell a futures contract at $f_0(T)$, store the asset and accumulate costs of FV(SC,0,T), and deliver the asset at expiration to receive the futures price. The total payoff is $f_0(T) - FV(SC,0,T)$.

---

[26] After all, oil has been stored by nature for millions of years.

[27] There may be reason to suggest that storage costs have an element of uncertainty in them, complicating the analysis.

This amount is risk free. To avoid an arbitrage opportunity, its present value should equal the initial outlay, S_0, required to establish the position. Thus,

$$[f_0(T) - FV(SC,0,T)]/(1 + r)^T = S_0$$

Solving for the futures price gives

$$f_0(T) = S_0(1 + r)^T + FV(SC,0,T) \tag{3-5}$$

This result says that *the futures price equals the spot price compounded over the life of the futures contract at the risk-free rate, plus the future value of the storage costs over the life of the contract.* In the previous example with no storage costs, we saw that the futures price was the spot price compounded at the risk-free rate. With storage costs, we must add the future value of the storage costs. The logic behind this adjustment should make sense. The futures price should be higher by enough to cover the storage costs when a trader buys the asset and sells a futures to create a risk-free position.[28]

Consider the following example. The spot price of the asset is $50, the interest rate is 6.25 percent, the future value of the storage costs is $1.35, and the futures expires in 15 months. Then $T = 15/12 = 1.25$. The futures price would, therefore, be

$$f_0(T) = S_0(1 + r)^T + FV(SC,0,T)$$
$$f_0(1.25) = 50(1.0625)^{1.25} + 1.35$$
$$= 55.29$$

If the futures is selling for more than $55.29, the arbitrageur would buy the asset and sell the futures, holding the position until expiration, at which time he would deliver the asset and collect the futures price, earning a return that covers the 6.25 percent cost of the money and the storage costs of $1.35. If the futures is selling for less than $55.29, the arbitrageur would sell short the asset and buy the futures, reinvesting the proceeds from the short sale at 6.25 percent and saving the storage costs. The net effect would be to generate a cash inflow today plus the storage cost savings and a cash outflow at expiration that would replicate a loan with a rate less than the risk-free rate. Only if the futures sells for exactly $55.29 do these arbitrage opportunities go away.

7.1.6   PRICING FUTURES CONTRACTS WHEN THERE ARE CASH FLOWS ON THE UNDERLYING ASSET

In each case we have considered so far, the underlying asset did not generate any positive cash flows to the holder. For some assets, there will indeed be positive cash flows to the holder. Recall that in Chapter 2, we examined the pricing and valuation of forward contracts on stocks and bonds and were forced to recognize that stocks pay dividends, bonds pay interest, and these cash flows affect the forward price. A similar concept applies here and does so in a symmetric manner to what we described in the previous section in which the asset incurs a cash cost. As we saw in that section, a cash cost incurred from holding the asset increases the futures price. Thus, we might expect that cash generated from holding the asset would result in a lower futures price and, as we shall see in this section, that

---

[28] We did not cover assets that are storable at significant cost when we studied forward contracts because such contracts are less widely used for these assets. Nonetheless, the formula given here would apply for forward contracts as well, given our assumption of no credit risk on forward contracts.

is indeed the case. But in the next section, we shall also see that it is even possible for an asset to generate nonmonetary benefits that must also be taken into account when pricing a futures contract on it.

Let us start by assuming that over the life of the futures contract, the asset generates positive cash flows of FV(CF,0,T). It is no coincidence that this notation is similar to the one we used in the previous section for the storage costs of the underlying asset over the life of the futures. Cash inflows and storage costs are just different sides of the same coin. We must remember, however, that FV(CF,0,T) represents a positive flow in this case. Now let us revisit our example.

We would buy the asset at S_0, sell a futures contract at $f_0(T)$, store the asset and generate positive cash flows of FV(CF,0,T), and deliver the asset at expiration, receiving the futures price. The total payoff is $f_0(T) + $ FV(CF,0,T). This amount is risk free and known at the start. To avoid an arbitrage opportunity, its present value should equal the initial outlay, S_0, required to establish the position. Thus,

$$[f_0(T) + FV(CF,0,T)]/(1 + r)^T = S_0$$

Solving for the futures price gives

$$f_0(T) = S_0(1 + r)^T - FV(CF,0,T) \tag{3-6}$$

In the previous example that included storage costs, we saw that the futures price was the spot price compounded at the risk-free rate plus the future value of the storage costs. With positive cash flows, we must subtract the future value of these cash flows. The logic behind this adjustment should make sense. The futures price should be reduced by enough to account for the positive cash flows when a trader buys the asset and sells a futures to create a risk-free position. Otherwise, the trader would receive risk-free cash flows from the asset *and* the equivalent amount from the sale of the asset at the futures price. Reduction of the futures price by this amount avoids overcompensating the trader.

As noted, these cash flows can be in the form of dividends from a stock or coupon interest from a bond. When we specifically examine the pricing of bond and stock futures, we shall make this specification a little more precise and work an example.

7.1.7 PRICING FUTURES CONTRACTS WHEN THERE IS A CONVENIENCE YIELD

Now consider the possibility that the asset might generate nonmonetary benefits that must also be taken into account. The notion of nonmonetary benefits that could affect futures prices might sound strange, but upon reflection, it makes perfect sense. For example, a house is a common and normally desirable investment made by individuals and families. The house generates no monetary benefits and incurs significant costs. As well as being a possible monetary investment if prices rise, the house generates some nonmonetary benefits in the form of serving as a place to live. These benefits are quite substantial; many people consider owning a residence preferable to renting, and people often sell their homes for monetary gains far less than any reasonable return on a risky asset. Clearly the notion of a nonmonetary benefit to owning an asset is one most people are familiar with.

In a futures contract on an asset with a nonmonetary gain, that gain must be taken into account. Suppose, for the purpose of understanding the effect of nonmonetary benefits on a futures contract, we create a hypothetical futures contract on a house. An individual purchases a house and sells a futures contract on it. We shall keep the arguments as simple as possible by ignoring the operating or carrying costs. What should be the futures price? If the futures is priced at the spot price plus the risk-free rate, as in the original case, the homeowner receives a guaranteed sale price, giving a return of the risk-free rate *and* the use of the home. This is clearly a good deal. Homeowners would be eager to sell futures contracts, leading to a decrease in the price of the futures. Thus, any nonmonetary benefits ought to be factored into the futures price and logically would lead to a lower futures price.

Of course, in the real world of standardized futures contracts, there are no futures contracts on houses. Nonetheless, there are futures contracts on assets that have nonmonetary benefits. Assets that are often in short supply, particularly those with seasonal and highly risky production processes, are commonly viewed as having such benefits. The nonmonetary benefits of these assets are referred to as the **convenience yield**. Formally, a convenience yield is the nonmonetary return offered by an asset when in short supply. When an asset is in short supply, its price tends to be high. Holders of the asset earn an implicit incremental return from having the asset on hand. This return enables them, as commercial enterprises, to avoid the cost and inconvenience of not having their primary product or resource input on hand. Because shortages are generally temporary, the spot price can be higher than the futures price, even when the asset incurs storage costs. If a trader buys the asset, sells a futures contract, and stores the asset, the return is risk free and will be sufficient to cover the storage costs and the opportunity cost of money, but it will be reduced by an amount reflecting the benefits of holding the asset during a period of shortage or any other nonmonetary benefits.

Now, let the notation FV(CB,0,T) represent the future value of the costs of storage minus the benefits:

FV(CB,0,T) = Costs of storage − Nonmonetary benefits (Convenience yield)

where all terms are expressed in terms of their future value at time T and are considered to be known at time 0. If the costs exceed the benefits, FV(CB,0,T) is a positive number.[29] We refer to FV(CB,0,T) as the **cost of carry**.[30] The general futures pricing formula is

$$f_0(T) = S_0(1 + r)^T + FV(CB,0,T) \tag{3-7}$$

The futures price is the spot price compounded at the risk-free rate plus the cost of carry. This model is often called the **cost-of-carry model**.

Consider an asset priced at \$75; the risk-free interest rate is 5.15 percent, the net of the storage costs, interest, and convenience yield is \$3.20, and the futures expires in nine months. Thus, T = 9/12 = 0.75. Then the futures price should be

$$f_0(T) = S_0(1 + r)^T + FV(CB,0,T)$$
$$f_0(0.75) = 75(1.0515)^{0.75} + 3.20$$
$$= 81.08$$

As we have always done, we assume that this price will prevail in the marketplace. If it does not, the forces of arbitrage will drive the market price to the model price. If the futures

---

[29] In other words, FV(CB,0,T) has to be positive to refer to it as a "cost."

[30] In some cases, such as in inventory storage, it is customary to include the opportunity cost in the definition of cost of carry; but we keep it separate in this text.

price exceeds \$81.08, the arbitrageur can buy the asset and sell the futures to earn a risk-free return in excess of the risk-free rate. If the futures price is less than \$81.08, the arbitrageur can either sell the asset short or sell it if he already owns it, and then also buy the futures, creating a risk-free position equivalent to a loan that will cost less than the risk-free rate. The gains from both of these transactions will have accounted for any nonmonetary benefits. This arbitrage activity will force the market price to converge to the model price.

The above equation is the most general form of the futures pricing formula we shall encounter. Exhibit 3-7 reviews and illustrates how we obtained this formula and provides another example.

EXHIBIT 3-7   Pricing a Futures Contract

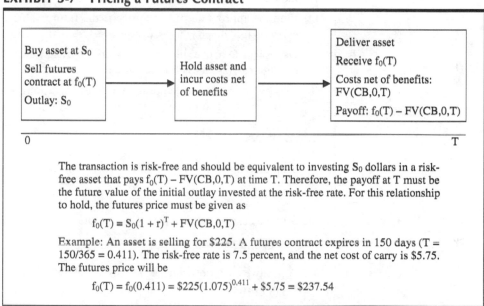

The transaction is risk-free and should be equivalent to investing S_0 dollars in a risk-free asset that pays $f_0(T) - FV(CB,0,T)$ at time T. Therefore, the payoff at T must be the future value of the initial outlay invested at the risk-free rate. For this relationship to hold, the futures price must be given as

$$f_0(T) = S_0(1 + r)^T + FV(CB,0,T)$$

Example: An asset is selling for \$225. A futures contract expires in 150 days (T = 150/365 = 0.411). The risk-free rate is 7.5 percent, and the net cost of carry is \$5.75. The futures price will be

$$f_0(T) = f_0(0.411) = \$225(1.075)^{0.411} + \$5.75 = \$237.54$$

Some variations of this general formula are occasionally seen. Sometimes the opportunity cost of interest is converted to dollars and imbedded in the cost of carry. Then we say that $f_0(T) = S_0 + FV(CB,0,T)$; the futures price is the spot price plus the cost of carry. This is a perfectly appropriate way to express the formula if the interest is imbedded in the cost of carry, but we shall not do so in this book.

Another variation of this formula is to specify the cost of carry in terms of a rate, such as y. Then we have $f_0(T) = S_0(1 + r)^T(1 + y)^T$. Again, this variation is certainly appropriate but is not the version we shall use.[31]

Note that when we get into the specifics of pricing certain types of futures contracts, we must fine-tune the formulas a little more. First, however, we explore some general characterizations of the relationship between futures and spot prices.

---

[31] Yet another variation of this formula is to use $(1 + r + y)^T$ as an approximation for $(1 + r)^T(1 + y)^T$. We do not, however, consider this expression an acceptable way to compute the futures price as it is an approximation of a formula that is simple enough to use without approximating.

PRACTICE PROBLEM 2

Consider an asset priced at $50. The risk-free interest rate is 8 percent, and a futures contract on the asset expires in 45 days. Answer the following, with questions A, B, C, and D independent of the others.

A. Find the appropriate futures price if the underlying asset has no storage costs, cash flows, or convenience yield.

B. Find the appropriate futures price if the future value of storage costs on the underlying asset at the futures expiration equals $2.25.

C. Find the appropriate futures price if the future value of positive cash flows on the underlying asset equals $0.75.

D. Find the appropriate futures price if the future value of the net overall cost of carry on the underlying asset equals $3.55.

E. Using Part D above, illustrate how an arbitrage transaction could be executed if the futures contract is trading at $60.

F. Using Part A above, determine the value of a long futures contract an instant before marking to market if the previous settlement price was $49.

SOLUTIONS

A. First determine that $T = 45/365 = 0.1233$. Then the futures price is

$$f_0(0.1233) = \$50(1.08)^{0.1233} = \$50.48$$

B. Storage costs must be covered in the futures price, so we add them:

$$f_0(0.1233) = \$50(1.08)^{0.1233} + \$2.25 = \$52.73$$

C. A positive cash flow, such as interest or dividends on the underlying, reduces the futures price:

$$f_0(0.1233) = \$50(1.08)^{0.1233} - \$0.75 = \$49.73$$

D. The net overall cost of carry must be covered in the futures price, so we add it:

$$f_0(0.1233) = \$50(1.08)^{0.1233} + \$3.55 = \$54.03$$

E. Follow these steps:
  - Sell the futures at $60.
  - Buy the asset at $50.
  - Because the asset price compounded at the interest rate is $50.48, the interest forgone is $0.48. So the asset price is effectively $50.48 by the time of the futures expiration.
  - Incur costs of $3.55.
  - At expiration, deliver the asset and receive $60. The net investment in the asset is $50.48 + $3.55 = $54.03. If the asset is sold for $60, the net gain is $5.97.

F. If the last settlement price was $49.00 and the price is now $50.48 (our answer in Part A), the value of a long futures contract equals the difference between these prices: $50.48 − $49.00 = $1.48.

7.1.8 BACKWARDATION AND CONTANGO

Because the cost of carry, FV(CB,0,T), can be either positive or negative, the futures price can be greater or less than the spot price. Because the costs plus the interest tend to exceed the benefits, it is more common for the futures price to exceed the spot price, a situation called **contango**. In contrast, when the benefits exceed the costs plus the interest, the futures price will be less than the spot price, called **backwardation**. These terms are not particularly important in understanding the necessary concepts, but they are so commonly used that they are worthwhile to remember.

7.1.9 FUTURES PRICES AND EXPECTED SPOT PRICES

An important concept when examining futures prices is the relationship between futures prices and expected spot prices. In order to fully understand the issue, let us first consider the relationship between spot prices and expected spot prices. Consider an asset with no risk, but which incurs carrying costs. At time 0, the holder of the asset purchases it with the certainty that she will cover her opportunity cost and carrying cost. Otherwise, she would not purchase the asset. Thus, the spot price at time 0 is the present value of the total of the spot price at time T less costs minus benefits:

$$S_0 = \frac{S_T - FV(CB,0,T)}{(1 + r)^T}$$

$$= \frac{S_T}{(1 + r)^T} - \frac{FV(CB,0,T)}{(1 + r)^T}$$

Because FV(CB,0,T) is the future value of the carrying cost, $FV(CB,0,T)/(1 + r)^T$ is the present value of the carrying cost. So on the one hand, we can say that the spot price is the future spot price minus the future value of the carrying cost, all discounted to the present. On the other hand, we can also say that the spot price is the discounted value of the future spot price minus the present value of the carrying cost.

If, however, the future price of the asset is uncertain, as it nearly always is, we must make some adjustments. For one, we do not know at time 0 what S_T will be. We must form an expectation, which we will denote as $E_0(S_T)$. But if we simply replace S_T above with $E_0(S_T)$ we would not be acting rationally. We would be paying a price today and expecting compensation only at the risk-free rate along with coverage of our carrying cost. Indeed, one of the most important and intuitive elements of all we know about finance is that risky assets require a risk premium. Let us denote this risk premium with the symbol, $\phi_0(S_T)$. It represents a discount off of the expected value that is imbedded in the current price, S_0. Specifically, the current price is now given as

$$S_0 = \frac{E_0(S_T) - FV(CB,0,T) - \phi_0(S_T)}{(1 + r)^T}$$

where we see that the risk premium lowers the current spot price. Intuitively, investors pay less for risky assets, all other things equal.

Until now, we have worked only with the spot price, but nothing we have said so far violates the rule of no arbitrage. Hence, our futures pricing formula, $f_0(T) = S_0(1 + r)^T + FV(CB,0,T)$, still applies. If we rearrange the futures pricing formula for FV(CB,0,T), substitute this result into the formula for S_0, and solve for the futures price, $f_0(T)$, we obtain $f_0(T) = E_0(S_T) - \phi_0(S_T)$. This equation says that the futures price equals the expected future spot price minus the risk premium.

An important conclusion to draw from this formula is that the futures price does not equal the expectation of the future spot price. The futures price would be biased on the high side. If one felt that the futures price were an unbiased predictor of the future spot price, $f_0(T) = E_0(S_T)$, one could expect on average to be able to predict the future spot price of oil by looking at the futures price of oil. But that is not likely to be the case.

The intuition behind this result is easy to see. We start with the assumption that all units of the asset must be held by someone. Holders of the asset incur the risk of its future selling price. If a holder of the asset wishes to transfer that risk by selling a futures contract, she must offer a futures contract for sale. But if the futures contract is offered at a price equal to the expected spot price, the buyer of the futures contract takes on the risk but expects to earn only a price equal to the price paid for the futures. Thus, the futures trader incurs the risk without an expected gain in the form of a risk premium. On the opposite side of the coin, the holder of the asset would have a risk-free position with an expected gain in excess of the risk-free rate. Clearly, the holder of the asset would not be able to do such a transaction. Thus, she must lower the price to a level sufficient to compensate the futures trader for the risk he is taking on. This process will lead to a futures price that equals the expected spot price minus the risk premium, as shown in the above equation. In effect, the risk premium transfers from the holder of the asset to the buyer of the futures contract.

In all fairness, however, we must acknowledge that this view is not without its opponents. Some consider the futures price an unbiased predictor of the future spot price. In such a case, the futures price would tend to overshoot and undershoot the future spot price but on average would be equal to it. For such a situation to exist would require the unreasonable assumption that there is no risk or that investors are risk neutral, meaning that they are indifferent to risk. There is, however, one other situation in which the risk premium could disappear or even turn negative. Suppose holders of the asset who want to hedge their holdings could find other parties who need to purchase the asset and who would like to hedge by going long. In that case, it should be possible for the two parties to consummate a futures transaction with the futures price equal to the expected spot price. In fact, if the parties going long exerted greater pressure than the parties going short, it might even be possible for the futures price to exceed the expected spot price.

When futures prices are lower than expected spot prices, the situation is called **normal backwardation**. When futures prices are higher than expected spot prices, it is called **normal contango**. Note the contrast with the terms backwardation and contango, which we encountered in Section 7.1.8. Backwardation means that the futures price is lower than the spot price; contango means that the futures price exceeds the spot price. Normal backwardation means that the futures price is lower than the expected spot price; normal contango means that the futures price exceeds the expected spot price.

Generally speaking, we should favor the notion that futures prices are biased predictors of future spot prices because of the transferal of the risk premium from holders of the asset to buyers of futures. Intuitively, this is the more likely case, but the other interpretations are possible. Fortunately, for our purposes, it is not critical to resolve the issue, but we do need to be aware of it.

7.2 Pricing Interest Rate Futures

We shall examine the pricing of three classes of interest rate futures contracts: Treasury bill futures, Eurodollar futures, and Treasury bond futures. In Section 6.1, we described the characteristics of these instruments and contracts. Now we look at their pricing, keeping in mind that we established the general foundations for pricing—the cost-of-carry model—in the previous section. Recall that in the cost-of-carry model, we buy the underlying asset, sell a futures contract, store the asset (which incurs costs and could generate benefits), and deliver the asset at expiration. To prevent arbitrage, the futures price is found in general as

Futures price = Spot price of underlying asset × Compounding factor
+ Costs net of monetary and nonmonetary benefits

When the underlying is a financial instrument, there will be no nonmonetary benefits and no costs other than the opportunity cost.

7.2.1 PRICING T-BILL FUTURES

Consider the following time line of our problem:

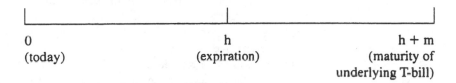

0	h	h + m
(today)	(expiration)	(maturity of underlying T-bill)

Time 0 is today, and time h is the expiration day of the futures contract. The T-bill underlying the contract is an m-day T-bill. Thus, when the futures expires, the T-bill is required to have m days to go before maturity. So from our perspective today, the underlying T-bill is an (h + m)-day T-bill.[32] As in Chapter 2 for FRAs, h and m represent a particular number of days. In accordance with common practice, m is traditionally 90. We now introduce some necessary notation. First, where necessary, we use a simple expression, r, for the risk-free interest rate. But when pricing Treasury bill futures, we need a more flexible notation. Here we need the rates for T-bills maturing on day h and on day h + m. In addition, because interest rates can change from day 0 to day h, we need notation that distinguishes rates for different maturities and rates at different points in time.[33]

To find the spot price of the underlying asset, we need the discount rate on an (h + m)-day T-bill. Suppose we have

$r_0^d(h), r_0^d(h + m)$ = Discount rates in effect on day 0 of h-day and (h + m)-day T-bills

As described in Section 6, these are discount rates and convert to prices by the following formula: $B_0(j) = 1 - r_0^d(j)(j/360)$, where in this case j will either be h or h + m. Thus, the prices of h- and (h + m)-day spot T-bills on day 0 (assuming $1 face amounts) are

$$B_0(h) = 1 - r_0^d(h)\left(\frac{h}{360}\right)$$

$$B_0(h + m) = 1 - r_0^d(h + m)\left(\frac{h + m}{360}\right)$$

In other words, the h- or (h + m)-day discount rate is multiplied by the number of days in the life of the T-bill over 360 and subtracted from the face value of $1.

Now let us turn to the futures market. We define

$r_0^{df}(h)$ = implied discount rate on day 0 of futures contract expiring on day h, where the deliverable instrument is an m-day T-bill

$f_0(h)$ = price on day 0 of futures contract expiring on day h

---

[32] It is common practice in the T-bill futures market to refer to the underlying as an m-day T-bill, but at time 0, the underlying must be an (h + m)-day T-bill in order for it to be an m-day T-bill at time h.

[33] When we assume that the interest rates are the same for all maturities and cannot change over time, which is considered acceptable when working with stock index and currency futures, we can use the simpler notation of r for the rate.

The relationship between $r_0^{df}(h)$ and $f_0(h)$ is

$$f_0(h) = 1 - r_0^{df}(h)\left(\frac{m}{360}\right)$$

It is important to note that the futures price, not the implied discount rate, is the more important variable. Like any price, the futures price is determined in a market of buyers and sellers. Any rate is simply a way of transforming a price into a number that can be compared with rates on various other fixed-income instruments.[34] Do not think that a futures contract pays an interest rate. It is more appropriate to think of such a rate imbedded in a futures price as an *implied rate*, hence our use of the term *implied discount rate*. Although knowing this rate does not tell us any more than knowing the futures price, traders often refer to the futures contract in terms of the rate rather than the price.

Finally, let us note that at expiration, the futures price is the price of the underlying T-bill

$$f_h(h) = B_h(h + m)$$

$$= 1 - r_h^d(h + m)\left(\frac{m}{360}\right)$$

where $B_h(h + m)$ is the price on day h of the T-bill maturing on day $h + m$, and $r_h^d(h + m)$ is the discount rate on day h on the T-bill maturing on day $h + m$.

We now derive the futures price by constructing a risk-free portfolio that permits no arbitrage profits to be earned. This transaction is referred to as a cash-and-carry strategy, because the trader buys the asset in the cash (spot) market and carries (holds) it.

On day 0, we buy the $(h + m)$-day T-bill, investing $B_0(h + m)$. We simultaneously sell a futures contract at the price $f_0(h)$. On day h, we are required to deliver an m-day T-bill. The bill we purchased, which originally had $h + m$ days to maturity, now has m days to maturity. We therefore deliver that bill and receive the original futures price. We can view this transaction as having paid $B_0(h + m)$ on day 0 and receiving $f_0(h)$. Because $f_0(h)$ is known on day 0, this transaction is risk free. It should thus earn the same return per dollar invested as would a T-bill purchased on day 0 that matures on day h. The return per dollar invested from the arbitrage transaction would be $f_0(h)/B_0(h + m)$, and the return per dollar invested in an h-day T-bill would be $1/B_0(h)$.[35] Consequently, we set these values equal:

$$\frac{f_0(h)}{B_0(h + m)} = \frac{1}{B_0(h)}$$

Solving for the futures price, we obtain

$$f_0(h) = \frac{B_0(h + m)}{B_0(h)}$$

---

[34] To further reinforce the notion that an interest rate is just a transformation of a price, consider a zero-coupon bond selling at $95 and using 360 days as a year. The price can be transformed into a rate in the manner of $1/0.95 - 1 = 0.0526$ or 5.26 percent. But using the convention of the Treasury bill market, the rate is expressed as a discount rate. Then $0.95 = 1 - \text{Rate} \times (360/360)$, and the rate would be 0.05 or 5 percent. A price can be converted into a rate in a number of other ways, such as by assuming different compound periods. The price of any asset is determined in a market-clearing process. The rate is just a means of transforming the price so that interest rate instruments and their derivatives can be discussed in a more comparable manner.

[35] For example, if a one-year $1 face value T-bill is selling for $0.90, the return per dollar invested is $1/\$0.90 = 1.1111$.

In words, the futures price is the ratio of the longer-term bill price to the shorter-term bill price. This price is, in fact, the same as the forward price from the term structure. In fact, as we noted above, futures prices and forward prices will be equal under the assumptions we have made so far and will follow throughout this book.

Recall that we previously demonstrated that the futures price should equal the spot price plus the cost of carry. Yet the above formula looks nothing like this result. In fact, however, it is consistent with the cost-of-carry formula. First, the above formula can be written as

$$f_0(h) = B_0(h + m)\left[\frac{1}{B_0(h)}\right]$$

As noted above, the expression $1/B_0(h)$ can be identified as the return per dollar invested over h days, which simplifies to $[1 + r_0(h)]^{h/365}$, which is essentially a compound interest factor for h days at the rate $r_0(h)$. Note that h is the number of days, assuming 365 in a year. For the period ending at day h, the above formula becomes

$$f_0(h) = B_0(h + m)[1 + r_0(h)]^{h/365} \tag{3-8}$$

and the futures price is seen to equal the spot price of the underlying compounded at the interest rate, which simply reflects the opportunity cost of the money tied up for h days.

Note that what we have been doing is deriving the appropriate price for a futures contract. In a market with no arbitrage opportunities, the actual futures price would be this theoretical price. Let us suppose for a moment, however, that the actual futures price is something else, say $f_0(h)^*$. The spot price is, of course, $B_0(h + m)$. Using these two numbers, we can infer the implied rate of return from a transaction involving the purchase of the T-bill and sale of the futures. We have

$$f_0(h)^* = B_0(h + m)[1 + r_0(h)^*]^{h/365}$$

where $r_0(h)^*$ is the implied rate of return. Solving for $r_0(h)^*$ we obtain

$$r_0(h)^* = \left[\frac{f_0(h)^*}{B_0(h + m)}\right]^{365/h} - 1 \tag{3-9}$$

This rate of return, $r_0(h)^*$, has a special name, the **implied repo rate**. It is the rate of return from a cash-and-carry transaction that is implied by the futures price relative to the spot price. Traders who engage in such transactions often obtain the funds to do so in the repurchase agreement (repo) market. The implied repo rate tells the trader what rate of return to expect from the strategy. If the financing rate available in the repo market is less than the implied repo rate, the strategy is worthwhile and would generate an arbitrage profit. If the trader could lend in the repo market at greater than the implied repo rate, the appropriate strategy would be to reverse the transaction—selling the T-bill short and buying the futures—turning the strategy into a source of financing that would cost less than the rate at which the funds could be lent in the repo market.[36]

The implied repo rate is the rate of return implied by the strategy of buying the asset and selling the futures. As noted above, the futures price is often expressed in terms of an implied discount rate. Remember that the buyer of a futures contract is committing to buy

---

[36] The concepts of a cash-and-carry strategy and the implied repo rate are applicable to any type of futures contract, but we cover them only with respect to T-bill futures.

a T-bill at the price $f_0(h)$. In the convention of pricing a T-bill by subtracting a discount rate from par value, the implied discount rate would be

$$r_0^{df}(h) = [1 - f_0(h)]\left(\frac{360}{m}\right) \tag{3-10}$$

We can also determine this implied discount rate from the discount rates on the h- and (h + m)-day T-bills as follows:[37]

$$r_0^{df}(h) = \left\{ 1 - \left[\frac{1 - r_0^d(h+m)\left(\dfrac{h+m}{360}\right)}{1 - r_0^d(h)\left(\dfrac{h}{360}\right)} \right] \right\}\left(\frac{360}{m}\right)$$

Now let us look at an example. We are interested in pricing a futures contract expiring in 30 days. A 30-day T-bill has a discount rate of 6 percent, and a 120-day T-bill has a discount rate of 6.6 percent. With h = 30 and h + m = 120, we have

$$r_0^d(h) = r_0^d(30) = 0.06$$

$$r_0^d(h+m) = r_0^d(120) = 0.066$$

The prices of these T-bills will, therefore, be

$$B_0(h) = 1 - r_0^d(h)\left(\frac{h}{360}\right)$$

$$B_0(30) = 1 - 0.06\left(\frac{30}{360}\right) = 0.9950$$

$$B_0(h+m) = 1 - r_0^d(h+m)\left(\frac{h+m}{360}\right)$$

$$B_0(120) = 1 - 0.066\left(\frac{120}{360}\right) = 0.9780$$

Using the formula we derived, we have the price of a futures expiring in 30 days as

$$f_0(h) = \frac{B_0(h+m)}{B_0(h)}$$

$$f_0(30) = \frac{B_0(120)}{B_0(30)} = \frac{0.9780}{0.9950} = 0.9829$$

The discount rate implied by the futures price would be

$$r_0^{df}(h) = [1 - f_0(h)]\left(\frac{360}{m}\right)$$

$$r_0^{df}(30) = (1 - 0.9829)\left(\frac{360}{90}\right) = 0.0684$$

---

[37] This formula is found by substituting $1 - r_0^d(h+m)[(h+m)/360]$ for $B_0(h+m)$ and $1 - r_0^d(h)(h/360)$ for $B_0(h)$ in the above equation for $r_0^{df}(h)$. This procedure expresses the spot prices in terms of their respective discount rates.

In other words, in the T-bill futures market, the rate would be stated as 6.84 percent, which would imply a futures price of 0.9829.[38] Alternatively, the implied futures discount rate could be obtained from the spot discount rates as

$$r_0^{df}(h) = \left\{ 1 - \left[\frac{1 - r_0^d(h + m)\left(\frac{h + m}{360}\right)}{1 - r_0^d(h)\left(\frac{h}{360}\right)} \right] \right\} \left(\frac{360}{m}\right)$$

$$r_0^{df}(30) = \left\{ 1 - \left[\frac{1 - 0.066\left(\frac{120}{360}\right)}{1 - 0.06\left(\frac{30}{360}\right)} \right] \right\} \left(\frac{360}{90}\right) = 0.0683$$

with a slight difference due to rounding.

To verify this result, one would buy the 120-day T-bill for 0.9780 and sell the futures at a price of 0.9829. Then, 30 days later, the T-bill would be a 90-day T-bill and would be delivered to settle the futures contract. The trader would receive the original futures price of 0.9829. The return per dollar invested would be

$$\frac{0.9829}{0.9780} = 1.0050$$

If, instead, the trader had purchased a 30-day T-bill at the price of 0.9950 and held it for 30 days, the return per dollar invested would be

$$\frac{1}{0.9950} = 1.0050$$

Thus, the purchase of the 120-day T-bill with its price in 30 days hedged by the sale of the futures contract is equivalent to purchasing a 30-day T-bill and holding it to maturity. Each transaction has the same return per dollar invested and is free of risk.

Suppose in the market, the futures price is 0.9850. The implied repo rate would be

$$r_0(h)* = \left[\frac{f_0(h)*}{B_0(h + m)} \right]^{365/h} - 1$$

$$= \left(\frac{0.9850}{0.9870}\right)^{365/30} - 1 = 0.0906$$

Buying the 120-day T-bill for 0.9780 and selling a futures for 0.9850 generates a rate of return of $0.9850/0.9780 - 1 = 0.007157$. Annualizing this rate, $(1.007157)^{365/30} - 1 = 0.0906$. If financing could be obtained in the repo market for less than this annualized rate, the strategy would be attractive. If the trader could lend in the repo market at higher than this rate, he should buy the futures and sell short the T-bill to implicitly borrow at 9.06 percent and lend in the repo market at a higher rate.

Let us now recap the pricing of Treasury bill futures. We buy an $(h + m)$-day bond and sell a futures expiring on day h, which calls for delivery of an m-day T-bill. The futures price should be the price of the $(h + m)$-day T-bill compounded at the h-day risk-free rate.

---

[38] We should also probably note that the IMM Index would be $100 - 6.84 = 93.16$. Thus, the futures price would be quoted in the market as 93.16.

That rate is the rate of return on an h-day bill. The futures price can also be obtained as the ratio of the price of the (h + m)-day T-bill to the price of the h-day T-bill. Alternatively, we can express the futures price in terms of an implied discount rate, and we can derive the price in terms of the discount rates on the (h + m)-day T-bill and the h-day T-bill. Finally, remember that the actual futures price in the market relative to the price of the (h + m)-day T-bill implies a rate of return called the implied repo rate. The implied repo rate can be compared with the rate in the actual repo market to determine the attractiveness of an arbitrage transaction.

Exhibit 3-8 summarizes the important formulas involved in the pricing of T-bill futures. We then turn to the pricing of another short-term interest rate futures contract, the Eurodollar futures.

EXHIBIT 3-8   Pricing Formulas for T-Bill Futures Contract

Futures price = Underlying T-bill price compounded at risk-free rate

Futures price in terms of spot T-bills:

$$f_0(h) = \frac{B_0(h + m)}{B_0(h)}$$

Futures price as spot price compounded at risk-free rate:

$$f_0(h) = B_0(h + m)[1 + r_0(h)]^{h/365}$$

Discount rate implied by futures price:

$$r_0^{df}(h) = [1 - f_0(h)]\left(\frac{360}{m}\right) = \left\{1 - \left[\frac{1 - r_0^d(h + m)\left(\frac{h + m}{360}\right)}{1 - r_0^d(h)\left(\frac{h}{360}\right)}\right]\right\}\left(\frac{360}{m}\right)$$

Implied repo rate:

$$r_0(h)^* = \left[\frac{f_0(h)^*}{B_0(h + m)}\right]^{365/h} - 1$$

PRACTICE PROBLEM 3

A futures contract on a Treasury bill expires in 50 days. The T-bill matures in 140 days. The discount rates on T-bills are as follows:

    50-day bill: 5.0 percent
    140-day bill: 4.6 percent

A. Find the appropriate futures price by using the prices of the 50- and 140-day T-bills.

B. Find the futures price in terms of the underlying spot price compounded at the appropriate risk-free rate.

C. Convert the futures price to the implied discount rate on the futures.

D. Now assume that the futures contract is trading in the market at an implied discount rate 10 basis points lower than is appropriate, given the pricing model and the rule of no arbitrage. Demonstrate how an arbitrage transaction could be executed and show the outcome. Calculate the implied repo rate and discuss how it would be used to determine the profitability of the arbitrage.

SOLUTIONS

A. First, find the prices of the 50- and 140-day bonds:

$$B_0(50) = 1 - 0.05(50/360) = 0.9931$$
$$B_0(140) = 1 - 0.046(140/360) = 0.9821$$

The futures price is, therefore,

$$f_0(50) - \frac{0.9821}{0.9931} = 0.9889$$

B. First, find the rate at which to compound the spot price of the 140-day T-bill. This rate is obtained from the 50-day T-bill:

$$[1 + r_0(h)]^{h/365} = \frac{1}{0.9931} = 1.0069$$

We actually do not need to solve for $r_0(h)$. The above says that based on the rate $r_0(h)$, every dollar invested should grow to a value of 1.0069. Thus, the futures price should be the spot price (the price of the 140-day T-bill) compounded by the factor 1.0069:

$$f_0(50) = 0.9821(1.0069) = 0.9889$$

Annualized, this rate would equal $(1.0069)^{365/50} - 1 = 0.0515$.

C. Given the futures price of 0.9889, the implied discount rate is

$$r_0^{df}(50) = (1 - 0.9889)\left(\frac{360}{90}\right)$$
$$= 0.0444$$

D. If the futures is trading for 10 basis points lower, it trades at a rate of 4.34 percent, so the futures price would be

$$f_0(50) = 1 - 0.0434\left(\frac{90}{360}\right)$$
$$= 0.9892$$

Do the following:
• Buy the 140-day bond at 0.9821
• Sell the futures at 0.9892
This strategy provides a return per dollar invested of

$$\frac{0.9892}{0.9821} = 1.0072$$

which compares favorably with a return per dollar invested of 1.0069 if the futures is correctly priced.

The implied repo rate is simply the annualization of this rate: $(1.0072)^{365/50} - 1 = 0.0538$. The cash-and-carry transaction would, therefore, earn 5.38 percent. Because the futures appears to be mispriced, we could likely obtain financing in the repo market at less than this rate.

7.2.2 PRICING EURODOLLAR FUTURES

Based on the T-bill case, it is tempting to argue that the interest rate implied by the Eurodollar futures price would be the forward rate in the term structure of LIBOR. Unfortunately, that is not quite the case. In fact, the unusual construction of the Eurodollar futures contract relative to the Eurodollar spot market means that no risk-free combination of a Eurodollar time deposit and a Eurodollar futures contract can be constructed. Recall that the Eurodollar time deposit is an add-on instrument. Using $L_0(j)$ as the rate (LIBOR) on a j-day Eurodollar time deposit on day 0, if one deposits \$1, the deposit will grow to a value of $1 + L_0(j)(j/360)$ j days later. So, the present value of \$1 in j days is $1/[1 + L_0(j)(j/360)]$. The Eurodollar futures contract, however, is structured like the T-bill contract—as though the underlying were a discount instrument. So its price is stated in the form of $1 - L_0(j)(j/360)$. If we try the same arbitrage with Eurodollars that we did with T-bills, we cannot get the LIBOR that determines the spot price of a Eurodollar at expiration to offset the LIBOR that determines the futures price at expiration.

In other words, suppose that on day 0 we buy an (h + m)-day Eurodollar deposit that pays \$1 on day (h + m) and sell a futures at a price of $f_0(h)$. On day h, the futures expiration, the Eurodollar deposit has m days to go and is worth $1/[1 + L_h(m)(m/360)]$. The futures price at expiration is $f_h(h) = 1 - L_h(m)(m/360)$. The profit from the futures is $f_0(h) - [1 - L_h(m)(m/360)]$. Adding this amount to the value of the m-day Eurodollar deposit we are holding gives a total position value of

$$\frac{1}{1 + L_h(m)\left(\dfrac{m}{360}\right)} + f_0(h) - [1 - L_h(m)]\left(\frac{m}{360}\right)$$

Although $f_0(h)$ is known when the transaction is initiated, $L_h(m)$ is not determined until the futures expiration. There is no way for the $L_h(m)$ terms to offset. This problem does not occur in the T-bill market because the spot price is a discount instrument and the futures contract is designed as a discount instrument.[39] It is, nonetheless, common for participants in the futures market to treat the Eurodollar rate as equivalent to the implied forward rate. Such an assumption would require the ability to conduct the risk-free arbitrage, which, as we have shown, is impossible. The differences are fairly small, but we shall not assume that the Eurodollar futures rate should equal the implied forward rate. In that case, it would take a more advanced model to solve the pricing problem. The essential points in pricing interest rate futures on short-term instruments can be understood by studying the T-bill futures market.

This mismatch in the design of spot and futures instruments in the Eurodollar market would appear to make the contract difficult to use as a hedging instrument. Although we cover hedging futures and forwards in Chapter 6, we should note that in the above equation for the payoff of the portfolio combining a spot Eurodollar time deposit and a short Eurodollar futures contract, an increase (decrease) in LIBOR lowers (raises) the value of the spot Eurodollar deposit and raises (lowers) the payoff from the short Eurodollar futures. Thus, the Eurodollar futures contract can still serve as a hedging tool. The hedge will not be perfect but can still be quite effective. Indeed, the Eurodollar futures contract is a major hedging tool of dealers in over-the-counter derivatives.

---

[39] It is not clear why the Chicago Mercantile Exchange designed the Eurodollar contract as a discount instrument when the underlying Eurodollar deposit is an add-on instrument. The most likely reason is that the T-bill futures contract was already trading, was successful, and its design was well understood and accepted by traders. The CME most likely felt that this particular design was successful and should be continued with the Eurodollar contract. Ironically, the Eurodollar contract became exceptionally successful and the T-bill contract now has virtually no trading volume.

We have now completed the treatment of futures contracts on short-term interest rate instruments. Now let us look at the pricing of Treasury bond futures.

7.2.3   PRICING TREASURY NOTE AND BOND FUTURES

Recall that in Section 6.2, we described the bond futures contract as one in which there are a number of deliverable bonds. When a given bond is delivered, the long pays the short the futures price times an adjustment term called the conversion factor. The conversion factor is the price of a $1 bond with coupon equal to that of the deliverable bond and yield equal to 6 percent, with calculations based on semiannual compounding. Bonds with a coupon greater (less) than 6 percent will have a conversion factor greater (less) than 1. Before we delve into the complexities added by this feature, however, let us start off by assuming a fairly generic type of contract: one in which the underlying is a single, specific bond.

When examining bond forward contracts in Chapter 2, we specified a time line and notation. We return to that specific time line and notation, which differs from those we used for examining short-term interest rate futures.

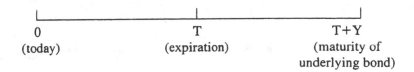

0	T	T+Y
(today)	(expiration)	(maturity of underlying bond)

Recall our notation from Chapter 2:

$B_0^c(T + Y)$ = price at time 0 of coupon bond that matures at time $T + Y$. The bond has a maturity of Y at the futures expiration.

CI_i = coupon at time t_i, where the coupons occur at times $t_1, t_2, \ldots, t_n$. Note that we care only about coupons prior to the futures expiration at T.

$f_0(T)$ = price at time 0 of futures expiring at time T.

$B_0(T)$ = price at time 0 of zero-coupon bond maturing at T.

We also need to know at time T the accumulated value of all coupons received over the period from 0 to T. We need the compound value from 0 to T of any coupons paid during the time the futures contract is alive. This value is denoted as $FV(CI,0,T)$. We introduced this variable in Chapter 2 and showed how to compute it, so you may wish to review that material. It is traditionally assumed that the interest rate at which these coupons are reinvested is known. We also assume that this interest rate applies to the period from 0 to T for money borrowed or lent. We denote this rate as

$r_0(T)$ = Interest rate at time 0 for period until time T

As described in the section on T-bill futures pricing, this is the rate that determines the price of a zero-coupon bond maturing at T.[40] Hence,

$$B_0(T) = \frac{1}{[1 + r_0(T)]^T}$$

---

[40] Keep in mind, however, that this rate is not the discount rate that determines the price of the zero-coupon bond maturing at T. It is the rate of return, expressed as an annual rate. When working with T-bills, the symbol "T" represented Days/365, which is consistent with its use here with T-bonds.

The futures price at expiration is the price of the deliverable bond at expiration:

$$f_T(T) = B_T(T + Y)$$

Now we are ready to price this bond futures contract. On day 0, we buy the bond at the price $B_0^c(T + Y)$ and sell the futures at the price $f_0(T)$. Because the futures does not require any cash up front, its initial value is zero. The current value of the overall transaction is, therefore, just the value of the bond, $B_0^c(T + Y)$. This value represents the amount of money we must invest to engage in this transaction.

We hold this position until the futures expiration. During this time, we collect and reinvest the coupons. On day T, the futures expires. We deliver the bond and receive the futures price, $f_0(T)$. We also have the reinvested coupons, which have a value at T of FV(CI,0,T). These two amounts, $f_0(T)$ and FV(CI,0,T), are known when the transaction was initiated at time 0, so the transaction is risk-free. Therefore, the current value of the transaction, $B_0^c(T + Y)$, should be the discounted value of its value at T of $f_0(T)$ + FV(CI,0,T):

$$B_0^c(T + Y) = \frac{f_0(T) + FV(CI, 0, T)}{[1 + r_0(T)]^T}$$

Note that we are simply discounting the known future value at T of the transaction at the risk-free rate of $r_0(T)$.[41]

We are, of course, more interested in the futures price, which is the only unknown in the above equation. Solving, we obtain

$$f_0(T) = B_0^c(T + Y)[1 + r_0(T)]^T - FV(CI,0,T) \qquad (3\text{-}11)$$

This equation is a variation of our basic cost-of-carry formula. The spot price, $B_0^c(T + Y)$, is compounded at the risk-free interest rate. We then subtract the compound future value of the reinvested coupons over the life of the contract. The coupon interest is like a negative cost of carry; it is a positive cash flow associated with holding the underlying bond.

Now let us work an example. Consider a $1 face value Treasury bond that pays interest at 7 percent semiannually. Thus, each coupon is $0.035. The bond has exactly five years remaining, so during that time it will pay 10 coupons, each six months apart. The yield on the bond is 8 percent. The price of the bond is found by calculating the present value of both the 10 coupons and the face value: The price is $0.9594.

Now consider a futures contract that expires in one year and three months: T = 1.25. The risk-free rate, $r_0(T)$, is 6.5 percent. The accumulated value of the coupons and the interest on them is

$$\$0.035(1.065)^{0.75} + \$0.035(1.065)^{0.25} = \$0.0722$$

The first coupon is paid in one-half a year and reinvests for three-quarters of a year. The second coupon is paid in one year and reinvests for one-quarter of a year.

Now the futures price is obtained as

$$f_0(T) = B_0^c(T + Y)[1 + r_0(T)]^T - FV(CI,0,T)$$

$$f_0(1.25) = \$0.9594(1.065)^{1.25} - \$0.0722 = \$0.9658$$

---

[41] We shall not take up the topic of the implied repo rate again, but note that if the futures is selling for $f_0(T)$, then $r_0(T)$ would be the implied repo rate.

This is the price at which the futures should trade, given current market conditions. To verify this result, buy the five-year bond for $0.9594 and sell the futures for $0.9658. Hold the position for 15 months until the futures expiration. Collect and reinvest the coupons. When the futures expires, deliver the bond and receive the futures price of $0.9658. Then add the reinvested coupons of $0.0722 for a total of $0.9658 + $0.0722 = $1.0380. If we invest $0.9594 and end up with $1.0380 15 months later, the return is $1.0380/$0.9594 = 1.0819. For comparison purposes, we should determine the annual equivalent of this rate, which is found as $(1.0819)^{1/1.25} - 1 = 0.065$. This is the same 6.5 percent risk-free rate. If the futures contract trades at a higher price, the above transaction would result in a return greater than 6.5 percent. The amount available at expiration would be higher, clearly leading to a rate of return higher than 6.5 percent. If the futures trades at a lower price, the arbitrageur would sell short the bond and buy the futures, which would generate a cash inflow today. The amount paid back would be at less than the risk-free rate of 6.5 percent.[42]

Unfortunately, we now must complicate the matter a little by moving to the more realistic case with a delivery option. Bond futures contracts traditionally permit the short to choose which bond to deliver. This feature reduces the possibility of unusual price behavior of the deliverable bond caused by holders of short positions scrambling to buy a single deliverable bond at expiration. By allowing more than one bond to be deliverable, such problems are avoided. The contract is structured as though there is a standard hypothetical deliverable bond, which has a given coupon rate. The Chicago Board of Trade's contract uses a 6 percent rate. If the short delivers a bond with a higher (lower) coupon rate, the price received at delivery is adjusted upward (downward). The conversion factor is defined and calculated as the price of a $1 face value bond with a coupon and maturity equal to that of the deliverable bond and a yield of 6 percent. Each deliverable bond has its own conversion factor. The short designates which bond he will deliver, and that bond's conversion factor is multiplied by the final futures price to determine the amount the long will pay the short for the bond.

The availability of numerous deliverable bonds creates some confusion in pricing the futures contract, arising from the fact that the underlying cannot be uniquely identified, at least not on the surface. This confusion has given rise to the concept that one bond is always the best one to deliver. If a trader buys a given bond and sells the futures, he creates a risk-free hedge. If there are no arbitrage opportunities, the return from that hedge cannot exceed the risk-free rate. That return can, however, be *less* than the risk-free rate. How can this be? In all previous cases, if a return from a risk-free transaction is less than the risk-free rate, it should be a simple matter to reverse the transaction and capture an arbitrage profit. In this case, however, a reverse transaction would not work. If the arbitrageur sells short the bond and buys the futures, she must be assured that the short will deliver the bond from which the potential arbitrage profit was computed. But the short makes the delivery decision and in all likelihood would not deliver that particular bond.

Thus, the short can be long a bond and short futures and earn a return less than the risk-free rate. One bond, however, results in a return closest to the risk-free rate. Clearly that bond is the best bond to deliver. The terminology in the business is that this bond is the cheapest to deliver.

The cheapest-to-deliver bond is determined by selecting a given bond and computing the rate of return from buying that bond and selling the futures to hedge its delivery at expiration. This calculation is performed for all bonds. The one with the highest rate of return is the cheapest to deliver.[43] The cheapest-to-deliver bond can change, however,

---

[42] Again, as in the section on T-bill futures, this analysis could be conducted in terms of the implied repo rate.

[43] As noted, this rate of return will not exceed the risk-free rate but will be the highest rate below the risk-free rate.

which can benefit the short and not the long. We ignore the details of determining the cheapest-to-deliver bond and assume that it has been identified. From here, we proceed to price the futures.

Let CF(T) be the conversion factor for the bond we have identified as the cheapest to deliver. Now we go back to the arbitrage transaction described for the case where there is only one deliverable bond. Recall that we buy the bond, sell a futures, and reinvest the coupons on the bond. At expiration, we deliver the bond, receive the futures price $f_0(T)$, and have the reinvested coupons, which are worth FV(CI,0,T). Now, in the case where the futures contract has many deliverable bonds, we must recognize that when the bond is delivered, the long pays $f_0(T)$ times CF(T). This adjustment does not add any risk to this risk-free transaction. Thus, the present value of the amount received at delivery, $f_0(T)CF(T) + FV(CI,0,T)$, should still equal the original price of the bond, which was the amount we invested to initiate the transaction:

$$B_0^c(T + Y) = \frac{f_0(T)CF(T) + FV(CI,0,T)}{[1 + r_0(T)]^T}$$

Solving for the futures price, we obtain

$$f_0(T) = \frac{B_0^c(T + Y)[1 + r_0(T)]^T - FV(CI,0,T)}{CF(T)} \qquad \text{(3-12)}$$

Note that when we had only one deliverable bond, the formula did not have the CF(T) term, but a better way to look at it is that for only one deliverable bond, the conversion factor is effectively 1, so Equation 3-12 would still apply.

Consider the same example we previously worked, but now we need a conversion factor. As noted above, the conversion factor is the price of a $1 bond with coupon and maturity equal to that of the deliverable bond on the expiration day and yield of 6 percent, with all calculations made assuming semiannual interest payments. As noted, we shall skip the specifics of this calculation here; it is simply a present value calculation. For this example, the 7 percent bond with maturity of three and three-quarter years on the delivery day would have a conversion factor of 1.0505. Thus, the futures price would be

$$f_0(T) = \frac{B_0^c(T + Y)[1 + r_0(T)]^T - FV(CI,0,T)}{CF(T)}$$

$$f_0(1.25) = \frac{0.9594(1.065)^{1.25} - 0.0722}{1.0505} = 0.9193$$

If the futures is priced higher than 0.9193, one can buy the bond and sell the futures to earn more than the risk-free rate. If the futures price is less than 0.9193, one can sell short the bond and buy the futures to end up borrowing at less than the risk-free rate. As noted previously, however, this transaction has a complication: If one goes short the bond and long the futures, this bond must remain the cheapest to deliver. Otherwise, the short will not deliver this particular bond and the arbitrage will not be successful.

Exhibit 3-9 reviews the important formulas for pricing Treasury bond futures contracts.

EXHIBIT 3-9 **Pricing Formulas for Treasury Bond Futures Contract**

Futures price = Underlying T-bond price compounded at risk-free rate less Compound future value of reinvested coupons.

Futures price if underlying bond is the only deliverable bond:

$$f_0(T) = B_0^c(T + Y)[1 + r_0(T)]^T - FV(CI,0,T)$$

Futures price when there are multiple deliverable bonds:

$$f_0(T) = \frac{B_0^c(T + Y)[1 + r_0(T)]^T - FV(CI,0,T)}{CF(T)}$$

PRACTICE PROBLEM 4

Consider a three year $1 par Treasury bond with a 7.5 percent annual yield and 8 percent semiannual coupon. Its price is $1.0132. A futures contract calling for delivery of this bond only expires in one year. The one-year risk-free rate is 7 percent.

A. Find the future value in one year of the coupons on this bond. Assume a reinvestment rate of 3.75 percent per six-month period.

B. Find the appropriate futures price.

C. Now suppose the bond is one of many deliverable bonds. The contract specification calls for the use of a conversion factor to determine the price paid for a given deliverable bond. Suppose the bond described here has a conversion factor of 1.0372. Now determine the appropriate futures price.

SOLUTIONS

A. One coupon of 0.04 will be invested for half a year at 3.75 percent (half of the rate of 7.5 percent). The other coupon is not reinvested but is still counted. Thus, $FV(CI,0,1) = 0.04(1.0375) + 0.04 = 0.0815$.

B. $f_0(1) = 1.0132(1.07) - 0.0815 = 1.0026$

C. $f_0(1) = \dfrac{1.0132(1.07) - 0.0815}{1.0372} = 0.9667$

7.3 **PRICING STOCK INDEX FUTURES**

Now let the underlying be either a portfolio of stocks or an individual stock.[44] The former are normally referred to as stock index futures, in which the portfolio is identical in composition to an underlying index of stocks. In this material, we focus on the pricing of stock index futures, but the principles are the same if the underlying is an individual stock.

In pricing stock index futures, we must account for the fact that the underlying stocks pay dividends.[45] Recall that in our previous discussions about the generic pricing of

---

[44] Futures on individual stocks have taken a long time to develop, primarily because of regulatory hurdles. They were introduced in the United States in late 2002 and, as of the publication date of this book, have achieved only modest trading volume. They currently trade in a few other countries such as the United Kingdom and Australia.

[45] Even if not all of the stocks pay dividends, at least some of the stocks almost surely pay dividends.

futures, we demonstrated that the futures price is lower as a result of the compound future value of any cash flows paid on the asset. Such cash flows consist of coupon interest payments if the underlying is a bond, or storage costs if the underlying incurs costs to store.[46] Dividends work exactly like coupon interest.

Consider the same time line we used before. Today is time 0, and the futures expires at time T. During the life of the futures, there are n dividends of D_j, $j = 1, 2, \ldots, n$. We assume these dividends are all known when the futures contract is initiated. Let

FV(D,0,T) = the compound value over the period of 0 to T of all dividends collected and reinvested

We introduced this variable in Chapter 2 and showed how to compute it, so you may wish to review that material. The other notation is the same we have previously used:

S_0 = current value of the stock index

$f_0(T)$ = futures price today of a contract that expires at T

r = risk-free interest rate over the period 0 to T

Now that we are no longer working with interest rate futures, we do not need the more flexible notation for interest rates on bonds of different maturities or interest rates at different time points. So we can use the simple notation of r as the risk-free interest rate, but we must keep in mind that it is the risk-free rate for the time period from 0 to T.

We undertake the following transaction: On day 0, we buy the stock portfolio that replicates the index. This transaction will require that we invest the amount S_0. We simultaneously sell the futures at the price $f_0(T)$.

On day T, the futures expires. We deliver the stock and receive the original futures price $f_0(T)$.[47] We also have the accumulated value of the reinvested dividends, FV(D,0,T) for a total of $f_0(T)$ + FV(D,0,T). Because this amount is known at time 0, the transaction is risk free. Therefore, we should discount its value at the risk-free rate and set this equal to the initial value of the portfolio, S_0, as follows:

$$S_0 = \frac{f_0(T) + FV(D,0,T)}{(1 + r)^T}$$

Solving for the futures price gives

$$f_0(T) = S_0(1 + r)^T - FV(D,0,T) \tag{3-13}$$

which is the cost-of-carry formula for stock index futures. Notice that it is virtually identical to that for bond futures. Ignoring the conversion factor necessitated by the delivery option, the only difference is that we use the compound future value of the dividends instead of the compound future value of the coupon interest.

Consider the following example. A stock index is at 1,452.45, and a futures contract on the index expires in three months. Thus, T = 3/12 = 0.25. The risk-free interest rate is

---

[46] We also allowed for the possibility of noncash costs, which we called the convenience yield, but there are no implicit costs or benefits associated with stock index futures.

[47] Virtually all stock index futures contracts call for cash settlement at expiration. See the explanation of the equivalence of delivery and cash settlement in Section 4 and Exhibit 3-2.

5.5 percent. The value of the dividends reinvested over the life of the futures is 7.26. The futures price should, therefore, be

$$f_0(T) = S_0(1 + r)^T - FV(D,0,T)$$

$$f_0(0.25) = 1{,}452.45(1.055)^{0.25} - 7.26$$

$$= 1{,}464.76$$

Thus, if the futures contract is selling for more than this price, an arbitrageur can buy the stocks and sell the futures. The arbitrageur would collect and reinvest the dividends and at expiration would receive a gain that would exceed the risk-free rate of 5.5 percent, a result of receiving more than 1,464.76 for the stocks. If the futures contract is selling for less than this price, the arbitrageur can sell short the stocks and buy the futures. After paying the dividends while holding the stocks,[48] the arbitrageur will end up buying back the stocks at a price that implies that he has borrowed money and paid it back at a rate less than the risk-free rate. The combined activities of all arbitrageurs will force the futures price to 1,464.76.

The stock index futures pricing formula has a number of variations. Suppose we define $FV(D,0,T)/(1 + r)^T$ as the present value of the dividends, $PV(D,0,T)$:

$$FV(D,0,T) = PV(D,0,T)(1 + r)^T$$

Substituting in the futures pricing formula above for $FV(D,0,T)$, we obtain

$$f_0(T) = [S_0 - PV(D,0,T)](1 + r)^T \tag{3-14}$$

Notice here that the stock price is reduced by the present value of the dividends. This adjusted stock price is then compounded at the risk-free rate over the life of the futures.

In the problem we worked above, the present value of the dividends is found as

$$PV(D,0,T) = \frac{FV(D,0,T)}{(1 + r)^T}$$

$$PV(D,0,0.25) = \frac{7.26}{(1.055)^{0.25}} = 7.16$$

Then the futures price would be

$$f_0(T) = [S_0 - PV(D,0,T)](1 + r)^T$$

$$f_0(0.25) = (1{,}452.45 - 7.16)(1.055)^{0.25}$$

$$= 1{,}464.76$$

Another variation of the formula defines the yield as δ in the following manner:

$$\frac{1}{(1 + \delta)^T} = 1 - \frac{FV(D,0,T)}{S_0(1 + r)^T}$$

The exact solution for δ is somewhat complex, so we shall just leave it in the form above. Using this specification, we find that the futures pricing formula would be

$$f_0(T) = \left(\frac{S_0}{(1 + \delta)^T}\right)(1 + r)^T \tag{3-15}$$

---

[48] Remember that a short seller must make restitution for any dividends paid while the position is short.

The stock price is, thus, discounted at the dividend yield, and this adjusted stock price is then compounded at the risk-free rate over the life of the futures.[49]

In the example above, the yield calculation is

$$\frac{1}{(1 + \delta)^T} = 1 - \frac{FV(D,0,T)}{S_0(1 + r)^T}$$

$$\frac{1}{(1 + \delta)^T} = 1 - \frac{7.26}{1,452.45(1.055)^{0.25}} = 0.9951$$

Then $(1 + \delta)^T$ is $1/0.9951 = 1.0049$ and the futures price is

$$f_0(T) = \left(\frac{S_0}{(1 + \delta)^T}\right)(1 + r)^T$$

$$f_0(0.25) = \left(\frac{1,452.45}{1.0049}\right)(1.055)^{0.25}$$

$$= 1,464.84$$

The difference between this and the answer we previously obtained is strictly caused by a rounding error.

Another variation of this formula is to express the yield as

$$\delta^* = \frac{PV(D,0,T)}{S_0} = \frac{FV(D,0,T)/(1 + r)^T}{S_0}$$

This means that $FV(D,0,T) = S_0(1 + r)^T\delta^*$. Substituting into our futures pricing formula for $FV(D,0,T)$, we obtain

$$f_0(T) = S_0(1 - \delta^*)(1 + r)^T \tag{3-16}$$

Here again, the stock price is reduced by the yield, and this "adjusted" stock price is compounded at the risk-free rate.

In the problem we worked above, the yield would be found as

$$\delta^* = \frac{PV(D,0,T)}{S_0}$$

$$\delta^* = \frac{7.16}{1,452.45} = 0.0049$$

Then the futures price would be

$$f_0(T) = S_0(1 - \delta^*)(1 + r)^T$$
$$f_0(0.25) = 1,452.45(1 - 0.0049)(1.055)^{0.25}$$

$$= 1,464.81$$

Again, the difference between the two prices comes from rounding.

---

[49] Sometimes the futures price is written as $f_0(T) = S_0(1 + r - \delta)^T$ where the dividend yield is simply subtracted from the risk-free rate to give a net cost of carry. This formula is a rough approximation that we do not consider acceptable.

A common variation uses the assumption of continuous compounding. The continuously compounded risk-free rate is defined as $r^c = \ln(1 + r)$. The continuously compounded dividend yield is $\delta^c = \ln(1 + \delta)$. When working with discrete dividends, we obtained the relationship

$$\frac{1}{(1 + \delta)^T} = 1 - \frac{FV(D,0,T)}{S_0(1 + r)^T}$$

We calculated $(1 + \delta)^T$. To obtain δ^c, we take the natural log of this value and divide by T: $\delta^c = (1/T)\ln[(1 + \delta)^T]$. The formula for the futures price is

$$f_0(T) = S_0 e^{(r^c - \delta^c)T}$$

In the above formula, the opportunity cost, expressed as the interest rate, is reduced by the dividend yield. Thus, the formula compounds the spot price by the interest cost less the dividend benefits. An equivalent variation of the above formula is

$$f_0(T) = (S_0 e^{-\delta^c T})e^{r^c T} \qquad (3\text{-}17)$$

The expression in parentheses is the stock price discounted at the dividend yield rate. The result is an adjusted stock price with the present value of the dividends removed. This adjusted stock price is then compounded at the risk-free rate. So, as we have previously seen, the stock price less the present value of the dividends is compounded at the risk-free rate to obtain the futures price.

In the previous problem, $(1 + \delta)^T = 1.0049$. Then $\delta^c = (1/0.25)\ln(1.0049) = 0.0196$. The continuously compounded risk-free rate is $\ln(1.055) = 0.0535$. The futures price is, therefore, $f_0(0.25) = (1452.45 e^{-0.0196(0.25)})e^{0.0535(0.25)} = 1464.81$; again the difference comes from rounding.

Exhibit 3-10 summarizes the formulas for pricing stock index futures contracts. Each of these formulas is consistent with the general formula for pricing futures. They are each based on the notion that a futures price is the spot price compounded at the risk-free rate, plus the compound future value of any other costs minus any cash flows and benefits. Alternatively, one can convert the compound future value of the costs net of benefits or cash flows of holding the asset to their current value and subtract this amount from the spot price before compounding the spot price at the interest rate. In this manner, the spot price adjusted for any costs or benefits is then compounded at the risk-free interest rate to give the futures price. These costs, benefits, and cash flows thus represent the linkage between spot and futures prices.

EXHIBIT 3-10   Pricing Formulas for Stock Index Futures Contract

Futures price = Stock index compounded at risk-free rate – Future value of dividends, or (Stock index – Present value of dividends) compounded at risk-free rate.

Futures price as stock index compounded at risk-free rate – Future value of dividends:

$$f_0(T) = S_0(1 + r)^T - FV(D,0,T)$$

Futures price as stock index – Present value of dividends compounded at risk-free rate:

$$f_0(T) = [S_0 - PV(D,0,T)](1 + r)^T$$

Futures price as stock index discounted at dividend yield, compounded at risk-free rate:

$$f_0(T) = \left(\frac{S_0}{(1 + \delta)^T}\right)(1 + r)^T \qquad \text{or}$$

$$f_0(T) = S_0(1 - \delta^*)^T(1 + r)^T$$

Futures price in terms of continuously compounded rate and yield:

$$f_0(T) = S_0 e^{(r^c - \delta^c)T} \qquad \text{or}$$

$$f_0(T) = (S_0 e^{-\delta^c T})e^{r^c T}$$

PRACTICE PROBLEM 5

A stock index is at 755.42. A futures contract on the index expires in 57 days. The risk-free interest rate is 6.25 percent. At expiration, the value of the dividends on the index is 3.94.

A. Find the appropriate futures price, using both the future value of the dividends and the present value of the dividends.

B. Find the appropriate futures price in terms of the two specifications of the dividend yield.

C. Using your answer in Part B, find the futures price under the assumption of continuous compounding of interest and dividends.

SOLUTIONS

A. $T = 57/365 = 0.1562$

$$f_0(0.1562) = 755.42(1.0625)^{0.1562} - 3.94 = 758.67$$

Alternatively, we can find the present value of the dividends:

$$PV(D,0,0.1562) = \frac{3.94}{(1.0625)^{0.1562}} = 3.90$$

Then we can find the futures price as $f_0(0.1562) = (755.42 - 3.90)(1.0625)^{0.1562} = 758.67$.

B. Under one specification of the yield, we have

$$\frac{1}{(1 + \delta)^T} = 1 - \frac{3.94}{755.42(1.0625)^{0.1562}} = 0.9948$$

We need the inverse of this amount, which is $1/0.9948 = 1.0052$. Then the futures price is

$$f_0(0.1562) = \left(\frac{755.42}{1.0052}\right)(1.0625)^{0.1562} = 758.66$$

Under the other specification of the dividend yield, we have

$$\delta^* = \frac{3.90}{755.42} = 0.0052$$

The futures price is $f_0(0.1562) = 755.42(1 - 0.0052)(1.0625)^{0.1562} = 758.64$, with the difference caused by rounding.

C. The continuously compounded risk-free rate is $r^c = \ln(1.0625) = 0.0606$. The continuously compounded dividend yield is

$$\frac{1}{0.1562}\ln(1.0052) = 0.0332$$

The futures price would then be

$$f_0(0.1562) = 755.42e^{(0.0606 - 0.0332)(0.1562)}$$
$$= 758.66$$

7.4 PRICING CURRENCY FUTURES

Given our assumptions about no marking to market, it will be a simple matter to learn how to price currency futures: We price them the same as currency forwards. Recall that in Chapter 2 we described a currency as an asset paying a yield of r^f, which can be viewed as the foreign risk-free rate. Thus, in this sense, a currency futures can also be viewed like a stock index futures, whereby the dividend yield is analogous to the foreign interest rate.

Therefore, an arbitrageur can buy the currency for the spot exchange rate of S_0 and sell a futures expiring at T for $f_0(T)$, holding the position until expiration, collecting the foreign interest, and delivering the currency to receive the original futures price. An important twist, however, is that the arbitrageur must be careful to have the correct number of units of the currency on hand to deliver.

Consider a futures contract on one unit of the currency. If the arbitrageur purchases one unit of the currency up front, the accumulation of interest on the currency will result in having more than one unit at the futures expiration. To adjust for this problem, the arbitrageur should take $S_0/(1 + r^f)^T$ units of his own currency and buy $1/(1 + r^f)^T$ units of the foreign currency.[50] The arbitrageur holds this position and collects interest at the foreign rate. The accumulation of interest is accounted for by multiplying by the interest factor $(1 + r^f)^T$. At expiration, the number of units of the currency will have grown to $[1/(1 + r^f)^T][1 + r^f]^T = 1$. So, the arbitrageur would then have 1 unit of the currency. He delivers that unit and receives the futures price of $f_0(T)$.

To avoid an arbitrage opportunity, the present value of the payoff of $f_0(T)$ must equal the amount initially invested. To find the present value of the payoff, we must discount at the domestic risk-free rate, because that rate reflects the opportunity cost of the arbitrageur's investment of his own money. So, first we equate the present value of the future payoff, discounting at the domestic risk-free rate, to the amount initially invested:

$$\frac{f_0(T)}{(1 + r)^T} = \frac{S_0}{(1 + r^f)^T}$$

Then we solve for the futures price to obtain

$$f_0(T) = \left(\frac{S_0}{(1 + r^f)^T}\right)(1 + r)^T \tag{3-18}$$

This formula is the same one we used for currency forwards.

An alternative variation of this formula would apply when we use continuously compounded interest rates. The adjustment is very slight. In the formula above, dividing S_0 by

---

[50] In other words, if S_0 buys 1 unit, then $S_0/(1 + r^f)^T$ buys $1/(1 + r^f)^T$ units.

$(1 + r^f)^T$ finds a present value by discounting at the foreign interest rate. Multiplying by $(1 + r)^T$ is finding a future value by compounding at the domestic interest rate. The continuously compounded analogs to those rates are $r^{fc} = \ln(1 + r^f)$ and $r^c = \ln(1 + r)$. Then the formula becomes

$$f_0(T) = (S_0 e^{-r^{fc}T}) e^{r^c T} \tag{3-19}$$

We also saw this formula in Chapter 2.

Consider a futures contract expiring in 55 days on the euro. Therefore, $T = 55/365 = 0.1507$. The spot exchange rate is \$0.8590. The foreign interest rate is 5.25 percent, and the domestic risk-free rate is 6.35 percent. The futures price should, therefore, be

$$f_0(T) = \left(\frac{S_0}{(1 + r^f)^T} \right)(1 + r)^T$$

$$f_0(0.1507) = \left(\frac{0.8590}{(1.0525)^{0.1507}} \right)(1.0635)^{0.1507} = 0.8603$$

If the futures is selling for more than this amount, the arbitrageur can buy the currency and sell the futures. He collects the foreign interest and converts the currency back at a higher rate than 0.8603, resulting in a risk-free return that exceeds the domestic risk-free rate. If the futures is selling for less than this amount, the arbitrageur can borrow the currency and buy the futures. The end result will be to receive money at the start and pay back money at a rate less than the domestic risk-free rate.

If the above problem were structured in terms of continuously compounded rates, the domestic rate would be $\ln(1.0635) = 0.0616$ and the foreign rate would be $\ln(1.0525) = 0.0512$. The futures price would then be

$$f_0(T) = (S_0 e^{-r^{fc}T}) e^{r^c T}$$

$$f_0(0.1507) = (0.85890 e^{-0.0512(0.1507)}) e^{0.0616(0.1507)} = 0.8603$$

which, of course, is the same price we calculated above.

Exhibit 3-11 summarizes the formulas for pricing currency futures.

EXHIBIT 3-11   Pricing Formulas for Currency Futures Contract

---

Futures price = (Spot exchange rate discounted by Foreign interest rate) compounded at Domestic interest rate:

Discrete interest: $f_0(T) = \left(\dfrac{S_0}{(1 + r^f)^T} \right)(1 + r)^T$

Continuous interest: $f_0(T) = (S_0 e^{-r^{fc}T}) e^{r^c T}$

PRACTICE PROBLEM 6

The spot exchange rate for the Swiss franc is \$0.60. The U.S. interest rate is 6 percent, and the Swiss interest rate is 5 percent. A futures contract expires in 78 days.

A. Find the appropriate futures price.

B. Find the appropriate futures price under the assumption of continuous compounding.

C. Using Part A, execute an arbitrage resulting from a futures price of $0.62.

SOLUTIONS

$T = 78/365 = 0.2137$

A. $f_0(0.2137) = \dfrac{\$0.60}{(1.05)^{0.2137}} (1.06)^{0.2137} = \$0.6012$

B. The continuously compounded equivalent rates are

$$r^{fc} = \ln(1.05) = 0.0488$$
$$r^c = \ln(1.06) = 0.0583$$

The futures price is

$$f_0(0.2137) = (\$0.60e^{-0.0488(0.2137)})e^{0.0583(0.2137)}$$
$$= \$0.6012$$

C. At $0.62, the futures price is too high, so we will need to sell the futures. First, however, we must determine how many units of the currency to buy. It should be

$$\dfrac{1}{(1.05)^{0.2137}} = 0.9896$$

So we buy this many units, which costs $0.9896(\$0.60) = \$0.5938$. We sell the futures at $0.62. We hold the position until expiration. During that time the accumulation of interest will make the 0.9896 units of the currency grow to 1.0000 unit. We convert the Swiss franc to dollars at the futures rate of $0.62. The return per dollar invested is

$$\dfrac{0.62}{0.5938} = 1.0441$$

This is a return of 1.0441 per dollar invested over 78 days. At the risk-free rate of 6 percent, the return over 78 days should be $(1.06)^{0.2137} = 1.0125$. Obviously, the arbitrage transaction is much better.

7.5 FUTURES PRICING: A RECAP

We have now examined the pricing of short-term interest rate futures, intermediate- and long-term interest rate futures, stock index futures, and currency futures. Let us recall the intuition behind pricing a futures contract and see the commonality in each of those special cases. First recall that under the assumption of no marking to market, at expiration the short makes delivery and we assume that the long pays the full futures price at that point. An arbitrageur buys the asset and sells a futures contract, holds the asset for the life of the futures, and delivers it at expiration of the futures, at which time he is paid the futures price. In addition, while holding the asset, the arbitrageur accumulates costs and accrues cash flows, such as interest, dividends, and benefits such as a convenience yield. The value of the position at expiration will be the futures price net of these costs minus benefits and cash flows. The overall value of this transaction at expiration is known when the transaction is initiated; thus, the value at expiration is risk-free. The return from a risk-free transaction should equal the risk-free rate, which is the rate on a zero-coupon bond whose maturity is the futures expiration day. If the return is indeed this risk-free rate, then the futures price must equal the spot price compounded at the risk-free rate plus the compound value of these costs net of benefits and cash flows.

It should also be noted that although we have taken the more natural approach of buying the asset and selling the futures, we could just as easily have sold short the asset and bought the futures. Because short selling is usually a little harder to do as well as to understand, the approach we take is preferable from a pedagogical point of view. It is important, nonetheless, to remember that the ability to sell short the asset or the willingness of parties who own the asset to sell it to offset the buying of the futures is critical to establishing the results we have shown here. Otherwise, the futures pricing formulas would be inequalities—limited on one side but not restricted on the other.

We should remind ourselves that this general form of the futures pricing model also applied in Chapter 2 in our discussion of forward contracts. Futures contracts differ from forward contracts in that the latter are subject to credit risk. Futures contracts are marked to market on a daily basis and guaranteed against losses from default by the futures clearinghouse, which has never defaulted. Although there are certain institutional features that distinguish futures from forwards, we consider those features separately from the material on pricing. Because the general economic and financial concepts are the same, for pricing purposes, we treat futures and forwards as the same.

8 THE ROLE OF FUTURES MARKETS AND EXCHANGES

We conclude this chapter with a brief look at the role that futures markets and exchanges play in global financial systems and in society. Virtually all participants in the financial markets have heard of futures markets, but many do not understand the role that futures markets play. Some participants do not understand how futures markets function in global financial systems and often look at futures with suspicion, if not disdain.

In Chapter 1, we discussed the purposes of derivative markets. We found that derivative markets provide price discovery and risk management, make the markets for the underlying assets more efficient, and permit trading at low transaction costs. These characteristics are also associated with futures markets. In fact, price discovery is often cited by others as the primary advantage of futures markets. Yet, all derivative markets provide these benefits. What characteristics do futures markets have that are not provided by comparable markets as forward markets?

First recall that a major distinction between futures and forwards is that futures are standardized instruments. By having an agreed-upon set of homogeneous contracts, futures markets can provide an orderly, liquid market in which traders can open and close positions without having to worry about holding these positions to expiration. Although not all futures contracts have a high degree of liquidity, an open position can nonetheless be closed on the exchange where the contract was initiated.[51] More importantly, however, futures contracts are guaranteed against credit losses. If a counterparty defaults, the clearinghouse pays and, as we have emphasized, no clearinghouse has ever defaulted. In this manner, a party can engage in a transaction to lock in a future price or rate without having

---

[51] Recall that there is no liquid market for previously opened forward contracts to be closed, but the holder of a forward contract can re-enter the market and establish a position opposite to the one previously established. If one holds a long forward contract to buy an asset in six months, one can then do a short forward contract to sell the asset in six months, and this transaction offsets the risk of changing market prices. The credit risk on both contracts remains. In some cases, the offsetting contract can be done with the same counterparty as in the original contract, permitting the two parties to arrange a single cash settlement to offset both contracts.

to worry about the credit quality of the counterparty. Forward contracts are subject to default risk, but of course they offer the advantage of customization, the tailoring of a contract's terms to meet the needs of the parties involved.

With an open, standardized, and regulated market for futures contracts, their prices can be disseminated to other investors and the general public. Futures prices are closely watched by a vast number of market participants, many trying to discern an indication of the direction of future spot prices and some simply trying to determine what price they could lock in for future purchase or sale of the underlying asset. Although forward prices provide similar information, forward contracts are private transactions and their prices are not publicly reported. Futures markets thus provide transparency to the financial markets. They reveal the prices at which parties contract for future transactions.

Therefore, futures prices contribute an important element to the body of information on which investors make decisions. In addition, they provide opportunities to transact for future purchase or sale of an underlying asset without having to worry about the credit quality of the counterparty.

In Chapters 2 and 3, we studied forward and futures contracts and showed that they have a lot in common. Both are commitments to buy or sell an asset at a future date at a price agreed on today. No money changes hands at the start of either transaction. We learned how to determine appropriate prices and values for these contracts. In Chapter 6, we shall look at a variety of strategies and applications using forward and futures contracts. For now, however, we take a totally different approach and look at contracts that provide not the obligation but rather the right to buy or sell an asset at a later date at a price agreed on today. To obtain such a right, in contrast to agreeing to an obligation, one must pay money at the start. These instruments, called options, are the subject of Chapter 4.

KEY POINTS

- Futures contracts are standardized instruments that trade on a futures exchange, have a secondary market, and are guaranteed against default by means of a daily settling of gains and losses. Forward contracts are customized instruments that are not guaranteed against default and are created anywhere off of an exchange.

- Modern futures markets primarily originated in Chicago out of a need for grain farmers and buyers to be able to transact for delivery at future dates for grain that would, in the interim, be placed in storage.

- Futures transactions are standardized and conducted in a public market, are homogeneous, have a secondary market giving them an element of liquidity, and have a clearinghouse, which collects margins and settles gains and losses daily to provide a guarantee against default. Futures markets are also regulated at the federal government level.

- Margin in the securities markets is the deposit of money, the margin, and a loan for the remainder of the funds required to purchase a stock or bond. Margin in the futures markets is much smaller and does not involve a loan. Futures margin is more like a performance bond or down payment.

- Futures trading occurs on a futures exchange, which involves trading either in a physical location called a pit or via a computer terminal off of the floor of the futures exchange as part of an electronic trading system. In either case, a party to a futures contract goes long, committing to buy the underlying asset at an agreed-upon price, or short, committing to sell the underlying asset at an agreed-upon price.

- A futures trader who has established a position can re-enter the market and close out the position by doing the opposite transaction (sell if the original position was long or buy if the original position was short). The party has offset the position, no longer has a contract outstanding, and has no further obligation.

- Initial margin is the amount of money in a margin account on the day of a transaction or when a margin call is made. Maintenance margin is the amount of money in a margin account on any day other than when the initial margin applies. Minimum requirements exist for the initial and maintenance margins, with the initial margin requirement normally being less than 10 percent of the futures price and the maintenance margin requirement being smaller than the initial margin requirement. Variation margin is the amount of money that must be deposited into the account to bring the balance up to the required level. The settlement price is an average of the last few trades of the day and is used to determine the gains and losses marked to the parties' accounts.

- The futures clearinghouse engages in a practice called marking to market, also known as the daily settlement, in which gains and losses on a futures position are credited and charged to the trader's margin account on a daily basis. Thus, profits are available for withdrawal and losses must be paid quickly before they build up and pose a risk that the party will be unable to cover large losses.

- The margin balance at the end of the day is determined by taking the previous balance and accounting for any gains or losses from the day's activity, based on the settlement price, as well as any money added or withdrawn.

- Price limits are restrictions on the price of a futures trade and are based on a range relative to the previous day's settlement price. No trade can take place outside of the price limits. A limit move is when the price at which two parties would like to trade is at or beyond the price limit. Limit up is when the market price would be at or above the upper limit. Limit down is when the market price would be at or below the lower limit. Locked limit occurs when a trade cannot take place because the price would be above the limit up or below the limit down prices.

- A futures contract can be terminated by entering into an offsetting position very shortly before the end of the expiration day. If the position is still open when the contract expires, the trader must take delivery (if long) or make delivery (if short), unless the contract requires that an equivalent cash settlement be used in lieu of delivery. In addition, two participants can agree to alternative delivery terms, an arrangement called exchange for physicals.

- Delivery options are features associated with a futures contract that permit the short some flexibility in what to deliver, where to deliver it, and when in the expiration month to make delivery.

- Scalpers are futures traders who take positions for very short periods of time and attempt to profit by buying at the bid price and selling at the ask price. Day traders close out all positions by the end of the day. Position traders leave their positions open overnight and potentially longer.

- Treasury bill futures are contracts in which the underlying is $1,000,000 of a U.S. Treasury bill. Eurodollar futures are contracts in which the underlying is $1,000,000 of a Eurodollar time deposit. Treasury bond futures are contracts in which the underlying is $100,000 of a U.S. Treasury bond with a minimum 15-year maturity. Stock index futures are contracts in which the underlying is a well-known stock index, such as the S&P 500 or FTSE 100. Currency futures are contracts in which the underlying is a foreign currency.

- An expiring futures contract is equivalent to a spot transaction. Consequently, at expiration the futures price must converge to the spot price to avoid an arbitrage opportunity in which one can buy the asset and sell a futures or sell the asset and buy a futures to capture an immediate profit at no risk.

- The value of a futures contract just prior to marking to market is the accumulated price change since the last mark to market. The value of a futures contract just after marking to market is zero. These values reflect the claim a participant has as a result of her position in the contract.

- The price of a futures contract will equal the price of an otherwise equivalent forward contract one day prior to expiration, or if interest rates are known or constant, or if interest rates are uncorrelated with futures prices.

- A futures price is derived by constructing a combination of a long position in the asset and a short position in the futures. This strategy guarantees that the price received from the sale of the asset is known when the transaction is initiated. The futures price is then derived as the unknown value that eliminates the opportunity to earn an arbitrage profit off of the transaction.

- Futures prices are affected by the opportunity cost of funds tied up in the investment in the underlying asset, the costs of storing the underlying asset, any cash flows paid on the underlying asset, such as interest or dividends, and nonmonetary benefits of holding the underlying asset, referred to as the convenience yield.

- Backwardation describes a condition in which the futures price is lower than the spot price. Contango describes a condition in which the futures price is higher than the spot price.

- The futures price will not equal the expected spot price if the risk premium in the spot price is transferred from hedgers to futures traders. If the risk premium is transferred, then the futures price will be biased high or low relative to the expected future spot price. When the futures price is biased low (high), it is called normal backwardation (normal contango).

- T-bill futures prices are determined by going short a futures contract and going long a T-bill that will have the desired maturity at the futures expiration. At expiration, the T-bill is delivered or cash settled to a price locked in when the transaction was initiated through the sale of the futures. The correct futures price is the one that prohibits this combination from earning an arbitrage profit. Under the assumptions we make, the T-bill futures price is the same as the T-bill forward price.

- The implied repo rate is the rate of return implied by a transaction of buying a spot asset and selling a futures contract. If financing can be obtained in the repo market at less than the implied repo rate, the transaction should be undertaken. If financing can be supplied to the repo market at greater than the implied repo rate, the transaction should be reversed.

- Eurodollar futures cannot be priced as easily as T-bill futures, because the expiration price of a Eurodollar futures is based on a value computed as 1 minus a rate, whereas the value of the underlying Eurodollar time deposit is based on 1 divided by a rate. The difference is small but not zero. Hence, Eurodollar futures do not lend themselves to an exact pricing formula based on the notion of a cost of carry of the underlying.

- Treasury bond futures prices are determined by first identifying the cheapest bond to deliver, which is the bond that the short would deliver under current market conditions. Then one must construct a combination of a short futures contract and a long position in that bond. The bond is held, and the coupons are collected and reinvested.

At expiration, the underlying bond is delivered and the futures price times the conversion factor for that bond is received. The correct futures price is the one that prevents this transaction from earning an arbitrage profit.

- Stock index futures prices are determined by constructing a combination of a long portfolio of stocks identical to the underlying index and a short futures contract. The stocks are held and the dividends are collected and reinvested. At expiration, the cash settlement results in the effective sale of the stock at the futures price. The correct futures price is the one that prevents this transaction from earning an arbitrage profit.

- Currency futures prices are determined by buying the underlying currency and selling a futures on the currency. The position is held, and the underlying currency pays interest at the foreign risk-free rate. At expiration, the currency is delivered and the futures price is received. The correct futures price is the one that prevents this transaction from earning an arbitrage profit.

- Futures markets serve our financial systems by making the markets for the underlying assets more efficient, by providing price discovery, by offering opportunities to trade at lower transaction costs, and by providing a means of managing risk. Futures markets also provide a homogeneous, standardized, and tradable instrument through which participants who might not have access to forward markets can make commitments to buy and sell assets at a future date at a locked-in price with no fear of credit risk. Because futures markets are so visible and widely reported on, they are also an excellent source of information, contributing greatly to the transparency of financial markets.

PROBLEMS

1. **A.** In February, Dave Parsons purchased a June futures contract on the Nasdaq 100 Index. He decides to close out his position in April. Describe how would he do so.

   B. Peggy Smith is a futures trader. In early August, she took a short position in an S&P 500 Index futures contract expiring in September. After a week, she decides to close out her position. Describe how would she do so.

2. A gold futures contract requires the long trader to buy 100 troy ounces of gold. The initial margin requirement is $2,000, and the maintenance margin requirement is $1,500.

   A. Matthew Evans goes long one June gold futures contract at the futures price of $320 per troy ounce. When could Evans receive a maintenance margin call?

   B. Chris Tosca sells one August gold futures contract at a futures price of $323 per ounce. When could Tosca receive a maintenance margin call?

3. A copper futures contract requires the long trader to buy 25,000 lbs of copper. A trader buys one November copper futures contract at a price of $0.75/lb. Theoretically, what is the maximum loss this trader could have? Another trader sells one November copper futures contract. Theoretically, what is the maximum loss this trader with a short position could have?

4. Consider a hypothetical futures contract in which the current price is $212. The initial margin requirement is $10, and the maintenance margin requirement is $8. You go long 20 contracts and meet all margin calls but do not withdraw any excess margin.

   A. When could there be a margin call?

   B. Complete the table below and explain any funds deposited. Assume that the contract is purchased at the settlement price of that day so there is no mark-to-market profit or loss on the day of purchase.

Day	Beginning Balance	Funds Deposited	Futures Price	Price Change	Gain/Loss	Ending Balance
0			212			
1			211			
2			214			
3			209			
4			210			
5			204			
6			202			

   C. How much are your total gains or losses by the end of day 6?

5. Sarah Moore has taken a short position in one Chicago Board of Trade Treasury bond futures contract with a face value of $100,000 at the price of 96 6/32. The initial margin requirement is $2,700, and the maintenance margin requirement is $2,000. Moore would meet all margin calls but would not withdraw any excess margin.

   A. Complete the table below and provide an explanation of any funds deposited. Assume that the contract is purchased at the settlement price of that day, so there is no mark-to-market profit or loss on the day of purchase.

Day	Beginning Balance	Funds Deposited	Futures Price	Price Change	Gain/Loss	Ending Balance
0			96-06			
1			96-31			
2			97-22			
3			97-18			
4			97-24			
5			98-04			
6			97-31			

    B. How much are Moore's total gains or losses by the end of day 6?

6. A. The IMM index price in yesterday's newspaper for a September Eurodollar futures contract is 95.23. What is the actual price of this contract?

    B. The IMM index price in today's newspaper for the contract mentioned above is 95.25. How much is the change in the actual futures price of the contract since the previous day?

7. Jason Hathaway, a speculator, has purchased a March Eurodollar futures contract at a price of 93.35.

    A. What is the annualized LIBOR rate priced into this contract?

    B. A month later, the interest rate has decreased to 6.5 percent. Would the futures price go up or down?

    C. How much is Hathaway's gain or loss in dollar terms?

8. Mary Craft is expecting large-capitalization stocks to rally close to the end of the year. She is pessimistic, however, about the performance of small-capitalization stocks. She decides to go long one December futures contract on the Dow Jones Industrial Average at a price of 9,020 and short one December futures contract on the S&P Midcap 400 Index at a price of 369.40. The multiplier for a futures contract on the Dow is $10, and the multiplier for a futures contract on the S&P Midcap 400 is $500. When Craft closes her position towards the end of the year, the Dow and S&P Midcap 400 futures prices are 9,086 and 370.20, respectively. How much is the net gain or loss to Craft?

9. A. The current price of gold is $300 per ounce. Consider the net cost of carry for gold to be zero. The risk-free interest rate is 6 percent. What should be the price of a gold futures contract that expires in 90 days?

    B. Using Part A above, illustrate how an arbitrage transaction could be executed if the futures contract is priced at $306 per ounce.

    C. Using Part A above, illustrate how an arbitrage transaction could be executed if the futures contract is priced at $303 per ounce.

10. Consider an asset priced at $90. A futures contract on the asset expires in 75 days. The risk-free interest rate is 7 percent. Answer the following questions, each of which is independent of the others, unless indicated otherwise.

    A. Find the appropriate futures price if the underlying asset has no storage costs, cash flows, or convenience yield.

    B. Find the appropriate futures price if the underlying asset's storage costs at the futures expiration equal $3.

    C. Find the appropriate futures price if the underlying asset has positive cash flows. The future value of these cash flows is $0.50 at the time of futures expiration.

    D. Find the appropriate futures price if the underlying asset's storage costs at the futures expiration equal $3.00 and the compound value at the time of the futures expiration of the positive cash flow from the underlying asset is $0.50.

    E. Using Part D above, illustrate how an arbitrage transaction could be executed if the futures contract is trading at $95.

    F. Using Part A above, determine the value of a long futures contract an instant before marking to market if the previous settlement price was $89.50.

    G. What happens to the value of the futures contract in Part F above as soon as it is marked to market?

11. A 45-day T-bill has a discount rate of 5.50 percent. A 135-day T-bill has a discount rate of 5.95 percent.

    A. What should be the price of a futures contract that expires in 45 days? Assume $1 par value.

    B. Show that the purchase of a 135-day T-bill, with its price in 45 days hedged by the sale of a 45-day futures contract that calls for the delivery of a 90-day T-bill, is equivalent to purchasing a 45-day T-bill and holding it to maturity.

12. The discount rate on a 60-day T-bill is 6.0 percent, and the discount rate on a 150-day T-bill is 6.25 percent.

    A. Based on the 60-day and 150-day T-bill discount rates, what should be the price of a 60-day futures contract? Assume $1 par value.

    B. If the actual price of a 60-day futures contract is 0.9853, outline the transactions necessary to take advantage of the arbitrage opportunity, and show the outcome.

    C. Calculate the implied repo rate and discuss how you interpret it to determine the profitability of the arbitrage strategy outlined in Part B.

13. A futures contract on a T-bill expires in 30 days. The T-bill matures in 120 days. The discount rates on T-bills are as follows:

30-day bill: 5.4 percent

120-day bill: 5.0 percent

    A. Find the appropriate futures price by using the prices of the 30- and 120-day T-bills.

    B. Find the futures price in terms of the underlying spot price compounded at the appropriate risk-free rate.

    C. Convert the futures price to the implied discount rate on the futures.

    D. Now assume that the futures is trading in the market at an implied discount rate 20 basis points lower than is appropriate, given the pricing model and the rule of no arbitrage. Demonstrate how an arbitrage transaction could be executed.

    E. Now assume that the futures is trading in the market at an implied discount rate 20 basis points higher than is appropriate, given the pricing model and the rule of no arbitrage. Demonstrate how an arbitrage transaction could be executed.

14. A $1 face value bond pays an 8 percent semiannual coupon. The annual yield is 6 percent. The bond has 10 years remaining until maturity, and its price is $1.1488. Consider a futures contract calling for delivery of this bond only. The contract expires in 18 months. The risk-free rate is 5 percent.

    A. Compute the appropriate futures price.

    B. Assuming that the futures contract is appropriately priced, show the riskless strategy involving the bond and the futures contract that would earn the risk-free rate of return.

15. Consider a six-year $1 par Treasury bond. The bond pays a 6 percent semiannual coupon, and the annual yield is 6 percent. The bond is priced at par. A futures contract expiring in 15 months calls for delivery of this bond only. The risk-free rate is 5 percent.

A. Find the future value in 15 months of the coupons on this bond.

B. Find the appropriate futures price.

C. Now suppose that the above bond is only one of many deliverable bonds. The contract specification calls for the use of a conversion factor to determine the price paid for a given deliverable bond. Suppose the bond described here has a conversion factor of 1.0567. Find the appropriate futures price.

16. A stock index is at 1,521.75. A futures contract on the index expires in 73 days. The risk-free interest rate is 6.10 percent. The value of the dividends reinvested over the life of the futures is 5.36.

A. Find the appropriate futures price.

B. Find the appropriate futures price in terms of the two specifications of the dividend yield.

C. Using your answer in Part B, find the futures price under the assumption of continuous compounding of interest and dividends.

17. A stock index is at 443.35. A futures contract on the index expires in 201 days. The price of the futures contract is 458.50. The risk-free interest rate is 6.50 percent. The value of the dividends reinvested over the life of the futures is 5.0.

A. Show that the futures contract above is mispriced by computing what the price of this futures contract should be.

B. Show how an arbitrageur could take advantage of the mispricing.

18. The spot exchange rate for the British pound is $1.4390. The U.S. interest rate is 6.3 percent, and the British interest rate is 5.8 percent. A futures contract on the exchange rate for the British pound expires in 100 days.

A. Find the appropriate futures price.

B. Find the appropriate futures price under the assumption of continuous compounding.

C. Suppose the actual futures price is $1.4650. Is the future contract mispriced? If yes, how could an arbitrageur take advantage of the mispricing? Use discrete compounding as in Part A.

SOLUTIONS

1. **A.** Parsons would close out his position in April by offsetting his long position with a short position. To do so, he would re enter the market and offer for sale a June futures contract on the Nasdaq 100 index. When he has a buyer, he has both a long and a short position in the June futures contract on the Nasdaq 100 index. From the point of view of the clearinghouse, he no longer has a position in the contract.

   B. Smith would close out her position in August by offsetting her short position with a long position. To do so, she would re-enter the market and purchase a September futures contract on the S&P 500. She then has both a short and a long position in the September futures contract on the S&P 500. From the point of view of the clearinghouse, she no longer has a position in the contract.

2. The difference between initial and maintenance margin requirements for one gold futures contract is $2,000 - $1,500 = $500. Because one gold futures contract is for 100 troy ounces, the difference between initial and maintenance margin requirements per troy ounce is $500/100, or $5.

   A. Because Evans has a long position, he would receive a maintenance margin call if the price were to *fall* below $320 - $5, or $315 per troy ounce.

   B. Because Tosca has a short position, he would receive a maintenance margin call if the price were to *rise* above $323 + $5, or $328 per troy ounce.

3. *Trader with a long position*: This trader loses if the price falls. The maximum loss would be incurred if the futures price falls to zero, and this loss would be $0.75/lb × 25,000 lbs, or $18,750. Of course, this scenario is only theoretical, not realistic.

   Trader with a short position: This trader loses if the price increases. Because there is no limit on the price increase, there is no theoretical upper limit on the loss that the trader with a short position could incur.

4. **A.** The difference between the initial margin requirement and the maintenance margin requirement is $2. Because the initial futures price was $212, a margin call would be triggered if the price falls below $210.

   B.

Day	Beginning Balance	Funds Deposited	Futures Price	Price Change	Gain/Loss	Ending Balance
0	0	200	212			200
1	200	0	211	−1	−20	180
2	180	0	214	3	60	240
3	240	0	209	−5	−100	140
4	140	60	210	1	20	220
5	220	0	204	−6	−120	100
6	100	100	202	−2	−40	160

On day 0, you deposit $200 because the initial margin requirement is $10 per contract and you go long 20 contracts ($10 per contract times 20 contracts equals $200). At the end of day 3, the balance is down to $140, $20 below the $160 maintenance margin requirement ($8 per contract times 20 contracts). You must deposit enough money to bring the balance up to the initial margin requirement of $200. So, the next day (day 4), you deposit $60. The price change on day 5 causes a gain/loss of −$120, leaving you with a balance of $100 at the end of day 5. Again, this amount is less than the $160 maintenance margin requirement. You must deposit enough money to bring the balance up to the initial margin requirement of $200. So on day 6, you deposit $100.

C. By the end of day 6, the price is $202, a decrease of $10 from your purchase price of $212. Your loss so far is $10 per contract times 20 contracts, or $200.

You could also look at your loss so far as follows. You initially deposited $200, followed by margin calls of $60 and $100. Thus, you have deposited a total of $360 so far and have not withdrawn any excess margin. The ending balance, however, is only $160. Thus, the total loss incurred by you so far is $360 − $160, or $200.

5. A.

Day	Beginning Balance	Funds Deposited	Futures Price	Price Change	Gain/Loss	Ending Balance
0	0	2,700.00	96-06			2,700.00
1	2,700.00	0	96-31	25/32	−781.25	1,918.75
2	1,918.75	781.25	97-22	23/32	−718.75	1,981.25
3	1,981.25	718.75	97-18	−4/32	125.00	2,825.00
4	2,825.00	0	97-24	6/32	−187.50	2,637.50
5	2,637.50	0	98-04	12/32	−375.00	2,262.50
6	2,262.50	0	97-31	−5/32	156.25	2,418.75

On day 0, Moore deposits $2,700 because the initial margin requirement is $2,700 per contract and she has gone short one contract. At the end of day 1, the price has increased from 96-06 to 96-31—that is, the price has increased from $96,187.50 to $96,968.75. Because Moore has taken a short position, this increase of $781.25 is an adverse price movement for her, and the balance is down by $781.25 to $1,918.75. Because this amount is less than the $2,000 maintenance margin requirement, she must deposit additional funds to bring her account back to the initial margin requirement of $2,700. So, the next day (day 2), she deposits $781.25. Another adverse price movement takes place on day 2 as the price further increases by $718.75 to $97,687.50. Her ending balance is again below the maintenance margin requirement of $2,000, and she must deposit enough money to bring her account back to the initial margin requirement of $2,700. So, the next day (day 3), she deposits $718.75. Subsequently, even though her balance falls below the initial margin requirement, it does not go below the maintenance margin requirement, and she does not need to deposit any more funds.

B. Moore bought the contract at a futures price of 96-06. By the end of day 6, the price is 97-31, an increase of 1 25/32. Therefore, her loss so far is 1.78125 percent of $100,000, which is $1,781.25.

You could also look at her loss so far as follows: She initially deposited $2,700, followed by margin calls of $781.25 and $718.75. Thus, she has deposited a total of $4,200 so far, and has not withdrawn any excess margin. Her ending balance is $2,418.75. Thus, the total loss so far is $4,200 − $2,418.75, or $1,781.25.

6. A. Because the IMM index price is 95.23, the annualized LIBOR rate priced into the contract is $100 − 95.23 = 4.77$ percent. With each contract based on $1 million notional principal of 90-day Eurodollars, the actual futures price is $1,000,000[1 − 0.0477(90/360)] = \$988,075$.

B. Because the IMM index price is 95.25, the annualized LIBOR rate priced into the contract is $100 - 95.25 = 4.75$ percent. The actual futures price is $\$1,000,000[1 - 0.0475(90/360)] = \$988,125$. So, the change in actual futures price is $\$988,125 - \$988,075 = \$50$.

You could also compute the change in price directly by noting that the IMM index price increased by 2 basis points. Because each basis point move in the rate moves the actual futures price by \$25, the increase in the actual futures price is 2 × \$25, or \$50.

7. A. Because the IMM index price is 93.35, the annualized LIBOR rate priced into the contract is $100 - 93.35 = 6.65$ percent.

B. Because the interest rate has decreased, the futures price would have increased.

C. With each contract based on \$1 million notional principal of 90-day Eurodollars, the actual futures price at the time of purchase was $\$1,000,000[1 - 0.0665(90/360)] = \$983,375$. The actual futures price a month later is $\$1,000,000[1 - 0.0650(90/360)] = \$983,750$. The increase in futures price is $\$983,750 - \$983,375 = \$375$. Thus, Jason Hathaway's gain is \$375.

You could also compute the change in price directly by noting that the interest rate decreased by 15 basis points (and the IMM index price increased by 15 basis points). Because each basis point move in the rate moves the actual futures price by \$25, the increase in actual futures price is 15 × \$25, or \$375.

8. Her gain caused by the increase in the price of Dow Jones Industrial Average futures is $\$10(9,086 - 9,020) = \$660$. Because Craft had a short position in S&P Midcap 400 futures, her loss caused by the increase in the price of S&P Midcap 400 futures is $\$500(370.20 - 369.40) = \$400$. Craft's net gain is $\$660 - \$400 = \$260$.

9. A. $T = 90/365 = 0.2466$. The futures price is

$$f_0(T) = S_0(1 + r)^T$$

$$f_0(0.2466) = 300(1.06)^{0.2466} = \$304.34 \text{ per ounce}$$

B. Do the following:
- Enter a short futures position—that is, sell the futures at \$306.
- Buy gold at \$300.
- At expiration, deliver an ounce of gold and receive \$306.

This amount is \$1.66 more than \$304.34, which is the sum of the cost of the asset (\$300) and the loss of interest on this amount at the rate of 6 percent a year (\$4.34). Thus, the overall strategy results in a riskless arbitrage profit of \$1.66 per futures contract. You can also look at this scenario in terms of returns: Investing \$300 and receiving \$306 90 days later is an annual return of 8.36 percent, because $300(1.0836)^{(90/365)} = 306$. This return is clearly greater than the risk-free return of 6 percent.

C. The steps in this case would be the reverse of the steps in Part B above. So, do the following:
- Enter a long futures position; that is, buy the futures at \$303.
- Sell short the gold at \$300.
- At expiration, take the delivery of an ounce of gold and pay \$303.

This amount paid is \$1.34 less than \$304.34, which is the sum of the funds received from the short sale of the asset (\$300) and the interest earned on this at the rate of 6 percent per year (\$4.34). Thus, the overall strategy results in a riskless arbitrage profit of \$1.34 per futures contract. In terms of rates, receiving \$300 up front and paying \$303 90 days later represents an annual rate of 4.12 percent, because $300(1.0412)^{(90/365)} = 303$. This rate is clearly less than the risk-free rate of 6 percent. Thus, the overall transaction is equivalent to borrowing at a rate less than the risk-free rate.

10. A. $T = 75/365 = 0.2055$. The futures price is $f_0(0.2055) = 90(1.07)^{0.2055} = 91.26$.

B. Storage costs must be covered in the futures price, so we add them:

$$f_0(0.2055) = 91.26 + 3 = 94.26$$

C. A positive cash flow, such as interest or dividends on the underlying, reduces the futures price:

$$f_0(0.2055) = 91.26 - 0.50 = 90.76$$

D. We add the storage costs and subtract the positive cash flow:

$$f_0(0.2055) = 91.26 + 3 - 0.50 = 93.76$$

E. We would do the following:
- Sell the futures at $95.
- Buy the asset at $90.
- Because the asset price compounded at the interest rate is $91.26, the interest forgone is 1.26. So the asset price is effectively $91.26 by the time of the futures expiration.
- We have incurred storage costs of $3 on the asset. We have received $0.50 from the asset. At expiration, we deliver the asset and receive $95. The net investment in the asset is $91.26 + $3.00 − $0.50 = $93.76. If we sell it for $95, we make a net gain of $1.24. Thus, the overall strategy results in a riskless arbitrage profit of $1.24 per futures contract. One can also look at this profit in terms of returns. Investing $90 and receiving a net of $95.00 − $3.00 + $0.50 = $92.50 75 days later is an annual return of 14.26 percent, because $90(1.14264)^{(75/365)} = $92.50. This return is clearly greater than the risk-free return of 7 percent.

F. The last settlement price was $89.50, and the price in our answer in Part A is $91.26. The value of a long futures contract is the difference between these prices, or $1.76.

G. When the futures contact is marked to market, the holder of the futures contract receives a gain of $1.76, and the value of the futures contract goes back to a value of zero.

11. A. $h = 45$ and $h + m = 135$

$$r_0^d(h) = r_0^d(45) = 0.055$$

$$r_0^d(h + m) = r_0^d(135) = 0.0595$$

The prices of these T-bills will, therefore, be

$$B_0(h) = 1 - r_0^d(h)\left(\frac{h}{360}\right)$$

$$B_0(45) = 1 - 0.055\left(\frac{45}{360}\right) = 0.9931$$

$$B_0(h + m) = 1 - r_0^d(h + m)\left(\frac{h + m}{360}\right)$$

$$B_0(135) = 1 - 0.0595\left(\frac{135}{360}\right) = 0.9777$$

So the price of a futures contract expiring in 45 days is

$$f_0(h) = \frac{B_0(h + m)}{B_0(h)}$$

$$f_0(45) = \frac{B_0(135)}{B_0(45)} = \frac{0.9777}{0.9931} - 0.9845$$

The discount rate implied in the futures would be

$$r_0^{df}(h) = [1 - f_0(h)]\left(\frac{360}{m}\right)$$

$$r_0^{df}(45) = [1 - 0.9845]\left(\frac{360}{90}\right) = 0.0620$$

In other words, in the T-bill futures market, the rate would be stated as 6.20 percent, which would imply a futures price of 0.9845. Alternatively, the implied futures discount rate could be obtained from the spot rates as

$$r_0^{df}(h) = \left\{1 - \left[\frac{1 - r_0^d(h + m)\left(\frac{h + m}{360}\right)}{1 - r_0^d\left(\frac{h}{360}\right)}\right]\right\}\left(\frac{360}{m}\right)$$

$$r_0^{df}(45) = \left\{1 - \left[\frac{1 - 0.0595\left(\frac{135}{360}\right)}{1 - 0.055\left(\frac{45}{360}\right)}\right]\right\}\left(\frac{360}{90}\right) = 0.0622$$

with the slight difference caused by rounding.

B. Suppose one purchases the 135-day T-bill for 0.9777 and sells the 45-day futures contract at a price of 0.9845. Then, 45 days later, the T-bill would be a 90-day T-bill and would be delivered to settle the futures contract. Thus, at that time, one would receive the original futures price of 0.9845. One initially paid 0.9777 and 45 days later received 0.9845. The return per dollar invested is

$$\frac{0.9845}{0.9777} = 1.00696$$

If instead one purchases a 45-day T-bill at the price of 0.9931 and holds it for 45 days, the return per dollar invested is

$$\frac{1}{0.9931} = 1.00695$$

Thus, the return per dollar invested is the same in both transactions (with a slight difference caused by rounding), and both transactions are free of risk.

12. A. First compute the prices of the 60-day and 150-day T-bills. With h = 60 and h + m = 150,

$$r_0^d(h) = r_0^d(60) = 0.060$$

$$r_0^d(h + m) = r_0^d(150) = 0.0625$$

The prices of these T-bills will, therefore, be

$$B_0(h) = 1 - r_0^d(h)\left(\frac{h}{360}\right)$$

$$B_0(60) = 1 - 0.06\left(\frac{60}{360}\right) = 0.99$$

$$B_0(h + m) = 1 - r_0^d(h + m)\left(\frac{h + m}{360}\right)$$

$$B_0(150) = 1 - 0.0625\left(\frac{150}{360}\right) = 0.974$$

So the price of a futures expiring in 60 days is

$$f_0(h) = \frac{B_0(h + m)}{B_0(h)}$$

$$f_0(45) = \frac{B_0(150)}{B_0(60)} = \frac{0.974}{0.990} = 0.9838$$

B. As the actual futures price of 0.9853 is more than the implied futures price computed in Part A, you should sell the futures contract. So, do the following.
  - Buy the 150-day T-bill at 0.974.
  - Sell the 60-day futures contract at 0.9853.
  The return per dollar would be

$$\frac{0.9853}{0.9740} = 1.0116$$

Note that this return is risk free. It compares favorably with return per dollar on purchasing a 60-day T-bill and holding it to maturity, which is

$$\frac{1}{0.99} = 1.0101$$

C. The repo rate is the annualization of the return per dollar because of the arbitrage transactions outlined in Part B:

$$1.0116^{365/60} - 1 = 0.0727$$

Thus, the rate of return from a cash-and-carry transaction implied by the futures price relative to the spot price is 7.27 percent. If the financing rate available in the repo market is less than this rate, the arbitrage strategy outlined in Part B is worthwhile, because the cost of funds is less than the return on the funds.

13. A. First, find the prices of 30- and 120-day bills:

$$B_0(30) = 1 - 0.054(30/360) = 0.9955$$

$$B_0(120) = 1 - 0.050(120/360) = 0.9833$$

$$f_0(h) = \frac{B_0(h + m)}{B_0(h)}$$

$$f_0(45) = \frac{B_0(120)}{B_0(30)} = \frac{0.9833}{0.9955} = 0.9877$$

B. We must find the rate at which to compound the spot price of the 120-day T-bill. The spot rate, obtained from the 30-day T-bill, is

$$[1 + r_0(h)]^{h/365} = \frac{1}{0.9955} = 1.0045$$

Based on the rate $r_0(h)$, every dollar invested should grow to a value of 1.0045. Thus, the futures price should be the spot price (price of the 120-day T-bill) compounded by the factor 1.0045:

$$f_0(30) = 0.9833(1.0045) = 0.9877$$

That is, $[1 + r_0(h)]^{h/365} = 1.0045$. Note that we do not actually need $r_0(h)$.

C. Given the futures price of 0.9877, the implied rate is

$$r_0^{df}(h) = (1 - 0.9877)\left(\frac{360}{90}\right) = 0.0492$$

D. If the futures contract is trading for 20 basis points lower, it is trading at a rate of 4.72 percent. So the futures price would be

$$f_0(30) = 1 - 0.0472\left(\frac{90}{360}\right) = 0.9882$$

Do the following:
- Buy the 120-day bill at 0.9833.
- Sell the futures at 0.9882.

This transaction produces a return per dollar invested of

$$\frac{0.9882}{0.9833} = 1.0050$$

which is a risk-free return and compares favorably with a return per dollar invested of 1.0045 (computed in Part B above) for a 30-day T-bill.

E. If the futures contract is trading for 20 basis points higher than is appropriate, it trades at a rate of 5.12 percent. So the futures price would be

$$f_0(30) = 1 - 0.0512\left(\frac{90}{360}\right) = 0.9872$$

Do the following:
- Sell the 120-day bill at 0.9833.
- Go long a 30-day futures contract at 0.9872.

Thus, at the beginning, you received 0.9833. At expiration 30 days later, the 120-day bill you sold short at the beginning is a 90-day bill. You would take care of this by paying 0.9872 and taking the delivery of a 90-day T-bill (because you had bought a 30-day futures contract at the beginning). Effectively, what you have done is borrowed at a rate of

$$\frac{0.9872}{0.9833} = 1.0040$$

which compares favorably with the risk-free rate of 1.0045 computed in Part B above.

You could also look at the above as follows. You go long a 30-day futures contract at 0.9872. You sell the 120-day bill at 0.9833. Invest this amount in a 30-day T-bill. At maturity, you will have 0.9833(1.0045), or 0.9877. This return compares favorably with the 0.9872 that you owe at expiration.

14. A. Because the futures contract expires in 18 months, $T = 1.5$. The risk-free rate, $r_0(T)$, is 0.05. When computing the accumulated value of the coupons on the bond and the interest on them until the futures contract expires, note that the first coupon is paid in exactly six months and reinvested for the one year remaining until expiration. Also, the second coupon is paid in exactly one year and reinvested

for the six months remaining until expiration, and the third coupon is paid in exactly one and a half years and not reinvested. So, the accumulated value of the coupons on the bond and the interest on them is

$$0.04(1.05)^1 + 0.04(1.05)^{0.5} + 0.04 = 0.1230$$

Because the underlying bond is the only deliverable bond in this simplistic problem, the conversion factor is 1.0, so no adjustment is required. Now the futures price is easily obtained as

$$f_0(T) = B_0^c(T + Y)[1 + r_0(T)]^T - FV(CI,0,T)$$

$$f_0(1.5) = 1.1488(1.05)^{1.5} - 0.1230$$

$$= 1.1130$$

B. Buy the five-year bond for $1.1488 and sell the futures for $1.1130. Hold the position for one and a half years until the futures expiration. Collect and reinvest the coupons in the meantime. When the futures contract expires, deliver the bond and receive the futures price of $1.1130. In addition, you will have the coupons and interest on them of $0.1230 for a total of $1.1130 + $0.1230 = $1.2360. You invested $1.1488 and end up with $1.2360 a year and a half later, so the return per dollar invested is $1.2360/$1.1488 = 1.0759. Because this amount is paid in 1.5 years, the annual equivalent of this is

$$1.0759^{1/1.5} = 1.05$$

This return is equivalent to the 5 percent risk-free rate.

15. A. Because the futures contract expires in 15 months, $T = 1.25$. The risk-free rate, $r_0(T)$, is 0.05. To compute the accumulated value of the coupons on the bond and the interest on them until the futures contract expires, we note that the first coupon is paid in exactly six months and reinvested for the nine months (0.75 years) remaining until expiration. Also, the second coupon is paid in exactly one year and reinvested for the three months (0.25 years) remaining until expiration. So, the accumulated value of the coupons on the bond and the interest on them is

$$0.03(1.05)^{0.75} + 0.03(1.05)^{0.25} = 0.0615$$

B. Because the underlying bond is the only deliverable bond in this part of the problem, the conversion factor is 1, and no adjustment is required. So, the futures price is

$$f_0(T) = B_0^c(T + Y)[1 + r_0(T)]^T - FV(CI,0,T)$$

$$f_0(1.25) = 1(1.05)^{1.25} - 0.0615$$

$$= 1.0014$$

C. The futures price now is the price computed in Part B above divided by the conversion factor. Because the conversion factor is 1.0567, the futures price is

$$\frac{1.0014}{1.0567} = 0.9477$$

16. A. $T = 73/365 = 0.20$. The futures price should be

$$f_0(T) = S_0(1 + r)^T - FV(D,0,T)$$

$$f_0(0.20) = 1,521.75(1.0610)^{0.20} - 5.36$$

$$= 1,534.52$$

Alternatively, we can find the present value of the dividends:

$$PV(D,0,T) = \frac{FV(D,0,T)}{(1 + r)^T}$$

$$PV(D,0,0.20) = \frac{5.36}{(1.0610)^{0.20}} = 5.30$$

Then the futures price would be

$$f_0(T) = [S_0 - PV(D,0,T)](1 + r)^T$$

$$f_0(0.20) = (1,521.75 - 5.30)(1.061)^{0.20}$$

$$= 1,534.52$$

B. One specification based on the yield δ is

$$\frac{1}{(1 + \delta)^T} = 1 - \frac{FV(D,0,T)}{S_0(1 + r)^T}$$

$$= 1 - \frac{5.36}{1,521.75(1.061)^{0.20}} = 0.9965$$

So, $(1 + \delta)^T$ is $1/0.9965 = 1.0035$. Then the futures price is

$$f_0(T) = \left(\frac{S_0}{(1 + \delta)^T}\right)(1 + r)^T$$

$$f_0(0.20) = \left(\frac{1,521.75}{1.0035}\right)(1.061)^{0.20}$$

$$= 1,534.51$$

The difference comes from rounding.

Under the other specification, the yield would be found as

$$\delta^* = \frac{PV(D,0,T)}{S_0}$$

$$= \frac{5.30}{1,521.75} = 0.0035$$

Then the futures price would be

$$f_0(T) = S_0(1 - \delta^*)(1 + r)^T$$

$$f_0(0.20) = 1,521.75(1 - 0.0035)(1.061)^{0.20}$$

$$= 1,534.49$$

The difference comes from rounding.

C. The continuously compounded risk-free rate is $r^c = \ln(1 + r) = \ln(1.061) = 0.0592$. The continuously compounded dividend yield is $\delta^c = \ln(1 + \delta) = (1/T)\ln[(1 + \delta)^T] = (1/0.20)\ln(1.0035) = 0.0175$. The futures price is

$$f_0(T) = S_0 e^{(r^c - \delta^c)T}$$

$$f_0(0.20) = 1,521.75 e^{(0.0592 - 0.0175)0.20}$$

$$= 1,534.49$$

The difference comes from rounding.

17. A. $T = 201/365 = 0.5507$. The futures price should be

$$f_0(T) = S_0(1 + r)^T - FV(D,0,T)$$

$$f_0(0.5507) = 443.35(1.0650)^{0.5507} - 5.0 = 454.0$$

Alternatively, we can find the present value of the dividends:

$$PV(D,0,T) = \frac{FV(D,0,T)}{(1 + r)^T}$$

$$PV(D,0,0.5507) = \frac{5.0}{(1.0650)^{0.5507}} = 4.83$$

Then the futures price would be

$$f_0(T) = [S_0 - PV(D,0,T)](1 + r)^T$$

$$f_0(0.5507) = (443.35 - 4.83)(1.065)^{0.5507}$$

$$= 454.0$$

Because the futures contract is selling at 458.50, which is higher than the price computed above, the futures contract is overpriced.

B. The arbitrageur will buy the stocks underlying the index at their current price of $443.35. Also, the arbitrageur will sell the futures contract at the settlement price of $458.50. The arbitrageur will collect and reinvest the dividends, which would be worth $5 at the time of the futures expiration. At the time of expiration, the arbitrageur will get the settlement price of $458.50. So, the arbitrageur invests $443.35 at the beginning and receives $5.00 + $458.50 = $463.50 at the expiration 201 days later. The return per dollar invested over the 201-day period is

$$\frac{463.50}{443.35} = 1.0454$$

The annual risk-free rate is 6.5 percent, equivalent to a return per dollar invested of $(1.065)^{0.5507} = 1.0353$ over the 201-day period. Thus, the return to the arbitrageur from the transactions described above exceeds the risk-free return. Alternatively, one could see that to the arbitrageur, the return per dollar invested, over a year, is $1.0454^{365/201} = 1.0832$. This annualized return of 8.32 percent is clearly greater than the annual risk-free rate of 6.5 percent.

18. $T = 100/365 = 0.274$

A. The futures price is

$$f_0(T) = \left(\frac{S_0}{(1 + r^f)^T}\right)(1 + r)^T$$

$$f_0(0.274) = \left(\frac{1.4390}{1.058^{0.274}}\right)(1.063)^{0.274}$$

$$= 1.4409$$

B. The continuously compounded equivalent rates are

$$r^{fc} = \ln(1.058) = 0.0564$$

$$r^c = \ln(1.063) = 0.0611$$

The futures price is

$$f_0(T) = (S_0 e^{-r^{fc}T})e^{r^c T}$$

$$f_0(T) = (1.4390 e^{-0.0564(0.274)})e^{0.0611(0.274)}$$

$$= 1.4409$$

C. The actual futures price of $1.4650 is higher than the price computed above—the futures contract is overpriced. To take advantage, the arbitrageur needs to buy the foreign currency and sell the futures contract. First, however, we must determine how many units of the currency to buy. Because we need to have 1 unit of currency, including the interest, the number of units to buy is

$$\frac{1}{(1.058)^{0.274}} = 0.9847$$

So we buy 0.9847 units, which costs 0.9847($1.4390) = $1.417. We sell the futures at $1.4650 and hold until expiration. During that time, the accumulation of interest will make the 0.9847 units of the currency grow to one unit. Using the futures contract, at expiration we convert this unit at the futures rate of $1.4650. The return per dollar invested is

$$\frac{1.4650}{1.417} = 1.0339$$

or a return of 3.39 percent over 100 days. The U.S. annual risk-free rate is 6.3 percent, which is equivalent to a return per dollar invested of $(1.063)^{0.274} = 1.0169$, over the 100-day period. Thus, the return to the arbitrageur from the transactions described above exceeds the risk-free return. Alternatively, one could see that to the arbitrageur, the return per dollar invested, over a year, is $(1.0339)^{365/100} = 1.1294$. This annualized return of 12.94 percent is more than double the annual risk-free rate of 6.3 percent.

CHAPTER

4

OPTION MARKETS AND CONTRACTS

LEARNING OUTCOMES

After completing this chapter, you will be able to do the following:

- Identify the basic elements and characteristics of option contracts.
- Define European option, American option, moneyness, payoff, intrinsic value, and time value.
- Differentiate between exchange-traded options and over-the-counter options.
- Identify the different varieties of options in terms of the types of instruments underlying them.
- Compare and contrast interest rate options to forward rate agreements (FRAs).
- Explain how option payoffs are determined, and show how interest rate option payoffs differ from the payoffs of other types of options.
- Define interest rate caps and floors.
- Identify the minimum and maximum values of European options and American options.
- Illustrate how the lower bounds of European calls and puts are determined by constructing portfolio combinations that prevent arbitrage, and calculate an option's lower bound.
- Determine the lowest prices of European and American calls and puts based on the rules for lower bounds.
- Illustrate how a portfolio (combination) of options establishes the relationship between options that differ only by exercise price.
- Explain how option prices are affected by differences in the time to expiration.
- Illustrate how put–call parity for European options is established by comparing the payoffs on a fiduciary call and a protective put, explain how to use this result to create synthetic instruments, and explain why an investor would want to do so.
- Illustrate how violations of put–call parity for European options can be exploited and how those violations are eliminated.
- Explain the relationship between American options and European options in terms of the lower bounds on option prices and the possibility of early exercise.
- Explain how cash flows on the underlying asset affect put–call parity and the lower bounds on option prices.
- Identify the directional effect of an interest rate change on an option's price.

- Explain how an option price is determined in a one-period binomial model.
- Illustrate how an arbitrage opportunity can be exploited in a one-period binomial model.
- Explain how an option price is determined in a two-period binomial model.
- Calculate prices of options on bonds and interest rate options in one- and two-period binomial models.
- Explain how the binomial model value converges as time periods are added.
- List and briefly explain the assumptions underlying the Black–Scholes–Merton model.
- Calculate the value of a European option using the Black–Scholes–Merton model.
- Explain how an option price, as represented by the Black–Scholes–Merton model, is affected by each of the input values (the Greeks).
- Explain and illustrate the concept of an option's delta and how it is used in dynamic hedging.
- Explain the gamma effect on an option's price and delta.
- Discuss how cash flows on the underlying asset affect an option's price.
- Explain and illustrate the two methods for estimating the volatility of the underlying.
- Illustrate how put–call parity for options on forwards (or futures) is established.
- Explain how American options on forwards and futures are alike, and explain how they differ from European options.
- Calculate the value of a European option on forwards (or futures) using the Black model.
- Calculate the value of a European interest rate option using the Black model.
- Discuss the role of options markets in financial systems and society.

1   INTRODUCTION

In Chapter 1, we provided a general introduction to derivative markets. In Chapter 2 we examined forward contracts, and in Chapter 3 we looked at futures contracts. We noted how similar forward and futures contracts are: Both are commitments to buy an underlying asset at a fixed price at a later date. Forward contracts, however, are privately created, over-the-counter customized instruments that carry credit risk. Futures contracts are publicly traded, exchange-listed standardized instruments that effectively have no credit risk. Now we turn to options. Like forwards and futures, they are derivative instruments that provide the opportunity to buy or sell an underlying asset with a specific expiration date. But in contrast, buying an option gives the *right*, not the obligation, to buy or sell an underlying asset. And whereas forward and futures contracts involve no exchange of cash up front, options require a cash payment from the option buyer to the option seller.

Yet options contain several features common to forward and futures contracts. For one, options can be created by any two parties with any set of terms they desire. In this sense, options can be privately created, over-the-counter, customized instruments that are subject to credit risk. In addition, however, there is a large market for publicly traded, exchange-listed, standardized options, for which credit risk is essentially eliminated by the clearinghouse.

Just as we examined the pricing of forwards and futures in the last two chapters, we shall examine option pricing in this chapter. We shall also see that options can be created out of forward contracts, and that forward contracts can be created out of options. With some simplifying assumptions, options can be created out of futures contracts and futures contracts can be created out of options.

Finally, we note that options also exist that have a futures or forward contract as the underlying. These instruments blend some of the features of both options and forwards/futures.

As background, we discuss the definitions and characteristics of options.

2 BASIC DEFINITIONS AND ILLUSTRATIONS OF OPTIONS CONTRACTS

In Chapter 1, we defined an option as a financial derivative contract that provides a party the right to buy or sell an underlying at a fixed price by a certain time in the future. The party holding the right is the option buyer; the party granting the right is the option seller. There are two types of options, a **call** and a **put**. A call is an option granting the right to buy the underlying; a put is an option granting the right to sell the underlying. With the exception of some advanced types of options, a given option contract is either a call, granting the right to buy, or a put, granting the right to sell, but not both.[1] We emphasize that this right to buy or sell is held by the option buyer, also called the long or option holder, and granted by the option seller, also called the short or option writer.

To obtain this right, the option buyer pays the seller a sum of money, commonly referred to as the **option price**. On occasion, this option price is called the **option premium** or just the **premium**. This money is paid when the option contract is initiated.

2.1 BASIC CHARACTERISTICS OF OPTIONS

The fixed price at which the option holder can buy or sell the underlying is called the **exercise price**, **strike price**, **striking price**, or **strike**. The use of this right to buy or sell the underlying is referred to as **exercise** or **exercising the option**. Like all derivative contracts, an option has an **expiration date**, giving rise to the notion of an option's **time to expiration**. When the expiration date arrives, an option that is not exercised simply expires.

What happens at exercise depends on the whether the option is a call or a put. If the buyer is exercising a call, she pays the exercise price and receives either the underlying or an equivalent cash settlement. On the opposite side of the transaction is the seller, who receives the exercise price from the buyer and delivers the underlying, or alternatively, pays an equivalent cash settlement. If the buyer is exercising a put, she delivers the stock and receives the exercise price or an equivalent cash settlement. The seller, therefore, receives the underlying and must pay the exercise price or the equivalent cash settlement.

As noted in the above paragraph, cash settlement is possible. In that case, the option holder exercising a call receives the difference between the market value of the underlying and the exercise price from the seller in cash. If the option holder exercises a put, she receives the difference between the exercise price and the market value of the underlying in cash.

---

[1] Of course, a party could buy both a call and a put, thereby holding the right to buy *and* sell the underlying.

There are two primary exercise styles associated with options. One type of option has **European-style exercise**, which means that the option can be exercised only on its expiration day. In some cases, expiration could occur during that day; in others, exercise can occur only when the option has expired. In either case, such an option is called a **European option**. The other style of exercise is **American-style exercise**. Such an option can be exercised on any day through the expiration day and is generally called an **American option**.[2]

Option contracts specify a designated number of units of the underlying. For exchange-listed, standardized options, the exchange establishes each term, with the exception of the price. The price is negotiated by the two parties. For an over-the-counter option, the two parties decide each of the terms through negotiation.

In an over-the-counter option—one created off of an exchange by any two parties who agree to trade—the buyer is subject to the possibility of the writer defaulting. When the buyer exercises, the writer must either deliver the stock or cash if a call, or pay for the stock or pay cash if a put. If the writer cannot do so for financial reasons, the option holder faces a credit loss. Because the option holder paid the price up front and is not required to do anything else, the seller does not face any credit risk. Thus, although credit risk is bilateral in forward contracts—the long assumes the risk of the short defaulting, and the short assumes the risk of the long defaulting—the credit risk in an option is unilateral. Only the buyer faces credit risk because only the seller can default. As we discuss later, in exchange-listed options, the clearinghouse guarantees payment to the buyer.

2.2   SOME EXAMPLES OF OPTIONS

Consider some call and put options on Sun Microsystems (SUNW). The date is 13 June and Sun is selling for $16.25. Exhibit 4-1 gives information on the closing prices of four options, ones expiring in July and October and ones with exercise prices of 15.00 and 17.50. The July options expire on 20 July and the October options expire on 18 October. In the parlance of the profession, these are referred to as the July 15 calls, July 17.50 calls, October 15 calls, and October 17.50 calls, with similar terminology for the puts. These particular options are American style.

EXHIBIT 4-1   Closing Prices of Selected Options on SUNW, 13 June

Exercise Price	July Calls	October Calls	July Puts	October Puts
15.00	2.35	3.30	0.90	1.85
17.50	1.00	2.15	2.15	3.20

Note: Stock price is $16.25; July options expire on 20 July; October options expire on 18 October.

Consider the July 15 call. This option permits the holder to buy SUNW at a price of $15 a share any time through 20 July. To obtain this option, one would pay a price of $2.35. Therefore, a writer received $2.35 on 13 June and must be ready to sell SUNW to the buyer for $15 during the period through 20 July. Currently, SUNW trades above $15 a share, but as we shall see in more detail later, the option holder has no reason to exercise the option

---

[2] It is worthwhile to be aware that these terms have nothing to do with Europe or America. Both types of options are found in Europe and America. The names are part of the folklore of options markets, and there is no definitive history to explain how they came into use.

right now.[3] To justify purchase of the call, the buyer must be anticipating that SUNW will increase in price before the option expires. The seller of the call must be anticipating that SUNW will not rise sufficiently in price before the option expires.

Note that the option buyer could purchase a call expiring in July but permitting the purchase of SUNW at a price of $17.50. This price is more than the $15.00 exercise price, but as a result, the option, which sells for $1.00, is considerably cheaper. The cheaper price comes from the fact that the July 17.50 call is less likely to be exercised, because the stock has a higher hurdle to clear. A buyer is not willing to pay as much and a seller is more willing to take less for an option that is less likely to be exercised.

Alternatively, the option buyer could choose to purchase an October call instead of a July call. For any exercise price, however, the October calls would be more expensive than the July calls because they allow a longer period for the stock to make the move that the buyer wants. October options are more likely to be exercised than July options; therefore, a buyer would be willing to pay more and the seller would demand more for the October calls.

Suppose the buyer expects the stock price to go down. In that case, he might buy a put. Consider the October 17.50 put, which would cost the buyer $3.20. This option would allow the holder to sell SUNW at a price of $17.50 any time up through 18 October.[4] He has no reason to exercise the option right now, because it would mean he would be buying the option for $3.20 and selling a stock worth $16.25 for $17.50. In effect, the option holder would part with $19.45 (the cost of the option of $3.20 plus the value of the stock of $16.25) and obtain only $17.50.[5] The buyer of a put obviously must be anticipating that the stock will fall before the expiration day.

If he wanted a cheaper option than the October 17.50 put, he could buy the October 15 put, which would cost only $1.85 but would allow him to sell the stock for only $15.00 a share. The October 15 put is less likely to be exercised than the October 17.50, because the stock price must fall below a lower hurdle. Thus, the buyer is not willing to pay as much and the seller is willing to take less.

For either exercise price, purchase of a July put instead of an October put would be much cheaper but would allow less time for the stock to make the downward move necessary for the transaction to be worthwhile. The July put is cheaper than the October put; the buyer is not willing to pay as much and the seller is willing to take less because the option is less likely to be exercised.

In observing these option prices, we have obtained our first taste of some principles involved in pricing options.

Call options have a lower premium the higher the exercise price.

Put options have a lower premium the lower the exercise price.

Both call and put options are cheaper the shorter the time to expiration.[6]

---

[3] The buyer paid $2.35 for the option. If he exercised it right now, he would pay $15.00 for the stock, which is worth only $16.25. Thus, he would have effectively paid $17.35 (the cost of the option of $2.35 plus the exercise price of $15) for a stock worth $16.25. Even if he had purchased the option previously at a much lower price, the current option price of $2.35 is the opportunity cost of exercising the option—that is, he can always sell the option for $2.35. Therefore, if he exercised the option, he would be throwing away the $2.35 he could receive if he sold it.

[4] Even if the option holder did not own the stock, he could use the option to sell the stock short.

[5] Again, even if the option were purchased in the past at a much lower price, the $3.20 current value of the option is an opportunity cost. Exercise of the option is equivalent to throwing away the opportunity cost.

[6] There is an exception to the rule that put options are cheaper the shorter the time to expiration. This statement is always true for American options but not always for European options. We explore this point later.

These results should be intuitive, but later in this chapter we show unequivocally why they must be true.

2.3 THE CONCEPT OF MONEYNESS OF AN OPTION

An important concept in the study of options is the notion of an option's **moneyness**, which refers to the relationship between the price of the underlying and the exercise price. We use the terms **in-the-money**, **out-of-the-money**, and **at-the-money**. We explain the concept in Exhibit 4-2 with examples from the SUNW options. Note that in-the-money options are those in which exercising the option would produce a cash inflow that exceeds the cash outflow. Thus, calls are in-the-money when the value of the underlying exceeds the exercise price. Puts are in-the-money when the exercise price exceeds the value of the underlying. In our example, there are no at-the-money SUNW options, which would require that the stock value equal the exercise price; however, an at-the-money option can effectively be viewed as an out-of-the-money option, because its exercise would not bring in more money than is paid out.

EXHIBIT 4-2   Moneyness of an Option

In-the-Money		Out-of-the-Money	
Option	Justification	Option	Justification
July 15 call	16.25 > 15.00	July 17.50 call	16.25 < 17.50
October 15 call	16.25 > 15.00	October 17.50 call	16.25 < 17.50
July 17.50 put	17.50 > 16.25	July 15 put	15.00 < 16.25
October 17.50 put	17.50 > 16.25	October 15 put	15.00 < 16.25

Notes: Sun Microsystems options on 13 June; stock price is 16.25. See Exhibit 4-1 for more details. There are no options with an exercise price of 16.25, so no options are at-the-money.

As explained above, *one would not necessarily exercise an in-the-money option, but one would never exercise an out-of-the-money option.*

We now move on to explore how options markets are organized.

3   THE STRUCTURE OF GLOBAL OPTIONS MARKETS

Although no one knows exactly how options first got started, contracts similar to options have been around for thousands of years. In fact, insurance is a form of an option. The insurance buyer pays the insurance writer a premium and receives a type of guarantee that covers losses. This transaction is similar to a put option, which provides coverage of a portion of losses on the underlying and is often used by holders of the underlying. The first true options markets were over-the-counter options markets in the United States in the 19th century.

3.1 OVER-THE-COUNTER OPTIONS MARKETS

In the United States, customized over-the-counter options markets were in existence in the early part of the 20th century and lasted well into the 1970s. An organization called the Put and Call Brokers and Dealers Association consisted of a group of firms that served as brokers and dealers. As brokers, they attempted to match buyers of options with sellers, thereby earning a commission. As dealers, they offered to take either side of the option transaction, usually laying off (hedging) the risk in another transaction. Most of these transactions were retail, meaning that the general public were their customers.

As we discuss in Section 3.2 below, the creation of the Chicago Board Options Exchange was a revolutionary event, but it effectively killed the Put and Call Brokers and Dealers Association. Subsequently, the increasing use of swaps facilitated a rebirth of the customized over-the-counter options market. Currency options, a natural extension to currency swaps, were in much demand. Later, interest rate options emerged as a natural outgrowth of interest rate swaps. Soon bond, equity, and index options were trading in a vibrant over-the-counter market. In contrast to the previous over-the-counter options market, however, the current one emerged as a largely wholesale market. Transactions are usually made with institutions and corporations and are rarely conducted directly with individuals. This market is much like the forward market described in Chapter 2, with dealers offering to take either the long or short position in options and hedging that risk with transactions in other options or derivatives. There are no guarantees that the seller will perform; hence, the buyer faces credit risk. As such, option buyers must scrutinize sellers' credit risk and may require some risk reduction measures, such as collateral.

As previously noted, customized options have *all* of their terms—such as price, exercise price, time to expiration, identification of the underlying, settlement or delivery terms, size of the contract, and so on—determined by the two parties.

Like forward markets, over-the-counter options markets are essentially unregulated. In most countries, participating firms, such as banks and securities firms, are regulated by the appropriate authorities but there is usually no particular regulatory body for the over-the-counter options markets. In some countries, however, there are regulatory bodies for these markets.

Exhibit 4-3 provides information on the leading dealers in over-the-counter currency and interest rate options as determined by *Risk* magazine in its annual surveys of banks and investment banks and also end users.

EXHIBIT 4-3 *Risk* **Magazine Surveys of Banks, Investment Banks, and Corporate End Users to Determine the Top Three Dealers in Over-the-Counter Currency and Interest Rate Options**

	Respondents	
Currencies	Banks and Investment Banks	Corporate End Users
Currency Options		
$/€	UBS Warburg	Citigroup
	Citigroup/Deutsche Bank	Royal Bank of Scotland
		Deutsche Bank
$/¥	UBS Warburg	Citigroup
	Credit Suisse First Boston	JP Morgan Chase
	JP Morgan Chase/Royal Bank of Scotland	UBS Warburg
$/£	Royal Bank of Scotland	Royal Bank of Scotland
	UBS Warburg	Citigroup
	Citigroup	Hong Kong Shanghai Banking Corp.
$/SF	UBS Warburg	UBS Warburg
	Credit Suisse First Boston	Credit Suisse First Boston
	Citigroup	Citigroup

Interest Rate Options

$	JP Morgan Chase	JP Morgan Chase
	Deutsche Bank	Citigroup
	Bank of America	Deutsche Bank/Lehman Brothers
€	JP Morgan Chase	JP Morgan Chase
	Credit Suisse First Boston/ Morgan Stanley	Citigroup UBS Warburg
¥	JP Morgan Chase/Deutsche Bank	UBS Warburg
	Bank of America	Barclays Capital Citigroup
£	Barclays Capital	Royal Bank of Scotland
	Societe Generale Groupe	Citigroup
	Bank of America/Royal Bank of Scotland	Hong Kong Shanghai Banking Corp.
SF	UBS Warburg	UBS Warburg
	JP Morgan Chase	JP Morgan
	Credit Suisse First Boston	Goldman Sachs

Notes: $ = U.S. dollar, € = euro, ¥ = Japanese yen, £ = U.K. pound sterling, SF = Swiss franc

Source: *Risk*, September 2002, pp. 30–67 for Banks and Investment Banking dealer respondents, and June 2002, pp. 24–34 for Corporate End User respondents.

Results for Corporate End Users for Interest Rate Options are from *Risk*, July 2001, pp. 38–46. *Risk* omitted this category from its 2002 survey.

3.2 EXCHANGE-LISTED OPTIONS MARKETS

As briefly noted above, the Chicago Board Options Exchange was formed in 1973. Created as an extension of the Chicago Board of Trade, it became the first organization to offer a market for standardized options. In the United States, standardized options also trade on the Amex–Nasdaq, the Philadelphia Stock Exchange, and the Pacific Stock Exchange.[7] On a worldwide basis, standardized options are widely traded on such exchanges as LIFFE (the London International Financial Futures and Options Exchange) in London, Eurex in Frankfurt, and most other foreign exchanges. Exhibit 4-4 shows the 20 largest options exchanges in the world. Note, perhaps surprisingly, that the leading options exchange is in Korea.

EXHIBIT 4-4   World's 20 Largest Options Exchanges

Exchange and Location	Volume in 2001
Korea Stock Exchange (Korea)	854,791,792
Chicago Board Options Exchange (United States)	306,667,851
MONEP (France)	285,667,686
Eurex (Germany and Switzerland)	239,016,516
American Stock Exchange (United States)	205,103,884
Pacific Stock Exchange (United States)	102,701,752
Philadelphia Stock Exchange (United States)	101,373,433
Chicago Mercantile Exchange (United States)	95,740,352

---

[7] You may wonder why the New York Stock Exchange is not mentioned. Standardized options did trade on the NYSE at one time but were not successful, and the right to trade these options was sold to another exchange.

Amsterdam Exchange (Netherlands)	66,400,654
LIFFE (United Kingdom)	54,225,652
Chicago Board of Trade (United States)	50,345,068
OM Stockholm (Sweden)	39,327,619
South African Futures Exchange (South Africa)	24,307,477
MEFF Renta Variable (Spain)	23,628,446
New York Mercantile Exchange (United States)	17,985,109
Korea Futures Exchange (Korea)	11,468,991
Italian Derivatives Exchange (Italy)	11,045,804
Osaka Securities Exchange (Japan)	6,991,908
Bourse de Montreal (Canada)	5,372,930
Hong Kong Futures Exchange (China)	4,718,880

Note: Volume given is in number of contracts.
Source: Data supplied by *Futures Industry* magazine.

As described in Chapter 2 on futures, the exchange fixes all terms of standardized instruments except the price. Thus, the exchange establishes the expiration dates and exercise prices as well as the minimum price quotation unit. The exchange also determines whether the option is European or American, whether the exercise is cash settlement or delivery of the underlying, and the contract size. In the United States, an option contract on an individual stock covers 100 shares of stock. Terminology such as "one option" is often used to refer to one option contract, which is really a set of options on 100 shares of stock. Index option sizes are stated in terms of a multiplier, indicating that the contract covers a hypothetical number of shares, as though the index were an individual stock. Similar specifications apply for options on other types of underlyings.

The exchange generally allows trading in exercise prices that surround the current stock price. As the stock price moves, options with exercise prices around the new stock price are usually added. The majority of trading occurs in options that are close to being at-the-money. Options that are far in-the-money or far out-of-the-money, called **deep-in-the-money** and **deep-out-of-the-money** options, are usually not very actively traded and are often not even listed for trading.

Most exchange-listed options have fairly short-term expirations, usually the current month, the next month, and perhaps one or two other months. Most of the trading takes place for the two shortest expirations. Some exchanges list options with expirations of several years, which have come to be called LEAPS, for **long-term equity anticipatory securities**. These options are fairly actively purchased, but most investors tend to buy and hold them and do not trade them as often as they do the shorter-term options.

The exchanges also determine on which companies they will list options for trading. Although specific requirements do exist, generally the exchange will list the options of any company for which it feels the options would be actively traded. The company has no voice in the matter. Options of a company can be listed on more than one exchange in a given country.

In Chapter 3, we described the manner in which futures are traded. The procedure is very similar for exchange-listed options. Some exchanges have pit trading, whereby parties meet in the pit and arrange a transaction. Some exchanges use electronic trading, in which transactions are conducted through computers. In either case, the transactions are guaranteed by the clearinghouse. In the United States, the clearinghouse is an independent company called the Options Clearing Corporation or OCC. The OCC guarantees to the buyer that the clearinghouse will step in and fulfill the obligation if the seller reneges at exercise.

When the buyer purchases the option, the premium, which one might think would go to the seller, instead goes to the clearinghouse, which maintains it in a margin account. In addition, the seller must post some margin money, which is based on a formula that reflects whether the seller has a position that hedges the risk and whether the option is in- or out-of-the-money. If the price moves against the seller, the clearinghouse will force the seller to put up additional margin money. Although defaults are rare, the clearinghouse has always been successful in paying when the seller defaults. Thus, exchange-listed options are effectively free of credit risk.

Because of the standardization of option terms and participants' general acceptance of these terms, exchange-listed options can be bought and sold at any time prior to expiration. Thus, a party who buys or sells an option can re-enter the market before the option expires and offset the position with a sale or a purchase of the identical option. From the clearinghouse's perspective, the positions cancel.

As in futures markets, traders on the options exchange are generally either market makers or brokers. Some slight technical distinctions exist between different types of market makers in different options markets, but the differences are minor and do not concern us here. Like futures traders, option market makers attempt to profit by scalping (holding positions very short term) to earn the bid–ask spread and sometimes holding positions longer, perhaps closing them overnight or leaving them open for days or more.

When an option expires, the holder decides whether or not to exercise it. When the option is expiring, there are no further gains to waiting, so in-the-money options are always exercised, assuming they are in-the-money by more than the transaction cost of buying or selling the underlying or arranging a cash settlement when exercising. Using our example of the SUNW options, if at expiration the stock is at 16, the calls with an exercise price of 15 would be exercised. Most exchange-listed stock options call for actual delivery of the stock. Thus, the seller delivers the stock and the buyer pays the seller, through the clearinghouse, $15 per share. If the exchange specifies that the contract is cash settled, the seller simply pays the buyer $1. For puts requiring delivery, the buyer tenders the stock and receives the exercise price from the seller. If the option is out-of-the-money, it simply expires unexercised and is removed from the books. If the put is cash settled, the writer pays the buyer the equivalent cash amount.

Some nonstandardized exchange-traded options exist in the United States. In an attempt to compete with the over-the-counter options market, some exchanges permit some options to be individually customized and traded on the exchange, thereby benefiting from the advantages of the clearinghouse's credit guarantee. These options are primarily available only in large sizes and tend to be traded only by large institutional investors.

Like futures markets, exchange-listed options markets are typically regulated at the federal level. In the United States, federal regulation of options markets is the responsibility of the Securities and Exchange Commission; similar regulatory structures exist in other countries.

4   TYPES OF OPTIONS

Almost anything with a random outcome can have an option on it. Note that by using the word *anything*, we are implying that the underlying does not even need to be an asset. In this section, we shall discover the different types of options, identified by the nature of the underlying. Our focus in this book is on financial options, but it is important, nonetheless, to gain some awareness of other types of options.

4.1 FINANCIAL OPTIONS

Financial options are options in which the underlying is a financial asset, an interest rate, or a currency.

4.1.1 STOCK OPTIONS

Options on individual stocks, also called **equity options**, are among the most popular. Exchange-listed options are available on most widely traded stocks and an option on any stock can potentially be created on the over-the-counter market. We have already given examples of stock options in an earlier section; we now move on to index options.

4.1.2 INDEX OPTIONS

Stock market indices are well known, not only in the investment community but also among many individuals who are not even directly investing in the market. Because a stock index is just an artificial portfolio of stocks, it is reasonable to expect that one could create an option on a stock index. Indeed, we have already covered forward and futures contracts on stock indices; options are no more difficult in structure.

For example, consider options on the S&P 500 Index, which trade on the Chicago Board Options Exchange and have a designated index contract multiplier of 250. On 13 June of a given year, the S&P 500 closed at 1241.60. A call option with an exercise price of $1,250 expiring on 20 July was selling for $28. The option is European style and settles in cash. The underlying, the S&P 500, is treated as though it were a share of stock worth $1,241.60, which can be bought, using the call option, for $1,250 on 20 July. At expiration, if the option is in-the-money, the buyer exercises it and the writer pays the buyer the $250 contract multiplier times the difference between the index value at expiration and $1,250.

In the United States, there are also options on the Dow Jones Industrial Average, the Nasdaq, and various other indices. There are nearly always options on the best-known stock indices in most countries.

Just as there are options on stocks, there are also options on bonds.

4.1.3 BOND OPTIONS

Options on bonds, usually called **bond options**, are primarily traded in the over-the-counter markets. Options exchanges have attempted to generate interest in options on bonds, but have not been very successful. Corporate bonds are not very actively traded; most are purchased and held to expiration. Government bonds, however, are very actively traded; nevertheless, options on them have not gained widespread acceptance on options exchanges. Options exchanges generate much of their trading volume from individual investors, who have far more interest in and understanding of stocks than bonds.

Thus, bond options are found almost exclusively in the over-the-counter market and are almost always options on government bonds. Consider, for example, a U.S. Treasury bond maturing in 27 years. The bond has a coupon of 5.50 percent, a yield of 5.75 percent, and is selling for $0.9659 per $1 par. An over-the-counter options dealer might sell a put or call option on the bond with an exercise price of $0.98 per $1.00 par. The option could be European or American. Its expiration day must be significantly before the maturity date of the bond. Otherwise, as the bond approaches maturity, its price will move toward par, thereby removing much of the uncertainty in its price. The option could be specified to settle with actual delivery of the bond or with a cash settlement. The parties would also specify that the contract covered a given notional principal, expressed in terms of a face value of the underlying bond.

Continuing our example, let us assume that the contract covers $5 million face value of bonds and is cash settled. Suppose the buyer exercises a call option when the bond price is at $0.995. Then the option is in-the-money by $0.995 − $0.98 = $0.015 per $1 par. The seller pays the buyer 0.015($5,000,000) = $75,000. If instead the contract called for delivery, the seller would deliver $5 million face value of bonds, which would be worth $5,000,000($0.995) = $4,975,000. The buyer would pay $5,000,000($0.98) = $4,900,000. Because the option is created in the over-the-counter market, the option buyer would assume the risk of the seller defaulting.

Even though bond options are not very widely traded, another type of related option is widely used, especially by corporations. This family of options is called **interest rate options**. These are quite different from the options we have previously discussed, because the underlying is not a particular financial instrument.

4.1.4 INTEREST RATE OPTIONS

In Chapter 2, we devoted considerable effort to understanding the Eurodollar spot market and forward contracts on the Eurodollar rate or LIBOR, called FRAs. In this chapter, we cover options on LIBOR. Although these are not the only interest rate options, their characteristics are sufficiently general to capture most of what we need to know about options on other interest rates. First recall that a Eurodollar is a dollar deposited outside of the United States. The primary Eurodollar rate is LIBOR, and it is considered the best measure of an interest rate paid in dollars on a nongovernmental borrower. These Eurodollars represent dollar-denominated time deposits issued by banks in London borrowing from other banks in London.

Before looking at the characteristics of interest rate options, let us set the perspective by recalling that FRAs are forward contracts that pay off based on the difference between the underlying rate and the fixed rate embedded in the contract when it is constructed. For example, consider a 3 × 9 FRA. This contract expires in three months. The underlying rate is six-month LIBOR. Hence, when the contract is constructed, the underlying Eurodollar instrument matures in nine months. *When the contract expires, the payoff is made immediately*, but the rate on which it is based, 180-day LIBOR, is set in the spot market, where it is assumed that interest will be paid 180 days later. Hence, the payoff on an FRA is discounted by the spot rate on 180-day LIBOR to give a present value for the payoff as of the expiration date.

Just as an FRA is a forward contract in which the underlying is an interest rate, an **interest rate option** is an option in which the underlying is an interest rate. Instead of an exercise price, it has an **exercise rate** (or **strike rate**), which is expressed on an order of magnitude of an interest rate. At expiration, the option payoff is based on the difference between the underlying rate in the market and the exercise rate. Whereas an FRA is a *commitment* to make one interest payment and receive another at a future date, an interest rate option is the *right* to make one interest payment and receive another. And just as there are call and put options, there is also an **interest rate call** and an **interest rate put**.

An interest rate call is an option in which the holder has the right to make a known interest payment and receive an unknown interest payment. The underlying is the unknown interest rate. If the unknown underlying rate turns out to be higher than the exercise rate at expiration, the option is in-the-money and is exercised; otherwise, the option simply expires. *An interest rate put is an option in which the holder has the right to make an unknown interest payment and receive a known interest payment*. If the unknown underlying rate turns out to be lower than the exercise rate at expiration, the option is in-the-money and is exercised; otherwise, the option simply expires. All interest rate option contracts have a specified size, which, as in FRAs, is called the notional principal. An interest rate option can be European or American style, but most tend to be European style. Interest rate options are settled in cash.

As with FRAs, these options are offered for purchase and sale by dealers, which are financial institutions, usually the same ones who offer FRAs. These dealers quote rates for options of various exercise prices and expirations. When a dealer takes an option position, it usually then offsets the risk with other transactions, often Eurodollar futures.

To use the same example we used in introducing FRAs, consider options expiring in 90 days on 180-day LIBOR. The option buyer specifies whatever exercise rate he desires. Let us say he chooses an exercise rate of 5.5 percent and a notional principal of $10 million.

Now let us move to the expiration day. Suppose that 180-day LIBOR is 6 percent. Then the call option is in-the-money. The payoff to the holder of the option is

$$(\$10{,}000{,}000)(0.06 - 0.055)\left(\frac{180}{360}\right) = \$25{,}000$$

This money is not paid at expiration, however; it is paid 180 days later. There is no reason why the payoff could not be made at expiration, as is done with an FRA. The delay of payment associated with interest rate options actually makes more sense, because these instruments are commonly used to hedge floating-rate loans in which the rate is set on a given day but the interest is paid later. We shall see examples of the convenience of this type of structure in Chapter 7.

Note that the difference between the underlying rate and the exercise rate is multiplied by 180/360 to reflect the fact that the rate quoted is a 180-day rate but is stated as an annual rate. Also, the interest calculation is multiplied by the notional principal.

In general, the payoff of an interest rate call is

$$\text{(Notional Principal)Max}\left(0, \text{Underlying rate at expiration} - \text{Exercise rate}\right)\left(\frac{\text{Days in underlying rate}}{360}\right) \quad \textbf{(4-1)}$$

The expression Max(0,Underlying rate at expiration − Exercise rate) is similar to a form that we shall commonly see throughout this chapter for all options. The payoff of a call option at expiration is based on the maximum of zero or the underlying minus the exercise rate. If the option expires out-of-the-money, then "Underlying rate at expiration − Exercise rate" is negative; consequently, zero is greater. Thus, the option expires with no value. If the option expires in-the-money, "Underlying rate at expiration − Exercise rate" is positive. Thus, the option expires worth this difference (multiplied by the notional principal and the Days/360 adjustment). The expression "Days in underlying rate," which we used in Chapter 2, refers to the fact that the rate is specified as the rate on an instrument of a specific number of days to maturity, such as a 90-day or 180-day rate, thereby requiring that we multiply by 90/360 or 180/360 or some similar adjustment.

For an interest rate put option, the general formula is

$$\text{(Notional Principal)Max}\left(0, \text{Exercise rate} - \text{Underlying rate at expiration}\right)\left(\frac{\text{Days in underlying rate}}{360}\right) \quad \textbf{(4-2)}$$

For an exercise rate of 5.5 percent and an underlying rate at expiration of 6 percent, an interest rate put expires out-of-the-money. Only if the underlying rate is less than the exercise rate does the put option expire in-the-money.

As noted above, borrowers often use interest rate call options to hedge the risk of rising rates on floating-rate loans. Lenders often use interest rate put options to hedge the risk of falling rates on floating-rate loans. The form we have seen here, in which the option expires with a single payoff, is not the more commonly used variety of interest rate option. Floating-rate loans usually involve multiple interest payments. Each of those payments is set on a given date. To hedge the risk of interest rates increasing, the borrower would need options expiring on each rate reset date. Thus, the borrower would require a combination of interest rate call options. Likewise, a lender needing to hedge the risk of falling rates on a multiple-payment floating-rate loan would need a combination of interest rate put options.

A combination of interest rate calls is referred to as an **interest rate cap** or sometimes just a **cap**. A combination of interest rate puts is called an **interest rate floor** or sometimes just a **floor**.[8] Specifically, *an interest rate cap is a series of call options on an interest rate, with each option expiring at the date on which the floating loan rate will be reset, and with each option having the same exercise rate.*[9] Each option is independent of the others; thus, exercise of one option does not affect the right to exercise any of the others. Each component call option is called a **caplet**. *An interest rate floor is a series of put options on an interest rate, with each option expiring at the date on which the floating loan rate will be reset, and with each option having the same exercise rate.* Each component put option is called a **floorlet**. The price of an interest rate cap or floor is the sum of the prices of the options that make up the cap or floor.

A special combination of caps and floors is called an **interest rate collar**. *An interest rate collar is a combination of a long cap and a short floor or a short cap and a long floor.* Consider a borrower in a floating rate loan who wants to hedge the risk of rising interest rates but is concerned about the requirement that this hedge must have a cash outlay up front: the option premium. A collar, which adds a short floor to a long cap, is a way of reducing and even eliminating the up-front cost of the cap. The sale of the floor brings in cash that reduces the cost of the cap. It is possible to set the exercise rates such that the price received for the sale of the floor precisely offsets the price paid for the cap, thereby completely eliminating the up-front cost. This transaction is sometimes called a **zero-cost collar**. The term is a bit misleading, however, and brings to mind the importance of noting the true cost of a collar. Although the cap allows the borrower to be paid from the call options when rates are high, the sale of the floor requires the borrower to pay the counterparty when rates are low. Thus, the cost of protection against rising rates is the loss of the advantage of falling rates. Caps, floors, and collars are popular instruments in the interest rate markets. We shall explore strategies using them in Chapter 7.

Although interest rate options are primarily written on such rates as LIBOR, Euribor, and Euroyen, the underlying can be any interest rate.

4.1.5 CURRENCY OPTIONS

As we noted in Chapter 2, the currency forward market is quite large. The same is true for the currency options market. A **currency option** allows the holder to buy (if a call) or sell (if a put) an underlying currency at a fixed exercise rate, expressed as an exchange rate. Many companies, knowing that they will need to convert a currency X at a future date into a currency Y, will buy a call option on currency Y specified in terms of currency X. For example, say that a U.S. company will be needing €50 million for an expansion project in three months. Thus, it will be buying euros and is exposed to the risk of the euro rising against the dollar. Even though it has that concern, it would also like to benefit if the euro weakens against the dollar. Thus, it might buy a call option on the euro. Let us say it specifies an exercise rate of $0.90. So it pays cash up front for the right to buy €50 million at a rate of $0.90 per euro. If the option expires with the euro above $0.90, it can buy euros

---

[8] It is possible to construct caps and floors with options on any other type of underlying, but they are very often used when the underlying is an interest rate.

[9] Technically, each option need not have the same exercise rate, but they generally do.

at $0.90 and avoid any additional cost over $0.90. If the option expires with the euro below $0.90, it does not exercise the option and buys euros at the market rate.

Note closely these two cases:

Euro expires above $0.90
Company buys €50 million at $0.90

Euro expires at or below $0.90
Company buys €50 million at the market rate

These outcomes can also be viewed in the following manner:

Dollar expires below €1.1111, that is, €1 > $0.90
Company sells $45 million (€50 million × $0.90) at €1.1111, equivalent to buying €50 million

Dollar expires above €1.1111, that is, €1 < $0.90
Company sells sufficient dollars to buy €50 million at the market rate

This transaction looks more like a put in which the underlying is the dollar and the exercise rate is expressed as €1.1111. Thus, the call on the euro can be viewed as a put on the dollar. Specifically, a call to buy €50 million at an exercise price of $0.90 is also a put to sell €50 million × $0.90 = $45 million at an exercise price of 1/$0.90, or €1.1111.

Most foreign currency options activity occurs on the customized over-the-counter markets. Some exchange-listed currency options trade on a few exchanges, but activity is fairly low.

4.2 OPTIONS ON FUTURES

In Chapter 2 we covered futures markets. One of the important innovations of futures markets is options on futures. These contracts originated in the United States as a result of a regulatory structure that separated exchange-listed options and futures markets. The former are regulated by the Securities and Exchange Commission, and the latter are regulated by the Commodity Futures Trading Commission (CFTC). SEC regulations forbid the trading of options side by side with their underlying instruments. Options on stocks trade on one exchange, and the underlying trades on another or on Nasdaq.

The futures exchanges got the idea that they could offer options in which the underlying is a futures contract; no such prohibitions for side-by-side trading existed under CFTC rules. As a result, the futures exchanges were able to add an attractive instrument to their product lines. The side-by-side trading of the option and its underlying futures made for excellent arbitrage linkages between these instruments. Moreover, some of the options on futures are designed to expire on the same day the underlying futures expires. Thus, the options on the futures are effectively options on the spot asset that underlies the futures.

A call option on a futures gives the holder the right to enter into a long futures contract at a fixed futures price. A put option on a futures gives the holder the right to enter into a short futures contract at a fixed futures price. The fixed futures price is, of course, the exercise price. Consider an option on the Eurodollar futures contract trading at the Chicago Mercantile Exchange. On 13 June of a particular year, an option expiring on 13 July was based on the July Eurodollar futures contract. That futures contract expires on 16 July, a few days after the option expires.[10] The call option with exercise price of 95.75 had a price of $4.60. The underlying futures price was 96.21. Recall that this price is the IMM index value, which means that the price is based on a discount rate of 100 − 96.21 = 3.79. The contract size is $1 million.

---

[10] Some options on futures expire a month or so before the futures expires. Others expire very close to, if not at, the futures expiration.

The buyer of this call option on a futures would pay 0.046($1,000,000) = $46,000 and would obtain the right to buy the July futures contract at a price of 95.75. Thus, at that time, the option was in the money by 96.21 − 95.75 = 0.46 per $100 face value. Suppose that when the option expires, the futures price is 96.00. Then the holder of the call would exercise it and obtain a long futures position at a price of 95.75. The price of the underlying futures is 96.00, so the margin account is immediately marked to market with a credit of 0.25 or $625.[11] The party on the short side of the contract is immediately set up with a short futures contract at the price of 95.75. That party will be charged the $625 gain that the long made. If the option is a put, exercise of it establishes a short position. The exchange assigns the put writer a long futures position.

4.3 COMMODITY OPTIONS

Options in which the asset underlying the futures is a commodity, such as oil, gold, wheat, or soybeans, are also widely traded. There are exchange-traded as well as over-the-counter versions. Over-the-counter options on oil are widely used.

Our focus in this book is on financial instruments so we will not spend any time on commodity options, but readers should be aware of the existence and use of these instruments by companies whose business involves the buying and selling of these commodities.

4.4 OTHER TYPES OF OPTIONS

As derivative markets develop, options (and even some other types of derivatives) have begun to emerge on such underlyings as electricity, various sources of energy, and even weather. These instruments are almost exclusively customized over-the-counter instruments. Perhaps the most notable feature of these instruments is how the underlyings are often instruments that cannot actually be held. For example, electricity is not considered a storable asset because it is produced and almost immediately consumed, but it is nonetheless an asset and certainly has a volatile price. Consequently, it is ideally suited for options and other derivatives trading.

Consider weather. It is hardly an asset at all but simply a random factor that exerts an enormous influence on economic activity. The need to hedge against and speculate on the weather has created a market in which measures of weather activity, such as economic losses from storms or average temperature or rainfall, are structured into a derivative instrument. Option versions of these derivatives are growing in importance and use. For example, consider a company that generates considerable revenue from outdoor summer activities, provided that it does not rain. Obviously a certain amount of rain will occur, but the more rain, the greater the losses for the company. It could buy a call option on the amount of rainfall with the exercise price stated as a quantity of rainfall. If actual rainfall exceeds the exercise price, the company exercises the option and receives an amount of money related to the excess of the rainfall amount over the exercise price.

Another type of option, which is not at all new but is increasingly recognized in practice, is the real option. A real option is an option associated with the flexibility inherent in capital investment projects. For example, companies may invest in new projects that have the option to defer the full investment, expand or contract the project at a later date, or even terminate the project. In fact, most capital investment projects have numerous elements of flex-

[11] If the contract is in-the-money by 96 − 95.75 = 0.25 per $100 par, it is in-the-money by 0.25/100 = 0.0025, or 0.25 percent of the face value. Because the face value is $1 million, the contract is in the money by (0.0025)(90/360)($1,000,000) = $625. (Note the adjustment by 90/360.) Another way to look at this calculation is that the futures price at 95.75 is 1 − (0.0425)(90/360) = $0.989375 per $1 par, or $989,375. At 96, the futures price is 1 − 0.04(90/360) = $0.99 per $1 par or $990,000. The difference is $625. So, exercising this option is like entering into a futures contract at a price of $989,375 and having the price immediately go to $990,000, a gain of $625. The call holder must deposit money to meet the Eurodollar futures margin, but the exercise of the option gives him $625. In other words, assuming he meets the minimum initial margin requirement, he is immediately credited with $625 more.

ibility that can be viewed as options. Of course, these options do not trade in markets the same way as financial and commodity options, and they must be evaluated much more carefully. They are, nonetheless, options and thus have the potential for generating enormous value.

Again, our emphasis is on financial options, but readers should be aware of the growing role of these other types of options in our economy. Investors who buy shares in companies that have real options are, in effect, buying real options. In addition, commodity and other types of options are sometimes found in investment portfolios in the form of "alternative investments" and can provide significant diversification benefits.

To this point, we have examined characteristics of options markets and contracts. Now we move forward to the all-important topic of how options are priced.

5 PRINCIPLES OF OPTION PRICING

In Chapters 2 and 3, we discussed the pricing and valuation of forward and futures contracts. Recall that the value of a contract is what someone must pay to buy into it or what someone would receive to sell out of it. A forward or futures contract has zero value at the start of the contract, but the value turns positive or negative as prices or rates change. A contract that has positive value to one party and negative value to the counterparty can turn around and have negative value to the former and positive value to the latter as prices or rates change. The forward or futures price is the price that the parties agree will be paid on the future date to buy and sell the underlying.

With options, these concepts are different. An option has a positive value at the start. The buyer must pay money and the seller receives money to initiate the contract. Prior to expiration, the option always has positive value to the buyer and negative value to the seller. In a forward or futures contract, the two parties agree on the fixed price the buyer will pay the seller. This fixed price is set such that the buyer and seller do not exchange any money. The corresponding fixed price at which a call holder can buy the underlying or a put holder can sell the underlying is the exercise price. It, too, is negotiated between buyer and seller but still results in the buyer paying the seller money up front in the form of an option premium or price.[12]

Thus, what we called the forward or futures price corresponds more to the exercise price of an option. The option price *is* the option value: With a few exceptions that will be clearly noted, in this chapter we do not distinguish between the option price and value.

In this section of the chapter, we examine the principles of option pricing. These principles are characteristics of option prices that are governed by the rationality of investors. These principles alone do not allow us to calculate the option price. We do that in Section 6.

Before we begin, it is important to remind the reader that we assume all participants in the market behave in a rational manner such that they do not throw away money and that they take advantage of arbitrage opportunities. As such, we assume that markets are sufficiently competitive that no arbitrage opportunities exist.

Let us start by developing the notation, which is very similar to what we have used previously. Note that time 0 is today and time T is the expiration.

S_0, S_T = price of the underlying asset at time 0 (today) and time T (expiration)

X   = exercise price

r   = risk-free rate

---

[12] For a call, there is no finite exercise price that drives the option price to zero. For a put, the unrealistic example of a zero exercise price would make the put price be zero.

T   = time to expiration, equal to number of days to expiration divided by 365

c_0, c_T = price of European call today and at expiration

C_0, C_T = price of American call today and at expiration

p_0, p_T = price of European put today and at expiration

P_0, P_T = price of American put today and at expiration

On occasion, we will introduce some variations of the above as well as some new notation. For example, we start off with no cash flows on the underlying, but we shall discuss the effects of cash flows on the underlying in Section 5.7.

5.1 PAYOFF VALUES

The easiest time to determine an option's value is at expiration. At that point, there is no future. Only the present matters. An option's value at expiration is called its **payoff**. We introduced this material briefly in our basic descriptions of types of options; now we cover it in more depth.

At expiration, a call option is worth either zero or the difference between the underlying price and the exercise price, whichever is greater:

$$c_T = \text{Max}(0, S_T - X)$$

$$C_T = \text{Max}(0, S_T - X)$$

(4-3)

Note that at expiration, a European option and an American option have the same payoff because they are equivalent instruments at that point.

The expression $\text{Max}(0, S_T - X)$ means to take the greater of zero or $S_T - X$. Suppose the underlying price exceeds the exercise price, $S_T > X$. In this case, the option is expiring in-the-money and the option is worth $S_T - X$. Suppose that at the instant of expiration, it is possible to buy the option for less than $S_T - X$. Then one could buy the option, immediately exercise it, and immediately sell the underlying. Doing so would cost c_T (or C_T) for the option and X to buy the underlying but would bring in S_T for the sale of the underlying. If c_T (or C_T) $< S_T - X$, this transaction would net an immediate risk-free profit. The collective actions of all investors doing this would force the option price up to $S_T - X$. The price could not go higher than $S_T - X$, because all that the option holder would end up with an instant later when the option expires is $S_T - X$. If $S_T < X$, meaning that the call is expiring out-of-the-money, the formula says the option should be worth zero. It cannot sell for less than zero because that would mean that the option seller would have to pay the option buyer. A buyer would not pay more than zero, because the option will expire an instant later with no value.

At expiration, a put option is worth either zero or the difference between the exercise price and the underlying price, whichever is greater:

$$p_T = \text{Max}(0, X - S_T)$$

$$P_T = \text{Max}(0, X - S_T)$$

(4-4)

Suppose $S_T < X$, meaning that the put is expiring in-the-money. At the instant of expiration, suppose the put is selling for less than $X - S_T$. Then an investor buys the put for p_T (or P_T) and the underlying for S_T and exercises the put, receiving X. If p_T (or P_T) $< X - S_T$, this transaction will net an immediate risk-free profit. The combined actions of participants doing this will force the put price up to $X - S_T$. It cannot go any higher, because the put buyer will end up an instant later with only $X - S_T$ and would not pay more than this. If $S_T > X$, meaning that the put is expiring out-of the-money, it is worth zero. It cannot be worth less than zero because the option seller would have to pay the option buyer.

It cannot be worth more than zero because the buyer would not pay for a position that, an instant later, will be worth nothing.

These important results are summarized along with an example in Exhibit 4-5. The payoff diagrams for the short positions are also shown and are obtained as the negative of the long positions. For the special case of $S_T = X$, meaning that both call and put are expiring at-the-money, we can effectively treat the option as out-of-the-money because it is worth zero at expiration.

EXHIBIT 4-5 Option Values at Expiration (Payoffs)

Option	Value	Example (X = 50)	
		$S_T = 52$	$S_T = 48$
European call	$c_T = \text{Max}(0, S_T - X)$	$c_T = \text{Max}(0, 52 - 50) = 2$	$c_T = \text{Max}(0, 48 - 50) = 0$
American call	$C_T = \text{Max}(0, S_T - X)$	$C_T = \text{Max}(0, 52 - 50) = 2$	$C_T = \text{Max}(0, 48 - 50) = 0$
European put	$p_T = \text{Max}(0, X - S_T)$	$p_T = \text{Max}(0, 50 - 52) = 0$	$p_T = \text{Max}(0, 50 - 48) = 2$
American put	$P_T = \text{Max}(0, X - S_T)$	$P_T = \text{Max}(0, 50 - 52) = 0$	$P_T = \text{Max}(0, 50 - 48) = 2$

Notes: Results for the European and American calls correspond to Graph A. Results for Graph B are the negative of Graph A. Results for the European and American puts correspond to Graph C, and results for Graph D are the negative of Graph C.

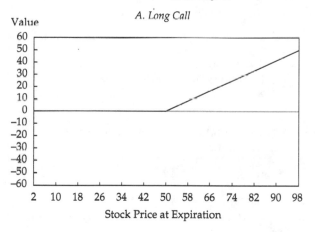

A. Long Call

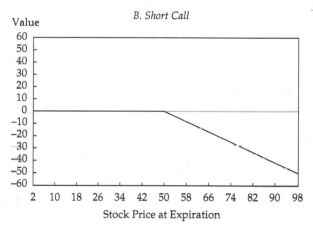

B. Short Call

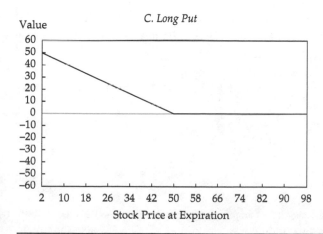

C. Long Put

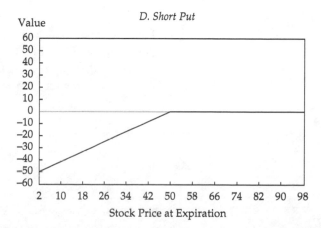

D. Short Put

The value $\text{Max}(0, S_T - X)$ for calls or $\text{Max}(0, X - S_T)$ for puts is also called the option's **intrinsic value** or **exercise value**. We shall use the former terminology. Intrinsic value is what the option is worth to exercise it based on current conditions. In this section, we have talked only about the option at expiration. Prior to expiration, an option will normally sell for more than its intrinsic value.[13] The difference between the market price of the option and its intrinsic value is called its **time value** or **speculative value**. We shall use the former terminology. The time value reflects the potential for the option's intrinsic value at expiration to be greater than its current intrinsic value. At expiration, of course, the time value is zero.

PRACTICE PROBLEM 1

For Parts A through E, determine the payoffs of calls and puts under the conditions given.

A. The underlying is a stock index and is at 5,601.19 when the options expire. The multiplier is 500. The exercise price is
   i. 5,500
   ii. 6,000

B. The underlying is a bond and is at $1.035 per $1 par when the options expire. The contract is on $100,000 face value of bonds. The exercise price is
   i. $1.00
   ii. $1.05

C. The underlying is a 90-day interest rate and is at 9 percent when the options expire. The notional principal is $50 million. The exercise rate is
   i. 8 percent
   ii. 10.5 percent

D. The underlying is the Swiss franc and is at $0.775 when the options expire. The options are on SF500,000. The exercise price is
   i. $0.75
   ii. $0.81

E. The underlying is a futures contract and is at 110.5 when the options expire. The options are on a futures contract covering $1 million of the underlying. These prices are percentages of par. The exercise price is
   i. 110
   ii. 115

For Parts F and G, determine the payoffs of the strategies indicated and describe the payoff graph.

F. The underlying is a stock priced at $40. A call option with an exercise price of $40 is selling for $7. You buy the stock and sell the call. At expiration, the stock price is
   i. $52
   ii. $38

---

[13] We shall later see an exception to this statement for European puts, but for now take it as the truth.

G. The underlying is a stock priced at $60. A put option with an exercise price of $60 is priced at $5. You buy the stock and buy the put. At expiration, the stock price is
  i. $68
  ii. $50

SOLUTIONS

A. **i.** Calls: Max(0,5601.19 − 5500) × 500 = 50,595
       Puts: Max(0,5500 − 5601.19) × 500 = 0
   ii. Calls: Max(0,5601.19 − 6000) × 500 = 0
       Puts: Max(0,6000 − 5601.19) × 500 = 199,405

B. **i.** Calls: Max(0,1.035 − 1.00) × $100,000 − $3,500
       Puts: Max(0,1.00 − 1.035) × $100,000 = $0
   ii. Calls: Max(0,1.035 − 1.05) × $100,000 = $0
       Puts: Max(0,1.05 − 1.035) × $100,000 = $1,500

C. **i.** Calls: Max(0,0.09 − 0.08) × (90/360) × $50,000,000 = $125,000
       Puts: Max(0,0.08 − 0.09) × (90/360) × $50,000,000 = $0
   ii. Calls: Max(0,0.09 − 0.105) × (90/360) × $50,000,000 = $0
       Puts: Max(0,0.105 − 0.09) × (90/360) × $50,000,000 = $187,500

D. **i.** Calls: Max(0,0.775 − 0.75) × SF500,000 = SF12,500
       Puts: Max(0,0.75 − 0.775) × SF500,000 = SF0
   ii. Calls: Max(0,0.775 − 0.81) × SF500,000 = SF0
       Puts: Max(0,0.81 − 0.775) × SF500,000 = SF17,500

E. **i.** Calls: Max(0,110.5 − 110) × (1/100) × $1,000,000 = $5,000
       Puts: Max(0,110 − 110.5) × (1/100) × $1,000,000 = $0
   ii. Calls: Max(0,110.5 − 115) × (1/100) × $1,000,000 = $0
       Puts: Max(0,115 − 110.5) × (1/100) × $1,000,000 = $45,000

F. **i.** 52 − Max(0,52 − 40) = 40
   ii. 38 − Max(0,38 − 40) = 38

For any value of the stock price at expiration of 40 or above, the payoff is constant at 40. For stock price values below 40 at expiration, the payoff declines with the stock price. The graph would look similar to the short put in Panel D of Exhibit 4-5. This strategy is known as a covered call and is discussed in Chapter 7.

G. **i.** 68 + Max(0,60 − 68) = 68
   ii. 50 + Max(0,60 − 50) = 60

For any value of the stock price at expiration of 60 or below, the payoff is constant at 60. For stock price values above 60 at expiration, the payoff increases with the stock price at expiration. The graph will look similar to the long call in Panel A of Exhibit 4-5. This strategy is known as a protective put and is covered later in this chapter and in Chapter 7.

There is no question that everyone agrees on the option's intrinsic value; after all, it is based on the current stock price and exercise price. It is the time value that we have more difficulty estimating. So remembering that *Option price = Intrinsic value + Time value*, let us move forward and attempt to determine the value of an option today, prior to expiration.

5.2 BOUNDARY CONDITIONS We start by examining some simple results that establish minimum and maximum values for options prior to expiration.

5.2.1   MINIMUM AND MAXIMUM VALUES

The first and perhaps most obvious result is one we have already alluded to: *The minimum value of any option is zero*. We state this formally as

$$c_0 \geq 0, C_0 \geq 0 \tag{4-5}$$

$$p_0 \geq 0, P_0 \geq 0$$

No option can sell for less than zero, for in that case the writer would have to pay the buyer.

Now consider the maximum value of an option. It differs somewhat depending on whether the option is a call or a put and whether it is European or American. *The maximum value of a call is the current value of the underlying*:

$$c_0 \leq S_0, C_0 \leq S_0 \tag{4-6}$$

A call is a means of buying the underlying. It would not make sense to pay more for the right to buy the underlying than the value of the underlying itself.

For a put, it makes a difference whether the put is European or American. One way to see the maximum value for puts is to consider the best possible outcome for the put holder. The best outcome is that the underlying goes to a value of zero. Then the put holder could sell a worthless asset for X. For an American put, the holder could sell it immediately and capture a value of X. For a European put, the holder would have to wait until expiration; consequently, we must discount X from the expiration day to the present. Thus, *the maximum value of a European put is the present value of the exercise price. The maximum value of an American put is the exercise price*,

$$p_0 \leq X/(1 + r)^T, P_0 \leq X \tag{4-7}$$

where r is the risk-free interest rate and T is the time to expiration. These results for the maximums and minimums for calls and puts are summarized in Exhibit 4-6, which also includes a numerical example.

EXHIBIT 4-6   Minimum and Maximum Values of Options

Option	Minimum Value	Maximum Value	Example (S_0 = 52, X = 50, r = 5%, T = 1/2 year)
European call	$c_0 \geq 0$	$c_0 \leq S_0$	$0 \leq c_0 \leq 52$
American call	$C_0 \geq 0$	$C_0 \leq S_0$	$0 \leq C_0 \leq 52$
European put	$p_0 \geq 0$	$p_0 \leq X/(1 + r)^T$	$0 \leq p_0 \leq 48.80$ [$48.80 = 50/(1.05)^{0.5}$]
American put	$P_0 \geq 0$	$P_0 \leq X$	$0 \leq P_0 \leq 50$

5.2.2   LOWER BOUNDS

The results we established in Section 5.2.1 do not put much in the way of restrictions on the option price. They tell us that the price is somewhere between zero and the maximum, which is either the underlying price, the exercise price, or the present value of the exercise price—a fairly wide range of possibilities. Fortunately, we can tighten the range up a little on the low side: We can establish a **lower bound** on the option price.

For American options, which are exercisable immediately, we can state that the lower bound of an American option price is its current intrinsic value:[14]

$$C_0 \geq \text{Max}(0, S_0 - X)$$

$$P_0 \geq \text{Max}(0, X - S_0)$$

(4-8)

The reason these results hold today is the same reason we have already shown for why they must hold at expiration. If the option is in-the-money and is selling for less than its intrinsic value, it can be bought and exercised to net an immediate risk-free profit.[15] The collective actions of market participants doing this will force the American option price up to at least the intrinsic value.

Unfortunately, we cannot make such a statement about European options—but we can show that the lower bound is either zero or the current underlying price minus the present value of the exercise price, whichever is greater. They cannot be exercised early; thus, there is no way for market participants to exercise an option selling for too little with respect to its intrinsic value. Fortunately, however, there is a way to establish a lower bound for European options. We can combine options with risk-free bonds and the underlying in such a way that a lower bound for the option price emerges.

First, we need the ability to buy and sell a risk-free bond with a face value equal to the exercise price and current value equal to the present value of the exercise price. This procedure is simple but perhaps not obvious. If the exercise price is X (say, 100), we buy a bond with a face value of X (100) maturing on the option expiration day. The current value of that bond is the present value of X, which is $X/(1 + r)^T$. So we buy the bond today for $X/(1 + r)^T$ and hold it until it matures on the option expiration day, at which time it will pay off X. We assume that we can buy or sell (issue) this type of bond. Note that this transaction involves borrowing or lending an amount of money equal to the present value of the exercise price with repayment of the full exercise price.

Exhibit 4-7 illustrates the construction of a special combination of instruments. We buy the European call and the risk-free bond and sell short the underlying asset. Recall that short selling involves borrowing the asset and selling it. At expiration, we shall buy back

EXHIBIT 4-7 A Lower Bound Combination for European Calls

Transaction	Current Value	Value at Expiration $S_T \leq X$	$S_T > X$
Buy call	c_0	0	$S_T - X$
Sell short underlying	$-S_0$	$-S_T$	$-S_T$
Buy bond	$X/(1 + r)^T$	X	X
Total	$c_0 - S_0 + X/(1 + r)^T$	$X - S_T \geq 0$	0

[14] Normally we have italicized sentences containing important results. This one, however, is a little different: We are stating it temporarily. We shall soon show that we can override one of these results with a lower bound that is higher and, therefore, is a better lower bound.

[15] Consider, for example, an in-the-money call selling for less than $S_0 - X$. One can buy the call for C_0, exercise it, paying X, and sell the underlying netting a gain of $S_0 - X - C_0$. This value is positive and represents an immediate risk-free gain. If the option is an in-the-money put selling for less than $X - S_0$, one can buy the put for P_0, buy the underlying for S_0, and exercise the put to receive X, thereby netting an immediate risk-free gain of $X - S_0 - P_0$.

the asset. In order to illustrate the logic behind the lower bound for a European call in the simplest way, we assume that we can sell short without any restrictions.

In Exhibit 4-7 the two right-hand columns contain the value of each instrument when the option expires. The rightmost column is the case of the call expiring in-the-money, in which case it is worth $S_T - X$. In the other column, the out-of-the-money case, the call is worth zero. The underlying is worth $-S_T$ (the negative of its current value) in either case, reflecting the fact that we buy it back to cover the short position. The bond is worth X in both cases. The sum of all the positions is positive when the option expires out-of-the-money and zero when the option expires in-the-money. Therefore, in no case does this combination of instruments have a negative value. That means that we never have to pay out any money at expiration. We are guaranteed at least no loss at expiration and possibly something positive.

If there is a possibility of a positive outcome from the combination and if we know we shall never have to pay anything out from holding a combination of instruments, the cost of that combination must be positive—it must cost us something to enter into the position. We cannot take in money to enter into the position. In that case, we would be receiving money up front and never having to pay anything out. The cost of entering the position is shown in the second column, labeled the "Current Value." Because that value must be positive, we therefore require that $c_0 - S_0 + X/(1 + r)^T \geq 0$. Rearranging this equation, we obtain $c_0 \geq S_0 - X/(1 + r)^T$. Now we have a statement about the minimum value of the option, which can serve as a lower bound. This result is solid, because if the call is selling for less than $S_0 - X/(1 + r)^T$, an investor can buy the call, sell short the underlying, and buy the bond. Doing so would bring in money up front and, as we see in Exhibit 4-7, an investor would not have to pay out any money at expiration and might even get a little more money. Because other investors would do the same, the call price would be forced up until it is at least $S_0 - X/(1 + r)^T$.

But we can improve on this result. Suppose $S_0 - X/(1 + r)^T$ is negative. Then we are stating that the call price is greater than a negative number. But we already know that the call price cannot be negative. So we can now say that

$$c_0 \geq \text{Max}[0, S_0 - X/(1 + r)^T]$$

In other words, *the lower bound on a European call price is either zero or the underlying price minus the present value of the exercise price, whichever is greater.* Notice how this lower bound differs from the minimum value for the American call, $\text{Max}(0, S_0 - X)$. For the European call, we must wait to pay the exercise price and obtain the underlying. Therefore, the expression contains the current underlying value—the present value of its future value—as well as the present value of the exercise price. For the American call, we do not have to wait until expiration; therefore, the expression reflects the potential to immediately receive the underlying price minus the exercise price. We shall have more to say, however, about the relationship between these two values.

To illustrate the lower bound, let $X = 50$, $r = 0.05$, and $T = 0.5$. If the current underlying price is 45, then the lower bound for the European call is

$$\text{Max}[0, 45 - 50/(1.05)^{0.5}] = \text{Max}(0, 45 - 48.80) = \text{Max}(0, -3.80) = 0$$

All this calculation tells us is that the call must be worth no less than zero, which we already knew. If the current underlying price is 54, however, the lower bound for the European call is

$$\text{Max}(0, 54 - 48.80) = \text{Max}(0, 5.20) = 5.20$$

which tells us that the call must be worth no less than 5.20. With European puts, we can also see that the lower bound differs from the lower bound on American puts in this same use of the present value of the exercise price.

EXHIBIT 4-8   A Lower Bound Combination for European Puts

Transaction	Current Value	Value at Expiration	
		$S_T < X$	$S_T \geq X$
Buy put	p_0	$X - S_T$	0
Buy underlying	S_0	S_T	S_T
Issue bond	$-X/(1 + r)^T$	$-X$	$-X$
Total	$p_0 + S_0 - X/(1 + r)^T$	0	$S_T - X \geq 0$

Exhibit 4-8 constructs a similar type of portfolio for European puts. Here, however, we buy the put and the underlying and borrow by issuing the zero-coupon bond. The payoff of each instrument is indicated in the two rightmost columns. Note that the total payoff is never less than zero. Consequently, the initial value of the combination must not be less than zero. Therefore, $p_0 + S_0 - X/(1 + r)^T \geq 0$. Isolating the put price gives us $p_0 \geq X/(1 + r)^T - S_0$. But suppose that $X/(1 + r)^T - S_0$ is negative. Then, the put price must be greater than a negative number. We know that the put price must be no less than zero. So we can now formally say that

$$p_0 > \text{Max}[0, X/(1 + r)^T - S_0]$$

In other words, *the lower bound of a European put is the greater of either zero or the present value of the exercise price minus the underlying price.* For the American put, recall that the expression was $\text{Max}(0, X - S_0)$. So for the European put, we adjust this value to the present value of the exercise price. The present value of the asset price is already adjusted to S_0.

Using the same example we did for calls, let $X = 50$, $r = 0.05$, and $T = 0.5$. If the current underlying price is 45, then the lower bound for the European put is

$$\text{Max}(0, 50/(1.05)^{0.5} - 45) = \text{Max}(0, 48.80 - 45) = \text{Max}(0, 3.80) = 3.80$$

If the current underlying price is 54, however, the lower bound is

$$\text{Max}(0, 48.80 - 54) = \text{Max}(0, -5.20) = 0$$

At this point let us reconsider what we have found. The lower bound for a European call is $\text{Max}[0, S_0 - X/(1 + r)^T]$. We also observed that an American call must be worth at least $\text{Max}(0, S_0 - X)$. But except at expiration, the European lower bound is greater than the minimum value of the American call.[16] We could not, however, expect an American call to be worth less than a European call. Thus the lower bound of the European call holds for American calls as well. Hence, we can conclude that

$$c_0 \geq \text{Max}[0, S_0 - X/(1 + r)^T] \tag{4-9}$$

$$C_0 \geq \text{Max}[0, S_0 - X/(1 + r)^T]$$

---

[16] We discuss this point more formally and in the context of whether it is ever worthwhile to exercise an American call early in Section 5.6.

For European puts, the lower bound is $\text{Max}[0, X/(1 + r)^T - S_0]$. For American puts, the minimum price is $\text{Max}(0, X - S_0)$. The European lower bound is lower than the minimum price of the American put, so the American put lower bound is not changed to the European lower bound, the way we did for calls. Hence,

$$p_0 \geq \text{Max}[0, X/(1 + r)^T - S_0] \tag{4-10}$$

$$P_0 \geq \text{Max}(0, X - S_0)$$

These results tell us the lowest possible price for European and American options.

Recall that we previously referred to an option price as having an intrinsic value and a time value. For American options, the intrinsic value is the value if exercised, $\text{Max}(0, S_0 - X)$ for calls and $\text{Max}(0, X - S_0)$ for puts. The remainder of the option price is the time value. For European options, the notion of a time value is somewhat murky, because it first requires recognition of an intrinsic value. Because a European option cannot be exercised until expiration, in a sense, all of the value of a European option is time value. The notion of an intrinsic value and its complement, a time value, is therefore inappropriate for European options, though the concepts are commonly applied to European options. Fortunately, understanding European options does not require that we separate intrinsic value from time value. We shall include them together as they make up the option price.

PRACTICE PROBLEM 2

Consider call and put options expiring in 42 days, in which the underlying is at 72 and the risk-free rate is 4.5 percent. The underlying makes no cash payments during the life of the options.

A. Find the lower bounds for European calls and puts with exercise prices of 70 and 75.

B. Find the lower bounds for American calls and puts with exercise prices of 70 and 75.

SOLUTIONS

A. 70 call: $\text{Max}[0, 72 - 70/(1.045)^{0.1151}] = \text{Max}(0, 2.35) = 2.35$
75 call: $\text{Max}[0, 72 - 75/(1.045)^{0.1151}] = \text{Max}(0, -2.62) = 0$
70 put: $\text{Max}[0, 70/(1.045)^{0.1151} - 72] = \text{Max}(0, -2.35) = 0$
75 put: $\text{Max}[0, 75/(1.045)^{0.1151} - 72] = \text{Max}(0, 2.62) = 2.62$

B. 70 call: $\text{Max}[0, 72 - 70/(1.045)^{0.1151}] = \text{Max}(0, 2.35) = 2.35$
75 call: $\text{Max}[0, 72 - 75/(1.045)^{0.1151}] = \text{Max}(0, -2.62) = 0$
70 put: $\text{Max}(0, 70 - 72) = 0$
75 put: $\text{Max}(0, 75 - 72) = 3$

5.3 **The Effect of a Difference in Exercise Price**

Now consider two options on the same underlying with the same expiration day but different exercise prices. Generally, the higher the exercise price, the lower the value of a call and the higher the price of a put. To see this, let the two exercise prices be X_1 and X_2, with X_1 being the smaller. Let $c_0(X_1)$ be the price of a European call with exercise price X_1 and $c_0(X_2)$ be the price of a European call with exercise price X_2. We refer to these as the X_1

call and the X_2 call. In Exhibit 4-9, we construct a combination in which we buy the X_1 call and sell the X_2 call.[17]

EXHIBIT 4-9 Portfolio Combination for European Calls Illustrating the Effect of Differences in Exercise Prices

Transaction	Current Value	Value at Expiration		
		$S_T \leq X_1$	$X_1 < S_T < X_2$	$S_T \geq X_2$
Buy call (X = X_1)	$c_0(X_1)$	0	$S_T - X_1$	$S_T - X_1$
Sell call (X = X_2)	$-c_0(X_2)$	0	0	$-(S_T - X_2)$
Total	$c_0(X_1) - c_0(X_2)$	0	$S_T - X_1 > 0$	$X_2 - X_1 > 0$

Note first that the three outcomes are all non-negative. This fact establishes that the current value of the combination, $c_0(X_1) - c_0(X_2)$ has to be non-negative. We have to pay out at least as much for the X_1 call as we take in for the X_2 call; otherwise, we would get money up front, have the possibility of a positive value at expiration, and never have to pay any money out. Thus, because $c_0(X_1) - c_0(X_2) \geq 0$, we restate this result as

$$c_0(X_1) \geq c_0(X_2)$$

This expression is equivalent to the statement that *a call option with a higher exercise price cannot have a higher value than one with a lower exercise price*. The option with the higher exercise price has a higher hurdle to get over; therefore, the buyer is not willing to pay as much for it. Even though we demonstrated this result with European calls, it is also true for American calls. Thus,[18]

$$C_0(X_1) \geq C_0(X_2)$$

In Exhibit 4-10 we construct a similar portfolio for puts, except that we buy the X_2 put (the one with the higher exercise price) and sell the X_1 put (the one with the lower exercise price).

EXHIBIT 4-10 Portfolio Combination for European Puts Illustrating the Effect of Differences in Exercise Prices

Transaction	Current Value	Value at Expiration		
		$S_T \leq X_1$	$X_1 < S_T < X_2$	$S_T \geq X_2$
Buy put (X = X_2)	$p_0(X_2)$	$X_2 - S_T$	$X_2 - S_T$	0
Sell put (X = X_1)	$-p_0(X_1)$	$-(X_1 - S_T)$	0	0
Total	$p_0(X_2) - p_0(X_1)$	$X_2 - X_1 > 0$	$X_2 - S_T > 0$	0

---

[17] In Chapter 7, when we cover option strategies, this transaction will be known as a bull spread.

[18] It is possible to use the results from this table to establish a limit on the difference between the prices of these two options, but we shall not do so here.

Observe that the value of this combination is never negative at expiration; therefore, it must be non-negative today. Hence, $p_0(X_2) - p_0(X_1) \geq 0$. We restate this result as

$$p_0(X_2) \geq p_0(X_1)$$

Thus, *the value of a European put with a higher exercise price must be at least as great as the value of a European put with a lower exercise price*. These results also hold for American puts. Therefore,

$$P_0(X_2) \geq P_0(X_1)$$

Even though it is technically possible for calls and puts with different exercise prices to have the same price, *generally we can say that the higher the exercise price, the lower the price of a call and the higher the price of a put*. For example, refer back to Exhibit 4-1 and observe how the most expensive calls and least expensive puts have the lower exercise prices.

5.4   THE EFFECT OF A DIFFERENCE IN TIME TO EXPIRATION

Option prices are also affected by the time to expiration of the option. Intuitively, one might expect that the longer the time to expiration, the more valuable the option. A longer-term option has more time for the underlying to make a favorable move. In addition, if the option is in-the-money by the end of a given period of time, it has a better chance of moving even further in-the-money over a longer period of time. If the additional time gives it a better chance of moving out-of-the-money or further out-of-the-money, the limitation of losses to the amount of the option premium means that the disadvantage of the longer time is no greater. In most cases, a longer time to expiration is beneficial for an option. We will see that longer-term American and European calls and longer-term American puts are worth no less than their shorter-term counterparts.

First let us consider each of the four types of options: European calls, American calls, European puts, and American puts. We shall introduce options otherwise identical except that one has a longer time to expiration than the other. The one expiring earlier has an expiration of T_1 and the one expiring later has an expiration of T_2. The prices of the options are $c_0(T_1)$ and $c_0(T_2)$ for the European calls, $C_0(T_1)$ and $C_0(T_2)$ for the American calls, $p_0(T_1)$ and $p_0(T_2)$ for the European puts, and $P_0(T_1)$ and $P_0(T_2)$ for the American puts.

When the shorter-term call expires, the European call is worth $Max(0, S_{T_1} - X)$, but we have already shown that the longer-term European call is worth *at least* $Max(0, S_{T_1} - X/(1 + r)^{(T_2-T_1)})$, which is at least as great as this amount.[19] Thus, the longer-term European call is worth at least the value of the shorter-term European call. These results are not altered if the call is American. When the shorter-term American call expires, it is worth $Max(0, S_{T_1} - X)$. The longer-term American call must be worth at least the value of the European call, so it is worth *at least* $Max[0, S - X/(1 + r)^{T_2-T_1}]$. Thus, the longer-term call, European or American, is worth no less than the shorter-term call when the shorter-term call expires. Because this statement is always true, the longer-term call, European or American, is worth no less than the shorter-term call at any time prior to expiration. Thus,

$$c_0(T_2) \geq c_0(T_1) \tag{4-11}$$

$$C_0(T_2) \geq C_0(T_1)$$

Notice that these statements do not mean that the longer-term call is always worth more; it means that the longer-term call can be worth no less. With the exception of the rare case

---

[19] Technically, we showed this calculation using a time to expiration of T, but here the time to expiration is $T_2 - T_1$.

in which both calls are so far out-of-the-money or in-the-money that the additional time is of no value, the longer-term call will be worth more.

For European puts, we have a slight problem. For calls, the longer term gives additional time for a favorable move in the underlying to occur. For puts, this is also true, but there is one disadvantage to waiting the additional time. When a put is exercised, the holder receives money. The lost interest on the money is a disadvantage of the additional time. For calls, there is no lost interest. In fact, a call holder earns additional interest on the money by paying out the exercise price later. Therefore, it is not always true that additional time is beneficial to the holder of a European put. It is true, however, that the additional time is beneficial to the holder of an American put. An American put can always be exercised; there is no penalty for waiting. Thus, we have

$p_0(T_2)$ can be either greater or less than $p_0(T_1)$

$$P_0(T_2) \geq P_0(T_1) \tag{4-12}$$

So for European puts, either the longer-term or the shorter-term option can be worth more. The longer-term European put will tend to be worth more when volatility is greater and interest rates are lower.

Referring back to Exhibit 4-1, observe that the longer-term put and call options are more expensive than the shorter-term ones. As noted, we might observe an exception to this rule for European puts, but these are all American options.

5.5 PUT–CALL PARITY

So far we have been working with puts and calls separately. To see how their prices must be consistent with each other and to explore common option strategies, let us combine puts and calls with each other or with a risk-free bond. We shall put together some combinations that produce equivalent results.

5.5.1 FIDUCIARY CALLS AND PROTECTIVE PUTS

First we consider an option strategy referred to as a **fiduciary call**. It consists of a European call and a risk-free bond, just like the ones we have been using, that matures on the option expiration day and has a face value equal to the exercise price of the call. The upper part of the table in Exhibit 4-11 shows the payoffs at expiration of the fiduciary call. We see that if the price of the underlying is below X at expiration, the call expires worthless and the bond is worth X. If the price of the underlying is above X at expiration, the call expires and is worth S_T (the underlying price) $- X$. So at expiration, the fiduciary call will end up worth X or S_T, whichever is greater.

EXHIBIT 4-11   Portfolio Combinations for Equivalent Packages of Puts and Calls

Transaction	Current Value	Value at Expiration $S_T \leq X$	$S_T > X$
Fiduciary Call			
Buy call	c_0	0	$S_T - X$
Buy bond	$X/(1 + r)^T$	X	X
Total	$c_0 + X/(1 + r)^T$	X	S_T
Protective Put			
Buy put	p_0	$X - S_T$	0
Buy underlying asset	S_0	S_T	S_T
Total	$p_0 + S_0$	X	S_T

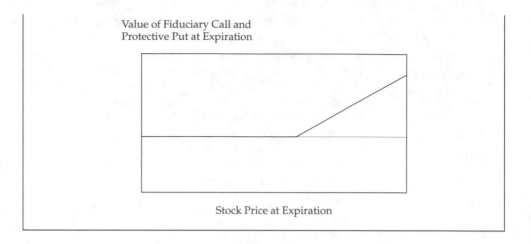

This type of combination is called a fiduciary call because it allows protection against downside losses and is thus faithful to the notion of preserving capital.

Now we construct a strategy known as a **protective put**, which consists of a European put and the underlying asset. If the price of the underlying is below X at expiration, the put expires and is worth $X - S_T$ and the underlying is worth S_T. If the price of the underlying is above X at expiration, the put expires with no value and the underlying is worth S_T. So at expiration, the protective put is worth X or S_T, whichever is greater. The lower part of the table in Exhibit 4-11 shows the payoffs at expiration of the protective put.

Thus, the fiduciary call and protective put end up with the same value. They are, therefore, identical combinations. To avoid arbitrage, their values today must be the same. The value of the fiduciary call is the cost of the call, c_0, and the cost of the bond, $X/(1 + r)^T$. The value of the protective put is the cost of the put, p_0, and the cost of the underlying, S_0. Thus,

$$c_0 + X/(1 + r)^T = p_0 + S_0 \tag{4-13}$$

This equation is called **put–call parity** and is one of the most important results in options. It does not say that puts and calls are equivalent, but it does show an equivalence (parity) of a call/bond portfolio and a put/underlying portfolio.

Put–call parity can be written in a number of other ways. By rearranging the four terms to isolate one term, we can obtain some interesting and important results. For example,

$$c_0 = p_0 + S_0 - X/(1 + r)^T$$

means that a call is equivalent to a long position in the put, a long position in the asset, and a short position in the risk-free bond. The short bond position simply means to borrow by issuing the bond, rather than lend by buying the bond as we did in the fiduciary call portfolio. We can tell from the sign whether we should go long or short. Positive signs mean to go long; negative signs mean to go short.

5.5.2 SYNTHETICS

Because the right-hand side of the above equation is equivalent to a call, we often refer to it as a **synthetic call**. To see that the synthetic call is equivalent to the actual call, look at Exhibit 4-12:

EXHIBIT 4-12   Call and Synthetic Call

Transaction	Current Value	Value at Expiration $S_T \leq X$	$S_T > X$
Call			
Buy call	c_0	0	$S_T - X$
Synthetic Call			
Buy put	p_0	$X - S_T$	0
Buy underlying asset	S_0	S_T	S_T
Issue bond	$-X/(1 + r)^T$	$-X$	X
Total	$p_0 + S_0 - X/(1 + r)^T$	0	$S_T - X$

The call produces the value of the underlying minus the exercise price or zero, whichever is greater. The synthetic call does the same thing, but in a different way. When the call expires in-the-money, the synthetic call produces the underlying value minus the payoff on the bond, which is X. When the call expires out-of-the-money, the put covers the loss on the underlying and the exercise price on the put matches the amount of money needed to pay off the bond.

Similarly, we can isolate the put as follows:

$$p_0 = c_0 - S_0 + X/(1 + r)^T$$

which says that a put is equivalent to a long call, a short position in the underlying, and a long position in the bond. Because the left-hand side is a put, it follows that the right-hand side is a **synthetic put**. The equivalence of the put and synthetic put is shown in Exhibit 4-13.

EXHIBIT 4-13   Put and Synthetic Put

Transaction	Current Value	Value at Expiration $S_T \leq X$	$S_T > X$
Put			
Buy put	p_0	$X - S_T$	0
Synthetic Put			
Buy call	c_0	0	$S_T - X$
Short underlying asset	$-S_0$	$-S_T$	$-S_T$
Buy bond	$X/(1 + r)^T$	X	X
Total	$c_0 - S_0 + X/(1 + r)^T$	$X - S_T$	0

As you can well imagine, there are numerous other combinations that can be constructed. Exhibit 4-14 shows a number of the more important combinations. There are two primary reasons that it is important to understand synthetic positions in option pricing. Synthetic positions enable us to price options, because they produce the same results as options and have known prices. Synthetic positions also tell how to exploit mispricing of options relative to their underlying assets. Note that we can not only synthesize a call or a put, but

EXHIBIT 4-14   Alternative Equivalent Combinations of Calls, Puts, the Underlying, and Risk-Free Bonds

Strategy	Consisting of	Worth	Equates to	Strategy	Consisting of	Worth
Fiduciary call	Long call + Long bond	$c_0 + X/(1 + r)^T$	=	Protective put	Long put + Long underlying	$p_0 + S_0$
Long call	Long call	c_0	=	Synthetic call	Long put + Long underlying + Short bond	$p_0 + S_0 - X/(1 + r)^T$
Long put	Long put	p_0	=	Synthetic put	Long call + Short underlying + Long bond	$c_0 - S_0 + X/(1 + r)^T$
Long underlying	Long underlying	S_0	=	Synthetic underlying	Long call + Long bond + Short put	$c_0 + X/(1 + r)^T - p_0$
Long bond	Long bond	$X/(1 + r)^T$	=	Synthetic bond	Long put + Long underlying + Short call	$p_0 + S_0 - c_0$

we can also synthesize the underlying or the bond. As complex as it might seem to do this, it is really quite easy. First, we learn that *a fiduciary call is a call plus a risk-free bond maturing on the option expiration day with a face value equal to the exercise price of the option.* Then we learn that *a protective put is the underlying plus a put.* Then we learn the basic put–call parity equation: *A fiduciary call is equivalent to a protective put*:

$$c_0 + X/(1 + r)^T = p_0 + S_0$$

Learn the put–call parity equation this way, because it is the easiest form to remember and has no minus signs.

Next, we decide which instrument we want to synthesize. We use simple algebra to isolate that instrument, with a plus sign, on one side of the equation, moving all other instruments to the other side. We then see what instruments are on the other side, taking plus signs as long positions and minus signs as short positions. Finally, to check our results, we should construct a table like Exhibits 4-11 or 4-12, with the expiration payoffs of the instrument we wish to synthesize compared with the expiration payoffs of the equivalent combination of instruments. We then check to determine that the expiration payoffs are the same.

5.5.3   AN ARBITRAGE OPPORTUNITY

In this section we examine the arbitrage strategies that will push prices to put–call parity. Suppose that in the market, prices do not conform to put–call parity. This is a situation in which price does not equal value. Recalling our basic equation, $c_0 + X/(1 + r)^T = p_0 + S_0$, we should insert values into the equation and see if the equality holds. If it does not, then obviously one side is greater than the other. We can view one side as overpriced and the other as underpriced, which suggests an arbitrage opportunity. To exploit this mispricing, we buy the underpriced combination and sell the overpriced combination.

Consider the following example involving call options with an exercise price of $100 expiring in half a year (T = 0.5). The risk-free rate is 10 percent. The call is priced at $7.50, and the put is priced at $4.25. The underlying price is $99.

The left-hand side of the basic put–call parity equation is $c_0 + X/(1 + r)^T = 7.50 + 100/(1.10)^{0.5} = 7.50 + 95.35 = 102.85$. The right-hand side is $p_0 + S_0 = 4.25 + 99 = 103.25$. So the right-hand side is greater than the left-hand side. This means that the protective put is overpriced. Equivalently, we could view this as the fiduciary call being underpriced. Either way will lead us to the correct strategy to exploit the mispricing.

We sell the overpriced combination, the protective put. This means that we sell the put and sell short the underlying. Doing so will generate a cash inflow of $103.25. We buy the fiduciary call, paying out $102.85. This series of transactions nets a cash inflow of $103.25 − $102.85 = $0.40. Now, let us see what happens at expiration.

The options expire with the underlying above 100:

   The bond matures, paying $100.

   Use the $100 to exercise the call, receiving the underlying.

   Deliver the underlying to cover the short sale.

   The put expires with no value.

   Net effect: No money in or out.

The options expire with the underlying below 100:

   The bond matures, paying $100.

   The put expires in-the-money; use the $100 to buy the underlying.

   Use the underlying to cover the short sale.

   The call expires with no value.

   Net effect: No money in our out.

So we receive $0.40 up front and do not have to pay anything out. The position is perfectly hedged and represents an arbitrage profit. The combined effects of other investors performing this transaction will result in the value of the protective put going down and/or the value of the covered call going up until the two strategies are equivalent in value. Of course, it is possible that transaction costs might consume any profit, so small discrepancies will not be exploited.

It is important to note that regardless of which put–call parity equation we use, we will arrive at the same strategy. For example, in the above problem, the synthetic put (a long call, a short position in the underlying, and a long bond) is worth $7.50 − $99 + $95.35 = $3.85. The actual put is worth $4.25. Thus, we would conclude that we should sell the actual put and buy the synthetic put. To buy the synthetic put, we would buy the call, short the underlying, and buy the bond—precisely the strategy we used to exploit this price discrepancy.

In all of these examples based on put–call parity, we used only European options. Put–call parity using American options is considerably more complicated. The resulting parity equation is a complex combination of inequalities. Thus, we cannot say that a given combination exactly equals another; we can say only that one combination is more valuable than another. Exploitation of any such mispricing is somewhat more complicated, and we shall not explore it here.

PRACTICE PROBLEM 3

European put and call options with an exercise price of 45 expire in 115 days. The underlying is priced at 48 and makes no cash payments during the life of the options. The risk-free rate is 4.5 percent. The put is selling for 3.75, and the call is selling for 8.00.

A. Identify the mispricing by comparing the price of the actual call with the price of the synthetic call.

B. Based on your answer in Part A, demonstrate how an arbitrage transaction is executed.

SOLUTIONS

A. Using put–call parity, the following formula applies:

$$c_0 = p_0 + S_0 - X/(1 + r)^T$$

The time to expiration is $T = 115/365 = 0.3151$. Substituting values into the right-hand side:

$$c_0 = 3.75 + 48 - 45/(1.045)^{0.3151} = 7.37$$

Hence, the synthetic call is worth 7.37, but the actual call is selling for 8.00 and is, therefore, overpriced.

B. Sell the call for 8.00 and buy the synthetic call for 7.37. To buy the synthetic call, buy the put for 3.75, buy the underlying for 48.00, and issue a zero-coupon bond paying 45.00 at expiration. The bond will bring in $45.00/(1.045)^{0.3151} = 44.38$ today. This transaction will bring in $8.00 - 7.37 = 0.63$.

At expiration, the following payoffs will occur:

	$S_T < 45$	$S_T \geq 45$
Short call	0	$-(S_T - 45)$
Long put	$45 - S_T$	0
Underlying	S_T	S_T
Bond	-45	-45
Total	0	0

Thus there will be no cash in or out at expiration. The transaction will net a risk-free gain of $8.00 - 7.37 = 0.63$ up front.

5.6 AMERICAN OPTIONS, LOWER BOUNDS, AND EARLY EXERCISE

As we have noted, American options can be exercised early and in this section we specify cases in which early exercise can have value. Because early exercise is never mandatory, the right to exercise early may be worth something but could never hurt the option holder. Consequently, the prices of American options must be no less than the prices of European options:

$$C_0 \geq c_0 \tag{4-14}$$

$$P_0 \geq p_0$$

Recall that we already used this result in establishing the minimum price from the lower bounds and intrinsic value results in Section 5.2.2. Now, however, our concern is understanding the conditions under which early exercise of an American option might occur.

Suppose today, time 0, we are considering exercising early an in-the-money American call. If we exercise, we pay X and receive an asset worth S_0. But we already determined that a European call is worth at least $S_0 - X/(1 + r)^T$—that is, the underlying price minus the present value of the exercise price, which is more than $S_0 - X$. Because we just argued that the American call must be worth no less than the European call, it therefore must also be worth at least $S_0 - X/(1 + r)^T$. This means that the value we could obtain by selling it to someone else is more than the value we could obtain by exercising it. Thus, there is no reason to exercise the call early.

Some people fail to see the logic behind not exercising early. Exercising a call early simply gives the money to the call writer and throws away the right to decide at expiration if you want the underlying. It is like renewing a magazine subscription before the current subscription expires. Not only do you lose the interest on the money, you also lose the right to decide later if you want to renew. Without offering an early exercise incentive, the American call would have a price equal to the European call price. Thus, we must look at another case to see the value of the early exercise option.

If the underlying makes a cash payment, there may be reason to exercise early. If the underlying is a stock and pays a dividend, there may be sufficient reason to exercise just before the stock goes ex-dividend. By exercising, the option holder throws away the time value but captures the dividend. We shall skip the technical details of how this decision is made and conclude by stating that

- *When the underlying makes no cash payments, $C_0 = c_0$.*
- *When the underlying makes cash payments during the life of the option, early exercise can be worthwhile and C_0 can thus be higher than c_0.*

We emphasize the word *can*. It is possible that the dividend is not high enough to justify early exercise.

For puts, there is nearly always a possibility of early exercise. Consider the most obvious case, an investor holding an American put on a bankrupt company. The stock is worth zero. It cannot go any lower. Thus, the put holder would exercise immediately. As long as there is a possibility of bankruptcy, the American put will be worth more than the European put. But in fact, bankruptcy is not required for early exercise. The stock price must be very low, although we cannot say exactly how low without resorting to an analysis using option pricing models. Suffice it to say that *the American put is nearly always worth more than the European put*: $P_0 > p_0$.

5.7 THE EFFECT OF CASH FLOWS ON THE UNDERLYING ASSET

Both the lower bounds on puts and calls and the put–call parity relationship must be modified to account for cash flows on the underlying asset. In Chapters 2 and 3, we discussed situations in which the underlying has cash flows. Stocks pay dividends, bonds pay interest, foreign currencies pay interest, and commodities have carrying costs. As we have done in the previous chapters, we shall assume that these cash flows are either known or can be expressed as a percentage of the asset price. Moreover, as we did previously, we can remove the present value of those cash flows from the price of the underlying and use this adjusted underlying price in the results we have obtained above.

In the previous chapters, we specified these cash flows in the form of the accumulated value at T of all cash flows incurred on the underlying over the life of the derivative contract. When the underlying is a stock, we specified these cash flows more precisely in the form of dividends, using the notation FV(D,0,T) as the future value, or alternatively PV(D,0,T) as the present value, of these dividends. When the underlying was a bond, we used the notation FV(CI,0,T) or PV(CI,0,T), where CI stands for "coupon interest." When the cash flows can be specified in terms of a yield or rate, we used the notation δ where $S_0/(1 + \delta)^T$ is the underlying price reduced by the present value of the cash flows.[20] Using

---

[20] We actually used several specifications of the dividend yield in Chapter 3, but we shall use just one here.

continuous compounding, the rate can be specified as δ^c so that $S_0 e^{-\delta^c T}$ is the underlying price reduced by the present value of the dividends. For our purposes in this chapter on options, let us just write this specification as PV(CF,0,T), which represents the present value of the cash flows on the underlying over the life of the options. Therefore, we can restate the lower bounds for European options as

$$c_0 \geq \text{Max}\{0,[S_0 - \text{PV(CF,0,T)}] - X/(1 + r)^T\}$$

$$p_0 \geq \text{Max}\{0,X/(1 + r)^T - [S_0 - \text{PV(CF,0,T)}]\}$$

and put–call parity as

$$c_0 + X/(1 + r)^T = p_0 + [S_0 - \text{PV(CF,0,T)}]$$

which reflects the fact that, as we said, we simply reduce the underlying price by the present value of its cash flows over the life of the option.

5.8 THE EFFECT OF INTEREST RATES AND VOLATILITY

It is important to know that interest rates and volatility exert an influence on option prices. *When interest rates are higher, call option prices are higher and put option prices are lower.* This effect is not obvious and strains the intuition somewhat. When investors buy call options instead of the underlying, they are effectively buying an indirect leveraged position in the underlying. When interest rates are higher, buying the call instead of a direct leveraged position in the underlying is more attractive. Moreover, by using call options, investors save more money by not paying for the underlying until a later date. For put options, however, higher interest rates are disadvantageous. When interest rates are higher, investors lose more interest while waiting to sell the underlying when using puts. Thus, the opportunity cost of waiting is higher when interest rates are higher. Although these points may not seem completely clear, fortunately they are not critical. Except when the underlying is a bond or interest rate, interest rates do not have a very strong effect on option prices.

Volatility, however, has an extremely strong effect on option prices. *Higher volatility increases call and put option prices because it increases possible upside values and increases possible downside values of the underlying.* The upside effect helps calls and does not hurt puts. The downside effect does not hurt calls and helps puts. The reasons calls are not hurt on the downside and puts are not hurt on the upside is that when options are out-of-the-money, it does not matter if they end up more out-of-the-money. But when options are in-the-money, it does matter if they end up more in-the-money.

Volatility is a critical variable in pricing options. It is the only variable that affects option prices that is not directly observable either in the option contract or in the market. It must be estimated. We shall have more to say about volatility later in this chapter.

5.9 OPTION PRICE SENSITIVITIES

Later in this chapter, we will study option price sensitivities in more detail. These sensitivity measures have Greek names:

- *Delta* is the sensitivity of the option price to a change in the price of the underlying.
- *Gamma* is a measure of how well the delta sensitivity measure will approximate the option price's response to a change in the price of the underlying.
- *Rho* is the sensitivity of the option price to the risk-free rate.
- *Theta* is the rate at which the time value decays as the option approaches expiration.
- *Vega* is the sensitivity of the option price to volatility.

6   DISCRETE-TIME OPTION PRICING: THE BINOMIAL MODEL

Until now, we have looked only at some basic principles of option pricing. Other than put–call parity, all we examined were rules and conditions, often suggesting limitations, on option prices. With put–call parity, we found that we could price a put or a call based on the prices of the combinations of instruments that make up the synthetic version of the instrument. If we wanted to determine a call price, we had to have a put; if we wanted to determine a put price, we had to have a call. What we need to be able to do is price a put or a call without the other instrument. In this section, we introduce a simple means of pricing an option. It may appear that we oversimplify the situation, but we shall remove the simplifying assumptions gradually, and eventually reach a more realistic scenario.

The approach we take here is called the **binomial model**. The word "binomial" refers to the fact that there are only two outcomes. In other words, we let the underlying price move to only one of two possible new prices. As noted, this framework oversimplifies things, but the model can eventually be extended to encompass all possible prices. In addition, we refer to the structure of this model as **discrete time**, which means that time moves in distinct increments. This is much like looking at a calendar and observing only the months, weeks, or days. Even at its smallest interval, we know that time moves forward at a rate faster than one day at a time. It moves in hours, minutes, seconds, and even fractions of seconds, and fractions of fractions of seconds. When we talk about time moving in the tiniest increments, we are talking about **continuous time**. We will see that the discrete time model can be extended to become a continuous time model. Although we present the continuous time model (Black–Scholes–Merton) in Section 7, we must point out that the binomial model has the advantage of allowing us to price American options. In addition, the binomial model is a simple model requiring a minimum of mathematics. Thus it is worthy of study in its own right.

6.1   THE ONE-PERIOD BINOMIAL MODEL

We start off by having only one binomial period. This means that the underlying price starts off at a given level, then moves forward to a new price, at which time the option expires. Here we need to change our notation slightly from what we have been using previously. We let S be the current underlying price. One period later, it can move up to S^+ or down to S^-. Note that we are removing the time subscript, because it will not be necessary here. We let X be the exercise price of the option and r be the one period risk-free rate. The option is European style.

6.1.1   THE MODEL

We start with a call option. If the underlying goes up to S^+, the call option will be worth c^+. If the underlying goes down to S^-, the option will be worth c^-. We know that if the option is expiring, its value will be the intrinsic value. Thus,

$$c^+ = \text{Max}(0, S^+ - X)$$

$$c^- = \text{Max}(0, S^- - X)$$

Exhibit 4-15 illustrates this scenario with a diagram commonly known as a **binomial tree**. Note how we indicate that the current option price, c, is unknown.

EXHIBIT 4-15   One-Period Binomial Model

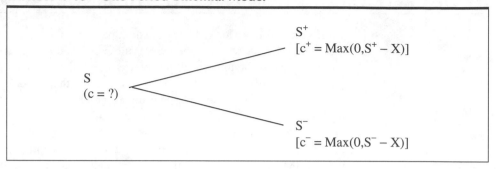

Now let us specify how the underlying moves. We identify a factor, u, as the up move on the underlying and d as the down move:

$$u = \frac{S^+}{S}$$

$$d = \frac{S^-}{S}$$

so that u and d represent 1 plus the rate of return if the underlying goes up and down, respectively. Thus, $S^+ = Su$ and $S^- = Sd$. To avoid an obvious arbitrage opportunity, we require that[21]

$$d < 1 + r < u$$

We are now ready to determine how to price the option. We assume that we have all information except for the current option price. In addition, we do not know in what direction the price of the underlying will move. We start by constructing an arbitrage portfolio consisting of one short call option. Let us now purchase an unspecified number of units of the underlying. Let that number be n. Although at the moment we do not know the value of n, we can figure it out quickly. We call this portfolio a hedge portfolio. In fact, n is sometimes called the **hedge ratio**. Its current value is H, where

$$H = nS - c$$

This specification reflects the fact that we own n units of the underlying worth S and we are short one call.[22] One period later, this portfolio value will go to either H^+ or H^-:

$$H^+ = nS^+ - c^+$$

$$H^- = nS^- - c^-$$

---

[21] This statement says that if the price of the underlying goes up, it must do so at a rate better than the risk-free rate. If it goes down, it must do so at a rate lower than the risk-free rate. If the underlying always does better than the risk-free rate, it would be possible to buy the underlying, financing it by borrowing at the risk-free rate, and be assured of earning a greater return from the underlying than the cost of borrowing. This would make it possible to generate an unlimited amount of money. If the underlying always does worse than the risk-free rate, one can buy the risk-free asset and finance it by shorting the underlying. This would also make it possible to earn an unlimited amount of money. Thus, the risky underlying asset cannot dominate or be dominated by the risk-free asset.

[22] Think of this specification as a plus sign indicating assets and a minus sign indicating liabilities.

Because we can choose the value of n, let us do so by setting H^+ equal to H^-. This specification means that regardless of which way the underlying moves, the portfolio value will be the same. Thus, the portfolio will be hedged. We do this by setting

$H^+ = H^-$, which means that

$nS^+ - c^+ = nS^- - c^-$

We then solve for n to obtain

$$n = \frac{c^+ - c^-}{S^+ - S^-} \tag{4-15}$$

Because the values on the right-hand side are known, we can easily set n according to this formula. If we do so, the portfolio will be hedged. A hedged portfolio should grow in value at the risk-free rate.

$H^+ = H(1 + r)$, or

$H^- = H(1 + r)$

We know that $H^+ = nS^+ - c^+$, $H^- = nS^- - c^-$, and $H = nS - c$. We know the values of n, S^+, S^-, c^+, and c^-, as well as r. We can substitute and solve either of the above for c to obtain

$$c = \frac{\pi c^+ + (1 - \pi)c^-}{1 + r} \tag{4-16}$$

where

$$\pi = \frac{1 + r - d}{u - d} \tag{4-17}$$

We see that the call price today, c, is a weighted average of the next two possible call prices, c^+ and c^-. The weights are π and $1 - \pi$. This weighted average is then discounted one period at the risk-free rate.

It might appear that π and $1 - \pi$ are probabilities of the up and down movements, but they are not. In fact, the probabilities of the up and down movements are not required. It is important to note, however, that π and $1 - \pi$ are the probabilities that would exist if investors were risk neutral. Risk-neutral investors value assets by computing the expected future value and discounting that value at the risk-free rate. Because we are discounting at the risk-free rate, it should be apparent that π and $1 - \pi$ would indeed be the probabilities if the investor were risk neutral. In fact, we shall refer to them as **risk-neutral probabilities** and the process of valuing an option is often called **risk-neutral valuation.**[23]

---

[23] It may be helpful to contrast risk neutrality with risk aversion, which characterizes nearly all individuals. People who are risk neutral value an asset, such as an option or stock, by discounting the expected value at the risk-free rate. People who are risk averse discount the expected value at a higher rate, one that consists of the risk-free rate plus a risk premium. In the valuation of options, we are not making the assumption that people are risk neutral, but the fact that options can be valued by finding the expected value, using these special probabilities, and discounting at the risk-free rate creates the *appearance* that investors are assumed to be risk neutral. We emphasize the word "appearance," because no such assumption is being made. The terms "risk neutral probabilities" and "risk neutral valuation" are widely used in options valuation, although they give a misleading impression of the assumptions underlying the process.

6.1.2   ONE-PERIOD BINOMIAL EXAMPLE

Suppose the underlying is a non-dividend-paying stock currently valued at \$50. It can either go up by 25 percent or go down by 20 percent. Thus, $u = 1.25$ and $d = 0.80$.

$$S^+ = Su = 50(1.25) = 62.50$$

$$S^- = Sd = 50(0.80) = 40$$

Assume that the call option has an exercise price of 50 and the risk-free rate is 7 percent. Thus, the option values one period later will be

$$c^+ = Max(0,S^+ - X) = Max(0,62.50 - 50) = 12.50$$

$$c^- = Max(0,S^- - X) = Max(0,40 - 50) = 0$$

Exhibit 4-16 depicts the situation.

EXHIBIT 4-16   One-Period Binomial Example

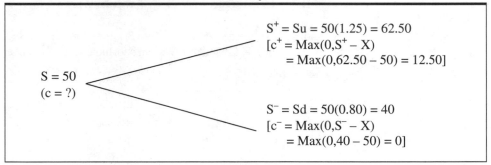

First we calculate π:

$$\pi = \frac{1 + r - d}{u - d} = \frac{1.07 - 0.80}{1.25 - 0.80} = 0.6$$

and, hence, $1 - \pi = 0.4$. Now, we can directly calculate the option price:

$$c = \frac{0.6(12.50) + 0.4(0)}{1.07} = 7.01$$

Thus, the option should sell for \$7.01.

6.1.3   ONE-PERIOD BINOMIAL ARBITRAGE OPPORTUNITY

Suppose the option is selling for \$8. If the option should be selling for \$7.01 and it is selling for \$8, it is overpriced—a clear case of price not equaling value. Investors would exploit this opportunity by selling the option and buying the underlying. The number of units of the underlying purchased for each option sold would be the value n:

$$n = \frac{c^+ - c^-}{S^+ - S^-} = \frac{12.50 - 0}{62.50 - 40} = 0.556$$

Thus, for every option sold, we would buy 0.556 units of the underlying. Suppose we sell 1,000 calls and buy 556 units of the underlying. Doing so would require an initial outlay of $H = 556(\$50) - 1,000(\$8) = \$19,800$. One period later, the portfolio value will be either

$$H^+ = nS^+ - c^+ = 556(\$62.50) - 1,000(\$12.50) = \$22,250, \text{ or}$$

$$H^- = nS^- - c^- = 556(\$40) - 1,000(\$0) = \$22,240$$

These two values are not exactly the same, but the difference is due only to rounding the hedge ratio, n. We shall use the $22,250 value. If we invest $19,800 and end up with $22,250, the return is

$$\frac{\$22,250}{\$19,800} - 1 = 0.1237$$

that is, a risk-free return of more than 12 percent in contrast to the actual risk-free rate of 7 percent. Thus we could borrow $19,800 at 7 percent to finance the initial net cash outflow, capturing a risk-free profit of $(0.1237 - 0.07) \times \$19,800 = \$1,063$ (to the nearest dollar) without any net investment of money. Other investors will recognize this opportunity and begin selling the option, which will drive down its price. When the option sells for $7.01, the initial outlay would be H = 556($50) − 1,000($7.01) = $20,790. The payoffs at expiration would still be $22,250. This transaction would generate a return of

$$\frac{\$22,250}{\$20,790} - 1 \approx 0.07$$

Thus, *when the option is trading at the price given by the model, a hedge portfolio would earn the risk-free rate*, which is appropriate because the portfolio would be risk free.

If the option sells for less than $7.01, investors would buy the option and sell short the underlying, which would generate cash up front. At expiration, the investor would have to pay back an amount less than 7 percent. All investors would perform this transaction, generating a demand for the option that would push its price back up to $7.01.

PRACTICE PROBLEM 4

Consider a one-period binomial model in which the underlying is at 65 and can go up 30 percent or down 22 percent. The risk-free rate is 8 percent.

A. Determine the price of a European call option with exercise prices of 70.

B. Assume that the call is selling for 9 in the market. Demonstrate how to execute an arbitrage transaction and calculate the rate of return. Use 10,000 call options.

SOLUTIONS

A. First find the underlying prices in the binomial tree. We have u = 1.30 and d = 1 − 0.22 = 0.78.

$$S^+ = Su = 65(1.30) = 84.50$$

$$S^- = Sd = 65(0.78) = 50.70$$

Then find the option values at expiration:

$$c^+ = Max(0, 84.50 - 70) = 14.50$$

$$c^- = Max(0, 50.70 - 70) = 0$$

The risk-neutral probability is

$$\pi = \frac{1.08 - 0.78}{1.30 - 0.78} = 0.5769$$

and $1 - \pi = 0.4231$. The call's price today is

$$c = \frac{0.5769(14.50) + 0.4231(0)}{1.08} = 7.75$$

B. We need the value of n for calls:

$$n = \frac{c^+ - c^-}{S^+ - S^-} = \frac{14.50 - 0}{84.50 - 50.70} = 0.4290$$

The call is overpriced, so we should sell 10,000 call options and buy 4,290 units of the underlying.

Sell 10,000 calls at 9	+90,000
Buy 4,290 units of the underlying at 65	−278,850
Net cash flow	−188,850

So we invest 188,850. The value of this combination at expiration will be

If $S_T = 84.50$,

$$4,290(84.50) - 10,000(14.50) = 217,505$$

If $S_T = 50.70$,

$$4,290(50.70) - 10,000(0) = 217,503$$

These values differ by only a rounding error.
The rate of return is

$$\frac{217,505}{188,850} - 1 = 0.1517$$

Thus, we receive a risk-free return almost twice the risk-free rate. We could borrow the initial outlay of $188,850 at the risk-free rate and capture a risk-free profit without any net investment of money.

6.2 THE TWO-PERIOD BINOMIAL MODEL

In the example above, the movements in the underlying were depicted over one period, and there were only two outcomes. We can extend the model and obtain more-realistic results with more than two outcomes. Exhibit 4-17 shows how to do so with a two-period binomial tree.

EXHIBIT 4-17   Two-Period Binomial Model

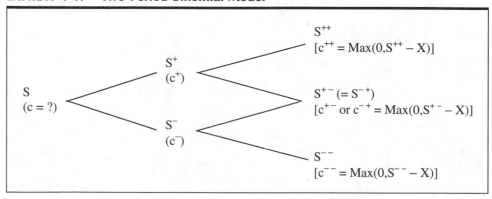

In the first period, we let the underlying price move from S to S^+ or S^- in the manner we did in the one-period model. That is, if u is the up factor and d is the down factor,

$$S^+ = Su$$

$$S^- = Sd$$

Then, with the underlying at S^+ after one period, it can either move up to S^{++} or down to S^{+-}. Thus,

$$S^{++} = S^+u$$

$$S^{+-} = S^+d$$

If the underlying is at S^- after one period, it can either move up to S^{-+} or down to S^{--}.

$$S^{-+} = S^-u$$

$$S^{--} = S^-d$$

We now have three unique final outcomes instead of two. Actually, we have four final outcomes, but S^{+-} is the same as S^{-+}. We can relate the three final outcomes to the starting price in the following manner:

$$S^{++} = S^+u = Suu = Su^2$$

$$S^{+-} \text{ (or } S^{-+}) = S^+d \text{ (or } S^-u) = Sud \text{ (or } Sdu)$$

$$S^{--} = S^-d = Sdd = Sd^2$$

Now we move forward to the end of the first period. Suppose we are at the point where the underlying price is S^+. Note that now we are back into the one-period model we previously derived. There is one period to go and two outcomes. The call price is c^+ and can go up to c^{++} or down to c^{+-}. Using what we know from the one-period model, the call price must be

$$c^+ = \frac{\pi c^{++} + (1 - \pi)c^{+-}}{1 + r} \tag{4-18}$$

where again we see that the call price is a weighted average of the next two possible call prices, then discounted back one period. If the underlying price is at S^-, the call price would be

$$c^- = \frac{\pi c^{-+} + (1 - \pi)c^{--}}{1 + r} \tag{4-19}$$

where in both cases the formula for π is still Equation 4-17:

$$\pi = \frac{1 + r - d}{u - d}$$

Now we step back to the starting point and find that the option price is still given as Equation 4-16:

$$c = \frac{\pi c^+ + (1 - \pi)c^-}{1 + r}$$

again, using the general form that the call price is a weighted average of the next two possible call prices, discounted back to the present. Other than requiring knowledge of the formula for π, the call price formula is simple and intuitive. It is an average, weighted by the risk-neutral probabilities, of the next two outcomes, then discounted to the present.[24]

Recall that the hedge ratio, n, was given as the difference in the next two call prices divided by the difference in the next two underlying prices. This will be true in all cases throughout the binomial tree. Hence, we have different hedge ratios at each time point:

$$n = \frac{c^+ - c^-}{S^+ - S^-}$$

$$n^+ = \frac{c^{++} - c^{+-}}{S^{++} - S^{+-}}$$

$$n^- = \frac{c^{-+} - c^{--}}{S^{-+} - S^{--}}$$

(4-20)

6.2.1   TWO-PERIOD BINOMIAL EXAMPLE

We can continue with the example presented in Section 6.1.2 in which the underlying goes up 25 percent or down 20 percent. Let us, however, alter the example a little. Suppose the underlying goes up 11.8 percent and down 10.56 percent, and we extend the number of periods to two. So, the up factor is 1.118 and the down factor is $1 - 0.1056 = 0.8944$. If the underlying goes up for two consecutive periods, it rises by a factor of $1.118(1.118) = 1.25$ (25 percent). If it goes down in both periods, it falls by a factor of $(0.8944)(0.8944) = 0.80$ (20 percent). This specification makes the highest and lowest prices unchanged. Let the risk-free rate be 3.44 percent per period. The π becomes $(1.0344 - 0.8944)/(1.118 - 0.8944) = 0.6261$. The underlying prices at expiration will be

$$S^{++} = Su^2 = 50(1.118)(1.118) = 62.50$$

$$S^{+-} = Sud = 50(1.118)(0.8944) = 50$$

$$S^{--} = Sd^2 = 50(0.8944)(0.8944) = 40$$

When the options expire, they will be worth

$$c^{++} = Max(0, S^{++} - 50) = Max(0, 62.50 - 50) = 12.50$$

$$c^{+-} = Max(0, S^{+-} - 50) = Max(0, 50 - 50) = 0$$

$$c^{--} = Max(0, S^{--} - 50) = Max(0, 40 - 50) = 0$$

The option values after one period are, therefore,

$$c^+ = \frac{\pi c^{++} + (1 - \pi)c^{+-}}{1 + r} = \frac{0.6261(12.50) + 0.3739(0)}{1.0344} = 7.57$$

$$c^- = \frac{\pi c^{-+} + (1 - \pi)c^{--}}{1 + r} = \frac{0.6261(0) + 0.3739(0)}{1.0344} = 0.0$$

---

[24] It is also possible to express the price today as a weighted average of the three final option prices discounted two periods, thereby skipping the intermediate step of finding c^+ and c^-; but little is gained by doing so and this approach is somewhat more technical.

So the option price today is

$$c = \frac{\pi c^+ + (1 - \pi)c^-}{1 + r} = \frac{0.6261(7.57) + 0.3739(0)}{1.0344} = 4.58$$

These results are summarized in Exhibit 4-18.

EXHIBIT 4-18   Two-Period Binomial Example

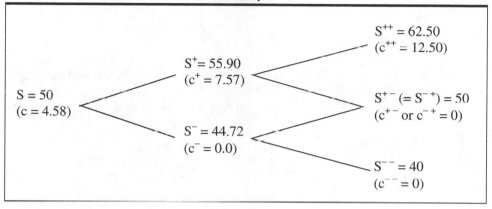

We shall not illustrate an arbitrage opportunity, because doing so requires a very long and detailed example that goes beyond our needs. Suffice it to say that if the option is mispriced, one can construct a hedged portfolio that will capture a return in excess of the risk-free rate.

PRACTICE PROBLEM 5

Consider a two-period binomial model in which the underlying is at 30 and can go up 14 percent or down 11 percent each period. The risk-free rate is 3 percent per period.

A. Find the value of a European call option expiring in two periods with an exercise price of 30.

B. Find the number of units of the underlying that would be required at each point in the binomial tree to construct a risk-free hedge using 10,000 calls.

SOLUTIONS

A. First find the underlying prices in the binomial tree: We have u = 1.14 and d = 1 − 0.11 = 0.89.

$$S^+ = Su = 30(1.14) = 34.20$$

$$S^- = Sd = 30(0.89) = 26.70$$

$$S^{++} = Su^2 = 30(1.14)^2 = 38.99$$

$$S^{+-} = Sud = 30(1.14)(0.89) = 30.44$$

$$S^{--} = Sd^2 = 30(0.89)^2 = 23.76$$

Then find the option prices at expiration:

$$c^{++} = \text{Max}(0, 38.99 - 30) = 8.99$$

$$c^{+-} = \text{Max}(0, 30.44 - 30) = 0.44$$

$$c^{--} = \text{Max}(0, 23.76 - 30) = 0$$

We will need the value of π:

$$\pi = \frac{1.03 - 0.89}{1.14 - 0.89} = 0.56$$

and $1 - \pi = 0.44$. Then step back and find the option prices at time 1:

$$c^+ = \frac{0.56(8.99) + 0.44(0.44)}{1.03} = 5.08$$

$$c^- = \frac{0.56(0.44) + 0.44(0)}{1.03} = 0.24$$

The price today is

$$c = \frac{0.56(5.08) + 0.44(0.24)}{1.03} = 2.86$$

B. The number of units of the underlying at each point in the tree is found by first computing the values of n.

$$n = \frac{5.08 - 0.24}{34.20 - 26.70} = 0.6453$$

$$n^+ = \frac{8.99 - 0.44}{38.99 - 30.44} = 1.00$$

$$n^- = \frac{0.44 - 0}{30.44 - 23.76} = 0.0659$$

The number of units of the underlying required for 10,000 calls would thus be 6,453 today, 10,000 at time 1 if the underlying is at 34.20, and 659 at time 1 if the underlying is at 26.70.

6.3   BINOMIAL PUT OPTION PRICING

In Section 6.2, the option was a call. It is a simple matter to make the option a put. We could step back through the entire example, changing all c's to p's and using the formulas for the payoff values of a put instead of a call. We should note, however, that if the same formula used for a call is used to calculate the hedge ratio, the minus sign should be ignored as it would suggest being long the stock (put) and short the put (stock) when the hedge portfolio should actually be long both instruments or short both instruments. The put moves opposite to the stock in the first place; hence, long or short positions in both instruments are appropriate.

PRACTICE PROBLEM 6

Repeating the data from Practice Problem 4, consider a one-period binomial model in which the underlying is at 65 and can go up 30 percent or down 22 percent. The risk-free rate is 8 percent. Determine the price of a European put option with exercise price of 70.

SOLUTION

First find the underlying prices in the binomial tree. We have $u = 1.30$ and $d = 1 - 0.22 = 0.78$.

$$S^+ = Su = 65(1.30) = 84.50$$

$$S^- = Sd = 65(0.78) = 50.70$$

Then find the option values at expiration:

$$p^+ = Max(0, 70 - 84.50) = 0$$

$$p^- = Max(0, 70 - 50.70) = 19.30$$

The risk-neutral probability is

$$\pi = \frac{1.08 - 0.78}{1.30 - 0.78} = 0.5769$$

and $1 - \pi = 0.4231$. The put price today is

$$p = \frac{0.5769(0) + 0.423(19.30)}{1.08} = 7.56$$

6.4 BINOMIAL INTEREST RATE OPTION PRICING

In the examples above, the applications were appropriate for options on a stock, currency, or commodity.[25] Now we take a brief look at options on bonds and interest rates. A model for pricing these options must start with a model for the one-period interest rate and the prices of zero-coupon bonds.

We look at such a model in Exhibit 4-19. Note that this binomial tree is the first one we have seen with more than two time periods. At each point in the tree, we see a group of numbers. The first number is the one-period interest rate. The second set of numbers, which are in parentheses, represents the prices of $1 face value zero-coupon bonds of various maturities. At time 0, 0.9048 is the price of a one-period zero-coupon bond, 0.8106 is the price of a two-period zero-coupon bond, 0.7254 is the price of a three-period zero-coupon bond, and 0.6479 is the price of a four-period zero-coupon bond. The one-period bond price can be determined from the one-period rate—that is, $0.9048 = 1/1.1051$, subject to some rounding off. The other prices cannot be determined solely from the one-period rate; we would have to see a tree of the two-, three-, and four-period rates. As we move forward in time, we lose one bond as the one-period bond matures.[26] Thus, at time 1, when the one-period rate is 13.04 percent, the two-period bond from the previous

---

[25] We have also been assuming that there are no cash flows on the underlying.

[26] Technically we could show the bond we are losing as a bond with a price of $1.00, its face value, at its point of maturity.

period, whose price was 0.8106, is now a one-period bond whose price is 1/1.1304 = 0.8846. Although we present these prices and rates here without derivation, they were determined using a model that prevents arbitrage opportunities in buying and selling bonds. We do not cover the actual derivation of the model here.

EXHIBIT 4-19   Binomial Interest Rate Tree

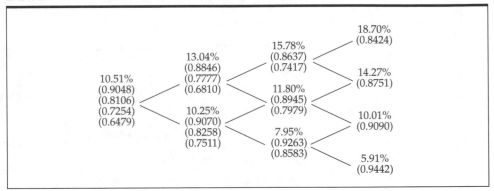

Now let us price a European option on a zero-coupon bond. First note that we need the option to expire before the bond matures, and it should have a reasonable exercise price. We shall work with the four-period zero-coupon bond. Exhibit 4-20 contains its price and the price of a two-period call option with an exercise price of $0.80 per $1 of par, as well as the one-period interest rate. The binomial interest rate tree in Exhibit 4-20 is based on the data in Exhibit 4-19. In parentheses in Exhibit 4-20 are the prices of the call option expiring at time 2.

EXHIBIT 4-20   Four-Period Zero-Coupon Bond and Two-Period Call Option with Exercise Price of 0.80

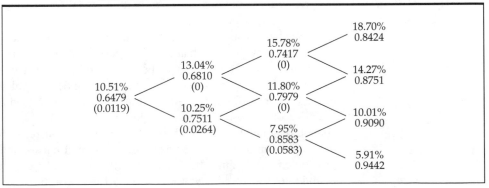

First note that in binomial term structure models, the models are usually fit such that the risk-neutral probability, π, is 0.5. Thus we do not have to calculate π, as in the examples above. We must, however, do one thing quite differently. Whereas we have used a constant interest rate, we must now discount at a different interest rate, the one-period rate, given in Exhibit 4-19, depending on where we are in the tree.

The payoff values at time 2 of the call with exercise price of 0.80 are

$$c^{++} = \text{Max}(0, 0.7417 - 0.80) = 0$$

$$c^{+-} = \text{Max}(0, 0.7979 - 0.80) = 0$$

$$c^{--} = \text{Max}(0, 0.8583 - 0.80) = 0.0583$$

These numbers appear in Exhibit 4-20 at time 2 along with the underlying bond prices and the one-period interest rates. Stepping back to time 1, we find the option prices as follows:

$$c^{+} = \frac{0.5(0) + 0.5(0)}{1.1304} = 0$$

$$c^{-} = \frac{0.5(0) + 0.5(0.0583)}{1.1025} = 0.0264$$

Note how we discount by the appropriate one-period rate, which is 10.25 percent for the bottom outcome at time 1 and 13.04 percent for the top outcome at time 1. Stepping back to time 0, the option price is, therefore,

$$c = \frac{0.5(0) + 0.5(0.0264)}{1.1051} = 0.0119$$

using the one-period rate of 10.51 percent. The call option is thus worth $0.0119 when the underlying zero-coupon bond paying $1 at time 4 is currently worth $0.6479.

Now let us price an option on a coupon bond. First, however, we must construct the tree of coupon bond prices. Exhibit 4-21 illustrates the price of a $1 face value, 11 percent coupon bond maturing at time 4 along with a call option expiring at time 2 with an exercise price of $0.95 per $1 of par.

EXHIBIT 4-21   Four-Period 11 Percent Coupon Bond and Two-Period Call Option with Exercise Price of 0.95

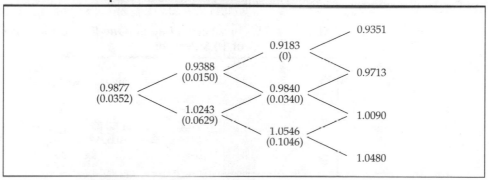

We obtain the prices of the coupon bond from the prices of zero-coupon bonds. For example, at time 0, a four-period 11 percent coupon bond is equivalent to a combination of zero-coupon bonds with face value of 0.11 maturing at times 1, 2, and 3, and a zero-coupon bond with face value of 1.11 maturing at time 4. Thus, its price can be found by multiplying these face values by the prices of one-, two-, three-, and four-period zero-coupon bonds respectively, the prices of which are taken from Exhibit 4-19.

$$0.11(0.9048) + 0.11(0.8106) + 0.11(0.7254) + 1.11(0.6479) = 0.9877$$

At any other point in the tree, we use the same procedure, but of course fewer coupons remain.[27] Of course, pricing a coupon bond by decomposing it into a combination of zero-coupon bonds is basic fixed income material, which you have learned elsewhere in the CFA curriculum.

Now let us find the option prices. At time 2, the prices are

$$c^{++} = \text{Max}(0, 0.9183 - 0.95) = 0$$

$$c^{+-} = \text{Max}(0, 0.9840 - 0.95) = 0.0340$$

$$c^{--} = \text{Max}(0, 1.0546 - 0.95) = 0.1046$$

Stepping back to time 1, the prices are

$$c^{+} = \frac{0.5(0.0) + 0.5(0.340)}{1.304} = 0.0150$$

$$c^{-} = \frac{0.5(0.340) + 0.5(0.1046)}{1.025} = 0.0629$$

Stepping back to time 0, the option price is

$$c = \frac{0.5(0.0150) + 0.5(0.0629)}{1.1051} = 0.0352$$

Now let us look at options on interest rates. Recall that in Section 4.1.4, we illustrated how these options work. Their payoffs are based on the difference between the interest rate and an exercise rate. When the option expires, the payoff does not occur for one additional period. Thus, we have to discount the intrinsic value at expiration by the one-period interest rate. Recall that an interest rate cap is a set of interest rate call options expiring at various points in the life of a loan. The cap is generally set up to hedge the interest rate risk on a floating rate loan.

Exhibit 4-22 illustrates the pricing of a two-period cap with an exercise rate of 10.5 percent. This contract consists of two caplets: a one-period call option on the one-period

EXHIBIT 4-22   Two-Period Cap on One-Period Interest Rate with Exercise Rate of 10.5 Percent

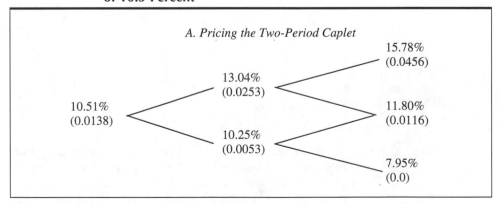

A. Pricing the Two-Period Caplet

---

[27] For example, consider the middle node at time 2. The coupon bond is now a two-period bond. The one- and two-period zero-coupon bond prices are 0.8945 and 0.7979, respectively (from Exhibit 4-19). Thus, the coupon bond price is 0.11(0.8945) + 1.11(0.7979) = 0.9840 as shown in Exhibit 4-21.

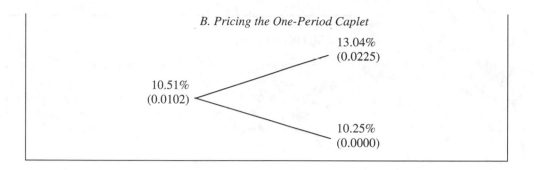

B. Pricing the One-Period Caplet

interest rate with an exercise rate of 10.5 percent, and a two-period call option on the one-period interest rate with an exercise rate of 10.5 percent. We price the cap by pricing these two component options.

In Panel A, we price the two-period caplet. The values at time 2 are

$$c^{++} = \frac{\text{Max}(0, 0.1578 - 0.105)}{1.1578} = 0.0456$$

$$c^{+-} = \frac{\text{Max}(0, 0.1180 - 0.105)}{1.1180} = 0.0116$$

$$c^{--} = \frac{\text{Max}(0, 0.0795 - 0.105)}{1.0795} = 0.0$$

Note especially that we discount the payoff one period at the appropriate one-period rate, because the payoff does not occur until one period later. Stepping back to time 1:

$$c^{+} = \frac{0.5(0.0456) + 0.5(0.0116)}{1.1304} = 0.0253$$

$$c^{-} = \frac{0.5(0.0116) + 0.5(0.0)}{1.1025} = 0.0053$$

At time 0, the option price is

$$c = \frac{0.5(0.0253) + 0.5(0.0053)}{1.1051} = 0.0138$$

Panel B illustrates the same procedure for the one-period caplet. We shall omit the details because they follow precisely the pattern above. The one-period caplet price is 0.0102; thus the cap costs $0.0138 + 0.0102 = 0.0240$.

If the option is a floor, the procedure is precisely the same but the payoffs are based on the payoffs of a put instead of a call. Pricing a zero-cost collar, however, is considerably more complex. Remember that a zero-cost collar is a long cap and a short floor with the exercise rates set such that the premium on the cap equals the premium on the floor. We can arbitrarily choose the exercise rate on the cap or the floor, but the exercise rate on the other would have to be found by trial and error so that the premium offsets the premium on the other instrument.

PRACTICE PROBLEM 7

The diagram below is a two-period binomial tree containing the one-period interest rate and the prices of zero-coupon bonds. The first price is a one-period zero-coupon bond, the second is a two-period zero-coupon bond, and the third is a three-period zero-coupon bond. As we move forward, one bond matures and its price is removed. The maturity of each bond is then shorter by one period.

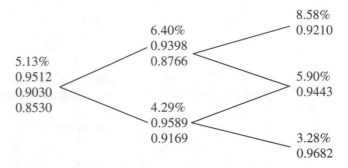

A. Find the price of a European put expiring in two periods with an exercise price of 1.01 on a three-period 6 percent coupon bond with $1.00 face value.

B. Find the price of a European put option expiring at time 2 with an exercise rate of 6 percent where the underlying is the one-period rate.

SOLUTIONS

A. First we have to find the price of the three-period $1.00 par, 6 percent coupon bond at expiration of the option (t = 2). We break the coupon bond up into zero-coupon bonds of one, two, and three periods to maturity. The face values of these zero-coupon bonds are 0.06, 0.06, and 1.06, respectively. The bond price at t = 2 is $1.06 discounted one period at the appropriate discount rate:
Bond prices at time 2:

$++$ outcome: $1.06(0.9210) = 0.9763$

$+-$ outcome: $1.06(0.9443) = 1.0010$

$--$ outcome: $1.06(0.9682) = 1.0263$

Now compute the put option values at expiration:

$++$ outcome: $Max(0, 1.01 - 0.9763) = 0.0337$

$+-$ outcome: $Max(0, 1.01 - 1.0010) = 0.0090$

$--$ outcome: $Max(0, 1.01 - 1.0263) = 0.0000$

Now step back and compute the option values at time 1:

$+$ outcome: $\dfrac{0.5(0.0337) + 0.5(0.0090)}{1.064} = 0.0201$

$-$ outcome: $\dfrac{0.5(0.0090) + 0.5(0.0000)}{1.0429} = 0.0043$

Now step back and compute the option values at time 0:

$$\frac{0.5(0.201) + 0.5(0.0043)}{1.0513} = 0.0116$$

B. First compute the put option values at expiration:

$$p^{++} = \frac{\text{Max}(0, 0.06 - 0.0858)}{1.0858} = 0.0000$$

$$p^{+-} = \frac{\text{Max}(0, 0.06 - 0.0590)}{1.059} = 0.0009$$

$$p^{--} = \frac{\text{Max}(0, 0.06 - 0.0328)}{1.0328} = 0.0263$$

Step back to time 2 and compute the option values:

$$p^{+} = \frac{0.5(0.0000) + 0.5(0.0009)}{1.064} = 0.0004$$

$$p^{-} = \frac{0.5(0.0009) + 0.5(0.0263)}{1.0429} = 0.0130$$

Now step back to time 0 and compute the option price as

$$p = \frac{0.5(0.0004) + 0.5(0.0130)}{1.0513} = 0.0064$$

6.5 AMERICAN OPTIONS

The binomial model is also well suited for handling American-style options. At any point in the binomial tree, we can see whether the calculated value of the option is exceeded by its value if exercised early. If that is the case, we replace the calculated value with the exercise value.[28]

6.6 EXTENDING THE BINOMIAL MODEL

In the examples in this chapter, we divided an option's life into a given number of periods. Suppose we are pricing a one-year option. If we use only one binomial period, it will give us only two prices for the underlying, and we are unlikely to get a very good result. If we use two binomial periods, we will have three prices for the underlying at expiration. This result would probably be better but still not very good. But as we increase the number of periods, the result should become more accurate. In fact, in the limiting case, we are likely to get a very good result. By increasing the number of periods, we are moving from discrete time to continuous time.

Consider the following example of a one-period binomial model for a nine-month option. The asset is priced at 52.75. It can go up by 35.41 percent or down by 26.15 percent, so u = 1.3541 and d = 1 − 0.2615 = 0.7385. The risk-free rate is 4.88 percent. A call option has an exercise price of 50 and expires in nine months. Using a one-period binomial model would obtain an option price of 10.0259. Exhibit 4-23 shows the results we obtain if we divide the nine-month option life into an increasing number of periods of smaller and smaller length. The manner in which we fit the binomial tree is not arbitrary, however, because we have to alter the values of u, d, and the risk-free rate so that the underlying price move is reasonable for the life of the option. How we alter u and d is related to the volatility, a topic we cover in the next section. In fact, we need not concern ourselves with exactly how to alter any of these values. We need only to observe that our binomial option price appears to be converging to a value of around 8.62.

In the same way a sequence of rapidly taken still photographs converges to what appears to be a continuous sequence of a subject's movements, the binomial model converges to a continuous-time model, the subject of which is in our next section.

---

[28] See Chapter 4 of *An Introduction to Derivatives and Risk Management*, 6th edition, Don M. Chance (South-Western College Publishing, 2004) for a treatment of this topic.

EXHIBIT 4-23   Binomial Option Prices for Different Numbers of Time Periods

Number of Time Periods	Option Price
1	10.0259
2	8.4782
5	8.8305
10	8.6983
25	8.5862
50	8.6438
100	8.6160
500	8.6162
1000	8.6190

Notes: Call option with underlying price of 52.75, up factor of 1.3541, down factor of 0.7385, risk-free rate of 4.88 percent, and exercise price of 50. The variables u, d, and r are altered accordingly as the number of time periods increases.

7 CONTINUOUS-TIME OPTION PRICING: THE BLACK–SCHOLES–MERTON MODEL

When we move to a continuous-time world, we price options using the famous Black–Scholes–Merton model. Named after its founders Fischer Black, Myron Scholes, and Robert Merton, this model resulted in the award of a Nobel Prize to Scholes and Merton in 1997.[29] (Fischer Black had died in 1995 and thus was not eligible for the prize.) The model can be derived either as the continuous limit of the binomial model, or through taking expectations, or through a variety of highly complex mathematical procedures. We are not concerned with the derivation here and instead simply present the model and its applications. First, however, let us briefly review its underlying assumptions.

7.1 ASSUMPTIONS OF THE MODEL

7.1.1 THE UNDERLYING PRICE FOLLOWS A GEOMETRIC LOGNORMAL DIFFUSION PROCESS

This assumption is probably the most difficult to understand, but in simple terms, *the underlying price follows a lognormal probability distribution as it evolves through time*. A lognormal probability distribution is one in which the log return is normally distributed. For example, if a stock moves from 100 to 110, the return is 10 percent but the log return is ln(1.10) = 0.0953 or 9.53 percent. Log returns are often called *continuously compounded returns*. If the log or continuously compounded return follows the familiar normal or bell-shaped distribution, the return is said to be lognormally distributed. The distribution of the return itself is skewed, reaching further out to the right and truncated on the left side, reflecting the limitation that an asset cannot be worth less than zero.

The lognormal distribution is a convenient and widely used assumption. It is almost surely not an exact measure in reality, but it suffices for our purposes.

---

[29] The model is more commonly called the Black–Scholes model, but we choose to give Merton the credit he is due that led to his co-receipt of the Nobel Prize.

7.1.2 The Risk-Free Rate Is Known and Constant

The Black–Scholes–Merton model does not allow interest rates to be random. Generally, we assume that *the risk-free rate is constant*. This assumption becomes a problem for pricing options on bonds and interest rates, and we will have to make some adjustments then.

7.1.3 The Volatility of the Underlying Asset Is Known and Constant

The volatility of the underlying asset, specified in the form of the standard deviation of the log return, is assumed to be known at all times and does not change over the life of the option. This assumption is the most critical, and we take it up again in a later section. In reality, the volatility is definitely not known and must be estimated or obtained from some other source. In addition, volatility is generally not constant. Obviously, the stock market is more volatile at some times than at others. Nonetheless, the assumption is critical for this model. Considerable research has been conducted with the assumption relaxed, but this topic is an advanced one and does not concern us here.

7.1.4 There Are No Taxes or Transaction Costs

We have made this assumption all along in pricing all types of derivatives. Taxes and transaction costs greatly complicate our models and keep us from seeing the essential financial principles involved in the models. It is possible to relax this assumption, but we shall not do so here.

7.1.5 There Are No Cash Flows on the Underlying

We have discussed this assumption at great length in pricing futures and forwards and earlier in this chapter in studying the fundamentals of option pricing. The basic form of the Black–Scholes–Merton model makes this assumption, but it can easily be relaxed. We will show how to do this in Section 7.4.

7.1.6 The Options Are European

With only a few very advanced variations, the Black–Scholes–Merton model does not price American options. Users of the model must keep this in mind, or they may badly misprice these options. For pricing American options, the best approach is the binomial model with a large number of time periods.

7.2 THE BLACK–SCHOLES–MERTON FORMULA

Although the mathematics underlying the Black–Scholes–Merton formula are quite complex, the formula itself is not difficult, although it may appear so at first glance. The input variables are some of those we have already used: S_0 is the price of the underlying, X is the exercise price, r^c is the continuously compounded risk-free rate, and T is the time to expiration. The one other variable we need is the standard deviation of the log return on the asset. We denote this as σ and refer to it as the volatility. Then, the Black–Scholes–Merton formulas for the prices of call and put options are

$$c = S_0 N(d_1) - Xe^{-r^c T} N(d_2) \qquad \textbf{(4-21)}$$

$$p = Xe^{-r^c T}[1 - N(d_2)] - S_0[1 - N(d_1)]$$

where

$$d_1 = \frac{\ln(S_0/X) + [r^c + (\sigma^2/2)]T}{\sigma\sqrt{T}} \qquad \textbf{(4-22)}$$

$$d_2 = d_1 - \sigma\sqrt{T}$$

σ = the annualized standard deviation of the continuously compounded return on the stock

r^c = the continuously compounded risk-free rate of return

Of course, we have already seen the terms "ln" and "e" in previous chapters. We do, however, introduce two new and somewhat unusual looking terms, $N(d_1)$ and $N(d_2)$. These terms represent normal probabilities based on the values of d_1 and d_2. We compute the normal probabilities associated with values of d_1 and d_2 using the second equation above and insert these values into the formula as $N(d_1)$ and $N(d_2)$. Exhibit 4-24 presents a brief review of the normal probability distribution and explains how to obtain a probability value. Once we know how to look up a number in a normal probability table, we can then easily calculate d_1 and d_2, look them up in the table to obtain $N(d_1)$ and $N(d_2)$, and then insert the values of $N(d_1)$ and $N(d_2)$ into the above formula.

EXHIBIT 4-24 The Normal Probability Distribution

The normal probability distribution, or bell-shaped curve, gives the probability that a standard normal random variable will be less than or equal to a given value. The graph below shows the normal probability distribution; note that the curve is centered around zero. The values on the horizontal axis run from $-\infty$ to $+\infty$. If we were interested in a value of x of positive infinity, we would have $N(+\infty) = 1$. This expression means that the probability is 1.0 that we would obtain a value less than $+\infty$. If we were interested in a value of x of negative infinity, then $N(-\infty) = 0.0$. This expression means that there is zero probability of a value of x of less than negative infinity. Below, we are interested in the probability of a value less than x, where x is not infinite. We want $N(x)$, which is the area under the curve to the left of x.

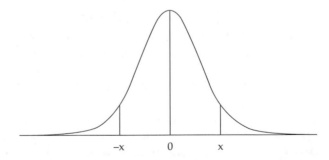

We obtain the values of $N(x)$ by looking them up in a table. Below is an excerpt from a table of values of x (the full table is given as Appendix 4A). Suppose $x = 1.12$. Then we find the

x	0	0.01	0.02	0.03	0.04	0.05	0.06	0.07	0.08	0.09
0.60	0.7257	0.7291	0.7324	0.7357	0.7389	0.7422	0.7454	0.7486	0.7517	0.7549
0.70	0.7580	0.7611	0.7642	0.7673	0.7704	0.7734	0.7764	0.7794	0.7823	0.7852
0.80	0.7881	0.7910	0.7939	0.7967	0.7995	0.8023	0.8051	0.8078	0.8106	0.8133
0.90	0.8159	0.8186	0.8212	0.8238	0.8264	0.8289	0.8315	0.8340	0.8365	0.8389
1.00	0.8413	0.8438	0.8461	0.8485	0.8508	0.8531	0.8554	0.8577	0.8599	0.8621
1.10	0.8643	0.8665	0.8686	0.8708	0.8729	0.8749	0.8770	0.8790	0.8810	0.8830
1.20	0.8849	0.8869	0.8888	0.8907	0.8925	0.8944	0.8962	0.8980	0.8997	0.9015

row containing the value 1.1 and move over to the column containing 0.02. The sum of the row value and the column value is the value of x. The corresponding probability is seen as the value 0.8686. Thus, $N(1.12) = 0.8686$. This means that the probability of obtaining a value of less than 1.12 in a normal distribution is 0.8686.

Now, suppose the value of x is negative. Observe in the figure above that the area to the left of $-x$ is the same as the area to the right of $+x$. Therefore, if x is a negative number, $N(x)$ is found as $1 - N(-x)$. For example, let $x = -0.75$. We simply look up $N(-x) = N[-(-0.75)] = N(0.75) = 0.7734$. Then $N(-0.75) = 1 - 0.7734 = 0.2266$.

Consider the following example. The underlying price is 52.75 and has a volatility of 0.35. The continuously compounded risk-free rate is 4.88 percent. The option expires in nine months; therefore, $T = 9/12 = 0.75$. The exercise price is 50. First we calculate the values of d_1 and d_2:

$$d_1 = \frac{\ln(52.75/50) + (0.0488 + (0.35)^2/2)0.75}{0.35\sqrt{0.75}} - 0.4489$$

$$d_2 = 0.4489 - 0.35\sqrt{0.75} = 0.1458$$

To use the normal probability table in Appendix 4A, we must round off d_1 and d_2 to two digits to the right of the decimal. Thus we have $d_1 = 0.45$ and $d_2 = 0.15$. From the table, we obtain

$$N(0.45) = 0.6736$$

$$N(0.15) = 0.5596$$

Then we plug everything into the equation for c:

$$c = 52.75(0.6736) - 50e^{-0.0488(0.75)}(0.5596) = 8.5580$$

The value of a put with the same terms would be

$$p = 50e^{-0.0488(0.75)}(1 - 0.5596) - 52.75(1 - 0.6736) = 4.0110$$

At this point, we should note that the Black–Scholes–Merton model is extremely sensitive to rounding errors. In particular, the process of looking up values in the normal probability table is a major source of error. A number of other ways exist to obtain $N(d_1)$ and $N(d_2)$, such as using Microsoft Excel's function "=normsdist()". Using a more precise method, such as Excel, the value of the call would be 8.619. Note that this is the value to which the binomial option price converged in the example we showed with 1,000 time periods in Exhibit 4-23. Indeed, the Black–Scholes–Merton model is said to be the continuous limit of the binomial model.

PRACTICE PROBLEM 8

Use the Black–Scholes–Merton model to calculate the prices of European call and put options on an asset priced at 68.5. The exercise price is 65, the continuously compounded risk-free rate is 4 percent, the options expire in 110 days, and the volatility is 0.38. There are no cash flows on the underlying.

SOLUTIONS

The time to expiration will be T = 110/365 = 0.3014. Then d_1 and d_2 are

$$d_1 = \frac{\ln(68.5/65) + (0.04 + (0.38)^2/2)(0.3014)}{0.38\sqrt{0.3014}} = 0.4135$$

$$d_2 = 0.4135 - 0.38\sqrt{0.3014} = 0.2049$$

Looking up in the normal probability table, we have

$$N(0.41) = 0.6591$$

$$N(0.20) = 0.5793$$

Plugging into the option price formula,

$$c = 68.5(0.6591) - 65e^{-0.04(0.3014)}(0.5793) = 7.95$$

$$p = 65e^{-0.04(0.3014)}(1 - 0.5793) - 68.5(1 - 0.6591) = 3.67$$

Let us now take a look at the various inputs required in the Black–Scholes–Merton model. We need to know where to obtain the inputs and how the option price varies with these inputs.

7.3 INPUTS TO THE BLACK–SCHOLES–MERTON MODEL

The Black–Scholes–Merton model has five inputs: the underlying price, the exercise price, the risk-free rate, the time to expiration, and the volatility.[30] As we have previously seen, call option prices should be higher the higher the underlying price, the longer the time to expiration, the higher the volatility, and the higher the risk-free rate. They should be lower the higher the exercise price. Put option prices should be higher the higher the exercise price and the higher the volatility. They should be lower the higher the underlying price and the higher the risk-free rate. As we saw, European put option prices can be either higher or lower the longer the time to expiration. American put option prices are always higher the longer the time to expiration, but the Black–Scholes–Merton model does not apply to American options.

These relationships are general to any European and American options and do not require the Black–Scholes–Merton model to understand them. Nonetheless, the Black–Scholes–Merton model provides an excellent opportunity to examine these relationships more closely. We can calculate and plot relationships such as those mentioned, which are usually called the option Greeks, because they are often referred to with Greek names. Let us now look at each of the inputs and the various option Greeks.

7.3.1 THE UNDERLYING PRICE: DELTA AND GAMMA

The price of the underlying is generally one of the easiest sources of input information. Suffice it to say that if an investor cannot obtain the price of the underlying, then she should not even be considering the option. The price should generally be obtained as a quote or trade price from a liquid, open market.

---

[30] Later we shall add one more input, cash flows on the underlying.

The relationship between the option price and the underlying price has a special name: It is called the option **delta**. In fact, the delta can be obtained approximately from the Black–Scholes–Merton formula as the value of $N(d_1)$ for calls and $N(d_1) - 1$ for puts. More formally, the delta is defined as

$$\text{Delta} = \frac{\text{Change in option price}}{\text{Change in underlying price}} \tag{4-23}$$

The above definition for delta is exact; the use of $N(d_1)$ for calls and $N(d_1) - 1$ for puts is approximate. Later in this section, we shall see why $N(d_1)$ and $N(d_2)$ are approximations and when they are good or bad approximations.

Let us consider the example we previously worked, where $S = 52.75$, $X = 50$, $r^c = 0.0488$, $T = 0.75$, and $\sigma = 0.35$. Using a computer to obtain a more precise Black–Scholes–Merton answer, we get a call option price of 8.6186 and a put option price of 4.0717. $N(d_1)$, the call delta, is 0.6733, so the put delta is $0.6733 - 1 = -0.3267$. Given that Delta = (Change in option price/Change in underlying price), we should expect that

Change in option price = Delta × Change in underlying price.

Therefore, for a $1 change in the price of the underlying, we should expect

Change in call option price = 0.6733(1) = 0.6733

Change in put option price = $-0.3267(1) = -0.3267$

This calculation would mean that

Approximate new call option price = 8.6186 + 0.6733 = 9.2919

Approximate new put option price = 4.0717 − 0.3267 = 3.7450

To test the accuracy of this approximation, we let the underlying price move up $1 to $53.75 and re-insert these values into the Black–Scholes–Merton model. We would then obtain

Actual new call option price = 9.3030

Actual new put option price = 3.7560

The delta approximation is fairly good, but not perfect.

Delta is important as a risk measure. *The delta defines the sensitivity of the option price to a change in the price of the underlying.* Traders, especially dealers in options, use delta to construct hedges to offset the risk they have assumed by buying and selling options. For example, recall from Chapter 2 that FRA dealers offer to take either side of an FRA transaction. They then usually hedge the risk they have assumed by entering into other transactions. These same types of dealers offer to buy and sell options, hedging that risk with other transactions. For example, suppose we are a dealer offering to sell the call option we have been working with above. A customer buys 1,000 options for 8.619. We now are short 1,000 call options, which exposes us to considerable risk if the underlying goes up. So we must buy a certain number of units of the underlying to hedge this risk. We previously showed that the delta is 0.6733, so we would buy 673 units of the underlying at 52.75.[31] Assume for the moment that the delta tells us precisely the movement in the option for a movement in the underlying. Then suppose the underlying moves up $1:

Change in value of 1,000 long units of the underlying: $673(+\$1) = \$673$

Change in value of 1,000 short options: $1,000(+\$1)(0.6733) \approx \$673$

Because we are long the underlying and short the options, these values offset. At this point, however, the delta has changed. If we recalculate it, we would find it to be 0.6953. This would require that we have 695 units of the underlying, so we would need to buy an additional 22 units. We would borrow the money to do this. In some cases, we would need to sell off units of the underlying, in which case we would invest the money in the risk-free asset.

We shall return to the topic of delta hedging in Chapter 7. For now, however, let us consider how changes in the underlying price will change the delta. In fact, even if the underlying price does not change, the delta would still change as the option moves toward expiration. For a call, the delta will increase toward 1.0 as the underlying price moves up and will decrease toward 0.0 as the underlying price moves down. For a put, the delta will decrease toward -1.0 as the underlying price moves down and increase towards 0.0 as the underlying price moves up.[32] If the underlying price does not move, a call delta will move toward 1.0 if the call is in-the-money or 0.0 if the call is out-of-the-money as the call moves toward the expiration day. A put delta will move toward -1.0 if the put is in-the-money or 0.0 if the put is out-of-the-money as it moves toward expiration.

So the delta is constantly changing, which means that delta hedging is a dynamic process. In fact, delta hedging is often referred to as **dynamic hedging**. In theory, the delta is changing continuously and the hedge should be adjusted continuously, but continuous adjustment is not possible in reality. When the hedge is not adjusted continuously, we are admitting the possibility of much larger moves in the price of the underlying. Let us see what happens in that case.

Using our previous example, we allow an increase in the underlying price of $10 to $62.75. Then the call price should change by $0.6733(10) = 6.733$, and the put option price should change by $-0.3267(10) = -3.267$. Thus, the approximate prices would be

Approximate new call option price $= 8.619 + 6.733 = 15.3520$

Approximate new put option price $= 4.0717 - 3.267 = 0.8047$

The actual prices are obtained by recalculating the option values using the Black–Scholes–Merton model with an underlying price of 62.75. Using a computer for greater precision, we find that these prices are

Actual new call option price $= 16.3026$

Actual new put option price $= 1.7557$

The approximations based on delta are not very accurate. In general, the larger the move in the underlying, the worse the approximation. This will make delta hedging less effective.

Exhibit 4-25 shows the relationship between the option price and the underlying price. Panel A depicts the relationship for calls and Panel B shows the corresponding relationship for puts. Notice the curvature in the relationship between the option price and the underlying price. Call option values definitely increase the greater the underlying value, and put

---

[31] This transaction would require $673(\$52.75) = \$35,500$, less the $1,000(\$8.619) = \$8,619$ received from the sale of the option, for a total investment required of $26,881. We would probably borrow this money.

[32] Remember that the put delta is negative; hence, its movement is down toward -1.0 or up toward 0.0.

option values definitely decrease. But the amount of change is not the same in each direction. $N(d_1)$ measures the slope of this line at a given point. As such, it measures only the slope for a very small change in the underlying. When the underlying changes by more than a very small amount, the curvature of the line comes into play and distorts the relationship between the option price and underlying price that is explained by the delta. The problem here is much like the relationship between a bond price and its yield. This first-order relationship between a bond price and its yield is called the duration; therefore, duration is similar to delta.

EXHIBIT 4-25   The Relationship between Option Price and Underlying Price
$X = 50$, $r^c - 0.0488$, $T = 0.75$, $\sigma = 0.35$

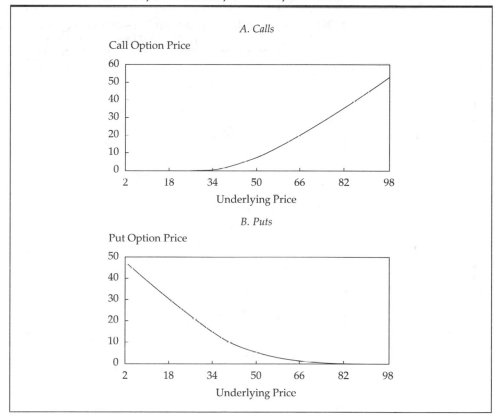

The curvature or second-order effect is known in the fixed income world as the convexity. In the options world, this effect is called **gamma**. Gamma is a numerical measure of how sensitive the delta is to a change in the underlying—in other words, how much the delta changes. When gamma is large, the delta changes rapidly and cannot provide a good approximation of how much the option moves for each unit of movement in the underlying. We shall not concern ourselves with measuring and using gamma, but we should know a few things about the gamma and, therefore, about the behavior of the delta.

Gamma is larger when there is more uncertainty about whether the option will expire in- or out-of-the-money. This means that *gamma will tend to be large when the option is at-the-money and close to expiration.* In turn, this statement means that delta will be a poor approximation for the option's price sensitivity when it is at-the-money and close to the expiration day. Thus, a delta hedge will work poorly. When the gamma is large, we may need to use a gamma-based hedge, which would require that we add a position in another option to the delta-hedge position of the underlying and the option. We shall not take up this advanced topic here.

7.3.2 THE EXERCISE PRICE

The exercise price is easy to obtain. It is specified in the option contract and does not change. Therefore, it is not worthwhile to speak about what happens when the exercise price changes, but we can talk about how the option price would differ if we choose an option with a different exercise price. As we have previously seen, the call option price will be lower the higher the exercise price and the put option price will be higher. This relationship is confirmed for our sample option in Exhibit 4-26.

EXHIBIT 4-26   **The Relationship between Option Price and Exercise Price**
$$S = 52.75, \; r^c = 0.0488, \; T = 0.75, \; \sigma = 0.35$$

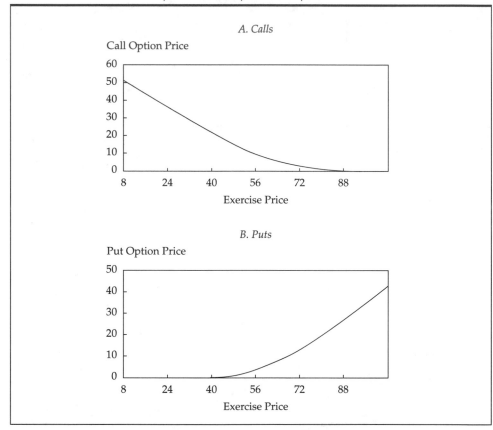

7.3.3 THE RISK-FREE RATE: RHO

The risk-free rate is the continuously compounded rate on the risk-free security whose maturity corresponds to the option's life. We have used the risk-free rate in previous chapters; sometimes we have used the discrete version and sometimes the continuous version. As we have noted, the continuously compounded risk-free rate is the natural log of 1 plus the discrete risk-free rate.

For example, suppose the discrete risk-free rate quoted in annual terms is 5 percent. Then the continuous rate is

$$r^c = \ln(1 + r) = \ln(1.05) = 0.0488$$

Let us recall the difference in these two specifications. Suppose we want to find the present value of $1 in six months using both the discrete and continuous risk-free rates.

$$\text{Present value using discrete rate} = \frac{1}{(1 + r)^T} = \frac{1}{(1.05)^{0.5}} = 0.9759$$

$$\text{Present value using continuous rate} = e^{-r^c T} = e^{-0.0488(0.5)} = 0.9759$$

Obviously either specification will work. Because of how it uses the risk-free rate in the calculation of d_1, however, the Black–Scholes–Merton model requires the continuous risk-free rate.

The sensitivity of the option price to the risk-free rate is called the **rho**. We shall not concern ourselves with the calculation of rho. Technically, the Black–Scholes–Merton model assumes a constant risk-free rate, so it is meaningless to talk about the risk-free rate changing over the life of the option. We can, however, explore how the option price would differ if the current rate were different. Exhibit 4-27 depicts this effect. Note how little change occurs in the option price over a very broad range of the risk-free rate. Indeed, *the price of a European option on an asset is not very sensitive to the risk-free rate.*[33]

EXHIBIT 4-27   The Relationship between Option Price and Risk-Free Rate
S = 52.75, X = 50, T = 0.75, σ = 0.35

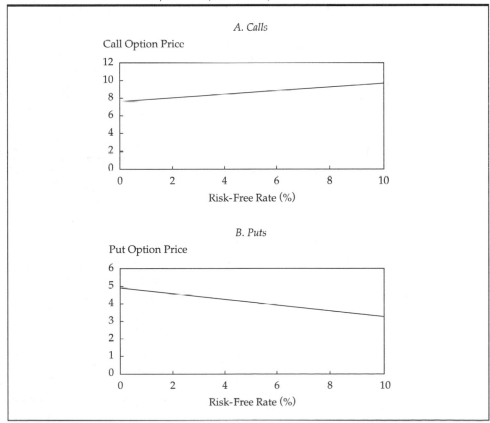

---

[33] When the underlying is an interest rate, however, there is a strong relationship between the option price and interest rates.

7.3.4   TIME TO EXPIRATION: THETA

Time to expiration is an easy input to determine. An option has a definite expiration date specified in the contract. We simply count the number of days until expiration and divide by 365, as we have done previously with forward and futures contracts.

Obviously, the time remaining in an option's life moves constantly towards zero. Even if the underlying price is constant, the option price will still change. We noted that American options have both an intrinsic value and a time value. For European options, all of the price can be viewed as time value. In either case, time value is a function of the option's moneyness, its time to expiration, and its volatility. The more uncertainty there is, the greater the time value. As expiration approaches, the option price moves toward the payoff value of the option at expiration, a process known as **time value decay**. The rate at which the time value decays is called the option's **theta**. We shall not concern ourselves with calculating the specific value of theta, but be aware that if the option price decreases as time moves forward, the theta will be negative. Exhibit 4-28 shows the time value decay for our sample option.

EXHIBIT 4-28   The Relationship between Option Price and Time to Expiration
S = 52.75, X = 50, r^c = 0.0488, σ = 0.35. T Starts at 0.75 and Goes toward 0.0

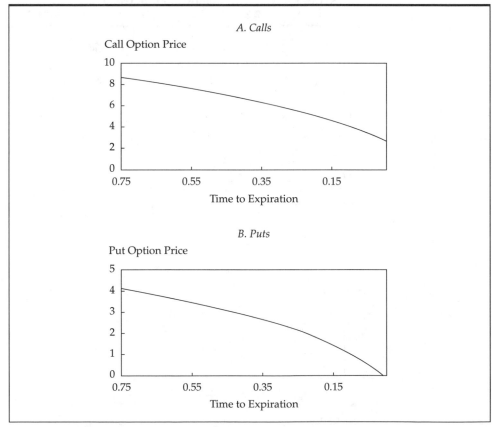

Note that both call and put values decrease as the time to expiration decreases. We previously noted that European put options do not necessarily do this. For some cases, European put options can increase in value as the time to expiration decreases, the case of a positive theta, but that is not so for our put.[34] *Most of the time, option prices are higher the longer the time to expiration. For European puts, however, some exceptions exist.*

7.3.5 VOLATILITY: VEGA

As we have previously noted, volatility is the standard deviation of the continuously compounded return on the stock. We have also noted that the volatility is an extremely important variable in the valuation of an option. It is the only variable that cannot be obtained easily and directly from another source. In addition, as we illustrate here, option prices are extremely sensitive to the volatility. We take up the subject of estimating volatility in Section 7.5.

The relationship between option price and volatility is called the **vega**, which—albeit considered an option Greek—is not actually a Greek word.[35] We shall not concern ourselves with the actual calculation of the vega, but know that the vega is positive for both calls and puts, meaning that if the volatility increases, both call and put prices increase. Also, the vega is larger the closer the option is to being at-the-money.

In the problem we previously worked (S_0 = \$52.75, X = \$50, r^c = 0.0488, T = 0.75), at a volatility of 0.35, the option price was 8.619. Suppose we erroneously use a volatility of 0.40. Then the call price would be 9.446. An error in the volatility of this magnitude would not be difficult to make, especially for a variable that is not directly observable. Yet the result is a very large error in the option price.

Exhibit 4-29 displays the relationship between the option price and the volatility. Note that this relationship is nearly linear and that the option price varies over a very wide range, although this near-linearity is not the case for all options.

**EXHIBIT 4-29   The Relationship between Option Price and Volatility
S = 52.75, X = 50, r^c = 0.0488, T = 0.75**

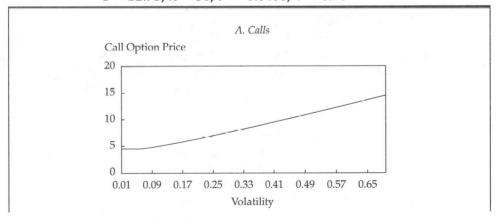

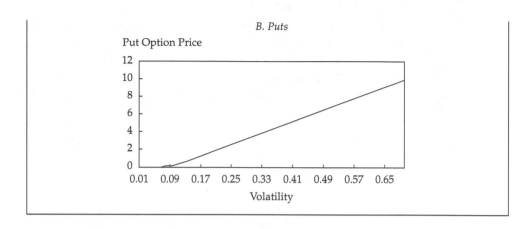

B. Puts

Put Option Price

7.4 THE EFFECT OF CASH FLOWS ON THE UNDERLYING

As we saw in Chapters 2 and 3, cash flows on the underlying affect the prices of forward and futures contracts. It should follow that they would affect the prices of options. In studying the option boundary conditions and put–call parity earlier in this chapter, we noted that we subtract the present value of the dividends from the underlying price and use this adjusted price to obtain the boundary conditions or to price the options using put–call parity. We do the same using the Black–Scholes–Merton model. Specifically, we introduced the expression PV(CF,0,T) for the present value of the cash flows on the underlying over the life of the option. So, we simply use $S_0 - PV(CF,0,T)$ in the Black–Scholes–Merton model instead of S_0.

Recall that in previous chapters, we also used continuous compounding to express the cash flows. For stocks, we used a continuously compounded dividend yield; for currencies, we used a continuously compounded interest rate. In the case of stocks, we let δ^c represent the continuously compounded dividend rate. Then we substituted for $S_0 e^{-\delta^c T}$ for S_0 in the Black–Scholes–Merton formula. For a foreign currency, we let S_0 represent the exchange rate, which we discount using r^{fc}, the continuously compounded foreign risk-free rate. Let us work an example involving a foreign currency option.

Let the exchange rate of U.S. dollars for euros be \$0.8575. The continuously compounded U.S. risk-free rate, which in this example is r^c, is 5.10 percent. The continuously compounded euro risk-free rate, r^{fc}, is 4.25 percent. A call option expires in 125 days (T = 125/365 = 0.3425) and has an exercise price of \$0.90. The volatility of the continuously compounded exchange rate is 0.055.

The first thing we do is obtain the adjusted price of the underlying: $0.8475 e^{-0.0425(0.3425)} = 0.8353$. We then use this value as S_0 in the formula for d_1 and d_2:

$$d_1 = \frac{\ln(0.8353/0.90) + [0.051 + (0.055)^2/2](0.3425)}{0.055\sqrt{0.3425}} = -1.7590$$

$$d_2 = -1.7590 - 0.055\sqrt{0.3425} = -1.7912$$

Using the normal probability table, we find that

$$N(d_1) = N(-1.76) = 1 - 0.9608 = 0.0392$$

$$N(d_2) = N(-1.79) = 1 - 0.9633 = 0.0367$$

In discounting the exercise rate to evaluate the second term in the Black–Scholes–Merton expression, we use the domestic (here, U.S.) continuously compounded risk-free rate. The call option price would thus be

$$c = 0.8353(0.0392) - 0.90e^{-0.051(0.3425)}(0.0367) = 0.0003$$

Therefore, this call option on an asset worth \$0.8575 would cost \$0.0003.

PRACTICE PROBLEM 9

Use the Black–Scholes–Merton model adjusted for cash flows on the underlying to calculate the price of a call option in which the underlying is priced at 225, the exercise price is 200, the continuously compounded risk-free rate is 5.25 percent, the time to expiration is three years, and the volatility is 0.15. The effect of cash flows on the underlying is indicated below for two alternative approaches:

A. The present value of the cash flows over the life of the option is 19.72.

B. The continuously compounded dividend yield is 2.7 percent.

SOLUTIONS

A. Adjust the price of the underlying to $S_0 = 225 - 19.72 = 205.28$. Then insert into the Black–Scholes–Merton formula as follows:

$$d_1 = \frac{\ln(205.28/200) + [0.0525 + (0.15)^2/2]3.0}{0.15\sqrt{3.0}} = 0.8364$$

$$d_2 = 0.8364 - 0.15\sqrt{3.0} = 0.5766$$

$$N(0.84) = 0.7995$$

$$N(0.58) = 0.7190$$

$$c = 205.28(0.7995) - 200e^{-0.0525(3.0)}(0.7190) = 41.28$$

B. Adjust the price of the underlying to $S_0 = 225e^{-0.027(3.0)} = 207.49$

$$d_1 = \frac{\ln(207.49/200) + [0.0525 + (0.15)^2/2]3.0}{0.15\sqrt{3.0}} = 0.8776$$

$$d_2 = 0.8776 - 0.15\sqrt{3.0} = 0.6178$$

$$N(0.88) = 0.8106$$

$$N(0.62) = 0.7324$$

$$c = 207.49(0.8106) - 200e^{-0.0525(3.0)}(0.7324) = 43.06$$

7.5 THE CRITICAL ROLE OF VOLATILITY

As we have previously stressed, volatility is an extremely important variable in the pricing of options. In fact, with the possible exception of the cash flows on the underlying, it is the only variable that cannot be directly observed and easily obtained. It is, after all, the volatility over the life of the option; therefore, it is not past or current volatility but rather the future volatility. Differences in opinion on option prices nearly always result from differences of opinion about volatility. But how does one obtain a number for the future volatility?

7.5.1   HISTORICAL VOLATILITY

The most logical starting place to look for an estimate of future volatility is past volatility. When the underlying is a publicly traded asset, we usually can collect some data over a recent past period and estimate the standard deviation of the continuously compounded return.

   Exhibit 4-30 illustrates this process for a sample of 12 monthly prices of a particular stock. We convert these prices to returns, convert the returns to continuously compounded returns, find the variance of the series of continuously compounded returns, and then convert the variance to the standard deviation. In this example, the data are monthly returns, so we must annualize the variance by multiplying it by 12. Then we take the square root to obtain the historical estimate of the annual standard deviation or volatility.

EXHIBIT 4-30   Estimating Historical Volatility

Month	Price	Return	Log Return	(Log Return − Average)^2
0	100			
1	102	0.020000	0.019803	0.000123
2	99	−0.029412	−0.029853	0.001486
3	97	−0.020202	−0.020409	0.000847
4	89	−0.082474	−0.086075	0.008982
5	103	0.157303	0.146093	0.018878
6	104	0.009709	0.009662	0.000001
7	102	−0.019231	−0.019418	0.000790
8	99	−0.029412	−0.029853	0.001486
9	104	0.050505	0.049271	0.001646
10	102	−0.019231	−0.019418	0.000790
11	105	0.029412	0.028988	0.000412
12	111	0.057143	0.055570	0.002197
		Sum	0.104360	0.037639
		Average	0.008697	

The variance is estimated as follows:

$$\sigma^2 = \frac{\displaystyle\sum_{i=1}^{N} (R_i^c - \bar{R}^c)^2}{N - 1}$$

where R_i^c is the continuously compounded return for observation i (shown above in the fourth column and calculated as $\ln(1 + R_i)$, where i goes from 1 to 12) and R_i is the ith return, $\bar{R}^c$ is the average return over the entire sample, and N is the number of observations in the sample (here, N = 12). Then

$$\sigma^2 = \frac{0.037639}{11} = 0.003422$$

Because this sample consists of monthly returns, to obtain the annual variance, we must multiply this number by 12 (or 52 for weekly, or 250—the approximate number of trading days in a year—for daily). Thus

$$\sigma^2 = 12(0.003422) = 0.041064$$

The annual standard deviation or volatility is, therefore,

$$\sigma^2 = \sqrt{0.041064} = 0.2026$$

So the historical volatility estimate is 20.26 percent.

The historical estimate of the volatility is based only on what happened in the past. To get the best estimate, we must use a lot of prices, but that means going back farther in time. The farther back we go, the less current the data become, and the less reliable our estimate of the volatility. We now look at a way of obtaining a more current estimate of the volatility, but one that raises questions as well as answers them.

7.5.2 IMPLIED VOLATILITY

In a market in which options are traded actively, we can reasonably assume that the market price of the option is an accurate reflection of its true value. Thus, by setting the Black–Scholes–Merton price equal to the market price, we can work backwards to infer the volatility. This procedure enables us to determine the volatility that option traders are using to price the option. This volatility is called the **implied volatility**.

Unfortunately, determining implied volatility is not a simple task. We cannot simply solve the Black–Scholes–Merton equation for the volatility. It is a complicated function with the volatility appearing several times, in some cases as σ^2. There are some mathematical techniques that speed up the estimation of the implied volatility. Here, however, we shall look at only the most basic method: trial and error.

Recall the option we have been working with. The underlying price is 52.75, the exercise price is 50, the risk-free rate is 4.88 percent, and the time to expiration is 0.75. In our previous examples, the volatility was 0.35. Using these values in the Black–Scholes–Merton model, we obtained a call option price of 8.619. Suppose we observe the option selling in the market for 9.25. What volatility would produce this price?

We have already calculated a price of 8.619 at a volatility of 0.35. Because the call price varies directly with the volatility, we know that it would take a volatility greater than 0.35 to produce a price higher than 8.619. We do not know how much higher, so we should just take a guess. Let us try a volatility of 0.40. Using the Black–Scholes–Merton formula with a volatility of 0.40, we obtain a price of 9.446. This is too high, so we try a lower volatility. We keep doing this in the following manner:

Volatility	Black–Scholes–Merton Price
0.35	8.619
0.40	9.446
0.39	9.280
0.38	9.114

So now we know that the correct volatility lies between 0.38 and 0.39, closer to 0.39. In solving for the implied volatility, we must decide either how close to the option price we want to be or how many significant digits we want in the implied volatility. If we choose four significant digits in the implied volatility, a value of 0.3882 would produce the option price of 9.2500. Alternatively, if we decide that we want to be within 0.01 of the option price, we would find that the implied volatility is in the range of 38.76 to 38.88 percent.

Thus, if the option is selling for about 9.25, we say that the market is pricing it at a volatility of 0.3882. This number represents the market's best estimate of the true volatility of the option; it can be viewed as a more current source of volatility information than the past volatility. Unfortunately, a circularity exists in the argument. If one uses the Black–Scholes–Merton model to determine if an futures option is over- or underpriced, the procedure for extracting the implied volatility assumes that the market correctly prices the option. The only way to use the implied volatility in identifying mispriced options is to interpret the implied volatility as either too high or too low, which would require an estimate of true volatility. Nonetheless, the implied volatility is a source of valuable information on the uncertainty in the underlying, and option traders use it routinely.

All of this material on continuous-time option pricing has been focused on options in which the underlying is an asset. As we described earlier in this chapter, there are also options on futures. Let us take a look at the pricing of options on futures, which will pave the way for a continuous-time pricing model for options on interest rates, another case in which the underlying is not an asset.

8   PRICING OPTIONS ON FORWARD AND FUTURES CONTRACTS AND AN APPLICATION TO INTEREST RATE OPTION PRICING

Earlier in this chapter, we discussed how options on futures contracts are active, exchange-traded options in which the underlying is a futures contract. In addition, there are over-the-counter options in which the underlying is a forward contract. In our treatment of these instruments, we assume constant interest rates. As we learned in Chapters 2 and 3, this assumption means that futures and forward contracts will have the same prices. European options on futures and forward contracts will, therefore, have the same prices. American options on forwards will differ in price from American options on futures, and we discuss this later.

First we take a quick look at the basic rules that we previously developed for options on underlying assets. If the underlying asset is a futures contract, the payoff values of the options at expiration are

$$c_T = \text{Max}[0, f_T(T) - X] \tag{4-24}$$

$$p_T = \text{Max}[0, X - f_T(T)]$$

where $f_T(T)$ is the price of a futures contract at T in which the contract expires at T. Thus, $f_T(T)$ is the futures price at expiration. These formulas are, of course, the same as for options when the underlying is an asset, with the futures price substituted for the asset price. When the option and the futures expire simultaneously, the futures price at expiration, $f_T(T)$, converges to the asset price, S_T, making the above payoffs precisely the same as those of the option on the underlying asset.

The minimum and maximum values for options on forwards or futures are the same as those we obtained for options on assets, substituting the futures price for the asset price. Specifically,

$$0 \le c_0 \le f_0(T)$$

$$0 \le C_0 \le f_0(T)$$

$$0 \le p_0 \le X/(1 + r)^T \tag{4-25}$$

$$0 \le P_0 \le X$$

We also established lower bounds for European options and intrinsic values for American options and used these results to establish the minimum prices of these options. For options on futures, the lower bounds are

$$c_0 \geq \text{Max}\{0,[f_0(T) - X]/(1 + r)^T\} \qquad (4\text{-}26)$$

$$p_0 \geq \text{Max}\{0,[X - f_0(T)]/(1 + r)^T\}$$

where $f_0(T)$ is the price at time 0 of a futures contract expiring at T. Therefore, the price of a European call or put on the futures is either zero or the difference between the futures price and exercise price, as formulated above, discounted to the present. For American options on futures, early exercise is possible. Thus, we express their lowest prices as the intrinsic values:

$$C_0 \geq \text{Max}[0,f_0(T) - X] \qquad (4\text{-}27)$$

$$P_0 \geq \text{Max}[0,X - f_0(T)]$$

Because these values are greater than the lower bounds, we maintain these values as the minimum prices of American calls.[36]

As we have previously pointed out, with the assumption of constant interest rates, futures prices and forward prices are the same. We can treat European options on futures the same way as options on forwards. American options on futures will differ from American options on forwards. Now we explore how put–call parity works for options on forwards.

8.1 PUT–CALL PARITY FOR OPTIONS ON FORWARDS

In an earlier section, we examined put–call parity. Now we take a look at the parity between puts and calls on forward contracts and their underlying forward contracts. First recall the notation: F(0,T) is the price established at time 0 for a forward contract expiring at time T. Let c_0 and p_0 be the prices today of calls and puts on the forward contract. We shall assume that the puts and calls expire when the forward contract expires. The exercise price of the options is X. The payoff of the call is $\text{Max}(0,S_T - X)$, and the payoff of the put is $\text{Max}(0,X - S_T)$.[37] We construct a combination consisting of a long call and a long position in a zero-coupon bond with face value of $X - F(0,T)$. We construct another combination consisting of a long position in a put and a long position in a forward contract. Exhibit 4-31 shows the results.

EXHIBIT 4-31 Portfolio Combinations for Equivalent Packages of Puts, Calls, and Forward Contracts (Put–Call Parity for Forward Contracts)

Transaction	Current Value	Value at Expiration	
		$S_T \leq X$	$S_T > X$
Call and Bond			
Buy call	c_0	0	$S_T - X$
Buy bond	$[X - F(0,T)]/(1 + r)^T$	$X - F(0,T)$	$X - F(0,T)$
Total	$c_0 + [X - F(0,T)]/(1 + r)^T$	$X - F(0,T)$	$S_T - F(0,T)$

---

[36] In other words, we cannot use the European lower bound as the lowest price of an American call or put, as we could with calls when the underlying was an asset instead of a futures.

[37] Recall that the option payoffs are given by the underlying price at expiration, because the forward contract expires when the option expires. Therefore, the forward price at expiration is the underlying price at expiration.

Put and Forward			
Buy put	p_0	$X - S_T$	0
Buy forward contract	0	$S_T - F(0,T)$	$S_T - F(0,T)$
Total	p_0	$X - F(0,T)$	$S_T - F(0,T)$

As the exhibit demonstrates, both combinations produce a payoff of either $X - F(0,T)$ or $S_T - F(0,T)$, whichever is greater. The call and bond combination is thus equivalent to the put and forward contract combination. Hence, to prevent an arbitrage opportunity, the initial values of these combinations must be the same. The initial value of the call and bond combination is $c_0 + [X - F(0,T)]/(1 + r)^T$. The forward contract has zero initial value, so the initial value of the put and forward contract combination is only the initial value of the put, p_0. Therefore,

$$c_0 + [X - F(0,T)]/(1 + r)^T = p_0 \tag{4-28}$$

This equation is **put–call parity for options on forward contracts**.

Note that we seem to have implied that the bond is a long position, but that might not be the case. The bond should have a face value of $X - F(0,T)$. We learned in Chapter 2 that $F(0,T)$ is determined in the market as the underlying price compounded at the risk-free rate.[38] Because there are a variety of options with different exercise prices, any one of which could be chosen, it is clearly possible for X to exceed or be less than $F(0,T)$. If $X > F(0,T)$, we are long the bond, because the payoff of $X - F(0,T)$ is greater than zero, meaning that we get back money from the bond. If $X < F(0,T)$, we issue the bond, because the payoff of $X - F(0,T)$ is less than zero, meaning that we must pay back money. Note the special case when $X = F(0,T)$. The bond is effectively out of the picture. Then $c_0 = p_0$.

Now recall from Chapter 2 that with discrete interest compounding and no storage costs, the forward price is the spot price compounded at the risk-free rate. So,

$$F(0,T) = S_0(1 + r)^T$$

If we substitute this result for $F(0,T)$ in the put–call parity equation for options on forwards, we obtain

$$p_0 + S_0 = c_0 + X/(1 + r)^T$$

which is the put–call parity equation for options on the underlying that we learned earlier in this chapter. Indeed, put–call parity for options on forwards and put–call parity for options on the underlying asset are the same. The only difference is that in the former, the forward contract and the bond replace the underlying. Given the equivalence of options on the forward contract and options on the underlying, we can refer to put–call parity for options on forwards as **put–call–forward parity**. The equation

$$c_0 + [X - F(0,T)]/(1 + r)^T = p_0$$

expresses the relationship between the forward price and the prices of the options on the underlying asset, or alternatively between the forward price and the prices of options on the forward contract. We can also rearrange the equation to isolate the forward price and obtain

$$F(0,T) = (c_0 - p_0)(1 + r)^T + X$$

---

[38] We are, of course, assuming no cash flows or costs on the underlying asset.

which shows how the forward price is related to the put and call prices and to the exercise price.

Now observe in Exhibit 4-32 how a synthetic forward contract can be created out of options.

EXHIBIT 4-32   Forward Contract and Synthetic Forward Contract

Transaction	Current Value	Value at Expiration	
		$S_T \leq X$	$S_T > X$
Forward Contract			
Long forward contract	0	$S_T - F(0,T)$	$S_T - F(0,T)$
Synthetic Forward Contract			
Buy call	c_0	0	$S_T - X$
Sell put	$-p_0$	$-(X - S_T)$	0
Buy (or sell) bond	$[X - F(0,T)]/(1 + r)^T$	$X - F(0,T)$	$X - F(0,T)$
Total	$c_0 - p_0 + [X - F(0,T)]/(1 + r)^T$	$S_T - F(0,T)$	$S_T - F(0,T)$

In the top half of the exhibit is a forward contract. Its payoff at expiration is $S_T - F(0,T)$. In the bottom half of the exhibit is a **synthetic forward contract**, which consists of a long call, a short put, and a long risk-free bond with a face value equal to the exercise price minus the forward price. Note that this bond can actually be short if the exercise price of these options is lower than the forward price. The forward contract and synthetic forward contract have the same payoffs, so their initial values must be equal. The initial value of the forward contract is zero, so the initial value of the synthetic forward contract must be zero. Thus,

$$c_0 - p_0 + [X - F(0,T)]/(1 + r)^T = 0$$

Solving for $F(0,T)$, we obtain the equation for the forward price in terms of the call, put, and bond that was given previously. So a synthetic forward contract is a combination consisting of a long call, a short put, and a zero-coupon bond with face value of $X - F(0,T)$.

Consider the following example: The options and a forward contract expire in 50 days, so $T = 50/365 = 0.1370$. The risk-free rate is 6 percent, and the exercise price is 95. The call price is 5.50, the put price is 10.50, and the forward price is 90.72. Substituting in the above equation, we obtain

$$5.50 - 10.50 + \frac{95 - 90.72}{(1.06)^{0.1370}} = -0.7540$$

which is supposed to be zero. The left-hand side replicates a forward contract. Thus, the synthetic forward is underpriced. We buy it and sell the actual forward contract. So if we buy the call, sell the put, and buy the bond with face value $95 - 90.72 = 4.28$, we bring in 0.7540. At expiration, the payoffs are as follows.

The options and forward expire with the underlying above 95:

The bond matures and pays off $95 - 90.72 = 4.28$.

Exercise the call, paying 95 and obtaining the underlying.

Deliver the underlying and receive 90.72 from the forward contract.

The put expires with no value.

Net effect: No money in or out.

The options and forward expire with the underlying at or below 95:

The bond matures and pays off 95 − 90.72 = 4.28.

Buy the underlying for 95 with the short put.

Deliver the underlying and receive 90.72 from the forward contract.

The call expires with no value.

Net effect: No money in or out.

So we take in 0.7540 up front and never have to pay anything out. The pressure of other investors doing this will cause the call price to increase and the put price to decrease until the above equation equals zero or is at least equal to the transaction costs that would be incurred to exploit any discrepancy from zero.

Similarly, an option can be created from a forward contract. If a long forward contract is equivalent to a long call, short put, and zero-coupon bond with face value of $X - F(0,T)$, then a long call is a long forward, long put, and a zero-coupon bond with face value of $F(0,T) - X$. A long put is a long call, short forward, and a bond with face value of $X - F(0,T)$. These results are obtained just by rearranging what we learned here about forwards and options.

These results hold strictly for European options; some additional considerations exist for American options, but we do not cover them here.

PRACTICE PROBLEM 10

Determine if a forward contract is correctly priced by using put–call–forward parity. The option exercise price is 90, the risk-free rate is 5 percent, the options and the forward contract expire in two years, the call price is 15.25, the put price is 3.00, and the forward price is 101.43.

SOLUTION

First note that the time to expiration is T = 2.0. There are many ways to express put–call–forward parity. We use the following specification:

$$p_0 = c_0 + [X - F(0,T)]/(1 + r)^T$$

The right-hand side is the synthetic put and consists of a long call, a short forward contract, and a bond with face value of $X - F(0,T)$. Substituting the values into the right-hand side, we obtain

$$p_0 = 15.25 + (90 - 101.43)/(1.05)^{2.0} = 4.88$$

Because the actual put is selling for 3.00, it is underpriced. So we should buy the put and sell the synthetic put. To sell the synthetic put we should sell the call, buy the forward contract, and hold a bond with face value $F(0,T) - X$. Doing so will generate the following cash flow up front:

Buy put: −3.00

Sell call: +15.25

Buy bond: $-(101.43 - 90)/(1.05)^{2.0} = -10.37$

Total: $+1.88$

Thus the transaction brings in 1.88 up front. The payoffs at expiration are

	$S_T < 90$	$S_T \geq 90$
Long put	$90 - S_T$	0
Short call	0	$-(S_T - 90)$
Long bond	$101.43 - 90$	$101.43 - 90$
Long forward	$S_T - 101.43$	$S_T - 101.43$
Total	0	0

Therefore, no money flows in or out at expiration.

8.2 EARLY EXERCISE OF AMERICAN OPTIONS ON FORWARD AND FUTURES CONTRACTS

As we noted earlier, the holder of an American put option may want to exercise it early. For American call options on underlying assets that make no cash payments, however, there is no justification for exercising the option early. If the underlying asset makes a cash payment, such as a dividend on a stock or interest on a bond, it may be justifiable to exercise the call option early.

For American options on futures, it may be worthwhile to exercise both calls and puts early. Even though early exercise is never justified for American calls on underlying assets that make no cash payments, early exercise can be justified for American call options on futures. Deep-in-the money American call options on futures behave almost identically to the underlying, but the investor has money tied up in the call. If the holder exercises the call and establishes a futures position, he earns interest on the futures margin account. A similar argument holds for deep-in-the-money American put options on futures. The determination of the timing of early exercise is a specialist topic so we do not explore it here.

If the option is on a forward contract instead of a futures contract, however, these arguments are overshadowed by the fact that a forward contract does not pay off until expiration, in contrast to the mark-to-market procedure of futures contracts. Thus, if one exercised either a call or a put on a forward contract early, doing so would only establish a long or short position in a forward contract. This position would not pay any cash until expiration. No justification exists for exercising early if one cannot generate any cash from the exercise. Therefore, an American call on a forward contract is the same as a European call on a forward contract, but American calls on futures are different from European calls on futures and carry higher prices.

8.3 THE BLACK MODEL

The usual model for pricing European options on futures is called the Black model, named after Fischer Black of Black–Scholes–Merton fame. The formula is

$$c = e^{-r^c T}[f_0(T)N(d_1) - XN(d_2)]$$
$$p = e^{-r^c T}(X[1 - N(d_2)] - f_0(T)[1 - N(d_1)])$$

where

$$d_1 = \frac{\ln(f_0(T)/X) + (\sigma^2/2)T}{\sigma\sqrt{T}}$$

$$d_2 = d_1 - \sigma\sqrt{T}$$

$f_0(T)$ = the futures price

and the other terms are those we have previously used. The volatility, σ, is the volatility of the continuously compounded change in the futures price.[39]

Although the Black model may appear to give a somewhat different formula, it can be obtained directly from the Black–Scholes–Merton formula. Recall that the futures price in terms of the underlying spot price would be $f_0(T) = S_0 e^{r^c T}$. If we substitute the right-hand-side for $f_0(T)$ in the Black formula for d_1, we obtain the Black–Scholes–Merton formula for d_1.[40] Then if we substitute the right-hand side of the above for $f_0(T)$ in the Black formula for c_0 and p_0, we obtain the Black–Scholes–Merton formula for c_0 and p_0. These substitutions should make sense: The prices of options on futures equal the prices of options on the asset when the options and futures expire simultaneously.

The procedure should be straightforward if you have mastered substituting the asset price and other inputs into the Black–Scholes–Merton formula. Also, note that as with the Black–Scholes–Merton formula, the formula applies only to European options. As we noted in the previous section, early exercise of American options on futures is often justified, so we cannot get away with using this formula for American options on futures. We can, however, use the formula for American options on forwards, because they are never exercised early.

PRACTICE PROBLEM 11

The price of a forward contract is 139.19. A European option on the forward contract expires in 215 days. The exercise price is 125. The continuously compounded risk-free rate is 4.25 percent. The volatility is 0.15.

A. Use the Black model to determine the price of the call option.

B. Determine the price of the underlying from the above information and use the Black–Scholes–Merton model to show that the price of an option on the underlying is the same as the price of the option on the forward.

SOLUTIONS

The time to expiration is $T = 215/365 = 0.5890$.

A. First find d_1 and d_2, then $N(d_1)$ and $N(d_2)$, and then the call price:

$$d_1 = \frac{\ln(139.19/125) + [(0.15)^2/2]0.5890}{0.15\sqrt{0.5890}} = 0.9916$$

$$d_2 = 0.9916 - 0.15\sqrt{0.5890} = 0.8765$$

---

[39] If we were using the model to price options on forward contracts, we would insert F(0,T), the forward price, instead of the futures price. Doing so would produce some confusion because we have never subscripted the forward price, arguing that it does not change. Therefore, although we could use the formula to price options on forwards at time 0, how could we use the formula to price options on forwards at a later time, say time t, prior to expiration? In that case, we would have to use the price of a newly constructed forward contract that expires at T, F(t,T). Of course, with constant interest rates, these forward prices, F(0,T) and F(t,T), would be identical to the analogous futures price, $f_0(T)$ and $f_t(T)$. So, for ease of exposition we use the futures price.

[40] This action requires us to recognize that $\ln(S_0 e^{r^c T}/X) = \ln(S_0/X) + r^c T$.

$$N(0.99) = 0.8389$$

$$N(0.88) = 0.8106$$

$$c = e^{-0.0425(0.5890)}[139.19(0.8389) - 125(0.8106)] = 15.06$$

B. We learned in Chapter 2 that if there are no cash flows on the underlying and the interest is compounded continuously, the forward price is given by the formula $F(0, T) = S_0 e^{rcT}$. We can thus find the spot price as

$$S_0 = F(0,T)e^{-rcT} = 139.19e^{-0.0425(0.5890)} = 135.75$$

Then we simply use the Black–Scholes–Merton formula:

$$d_1 = \frac{\ln(135.75/125) + (0.0425 + (0.15)^2/2)(0.5890)}{0.15\sqrt{0.5890}} = 0.9916$$

$$d_2 = 0.9916 - 0.15\sqrt{0.5890} = 0.8765$$

These are the same values as in Part A, so $N(d_1)$ and $N(d_2)$ will be the same. Plugging into the formula for the call price gives

$$c = 135.75(0.8389) - 125e^{-0.0425(0.5890)}(0.8106) = 15.06$$

This price is the same as in Part A.

8.4 APPLICATION OF THE BLACK MODEL TO INTEREST RATE OPTIONS

Earlier in this chapter, we described options on interest rates. These derivative instruments parallel the FRAs that we covered in Chapter 2, in that they are derivatives in which the underlying is not a bond but rather an interest rate. Pricing options on interest rates is a challenging task. We showed how this is done using binomial trees. It would be nice if the Black–Scholes–Merton model could be easily used to price interest rate options, but the process is not so straightforward. Pricing options on interest rates requires a sophisticated model that prohibits arbitrage among interest-rate related instruments and their derivatives. The Black–Scholes–Merton model is not sufficiently general to use in this manner. Nonetheless, practitioners often employ the Black model to price interest rate options. Somewhat remarkably, perhaps, it is known to give satisfactory results. Therefore, we provide a quick overview of this practice here.

Suppose we wish to price a one-year interest rate cap, consisting of three caplets. One caplet expires in 90 days, one 180 days, and one in 270 days.[41] The exercise rate is 9 percent. To use the Black model, we use the forward rate as though it were $f_0(T)$.

---

[41] A one-year cap will have three individual caplets. The first expires in 90 days and pays off in 180 days, the second expires in 180 days and pays off in 270 days, and the third expires in 270 days and pays off in 360 days. The tendency to think that a one-year cap using quarterly periods should have four caplets is incorrect because there is no caplet expiring right now and paying off in 90 days. It would make no sense to create an option that expires immediately. Also, in a one-year loan, the rate is set at the start and reset only three times; hence, only three caplets are required.

Therefore, we also require its volatility and the risk-free rate for the period to the option's expiration.[42] Recalling that there are three caplets and we have to price each one individually, let us first focus on the caplet expiring in 90 days. We first specify that T = 90/365 = 0.2466. Then we need the forward rate today for the period day 90 to day 180. Let this rate be 9.25 percent. We shall assume its volatility is 0.03. We then need the continuously compounded risk-free rate for 90 days, which we assume to be 9.60 percent. So now we have the following input variables:

$$T = 0.2466$$

$$f_0(T) = 0.0925$$

$$\sigma = 0.03$$

$$X = 0.09$$

$$r^c = 0.096$$

Inserting these inputs into the Black model produces

$$d_1 = \frac{\ln(0.0925/0.09) + [(0.03)^2/2](0.2466)}{0.03\sqrt{0.2466}} = 1.8466$$

$$d_2 = 1.8466 - 0.03\sqrt{0.2466} = 1.8317$$

$$N(1.85) = 0.9678$$

$$N(1.83) = 0.9664$$

$$c_0 = e^{-0.096(0.2466)}[0.0925(0.9678) - 0.09(0.9664)] = 0.00248594$$

(Because of the order of magnitude of the inputs, we carry the answer out to eight decimal places.) But this answer is not quite what we need. The formula gives the answer under the assumption that the option payoff occurs at the option expiration. As we know, interest rate options pay off later than their expirations. This option expires in 90 days and pays off 90 days after that. Therefore, we need to discount this result back from day 180 to day 90 using the forward rate of 9.25 percent.[43] We thus have

$$0.00248594e^{-0.0925(0.2466)} = 0.00242988$$

Another adjustment is necessary. Because the underlying price and exercise price are entered as rates, the resulting answer is a rate. Moreover, the underlying rate and exercise rate are expressed as annual rates, so the answer is an annual rate. Interest rate option

---

[42] It is important to note here that the Black model requires that all inputs be in continuous compounding format. Therefore, the forward rate and risk-free rate would need to be the continuously compounded analogs to the discrete rates. Because the underlying is usually LIBOR, which is a discrete rate quoted on the basis of a 360-day year, some adjustments must be made to convert to a continuous rate quoted on the basis of a 365-day year. We will not address these adjustments here.

[43] Be very careful in this discounting procedure. The exponent in the exponential should have a time factor of the number of days between the option expiration and its payoff. Because there are 90 days between days 90 and 180, we use 90/365 = 0.2466. This value is not quite the same as the time until the option expiration, which today is 90 but which will count down to zero.

prices are always quoted as periodic rates (which are prices for $1 notional principal). We would adjust this rate by multiplying by 90/360.[44] The price would thus be

$$0.00242988(90/360) = 0.00060747$$

Finally, we should note that this price is valid for a $1 notional principal option. If the notional principal were $1 million, the option price would be

$$\$1,000,000(0.00060747) = \$607.47$$

We have just priced the first caplet of this cap. To price the second caplet, we need the forward rate for the period 180 days to 270 days, we would use 180/365 = 0.4932 as the time to expiration, and we need the risk-free rate for 180 days. To price the third caplet, we need the forward rate for the period 270 days to 360 days, we would use 270/365 = 0.7397 as the time to expiration, and we need the risk-free rate for 270 days. The price of the cap would be the sum of the prices of the three component caplets. If we were pricing a floor, we would price the component floorlets using the Black model for puts.

Although the Black model is frequently used to price interest rate options, binomial models, as we illustrated earlier, are somewhat more widely used in this area. These models are more attuned to deriving prices that prohibit arbitrage opportunities using any of the diverse instruments whose prices are given by the term structure. When you use the Black model to price interest rate options, there is some risk, perhaps minor, of having a counterparty be able to do arbitrage against you. Yet somehow the Black model is used often, and professionals seem to agree that it works remarkably well.

PRACTICE PROBLEM 12

Use the Black model to price an interest rate put that expires in 280 days. The forward rate is currently 6.8 percent, the 280-day continuously compounded risk-free rate is 6.25 percent, the exercise rate is 7 percent, and the volatility is 0.02. The option is based on a 180-day underlying rate, and the notional principal is $10 million.

SOLUTION

The time to expiration is T = 280/365 = 0.7671. Calculate the value of d_1, d_2, and $N(d_1)$, $N(d_2)$, and p_0 using the Black model:

$$d_1 = \frac{\ln(0.068/0.07) + [(0.02)^2/2]0.7671}{0.02\sqrt{0.7671}} = 1.6461$$

$$d_2 = -1.6461 - 0.02\sqrt{0.7671} = -1.6636$$

$$N(-1.65) = 1 - N(1.65) = 1 - 0.9505 = 0.0495$$

$$N(-1.66) = 1 - N(1.66) = 1 - 0.9515 = 0.0485$$

$$p_0 = e^{-0.0625(0.7671)}[0.07(1 - 0.0485) - 0.068(1 - 0.0495)] = 0.00187873$$

---

[44] It is customary in the interest rate options market to use 360 in the denominator to make this adjustment, even though we have used 365 in other places.

This formula assumes the option payoff is made at expiration. For an interest rate option, that assumption is false. This is a 180-day rate, so the payoff is made 180 days later. Therefore, we discount the payoff over 180 days using the forward rate:

$$e^{-0.068(180/365)}(0.00187873) = 0.00181677$$

Interest rate option prices must reflect the fact that the rate used in the formula is quoted as an annual rate. So, we must multiply by 180/360 because the transaction is based on a 180-day rate:

$$0.00181677(180/360) = 0.00090839$$

Then we multiply by the notional principal:

$$\$10,000,000(0.00090839) = \$9,084$$

9   THE ROLE OF OPTIONS MARKETS

As we did with futures markets, we conclude the chapter by looking at the important role options markets play in the financial system. Recall from Chapter 1 that we looked at the purposes of derivative markets. We noted that derivative markets provide price discovery and risk management, make the markets for the underlying assets more efficient, and permit trading at low transaction costs. These features are also associated with options markets. Yet, options offer further advantages that some other derivatives do not offer.

For example, forward and futures contracts have bidirectional payoffs. They have the potential for a substantial gain in one direction and a substantial loss in the other direction. The advantage of taking such a position lies in the fact that one need pay no cash up front. In contrast, options offer the feature that, if one is willing to pay cash up front, one can limit the loss in a given direction. In other words, options have unidirectional payoffs. This feature can be attractive to the holder of an option. To the writer, options offer the opportunity to be paid cash up front for a willingness to assume the risk of the unidirectional payoff. An option writer can assume the risk of potentially a large loss unmatched by the potential for a large gain. In fact, the potential gain is small. But for this risk, the option writer receives money up front.

Options also offer excellent devices for managing the risk of various exposures. An obvious one is the protective put, which we saw earlier and which can protect a position against loss by paying off when the value of the underlying is down. We shall see this and other such applications in Chapter 7.

Recall that futures contracts offer price discovery, the revelation of the prices at which investors will contract today for transactions to take place later. Options, on the other hand, provide volatility discovery. Through the implied volatility, investors can determine the market's assessment of how volatile it believes the underlying asset is. This valuable information can be difficult to obtain from any other source.

Futures offer advantages over forwards, in that futures are standardized, tend to be actively traded in a secondary market, and are protected by the exchange's clearinghouse against credit risk. Although some options, such as interest rate options, are available only in over-the-counter forms, many options exist in both over-the-counter and exchange-listed forms. Hence, one can often customize an option if necessary or trade it on an exchange.

In Chapter 2, we covered forward contracts; in Chapter 3, we covered futures contracts; and in this chapter we covered option contracts. We have one more major class of derivative instruments, swaps, which we now turn to in Chapter 5. We shall return to options in Chapter 7, where we explore option trading strategies.

KEY POINTS

- Options are rights to buy or sell an underlying at a fixed price, the exercise price, for a period of time. The right to buy is a call; the right to sell is a put. Options have a definite expiration date. Using the option to buy or sell is the action of exercising it. The buyer or holder of an option pays a price to the seller or writer for the right to buy (a call) or sell (a put) the underlying instrument. The writer of an option has the corresponding potential obligation to sell or buy the underlying.

- European options can be exercised only at expiration; American options can be exercised at any time prior to expiration. Moneyness refers to the characteristic that an option has positive intrinsic value. The payoff is the value of the option at expiration. An option's intrinsic value is the value that can be captured if the option is exercised. Time value is the component of an option's price that reflects the uncertainty of what will happen in the future to the price of the underlying.

- Options can be traded as standardized instruments on an options exchange, where they are protected from default on the part of the writer, or as customized instruments on the over-the-counter market, where they are subject to the possibility of the writer defaulting. Because the buyer pays a price at the start and does not have to do anything else, the buyer cannot default.

- The underlying instruments for options are individual stocks, stock indices, bonds, interest rates, currencies, futures, commodities, and even such random factors as the weather. In addition, a class of options called real options is associated with the flexibility in capital investment projects.

- Like FRAs, which are forward contracts in which the underlying is an interest rate, interest rate options are options in which the underlying is an interest rate. However, FRAs are commitments to make one interest payment and receive another, whereas interest rate options are rights to make one interest payment and receive another.

- Option payoffs, which are the values of options when they expire, are determined by the greater of zero or the difference between underlying price and exercise price, if a call, or the greater of zero or the difference between exercise price and underlying price, if a put. For interest rate options, the exercise price is a specified rate and the underlying price is a variable interest rate.

- Interest rate options exist in the form of caps, which are call options on interest rates, and floors, which are put options on interest rates. Caps consist of a series of call options, called caplets, on an underlying rate, with each option expiring at a different time. Floors consist of a series of put options, called floorlets, on an underlying rate, with each option expiring at a different time.

- The minimum value of European and American calls and puts is zero. The maximum value of European and American calls is the underlying price. The maximum value of a European put is the present value of the exercise price. The maximum value of an American put is the exercise price.

- The lower bound of a European call is established by constructing a portfolio consisting of a long call and risk-free bond and a short position in the underlying asset. This combination produces a non-negative value at expiration, so its current value must be non-negative. For this situation to occur, the call price has to be worth at least the underlying price minus the present value of the exercise price. The lower bound of a European put is established by constructing a portfolio consisting of a long put, a long position in the underlying, and the issuance of a zero-coupon bond. This combination produces a non-negative value at expiration so its current value must be non-negative. For this to occur, the put price has to be at least as much as the present value of the exercise price minus the underlying price. For both calls and puts, if this lower bound is negative, we invoke the rule that an option price can be no lower than zero.

- The lowest price of a European call is referred to as the lower bound. The lowest price of an American call is also the lower bound of a European call. The lowest price of a European put is also referred to as the lower bound. The lowest price of an American put, however, is its intrinsic value.

- Buying a call with a given exercise price and selling an otherwise identical call with a higher exercise price creates a combination that always pays off with a non-negative value. Therefore, its current value must be non-negative. For this to occur, the call with the lower exercise price must be worth at least as much as the other call. A similar argument holds for puts, except that one would buy the put with the higher exercise price. This line of reasoning shows that the put with the higher exercise price must be worth at least as much as the one with the lower exercise price.

- A longer-term European or American call must be worth at least as much as a corresponding shorter-term European or American call. A longer-term American put must be worth at least as much as a shorter-term American put. A longer-term European put, however, can be worth more or less than a shorter-term European put.

- A fiduciary call, consisting of a European call and a zero-coupon bond, produces the same payoff as a protective put, consisting of the underlying and a European put. Therefore, their current values must be the same. For this equivalence to occur, the call price plus bond price must equal the underlying price plus put price. This relationship is called put–call parity and can be used to identify combinations of instruments that synthesize another instrument by rearranging the equation to isolate the instrument you are trying to create. Long positions are indicated by positive signs, and short positions are indicated by negative signs. One can create a synthetic call, a synthetic put, a synthetic underlying, and a synthetic bond, as well as synthetic short positions in these instruments for the purpose of exploiting mispricing in these instruments.

- Put–call parity violations exist when one side of the equation does not equal the other. An arbitrageur buys the lower-priced side and sells the higher-priced side, thereby earning the difference in price, and the positions offset at expiration. The combined actions of many arbitrageurs performing this set of transactions would increase the demand and price for the underpriced instruments and decrease the demand and price for the overpriced instruments, until the put–call parity relationship is upheld.

- American option prices must always be no less than those of otherwise equivalent European options. American call options, however, are never exercised early unless there is a cash flow on the underlying, so they can sell for the same as their European counterparts in the absence of such a cash flow. American put options nearly always have a possibility of early exercise, so they ordinarily sell for more than their European counterparts.

- Cash flows on the underlying affect an option's boundary conditions and put–call parity by lowering the underlying price by the present value of the cash flows over the life of the option.

- A higher interest rate increases a call option's price and decreases a put option's price.

- In a one-period binomial model, the underlying asset can move up to one of two prices. A portfolio consisting of a long position in the underlying and a short position in a call option can be made risk-free and, therefore, must return the risk-free rate. Under this condition, the option price can be obtained by inferring it from a formula that uses the other input values. The option price is a weighted average of the two option prices at expiration, discounted back one period at the risk-free rate.

- If an option is trading for a price higher than that given in the binomial model, one can sell the option and buy a specific number of units of the underlying, as given by the model. This combination is risk free but will earn a return higher than the risk-free rate. If the option is trading for a price lower than the price given in the binomial model, a short position in a specific number of units of the underlying and a long position in the option will create a risk-free loan that costs less than the risk-free rate.

- In a two-period binomial model, the underlying can move to one of two prices in each of two periods; thus three underlying prices are possible at the option expiration. To price an option, start at the expiration and work backward, following the procedure in the one-period model in which an option price at any given point in time is a weighted average of the next two possible prices discounted at the risk-free rate.

- To calculate the price of an option on a zero-coupon bond or a coupon bond, one must first construct a binomial tree of the price of the bond over the life of the option. To calculate the price of an option on an interest rate, one should use a binomial tree of interest rates. Then the option price is found by starting at the option expiration, determining the payoff and successively working backwards by computing the option price as the weighted average of the next two option prices discounted back one period. For the case of options on bonds or interest rates, a different discount rate is used at different parts of the tree.

- For an option of a given expiration, a greater pricing accuracy is obtained by dividing the option's life into a greater number of time periods in a binomial tree. As more time periods are added, the discrete-time binomial price converges to a stable value as though the option is being modeled in a continuous-time world.

- The assumptions under which the Black–Scholes–Merton model is derived state that the underlying asset follows a geometric lognormal diffusion process, the risk-free rate is known and constant, the volatility of the underlying asset is known and constant, there are no taxes or transaction costs, there are no cash flows on the underlying, and the options are European.

- To calculate the value of an option using the Black–Scholes–Merton model, enter the underlying price, exercise price, risk-free rate, volatility, and time to expiration into a formula. The formula will require you to look up two normal probabilities, obtained from either a table or preferably a computer routine.

- The change in the option price for a change in the price of the underlying is called the delta. The change in the option price for a change in the risk-free rate is called the rho. The change in the option price for a change in the time to expiration is called the theta. The change in the option price for a change in the volatility is called the vega.

- The delta is defined as the change in the option price divided by the change in the underlying price. The option price change can be approximated by the delta times the change in the underlying price. To construct a delta-hedged position, a short (long) position in each option is matched with a long (short) position in delta units of the underlying. Changes in the underlying price will generate offsetting changes in the value of the option position, provided the changes in the underlying price are small and occur over a short time period. A delta-hedged position should be adjusted as the delta changes and time passes.

- If changes in the price of the underlying are large or the delta hedge is not adjusted over a longer time period, the hedge may not be effective. This effect is due to the instability of the delta and is called the gamma effect. If the gamma effect is large, option price changes will not be very close to the changes as approximated by the delta times the underlying price change.

- Cash flows on the underlying are accommodated in option pricing models by reducing the price of the underlying by the present value of the cash flows over the life of the option.

- Volatility can be estimated by calculating the standard deviation of the continuously compounded returns from a sample of recent data for the underlying. This is called the historical volatility. An alternative measure, called the implied volatility, can be obtained by setting the Black–Scholes–Merton model price equal to the market price and inferring the volatility. The implied volatility is a measure of the volatility the market is using to price the option.

- The payoffs of a call on a forward contract and an appropriately chosen zero-coupon bond are equivalent to the payoffs of a put on the forward contract and the forward contract. Thus, their current values must be the same. For this equality to occur, the call price plus the bond price must equal the put price. The appropriate zero-coupon bond is one with a face value equal to the exercise price minus the forward price. This relationship is called put–call–forward (or futures) parity.

- There is no justification for exercising American options on forward contracts early, so they are equivalent to European options on forwards. American options on futures, both calls and puts, can sometimes be exercised early, so they are different from European options on futures and carry a higher price.

- The Black model can be used to price European options on forwards or futures by entering the forward price, exercise price, risk-free rate, time to expiration, and volatility into a formula that will also require the determination of two normal probabilities.

- The Black model can be used to price European options on interest rates by entering the forward interest rate into the model for the forward or futures price and the exercise rate for the exercise price.

- Options are useful in financial markets because they provide a way to limit losses to the premium paid while permitting potentially large gains. They can be used for hedging purposes, especially in the case of puts, which can be used to limit the loss on a long position in an asset. Options also provide information on the volatility of the underlying asset. Options can be standardized and exchange-traded or customized in the over-the-counter market.

APPENDIX 4A Cumulative Probabilities for a Standard Normal Distribution
$P(X \leq x) = N(x)$ for $x \geq 0$ or $1 - N(-x)$ for $x < 0$

x	0	0.01	0.02	0.03	0.04	0.05	0.06	0.07	0.08	0.09
0.00	0.5000	0.5040	0.5080	0.5120	0.5160	0.5199	0.5239	0.5279	0.5319	0.5359
0.10	0.5398	0.5438	0.5478	0.5517	0.5557	0.5596	0.5636	0.5675	0.5714	0.5753
0.20	0.5793	0.5832	0.5871	0.5910	0.5948	0.5987	0.6026	0.6064	0.6103	0.6141
0.30	0.6179	0.6217	0.6255	0.6293	0.6331	0.6368	0.6406	0.6443	0.6480	0.6517
0.40	0.6554	0.6591	0.6628	0.6664	0.6700	0.6736	0.6772	0.6808	0.6844	0.6879
0.50	0.6915	0.6950	0.6985	0.7019	0.7054	0.7088	0.7123	0.7157	0.7190	0.7224
0.60	0.7257	0.7291	0.7324	0.7357	0.7389	0.7422	0.7454	0.7486	0.7517	0.7549
0.70	0.7580	0.7611	0.7642	0.7673	0.7704	0.7734	0.7764	0.7794	0.7823	0.7852
0.80	0.7881	0.7910	0.7939	0.7967	0.7995	0.8023	0.8051	0.8078	0.8106	0.8133
0.90	0.8159	0.8186	0.8212	0.8238	0.8264	0.8289	0.8315	0.8340	0.8365	0.8389
1.00	0.8413	0.8438	0.8461	0.8485	0.8508	0.8531	0.8554	0.8577	0.8599	0.8621
1.10	0.8643	0.8665	0.8686	0.8708	0.8729	0.8749	0.8770	0.8790	0.8810	0.8830
1.20	0.8849	0.8869	0.8888	0.8907	0.8925	0.8944	0.8962	0.8980	0.8997	0.9015
1.30	0.9032	0.9049	0.9066	0.9082	0.9099	0.9115	0.9131	0.9147	0.9162	0.9177
1.40	0.9192	0.9207	0.9222	0.9236	0.9251	0.9265	0.9279	0.9292	0.9306	0.9319
1.50	0.9332	0.9345	0.9357	0.9370	0.9382	0.9394	0.9406	0.9418	0.9429	0.9441
1.60	0.9452	0.9463	0.9474	0.9484	0.9495	0.9505	0.9515	0.9525	0.9535	0.9545
1.70	0.9554	0.9564	0.9573	0.9582	0.9591	0.9599	0.9608	0.9616	0.9625	0.9633
1.80	0.9641	0.9649	0.9656	0.9664	0.9671	0.9678	0.9686	0.9693	0.9699	0.9706
1.90	0.9713	0.9719	0.9726	0.9732	0.9738	0.9744	0.9750	0.9756	0.9761	0.9767
2.00	0.9772	0.9778	0.9783	0.9788	0.9793	0.9798	0.9803	0.9808	0.9812	0.9817
2.10	0.9821	0.9826	0.9830	0.9834	0.9838	0.9842	0.9846	0.9850	0.9854	0.9857
2.20	0.9861	0.9864	0.9868	0.9871	0.9875	0.9878	0.9881	0.9884	0.9887	0.9890
2.30	0.9893	0.9896	0.9898	0.9901	0.9904	0.9906	0.9909	0.9911	0.9913	0.9916
2.40	0.9918	0.9920	0.9922	0.9925	0.9927	0.9929	0.9931	0.9932	0.9934	0.9936
2.50	0.9938	0.9940	0.9941	0.9943	0.9945	0.9946	0.9948	0.9949	0.9951	0.9952
2.60	0.9953	0.9955	0.9956	0.9957	0.9959	0.9960	0.9961	0.9962	0.9963	0.9964
2.70	0.9965	0.9966	0.9967	0.9968	0.9969	0.9970	0.9971	0.9972	0.9973	0.9974
2.80	0.9974	0.9975	0.9976	0.9977	0.9977	0.9978	0.9979	0.9979	0.9980	0.9981
2.90	0.9981	0.9982	0.9982	0.9983	0.9984	0.9984	0.9985	0.9985	0.9986	0.9986
3.00	0.9987	0.9987	0.9987	0.9988	0.9988	0.9989	0.9989	0.9989	0.9990	0.9990

PROBLEMS

1. A. Calculate the payoff at expiration for a call option on the S&P 100 stock index in which the underlying price is 579.32 at expiration, the multiplier is 100, and the exercise price is

    i. 450

    ii. 650

  B. Calculate the payoff at expiration for a put option on the S&P 100 in which the underlying is at 579.32 at expiration, the multiplier is 100, and the exercise price is

    i. 450

    ii. 650

2. A. Calculate the payoff at expiration for a call option on a bond in which the underlying is at $0.95 per $1 par at expiration, the contract is on $100,000 face value bonds, and the exercise price is

    i. $0.85

    ii. $1.15

  B. Calculate the payoff at expiration for a put option on a bond in which the underlying is at $0.95 per $1 par at expiration, the contract is on $100,000 face value bonds, and the exercise price is

    i. $0.85

    ii. $1.15

3. A. Calculate the payoff at expiration for a call option on an interest rate in which the underlying is a 180-day interest rate at 6.53 percent at expiration, the notional principal is $10 million, and the exercise price is

    i. 5 percent

    ii. 8 percent

  B. Calculate the payoff at expiration for a put option on an interest rate in which the underlying is a 180-day interest rate at 6.53 percent at expiration, the notional principal is $10 million, and the exercise price is

    i. 5 percent

    ii. 8 percent

4. A. Calculate the payoff at expiration for a call option on the British pound in which the underlying is at $1.438 at expiration, the options are on 125,000 British pounds, and the exercise price is

    i. $1.35

    ii. $1.55

  B. Calculate the payoff at expiration for a put option on the British pound where the underlying is at $1.438 at expiration, the options are on 125,000 British pounds, and the exercise price is

    i. $1.35

    ii. $1.55

5. A. Calculate the payoff at expiration for a call option on a futures contract in which the underlying is at 1136.76 at expiration, the options are on a futures contract for $1,000, and the exercise price is

    i. 1130

    ii. 1140

  B. Calculate the payoff at expiration for a put option on a futures contract in which the underlying is at 1136.76 at expiration, the options are on a futures contract for $1000, and the exercise price is

    i. 1130

    ii. 1140

6. Consider a stock index option that expires in 75 days. The stock index is currently at 1240.89 and makes no cash payments during the life of the option. Assume that the stock index has a multiplier of 1. The risk-free rate is 3 percent.
   A. Calculate the lowest and highest possible prices for European-style call options on the above stock index with exercise prices of
      i. 1225
      ii. 1255
   B. Calculate the lowest and highest possible prices for European-style put options on the above stock index with exercise prices of
      i. 1225
      ii. 1255

7. A. Consider American-style call and put options on a bond. The options expire in 60 days. The bond is currently at $1.05 per $1 par and makes no cash payments during the life of the option. The risk-free rate is 5.5 percent. Assume that the contract is on $1 face value bonds. Calculate the lowest and highest possible prices for the calls and puts with exercise prices of
      i. $0.95
      ii. $1.10
   B. Consider European style call and put options on a bond. The options expire in 60 days. The bond is currently at $1.05 per $1 par and makes no cash payments during the life of the option. The risk-free rate is 5.5 percent. Assume that the contract is on $1 face value bonds. Calculate the lowest and highest possible prices for the calls and puts with exercise prices of
      i. $0.95
      ii. $1.10

8. You are provided with the following information on put and call options on a stock:
   Call price, $c_0 = \$6.64$
   Put price, $p_0 = \$2.75$
   Exercise price, X = $30
   Days to option expiration = 219
   Current stock price, $S_0 = \$33.19$
   Put–call parity shows the equivalence of a call/bond portfolio (fiduciary call) and a put/underlying portfolio (protective put). Illustrate put–call parity assuming stock prices at expiration (S_T) of $20 and of $40. Assume that the risk-free rate, r, is 4 percent.

9. Consider the following information on put and call options on a stock:
   Call price, $c_0 = \$4.50$
   Put price, $p_0 = \$6.80$
   Exercise price, X = $70
   Days to option expiration = 139
   Current stock price, $S_0 = \$67.32$
   Risk-free rate, r = 5 percent
   A. Use put–call parity to calculate prices of the following:
      i. Synthetic call option
      ii. Synthetic put option
      iii. Synthetic bond
      iv. Synthetic underlying stock
   B. For each of the synthetic instruments in Part A, identify any mispricing by comparing the actual price with the synthetic price.
   C. Based on the mispricing in Part B, illustrate an arbitrage transaction using a synthetic call.

   D. Based on the mispricing in Part B, illustrate an arbitrage transaction using a synthetic put.

10. A stock currently trades at a price of $100. The stock price can go up 10 percent or down 15 percent. The risk-free rate is 6.5 percent.
   A. Use a one-period binomial model to calculate the price of a call option with an exercise price of $90.
   B. Suppose the call price is currently $17.50. Show how to execute an arbitrage transaction that will earn more than the risk-free rate. Use 100 call options.
   C. Suppose the call price is currently $14. Show how to execute an arbitrage transaction that replicates a loan that will earn less than the risk-free rate. Use 100 call options.

11. Suppose a stock currently trades at a price of $150. The stock price can go up 33 percent or down 15 percent. The risk-free rate is 4.5 percent.
   A. Use a one-period binomial model to calculate the price of a put option with exercise price of $150.
   B. Suppose the put price is currently $14. Show how to execute an arbitrage transaction that will earn more than the risk-free rate. Use 10,000 put options.
   C. Suppose the put price is currently $11. Show how to execute an arbitrage transaction that will earn more than the risk-free rate. Use 10,000 put options.

12. Consider a two-period binomial model in which a stock currently trades at a price of $65. The stock price can go up 20 percent or down 17 percent each period. The risk-free rate is 5 percent.
   A. Calculate the price of a call option expiring in two periods with an exercise price of $60.
   B. Based on your answer in Part A, calculate the number of units of the underlying stock that would be needed at each point in the binomial tree to construct a risk-free hedge. Use 10,000 calls.
   C. Calculate the price of a call option expiring in two periods with an exercise price of $70.
   D. Based on your answer in Part C, calculate the number of units of the underlying stock that would be needed at each point in the binomial tree to construct a risk-free hedge. Use 10,000 calls.

13. Consider a two-period binomial model in which a stock currently trades at a price of $65. The stock price can go up 20 percent or down 17 percent each period. The risk-free rate is 5 percent.
   A. Calculate the price of a put option expiring in two periods with exercise price of $60.
   B. Based on your answer in Part A, calculate the number of units of the underlying stock that would be needed at each point in the binomial tree in order to construct a risk-free hedge. Use 10,000 puts.
   C. Calculate the price of a put option expiring in two periods with an exercise price of $70.
   D. Based on your answer in Part C, calculate the number of units of the underlying stock that would be needed at each point in the binomial tree in order to construct a risk-free hedge. Use 10,000 puts.

14. The three-period binomial interest rate tree provided below gives one-period interest rates and prices of zero-coupon bonds. Starting at t = 0, you are provided with the one-period interest rate and prices of zero-coupon bonds with maturities of one period, two periods, three periods, and four periods. At t = 1, you are provided with the one-period interest rate and prices of zero-coupon bonds with maturities of one period, two periods, and three periods. At t = 2, you are provided with the one-period interest rate and prices of zero-coupon bonds with maturities of one period and two periods. At t = 3, you are provided with the one-period interest rate and prices of zero-coupon bonds with maturity of one period.

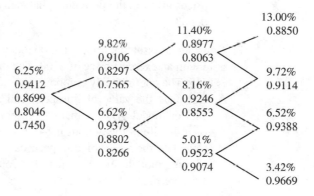

A. Calculate the value of a European call option on a four-period zero-coupon bond. The call option expires in two periods and has an exercise price of 0.85.

B. Calculate the value of a European call option on a four-period 8 percent coupon bond with a 1.0 face value. The call option expires in two periods and has an exercise price of 0.95.

C. Calculate the value of a European put option on a four-period zero-coupon bond. The call option expires in two periods and has an exercise price of 0.85.

D. Calculate the value of a European put option on a four-period 8 percent coupon bond with a 1.0 face value. The put option expires in two periods and has an exercise price of 1.

15. Assume that the evolution of one-period spot rates is still the same as in Problem 14; that is, the same three-period binomial interest rate tree still applies.

A. Calculate the price of a two-period cap with an exercise rate of 8 percent. The underlying is the one-period rate.

B. Calculate the price of a two-period floor with an exercise rate of 9 percent. The underlying is the one-period rate.

16. Call and put options on an asset are available with an exercise price of $30. The options expire in 75 days, and the volatility is 0.40. The continuously compounded risk-free rate is 3.5 percent, and there are no cash flows on the underlying. The precise Black–Scholes–Merton values of these options at different underlying prices are as follows.

Asset Price	Call Price	Put Price
$28	1.3144	3.0994
$29	1.7538	2.5388
$33	4.2270	1.0120

    A. From the Black–Scholes–Merton model, obtain the approximate values of the call delta and put delta if the underlying asset price is $28.

    B. Using the call delta and put delta obtained in Part A and the call and put prices given in the problem for the asset price of $28, calculate the approximate new call and put prices for a

      i. $1 increase in the price of the underlying asset

      ii. $5 increase in the price of the underlying asset

    C. Based on a comparison of your answers in Part B with the actual call and put prices given in the problem, what can you say about the approximations based on delta?

17. Consider an asset that trades at $100 today. Call and put options on this asset are available with an exercise price of $100. The options expire in 275 days, and the volatility is 0.45. The continuously compounded risk-free rate is 3 percent.

    A. Calculate the value of European call and put options using the Black–Scholes–Merton model. Assume that the present value of cash flows on the underlying asset over the life of the options is $4.25.

    B. Calculate the value of European call and put options using the Black–Scholes–Merton model. Assume that the continuously compounded dividend yield is 1.5 percent.

18. Consider the following information on put and call options on an asset:

Call price, $c_0 = \$3.50$

Put price, $p_0 = \$9$

Exercise price, $X = \$50$

Forward price, $F(0,T) = \$45$

Days to option expiration $= 175$

Risk-free rate, $r = 4$ percent

    A. Use put–call–forward parity to calculate prices of the following:

      i. Synthetic call option

      ii. Synthetic put option

      iii. Synthetic forward contract

    B. For each of the synthetic instruments in Part A, identify any mispricing by comparing the actual price with the synthetic price.

    C. Based on the mispricing in Part B, illustrate how to earn a risk-free profit using a synthetic call.

    D. Based on the mispricing in Part B, illustrate how to earn a risk-free profit using a synthetic put.

19. A forward contract is priced at 145. European options on the forward contract have an exercise price of 150 and expire in 65 days. The continuously compounded risk-free rate is 3.75 percent, and volatility is 0.33.

    A. Calculate the price of a call option on the forward contract using the Black model.

    B. Calculate the price of the underlying asset. Calculate the price of a call option on the underlying asset using the Black–Scholes–Merton model. Compare your answer here with the answer in Part A.

    C. Calculate the price of a put option on the forward contract using the Black model.

    D. Now calculate the price of a put option on the underlying asset using the Black–Scholes–Merton model. Compare your answer here with the answer in Part C.

20. A. An interest rate call option based on a 90-day underlying rate has an exercise rate of 7.5 percent and expires in 180 days. The forward rate is 7.25 percent, and the volatility is 0.04. The continuously compounded risk-free rate is 5 percent. Calculate the price of the interest rate call option using the Black model.

   B. An interest rate put option based on a 90-day underlying rate has an exercise rate of 7.5 percent and expires in 180 days. The forward rate is 7.25 percent, and the volatility is 0.04. The continuously compounded risk-free rate is 5 percent. Calculate the price of the interest rate put option using the Black model.

SOLUTIONS

1. **A.** $S_T = 579.32$
   i. Call payoff, $X = 450$: $\text{Max}(0,579.32 - 450) \times 100 = \$12,932$
   ii. Call payoff, $X = 650$: $\text{Max}(0,579.32 - 650) \times 100 = 0$
   B. $S_T = 579.32$
   i. Put payoff, $X = 450$: $\text{Max}(0,450 - 579.32) \times 100 = 0$
   ii. Put payoff, $X = 650$: $\text{Max}(0,650 - 579.32) \times 100 = \$7,068$

2. **A.** $S_T = \$0.95$
   i. Call payoff, $X = 0.85$: $\text{Max}(0,0.95 - 0.85) \times 100,000 = \$10,000$
   ii. Call payoff, $X = 1.15$: $\text{Max}(0,0.95 - 1.15) \times 100,000 = \$0$
   B. $S_T = \$0.95$
   i. Put payoff, $X = 0.85$: $\text{Max}(0,0.85 - 0.95) \times 100,000 = \$0$
   ii. Put payoff, $X = 1.15$: $\text{Max}(0,1.15 - 0.95) \times 100,000 = \$20,000$

3. **A.** $S_T = 0.0653$
   i. Call payoff, $X = 0.05$: $\text{Max}(0,0.0653 - 0.05) \times (180/360) \times 10,000,000 = \$76,500$
   ii. Call payoff, $X = 0.08$: $\text{Max}(0,0.0653 - 0.08) \times (180/360) \times 10,000,000 = 0$
   B. $S_T = 0.0653$
   i. Put payoff, $X = 0.05$: $\text{Max}(0,0.05 - 0.0653) \times (180/360) \times 10,000,000 = 0$
   ii. Put payoff, $X = 0.08$: $\text{Max}(0,0.08 - 0.0653) \times (180/360) \times 10,000,000 = \$73,500$

4. **A.** $S_T = \$1.438$
   i. Call payoff, $X = 1.35$: $\text{Max}(0,1.438 - 1.35) \times 125,000 = \$11,000$
   ii. Call payoff, $X = 1.55$: $\text{Max}(0,1.438 - 1.55) \times 125,000 = \$0$
   B. $S_T = \$1.438$
   i. Put payoff, $X = 1.35$: $\text{Max}(0,1.35 - 1.438) \times 125,000 = \$0$
   ii. Put payoff, $X = 1.55$: $\text{Max}(0,1.55 - 1.438) \times 125,000 = \$14,000$

5. **A.** $S_T = 1136.76$
   i. Call payoff, $X = 1130$: $\text{Max}(0,1136.76 - 1130) \times 1,000 = \$6,760$
   ii. Call payoff, $X = 1140$: $\text{Max}(0,1136.76 - 1140) \times 1,000 = 0$
   B. $S_T = 1136.76$
   i. Put payoff, $X = 1130$: $\text{Max}(0,1130 - 1136.76) \times 1,000 = 0$
   ii. Put payoff, $X = 1140$: $\text{Max}(0,1140 - 1136.76) \times 1,000 = \$3,240$

6. **A.** $S_0 = 1240.89$, $T = 75/365 = 0.2055$, $X = 1225$ or 1255, call options
   i. $X = 1225$
   Maximum value for the call: $c_0 = S_0 = 1240.89$
   Lower bound for the call: $c_0 = \text{Max}[0,1240.89 - 1225/(1.03)^{0.2055}] = 23.31$
   ii. $X = 1255$
   Maximum value for the call: $c_0 = S_0 = 1240.89$
   Lower bound for the call: $c_0 = \text{Max}[0,1240.89 - 1255/(1.03)^{0.2055}] = 0$
   B. $S_0 = 1240.89$, $T = 75/365 = 0.2055$, $X = 1225$ or 1255, put options
   i. $X = 1225$
   Maximum value for the put: $p_0 = 1225/(1.03)^{0.2055} = 1217.58$
   Lower bound for the put: $p_0 = \text{Max}[0,1225/(1.03)^{0.2055} - 1240.89] = 0$
   ii. $X = 1255$
   Maximum value for the put: $p_0 = 1255/(1.03)^{0.2055} = 1247.40$
   Lower bound for the put: $p_0 = \text{Max}[0,1255/(1.03)^{0.2055} - 1240.89] = 6.51$

7. **A.** $S_0 = 1.05$, $T = 60/365 = 0.1644$, $X = 0.95$ or 1.10, American-style options
   i. $X = \$0.95$

Maximum value for the call: $C_0 = S_0 = \$1.05$
Lower bound for the call: $C_0 = \text{Max}[0, 1.05 - 0.95/(1.055)^{0.1644}] = \$0.11$
Maximum value for the put: $P_0 = X = \$0.95$
Lower bound for the put: $P_0 = \text{Max}(0, 0.95 - 1.05) = \$0$

ii. $X - \$1.10$

Maximum value for the call: $C_0 = S_0 = \$1.05$
Lower bound for the call: $C_0 = \text{Max}[0, 1.05 - 1.10/(1.055)^{0.1644}] = \$0$
Maximum value for the put: $P_0 = X = \$1.10$
Lower bound for the put: $P_0 - \text{Max}(0, 1.10 - 1.05) = \$0.05$

B. $S_0 = 1.05$, $T = 60/365 = 0.1644$, $X = 0.95$ or 1.10, European-style options

i. $X = \$0.95$

Maximum value for the call: $c_0 = S_0 = \$1.05$
Lower bound for the call: $c_0 = \text{Max}[0, 1.05 - 0.95/(1.055)^{0.1644}] = \$0.11$
Maximum value for the put: $p_0 = 0.95/(1.055)^{0.1644} = \$0.94$
Lower bound for the put: $p_0 = \text{Max}[0, 0.95/(1.055)^{0.1644} - 1.05] = \$0$

ii. $X = \$1.10$

Maximum value for the call: $c_0 = S_0 = \$1.05$
Lower bound for the call: $c_0 = \text{Max}[0, 1.05 - 1.10/(1.055)^{0.1644}] = \$0$
Maximum value for the put: $p_0 = 1.10/(1.055)^{0.1644} - \$1.09$
Lower bound for the put: $p_0 = \text{Max}[0, 1.10/(1.055)^{0.1644} - 1.05] = \$0.04$

8. We can illustrate put–call parity by showing that for the fiduciary call and the protective put, the current values and values at expiration are the same.

Call price, $c_0 = \$6.64$
Put price, $p_0 = \$2.75$
Exercise price, $X = \$30$
Risk-free rate, $r = 4$ percent
Time to expiration $= 219/365 = 0.6$
Current stock price, $S_0 = \$33.19$
Bond price, $X/(1 + r)^T = 30/(1 + 0.04)^{0.6} = \$29.3$

Transaction	Current Value	Value at Expiration	
		$S_T = 20$	$S_T = 40$
Fiduciary call			
Buy call	6.64	0	$40 - 30 = 10$
Buy bond	29.30	30	30
Total	35.94	30	40
Protective put			
Buy put	2.75	$30 - 20 = 10$	0
Buy stock	33.19	20	40
Total	35.94	30	40

The values in the table above show that the current values and values at expiration for the fiduciary call and the protective put are the same. That is, $c_0 + X/(1 + r)^T = p_0 + S_0$.

9. Call price, $c_0 = \$4.50$
Put price, $p_0 = \$6.80$
Exercise price, $X = \$70$
Risk-free rate, $r = 5$ percent

Time to expiration = 139/365 = 0.3808
Current stock price, S_0 = \$67.32
Bond price = $X/(1 + r)^T$ = $70/(1 + 0.05)^{0.3808}$ = \$68.71
A. Synthetic call = $p_0 + S_0 - X/(1 + r)^T$ = $6.8 + 67.32 - 68.71$ = \$5.41
    Synthetic put = $c_0 + X/(1 + r)^T - S_0$ = $4.5 + 68.71 - 67.32$ = \$5.89
    Synthetic bond = $p_0 + S_0 - c_0$ = $6.8 + 67.32 - 4.5$ = \$69.62
    Synthetic underlying = $c_0 + X/(1 + r)^T - p_0$ = $4.5 + 68.71 - 6.8$ = \$66.41

B.

Instrument	Actual Price	Synthetic Price	Mispricing/Profit
Call	4.50	5.41	0.91
Put	6.80	5.89	0.91
Bond	68.71	69.62	0.91
Stock	67.32	66.41	0.91

Thus, the mispricing is the same regardless of the instrument used to look at it.

C. The actual call is cheaper than the synthetic call. Therefore, an arbitrage transaction where you buy the call (underpriced) and sell the synthetic call (overpriced) will yield a risk-free profit of \$5.41 − \$4.50 = \$0.91.

As shown below, at expiration no cash will be received or paid out.

	Value at Expiration	
Transaction	$S_T < 70$	$S_T > 70$
Buy call	0	$S_T - 70$
Sell synthetic call		
Short put	$-(70 - S_T)$	0
Short stock	$-S_T$	$-S_T$
Long bond	70	70
Total	0	0

D. The actual put is more expensive than the synthetic put. Therefore, an arbitrage transaction in which you buy the synthetic put (underpriced) and sell the put (overpriced) will yield a risk-free profit of \$6.80 − \$5.89 = \$0.91. As shown below, at expiration no cash will be received or paid out.

	Value at Expiration	
Transaction	$S_T < 70$	$S_T > 70$
Sell put	$-(70 - S_T)$	0
Buy synthetic put		
Long call	0	$S_T - 70$
Long bond	70	70
Short stock	$-S_T$	$-S_T$
Total	0	0

10. Current stock price, $S = \$100$
Up move, $u = 1.1$
Down move, $d = 0.85$
Exercise price, $X = \$90$
Risk-free rate, $r = 6.5$ percent

A. Stock prices one period from now are

$$S^+ = Su = 100(1.1) = \$110$$

$$S^- = Sd = 100(0.85) = \$85$$

Call option values at expiration one period from now are

$$c^+ = Max(0, 110 - 90) = \$20$$

$$c^- = Max(0, 85 - 90) = \$0$$

The risk-neutral probability is

$$\pi = \frac{1.065 - 0.85}{1.1 - 0.85} = 0.86 \text{ and } 1 - \pi = 0.14$$

The call price today is

$$c = \frac{0.86(20) + 0.14(0)}{1.065} = 16.15$$

B. If the current call price is $17.50, it is overpriced. Therefore, we should sell the call and buy the underlying stock. The hedge ratio is

$$n = \frac{20 - 0}{110 - 85} = 0.8$$

For every option sold we should purchase 0.8 shares of stock. If we sell 100 calls we should buy 80 shares of stock.

Sell 100 calls at 17.50 =   1,750
Buy 80 shares at 100   = −8,000
Net cash flow   = −6,250

At expiration the value of this combination will be

$$80(110) - 100(20) = \$6,800 \text{ if } S_T = 110$$

$$80(85) - 100(0) = \$6,800 \text{ if } S_T = 85$$

We invested $6,250 for a payoff of $6,800. The rate of return is (6,800/6,250) − 1 = 0.088. This rate is higher than the risk-free rate of 0.065.

C. If the current call price is $14, it is underpriced. Therefore, we should buy the call and sell the underlying stock. The hedge ratio is

$$n = \frac{20 - 0}{110 - 85} = 0.8$$

For every option purchased we should sell 0.8 shares of stock. If we buy 100 calls we should sell 80 shares of stock.

Buy 100 calls at 14   = −1,400
Sell 80 shares at 100 −   8,000
Net cash flow   =   6,600

Thus, we generate $6,600 up front.

At expiration the value of this combination will be

$$100(20) - 80(110) = -\$6,800 \text{ if } S_T = 110$$

$$100(0) - 80(85) = -\$6,800 \text{ if } S_T = 85$$

We generated \$6,600 up front and pay back \$6,800. The rate of return is $(6,800/6,600) - 1 = 0.0303$. This borrowing rate is lower than the risk-free rate of 0.065.

11. Current stock price, S = \$150
Up move, u = 1.33
Down move, d = 0.85
Exercise price, X = \$150
Risk-free rate, r = 4.5 percent

A. Stock prices one period from now are

$$S^+ = Su = 150(1.33) = \$199.5$$

$$S^- = Sd = 150(0.85) = \$127.5$$

Put option values at expiration one period from now are

$$p^+ = \text{Max}(0, 150 - 199.5) = \$0$$

$$p^- = \text{Max}(0, 150 - 127.5) = \$22.5$$

The risk-neutral probability is

$$\pi = \frac{1.045 - 0.85}{1.33 - 0.85} = 0.4063, \text{ and } 1 - \pi = 0.5937$$

The put price today is

$$\pi = \frac{0.4063(0) + 0.5937(22.50)}{1.045} = 12.78$$

B. If the current put price is \$14, it is overpriced. In order to create a hedge portfolio, we should sell the put and short the underlying stock. The hedge ratio is

$$n = \frac{p^+ - p^-}{S^+ - S^-} = \frac{0 - 22.5}{199.5 - 127.5} = -0.3125$$

For every option sold, we should sell 0.3125 shares of stock. If we sell 10,000 puts, we should sell 3,125 shares of stock.

Sell 10,000 puts at 14	= 140,000
Sell 3,125 shares at 150	= 468,750
Net cash flow	= 608,750

Thus, we generate \$608,750 up front.

At expiration, the value of this combination will be

$$-3,125(199.5) - 10,000(0) = -\$623,437 \text{ if } S_T = \$199.5$$

$$-3,125(127.5) - 10,000(22.5) = -\$623,437 \text{ if } S_T = \$127.5$$

We generated \$608,750 up front and pay back \$623,437. The rate of return is

$$\frac{623,437}{608,750} - 1 = 0.0241$$

This borrowing rate is lower than the risk-free rate of 0.045.

C. If the current put price is $11, it is underpriced. In order to create a hedge portfolio, we should buy the put and buy the underlying stock. The hedge ratio is

$$n = \frac{p^+ - p^-}{S^+ - S^-} = \frac{0 - 22.5}{199.5 - 127.5} = -0.3125$$

For every option purchased we should buy 0.3125 shares of stock. If we buy 10,000 puts we should buy 3,125 shares of stock.

Buy 10,000 puts at 11   = −110,000
Buy 3,125 shares at 150 = −468,750
Net cash flow   = −578,750

That is, we invest $578,750.

At expiration, the value of this combination will be

$$3{,}125(199.5) + 10{,}000(0) = \$623{,}437 \text{ if } S_T = \$199.5$$

$$3{,}125(127.5) + 10{,}000(22.5) = \$623{,}437 \text{ if } S_T = \$127.5$$

We invested $578,750 for a payoff of $623,437. The rate of return is $\frac{623{,}437}{578{,}750} - 1 = 0.0772$. This rate is higher than the risk-free rate of 0.045.

12. Current stock price, $S = \$65$
Up move, $u = 1.20$
Down move, $d = 0.83$
Risk-free rate, $r = 5$ percent
A. Exercise price, $X = \$60$
Stock prices in the binomial tree one and two periods from now are

$$S^+ = Su = 65(1.20) = \$78$$

$$S^- = Sd = 65(0.83) = \$53.95$$

$$S^{++} = Su^2 = 65(1.20)(1.20) = \$93.60$$

$$S^{+-} = Sud = 65(1.20)(0.83) = \$64.74$$

$$S^{--} = Sd^2 = 65(0.83)(0.83) = \$44.78$$

Call option values at expiration two periods from now are

$$c^{++} = \text{Max}(0, 93.60 - 60) = \$33.6$$

$$c^{+-} = \text{Max}(0, 64.74 - 60) = \$4.74$$

$$c^{--} = \text{Max}(0, 44.78 - 60) = \$0$$

The risk-neutral probability is

$$\pi = \frac{1.05 - 0.83}{1.20 - 0.83} = 0.5946, \text{ and } 1 - \pi = 0.4054$$

Now find the option prices at time 1:

$$c^+ = \frac{0.5946(33.6) + 0.4054(4.74)}{1.05} = \$20.86$$

$$c^- = \frac{0.5946(4.74) + 0.4054(0)}{1.05} = \$2.68$$

The call price today is

$$c = \frac{0.5946(20.86) + 0.4054(2.68)}{1.05} = \$12.85$$

B. The hedge ratios at each point in the binomial tree are calculated as follows:

At the current stock price of $65,

$$n = \frac{c^+ - c^-}{S^+ - S^-} = \frac{20.86 - 2.68}{78 - 53.95} = 0.7559$$

Therefore, today at time 0, the risk-free hedge would consist of a short position in 10,000 calls and a long position in 7,559 shares of the underlying stock.

At a stock price of $78,

$$n^+ = \frac{c^{++} - c^{+-}}{S^{++} - S^{+-}} = \frac{33.6 - 4.74}{93.6 - 64.74} = 1$$

Now the risk-free hedge would consist of a short position in 10,000 calls and a long position in 10,000 shares of the underlying stock.

At a stock price of $53.95,

$$\frac{n^- = c^{+-} - c^{--}}{S^{+-} - S^{--}} = \frac{4.74 - 0}{64.74 - 44.78} = 0.2375$$

Now the risk-free hedge would consist of a short position in 10,000 calls and a long position in 2,375 shares of the underlying stock.

C. Exercise price, X = $70

Stock prices in the binomial tree one and two periods from now are

$$S^+ = Su = 65(1.20) = \$78$$

$$S^- = Sd = 65(0.83) = \$53.95$$

$$S^{++} = Su^2 = 65(1.20)(1.20) = \$93.6$$

$$S^{+-} = Sud = 65(1.20)(0.83) = \$64.74$$

$$S^{--} = Sd^2 = 65(0.83)(0.83) = \$44.78$$

Call option values at expiration two periods from now are

$$c^{++} = Max(0, 93.6 - 70) = \$23.6$$

$$c^{+-} = Max(0, 64.74 - 70) = \$0$$

$$c^{--} = Max(0, 44.78 - 70) = \$0$$

The risk-neutral probability is

$$\pi = \frac{1.05 - 0.83}{1.20 - 0.83} = 0.5946, \text{ and } 1 - \pi = 0.4054$$

Now find the option prices at time 1:

$$c^+ = \frac{0.5946(23.6) + 0.4054(0)}{1.05} = \$13.36$$

$$c^- = \frac{0.5946(0) + 0.4054(0)}{1.05} = \$0$$

The call price today is

$$c = \frac{0.5946(13.36) + 0.4054(0)}{1.05} = \$7.57$$

D. The hedge ratios at each point in the binomial tree are calculated as follows.

At the current stock price of $65,

$$n = \frac{c^+ - c^-}{S^+ - S^-} = \frac{13.36 - 0}{78 - 53.95} = 0.5555$$

Therefore, today at time 0, the risk-free hedge would consist of a short position in 10,000 calls and a long position in 5,555 shares of the underlying stock.

At a stock price of $78,

$$n^+ = \frac{c^{++} - c^{+-}}{S^{++} - S^{+-}} = \frac{23.6 - 0}{93.6 - 64.74} = 0.8177$$

Now, the risk-free hedge would consist of a short position in 10,000 calls and a long position in 8,177 shares of the underlying stock.

At a stock price of $53.95,

$$n^- = \frac{c^{+-} - c^{--}}{S^{+-} - S^{--}} = \frac{0 - 0}{64.74 - 44.78} = 0$$

Zero shares of the underlying stock are needed for the short position in calls.

13. Current stock price, $S_0 = \$65$
Up move, $u = 1.20$
Down move, $d = 0.83$
Risk-free rate, $r = 5$ percent
A. Exercise price, $X = \$60$

Stock prices in the binomial tree one and two periods from now are

$$S^+ = Su = 65(1.20) = \$78$$

$$S^- = Sd = 65(0.83) = \$53.95$$

$$S^{++} = Su^2 = 65(1.20)(1.20) = \$93.6$$

$$S^{+-} = Sud = 65(1.20)(0.83) = \$64.74$$

$$S^{--} = Sd^2 = 65(0.83)(0.83) = \$44.78$$

Put option values at expiration two periods from now are

$$p^{++} = Max(0, 60 - 93.6) = \$0$$

$$p^{+-} = Max(0, 60 - 64.74) = \$0$$

$$p^{--} = Max(0, 60 - 44.78) = \$15.22$$

The risk-neutral probability is

$$\pi = \frac{1.05 - 0.83}{1.20 - 0.83} = 0.5946 \text{ and } 1 - \pi = 0.4054$$

Now find the option prices at time 1:

$$p^+ = \frac{0.5946(0) + 0.4054(0)}{1.05} = \$0$$

$$p^- = \frac{0.5946(0) + 0.4054(15.22)}{1.05} = \$5.88$$

The put price today is

$$p = \frac{0.5946(0) + 0.4054(5.88)}{1.05} = \$2.27$$

B. Unlike the hedge portfolio for calls, which has the opposite positions in the two instruments (calls and underlying stock), the hedge portfolio for puts has the same positions in the two instruments. Therefore, the current value of the hedge portfolio for puts is

$$H = nS + p$$

The possible values of the hedge portfolio one period later are

$$H^+ = nS^+ + p^+$$

$$H^- = nS^- + p^-$$

Setting H^+ equal to H^- and solving for n,

$$n = \frac{p^- - p^+}{S^+ - S^-}$$

Note that the above formula is the same as that for the hedge portfolio for calls, except that the p^+ and p^- have switched positions in the numerator. Similarly, the hedge ratios for the next time point are

$$n^+ = \frac{p^{+-} - p^{++}}{S^{++} - S^{+-}}$$

$$n^- = \frac{p^{--} - p^{+-}}{S^{+-} - S^{--}}$$

At the current stock price of $65,

$$n = \frac{p^- - p^+}{S^+ - S^-} = \frac{5.88 - 0}{78 - 53.95} = 0.2445$$

Therefore, today at time 0, the risk-free hedge would consist of a long position in 10,000 puts and a long position in 2,445 shares of the underlying stock.

At a stock price of $78,

$$n^+ = \frac{p^{+-} - p^{++}}{S^{++} - S^{+-}} = \frac{0 - 0}{93.6 - 64.74} = 0$$

Zero shares of the underlying stock are needed for the long position in puts.

At a stock price of $53.95,

$$n^- = \frac{p^{--} - p^{+-}}{S^{+-} - S^{--}} = \frac{15.22 - 0}{64.74 - 44.78} = 0.7625$$

Now the risk-free hedge would consist of a long position in 10,000 puts and a long position in 7,625 shares of the underlying stock.

C. Exercise price, X = $70

Stock prices in the binomial tree, one and two periods from now are

$$S^+ = Su - 65(1.20) - \$78$$

$$S^- = Sd = 65(0.83) = \$53.95$$

$$S^{++} = Su^2 = 65(1.20)(1.20) = \$93.6$$

$$S^{+-} = Sud = 65(1.20)(0.83) = \$64.74$$

$$S^{--} = Sd^2 = 65(0.83)(0.83) = \$44.78$$

Put option values at expiration two periods from now are

$$p^{++} = Max(0, 70 - 93.6) = \$0$$

$$p^{+-} = Max(0, 70 - 64.74) = \$5.26$$

$$p^{--} = Max(0, 70 - 44.78) = \$25.22$$

The risk-neutral probability is

$$\pi = \frac{1.05 - 0.83}{1.20 - 0.83} = 0.5946, \text{ and } 1 - \pi = 0.4054$$

Now find the option prices at time 1:

$$p^+ = \frac{0.5946(0) + 0.4054(5.26)}{1.05} = \$2.03$$

$$p^- = \frac{0.5946(5.26) + 0.4054(25.22)}{1.05} = \$12.72$$

The put price today is

$$p = \frac{0.5946(2.03) + 0.4054(12.72)}{1.05} = \$6.06$$

D. The hedge ratios at each point in the binomial tree are calculated as follows:

At the current stock price of $65,

$$n = \frac{p^- - p^+}{S^1 - S} = \frac{12.72 - 2.03}{78 - 53.95} = 0.4445$$

Therefore, today at time 0, the risk-free hedge would consist of a long position in 10,000 puts and a long position in 4,445 shares of the underlying stock.

At stock price $78,

$$n^+ = \frac{p^{+-} - p^{++}}{S^{++} - S^{+-}} = \frac{5.26 - 0}{93.6 - 64.74} = 0.1823$$

Therefore, today at time 0, the risk-free hedge would consist of a long position in 10,000 puts and a long position in 1,823 shares of the underlying stock.

At stock price $53.95,

$$n^- = \frac{p^{--} - p^{+-}}{S^{+-} - S^{--}} = \frac{25.22 - 5.26}{64.74 - 44.78} = 1$$

Now, the risk-free hedge would consist of a long position in 10,000 puts and a long position in 10,000 shares of the underlying stock.

14. A. Because the underlying is a four-period bond, redraw the interest rate tree to include only the four-year maturity bond prices.

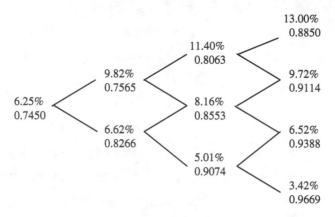

Because the call expires in two periods, first we must calculate the payoff values of the call at expiration in two periods using the bond prices at time 2 in the above tree.

$$c^{++} = \text{Max}(0, 0.8063 - 0.85) = 0$$

$$c^{+-} = \text{Max}(0, 0.8553 - 0.85) = 0.0053$$

$$c^{--} = \text{Max}(0, 0.9074 - 0.85) = 0.0574$$

The risk-neutral probability is

$$\pi = 0.5 \text{ and } 1 - \pi = 0.5$$

Now find the option prices at time 1:

$$c^{+} = \frac{0.5(0) + 0.5(0.0053)}{1.0982} = 0.0024$$

$$c^{-} = \frac{0.5(0.0053) + 0.5(0.0574)}{1.0662} = 0.0294$$

The call price today is

$$c = \frac{0.5(0.0024) + 0.5(0.0294)}{1.0625} = 0.0150$$

B. Because the bond expires in two periods, first we have to calculate the prices of the 8 percent coupon bond with $1 face value at t = 2. At t = 2, the bond is a two-period bond. Consider the top node at t = 2. The one-and two-period zero-coupon bond prices are 0.8977 and 0.8063, respectively. Therefore, the coupon bond price at the top node at t = 2 is

$$0.9426 = 0.08(0.8977) + 1.08(0.8063)$$

Similarly, the coupon bond prices at the middle and bottom nodes at t = 2 are

$$0.9977 = 0.08(0.9246) + 1.08(0.8553)$$

$$1.0562 = 0.08(0.9523) + 1.08(0.9074)$$

Now compute the option prices. At time 2, the prices are

$$c^{++} = Max(0, 0.9426 - 0.95) = 0$$

$$c^{+-} = Max(0, 0.9977 - 0.95) = 0.0477$$

$$c^{--} = Max(0, 1.0562 - 0.95) = 0.1062$$

The risk-neutral probability is

$$\pi = 0.5 \text{ and } 1 - \pi = 0.5$$

Now find the option prices at time 1:

$$c^+ = \frac{0.5(0) + 0.5(0.0477)}{1.0982} = 0.0217$$

$$c^- = \frac{0.5(0.0477) + 0.5(0.1062)}{1.0662} = 0.0722$$

The call price today is

$$c = \frac{0.5(0.0217) + 0.5(0.0722)}{1.0625} = 0.0442$$

C. First calculate the payoff values of the put at expiration in two periods.

$$p^{++} = Max(0, 0.85 - 0.8063) = 0.0437$$

$$p^{+-} = Max(0, 0.85 - 0.8553) = 0$$

$$p^{--} = Max(0, 0.85 - 0.9074) = 0$$

The risk-neutral probability is

$$\pi = 0.5 \text{ and } 1 - \pi = 0.5$$

Now find the option prices at time 1:

$$p^+ = \frac{0.5(0.0437) + 0.5(0)}{1.0982} = 0.0199$$

$$p^- = \frac{0.5(0) + 0.5(0)}{1.0662} = 0$$

The put price today is

$$p = \frac{0.5(0.0199) + 0.5(0)}{1.0625} = 0.0094$$

D. The prices at time 2 of the 8 percent coupon bond with \$1 face value are the same as in Part B.

The payoff values of the put at expiration in two periods at t = 2 are

$$p^{++} = Max(0, 1 - 0.9426) = 0.0574$$

$$p^{+-} = Max(0, 1 - 0.9977) = 0.0023$$

$$p^{--} = Max(0, 1 - 1.0562) = 0$$

The risk-neutral probability is

$$\pi = 0.5 \text{ and } 1 - \pi = 0.5$$

Now find the option prices at time 1:

$$p^+ = \frac{0.5(0.0574) + 0.5(0.0023)}{1.0982} = 0.0272$$

$$p^- = \frac{0.5(0.0023) + 0.5(0)}{1.0662} = 0.0011$$

The put price today is

$$p = \frac{0.5(0.0272) + 0.5(0.0011)}{1.0625} = 0.0133$$

15. **A.** The two-period cap with an exercise rate of 8 percent consists of two caplets, a one-period call on the one-period interest rate with an exercise rate of 8 percent, and a two-period call on the one-period interest rate with an exercise rate of 8 percent. Price these caplets separately and sum them to obtain the price of the cap.

Pricing the two-period caplet
The option values at expiration at t = 2 are

$$c^{++} = \text{Max}(0, 0.114 - 0.08)/1.114 = 0.0305$$

$$c^{+-} = \text{Max}(0, 0.0816 - 0.08)/1.0816 = 0.0015$$

$$c^{--} = \text{Max}(0, 0.0501 - 0.08)/1.0501 = 0$$

The risk-neutral probability is

$$\pi = 0.5 \text{ and } 1 - \pi = 0.5$$

Now find the option prices at time 1

$$c^+ = \frac{0.5(0.0305) + 0.5(0.0015)}{1.0982} = 0.0146$$

$$c^- = \frac{0.5(0.0015) + 0.5(0)}{1.0662} = 0.0007$$

The price of the two-period caplet today is

$$c = \frac{0.5(0.0146) + 0.5(0.0007)}{1.0625} = 0.0072$$

Pricing the one-period caplet
The option values at expiration at t = 1 are

$$c^+ = \text{Max}(0, 0.0982 - 0.08)/1.0982 = 0.0166$$

$$c^- = \text{Max}(0, 0.0662 - 0.08)/1.0662 = 0$$

The price of the one-period caplet today is

$$c = \frac{0.5(0.0166) + 0.5(0)}{1.0625} = 0.0078$$

The price of the two-period cap = 0.0072 + 0.0078 = 0.0150

B. The two-period floor with an exercise rate of 9 percent consists of two floorlets, a one-period put on the one-period interest rate with an exercise rate of 9 percent, and a two-period put on the one-period interest rate with an exercise rate of 9 percent. Price these floorlets separately and sum them to obtain the price of the floor.

Pricing the two-period floorlet

The option values at expiration at t = 2 are

$$p^{++} = Max(0,0.09 - 0.114)/1.114 = 0$$

$$p^{+-} = Max(0,0.09 - 0.0816)/1.0816 = 0.0078$$

$$p^{--} = Max(0,0.09 - 0.0501)/1.0501 = 0.0380$$

The risk-neutral probability is

$$\pi = 0.5 \text{ and } 1 - \pi = 0.5$$

Now find the option prices at time 1:

$$p^+ = \frac{0.5(0) + 0.5(0.0078)}{1.0982} = 0.0036$$

$$p^- = \frac{0.5(0.0078) + 0.5(0.0380)}{1.0662} = 0.0215$$

The price of the two-period floorlet today is

$$p = \frac{0.5(0.0036) + 0.5(0.0215)}{1.0625} = 0.0118$$

Pricing the one-period floorlet

The option values at expiration at t = 1 are

$$p^+ = Max(0,0.09 - 0.0982)/1.0982 = 0$$

$$p^- = Max(0,0.09 - 0.0662)/1.0662 = 0.0223$$

The price of the one-period floorlet today is

$$p = \frac{0.5(0) + 0.5(0.0223)}{1.0625} = 0.0105$$

The price of the two period floor $-$ 0.0118 + 0.0105 = 0.0223

16. **A.** The value of $N(d_1)$ is the approximate value of delta for calls and $N(d_1) - 1$ is the approximate value of delta for puts. So, first calculate the value of d_1. The time to expiration is T = 75/365 = 0.2055.

$$d_1 = \frac{\ln(28/30) + [0.035 + (0.40)^2/2](0.2055)}{0.40\sqrt{0.2055}} = -0.25$$

Using the normal probability table,

$$N(-0.25) = 1 - N(0.25) = 1 - 0.5987 = 0.4013 = N(d_1)$$

Therefore, the approximate value of delta for calls is 0.4013 and the approximate value of delta for puts is 0.4013 − 1 = − 0.5987.

B. Change in option price = Delta × Change in underlying asset price

Call delta = 0.4013

Put delta = −0.5987

i. For a $1 change in the price of the underlying:

Change in call price = 0.4013(1) = $0.4013

Change in put price = −0.5987(1) = −$0.5987

Approximate new call price = 1.3144 + 0.4013 = $1.7157

Approximate new put price = 3.0994 − 0.5987 = $2.5007

    ii. For a \$5 change in the price of the underlying:

      Change in call price = 0.4013(5) = \$2.0065

      Change in put price = −0.5987(5) = −\$2.9935

      Approximate new call price = 1.3144 + 2.0065 = \$3.3209

      Approximate new put price = 3.0994 − 2.9935 = \$0.1059

C. For a \$1 change in the price of the underlying, the approximate new call price of \$1.7157 is different from but not too far off the actual call price of \$1.7538. Similarly, the approximate new put price of \$2.5007 is different from but not too far off the actual put price of \$2.5388. Therefore, the delta approximation is good but not perfect.

For a \$5 change in the price of the underlying, the approximate new call price of \$3.3209 is fairly far off the actual call price of \$4.2270. Similarly, the approximate new put price of \$0.1059 is quite far off the actual put price of \$1.0120. Therefore, the delta approximation is not particularly good.

The above comparisons indicate that the approximations based on delta are worse for larger moves in the underlying price.

17. A. First calculate the values of d_1 and d_2. The time to expiration is T = 275/365 = 0.7534. Adjust the price of the asset S_0 = \$100 − \$4.25 = \$95.75

$$d_1 = \frac{\ln(95.75/100) + [0.03 + (0.45)^2/2](0.7534)}{0.45\sqrt{0.7534}} = 0.1420$$

$$d_2 = 0.1420 - 0.45\sqrt{0.7534} = -0.2486$$

Using the normal probability table,

$$N(0.14) = 0.5557 = N(d_1)$$

$$N(-0.25) = 1 - N(0.25) = 1 - 0.5987 = 0.4013 = N(d_2)$$

The value of the call option is

$$c = 95.75(0.5557) - 100e^{-0.03(0.7534)}(0.4013) = 13.975$$

The value of the put option is

$$p = 100e^{-0.03(0.7534)}(1 - 0.4013) - 95.75(1 - 0.5557) = 15.990$$

B. First calculate the values of d_1 and d_2. The time to expiration is T = 275/365 = 0.7534. Adjust the price of the asset S_0 = $100e^{-0.015(0.7534)}$ = 98.87626

$$d_1 = \frac{\ln(98.876/100) + [0.03 + (0.45)^2/2](0.7534)}{0.45\sqrt{0.7534}} = 0.2242$$

$$d_2 = 0.22423 - 0.45\sqrt{0.7534} = -0.1664$$

Using the normal probability table,

$$N(0.22) = 0.5871 = N(d_1)$$

$$N(-0.17) = 1 - N(0.17) = 1 - 0.5675 = 0.4325 = N(d_2)$$

The value of the call option is

$$c = 98.876(0.5871) - 100e^{-0.03(0.7534)}(0.4325) = \$15.767$$

The value of the put option is

$$p = 100e^{-0.03(0.7534)}(1 - 0.4325) - 98.876(1 - 0.5871) = \$14.656$$

18. Call price, $c_0 = \$3.50$
Put price, $p_0 = \$9$
Exercise price, $X = \$50$
Forward price, $F(0,T) = \$45$
Days to option expiration $= 175$
Risk-free rate, $r = 4$ percent
Time to expiration $= 175/365 = 0.4795$
Bond price $= [X - F(0,T)]/(1 + r)^T = (50 - 45)/(1 + .04)^{0.4795} = \$4.91$
A. Synthetic call $=$ Long forward $+ p_0 - [X - F(0,T)]/(1 + r)^T = 0 + 9 - 4.91 = 4.09$
Synthetic put $= c_0 +$ Short forward $+ [X - F(0,T)]/(1 + r)^T = 3.5 + 0 + 4.91 = 8.41$
Synthetic forward $= c_0 - p_0 + [X - F(0,T)]/(1 + r)^T = 3.5 - 9 + 4.91 = -0.59$

B.

Instrument	Actual Price	Synthetic Price	Mispricing/Profit
Call	3.50	4.09	0.59
Put	9	8.41	0.59
Forward	0	−0.59	0.59

C. The actual call is cheaper than the synthetic call. Therefore, an arbitrage transaction in which you buy the actual call (underpriced) and sell the synthetic call (overpriced) will yield a risk-free profit up front of $\$4.09 - \$3.50 = \$0.59$. The initial up-front cash is generated as follows:

Transaction	
Buy call	−3.5
Sell synthetic call	
Short forward	0
Short put	9
Long bond	−4.91
Total	0.59

As shown below, at expiration no cash will be received or paid out.

	Value at Expiration	
Transaction	$S_T < 50$	$S_T > 50$
Buy call	0	$S_T - 50$
Sell synthetic call		
Short forward	$-(S_T - 45)$	$-(S_T - 45)$
Short put	$-(50 - S_T)$	0
Long bond	$50 - 45$	$50 - 45$
Total	0	0

D. The actual put is more expensive than the synthetic put. Therefore, an arbitrage transaction in which you buy the synthetic put (underpriced) and sell the actual put (overpriced) will yield a risk-free profit of $9 - \$8.41 = \$0.59$. The initial up-front cash is generated as follows:

Transaction	
Sell put	9
Buy synthetic put	
Long call	-3.5
Short forward	0
Long bond	-4.91
Total	0.59

As shown below, at expiration no cash will be received or paid out.

	Value at Expiration	
Transaction	$S_T < 50$	$S_T > 50$
Sell put	$-(50 - S_T)$	0
Buy synthetic put		
Long call	0	$S_T - 50$
Short forward	$-(S_T - 45)$	$-(S_T - 45)$
Long bond	$50 - 45$	$50 - 45$
Total	0	0

19. A. First calculate the values of d_1 and d_2. The time to expiration, $T = 65/365 = 0.1781$.

$$d_1 = \frac{\ln(145/150) + [(0.03)^2/2](0.1781)}{0.33\sqrt{0.1781}} = -0.1738$$

$$d_2 = -0.1738 - 0.33\sqrt{0.1781} = -0.3131$$

Using the normal probability table,

$$N(-0.17) = 1 - N(0.17) = 1 - 0.5675 = 0.4325 = N(d_1)$$

$$N(-0.31) = 1 - N(0.31) = 1 - 0.6217 = 0.3783 = N(d_2)$$

The value of the call option is

$$c = e^{-0.0375(0.1781)}[145(0.4325) - 150(0.3783)] = 5.928$$

B. With no cash flows on the underlying and continuously compounded interest, the price of the underlying asset can be calculated as

$$S_0 = 145e^{-0.0375(0.1781)} = 144.03$$

Now use the Black–Scholes–Merton model:

$$d_1 = \frac{\ln(144.03/150) + [0.0375 + (0.33)^2/2](0.1781)}{0.33\sqrt{0.1781}} = -0.1740$$

$$d_2 = -0.174 - 0.33\sqrt{0.1781} = -0.3133$$

Using the normal probability table,

$$N(-0.17) = 1 - N(0.17) = 1 - 0.5675 = 0.4325 = N(d_1)$$

$$N(-0.31) = 1 - N(0.31) = 1 - 0.6217 = 0.3783 = N(d_2)$$

The value of the call option is

$$c = 144.03(0.4325) - 150e^{-0.0375(0.1781)}(0.3783) = 5.926$$

Consistent with the equivalence of options on the underlying and options on the forward contract, this value is the same as the value of the call option on the forward contract in Part A (the slight difference comes from rounding).

C. The values for $N(d_1)$ and $N(d_2)$ are the same as in Part A. Putting these values into the formula for the put option in the Black model produces

$$p = e^{-0.0375(0.1781)}[150(1 - 0.3783) - 145(1 - 0.4325)] = 10.894$$

D. The values for $N(d_1)$ and $N(d_2)$ are the same as in Part B. Putting these values into the formula for the put option in the Black–Scholes–Merton model produces

$$p = 150e^{-0.0375(0.1781)}(1 - 0.3783) - 144.03(1 - 0.4325) = 10.897$$

Consistent with the equivalence of options on the underlying and options on the forward contract, this value is the same as the value of the put option on the forward contract in Part C (the slight difference comes from rounding).

20. A. Calculate the values of d_1 and d_2. The time to expiration is $T = 180/365 = 0.4932$.

$$d_1 = \frac{\ln(0.0725/0.075) + [(0.04)^2/2](0.4932)}{0.04\sqrt{0.4932}} = -1.1928$$

$$d_2 = -1.1928 - 0.04\sqrt{0.4932} = -1.2209$$

Using the normal probability table,

$$N(-1.19) = 1 - N(1.19) = 1 - 0.8830 = 0.1170 = N(d_1)$$

$$N(-1.22) = 1 - N(1.22) = 1 - 0.8888 = 0.1112 = N(d_2)$$

The value of the call option is

$$c = e^{-0.05(0.4932)}[0.0725(0.1170) - 0.075(0.1112)] = 0.00013903$$

This value is computed based on the assumption that the option payoff is made at expiration. For the 90-day interest rate option, however, the payment is made 90 days after expiration. So, discount back 90 days:

$$0.00013903e^{-0.0725(90/365)} = 0.00013657$$

Convert to periodic rate based on a 90-day rate and using the customary 360-day year.

$$0.00013657(90/360) = 0.00003414$$

B. The values of $N(d_1)$ and $N(d_2)$ are the same as in Part A. Plug these values into the Black model for the put option.

$$p = e^{-0.05(0.4932)}[0.075(1 - 0.1112) - 0.0725(1 - 0.1170)] = 0.00257813$$

Now discount back 90 days:

$$0.00257813e^{-0.0725(90/365)} = 0.00253245$$

Convert to periodic rate based on 90-day rate:

$$0.00253245(90/360) = 0.00063311$$

5

SWAP MARKETS AND CONTRACTS

LEARNING OUTCOMES

After completing this chapter, you will be able to do the following:

- Describe the characteristics of swap contracts.
- Explain how swaps are terminated.
- Define and give examples of the types of currency swaps.
- Calculate the payments on a currency swap.
- Define and give an example of a plain vanilla interest rate swap.
- Calculate the payments on an interest rate swap.
- Define and give examples of the types of equity swaps.
- Calculate the payments on an equity swap.
- Distinguish between the pricing and valuation of swaps.
- Explain the equivalence of swaps to combinations of other instruments.
- Explain how interest rate swaps are equivalent to a series of off-market forward rate agreements (FRAs).
- Explain how a plain vanilla swap is equivalent to a combination of an interest rate call and an interest rate put.
- Determine the fixed rate on a plain vanilla interest rate swap and the market value of the swap during its life.
- Determine the fixed rate, if applicable, and the foreign notional principal for a given domestic notional principal on a currency swap, and determine the market values of each of the different types of currency swaps during their lives.
- Determine the fixed rate, if applicable, on an equity swap and the market values of the different types of equity swaps during their lives.
- Define, explain, and interpret the characteristics of swaptions, including the difference between payer and receiver swaptions.
- Explain why swaptions exist and give examples of how they are used.
- Show how the payoffs of an interest rate swaption are like those of an option on a coupon-bearing bond.
- Calculate the value of an interest rate swaption on the expiration day.
- Explain how the market value of a swaption at expiration can be received in different ways.

- Define forward swaps and distinguish between forward swaps and swaptions.

- Explain how credit risk arises in a swap and distinguish between current credit risk and potential credit risk.

- Identify and explain at what point in a swap's life credit risk is the greatest.

- Define the swap spread and explain what it represents.

- Illustrate how swap credit risk is reduced by both netting and marking to market.

- Explain the role that swaps play in the financial system.

1   INTRODUCTION

This chapter completes the survey of the main types of derivative instruments. The three preceding chapters covered forward contracts, futures contracts, and options. This chapter covers swaps. Although swaps were the last of the main types of derivatives to be invented, they are clearly not the least important. In fact, judging by the size of the swap market, they are probably the most important. In Chapter 1, we noted that the Bank for International Settlements had estimated the notional principal of the global over-the-counter derivatives market as of 30 June 2001 at $100 trillion. Of that amount, interest rate and currency swaps account for about $61 trillion, with interest rate swaps representing about $57 trillion of that total.[1] Indeed, interest rate swaps have had overwhelming success as a derivative product. They are widely used by corporations, financial institutions, and governments.

In Chapter 1, we briefly described the characteristics of swaps, but now we explore this subject in more detail. Recall first that *a swap is an agreement between two parties to exchange a series of future cash flows*. For most types of swaps, one party makes payments that are determined by a random outcome, such as an interest rate, a currency rate, an equity return, or a commodity price. These payments are commonly referred to as variable or *floating*. The other party either makes variable or floating payments determined by some other random factor or makes fixed payments. At least one type of swap involves both parties making fixed payments, but the values of those payments vary due to random factors.

In forwards, futures, and options, the terminology of *long* and *short* has been used to describe buyers and sellers. These terms are not used as often in swaps. The preferred terminology usually designates a party as being the floating- (or variable-) rate payer or the fixed-rate payer. Nonetheless, in swaps in which one party receives a floating rate and the other receives a fixed rate, the former is usually said to be long and the latter is said to be short. This usage is in keeping with the fact that parties who go long in other instruments pay a known amount and receive a claim on an unknown amount. In some swaps, however, both sides are floating or variable, and this terminology breaks down.

**1.1
CHARACTERISTICS
OF SWAP
CONTRACTS**

Although technically a swap can have a single payment, most swaps involve multiple payments. Thus, we refer to a swap as a *series* of payments. In fact, we have already covered a swap with one payment, which is just a forward contract. Hence, a swap is basically a series of forward contracts. We will elaborate further in Section 4.1.2, but with this idea in mind, we can see that a swap is like an agreement to buy something over a period of time.

---

[1] Equity and commodity swaps account for less than the notional principal of currency swaps.

We might be paying a variable price or a price that has already been fixed; we might be paying an uncertain price, or we might already know the price we shall pay.

When a swap is initiated, neither party pays any amount to the other. Therefore, a swap has zero value at the start of the contract. Although it is not absolutely necessary for this condition to be true, swaps are typically done in this fashion. Neither party pays anything up front. There is, however, a technical exception to this point in regard to currency swaps. Each party pays the notional principal to the other, but the amounts exchanged are equivalent, though denominated in two different currencies.

Each date on which the parties make payments is called a **settlement date**, sometimes called a payment date, and the time between settlement dates is called the **settlement period**. On a given settlement date when payments are due, one party makes a payment to the other, which in turn makes a payment to the first party. With the exception of currency swaps and a few variations associated with other types of swaps, both sets of payments are made in the same currency. Consequently, the parties typically agree to exchange only the net amount owed from one party to the other, a practice called **netting**. In currency swaps and a few other special cases, the payments are not made in the same currency; hence, the parties usually make separate payments without netting. Note the implication that swaps are generally settled in cash. It is quite rare for swaps to call for actual physical delivery of an underlying asset.

A swap always has a **termination date**, the date of the final payment. We can think of this date as its expiration date, as we do with other derivatives. The original time to maturity is sometimes called the *tenor* of a swap.

The swap market is almost exclusively an over-the-counter market, so swaps contracts are customized to the parties' specific needs. Several of the leading futures exchanges have created futures contracts on swaps. These contracts allow participants to hedge and speculate on the rates that will prevail in the swap market at future dates. Of course, these contracts are not swaps themselves but, as derivatives of swaps, they can in some ways serve as substitutes for swaps. These futures contracts have been moderately successful, but their volume is insignificant compared with the over-the-counter market for swaps.

As we have discussed in previous chapters, over-the-counter instruments are subject to default risk. Default is possible whenever a payment is due. When a series of payments is made, there is default risk potential throughout the life of the contract, depending on the financial condition of the two parties. But default can be somewhat complicated in swaps. Suppose, for example, that on a settlement date, Party A owes Party B a payment of $50,000 and Party B owes Party A a payment of $12,000. Agreeing to net, Party A owes Party B $38,000 for that particular payment. Party A may be illiquid, or perhaps even bankrupt, and unable to make the payment. But it may be the case that the market value of the swap, which reflects the present value of the remaining payments, could be positive from the perspective of Party A and negative from the perspective of Party B. In that case, Party B owes Party A more for the remaining payments. We will learn how to determine the market value of a swap in Section 4.2 of this chapter.

The handling of default in swaps can be complicated, depending on the contract specifications and the applicable laws under which the contract was written. In most cases, the above situation would be resolved by having A be in default but possessing an asset, the swap, that can be used to help settle its other liabilities. We shall discuss the default risk of swaps in more detail in Section 7.

1.2 TERMINATION OF A SWAP

As we noted earlier, a swap has a termination or expiration date. Sometimes, however, a party could want to terminate a swap before its formal expiration. This scenario is much like a party selling a bond before it matures or selling an exchange-traded option or futures contract before its expiration. With swaps, early termination can take place in several ways.

As we mentioned briefly and will cover in more detail later, a swap has a market value that can be calculated during its life. If a party holds a swap with a market value of $125,000, for example, it can settle the swap with the counterparty by having the counterparty pay it $125,000 in cash. This payment terminates the transaction for both parties. From the opposite perspective, a party holding a swap with a negative market value can terminate the swap by paying the market value to the counterparty. Terminating a swap in this manner is possible only if the counterparties specify in advance that such a transaction can be made, or if they reach an agreement to do so without having specified in advance. In other words, this feature is not automatically available and must be agreed to by both parties.

Many swaps are terminated early by entering into a separate and offsetting swap. For example, suppose a corporation is engaged in a swap to make fixed payments of 5 percent and receive floating payments based on LIBOR, with the payments made each 15 January and 15 July. Three years remain on the swap. That corporation can offset the swap by entering into an entirely new swap in which it makes payments based on LIBOR and receives a fixed rate with the payments made each 15 January and 15 July for three years. The swap fixed rate is determined by market conditions at the time the swap is initiated. Thus, the fixed rate on the new swap is not likely to match the fixed rate on the old swap, but the effect of this transaction is simply to have the floating payments offset; the fixed payments will net out to a known amount. Hence, the risk associated with the floating rate is eliminated. The default risk, however, is not eliminated because both swaps remain in effect.

Another way to terminate a swap early is sell the swap to another counterparty. Suppose a corporation holds a swap worth $75,000. If it can obtain the counterparty's permission, it can find another party to take over its payments. In effect, it sells the swap for $75,000 to that party. This procedure, however, is not commonly used.

A final way to terminate a swap early is by using a swaption. This instrument is an option to enter into a swap at terms that are established in advance. Thus, a party could use a swaption to enter into an offsetting swap, as described above. We shall cover swaptions in more detail in Section 6.

2   THE STRUCTURE OF GLOBAL SWAP MARKETS

The global swaps market is much like the global forward and over-the-counter options markets, which we covered in some detail in Chapters 1, 2, and 4. It is made up of dealers, which are banks and investment banking firms. These dealers make markets in swaps, quoting bid and ask prices and rates, thereby offering to take either side of a swap transaction. Upon taking a position in a swap, the dealer generally offsets the risk by making transactions in other markets. The counterparties to swaps are either end users or other dealers. The end users are often corporations with risk management problems that can be solved by engaging in a swap—a corporation or other end user is usually exposed to or needs an exposure to some type of risk that arises from interest rates, exchange rates, stock prices, or commodity prices. The end user contacts a dealer that makes a market in swaps. The two engage in a transaction, at which point the dealer assumes some risk from the end user. The dealer then usually lays off the risk by engaging in a transaction with another party. That transaction could be something as simple as a futures contract, or it could be an over-the-counter transaction with another dealer.

Risk magazine conducts annual surveys of participants in various derivative products. Exhibit 5-1 presents the results of those surveys for currency and interest rate swaps. One survey provides opinions of banks and investment banks that are swaps dealers. In the other survey, the respondents are end users. The results give a good idea of the major players in this market. It is interesting to note the disagreement between how dealers view themselves and how end users view them. Also, note that the rankings change, sometimes drastically, from year to year.

EXHIBIT 5-1 *Risk* Magazine Surveys of Banks, Investment Banks, and Corporate End Users to Determine the Top Three Dealers in Currency and Interest Rate Swaps

	Respondents	
Currencies	Banks and Investment Banks	Corporate End Users
Currency Swaps		
$/€	UBS Warburg	Citigroup
	JP Morgan Chase	Royal Bank of Scotland
	Deutsche Bank	Bank of America
$/¥	JP Morgan Chase	Citigroup
	UBS Warburg	Bank of America
	Credit Suisse First Boston/Deutsche Bank	JP Morgan Chase
$/£	Royal Bank of Scotland	Royal Bank of Scotland
	JP Morgan Chase	Citigroup
	Goldman Sachs	Deutsche Bank
$/SF	UBS Warburg	UBS Warburg
	Goldman Sachs	Citigroup
	Credit Suisse First Boston	Credit Suisse First Boston
Interest Rate Swaps (2–10 years)		
$	JP Morgan Chase	JP Morgan Chase
	Bank of America	Bank of America
	Morgan Stanley	Royal Bank of Scotland
€	JP Morgan Chase	Royal Bank of Scotland
	Deutsche Bank	Deutsche Bank
	Morgan Stanley	Citigroup
¥	JP Morgan Chase	Royal Bank of Scotland
	Deutsche Bank	Barclays Capital
	Bank of America	Citigroup/JP Morgan Chase
£	Royal Bank of Scotland	Royal Bank of Scotland
	Barclays Capital	Barclays Capital
	UBS Warburg	Deutsche Bank
SF	UBS Warburg	UBS Warburg
	Credit Suisse First Boston	Credit Suisse First Boston
	Zürcher Kantonalbank	Zürcher Kantonalbank

Note: $ = U.S. dollar, € = euro, ¥ = Japanese yen, £ = U.K. pound sterling, SF = Swiss franc

Source: *Risk*, September 2002, pp. 30–67 for banks and investment banking dealer respondents, and June 2002, pp. 24–34 for corporate end user respondents. Ratings for swaps with maturities less than 2 years and greater than 10 years are also provided in the September 2002 issue of *Risk*.

3 TYPES OF SWAPS

We alluded to the fact that the underlying asset in a swap can be a currency, interest rate, stock, or commodity. We now take a look at these types of swaps in more detail.

3.1 CURRENCY SWAPS

In a currency swap, each party makes interest payments to the other in different currencies.[2] Consider this example. The U.S. retailer Target Corporation (NYSE: TGT) does not have an established presence in Europe. Let us say that it has decided to begin opening a few stores in Germany and needs €9 million to fund construction and initial operations. TGT would like to issue a fixed-rate euro-denominated bond with face value of €9 million, but the company is not very well known in Europe. European investment bankers have given it a quote for such a bond. Deutsche Bank, AG (NYSE: DB), however, tells TGT that it should issue the bond in dollars and use a swap to convert it into euros.

Suppose TGT issues a five-year US$10 million bond at a rate of 6 percent. It then enters into a swap with DB in which DB will make payments to TGT in U.S. dollars at a fixed rate of 5.5 percent and TGT will make payments to DB in euros at a fixed rate of 4.9 percent each 15 March and 15 September for five years. The payments are based on a notional principal of 10 million in dollars and 9 million in euros. We assume the swap starts on 15 September of the current year. The swap specifies that the two parties exchange the notional principal at the start of the swap and at the end. Because the payments are made in different currencies, netting is not practical, so each party makes its respective payments.[3]

Thus, the swap is composed of the following transactions:

15 September:

- DB pays TGT €9 million
- TGT pays DB $10 million

Each 15 March and 15 September for five years:

- DB pays TGT 0.055(180/360)$10 million = $275,000
- TGT pays DB 0.049(180/360) €9 million = €220,500

15 September five years after initiation:

- DB pays TGT $10 million
- TGT pays DB €9 million

---

[2] It is important at this point to clear up some terminology confusion. Foreign currency is often called *foreign exchange* or sometimes *FX*. There is another transaction called an *FX swap*, which sounds as if it might be referring to a currency swap. In fact, an FX swap is just a long position in a forward contract on a foreign currency and a short position in a forward contract on the same currency with a different expiration. Why this transaction is called a swap is not clear, but this transaction existed before currency swaps were created. In futures markets, the analogous transaction is called a *spread*, reflecting as it does the risk associated with the spread between the prices of futures contracts with different expirations.

[3] In this example, we shall assume 180 days between payment dates. In practice, exact day counts are usually used, leading to different fixed payment amounts in one six-month period from those of another. In the example here, we are only illustrating the idea behind swap cash flows, so it is convenient to keep the fixed payments the same. Later in the chapter, we shall illustrate situations in which the exact day count is used, leading to fixed payments that vary slightly.

Note that we have simplified the interest calculations a little. In this example, we calculated semiannual interest using the fraction 180/360. Some parties might choose to use the exact day count in the six-month period divided by 365 days. LIBOR and Euribor transactions, the predominant rates used in interest rate swaps, nearly always use 360 days, as mentioned in previous chapters. Exhibit 5-2 shows the stream of cash flows from TGT's perspective.

EXHIBIT 5-2   Cash Flows to TGT on Swap with DB

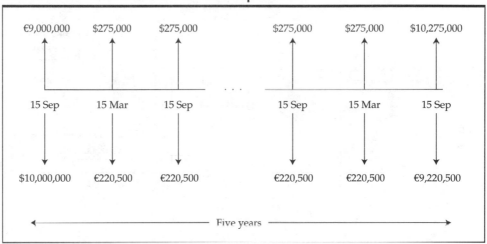

Note that the Target–Deutsche Bank transaction looks just like TGT is issuing a bond with face value of €9 million and that bond is purchased by DB. TGT converts the €9 million to $10 million and buys a dollar-denominated bond issued by DB. Note that TGT, having issued a bond denominated in euros, accordingly makes interest payments to DB in euros. DB, appropriately, makes interest payments in dollars to TGT. At the end, they each pay off the face values of the bonds they have issued. We emphasize that the Target–Deutsche Bank transaction *looks like* what we have just described. In fact, neither TGT nor DB actually issues or purchases a bond. They exchange only a series of cash flows that replicated the issuance and purchase of these bonds.

Exhibit 5-3 illustrates how such a combined transaction would work. TGT issues a bond in dollars (Exhibit 5-3, Panel A). It takes the dollars and passes them through to DB, which gives TGT the €9 million it needs. On the interest payment dates, the swap generates $275,000 of the $300,000 in interest TGT needs to pay its bondholders (Panel B). In turn, TGT makes interest payments in euros. Still, small dollar interest payments are necessary because TGT cannot issue a dollar bond at the swap rate. At the end of the transaction, TGT receives $10 million back from DB and passes it through to its bondholders (Panel C). TGT pays DB €9 million, thus effectively paying off a euro-denominated bond.

TGT has effectively issued a dollar-denominated bond and converted it to a euro-denominated bond. In all likelihood, it can save on interest expense by funding its need for euros in this way, because TGT is better known in the United States than in Europe. Its swap dealer, DB, knows TGT well and also obviously has a strong presence in Europe. Thus, DB can pass on its advantage in euro bond markets to TGT. In addition, had TGT issued a euro-denominated bond, it would have assumed no credit risk. By entering into the swap, TGT assumes a remote possibility of DB defaulting. Thus, TGT saves a little money by assuming some credit risk.

EXHIBIT 5-3   Issuing a Dollar-Denominated Bond and Using a Currency Swap to Convert a Euro-Denominated Bond

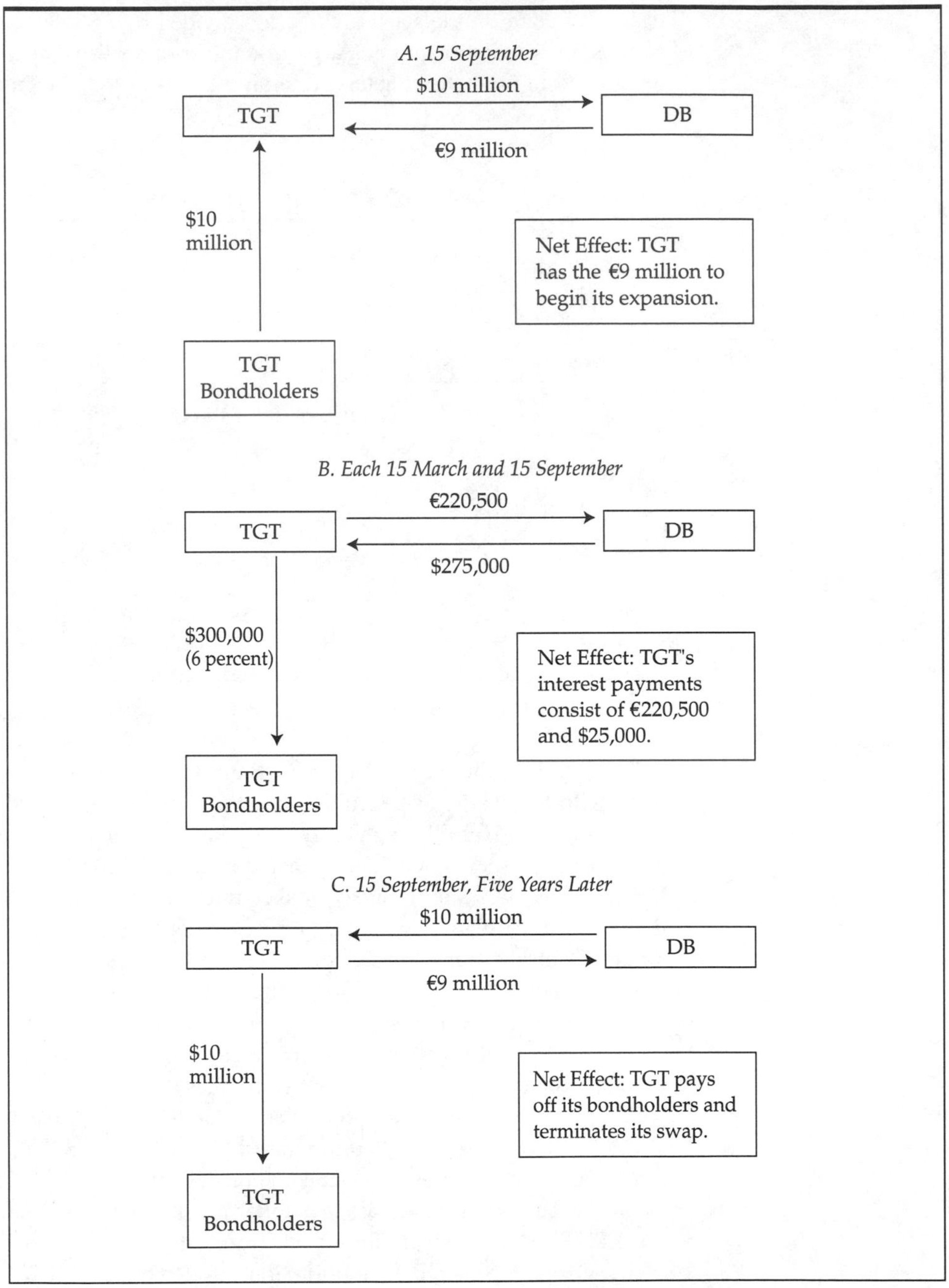

A. 15 September

$10 million →

TGT ←———— DB

€9 million

$10 million ↑ (from TGT Bondholders)

TGT Bondholders

Net Effect: TGT has the €9 million to begin its expansion.

B. Each 15 March and 15 September

€220,500 →

TGT ←———— DB

$275,000

$300,000 (6 percent) ↓

TGT Bondholders

Net Effect: TGT's interest payments consist of €220,500 and $25,000.

C. 15 September, Five Years Later

$10 million ←

TGT ———→ DB

€9 million

$10 million ↓

TGT Bondholders

Net Effect: TGT pays off its bondholders and terminates its swap.

PRACTICE PROBLEM 1

Consider a currency swap in which the domestic party pays a fixed rate in the foreign currency, the British pound, and the counterparty pays a fixed rate in U.S. dollars. The notional principals are $50 million and £30 million. The fixed rates are 5.6 percent in dollars and 6.25 percent in pounds. Both sets of payments are made on the basis of 30 days per month and 365 days per year, and the payments are made semiannually.

A. Determine the initial exchange of cash that occurs at the start of the swap.

B. Determine the semiannual payments.

C. Determine the final exchange of cash that occurs at the end of the swap.

D. Give an example of a situation in which this swap might be appropriate.

SOLUTIONS

A. At the start of the swap:
Domestic party pays counterparty $50 million
Counterparty pays domestic party £30 million

B. Semiannually:
Domestic party pays counterparty £30,000,000(0.0625)(180/365) = £924,658
Counterparty pays domestic party $50,000,000(0.056)(180/365) = $1,380,822

C. At the end of the swap:
Domestic party pays counterparty £30,000,000
Counterparty pays domestic party $50,000,000

D. This swap would be appropriate for a U.S. company that issues a dollar-denominated bond but would prefer to borrow in British pounds.

Returning to the Target swap, recall that Target effectively converted a fixed-rate loan in dollars to a fixed-rate loan in euros. Suppose instead that TGT preferred to borrow in euros at a floating rate. It then would have specified that the swap required it to make payments to DB at a floating rate. Had TGT preferred to issue the dollar-denominated bond at a floating rate, it would have specified that DB pay it dollars at a floating rate.

Although TGT and DB exchanged notional principal, some scenarios exist in which the notional principals are not exchanged. For example, suppose many years later, TGT is generating €10 million in cash annually and converting it back to dollars twice a year on 15 January and 15 July. It might then wish to lock in the conversion rate by entering into a currency swap that would require it to pay a dealer €10 million and receive a fixed amount of dollars. If the euro fixed rate were 5 percent, a notional principal of €400 million would generate a payment of 0.05(180/360)€400 million = €10 million. If the exchange rate is, for example, $0.85, the equivalent dollar notional principal would be $340 million. If the dollar fixed rate is 6 percent, TGT would receive 0.06(180/360)$340 million = $10.2 million.[4] These payments would occur twice a year for the life of the swap. TGT might then lock in the conversion rate by entering into a currency swap with notional principal amounts that would allow it to receive a fixed amount of dollars on 15 January and 15 July. There would be no reason to specify an exchange of notional principal.

---

[4] It might appear that TGT has somehow converted cash flows worth €10million($0.085) = $8.5 million into cash flows worth $10.2 million. Recall, however, that the €10 million cash flows are generated yearly and $0.85 is the *current* exchange rate. We cannot apply the current exchange rate to a series of cash flows over various future dates. We would apply the respective forward exchange rates, not the spot rate, to the series of future euro cash flows.

As we previously described, there are four types of currency swaps. Using the original Target–Deutsche Bank swap as an example, the semiannual payments would be

  A. TGT pays euros at a fixed rate; DB pays dollars at a fixed rate.
  B. TGT pays euros at a fixed rate; DB pays dollars at a floating rate.
  C. TGT pays euros at a floating rate; DB pays dollars at a floating rate.
  D. TGT pays euros at a floating rate; DB pays dollars at a fixed rate.

Or, reversing the flow, TGT could be the payer of dollars and DB could be the payer of euros:

  E. TGT pays dollars at a fixed rate; DB pays euros at a fixed rate.
  F. TGT pays dollars at a fixed rate; DB pays euros at a floating rate.
  G. TGT pays dollars at a floating rate; DB pays euros at a floating rate.
  H. TGT pays dollars at a floating rate; DB pays euros at a fixed rate.

Suppose we combine Swap A with Swap H. With TGT paying euros at a fixed rate and DB paying euros at a fixed rate, the euro payments wash out and the net effect is

  I. TGT pays dollars at a floating rate; DB pays dollars at a fixed rate.

Suppose we combine Swap B with Swap E. Similarly, the euro payments again wash out, and the net effect is

  J. TGT pays dollars at a fixed rate; DB pays dollars at a floating rate.

Suppose we combine Swap C with Swap F. Likewise, the euro floating payments wash out, and the net effect is

  K. TGT pays dollars at a fixed rate; DB pays dollars at a floating rate.

Lastly, suppose we combine Swap D with Swap G. Again, the euro floating payments wash out, and the net effect is

  L. TGT pays dollars at a floating rate; DB pays dollars at a fixed rate.

Of course, the net results of I and L are equivalent, and the net results of J and K are equivalent. What we have shown here, however, is that combinations of currency swaps eliminate the currency flows and leave us with transactions in only one currency. A swap in which both sets of interest payments are made in the same currency is an interest rate swap.

3.2 INTEREST RATE SWAPS

As we discovered in the above paragraph, an interest rate swap can be created as a combination of currency swaps. Of course, no one would create an interest rate swap that way; doing so would require two transactions when only one would suffice. Interest rate swaps evolved into their own market. In fact, the interest rate swap market is much bigger than the currency swap market, as we have seen in the notional principal statistics.

As previously noted, one way to look at an interest rate swap is that it is a currency swap in which both currencies are the same. Consider a swap to pay Currency A fixed and Currency B floating. Currency A could be dollars, and B could be euros. But what if A and

B are both dollars, or A and B are both euros? The first case is a dollar-denominated plain vanilla swap; the second is a euro-denominated plain vanilla swap. *A **plain vanilla swap** is simply an interest rate swap in which one party pays a fixed rate and the other pays a floating rate, with both sets of payments in the same currency.* In fact, the plain vanilla swap is probably the most common derivative transaction in the global financial system.

Note that because we are paying in the same currency, there is no need to exchange notional principals at the beginning and at the end of an interest rate swap. In addition, the interest payments can be, and nearly always are, netted. If one party owes $X and the other owes $Y, the party owing the greater amount pays the net difference, which greatly reduces the credit risk (as we discuss in more detail in Section 7). Finally, we note that there is no reason to have both sides pay a fixed rate. The two streams of payments would be identical in that case. So in an interest rate swap, either one side always pays fixed and the other side pays floating, or both sides paying floating, but never do both sides pay fixed.[5]

Thus, in a plain vanilla interest rate swap, one party makes interest payments at a fixed rate and the other makes interest payments at a floating rate. Both sets of payments are on the same notional principal and occur on regularly scheduled dates. For each payment, the interest rate is multiplied by a fraction representing the number of days in the settlement period over the number of days in a year. In some cases, the settlement period is computed assuming 30 days in each month; in others, an exact day count is used. Some cases assume a 360-day year; others use 365 days.

Let us now illustrate an interest rate swap. Suppose that on 15 December, General Electric Company (NYSE: GE) borrows money for one year from a bank such as Bank of America (NYSE: BAC). The loan is for $25 million and specifies that GE will make interest payments on a quarterly basis on the 15th of March, June, September, and December for one year at the rate of LIBOR plus 25 basis points. At the end of the year, it will pay back the principal. On the 15th of December, March, June, and September, LIBOR is observed and sets the rate for that quarter. The interest is then paid at the end of the quarter.[6]

GE believes that it is getting a good rate, but fearing a rise in interest rates, it would prefer a fixed-rate loan. It can easily convert the floating-rate loan to a fixed-rate loan by engaging in a swap. Suppose it approaches JP Morgan Chase (NYSE: JPM), a large dealer bank, and requests a quote on a swap to pay a fixed rate and receive LIBOR, with payments on the dates of its loan payments. The bank prices the swap (a procedure we cover in Section 4) and quotes a fixed rate of 6.2 percent.[7] The fixed payments will be made based on a day count of 90/365, and the floating payments will be made based on 90/360. Current LIBOR is 5.9 percent. Therefore, the first fixed payment, which GE makes to JPM, is $25,000,000(0.062)(90/365) = $382,192. This is also the amount of each remaining fixed payment.

The first floating payment, which JPM makes to GE, is $25,000,000(0.059)(90/360) = $368,750. Of course, the remaining floating payments will not be known until later. Exhibit 5-4 shows the pattern of cash flows on the swap from GE's perspective.

---

[5] The case of both sides paying floating is called a basis swap, which we shall cover in Section 5.

[6] Again, we assume 90 days in each interest payment period for this example. The exact payment dates are not particularly important for illustrative purposes.

[7] Typically the rate is quoted as a spread over the rate on a U.S. Treasury security with a comparable maturity. Suppose the yield on a two-year Treasury note is 6 percent. Then the swap would be quoted as 20 basis points over the two-year Treasury rate. By quoting the rate in the this manner, GE knows what it is paying over the Treasury rate, a differential called the swap spread, which is a type of credit risk premium we discuss in Section 7. In addition, a quote in this form protects the bank from the rate changing drastically either during the phone conversation or shortly thereafter. Thus, the quote can stay in effect for a reasonable period of time while GE checks out quotes from other dealers.

EXHIBIT 5-4   Cash Flows to GE on Swap with JPM

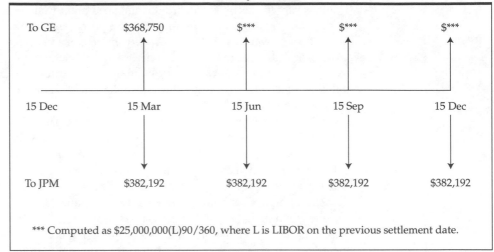

*** Computed as $25,000,000(L)90/360, where L is LIBOR on the previous settlement date.

PRACTICE PROBLEM 2

Determine the upcoming payments in a plain vanilla interest rate swap in which the notional principal is €70 million. The end user makes semiannual fixed payments at the rate of 7 percent, and the dealer makes semiannual floating payments at Euribor, which was 6.25 percent on the last settlement period. The floating payments are made on the basis of 180 days in the settlement period and 360 days in a year. The fixed payments are made on the basis of 180 days in the settlement period and 365 days in a year. Payments are netted, so determine which party pays which and what amount.

SOLUTION

The fixed payments are €70,000,000(0.07)(180/365) = €2,416,438.

The upcoming floating payment is €70,000,000(0.0625)(180/360) = €2,187,500.

The net payment is that the party paying fixed will pay the party paying floating
€2,416,438 − €2,187,500 = €228,938.

Note in Exhibit 5-4 that we did not show the notional principal, because it was not exchanged. We could implicitly show that GE received $25 million from JPM and paid $25 million to JPM at the start of the swap. We could also show that the same thing happens at the end. If we look at it that way, it appears as if GE has issued a $25 million fixed-rate bond, which was purchased by JPM, which in turn issued a $25 million floating-rate bond, which was in turn purchased by GE. We say that *it appears* as if this is what happened: In fact, neither party actually issued a bond, but they have generated the cash flows that would occur if GE had issued such a fixed-rate bond, JPM had issued such a floating-rate bond, and each purchased the bond of the other. In other words, we could include the principals on both sides to make each set of cash flows look like a bond, yet the overall cash flows would be the same as on the swap.

So let us say that GE enters into this swap. Exhibit 5-5 shows the net effect of the swap and the loan. GE pays LIBOR plus 25 basis points to Bank of America on its loan,

EXHIBIT 5-5   GE's Conversion of a Floating-Rate Loan to a Fixed-Rate Loan Using an Interest Rate Swap with JPM

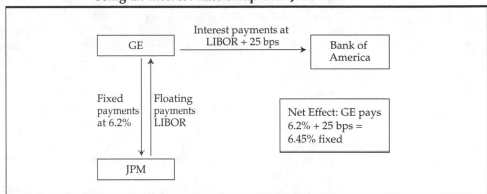

pays 6.2 percent to JPM, and receives LIBOR from JPM. The net effect is that GE pays 6.2 + 0.25 = 6.45 percent fixed.

Now, JPM is engaged in a swap to pay LIBOR and receive 6.2 percent. It is exposed to the risk of LIBOR increasing. It would, therefore, probably engage in some other type of transaction to offset this risk. One transaction commonly used in this situation is to sell Eurodollar futures. As discussed in Chapter 3, Eurodollar futures prices move $25 in value for each basis point move in LIBOR. JPM will determine how sensitive its position is to a move in LIBOR and sell an appropriate number of futures to offset the risk. Note that Bank of America is exposed to LIBOR as well, but in the banking industry, floating-rate loans are often made because the funding that the bank obtained to make the loan was probably already at LIBOR or a comparable floating rate.

It is possible but unlikely that GE could get a fixed-rate loan at a better rate. The swap involves some credit risk: the possibility, however small, that JPM will default. In return for assuming that risk, GE in all likelihood would get a better rate than it would if it borrowed at a fixed rate. JPM is effectively a wholesaler of risk, using its powerful position as one of the world's leading banks to facilitate the buying and selling of risk for companies such as GE. Dealers profit from the spread between the rates they quote to pay and the rates they quote to receive. The swaps market is, however, extremely competitive and the spreads have been squeezed very tight, which makes it very challenging for dealers to make a profit. Of course, this competition is good for end users, because it gives them more attractive rates.

3.3 EQUITY SWAPS

By now, it should be apparent that a swap requires at least one variable rate or price underlying it. So far, that rate has been an interest rate.[8] In an equity swap, the rate is the return on a stock or stock index. This characteristic gives the equity swap two features that distinguish it from interest rate and currency swaps.

First, the party making the fixed-rate payment could also have to make a variable payment based on the equity return. Suppose the end user pays the equity payment and receives the fixed payment, i.e., it pays the dealer the return on the S&P 500 Index, and the dealer pays the end user a fixed rate. If the S&P 500 increases, the return is positive and the end user pays that return to the dealer. If the S&P 500 goes down, however, its return is obviously negative. In that case, the end user would pay the dealer the *negative return on the*

---

[8] Currency swaps also have the element that the exchange rate is variable.

S&P 500, which means that it would receive that return from the dealer. For example, if the S&P 500 falls by 1 percent, the dealer would pay the end user 1 percent, in addition to the fixed payment the dealer makes in any case. So the dealer, or in general the party receiving the equity return, could end up making *both* a fixed-rate payment and an equity payment.

The second distinguishing feature of an equity swap is that the payment is not known until the end of the settlement period, at which time the return on the stock is known. In an interest rate or currency swap, the floating interest rate is set at the beginning of the period.[9] Therefore, one always knows the amount of the upcoming floating interest payment.[10]

Another important feature of some equity swaps is that the rate of return is often structured to include both dividends and capital gains. In interest rate and currency swaps, capital gains are not paid.[11] Finally, we note that in some equity swaps, the notional principal is indexed to change with the level of the stock, although we will not explore such swaps in this book.[12]

Equity swaps are commonly used by asset managers. Let us consider a situation in which an asset manager might use such a swap. Suppose that the Vanguard Asset Allocation Fund (Nasdaq: VAAPX) is authorized to use swaps. On the last day of December, it would like to sell $100 million in U.S. large-cap equities and invest the proceeds at a fixed rate. It believes that a swap allowing it to pay the total return on the S&P 500, while receiving a fixed rate, would achieve this objective. It would like to hold this position for one year, with payments to be made on the last day of March, June, September, and December. It enters into such a swap with Morgan Stanley (NYSE: MWD).

Specifically, the swap covers a notional principal of $100 million and calls for VAAPX to pay MWD the return on the S&P 500 Total Return Index and for MWD to pay VAAPX a fixed rate on the last day of March, June, September, and December for one year. MWD prices the swap at a fixed rate of 6.5 percent. The fixed payments will be made using an actual day count/365 days convention. There are 90 days between 31 December and 31 March, 91 days between 31 March and 30 June, 92 days between 30 June and 30 September, and 92 days between 30 September and 31 December. Thus, the fixed payments will be

31 March: $100,000,000(0.065)(90/365) = $1,602,740

30 June: $100,000,000(0.065)(91/365) = $1,620,548

30 September: $100,000,000(0.065)(92/365) = $1,638,356

31 December: $100,000,000(0.065)(92/365) = $1,638,356

Exhibit 5-6 shows the cash flow stream to VAAPX.

Suppose that on the day the swap is initiated, 31 December, the S&P 500 Total Return Index is at 3,517.76. Now suppose that on 31 March, the index is at 3,579.12. The return on the index is

$$\frac{3,579.12}{3,517.76} - 1 = 0.0174$$

---

[9] Technically, there are interest rate swaps in which the floating rate is set at the end of the period, at which time the payment is made. We shall briefly mention these swaps in Section 5.

[10] In a currency swap, however, one does not know the exchange rate until the settlement date.

[11] In some kinds of interest rate swaps, the total return on a bond, which includes dividends and capital gains, is paid. This instrument is called a **total return swap** and is a common variety of a credit derivative, which we cover in Chapter 9.

[12] Some interest rate swaps also have a notional principal that changes, which we shall briefly discuss in Section 5.

EXHIBIT 5-6   Cash Flows to VAAPX on Equity Swap with MWD

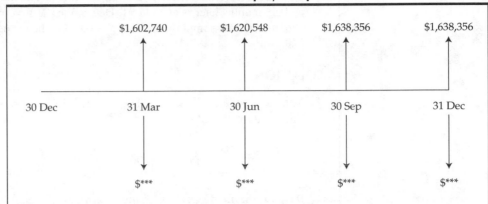

*** Computed as $100,000,000R, where R is the return on the S&P 500 Total Return Index from the previous settlement date.

Thus, the return is 1.74 percent. The equity payment that VAAPX would make to MWD would be $100,000,000(0.0174) = $1,740,000.

Of course, this amount would not be known until 31 March, and only the difference between this amount and the fixed payment would be paid. Then on 31 March, the index value of 3,579.12 would be the base for the following period. Suppose that on 30 June, the index declines to 3,452.78. Then the return for the second quarter would be

$$\frac{3,452.78}{3,579.12} - 1 = -0.0353$$

Therefore, the loss is 3.53 percent, requiring a payment of $100,000,000(0.0353) = $3,530,000.

Because this amount represents a loss on the S&P 500, MWD would make a payment to VAAPX. In addition, MWD would also owe VAAPX the fixed payment of $1,620,548. It is as though VAAPX sold out of its position in stock, thereby avoiding the loss of about $3.5 million, and moved into a fixed-income position, thereby picking up a gain of about $1.6 million.

PRACTICE PROBLEM 3

A mutual fund has arranged an equity swap with a dealer. The swap's notional principal is $100 million, and payments will be made semiannually. The mutual fund agrees to pay the dealer the return on a small-cap stock index, and the dealer agrees to pay the mutual fund based on one of the two specifications given below. The small-cap index starts off at 1,805.20; six months later, it is at 1,796.15.

A. The dealer pays a fixed rate of 6.75 percent to the mutual fund, with payments made on the basis of 182 days in the period and 365 days in a year. Determine the first payment for both parties and, under the assumption of netting, determine the net payment and which party makes it.

B. The dealer pays the return on a large-cap index. The index starts off at 1155.14 and six months later is at 1148.91. Determine the first payment for both parties and, under the assumption of netting, determine the net payment and which party makes it.

SOLUTIONS

A. The fixed payment is $100,000,000(0.0675)182/365 = $3,365,753
The equity payment is

$$\left(\frac{1796.15}{1805.20} - 1\right)\$100,000,000 = -\$501,329$$

Because the fund pays the equity return and the equity return is negative, the dealer must pay the equity return. The dealer also pays the fixed return, so the dealer makes both payments, which add up to $3,365,753 + $501,329 = $3,867,082. The net payment is $3,867,082, paid by the dealer to the mutual fund.

B. The large-cap equity payment is

$$\left(\frac{1148.91}{1155.14} - 1\right)\$100,000,000 = -\$539,329$$

The fund owes −$501,329, so the dealer owes the fund $501,329. The dealer owes −$539,329, so the fund owes the dealer $539,329. Therefore, the fund pays the dealer the net amount of $539,329 − $501,329 = $38,000.

Exhibit 5-7 illustrates what VAAPX has accomplished. It is important to note that the conversion of its equity assets into fixed income is not perfect. VAAPX does not hold a portfolio precisely equal to the S&P 500 Total Return Index. To the extent that VAAPX's portfolio generates a return that deviates from the index, some mismatching can occur, which can be a problem. As an alternative, VAAPX can request that MWD give it a swap based on

EXHIBIT 5-7   VAAPX's Conversion of an Equity Position into a Fixed-Income Position

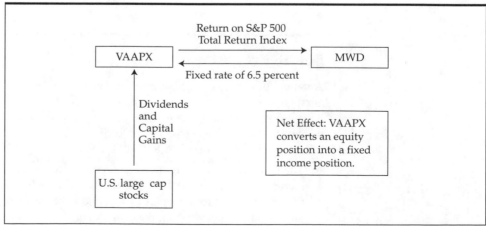

the precise portfolio that VAAPX wishes to sell off. In that case, however, MWD would assess a charge by lowering the fixed rate it pays or raising the rate VAAPX pays to it.[13]

In our previous VAAPX example, the fund wanted to move some money out of a large-cap equity position and invest the proceeds at a fixed rate. Suppose instead that they do not want to move the proceeds into a fixed-rate investment. VAAPX could structure a swap to pay it a floating rate or the return on some other equity index. For example, an asset allocation from U.S. large-cap stocks to U.S. small-cap stocks could be accomplished by having MWD pay the return on the S&P 500 Small Cap 600 Index.

Suppose VAAPX wanted to move out of a position in U.S. stocks and into a position in U.K. large-cap stocks. It could structure the swap to have MWD pay it the return on the FTSE (Financial Times Stock Exchange) 100 Index. Note, however, that this index is based on the prices of U.K. stocks as quoted in pounds sterling. If VAAPX wanted the exposure in pounds—that is, it wanted the currency risk as well as the risk of the U.K. stock market—the payments from MWD to VAAPX would be made in pounds. VAAPX could, however, ask for the payments in dollars. In that case, MWD would hedge the currency risk and make payments in dollars.

Although our focus in this book is on currency, interest rate, and equity products, we shall take a very brief look at some other types of swaps.

3.4 COMMODITY AND OTHER TYPES OF SWAPS

Just as currencies, interest rates, and equities can be used to structure swaps, so too can commodities and just about anything that has a random outcome and to which a corporation, financial institution, or even an individual is exposed. Commodity swaps are very commonly used. For example, airlines enter into swaps to hedge their future purchases of jet fuel. They agree to make fixed payments to a swap dealer on regularly scheduled dates and receive payments determined by the price of jet fuel. Gold mining companies use swaps to hedge future deliveries of gold. Other parties dealing in such commodities as natural gas and precious metals often use swaps to lock in prices for future purchases and sales. In addition, swaps can be based on non-storable commodities, like electricity and the weather. In the case of the weather, payments are made based on a measure of a particular weather factor, such as amounts of rain, snowfall, or weather-related damage.

We have now introduced and described the basic structure of swaps. We have made many references to the pricing and valuation of swaps, and we now move on to explore how this is done.

4 PRICING AND VALUATION OF SWAPS

In Chapter 2, we took our first look at the concepts of pricing and valuation when we examined forward contracts on assets and FRAs, which are essentially forward contracts on interest rates. Recall that a forward contract requires no cash payment at the start and commits one party to buy and another to sell an asset at a later date. An FRA commits one party to make a single fixed-rate interest payment and the other to make a single floating-rate interest payment. A swap extends that concept by committing one party to making a series of floating payments. The other party commits to making a series of fixed or floating payments. For swaps containing any fixed terms, such as a fixed rate, pricing the swap means to determine those terms at the start of the swap. Some swaps do not contain any fixed terms; we explore examples of both types of swaps.

---

[13] Note, however, that VAAPX is converting not its entire portfolio but simply a $100 million portion of it.

All swaps have a market value. Valuation of a swap means to determine the market value of the swap based on current market conditions. The fixed terms, such as the fixed rate, are established at the start to give the swap an initial market value of zero. As we have already discussed, a zero market value means that neither party pays anything to the other at the start. Later during the life of the swap, as market conditions change, the market value will change, moving from zero from both parties' perspective to a positive value for one party and a negative value for the other. When a swap has zero value, it is neither an asset nor a liability to either party. When the swap has positive value to one party, it is an asset to that party; from the perspective of the other party, it thus has negative value and is a liability.

We begin the process of pricing and valuing swaps by learning how swaps are comparable to other instruments. If we know that one financial instrument is equivalent to another, we can price one instrument if we know or can determine the price of the other instrument.

4.1 EQUIVALENCE OF SWAPS AND OTHER INSTRUMENTS

In this section, we look at how swaps are similar to other instruments. Because our focus is on currency, interest rate, and equity swaps, we do not discuss commodity swaps here.

4.1.1 SWAPS AND ASSETS

We have already alluded to the similarity between swaps and assets. For example, a currency swap is identical to issuing a fixed- or floating-rate bond in one currency, converting the proceeds to the other currency, and using the proceeds to purchase a fixed- or floating-rate bond denominated in the other currency. An interest rate swap is identical to issuing a fixed- or floating-rate bond and using the proceeds to purchase a floating- or fixed-rate bond. The notional principal is equivalent to the face value on these hypothetical bonds.

Equity swaps appear to be equivalent to issuing one type of security and using the proceeds to purchase another, where at least one of the types of securities is a stock or stock index. For example, a pay-fixed, receive-equity swap looks like issuing a fixed-rate bond and using the proceeds to buy a stock or index portfolio. As it turns out, however, these two transactions are not exactly the same, although they are close. The stock position in the transaction is not the same as a buy-and-hold position; some adjustments are required on the settlement dates to replicate the cash flows of a swap. We shall take a look at this process of replicating an equity swap in Section 4.2.3. For now, simply recognize that an equity swap is like issuing bonds and buying stock, but not buying and holding stock.

The equivalence of a swap to transactions we are already familiar with, such as owning assets, is important because it allows us to price and value the swap using simple instruments, such as the underlying currency, interest rate, or stock. We do not require other derivatives to replicate the cash flows of a swap. Nonetheless, other derivatives can be used to replicate the cash flows of a swap, and it is worth seeing why this is true.

4.1.2 SWAPS AND FORWARD CONTRACTS

Recall that a forward contract, whether on an interest rate, a currency, or an equity, is an agreement for one party to make a fixed payment to the other, while the latter party makes a variable payment to the former. A swap extends this notion by combining a series of forward contracts into a single transaction. There are, however, some subtle differences between swaps and forward contracts. For example, swaps are a series of equal fixed payments, whereas the component contracts of a series of forward contracts would almost always be priced at different fixed rates.[14] In this context we often refer to a swap as a series of off-market forward contracts, reflecting the fact that the implicit forward con-

---

[14] For example, a series of FRAs would have different fixed rates unless the term structure is flat.

tracts that make up the swap are all priced at the swap fixed rate and not at the rate at which they would normally be priced in the market. In addition, in interest rate swaps, the next payment that each party makes is known. That would obviously not be the case for a single forward contract. Other subtleties distinguish currency swaps from a series of currency forwards and equity swaps from a series of equity forwards, but in general, it is acceptable to view a swap as a series of forward contracts.

4.1.3 SWAPS AND FUTURES CONTRACTS

It is a fairly common practice to equate swaps to futures contracts. This practice is partially correct, but only to the extent that futures contracts can be equated to forward contracts. We saw in Chapter 3 that futures contracts are equivalent to forward contracts only when future interest rates are known. Obviously this condition can never truly be met, and because swaps are often used to manage uncertain interest rates, the equivalence of futures with swaps is not always appropriate. Moreover, swaps are highly customized contracts, whereas futures are standardized with respect to expiration and the underlying instrument. Although it is common to equate a swap with a series of futures contracts, this equality holds true only in very limited cases.[15]

4.1.4 SWAPS AND OPTIONS

Finally, we note that swaps can be equated to combinations of options. Buying a call and selling a put would force the transacting party to make a net payment if the underlying is below the exercise rate at expiration, and would result in receipt of a payment if the underlying is above the exercise rate at expiration. This payment will be equivalent to a swap payment if the exercise rate is set at the fixed rate on the swap. Therefore, a swap is equivalent to a combination of options with expirations at the swap payment dates. The connection between swaps and options is relatively straightforward for interest rate instruments, but less so for currency and equity instruments. Nonetheless, we can generally consider swaps as equivalent to combinations of options.

In this section, we have learned that swaps can be shown to be equivalent to combinations of assets, combinations of forward contracts, combinations of futures contracts, and combinations of options. Thus, to price and value swaps we can choose any of these approaches. We choose the simplest: swaps and assets.

4.2 PRICING AND VALUATION

As in previous chapters, our goal is to determine the market value of the derivative transaction of interest, in this case, swaps. At the start of a swap, the market value is set to zero. The process of pricing the swap involves finding the terms that force that market value to zero. To determine the market value of a swap, we replicate the swap using other instruments that produce the same cash flows. Knowing the values of these other instruments, we are able to value the swap. This value can be thought of as what the swap is worth if we were to sell it to someone else. In addition, we can think of the value as what we might assign to it on our balance sheet. The swap can have a positive value, making it an asset, or a negative value, making it a liability.

---

[15] It is possible only in extremely rare circumstances for futures expirations to line up with swap settlement dates and thereby provide perfect equivalence. That does not mean, however, that futures cannot be used to hedge in a delta-hedging sense, as described in Chapter 4. A futures price has a given sensitivity to the underlying, and futures are often highly liquid. A dealer, having entered into a swap, can determine the swap's sensitivity to the underlying and execute the appropriate number of futures transactions to balance the volatility of the swap to that of the futures. Indeed, this method is standard for hedging plain vanilla swaps using the Eurodollar futures contract.

As we noted in Section 4.1, swaps are equivalent to a variety of instruments, but we prefer to use the simplest instruments to replicate the swap. The simplest instruments are the underlying assets: bonds, stocks, and currencies. Therefore, we shall use these underlying instruments to replicate the swap.

To understand the pricing of currency, interest rate, and equity swaps, we shall have to first take a brief digression to examine an instrument that plays an important role in their pricing. We shall see that the floating-rate security will have a value of 1.0, its par, at the start and on any coupon reset date. Recall that we have made numerous references to floating rates and floating payments. Accordingly, we must first obtain a solid understanding of floating-rate notes.

As we did in Chapter 2, let us first set up a time line that indicates where we are and where the interest payments on the floating-rate note will occur:

We start at time 0. The interest payments will occur on days $h_1, h_2, \ldots, h_{n-1}$, and h_n, so there are n interest payments in all. Day h_n is the maturity date of the floating-rate note. The time interval between payments is m days. The underlying rate is an m-day interest rate.

For simplicity, we will use LIBOR as the underlying rate and denote it with the symbol we have previously used, $L_i(m)$, which stands for the m-day LIBOR on day i. If i = 1, we are referring to day h_1, which might, for example, be 180 days after day 0. Thus, $h_1 = 180$. $L_0(180)$ is the 180-day LIBOR on day 0. Then h_2 would likely be 360 and $L_0(2m) = L_0(360)$, the 360-day LIBOR on day 0. We denote $B_0(h_j)$ as the present value factor on a zero-coupon instrument paying \$1 at its maturity date. As an example, to discount payments 180 and 360 days later, we multiply the payment amount by the following respective factors:

$$B_0(180) = \frac{1}{1 + L_0(180) \times (180/360)}$$

$$B_0(360) = \frac{1}{1 + L_0(360) \times (360/360)}$$

We can think of these discount factors as the values of spot LIBOR deposits that pay \$1 at maturity, 180 and 360 days later.

On day 0, the floating rate is set for the first period and the interest to be paid at that rate is paid on day h_1. Then on day h_1, the rate is set for the second period and the interest is paid on day h_2. This process continues so that on day h_{n-1} the rate is set for the last period, and the final interest payment and the principal are paid on day h_n. Let the principal be 1.0.

Suppose today is day h_{n-1} and LIBOR on that day is $L_{n-1}(m)$. Remember that this rate is the m-day LIBOR in the market at that time. Therefore, looking ahead to day h_n, we anticipate receiving 1.0, the final principal payment, plus $L_{n-1}(m) \times (m/360)$. What is the value of this amount on day h_{n-1}? We would discount it by the appropriate m-day LIBOR in the following manner:

Value at h_{n-1} = (Payment at h_n)(One-period discount factor)

$$= [1.0 + L_{n-1}(m) \times (m/360)]\left[\frac{1}{1.0 + L_{n-1}(m) \times (m/360)}\right] = 1.0$$

The value is 1.0, its par value. Now step back to day h_{n-2}, at which time the rate is $L_{n-2}(m)$. Looking ahead to day h_{n-1} we shall receive an interest payment of $L_{n-2}(m) \times (m/360)$. We do not receive the principal on day h_{n-1}, but it is appropriate to discount the market value on day h_{n-1}, which we just determined is 1.0.[16] Thus, the value of the floating-rate security will be

$$\text{Value at } h_{n-2} = (\text{Payment at } h_{n-1})(\text{One-period discount factor})$$

$$= [1.0 + L_{n-2}(m) \times (m/360)]\left[\frac{1}{1.0 + L_{n-2}(m) \times (m/360)}\right] = 1.0$$

We continue this procedure, stepping back until we reach time 0. The floating-rate security will have a value of 1.0, its par, at the start and on any coupon reset date.[17] We shall use this result to help us price and value swaps.

In previous material in this chapter, we have covered currency swaps first. We did so because we showed that an interest rate swap is just a currency swap in which both currencies are the same. A currency swap is thus the more general instrument of the two. For the purposes of this section, however, it will be easier to price and value a currency swap if we first price and value an interest rate swap.

4.2.1 INTEREST RATE SWAPS

Pricing an interest rate swap means finding the fixed rate that equates the present value of the fixed payments to the present value of the floating payments, a process that sets the market value of the swap to zero at the start. Using the time line illustrated earlier, the swap cash flows will occur on days $h_1, h_2, \ldots, h_{n-1}$, and h_n, so there are n cash flows in the swap. Day h_n is the expiration date of the swap. The time interval between payments is m days. We can thus think of the swap as being on an m-day interest rate, which will be LIBOR in our examples.

As previously mentioned, the payments in an interest rate swap are a series of fixed and floating interest payments. They do not include an initial and final exchange of notional principals. As we already observed, such payments would be only an exchange of the same money. But if we introduce the notional principal payments as though they were actually made, we have not done any harm. The cash flows on the swap are still the same. The advantage of introducing the notional principal payments is that we can now treat the fixed and floating sides of the swap as though they were fixed- and floating-rate bonds.

So we introduce a hypothetical final notional principal payment of $1 on a swap starting at day 0 and ending on day h_n, in which the underlying is an m-day rate. The fixed swap interest payment *rate*, FS(0,n,m), gives the fixed payment *amount* corresponding to the $1 notional principal. Thus, the present value of a series of fixed interest payments at the swap rate FS(0,n,m) plus a final principal payment of 1.0 is

---

[16] All we are doing here is discounting the upcoming cash flow and the market value of the security on the next payment date. This procedure is not unique to floating-rate securities; it is standard valuation procedure for any type of security. What is special and different for floating-rate securities is that the market value goes back to par on each payment date.

[17] Floating-rate securities are designed to allow the coupon to catch up with market interest rates on a regularly scheduled basis. The price can deviate from par during the period between reset dates. In addition, if there is any credit risk and that risk changes during the life of the security, its price can deviate from par at any time, including at the coupon reset date. We are assuming no credit risk here.

$$\sum_{j=1}^{n} FS(0, n, m)B_0(h_j) + \$1 \times B_0(h_n), \text{ or}$$

$$FS(0, n, m) \sum_{j=1}^{n} B_0(h_j) + B_0(h_n)$$

Here the summation simply represents the sum of the present value factors for each payment. The expression $B_0(h_n)$ is the present value factor for the final hypothetical notional principal payment of 1.0.

Now we must find the present value of the floating payments, and here we use what we learned about floating-rate notes. Remember that a floating-rate note with $1 face will have a value of $1 at the start and at any coupon reset date. If the swap's floating payments include a final principal payment, we can treat them like a floating-rate note. Hence, we know their value is $1.

Now all we have to do is equate the present value of the fixed payments to the present value of the floating payments

$$FS(0, n, m) \sum_{j=1}^{n} B_0(h_j) + B_0(h_n) = 1.0$$

and solve for the fixed rate FS(0,n,m) that will result in equality of these two streams of payments. The solution is as follows:

$$FS(0, n, m) = \frac{1.0 - B_0(h_n)}{\sum_{j=1}^{n} B_0(h_j)} \tag{5-1}$$

The swap fixed payment is 1.0 minus the last present value factor divided by the sum of the present value factors for each payment. Thus, we have priced the swap.

One can use several other ways to find the fixed payment on a swap, but this method is unquestionably the simplest. In fact, this formulation shows that the fixed rate on a swap is simply the coupon rate on a par bond whose payments coincide with those on the swap.[18]

Let us now work a problem. Consider a one-year swap with quarterly payments on days 90, 180, 270, and 360. The underlying is 90-day LIBOR. The annualized LIBOR spot rates today are

$$L_0(90) \ \ = 0.0345$$

$$L_0(180) = 0.0358$$

$$L_0(270) = 0.0370$$

$$L_0(360) = 0.0375$$

---

[18] Technically, bond interest payments are usually found by dividing the annual rate by 2 if the payments are semiannual, whereas swap payments do, on occasion, use day counts such as 181/365 to determine semiannual payments. When we refer to a par bond, we are assuming the payments are structured exactly like those on the swap.

The present value factors are obtained as follows:

$$B_0(90) = \frac{1}{1 + 0.0345(90/360)} = 0.9914$$

$$B_0(180) = \frac{1}{1 + 0.0358(180/360)} = 0.9824$$

$$B_0(270) = \frac{1}{1 + 0.0370(270/360)} = 0.9730$$

$$B_0(360) = \frac{1}{1 + 0.0375(360/360)} = 0.9639$$

The fixed payment is found as

$$FS(0, n, m) = FS(0,4,90) = \frac{1 - 0.9639}{0.9914 + 0.9824 + 0.9730 + 0.9639} = 0.0092$$

Therefore, the quarterly fixed payment will be 0.0092 for each \$1 notional principal. Of course, this rate is quarterly; it is customary to quote it as an annual rate. We would thus see the rate quoted as $0.0092 \times (360/90) = 0.0368$, or 3.68 percent. We would also have to adjust our payment by multiplying by the actual notional principal. For example, if the actual notional principal were \$30 million, the payment would be (0.0092)\$30 million = \$276,000.

In determining the fixed rate on the swap, we have essentially found the fixed payment that sets the present value of the floating payments plus a hypothetical notional principal of 1.0 equal to the present value of the fixed payments plus a hypothetical notional principal of 1.0. We have thus made the market value of the swap equal to zero at the start of the transaction. This equality makes sense, because neither party pays any money to the other.

Now suppose we have entered into the swap. Let us move forward into the life of the swap, at which time interest rates have changed, and determine its market value. Rather than present mathematical equations for determining its value, we shall work through this example informally. We shall see that the procedure is simple and intuitive. Suppose we have now moved 60 days into the life of the swap. At day 60, we face a new term structure of LIBORs. Because the upcoming payments occur in 30, 120, 210, and 300 days, we want the term structure for 30, 120, 210, and 300 days, which is given as follows:

$$L_{60}(30) = 0.0425$$

$$L_{60}(120) = 0.0432$$

$$L_{60}(210) = 0.0437$$

$$L_{60}(300) = 0.0444$$

The new set of discount factors is

$$B_{60}(90) = \frac{1}{1 + 0.0425(30/360)} = 0.9965$$

$$B_{60}(180) = \frac{1}{1 + 0.0432(120/360)} = 0.9858$$

$$B_{60}(270) = \frac{1}{1 + 0.0437(210/360)} = 0.9751$$

$$B_{60}(360) = \frac{1}{1 + 0.0444(300/360)} = 0.9643$$

We must value the swap from the perspective of one of the parties. Let us look at it as though we were the party paying fixed and receiving floating. Finding the present value of the remaining fixed payments of 0.0092 is straightforward. This present value, including the hypothetical notional principal, is 0.0092(0.9965 + 0.9858 + 0.9751 + 0.9643) + 1.0(0.9643) = 1.0004.

Now we must find the present value of the floating payments. Recall that on day 0, the 90-day LIBOR was 3.45 percent. Thus, the first floating payment will be 0.0345(90/360) = 0.0086. We know that we should discount this payment back 30 days, but what about the remaining floating payments? Remember that we know that the market value of the remaining payments on day 90, including the hypothetical final notional principal, is 1.0. So, we can discount 1.00 + 0.0086 = 1.0086 back 30 days to obtain 1.0086(0.9965) = 1.0051.

The present value of the remaining floating payments, plus the hypothetical notional principal, is 1.0051, and the present value of the remaining fixed payments, plus the hypothetical notional principal, is 1.0004. Therefore, the value of the swap is 1.0051 − 1.0004 = 0.0047 per $1 notional principal. If, for example, the actual swap were for a notional principal of $30 million, the market value would be $30 million(0.0047) = $141,000.

PRACTICE PROBLEM 4

Consider a one-year interest rate swap with semiannual payments.

A. Determine the fixed rate on the swap and express it in annualized terms. The term structure of LIBOR spot rates is given as follows:

Days	Rate
180	7.2%
360	8.0%

B. Ninety days later, the term structure is as follows:

Days	Rate
90	7.1%
270	7.4%

Determine the market value of the swap from the perspective of the party paying the floating rate and receiving the fixed rate. Assume a notional principal of $15 million.

SOLUTIONS

A. First calculate the present value factors for 180 and 360 days:

$$B_0(180) = \frac{1}{1 + 0.072(180/360)} = 0.9753$$

$$B_0(360) = \frac{1}{1 + 0.08(360/360)} = 0.9259$$

The fixed rate is $\dfrac{1 - 0.9259}{0.9653 + 0.9259} = 0.0392$. The fixed payment would, therefore, be 0.0392 per \$1 notional principal. The annualized rate would be 0.0392(360/180) = 0.0784.

B. Calculate the new present value factors for 90 and 270 days:

$$B_{90}(180) = \frac{1}{1 + 0.071(90/360)} = 0.9826$$

$$B_{90}(360) = \frac{1}{1 + 0.0074(270/360)} = 0.9474$$

The present value of the remaining fixed payments plus hypothetical \$1 notional principal is 0.0392(0.9826 + 0.9474) + 1.0(0.9474) = 1.0231.

The 180-day rate at the start was 7.2 percent, so the first floating payment would be 0.072(180/360) = 0.036. The present value of the floating payments plus hypothetical \$1 notional principal will be 1.036(0.9826) = 1.0180. The market value of a pay-floating, receive-fixed swap is, therefore, 1.0231 − 1.0180 = 0.0051. For a notional principal of \$15 million, the market value is \$15,000,000(0.0051) = \$76,500.

Note that we valued the swap from the perspective of the party paying the fixed rate. From the counterparty's perspective, the value of the swap would be the negative of the value to the fixed-rate payer.

Although an interest rate swap is like a series of FRAs, or a long position in an interest rate cap and a short position in an interest rate floor with the exercise rate set at the fixed rate on a swap, pricing and valuing an interest rate swap as either of these instruments is more difficult than what we have done here. To price the swap as a series of FRAs, we would need to calculate the forward rates, which is not difficult but would add another step. If we priced a swap as a combination of caps and floors, we would need to price these options. As we saw in Chapter 4, interest rate option pricing can be somewhat complex. In addition, we would have to find the exercise rate on the cap and floor that equated their values, which would require trial and error. What we have seen here is the trick that if we add the notional principal to both sides of an interest rate swap, we do not change the swap payments, but we make the cash flows on each side of the swap equivalent to those of a bond. Then we can price the swap as though it were a pair of bonds, one long and the other short. One side is like a floating-rate bond, which we know is priced at par value at the time of issuance as well as on any reset date. The other side is like a fixed-rate bond.

Because the value of the fixed-rate bond must equal that of the floating-rate bond at the start, we know that the coupon on a par value bond is the fixed rate on the swap.

Having discussed the pricing and valuation of interest rate swaps, we can now move on to currency swaps, taking advantage of what we know about pricing interest rate swaps. As we have already noted, an interest rate swap is just like a currency swap in which both currencies are the same.

4.2.2   CURRENCY SWAPS

Recall the four types of currency swaps: (1) pay one currency fixed, receive the other fixed, (2) pay one currency fixed, receive the other floating, (3) pay one currency floating, receive the other fixed, and (4) pay one currency floating, receive the other floating. In determining the fixed rate on a swap, we must keep in mind one major point: The fixed rate is the rate that makes the present value of the payments made equal the present value of the payments received. In the fourth type of currency swap mentioned here, both sides pay floating so there is no need to find a fixed rate. But all currency swaps have two notional principals, one in each currency. We can arbitrarily set the notional principal in the domestic currency at one unit. We then must determine the equivalent notional principal in the other currency. This task is straightforward: We simply convert the one unit of domestic currency to the equivalent amount of foreign currency, dividing 1.0 by the exchange rate.

Consider the first type of currency swap, in which we pay the foreign currency at a fixed rate and receive the domestic currency at a fixed rate. What are the two fixed rates? We will see that they are the fixed rates on plain vanilla interest rate swaps in the respective countries.

Because we know that the value of a floating-rate security with \$1 face value is \$1, we know that the fixed rate on a plain vanilla interest rate swap is the rate on a \$1 par bond in the domestic currency. That rate results in the present value of the interest payments and the hypothetical notional principal being equal to 1.0 unit of the domestic currency. Moreover, for a currency swap, the notional principal is typically paid, so we do not even have to call it hypothetical. We know that the fixed rate on the domestic leg of an interest rate swap is the appropriate domestic fixed rate for a currency swap in which the domestic notional principal is 1.0 unit of the domestic currency.

What about the fixed rate for the foreign payments on the currency swap? To answer that question, let us assume the point of view of a resident of the foreign country. Given the term structure in the foreign country, we might be interested in first pricing plain vanilla interest rate swaps in that country. So, we know that the fixed rate on interest rate swaps in that country would make the present value of the interest and principal payments equal 1.0 unit of that currency.

Now let us return to our domestic setting. We know that the fixed rate on interest rate swaps in the foreign currency makes the present value of the foreign interest and principal payments equal to 1.0 unit of the foreign currency. We multiply by the spot rate, S_0, to obtain the value of those payments in our domestic currency: 1.0 times S_0 equals S_0, which is now in terms of the domestic currency. This amount does not equal the present value of the domestic payments, but if we set the notional principal on the foreign side of the swap equal to $1/S_0$, then the present value of the foreign payments will be $S_0(1/S_0) = 1.0$ unit of our domestic currency, which is what we want.

Let us now summarize this argument:

- *The fixed rate on plain vanilla swaps in our country makes the present value of the domestic interest and principal payments equal 1.0 unit of the domestic currency.*

- *The fixed rate on plain vanilla swaps in the foreign country makes the present value of the foreign interest and principal payments equal 1.0 unit of the foreign currency.*

- *A notional principal of $1/S_0$ units of foreign currency makes the present value of the foreign interest and principal payments equal $1/S_0$ units of the foreign currency.*

- *Conversion of $1/S_0$ units of foreign currency at the current exchange rate of S_0 gives 1.0 unit of domestic currency.*

- *Therefore, the present value of the domestic payments equals the present value of the foreign payments.*

- *The fixed rates on a currency swap are, therefore, the fixed rates on plain vanilla interest rate swaps in the respective countries.*

Of course, if the domestic notional principal is any amount other than 1.0, we multiply the domestic notional principal by $1/S_0$ to obtain the foreign notional principal. Then the actual swap payments are calculated by multiplying by the overall respective notional principals.

The second and third types of currency swaps each involve one side paying fixed and the other paying floating. The rate on the fixed side of each of these swaps is, again, just the fixed rate on an interest rate swap in the given country. The payments on the floating side automatically have the same present value as the payments on the fixed side. We again use 1.0 unit of domestic currency and $1/S_0$ units of foreign currency as the notional principal.

For the last type of currency swap, in which both sides pay floating, we do not need to price the swap because both sides pay a floating rate. Again, the notional principals are 1.0 unit of domestic currency and $1/S_0$ units of foreign currency.

In the example we used in pricing interest rate swaps, we were given a term structure for a one-year swap with quarterly payments. We found that the fixed payment was 0.0092, implying an annual rate of 3.68 percent. Let us now work through a currency swap in which the domestic currency is the dollar and the foreign currency is the Swiss franc. The current exchange rate is \$0.80. We shall use the same term structure used previously for the domestic term structure: $L_0(90) = 0.0345$, $L_0(180) = 0.0358$, $L_0(270) = 0.0370$, and $L_0(360) = 0.0375$. The Swiss term structure, denoted with a superscript SF, is

$$L_0^{SF}(90) \ = 0.0520$$

$$L_0^{SF}(180) = 0.0540$$

$$L_0^{SF}(270) = 0.0555$$

$$L_0^{SF}(360) = 0.0570$$

The present value factors are

$$B_0^{SF}(90) = \frac{1}{1 + 0.0520(90/360)} = 0.9872$$

$$B_0^{SF}(180) = \frac{1}{1 + 0.0540(180/360)} = 0.9737$$

$$B_0^{SF}(270) = \frac{1}{1 + 0.0555(270/360)} = 0.9600$$

$$B_0^{SF}(360) = \frac{1}{1 + 0.0570(360/360)} = 0.9461$$

The fixed payment is easily found as

$$FS^{SF}(0, n, m) = FS^{SF}(0,4,90) = \frac{1 - 0.9461}{0.9872 + 0.9737 + 0.9600 + 0.9461} = 0.0139$$

The quarterly fixed payment is thus SF0.0139 for each SF1.00 of notional principal. This translates into an annual rate of $0.0139(360/90) = 0.0556$ or 5.56 percent, so in Switzerland we would quote the fixed rate on a plain vanilla interest rate swap in Swiss francs as 5.56 percent.

Our currency swap involving dollars for Swiss francs would have a fixed rate of 3.68 percent in dollars and 5.56 percent in Swiss francs. The notional principal would be $1.0 and $1/\$0.80 = SF1.25$. Summarizing, we have the following terms for the four swaps:

Swap 1: Pay dollars fixed at 3.68 percent, receive SF fixed at 5.56 percent.

Swap 2: Pay dollars fixed at 3.68 percent, receive SF floating.

Swap 3: Pay dollars floating, receive SF fixed at 5.56 percent.

Swap 4: Pay dollars floating, receive SF floating.

In each case, the notional principal is $1 and SF1.25, or more generally, SF1.25 for every dollar of notional principal.

As we did with interest rate swaps, we move 60 days forward in time. We have a new U.S. term structure, given in the interest rate swap problem, and a new Swiss franc term structure, which is given below:

$$L_{60}^{SF}(30)\ \ = 0.0600$$
$$L_{60}^{SF}(120) = 0.0615$$
$$L_{60}^{SF}(210) = 0.0635$$
$$L_{60}^{SF}(300) = 0.0653$$

The new set of discount factors is

$$B_{60}^{SF}(90) = \frac{1}{1 + 0.0600(30/360)} = 0.9950$$

$$B_{60}^{SF}(180) = \frac{1}{1 + 0.0615(120/360)} = 0.9799$$

$$B_{60}^{SF}(270) = \frac{1}{1 + 0.0635(210/360)} = 0.9643$$

$$B_{60}^{SF}(360) = \frac{1}{1 + 0.0653(300/360)} = 0.9484$$

The new exchange rate is $0.82. Now let us value each swap in turn, taking advantage of what we already know about the values of the U.S. dollar interest rate swaps calculated in the previous section. Recall we found that

Present value of dollar fixed payments = 1.0004

Present value of dollar floating payments = 1.0051

Let us find the comparable numbers for the Swiss franc payments. In other words, we position ourselves as a Swiss resident or institution and obtain the values of the fixed and floating streams of Swiss franc payments per SF1 notional principal. The present value of the remaining Swiss fixed payments is

$$0.0139(0.9950 + 0.9799 + 0.9643 + 0.9484) + 1.0(0.9484) = 1.0024$$

Recall that in finding the present value of the floating payments, we simply recognize that on the next payment date, we shall receive a floating payment of $0.052(90/360) = 0.013$, and the market value of the remaining payments will be 1.0.[19] Thus, we can discount 1.0130 back 30 days to obtain $1.0130(0.9950) = 1.0079$.

These two figures are based on SF1 notional principal. We convert them to the actual notional principal in Swiss francs by multiplying by SF1.25. Thus,

Present value of SF fixed payments = 1.0024(1.25) = SF1.2530

Present value of SF floating payments = 1.0079(1.25) = SF1.2599

Now we need to convert these figures to dollars by multiplying by the current exchange rate of $0.82. Thus,

Present value of SF fixed payments in dollars = 1.2530($0.82) = $1.0275

Present value of SF floating payments in dollars = 1.2599($0.82) = $1.0331

Now we can value the four currency swaps:

Value of swap to pay SF fixed, receive $ fixed = $-$1.0275 + $1.0004 = -$0.0271

Value of swap to pay SF floating, receive $ fixed = $-$1.0331 + $1.0004 = -$0.0327

Value of swap to pay SF fixed, receive $ floating = $-$1.0275 + $1.0051 = -$0.0224

Value of swap to pay SF floating, receive $ floating = $-$1.0331 + $1.0051 = -$0.0280

Note that all of these numbers are negative. Therefore, our swaps are showing losses as a result of the combination of interest rate changes in the two countries as well as the exchange rate change. To the counterparty, the swaps are worth these same numerical amounts, but the signs are positive.

PRACTICE PROBLEM 5

Consider a one-year currency swap with semiannual payments. The two currencies are the U.S. dollar and the euro. The current exchange rate is $0.75.

A. The term structure of interest rates for LIBOR and Euribor are

Days	LIBOR	Euribor
180	7.2%	6.0%
360	8.0%	6.6%

---

[19] The first floating payment was set when the swap was initiated at the 90-day rate of 5.2 percent times 90/360.

Determine the fixed rate in euros and express it in annualized terms. Note that the LIBOR rates are the same as in Practice Problem 4, in which we found that the fixed payment in dollars was 0.0392.

B. Ninety days later, the term structure is as follows:

Days	LIBOR	Euribor
90	7.1%	5.5%
270	7.4%	6.0%

The new exchange rate is $0.70. Determine the market values of swaps to pay dollars and receive euros. Consider all four swaps that are covered in the chapter. Assume a notional principal of $20 million and the appropriate amount for euros. Note that the LIBOR rates are the same as in Practice Problem 4, in which we found that the present value of the fixed payments (floating payments) plus the hypothetical $1 notional principal was $1.0231 ($1.0180).

SOLUTIONS

A. The fixed payment in dollars is the same as in Practice Problem 4: 0.0392. To determine the fixed rate in euros, we first compute the discount factors:

$$B_0^€(180) = \frac{1}{1 + 0.06(180/360)} = 0.9709$$

$$B_0^€(360) = \frac{1}{1 + 0.066(360/360)} = 0.9381$$

The fixed rate in euros is, therefore, $\dfrac{1 - 0.9381}{0.9709 + 0.9381} = 0.0324$.

On an annual basis, this rate would be $0.0324(360/180) = 0.0648$.

B. Recalculate the euro discount factors:

$$B_{90}^€(90) = \frac{1}{1 + 0.055(90/360)} = 0.9864$$

$$B_{90}^€(270) = \frac{1}{1 + 0.060(270/360)} = 0.9569$$

The present value of the fixed payments plus hypothetical €1 notional principal is €0.0324(0.9864 + 0.9569) + €1.0(0.9569) = €1.0199.

The 180-day rate at the start of the swap was 6 percent, so the first floating payment would be 0.06(180/360) = 0.03. The present value of the floating payments plus hypothetical notional principal of €1 is €1.03(0.9864) = €1.0160.

The euro notional principal, established at the start of the swap, is 1/$0.75 = €1.3333. Converting the euro payments to dollars at the new exchange rate and multiplying by the euro notional principal, we obtain the following values for the four swaps (where we use the present values of U.S. dollar fixed and floating payments as found in Practice Problem 4, repeated in the statement of Part B above).

- Pay $ fixed, receive € fixed = −$1.0231 + €1.3333($0.70)1.0199 = −$0.0712

- Pay \$ fixed, receive € floating $= -\$1.0231 + €1.3333(\$0.70)1.0160 = -\$0.0749$

- Pay \$ floating, receive € fixed $= -\$1.0180 + €1.3333(\$0.70)1.0199 = -\$0.0661$

- Pay \$ floating, receive € floating $= -\$1.0180 + €1.3333(\$0.70)1.0160 = -\$0.0698$

Now we turn to equity swaps. It is tempting to believe that we will not use any more information regarding the term structure in pricing and valuing equity swaps. In fact, for equity swaps in which one side pays either a fixed or floating rate, the results we have obtained for interest rate swaps will be very useful.

4.2.3 Equity Swaps

In this section, we explore how to price and value three types of equity swaps: (1) a swap to pay a fixed rate and receive the return on the equity, (2) a swap to pay a floating rate and receive the return on the equity, and (3) a swap to pay the return on one equity and receive the return on another.

To price or value an equity swap, we must determine a combination of stock and bonds that replicates the cash flows on the swap. As we saw with interest rate and currency swaps, such a replication is not difficult to create. We issue a bond and sell a bond, with one being a fixed-rate bond and the other being a floating-rate bond. If we are dealing with a currency swap, we require that one of the bonds be denominated in one currency and the other be denominated in the other currency. With an equity swap, it would appear that a replicating strategy would involve issuing a bond and buying the stock or vice versa, but this is not exactly how to replicate an equity swap. Remember that in an equity swap, we receive cash payments representing the return on the stock, and that is somewhat different from payments based on the price.

Pricing a Swap to Pay a Fixed Rate and Receive the Return on the Equity: By example, we will demonstrate how to price an n-payment m-day rate swap to pay a fixed rate and receive the return on equity. Suppose the notional principal is \$1, the swap involves annual settlements and lasts for two years (n = 2), and the returns on the stock for each of the two years are 10 percent for the first year and 15 percent for the second year. The equity payment on the swap would be \$0.10 the first year and \$0.15 the second. If, however, we purchased the stock instead of doing the equity swap, we would have to sell the stock at the end of the first year or we would not generate any cash. Suppose at the end of the first year, the stock is at \$1.10. We sell the stock, withdraw \$0.10, and reinvest \$1.00 in the stock. At the end of the second year the stock would be at \$1.15. We then sell the stock, taking cash of \$0.15. But we have \$1.00 left over. To get rid of, or offset, this cash flow, suppose that when we purchased the stock we borrowed the present value of \$1.00 for two years. Then two years later, we would pay back \$1.00 on that loan. This procedure would offset the \$1.00 in cash we have from the stock. The fixed payments on the swap can be easily replicated. If the fixed payment is denoted as FS(0,n,m), we simply borrow the present value of FS(0,n,m) for one year and also borrow the present value of FS(0,n,m) for two years. When we pay those loans back, we will have replicated the fixed payments on the swap.

For the more general case of n payments, we do the following to replicate the swap whose fixed payments are FS(0,n,m):

1. Invest $1.00 in the stock.

2. Borrow the present value of $1.00 to be paid back at the swap expiration, day h_n. This is the amount $B_0(h_n)$.

3. Take out a series of loans requiring that we pay back FS(0,n,m) at time h_1, and also at time h_2, and at all remaining times through time h_n.

Note that this transaction is like issuing debt and buying stock. The amount of money required to do this is

$$\$1 - B_0(h_n) - FS(0, n, m) \sum_{j=1}^{n} B_0(h_j)$$

Because no money changes hands at the start, the initial value of the swap is zero. We set the expression above to zero and solve for the fixed payment FS(0,n,m) to obtain

$$FS(0, n, m) = \frac{1.0 - B_0(h_n)}{\sum_{j=1}^{n} B_0(h_j)}$$

This is precisely the formula (Equation 5-1) for the fixed rate on an interest rate swap or a currency swap.

Pricing a Swap to Pay a Floating Rate and Receive the Return on the Equity: If, instead, the swap involves the payment of a floating rate for the equity return, no further effort is needed because there is no fixed rate for which we must solve. We know from our understanding of interest rate swaps that the present value of the floating payments equals the present value of the fixed payments, which equals the notional principal of 1.0. The market value of the swap is zero at the start, as it should be.

Pricing a Swap to Pay the Return on One Equity and Receive the Return on Another Equity: Let $S_0(1)$ and $S_1(1)$ be the level of Stock Index 1 at times 0 and 1, and let $S_0(2)$ and $S_1(2)$ be the level of Stock Index 2 at times 0 and 1. Assume we pay the return on Index 2 and receive the return on Index 1. We need to replicate the cash flows on this swap by investing in these two stocks using some type of strategy. Suppose we sell short $1.00 of Index 2, taking the proceeds and investing in $1.00 of Index 1. Then at time 1, we liquidate the position in Index 1, as described above, withdrawing the cash and reinvesting the $1.00 back into Index 1. We cover the short position in Index 2, taking the proceeds and re-shorting Index 2. We continue in this manner throughout the life of the swap. This strategy replicates the cash flows on the swap. Thus, going long one stock and short the other replicates this swap. Of course, there is no fixed rate and thus no need to price the swap. The market value at the start is zero as it should be.

Now let us look at how to determine the market values of each of these swaps during their lives. In other words, after the swap has been initiated, we move forward in time. We must take into account where we are in the life of the swap and how interest rates and the equity price have changed.

Valuing a Swap to Pay the Fixed Rate and Receive the Return on the Equity: Let us use the same U.S. term structure we have already been using for interest rate and currency swaps.

Our equity swap is for one year and will involve fixed quarterly payments. Recall that the fixed payment on the interest rate swap is 0.0092, corresponding to an annual rate of 3.68 percent. This will be the rate on the swap to pay fixed and receive the equity payment.

Now let us move 60 days into the life of the swap, at which time we have a new term structure as given in the interest rate swap example. We started off with a stock price of S_0, and now the stock price is S_{60}. The stock payment we will receive at the first settlement in 30 days is $S_{90}/S_0 - 1$. Let us write this amount as

$$\left(\frac{1}{S_0}\right)S_{90} - 1$$

Sixty days into the life of the swap, we could replicate this payment by purchasing $1/S_0$ shares of stock, currently at S_{60}. Doing so will cost $(1/S_0)S_{60}$. Then at the first settlement, we shall have stock worth $(1/S_0)S_{90}$. We sell that stock, withdrawing cash of $(1/S_0)S_{90} - 1$. We then take the $1 left over and roll it into the stock again, which will replicate the return the following period, as described above. This procedure will leave $1 left over at the end. Thus, sixty days into the swap, to replicate the remaining cash flows, we do the following:

1. Invest $(1/S_0)S_{60}$ in the stock.
2. Borrow the present value of $1.00 to be paid back at the swap expiration, time h_n. This is the amount $B_{60}(h_n)$.
3. Take out a series of loans requiring that we pay back $FS(0,n,m)$ at time h_1, and also at time h_2, and at all remaining times through time h_n.

For the general case of day t, the market value of the swap is

$$\left(\frac{S_t}{S_0}\right) - B_t(h_n) - FS(0,n,m)\sum_{j=1}^{n} B_t(h_j) \tag{5-2}$$

The first term reflects the investment in the stock necessary to replicate the equity return. The second term is the loan for the present value of $1.00 due at the expiration date of the swap. The third term is the series of loans of the amount $FS(0,n,m)$ due at the various swap settlement dates. Note that all discounting is done using the new term structure. Of course, the overall market value figure would then be multiplied by the notional principal.

Let us calculate these results for our pay-fixed, receive-equity swap 60 days into its life. Suppose the stock index was at 1405.72 when the swap was initiated. Now it is at 1436.59. We use the same term structure at 60 days that we used for the interest rate swap example. The market value of the swap is

$$\left(\frac{1436.59}{1405.72}\right) - 0.9643 - (0.0092)(0.9965 + 0.9858 + 0.9751 + 0.9643) = 0.0216$$

Thus, 60 days into its life, the market value of this fixed-for-equity swap is positive at $0.0216 per $1 notional principal.

Valuing a Swap to Pay a Floating Rate and Receive the Return on the Equity: We can value this swap in two ways. The first will require that we discount the next floating rate and the par value, as we did with interest rate swaps. We can do this because we recognize that a floating-rate security is worth its par value on the payment date. As long as we add the notional principal, we can assume the floating payments are those of a floating-rate bond. The notional principal offsets the $1 left over at the end from holding the stock and withdrawing all of the profits on each settlement date. The calculation of the market value of this swap is simple. We just determine the value of $1 invested in the stock since the last settlement period, minus the present value of the floating leg. With the upcoming floating payment being 0.0086, the market value of the swap is, therefore,

$$\left(\frac{1436.59}{1405.72}\right) - (1.0086)(0.9965) = 0.0169$$

Another, and probably easier, way to arrive at this answer is to recognize that

- a swap to pay fixed and receive the equity return is worth 0.0216, and
- a swap to pay floating and receive fixed is worth −0.0047.[20]

If we did both of these swaps, the fixed payments would offset and would leave the equivalent of the equity swap. The value would then be $0.0216 - 0.0047 = 0.0169$.

Valuing a Swap to Pay One Equity Return and Receive Another: Now we need to value the swap to pay the return on Index 2 and receive the return on Index 1, 60 days into the swap's life. Let the following be the values of the indices on days 0 and 60.

	Day 0	Day 60
Index 1	1405.72	1436.59
Index 2	5255.18	5285.73

As we previously described, this swap can be replicated by going long Index 1 and short Index 2. The market value calculation is simple: We find the value of $1 invested in Index 1 since the last settlement day minus the value of $1 invested in Index 2 since the last settlement day. Thus, the market value of the position is

$$\left(\frac{1436.59}{1405.72}\right) - \left(\frac{5285.73}{5255.18}\right) = 0.0161$$

Of course, all of these results are per $1 notional principal, so we would have to multiply by the actual notional principal to get the overall market value of this equity-for-equity swap.

PRACTICE PROBLEM 6

Consider an equity swap that calls for semiannual payments for one year. The party will receive the return on the Dow Jones Industrial Average (DJIA), which starts off at 10033.27. The current LIBOR term structure is

Days	Rate
180	7.2%
360	8.0%

---

[20] In Section 4.2.1, we found the value of a swap to pay fixed and receive floating to be 0.0047. Therefore, a swap to pay floating and receive fixed is worth −0.0047.

A. In Practice Problem 4, we determined that the fixed rate for a one-year interest rate swap given the above term structure was 0.0392. Given this term structure data, what is the fixed rate in an equity swap calling for the party to pay a fixed rate and receive the return on the DJIA?

B. Find the market value of the swap 90 days later if the new term structure is

Days	Rate
90	7.1%
270	7.4%

The notional principal of the swap is $60 million. The DJIA is at 9955.14. Again, these are the same rates as in Practice Problem 4, for which we computed $B_{90}(180) = 0.9826$ and $B_{90}(360) = 0.9474$.

C. Recompute the market value under the assumption that the counterparty pays a floating rate instead of a fixed rate.

D. Recompute the market value under the assumption that the counterparty pays the return on the Dow Jones Transportation Index, which started off at 2835.17 and 90 days later is 2842.44.

SOLUTIONS

A. Because this term structure is the same as in Practice Problem 4, the fixed rate is the same at 0.0392. The fact that the party here receives an equity return rather than a floating interest rate does not affect the magnitude of the fixed payment.

B. Using the 180- and 360-day discount factors at 180 days from Practice Problem 4, the market value of the swap to pay a fixed rate and receive the equity return is

$$\left(\frac{9955.14}{10033.27} \right) - 0.9474 - 0.0392(0.9826 + 0.9474) = -0.0309$$

Multiplying by the notional principal of $60 million, we obtain a market value of $60,000,000(-0.0309) = -\$1,854,000$.

C. Because the first floating payment would be at the rate of 7.2 percent and is, therefore, 0.036, the market value of the swap to pay a floating rate and receive the equity return is

$$\left(\frac{9955.14}{10033.27} \right) - 1.036(0.9826) = -0.0258$$

Adjusting for the notional principal, the market value is $60,000,000(-0.0258) = -\$1,548,000$.

D. The market value of the swap to pay the return on the Dow Jones Transportation Average and receive the return on the DJIA is

$$\left(\frac{9955.14}{10033.27} \right) - \left(\frac{2842.44}{2835.17} \right) = -0.0104$$

Adjusting for the notional principal, the market value is $60,000,000(-0.0104) = -\$624,000$.

4.3 SOME CONCLUDING COMMENTS ON SWAP VALUATION

Let us review some important results on swap valuation and pricing. Because the market value of the swap when initiated is zero, pricing the swap means to find the terms of the swap that will make its market value be zero. If the swap pays a fixed rate, we must find the fixed rate that makes the present value of the fixed payments equal the present value of the floating payments. If both sides of the swap involve floating payments, there are no terms to determine. For currency swaps, we also have to determine the notional principal in one currency that is equivalent to a given notional principal in another currency.

The market value of a swap starts off at zero but changes to either a positive or negative value as the swap evolves through its life and market conditions change. To determine the market value of a swap, we must determine the present value of the remaining stream of payments, netting one against the other.

The market value of a swap gives a number that represents what the swap is worth to each party. If the market value is positive, the swap is like an asset. The amount due to one party is worth more than the amount that party owes. If it is negative, the swap is like a liability. The amount that party owes is worth more than the amount owed to it. The market value of a swap is also sometimes known as the **replacement value**. This notion views the swap as an instrument whose value can potentially be lost through default. If a party is holding a positive value swap and the other party defaults, that value is lost and would require that amount of money to replace it. We discuss this point further in Section 7.

5 VARIATIONS OF SWAPS

So far we have covered the most common types of swaps: fixed-for-floating interest rate swaps, various combinations of fixed and floating currency swaps, and equity swaps involving fixed payments, floating payments, or the returns on another equity. We must also mention some other types of swaps.

We briefly referred to the **basis swap**, in which both sides pay a floating rate. A typical basis swap involves one party paying LIBOR and the other paying the T-bill rate. As we learned in Chapter 3, the term *basis* refers to the spread between two prices, usually the spot and futures prices. Here it is simply the spread between two rates, LIBOR and the T-bill rate. Because LIBOR is always more than the T-bill rate, the two parties negotiate a fixed spread such that the party paying LIBOR actually pays LIBOR minus the spread.[21] LIBOR is the borrowing rate of high-quality London banks, and the T-bill rate is the default-free borrowing rate of the U.S. government. The difference between LIBOR and the T-bill rate is thus a reflection of investors' perception of the general level of credit risk in the market. Basis swaps are usually employed for speculative purposes by end users who believe the spread between LIBOR and the T-bill rate will change.[22] A basis swap of this type is, therefore, usually a position taken in anticipation of a change in the relative level of credit risk in the market. As noted, both sides are floating, and typically both sides use 360-day years in their calculations.[23]

Another type of swap we sometimes encounter is not all that different from a plain vanilla or basis swap. In a **constant maturity swap**, one party pays a fixed rate, or a short-

---

[21] Alternatively, the counterparty could pay the T-bill rate plus the spread.

[22] The spread between LIBOR and the T-bill rate is called the TED spread. It is considered an indicator of the relative state of credit risk in the markets. LIBOR represents the rate on a private borrower (London banks); the T-bill rate is the U.S. government borrowing rate. When the global economy weakens, the TED spread tends to widen because rates based on the credit risk of private borrowers will increase while the U.S. government remains a risk-free borrower.

[23] Of course, a basis swap need not be based on LIBOR and the T-bill rate, so other conventions can be used.

term floating rate such as LIBOR, and the other party pays a floating rate that is the rate on a security known as a **constant maturity treasury (CMT)** security. The transaction is also sometimes known as a CMT swap. This underlying instrument is a hypothetical U.S. Treasury note, meaning that its maturity is in the 2- to 10-year range, with a constant maturity. Obviously the reference to a particular CMT cannot be referring to a single note, because the maturity of any security decreases continuously. As mentioned, the note is hypothetical. For example, for a two-year CMT security, when there is an actual two-year note, that note is the CMT security. Otherwise, the yield on a CMT security is interpolated from the yields of securities with surrounding maturities. The distinguishing characteristic of a constant maturity swap is that the maturity of the underlying security exceeds the length of the settlement period. For example, a CMT swap might call for payments every six months, with the rate based on the one-year CMT security. In contrast, a standard swap settling every six months would nearly always be based on a six-month security. Otherwise, however, a constant maturity swap possesses the general characteristics of a plain vanilla swap.

One interesting variant of an interest rate swap is an **overnight index swap (OIS)**. This instrument commits one party to paying a fixed rate as usual. The floating rate, however, is the cumulative value of a single unit of currency invested at an overnight rate during the settlement period. The overnight rate changes daily. This instrument is used widely in Europe but not in the United States.

Amortizing and **accreting swaps** are those in which the notional principal changes according to a formula related to the underlying. The more common of the two is the amortizing swap, sometimes called an **index amortizing swap**. In this type of interest rate swap, the notional principal is indexed to the level of interest rates. The notional principal declines with the level of interest rates according to a predefined schedule. This feature makes the swap similar to certain asset-backed securities, such as mortgage-backed securities, which prepay some of their principal as rates fall. An index amortizing swap is often used to hedge this type of security.

Diff swaps combine elements of interest rate, currency, and equity swaps. In a typical diff swap, one party pays the floating interest rate of one country and the other pays the floating interest rate of another country. Both sets of payments, however, are made in a single currency. So one set of payments is based on the interest rate of one country, but the payment is made in the currency of another country. This swap is a pure play on the interest rate differential between two countries and is basically a currency swap with the currency risk hedged. Alternatively, in equity diff swaps, the return on a foreign stock index is paid in the domestic currency.

An **arrears swap** is a special type of interest rate swap in which the floating payment is set at the end of the period and the interest is paid at that same time. This procedure stands in contrast to the typical interest rate swap, in which the payment is set on one settlement date and the interest is paid on the next settlement date.

In a **capped swap**, the floating payments have a limit as to how high they can be. Similarly, a **floored swap** has a limit on how low the floating payments can be.

There is no limit to the number of variations that can be found in swaps, and it is not worthwhile to examine them beyond the basic, most frequently used types. We must, however, cover an important variation of a swap that combines elements of both swaps and options.

6   SWAPTIONS

A **swaption** *is an option to enter into a swap*. Although swaptions can be designed in a variety of ways, we shall focus exclusively on the most widely used swaption, the plain vanilla interest rate swaption. This is a swaption to pay the fixed rate and receive the floating rate or the other way around. It allows the holder to establish a fixed rate on the underlying swap in advance and have the option of entering into the swap with that fixed rate or allowing the swaption to expire and entering into the swap at the fixed rate that prevails in the market.

6.1   BASIC CHARACTERISTICS OF SWAPTIONS

The two types of swaptions are a **payer swaption** and a **receiver swaption**. A payer swaption allows the holder to enter into a swap as the fixed-rate payer and floating-rate receiver. A receiver swaption allows the holder to enter into a swap as the fixed-rate receiver and floating-rate payer. Therefore, these terms refer to the fixed rate and are comparable to the terms *call* and *put* used for other types of options. Although it is not apparent at this point, a payer swaption is a put and a receiver swaption is a call.

Swaptions have specific expiration dates. Like ordinary options, swaptions can be European style (exercisable only at expiration) or American style (exercisable at any time prior to expiration). A swaption is based on a specific underlying swap. For example, consider a European payer swaption that expires in two years and allows the holder to enter into a three-year swap with semiannual payments every 15 January and 15 July. The payments will be made at the rate of 6.25 percent and will be computed using the 30/360 adjustment. The underlying swap is based on LIBOR, and the notional principal is $10 million. Of course, a swaption has a price or premium, which is an amount paid by the buyer to the seller up front.

Note that this swaption expires in two years and the underlying swap expires three years after that. This arrangement is called a 2×5 swaption, a terminology we used in explaining FRAs. The underlying can be viewed as a five-year swap at the time the swaption is initiated and will be a three-year swap when the swaption expires.

Finally, there are a number of ways to settle a swaption at expiration. Recall that ordinary options can allow for either physical delivery or cash settlement. We will explore the comparable concepts for swaptions in Section 6.3.

6.2   USES OF SWAPTIONS

Swaptions have a variety of purposes, which we shall cover in more detail in Chapter 8 when we discuss swap applications and strategies. For right now, however, we take a brief glance at why swaptions exist.

Swaptions are used by parties who anticipate the need for a swap at a later date but would like to establish the fixed rate today, while providing the flexibility to not engage in the swap later or engage in the swap at a more favorable rate in the market. These parties are often corporations that expect to need a swap later and would like to hedge against unfavorable interest rate moves while preserving the flexibility to gain from favorable moves.

Swaptions are used by parties entering into a swap to give them the flexibility to terminate the swap. In Section 1.2, we discussed why a party engaged in a swap might wish to terminate it before expiration. Suppose the party in a swap is paying fixed and receiving floating. If it owned a receiver swaption, it could exercise the swaption, thereby entering into a swap to receive a fixed rate and pay a floating rate. It would then have offset the floating parts of the swap, effectively removing any randomness from the position.[24] But the only way the party could do so would require having previously purchased a swaption. Similarly, parties engaged in a receive-fixed, pay-floating swap can effectively offset it by exercising a payer swaption.

Swaptions are used by parties to speculate on interest rates. As with any interest rate sensitive instrument, swaptions can be used to speculate. Their prices move with interest rates and, like all options, they contain significant leverage. Thus, they are appropriate instruments for interest rate speculators.

---

[24] Note, however, that both swaps are still in effect even though the floating sides offset. Because both swaps remain in effect, there is credit risk on the two transactions.

6.3 SWAPTION PAYOFFS

When a swaption is exercised, it effectively creates a stream of equivalent payments, commonly referred to in the financial world as an annuity. This stream is a series of interest payments equal to the difference between the exercise rate and the market rate on the underlying swap when the swaption is exercised.

Consider a European payer swaption that expires in two years and is exercisable into a one-year swap with quarterly payments, using 90/360 as the day-count adjustment. The exercise rate is 3.60 percent. The notional principal is $20 million. Now, suppose we are at the swaption expiration and the term structure is the one we obtained when pricing the interest rate swap earlier in this chapter. We repeat that information here:

Maturity	Rate	Discount Factor
90 days	3.45%	0.9914
180 days	3.58%	0.9824
270 days	3.70%	0.9730
360 days	3.75%	0.9639

Under these conditions, we found that the swap fixed payment is 0.0092, equating to an annual fixed rate of 3.68 percent.

The holder of the swaption has the right to enter into a swap to pay 3.60 percent, whereas in the market such a swap would require payment at a rate of 3.68 percent. Therefore, here at expiration this swaption does appear to offer an advantage over the market rate. Let us consider the three possible ways to exercise this swaption.

The holder can exercise the swaption, thereby entering into a swap to pay 3.60 percent. The quarterly payment at the rate of 3.60 percent would be $20,000,000(0.0360)(90/360) = $180,000. The swaption holder would then be engaged in a swap to pay $180,000 quarterly and receive LIBOR. The first floating payment would be at 3.45 percent[25] and would be $20,000,000(0.0345)(90/360) = $172,500. The remaining floating payments would, of course, be determined later. The payment stream is illustrated in Exhibit 5-8, Panel A.

Alternatively, the holder can exercise the swaption, thereby entering into a swap to pay 3.60 percent, and then enter into a swap in the market to receive fixed and pay floating. The fixed rate the holder would receive is 3.68 percent, the market-determined fixed rate at the time the swaption expires. The quarterly fixed payment at 3.68 percent would be $20,000,000(0.0368)(90/360) = $184,000. Technically, the LIBOR payments are still made, but the same amount is paid and received. Hence, they effectively offset. Panel B illustrates this payment stream. This arrangement would be common if the counterparty to the second swap is not the same as the counterparty to the swaption.

The holder can arrange to receive a net payment stream of $184,000 − $180,000 = $4,000. Panel C illustrates this payment stream. In this case, the counterparty to the second swap is probably the same as the counterparty to the swap created by exercising the swaption, who would be the counterparty to the swaption. Because the floating payments are eliminated, the amount of cash passing between the parties is reduced, which mitigates the credit risk.

The holder can receive an up-front cash payment. We can easily determine the amount. It is simply the present value of the payment stream shown in Panel C, which we can obtain using the discount factors shown above:

$$\$4,000(0.9914 + 0.9824 + 0.9730 + 0.9639) = \$15,643$$

This pure cash settlement is illustrated in Panel D.

---

[25] The first floating payment is at 3.45 percent because this is the 90-day rate in effect at the time the swap is initiated.

EXHIBIT 5-8   Cash Flows from Swaptions

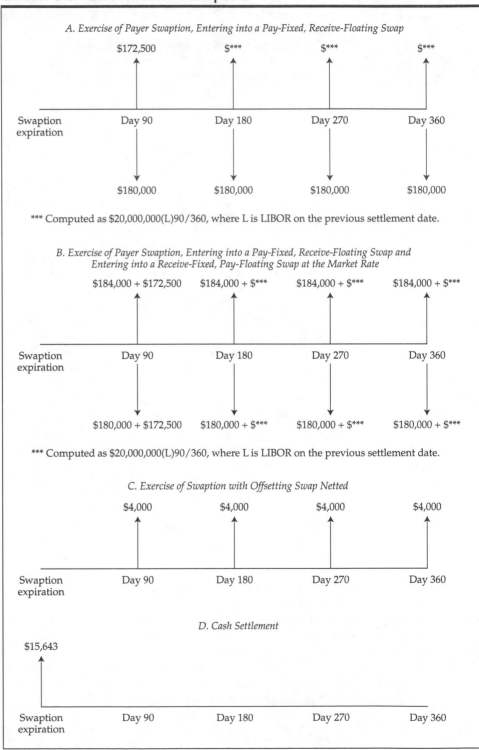

A. Exercise of Payer Swaption, Entering into a Pay-Fixed, Receive-Floating Swap

	$172,500	$***	$***	$***

| Swaption expiration | Day 90 | Day 180 | Day 270 | Day 360 |

| | $180,000 | $180,000 | $180,000 | $180,000 |

*** Computed as $20,000,000(L)90/360, where L is LIBOR on the previous settlement date.

*B. Exercise of Payer Swaption, Entering into a Pay-Fixed, Receive-Floating Swap and
Entering into a Receive-Fixed, Pay-Floating Swap at the Market Rate*

	$184,000 + $172,500	$184,000 + $***	$184,000 + $***	$184,000 + $***

| Swaption expiration | Day 90 | Day 180 | Day 270 | Day 360 |

| | $180,000 + $172,500 | $180,000 + $*** | $180,000 + $*** | $180,000 + $*** |

*** Computed as $20,000,000(L)90/360, where L is LIBOR on the previous settlement date.

C. Exercise of Swaption with Offsetting Swap Netted

	$4,000	$4,000	$4,000	$4,000

| Swaption expiration | Day 90 | Day 180 | Day 270 | Day 360 |

D. Cash Settlement

$15,643

| Swaption expiration | Day 90 | Day 180 | Day 270 | Day 360 |

Other than transaction costs and the credit risk associated with the newly created swaps, each of these means of exercising a swaption has the same value. Of course, the two parties would have to agree up front which of these means to use at expiration. Cash settlement is the most common.

Therefore, the payoff of a payer swaption in which the exercise rate is x and the market rate on the underlying swap is FS(0,n,m) is

$$\text{Max}[0, \text{FS}(0, n, m) - x] \sum_{j=1}^{n} B_0(h_j) \tag{5-3}$$

Similarly, the payoff of a receiver swaption would be

$$\text{Max}[0, x - \text{FS}(0, n, m)] \sum_{j=1}^{n} B_0(h_j) \tag{5-4}$$

Of course, these figures would be multiplied by the actual notional principal. So we see that a swaption effectively creates an annuity. The present value factors are not relevant in determining whether the swaption will be exercised. Exercise is determined solely on the relationship between the swap rate at expiration and the exercise rate. The present value factors are used to convert the stream of net payments obtained upon exercise of the swap into a current value. Now, let us take a brief look at how a swaption is priced.

6.4 PRICING AND VALUATION OF SWAPTIONS

We shall show here, perhaps somewhat surprisingly, that an interest rate swaption is like an option on a coupon bond. Restating our result given above, the payoff of a payer swaption is

$$\text{Max}[0, \text{FS}(0, n, m) - x] \sum_{j=1}^{n} B_0(h_j)$$

This expression finds the present value of the difference between the fixed rate on the swap and the exercise rate on the swaption if that difference is positive. Otherwise, the payoff is zero. Recall from Section 4.2.1 (Equation 5-1) that the fixed rate on an interest rate swap is

$$\text{FS}(0, n, m) = \frac{1.0 - B_0(h_n)}{\sum_{j=1}^{n} B_0(h_j)}$$

Substituting the fixed rate into the payoff equation, we obtain

$$\text{Max}\left[0, \frac{1.0 - B_0(h_n)}{\sum_{j=1}^{n} B_0(h_j)} - x \right] \sum_{j=1}^{n} B_0(h_j)$$

which can be rewritten as

$$\text{Max}\left\{ 0, 1.0 - \left[x \sum_{j=1}^{n} B_0(h_j) + B_0(h_N) \right] \right\}$$

Note the term in brackets,

$$x \sum_{j=1}^{n} B_0(h_j) + B_0(h_N)$$

which is the same as the market value at the swaption expiration of a coupon bond of $1.00 par value, in which the coupon is x. Thus, the swaption payoff is effectively Max(0,1.0 − Market value of coupon bond). This amount is the payoff of a put option on a coupon bond with coupon of x, a face value of 1.0, and a maturity of the swap expiration date. The exercise price is the par value of 1.0, and the exercise rate of the swaption is the coupon rate on the bond. Hence, we can value the swaption as though it were simply a put on a bond. In a similar manner, the payoff of a receiver swaption can be shown to be that of a call option on this coupon bond.

Now you can see why, as we stated earlier, a payer swaption is a put option and a receiver swaption is a call option. More specifically, a payer swaption is a put option on a bond and a receiver swaption is a call option on a bond.

PRACTICE PROBLEM 7

Calculate the market value of a receiver swaption at the expiration if the exercise rate is 4 percent and the term structure is given below:

Days	Rate
180	7.2%
360	8.0%

These are the same rates as in Practice Problem 4. The swaption is on a swap that will make payments in 180 and 360 days, and the notional principal is $25 million. Also, show that this payoff is equivalent to that of a call option on a bond.

SOLUTION

Based on a fixed rate of 0.0392 from Practice Problem 4, the market value is Max(0,0.04 − 0.0392)(0.9653 + 0.9259) = 0.0015.

Based on a notional principal of $25 million, this is a market value of 25,000,000(0.0015) = $37,500.

This payoff is equivalent to that of a call option on a bond with an exercise price of 1.0, its par value. At this point in time, the expiration of the option, the bond on which this call is based would have a market value of 0.04(0.9653 + 0.9259) + 1.0(0.9259) = 1.0015.

Therefore, the payoff of a call on this bond is Max(0,1.0015 − 1.0) = 0.0015—the same as that of the swaption.

With that result in mind, we could value the swaption using any of a number of approaches to valuing bond options. We shall not take up the pricing of swaptions here, as it is a somewhat advanced topic and the issues are somewhat complicated. It is not a straightforward matter to apply the Black–Scholes–Merton or Black models to pricing bond options. We discussed the valuation of options on bonds in Chapter 4, noting that the binomial model is probably the best way to do so.

6.5 FORWARD SWAPS

We have seen in this book that options represent rights and forward contracts represent commitments. Just as there are options to enter swaps, there are also forward contracts to enter into swaps, called **forward swaps**. They are not as widely used as swaptions but do offer the advantage, as is always the case with forwards, that one does not have to pay any cash up front as with an option premium. Forward swaps are priced by pricing the swap off of the forward term structure instead of the spot term structure.

7 CREDIT RISK AND SWAPS

In this chapter, we have mentioned on a few occasions that swaps are subject to credit risk. Indeed, as we have emphasized throughout the book, *all* over-the-counter derivatives are subject to credit risk. In this section, we examine some of the issues involved in the credit risk of swaps.

Recall that a swap has zero market value at the start. It starts off as neither an asset nor a liability. Once the swap is engaged and market conditions change, the market value becomes positive for one party and negative for the other. The party holding the positive value swap effectively owns an asset, which represents a claim against the counterparty. This claim is a netting of the amount owed by the counterparty and the amount that the party owes, with the former exceeding the latter. The party holding the positive-value swap thus assumes credit risk. The counterparty could declare bankruptcy, leaving the party holding the positive-value swap with a claim that is subject to the legal process of bankruptcy. In most swap arrangements, netting is legally recognized, so the claim has a value based on the net amount. Of course, as we described in the chapter, currency swaps are generally not netted so the credit risk is greater on currency swaps.

The party to which the swap has a negative value is not subject to credit risk. It owes more than is owed to it, so the other party faces the risk.

During the life of the swap, however, the market value to a given party can change from positive to negative or vice versa. Hence, the party not facing credit risk at a given moment is not entirely free of risk, because the swap value could turn positive for it later.

The timing of credit risk is in the form of immediate or **current credit risk** and deferred or **potential credit risk**. The former arises when a payment is immediately due and cannot be made by one party. The latter reflects the ever-present possibility that, although a counterparty may currently be able to make payments, it may be unable to make future payments.

Let us work through an example illustrating these points. Consider two parties A and B who are engaged in a swap. At a given payment date, the payment of Party A to Party B is $100,000 and the payment of Party B to Party A is $35,000. As is customarily the case, Party A must pay $65,000 to Party B. Once the payment is made, we shall assume that the market value of the swap is $1,250,000, which is an asset to A and a liability to B.

Suppose Party A is unable to pay and declares bankruptcy. Then Party B does not make any payment to Party A. Party A is bankrupt, but the swap is an asset to A. Given the $65,000 owed by A to B, the claim of A against B is $1,250,000 − $65,000 = $1,185,000. We emphasize in this example that A is the bankrupt party, but the swap is an asset to A, representing its claim against B. If B were holding the positive market value of the swap, it would have a claim of $1,250,000 + $65,000 = $1,315,000 on A as A enters into the bankruptcy process.

Let us change the example a little by having A not be bankrupt on the payment date. It makes its payment of $65,000 to B and moves forward. But a few months later, before the next payment, A declares bankruptcy. Its payment is not immediately due, but it has essentially stated that it will not make its next payment or any payments thereafter. To determine the financial implications of the event, the two parties must compute the market value of the swap. Suppose the value is now $1,100,000 and is positive to A. Then A, the bankrupt party, holds a claim against B of $1,100,000. The fact that A is bankrupt does not mean that it cannot have a claim against someone else, just as a bankrupt corporation can be owed money for inventory it has sold but on which it has not yet collected payment.

Of course, A could be bankrupt and B's claim against A could be the greater. In fact, with A bankrupt, there is a very good possibility that this scenario would be the case. Then, of course, B would simply be another of A's many creditors.

Exactly what happens to resolve these claims in each of these situations is a complex legal issue and is beyond the scope of our level of treatment. In addition, the bankruptcy laws vary somewhat around the world, so the potential exists for different treatments of the same situation. Most countries do recognize the legality of netting, however, so it would be rare that a party would be able to claim the full amount owed it without netting out the amount it owes.

The credit risk in a swap varies during its life. An interest rate or equity swap has no final principal payments. The credit risk in either of these swap types is greater during the middle of its life. This occurs because near the end of the life of the swap, not many payments remain, so there is not much money at risk. And at the beginning of the life of the swap, the credit risk is usually low because the parties would probably not engage in the swap if a great deal of credit risk already were present at the start. Therefore, the greatest potential for credit losses is during the middle of the life of the swap. For currency swaps, in which the notional principals are typically exchanged at the end of the life of the swap, the credit risk is concentrated between the middle and the end of its life.

The parties that engage in swaps are generally of good credit quality, but the fear of default is still a significant concern. Yet, perhaps surprisingly, the rates that all parties pay on swaps are the same, regardless of either party's credit quality. As we have illustrated here, a plain vanilla swap, in which one party pays a floating rate and the other pays a fixed rate, has the fixed rate determined by the term structure for that underlying rate. Therefore, if a party wanted to engage in a swap to pay LIBOR and receive a fixed rate, it would get the fixed rate based on the LIBOR term structure, regardless of its credit quality or that of the counterparty, provided that the two parties agreed to do the transaction. Implicit in the fixed rate, however, is the spread between LIBOR and the default-free rate. As we described earlier in the chapter, swap rates are quoted with respect to a spread over the equivalent default-free rate. Thus, a one-year swap rate of 3.68 percent as in our example might be quoted as 50 basis points over the rate on a one-year U.S. Treasury note, implying that the one-year U.S. Treasury note rate was 3.18 percent. This differential is called the **swap spread**.

It is important to note that the swap spread is not a measure of the credit risk on a given swap but rather a reflection of the general level of credit risk in the global economy. The LIBOR term structure reflects the borrowing rate for London banks, which are generally highly rated but not default free. Whenever a recession approaches or credit concerns arise, this spread widens and fixed-rate payers on swaps end up paying more. Of course, floating-rate payers end up paying more as well, but the additional cost to them is less obvious up front because the floating rates change over the life of the swap.

So all parties pay the same rate, but clearly some parties are better credit risks than others. In addition, virtually no parties are default free, and many are of lower credit quality than the typical London bank on which LIBOR is based. How do parties manage the credit risk in swaps? There are a number of methods, which we shall discuss in more detail in Chapter

9. For right now, however, we cover one such method that we have seen before with respect to forward contracts and that is routinely used in the futures market: marking to market.

Reconsider the interest rate swap we covered earlier in the chapter in which the payments are made quarterly in the amount of 0.0092 per $1 notional principal. The swap lasts for one year, so there are four payments. Suppose the parties agree to mark the contract to market halfway through its life—that is, in six months, immediately after the payment is made. Suppose we are at that point and the term structure is as follows:

$$L_{180}(90) = 0.0390$$

$$L_{180}(180) = 0.0402$$

Note that we are at day 180, and the upcoming payments occur in 90 and 180 days. We thus need to calculate $B_{180}(270)$ and $B_{180}(360)$. These present value factors are

$$B_{180}(270) = \frac{1}{1 + 0.039(90/360)} = 0.9903$$

$$B_{180}(360) = \frac{1}{1 = 0.0402(180/360)} = 0.9803$$

Now we can compute the market value of the swap. The present value of the remaining fixed payments, plus the hypothetical notional principal, is $0.0092(0.9903 + 0.9803) + 1.0(0.9803) = 0.9984$.

Because the 90-day floating rate is 3.90 percent, the next floating payment will be $0.0390(90/360) = 0.00975$. Of course, we do not know the last floating payment, but it does not matter because the present value of the remaining floating payments, plus hypothetical notional principal, is automatically 1.0 because we are on the coupon reset date. Therefore, the market value of the swap to the party receiving floating and paying fixed is the present value of the floating payments, 1.0, minus the present value of the fixed payments, 0.9984, or $1.0 - 0.9984 = 0.0016$.

If the two parties marked this swap to market, the party paying floating and receiving fixed would pay the other party a lump sum cash payment of $0.0016 per $1 notional principal. The two parties would then reprice the swap. The new payment would be

$$FS(0, n, m) = FS(0,2,90) = \frac{1 - 0.9803}{0.9903 + 0.9803} = 0.01$$

Thus, the fixed payment would be 0.01 for the rest of the swap.

PRACTICE PROBLEM 8

Consider a two-year swap to pay a fixed rate and receive a floating rate with semi-annual payments. The fixed rate is 0.0462. Now, 360 days later, the term structure is

Days	Rate
180	10.1%
360	10.4%

The next floating payment will be 0.045. The swap calls for marking to market after 180 days, and, therefore, will now be marked to market. Determine the market value, identify which party pays which, and calculate the new fixed rate.

SOLUTION

First find the discount factors:

$$B_{360}(540) = \frac{1}{1 + 0.101(180/360)} = 0.9519$$

$$B_{360}(720) = \frac{1}{1 + 0.104(360/360)} = 0.9058$$

The market value of the fixed payments plus $1 hypothetical notional principal is $0.0462(0.9519 + 0.9058) + 1.0(0.9058) = 0.9916$.

The market value of the floating payments plus $1 hypothetical notional principal is $1.045(0.9519) = 0.9947$.

Therefore, the market value to the party paying fixed and receiving floating is $0.9947 - 0.9916 = 0.0031$.

This amount would be paid by the party paying floating and receiving fixed. The new fixed rate would then be

$$\frac{1 - 0.9058}{0.9519 + 0.9058} = 0.0507$$

This rate would be quoted as an annual rate of $5.07\%(360/180) = 10.14\%$.

As in the futures market, marking a swap contract to market results in the two parties terminating the contract and automatically engaging in a new swap. In essence, the arrangement commits the two parties to terminating the swap and re-establishing it on a predetermined schedule. This process reduces the credit risk by requiring one party to pay the other any amount due at a time prior to the expiration date of the swap. The effect is to reduce the extent to which the swap can go deeply underwater to one of the parties, who may be facing financial problems.

A number of other techniques can be used to control credit risk in swaps. We shall return to the general subject of credit risk and derivatives in Chapter 9.

8 THE ROLE OF SWAP MARKETS

In each of the preceding three chapters, we have discussed the role played by the markets represented by the various derivative instruments. The swap market is extremely large, consisting of dealers and end users engaging in customized transactions that involve a series of payments. As we showed in this chapter, swaps can be equivalent to various other derivative instruments. Moreover, we used transactions in assets to replicate swaps. Hence, an obvious question is why swaps exist when the same results can be obtained using other instruments.

First let us ignore the obvious counter-question of why other instruments exist when swaps serve the same purpose. In the race to see which derivative instrument is more popular, swaps have clearly won. We can only surmise the reason why.

The tremendous popularity of swaps results largely from the popularity of interest rate swaps. For several reasons, these instruments have been embraced by corporations as tools for managing interest rate risk. One is that interest rate swaps, certainly the plain vanilla type, are simple instruments, rarely requiring technology, computational skills, or financial know-how beyond what exists in most corporate treasury offices. In short, they are easy to understand. In addition, interest rate swaps can easily be viewed as a pair of loans. Borrowing and lending money is second nature to corporations. Corporations view engaging in swaps as nothing more than an extension of their regular practice of borrowing and lending money. Many corporations are restricted in their use of options and futures, but they can usually justify swaps as nothing more than variations of loans. Also, swaps are so easily tailored to alter the interest rate patterns on most corporate loans that they seem to go hand in hand with the typical fixed- and floating-rate loans that corporations take out. Many corporations borrow money and combine the loan with a swap right from the start. Finally, we should note that some dealer firms have exploited the attractions of swaps by aggressive selling. In some cases, corporations entered into ill-advised and occasionally complex, exotic swaps. We do not suggest that most dealers have engaged in unethical actions (although some certainly have) but rather that, as in all sales-oriented activities, customers do not always get impartial advice from sales personnel. In some cases, corporations have used swaps to step over the line from good risk management into speculation on risks they know nothing about. In short, at least part of the success of swaps has probably not been for the right reasons.

But using swaps for the wrong reason does not sufficiently explain the success of these instruments. If it were the primary motivation for their use, swaps would die out as a risk management tool. Instead, swaps have grown in popularity. Swaps provide a mechanism for managing the risks associated with a series of payments. Although forward contracts and other instruments can manage that risk, a swap is more of a portfolio approach to managing risk—a package of risk management tools all rolled up into one. Given that risk often exists in a series, swaps are ideal instruments for managing it. Other instruments may be able to do the job, but they must be carefully constructed with a certain amount of financial ingenuity.

We have now completed Chapters 2, 3, 4, and 5, each of which deals with specific types of derivatives. We have obtained a good description of each derivative and examined how to price and value them. We have briefly alluded to how they are used. In the following three chapters we shall examine strategies and applications using these instruments.

KEY POINTS

- Swaps are over-the-counter contracts in which two parties agree to pay a series of cash flows to each other. At least one series is floating or variable and related to an interest rate, exchange rate, equity price, or commodity price; the other can be fixed or floating. Swaps have zero value at the start and have payments made on scheduled payment or settlement dates and a final termination or expiration date. When swap payments are made in the same currency, the payments are usually netted. Swaps are subject to default on the part of either party.

- Swaps can be terminated by having one party pay the market value of the swap to the other party, by entering into a swap in which the variable payments offset, by selling the swap to another party, or by exercising a swaption to enter into an offsetting swap.

- In a currency swap, each party makes payments to the other in different currencies. A currency swap can have one party pay a fixed rate in one currency and the other pay a fixed rate in the other currency; have both pay a floating rate in their respective currencies; have the first party pay a fixed rate in one currency and the second party pay a floating rate in the other currency; or have the first party pay a floating rate in one currency and the second pay a fixed rate in the other currency. In currency swaps, the notional principal is usually exchanged at the beginning and at the end of the life of the swap, although this exchange is not mandatory.

- The payments on a currency swap are calculated by multiplying the notional principal by the fixed or floating interest rate times a day-count adjustment. This procedure is done in each currency, and the respective parties make their separate payments to each other. The payments are not netted.

- In a plain vanilla interest rate swap, one party makes payments at a fixed rate and the other makes payments at a floating rate, with no exchange of notional principal. A typical plain vanilla swap involves one party paying a fixed rate and the other paying a floating rate such as LIBOR. Swaps are often done by a party borrowing floating at a rate tied to LIBOR; that party then uses a pay-fixed, receive-floating swap to offset the risk of its exposure to LIBOR and effectively convert its loan to a fixed-rate loan.

- The payments on an interest rate swap are calculated by multiplying the notional principal by the fixed or floating interest rate times a day-count adjustment. The respective amounts are netted so that the party owing the greater amount makes a net payment to the other.

- The three types of equity swaps involve one party paying a fixed rate, a floating rate, or the return on another equity, while the other party pays an equity return. Therefore, an equity swap is a swap in which at least one party pays the return on a stock or stock index.

- The equity payment (or payments, if both sides of the swap are related to an equity return) on an equity swap is calculated by multiplying the return on the stock over the settlement period by the notional principal. If there is a fixed or floating payment, it is calculated in the same manner as in an interest rate swap. With payments in a single currency, the two sets of payments are netted.

- Swap pricing means to determine the fixed rate and any relevant terms, such as the foreign notional principal on a currency swap, at the start of the swap. Valuation means to determine the market value of the swap, which is the present value of one stream of payments less the present value of the other stream of payments. The market value of a swap is zero at the start but will change to positive for one party and negative for the other during the life of the swap, as market conditions change and time passes.

- Swaps can be viewed as combinations of assets. Currency swaps are like issuing a bond denominated in one currency and using the proceeds to buy a bond denominated in another currency. Interest rate swaps are like issuing a fixed-rate bond and using the proceeds to buy a floating-rate bond or vice versa. Equity swaps are like issuing a bond and using the proceeds to buy stock or vice versa. Equity swaps with both sides paying an equity return are like selling short one stock and using the proceeds to buy another stock. The stock position is not, however, a buy-and-hold position and requires some rebalancing.

- An interest rate swap is like a series of off-market FRAs, meaning that the rate on each FRA is set at the swap rate, not at the rate it would be set at if priced as an FRA with zero market value at the start. In addition, the first payment on a swap is just an exchange of known amounts of cash. Currency swaps and equity swaps are similar to forward contracts, but the connection is not as straightforward as in interest rate swaps.

- Interest rate swaps are like being long (short) interest rate calls and short (long) interest rate puts. Currency swaps and equity swaps are also similar to combinations of options, but the connection is not as straightforward.

- The fixed rate on an interest rate swap equates the present value of the fixed payments plus a hypothetical notional principal to the present value of the floating payments plus a hypothetical notional principal. The notional principals offset but permit these swaps to be treated like bonds. The fixed rate is then equivalent to the fixed rate on a par bond with the same payments as on the swap. The market value of the swap during its life is found by determining the difference in the market values of the floating- and fixed-rate bonds later during their lives under the new term structure.

- The fixed rates on a currency swap are the same as the fixed rates on plain vanilla interest rate swaps in the given countries. The foreign notional principal for a domestic notional principal of one unit is the inverse of the exchange rate. In other words, it is the foreign currency equivalent of the domestic notional principal. Because a currency swap is like issuing a bond in one currency and using the proceeds to buy a bond in another currency, the market value of a currency swap during its life is found by determining the difference in the market values of the two bonds during their lives using the new term structures in the two countries. The foreign bond value must be converted to its domestic equivalent by using the new exchange rate.

- The fixed rate on an equity swap is the same as the fixed rate on a plain vanilla interest rate swap. The market value of an equity swap involving fixed or floating payments during its life is found as the present value of the equity payments less the present value of the fixed or floating payments necessary to replicate the equity swap payment. The market value of an equity swap in which both sides make equity payments is the market value of a long position in one equity and a short position in the other, assuming the positions are liquidated at each settlement date and gains and losses are paid out.

- A swaption is an option to enter into a swap. The two types of interest rate swaptions are payer swaptions, which allow the holder to enter into a swap to pay the fixed rate and receive the floating rate, and receiver swaptions, which allow the holder to enter into a swap to receive the fixed rate and pay the floating rate. Swaptions are based on a specific underlying swap and have an exercise rate and an expiration date. At expiration, they can be exercised to enter into the underlying swap. Swaptions require an up-front premium.

- Swaptions exist to allow users the flexibility to enter into swaps at later dates but establish the terms in advance. If market conditions are not favorable to exercising a swaption, the holder can allow the swaption to expire and obtain more favorable terms by entering into a swap at the market rate. Swaptions are used by parties who anticipate a need to enter into a swap at a later date, who anticipate the need to terminate an already-existing swap, or who wish to speculate on interest rates.

- The payoffs of an interest rate swaption are like those of an option on a coupon-bearing bond. The option has an exercise price of par value, and the coupon rate is the exercise rate on the swaption. A payer swaption is like a put on the bond, and a receiver swaption is like a call on the bond.

- At expiration, an interest rate payer swaption is worth the maximum of zero or the present value of the difference between the market swap rate and the exercise rate, valued as an annuity extending over the remaining life of the underlying swap. To value a receiver swaption at expiration, we take the difference between the exercise rate and the market swap rate, adjusted for its present value over the life of the underlying swap. These figures must be multiplied by the notional principal.

- The market value of a swaption at expiration can be received in one of four ways: by exercising the swaption to enter into the underlying swap, by exercising the swaption and entering into an offsetting swap that keeps both swaps in force, by exercising the swaption and entering into an offsetting swap that eliminates both swaps and pays a series of payments equal to the net difference in the fixed rates on the two swaps, or by exercising the swaption and receiving a lump sum cash payment.

- A forward swap is a forward contract to enter into a swap. It commits both parties to entering into a swap at a later date at a fixed rate agreed on today. In contrast to a swaption, which is the right to enter into a swap, a forward swap is a binding commitment to enter into a swap.

- Credit risk arises in a swap due to the possibility that a party will not be able to make its payments. Current credit risk is the risk of a party being unable to make the upcoming payment. Potential credit risk is the risk of a party being unable to make future payments. Credit risk is faced only by the party that is owed the greater amount.

- The credit risk in an interest rate or equity swap is greatest during the middle of the swap's life. The risk is small at the beginning of the swap because the parties would not engage in the swap if the credit risk were significant at the start. The risk is low at the end of the life of the swap because of the small number of remaining payments. For currency swaps, the payment of notional principal shifts the credit risk more toward the end of the life of the swap. In addition, because the payments are typically not netted, the credit risk on currency swaps is greater than on interest rate swaps.

- The swap spread is the difference between the fixed rate on a swap and the yield on a default-free security of the same maturity as the swap. The spread indicates the average credit risk in the global economy but not the credit risk in a given swap.

- Netting reduces the credit risk in a swap by reducing the amount of money passing from any one party to another. The amount owed by a party is deducted from the amount due to a party, and only the net is paid. Marking a swap to market is a process in which the parties agree to periodically calculate the market value of the swap and have the party owing the greater amount pay the market value to the other party. The fixed rate is then reset on the swap until it is marked to market again or terminates. This procedure forces the party to which the swap is losing money to pay the other party before getting too deeply in debt.

- Swaps play an important role in the financial system by providing a simple means of managing a series of risks. Their popularity has arisen largely from corporate use in managing interest rate exposure.

PROBLEMS

1. A U.S. company enters into a currency swap in which it pays a fixed rate of 5.5 percent in euros and the counterparty pays a fixed rate of 6.75 percent in dollars. The notional principals are $100 million and €116.5 million. Payments are made semiannually and on the basis of 30 days per month and 360 days per year.
   A. Calculate the initial exchange of payments that takes place at the beginning of the swap.
   B. Calculate the semiannual payments.
   C. Calculate the final exchange of payments that takes place at the end of the swap.

2. A British company enters into a currency swap in which it pays a fixed rate of 6 percent in dollars and the counterparty pays a fixed rate of 5 percent in pounds. The notional principals are £75 million and $105 million. Payments are made semiannually and on the basis of 30 days per month and 360 days per year.
   A. Calculate the initial exchange of payments that takes place at the beginning of the swap.
   B. Calculate the semiannual payments.
   C. Calculate the final exchange of payments that takes place at the end of the swap.

3. A U.S. company has entered into an interest rate swap with a dealer in which the notional principal is $50 million. The company will pay a floating rate of LIBOR and receive a fixed rate of 5.75 percent. Interest is paid semiannually, and the current LIBOR is 5.15 percent. Calculate the first payment and indicate which party pays which. Assume that floating-rate payments will be made on the basis of 180/360 and fixed-rate payments will be made on the basis of 180/365.

4. A German company that has issued floating-rate notes now believes that interest rates will rise. It decides to protect itself against this possibility by entering into an interest rate swap with a dealer. In this swap, the notional principal is €25 million and the company will pay a fixed rate of 5.5 percent and receive Euribor. The current Euribor is 5 percent. Calculate the first payment and indicate which party pays which. Assume that floating-rate payments will be made on the basis of 90/360 and fixed-rate payments will be made on the basis of 90/365.

5. An asset manager wishes to reduce his exposure to large-cap stocks and increase his exposure to small-cap stocks. He seeks to do so using an equity swap. He agrees to pay a dealer the return on a large-cap index, and the dealer agrees to pay the manager the return on a small-cap index. For each of the scenarios listed below, calculate the first overall payment and indicate which party makes the payment. Assume that payments are made semiannually. The notional principal is $100 million.
   A. The value of the small-cap index starts off at 689.40, and the large-cap index starts at 1130.20. In six months, the small-cap index is at 625.60 and the large-cap index is at 1251.83.
   B. The value of the small-cap index starts off at 689.40 and the large-cap index starts at 1130.20. In six months, the small-cap index is at 703.23 and the large-cap index is at 1143.56.

6. An asset manager wishes to reduce her exposure to small-cap stocks and increase her exposure to fixed-income securities. She seeks to do so using an equity swap. She agrees to pay a dealer the return on a small-cap index and the dealer agrees to pay the manager a fixed rate of 5.5 percent. For each of the scenarios listed below, calculate the overall payment six months later and indicate which party makes the payment. Assume that payments are made semiannually (180 days per period) and there are 365 days in each year. The notional principal is $50 million.

   A. The value of the small-cap index starts off at 234.10 and six months later is at 238.41.

   B. The value of the small-cap index starts off at 234.10 and six months later is at 241.27.

7. An asset manager wishes to reduce his exposure to fixed-income securities and increase his exposure to large-cap stocks. He seeks to do so using an equity swap. He agrees to pay a dealer a fixed rate of 4.5 percent, and the dealer agrees to pay the manager the return on a large-cap index. For each of the scenarios listed below, calculate the overall payment six months later and indicate which party makes it. Assume that payments are made semiannually (180 days per period) and there are 365 days in a year. The notional principal is $25 million.

   A. The value of the large-cap index starts off at 578.50 and six months later is at 622.54.

   B. The value of the large-cap index starts off at 578.50 and six months later is at 581.35.

8. Consider a two-year interest rate swap with semiannual payments. Assume a notional principal of $25 million.

   A. Calculate the annualized fixed rate on the swap. The current term structure of LIBOR interest rates is as follows:

   $$L_0(180) = 0.0585$$

   $$L_0(360) = 0.0605$$

   $$L_0(540) = 0.0624$$

   $$L_0(720) = 0.0665$$

   B. Calculate the market value of the swap 120 days later 1) from the point of view of the party paying the floating rate and receiving the fixed rate and 2) from the point of view of the party paying the fixed rate and receiving the floating rate. The term structure 120 days later is as follows:

   $$L_{120}(60) = 0.0613$$

   $$L_{120}(240) = 0.0629$$

   $$L_{120}(420) = 0.0653$$

   $$L_{120}(600) = 0.0697$$

9. Consider a one-year interest rate swap with quarterly payments. Assume a notional principal of $15 million.

   A. Calculate the annualized fixed rate on the swap. The current term structure of LIBOR interest rates is as follows:

   $$L_0(90) = 0.0656$$

   $$L_0(180) = 0.0640$$

   $$L_0(270) = 0.0621$$

   $$L_0(360) = 0.0599$$

   B. Calculate the market value of the swap 30 days later 1) from the point of view of the party paying the floating rate and receiving the fixed rate and 2) from the point of view of the party paying the fixed rate and receiving the floating rate. The term structure 30 days later is as follows:

$$L_{30}(60) = 0.0384$$

$$L_{30}(150) = 0.0379$$

$$L_{30}(240) = 0.0382$$

$$L_{30}(330) = 0.0406$$

10. Consider a two-year currency swap with semiannual payments. The domestic currency is the U.S. dollar, and the foreign currency is the U.K. pound. The current exchange rate is $1.41 per pound.

   A. Calculate the annualized fixed rates for dollars and pounds. The current U.S. term structure is the same as in Problem 8, Part A:

   $$L_0(180) = 0.0585$$

   $$L_0(360) = 0.0605$$

   $$L_0(540) = 0.0624$$

   $$L_0(720) = 0.0665$$

   The U.K. term structure is

   $$L_0^{\pounds}(180) = 0.0493$$

   $$L_0^{\pounds}(360) = 0.0505$$

   $$L_0^{\pounds}(540) = 0.0519$$

   $$L_0^{\pounds}(720) = 0.0551$$

   B. Now move forward 120 days. The new exchange rate is $1.35 per pound, and the new U.S. term structure is the same as in Problem 8, Part B:

   $$L_{120}(60) = 0.0613$$

   $$L_{120}(240) = 0.0629$$

   $$L_{120}(420) = 0.0653$$

   $$L_{120}(600) = 0.0697$$

   The new U.K. term structure is

   $$L_{120}^{\pounds}(60) = 0.0517$$

   $$L_{120}^{\pounds}(240) = 0.0532$$

   $$L_{120}^{\pounds}(420) = 0.0568$$

   $$L_{120}^{\pounds}(600) = 0.0583$$

   Assume that the notional principal is $1 or the corresponding amount in British pounds. Calculate the market values of the following swaps:

   i. Pay £ fixed and receive $ fixed.
   ii. Pay £ floating and receive $ fixed.
   iii. Pay £ floating and receive $ floating.
   iv. Pay £ fixed and receive $ floating.

11. Consider a one-year currency swap with quarterly payments. The domestic currency is the U.S. dollar, and the foreign currency is the euro. The current exchange rate is $0.86 per euro.

A. Calculate the annualized fixed rates for dollars and euros. The current U.S. term structure is the same as in Problem 9, Part A:

$$L_0(90) = 0.0656$$

$$L_0(180) = 0.0640$$

$$L_0(270) = 0.0621$$

$$L_0(360) = 0.0599$$

The Euribor term structure is

$$L_0^{€}(90) = 0.0682$$

$$L_0^{€}(180) = 0.0673$$

$$L_0^{€}(270) = 0.0661$$

$$L_0^{€}(360) = 0.0668$$

B. Now move forward 30 days. The new exchange rate is $0.82 per euro, and the new U.S. term structure is the same as in Problem 9, Part B:

$$L_{30}(60) = 0.0384$$
$$L_{30}(150) = 0.0379$$
$$L_{30}(240) = 0.0382$$
$$L_{30}(330) = 0.0406$$

The new Euribor term structure is

$$L_{30}^{€}(60) = 0.0583$$

$$L_{30}^{€}(150) = 0.0605$$

$$L_{30}^{€}(240) = 0.0613$$

$$L_{30}^{€}(330) = 0.0651$$

Assume that the notional principal is $1 or the corresponding amount in euros. Calculate the market values of the following swaps:
  i. Pay € fixed and receive $ fixed.
  ii. Pay € floating and receive $ fixed.
  iii. Pay € floating and receive $ floating.
  iv. Pay € fixed and receive $ floating.

12. Consider a one-year currency swap with semiannual payments. The two currencies are the U.K. pound and the euro. The current exchange rate is £0.61 per euro.
  A. Calculate the annualized fixed rates for pounds and euros. The current U.K. term structure is

$$L_0^{€}(180) = 0.0623$$

$$L_0^{€}(360) = 0.0665$$

The Euribor term structure is

$$L_0^{€}(180) = 0.0563$$

$$L_0^{€}(360) = 0.0580$$

  B. Now move forward 60 days. The new exchange rate is £0.57 per euro, and the new British term structure is

$$L_{60}^{£}(120) = 0.0585$$

$$L_{60}^{£}(300) = 0.0605$$

The new Euribor term structure is

$$L_{60}^{€}(120) = 0.0493$$

$$L_{60}^{€}(300) = 0.0505$$

Assume that the notional principal is £1 or the corresponding amount in euros. Calculate the market values in pounds of the following swaps:

   i. Pay £ fixed and receive € fixed.

  ii. Pay £ floating and receive € fixed.

 iii. Pay £ floating and receive € floating.

  iv. Pay £ fixed and receive € floating.

13. An asset manager wishes to enter into a two-year equity swap in which he will receive the rate of return on the S&P 500 Index in exchange for paying a fixed interest rate. The S&P 500 stock index is at 1150.89 at the beginning of the swap. The swap calls for semiannual payments.

   A. Calculate the annualized fixed rate on the swap. The current term structure of interest rates is as follows:

$$L_0(180) = 0.0458$$

$$L_0(360) = 0.0528$$

$$L_0(540) = 0.0624$$

$$L_0(720) = 0.0665$$

   B. Calculate the market value of the swap 160 days later if the new term structure is

$$L_{160}(20) = 0.0544$$

$$L_{160}(200) = 0.0629$$

$$L_{160}(380) = 0.0679$$

$$L_{160}(560) = 0.0697$$

The S&P 500 is at 1204.10. The notional principal of the swap is $100 million.

14. Assume an asset manager enters into a one-year equity swap in which he will receive the return on the Nasdaq 100 Index in return for paying a floating interest rate. The swap calls for quarterly payments. The Nasdaq 100 is at 1561.27 at the beginning of the swap. Ninety days later, the rate $L_{90}(90)$ is 0.0432. Calculate the market value of the swap 100 days from the beginning of the swap if the Nasdaq 100 is at 1595.72 and the term structure is

$$L_{100}(80) = 0.0427$$

$$L_{100}(170) = 0.0481$$

$$L_{100}(260) = 0.0544$$

The notional principal of the swap is $50 million.

15. Consider an equity swap in which the asset manager receives the return on the Russell 2000 Index in return for paying the return on the DJIA. At the inception of the equity swap, the Russell 2000 is at 478.19 and the DJIA is at 9867.33. Calculate the market value of the swap a few months later when the Russell 2000 is at 524.29 and the DJIA is at 10016. The notional principal of the swap is $15 million.

16. Consider a European receiver swaption that expires in one year and is on a two-year swap that will make semiannual payments. The swaption has an exercise rate of 7 percent. The notional principal is $50 million. At expiration, the term structure of interest rates is as follows:

$$L_0(180) = 0.0420$$

$$L_0(360) = 0.0474$$

$$L_0(540) = 0.0544$$

$$L_0(720) = 0.0661$$

   A. List the four possible ways this swaption could be exercised, and indicate the relevant cash flows in each case.
   B. Show that the payoff on the swaption is equivalent to that of a call option on a bond with exercise price of $1 (the par value of the bond).

17. Consider a European payer swaption that expires in one year and is on a two-year swap that will make semiannual payments. The swaption has an exercise rate of 5 percent. The notional principal is $10 million. At expiration, the term structure of interest rates is as follows:

$$L_0(180) = 0.0583$$

$$L_0(360) = 0.0605$$

$$L_0(540) = 0.0614$$

$$L_0(720) = 0.0651$$

   A. List the four possible ways this swaption could be exercised, and indicate the relevant cash flows in each case.
   B. Show that the payoff on the swaption is equivalent to that of a put option on a bond with exercise price of $1 (the par value of the bond).

18. Consider a European receiver swaption that expires in two years and is on a one-year swap that will make quarterly payments. The swaption has an exercise rate of 6.5 percent. The notional principal is $100 million. At expiration, the term structure of interest rates is as follows:

$$L_0(90) = 0.0373$$

$$L_0(180) = 0.0429$$

$$L_0(270) = 0.0477$$

$$L_0(360) = 0.0538$$

   A. Calculate the market value of the swaption at expiration.
   B. Show that the payoff is equivalent to that of a call option on a bond with exercise price of $1 (the par value of the bond).

19. A two-year swap with semiannual payments pays a floating rate and receives a fixed rate. The term structure at the beginning of the swap is

$$L_0(180) = 0.0583$$

$$L_0(360) = 0.0616$$

$$L_0(540) = 0.0680$$

$$L_0(720) = 0.0705$$

In order to mitigate the credit risk of the parties engaged in the swap, the swap will be marked to market in 180 days. Suppose it is now 180 days later and the swap is being marked to market. The new term structure is

$$L_{180}(180) = 0.0429$$

$$L_{180}(360) = 0.0538$$

$$L_{180}(540) = 0.0618$$

    A. Calculate the market value of the swap per \$1 notional principal and indicate which party pays which.

    B. Calculate the new fixed rate on the swap at which the swap would proceed after marking to market.

20. A one-year swap with quarterly payments pays a fixed rate and receives a floating rate. The term structure at the beginning of the swap is

$$L_0(90) = 0.0252$$

$$L_0(180) = 0.0305$$

$$L_0(270) = 0.0373$$

$$L_0(360) = 0.0406$$

In order to mitigate the credit risk of the parties engaged in the swap, the swap will be marked to market in 90 days. Suppose it is now 90 days later and the swap is being marked to market. The new term structure is

$$L_{90}(90) = 0.0539$$

$$L_{90}(180) = 0.0608$$

$$L_{90}(270) = 0.0653$$

    A. Calculate the market value of the swap per \$1 notional principal and indicate which party pays which.

    B. Calculate the new fixed rate on the swap at which the swap would proceed after marking to market.

SOLUTIONS

1. **A.** The payments at the beginning of the swap are as follows:
   The U.S. company (domestic party) pays the counterparty $100 million.
   The counterparty pays the U.S. company €116.5 million.
   B. The semiannual payments are as follows:
   The U.S. company (domestic party) pays the counterparty
   €116,500,000(0.055)(180/360) = €3,203,750.
   The counterparty pays the U.S. company $100,000,000(0.0675)(180/360) = $3,375,000.
   C. The payments at the end of the swap are as follows:
   The U.S. company (domestic party) pays the counterparty €116.5 million.
   The counterparty pays the U.S. company $100 million.

2. **A.** The payments at the beginning of the swap are as follows:
   The British company (domestic party) pays the counterparty £75 million.
   The counterparty pays the British company $105 million.
   B. The semiannual payments are as follows:
   The British company (domestic party) pays the counterparty
   $105,000,000(0.06)(180/360) = $3,150,000.
   The counterparty pays the British company £75,000,000(0.05)(180/360) = £1,875,000.
   C. The payments at the end of the swap are as follows:
   The British company (domestic party) pays the counterparty $105 million.
   The counterparty pays the British company £75 million.

3. The fixed payments are $50,000,000(0.0575)(180/365) = $1,417,808.
   The floating payments are $50,000,000(0.0515)(180/360) = $1,287,500.
   The net payment is $130,308, made by the party paying fixed—that is, the dealer pays the company.

4. The fixed payments are €25,000,000(0.055)(90/365) = €339,041.
   The floating payments are €25,000,000(0.05)(90/360) = €312,500.
   The net payment is €26,541, made by the party paying fixed—that is, the company pays the dealer.

5. **A.** The small-cap equity payment is $\left(\dfrac{625.60}{689.40} - 1\right)(100,000,000) = -\$9,254,424$.

   The asset manager owes $9,254,424 to the dealer.

   The large-cap equity payment is $\left(\dfrac{1251.83}{1130.20} - 1\right)(100,000,000) = \$10,761,812$.

   The asset manager owes this amount to the dealer.
   The overall payment made by the asset manager to the dealer is $9,254,424 + $10,761,812 = $20,016,236.
   B. The small-cap equity payment is $\left(\dfrac{703.23}{689.40} - 1\right)(100,000,000) = \$2,006,092$.

   The dealer owes the asset manager this amount.

   The large-cap equity payment is $\left(\dfrac{1143.56}{1130.20} - 1\right)(100,000,000) = \$1,182,092$.

   The asset manager owes this amount to the dealer.
   The overall payment made by the dealer to the asset manager is $2,006,092 − $1,182,092 = $824,000.

6. A. The small-cap equity payment is $\left(\dfrac{238.41}{234.10} - 1\right)(50{,}000{,}000) = \$920{,}547$.

The asset manager owes the dealer this amount.
The fixed interest payment is $(50{,}000{,}000)(0.055)(180/365) = \$1{,}356{,}164$.
The dealer owes this amount to the asset manager.
So the dealer pays to the asset manager $\$1{,}356{,}164 - \$920{,}547 = \$435{,}617$.

B. The small-cap equity payment is $\left(\dfrac{241.27}{234.10} - 1\right)(50{,}000{,}000) = \$1{,}531{,}397$.

The asset manager owes the dealer this amount.
The fixed interest payment is $(50{,}000{,}000)(0.055)(180/365) = \$1{,}356{,}164$.
The dealer owes this amount to the asset manager.
So the asset manager pays to the dealer $\$1{,}531{,}397 - \$1{,}356{,}164 = \$175{,}233$.

7. A. The large-cap equity payment is $\left(\dfrac{622.54}{578.50} - 1\right)(25{,}000{,}000) = \$1{,}903{,}198$.

The dealer owes this amount to the asset manager.
The fixed interest payment is $(25{,}000{,}000)(0.045)(180/365) = \$554{,}795$.
The asset manager owes this amount to the dealer.

So the dealer pays to the asset manager $\$1{,}903{,}198 - \$554{,}795 = 1{,}348{,}403$.

B. The large-cap equity payment is $\left(\dfrac{581.35}{578.50} - 1\right)(25{,}000{,}000) = \$123{,}163$.

The dealer owes this amount to the asset manager.
The fixed interest payment is $(25{,}000{,}000)(0.045)(180/365) = \$554{,}795$.
The asset manager owes this amount to the dealer.
So the asset manager pays to the dealer $\$554{,}795 - \$123{,}163 = \$431{,}632$.

8. A. The present value factors for 180, 360, 540, and 720 days are as follows:

$$B_0(180) = \frac{1}{1 + 0.0585(180/360)} = 0.9716$$

$$B_0(360) = \frac{1}{1 + 0.0605(360/360)} = 0.9430$$

$$B_0(540) = \frac{1}{1 + 0.0624(540/360)} = 0.9144$$

$$B_0(720) = \frac{1}{1 + 0.0665(720/360)} = 0.8826$$

The semiannual fixed rate (or payment per \$1 of notional principal) is calculated as

$$\text{FS}(0, n, m) = \text{FS}(0,4,180) = \frac{1 - 0.8826}{0.9716 + 0.9430 + 0.9144 + 0.8826} = 0.0316$$

The annualized fixed rate (or payment per \$1 of notional principal) is $0.0316(360/180) = 0.0632$. Because the notional principal is \$25,000,000, the semiannual fixed payment is $25{,}000{,}000(0.0316) = \$790{,}000$.

B. The new present value factors for 60, 240, 420, and 600 days are as follows:

$$B_{120}(180) = \frac{1}{1 + 0.0613(60/360)} = 0.9899$$

$$B_{120}(360) = \frac{1}{1 + 0.0629(240/360)} = 0.9598$$

$$B_{120}(540) = \frac{1}{1 + 0.0653(420/360)} = 0.9292$$

$$B_{120}(720) = \frac{1}{1 + 0.0697(600/360)} = 0.8959$$

The present value of the remaining fixed payments plus the $1 hypothetical notional principal is $0.0316(0.9899 + 0.9598 + 0.9292 + 0.8959) + 1(0.8959) = 1.0152$.

The present value of the floating payments plus the hypothetical $1 notional principal is $1.0293(0.9899) = 1.0189$, where
- 1.0293 is the first floating payment, $0.0585(180/360) + 1$, which is the market value of the remaining payments plus the $1 notional principal, and
- 0.9899 is the discount factor.

Based on a notional principal of $25,000,000, the market value of the swap to the pay-floating, receive-fixed party is $(1.0152 - 1.0189)25,000,000 = -\$92,500$. Thus, the market value of the swap to opposite party that pays fixed and receives floating is $92,500.

9. A. The present value factors for 90, 180, 270, and 360 days are as follows:

$$B_0(90) = \frac{1}{1 + 0.0656(90/360)} = 0.9839$$

$$B_0(180) = \frac{1}{1 + 0.0640(180/360)} = 0.9690$$

$$B_0(270) = \frac{1}{1 + 0.0621(270/360)} = 0.9555$$

$$B_0(360) = \frac{1}{1 + 0.0599(360/360)} = 0.9435$$

The quarterly fixed rate (or payment per $1 of notional principal) is calculated as

$$FS(0, n, m) = FS(0,4,90) = \frac{1 - 0.9435}{0.9839 + 0.9690 + 0.9555 + 0.9435} = 0.0147$$

The annualized fixed rate (or payment per $1 of notional principal) is $0.0147(360/90) = 0.0588$. Because the notional principal is $15,000,000, the quarterly fixed payment is $15,000,000(0.0147) = \$220,500$.

B. The new present value factors for 60, 150, 240, and 330 days are as follows:

$$B_{30}(90) = \frac{1}{1 + 0.0384(60/360)} = 0.9936$$

$$B_{30}(180) = \frac{1}{1 + 0.0379(150/360)} = 0.9845$$

$$B_{30}(270) = \frac{1}{1 + 0.0382(240/360)} = 0.9752$$

$$B_{30}(360) = \frac{1}{1 + 0.0406(330/360)} = 0.9641$$

The present value of the remaining fixed payments plus the $1 notional principal is $0.0147(0.9936 + 0.9845 + 0.9752 + 0.9641) + 1(0.9641) = 1.0217$.

The present value of the floating payments plus hypothetical $1 notional principal is $1.0164(0.9936) = 1.0099$, where

- 1.0164 is the first floating payment, $0.0656(90/360) + 1$, which is the market value of the remaining payments plus the $1 notional principal, and
- 0.9936 is the discount factor.

Based on a notional principal of $15,000,000, the market value of the swap to the pay-floating, receive-fixed party is $(1.0217 - 1.0099)15,000,000 = \$177,000$. Thus, the market value of the swap to the pay-fixed, receive-floating party is $-\$177,000$.

10. A. First calculate the fixed payment in dollars. The dollar present value factors for 180, 360, 540, and 720 days are as follows:

$$B_0(180) = \frac{1}{1 + 0.0585(180/360)} = 0.9716$$

$$B_0(360) = \frac{1}{1 + 0.0605(360/360)} = 0.9430$$

$$B_0(540) = \frac{1}{1 + 0.0624(540/360)} = 0.9144$$

$$B_0(720) = \frac{1}{1 + 0.0665(720/360)} = 0.8826$$

The semiannual fixed payment per $1 of notional principal is calculated as

$$FS(0, n, m) = FS(0,4,180) = \frac{1 - 0.8826}{0.9716 + 0.9430 + 0.9144 + 0.8826} = 0.0316$$

The annualized fixed payment per $1 of notional principal is calculated as $0.0316(360/180) = 0.0632$.

Now calculate the fixed payment in pounds. The pound present value factors for 180, 360, 540, and 720 days are as follows:

$$B_0^£(180) = \frac{1}{1 + 0.0493(180/360)} = 0.9759$$

$$B_0^£(360) = \frac{1}{1 + 0.0505(360/360)} = 0.9519$$

$$B_0^£(540) = \frac{1}{1 + 0.0519(540/360)} = 0.9278$$

$$B_0^£(720) = \frac{1}{1 + 0.0551(720/360)} = 0.9007$$

The semiannual fixed payment per £1 of notional principal is calculated as

$$FS(0, n, m) = FS(0,4,180) = \frac{1 - 0.9007}{0.9759 + 0.9519 + 0.9278 + 0.9007} = 0.0264$$

The annualized fixed payment per £1 of notional principal is calculated as $0.0264(360/180) = 0.0528$.

B. The new dollar discount factors for 60, 240, 420, and 600 days are as follows:

$$B_{120}(180) = \frac{1}{1 + 0.0613(60/360)} = 0.9899$$

$$B_{120}(360) = \frac{1}{1 + 0.0629(240/360)} = 0.9598$$

$$B_{120}(540) = \frac{1}{1 + 0.0653(420/360)} = 0.9292$$

$$B_{120}(720) = \frac{1}{1 + 0.0697(600/360)} = 0.8959$$

The present value of the remaining fixed payments plus the $1 notional principal is 0.0316(0.9899 + 0.9598 + 0.9292 + 0.8959) + 1(0.8959) = 1.0152.

The present value of the floating payments plus hypothetical $1 notional principal discounted back 120 days is 1.0293(0.9899) = 1.0189, where
- 1.0293 is the first floating payment, 0.0585(180/360) + 1, which is the market value of the remaining payments plus the $1 notional principal, and
- 0.9899 is the discount factor.

The new pound discount factors for 60, 240, 420, and 600 days are as follows:

$$B_{120}^{£}(180) = \frac{1}{1 + 0.0517(60/360)} = 0.9915$$

$$B_{120}^{£}(360) = \frac{1}{1 + 0.0532(240/360)} = 0.9657$$

$$B_{120}^{£}(540) = \frac{1}{1 + 0.0568(420/360)} = 0.9379$$

$$B_{120}^{£}(720) = \frac{1}{1 + 0.0583(600/360)} = 0.9114$$

The present value of the remaining fixed payments plus the £1 notional principal is 0.0264(0.9915 + 0.9657 + 0.9379 + 0.9114) + 1(0.9114) = 1.0119. Convert this amount to the equivalent of $1 notional principal; that is, 1/$1.41: 1.0119(1/1.41) = £0.7177. Now convert to dollars at the current exchange rate $1.35/£: 0.7177(1.35) = $0.9688.

The present value of the floating payments plus hypothetical £1 notional principal is 1.0247(0.9915) = 1.016, where
- 1.0247 is the first floating payment, 0.0493(180/360) + 1, which is the market value of the remaining payments plus the £1 notional principal, and
- 0.9915 is the discount factor.

Convert this amount to the equivalent of $1 notional principal; that is, 1/$1.41: 1.016(1/1.41) = £0.7206. Now convert to dollars at the current exchange rate $1.35/£: 0.7206(1.35) = $0.9728.

The market values based on notional principal of $1 are as follows:
  i. Pay £ fixed and receive $ fixed = $0.0464 = 1.0152 − 0.9688
 ii. Pay £ floating and receive $ fixed = $0.0424 = 1.0152 − 0.9728
iii. Pay £ floating and receive $ floating = $0.0461 = 1.0189 − 0.9728
 iv. Pay £ fixed and receive $ floating = $0.0501 = 1.0189 −0.9688

11. A. First calculate the fixed payment in dollars. The dollar present value factors for 90, 180, 270, and 360 days are as follows:

$$B_0(90) = \frac{1}{1 + 0.0656(90/360)} = 0.9839$$

$$B_0(180) = \frac{1}{1 + 0.0640(180/360)} = 0.9690$$

$$B_0(270) = \frac{1}{1 + 0.0621(270/360)} = 0.9555$$

$$B_0(360) = \frac{1}{1 + 0.0599(360/360)} = 0.9435$$

The quarterly fixed payment per \$1 of notional principal is calculated as

$$FS(0, n, m) = FS(0,4,90) = \frac{1 - 0.9435}{0.9839 + 0.9690 + 0.9555 + 0.9435} = 0.0147$$

The annualized fixed payment per \$1 of notional principal is $0.0147(360/90) = 0.0588$.

Now calculate the fixed payment in euros. The euro present value factors for 90, 180, 270, and 360 days are as follows:

$$B_0^{€}(90) = \frac{1}{1 + 0.0682(90/360)} = 0.9832$$

$$B_0^{€}(180) = \frac{1}{1 + 0.0673(180/360)} = 0.9674$$

$$B_0^{€}(270) = \frac{1}{1 + 0.0661(270/360)} = 0.9528$$

$$B_0^{€}(360) = \frac{1}{1 + 0.0668(360/360)} = 0.9374$$

The quarterly fixed payment per €1 of notional principal is calculated as

$$FS(0, n, m) = FS(0,4,90) = \frac{1 - 0.9374}{0.9832 + 0.9674 + 0.9528 + 0.9374} = 0.0163$$

The annualized fixed payment per €1 of notional principal is $0.0163(360/90) = 0.0652$.

B. The new dollar discount factors for 60, 150, 240, and 330 days are as follows:

$$B_{30}(90) = \frac{1}{1 + 0.0384(60/360)} = 0.9936$$

$$B_{30}(180) = \frac{1}{1 + 0.0379(150/360)} = 0.9845$$

$$B_{30}(270) = \frac{1}{1 + 0.0382(240/360)} = 0.9752$$

$$B_{30}(360) = \frac{1}{1 + 0.0406(330/360)} = 0.9641$$

The present value of the remaining fixed payments plus the \$1 notional principal is $0.0147(0.9936 + 0.9845 + 0.9752 + 0.9641) + 1(0.9641) = 1.0217$.

The present value of the floating payments plus hypothetical \$1 notional principal is $1.0164(0.9936) = 1.0099$, where

- 1.0164 is the first floating payment, $0.0656(90/360) + 1$, which is the market value of the remaining payments plus the \$1 notional principal, and
- 0.9936 is the discount factor.

The new euro discount factors for 60, 150, 240, and 330 days are as follows:

$$B_{30}^{\euro}(90) = \frac{1}{1 + 0.0583(60/360)} = 0.9904$$

$$B_{30}^{\euro}(180) = \frac{1}{1 + 0.0605(150/360)} = 0.9754$$

$$B_{30}^{\euro}(270) = \frac{1}{1 + 0.0613(240/360)} = 0.9604$$

$$B_{30}^{\euro}(360) = \frac{1}{1 + 0.0651(330/360)} = 0.9437$$

The present value of the remaining fixed payments plus the €1 notional principal is $0.0163(0.9904 + 0.9754 + 0.9604 + 0.9437) + 1(0.9437) = 1.0068$. Convert this amount to the equivalent of \$1 notional principal; that is, 1/\$0.86: $1.0068(1/0.86) = €1.1707$. Now convert to dollars at the current exchange rate of \$0.82 per euro: $1.1707(0.82) = \$0.96$.

    The present value of the floating payments plus hypothetical €1 notional principal is $1.0171(0.9904) = 1.0073$, where

- 1.0171 is the first floating payment, $0.0682(90/360) + 1$, which is the market value of the remaining payments plus the €1 notional principal, and
- 0.9904 is the discount factor.

Convert this amount to the equivalent of \$1 notional principal; that is, 1/\$0.86: $1.0073(1/0.86) = €1.1713$. Now convert to dollars at the current exchange rate of \$0.82 per euro: $1.1713(0.82) = \$0.9605$. The market values based on notional principal of \$1 are

  i. Pay € fixed and receive \$ fixed = \$0.0617 = $1.0217 - 0.96$

 ii. Pay € floating and receive \$ fixed = \$0.0612 = $1.0217 - 0.9605$

iii. Pay € floating and receive \$ floating = \$0.0494 = $1.0099 - 0.9605$

iv. Pay € fixed and receive \$ floating = \$0.0499 = $1.0099 - 0.96$

12. A. First calculate the fixed payment in pounds. The pound present value factors for 180 and 360 days are as follows:

$$B_0^{\pounds}(180) = \frac{1}{1 + 0.0623(180/360)} = 0.9698$$

$$B_0^{\pounds}(360) = \frac{1}{1 + 0.0665(360/360)} = 0.9376$$

The semiannual fixed payment per £1 of notional principal is calculated as

$$FS(0, n, m) = FS(0,2,180) = \frac{1 - 0.9376}{0.9698 + 0.9376} = 0.0327$$

The annualized fixed payment per £1 of notional principal is calculated as $0.0327(360/180) = 0.0654$.

Now calculate the fixed payment in euros. The euro present value factors for 180 and 360 days are as follows:

$$B_0^{\text{€}}(180) = \frac{1}{1 + 0.0563(180/360)} = 0.9726$$

$$B_0^{\text{€}}(360) = \frac{1}{1 + 0.0580(360/360)} = 0.9452$$

The quarterly fixed payment per €1 of notional principal is calculated as

$$FS(0, n, m) = FS(0,2,180) = \frac{1 - 0.9452}{0.9726 + 0.9452} = 0.0286$$

The annualized fixed payment per €1 of notional principal is $0.0286(360/180) = 0.0572$.

B. The new pound present value factors for 120 and 300 days are as follows:

$$B_{60}^{\text{£}}(180) = \frac{1}{1 + 0.0585(120/360)} = 0.9809$$

$$B_{60}^{\text{£}}(360) = \frac{1}{1 + 0.0605(300/360)} = 0.9520$$

The present value of the remaining fixed payments plus the £1 notional principal is $0.0327(0.9809 + 0.9520) + 1(0.9520) = 1.0152$.

The present value of the floating payments plus hypothetical £1 notional principal is $1.0312(0.9809) = 1.0115$, where
- 1.0312 is the first floating payment, $0.0623(180/360) + 1$, which is the market value of the remaining payments plus the £1 notional principal, and
- 0.9809 is the discount factor.

The new euro discount factors for 120 and 300 days are as follows:

$$B_{60}^{\text{€}}(180) = \frac{1}{1 + 0.0493(120/360)} = 0.9838$$

$$B_{60}^{\text{€}}(360) = \frac{1}{1 + 0.0505(300/360)} = 0.9596$$

The present value of the remaining fixed payments plus the €1 notional principal is $0.0286(0.9838 + 0.9596) + 1(0.9596) = 1.0152$. Convert this to the equivalent of £1 notional principal; that is, $1/£0.61$: $1.0152(1/0.61) = $ €1.6643.

Now convert to pounds at the current exchange rate of £0.57 per euro: $1.6643(0.57) = £0.9487$. The present value of the floating payments plus hypothetical €1 notional principal is $1.0282(0.9838) = 1.0115$, where
- 1.0282 is the first floating payment, $0.0563(180/360) + 1$, which is the market value of the remaining payments plus the €1 notional principal, and
- 0.9838 is the discount factor.

Convert this amount to the equivalent of £1 notional principal; that is, $1/£0.61$: $1.0115(1/0.61) = $ €1.6582. Now convert to pounds at the current exchange rate of £0.57 per euro: 1.6582(0.57) = £0.9452. The market values based on notional principal of £1 are:

  i. Pay £ fixed and receive € fixed = −£0.0665 = 0.9487 − 1.0152
  ii. Pay £ floating and receive € fixed = −£0.0628 = 0.9487 − 1.0115
  iii. Pay £ floating and receive € floating = −£0.0663 = 0.9452 − 1.0115
  iv. Pay £ fixed and receive € floating = −£0.07 = 0.9452 − 1.0152

13. A. The present value factors for 180, 360, 540, and 720 days are as follows:

$$B_0(180) = \frac{1}{1 + 0.0458(180/360)} = 0.9776$$

$$B_0(360) = \frac{1}{1 + 0.0528(360/360)} = 0.9499$$

$$B_0(540) = \frac{1}{1 + 0.0624(540/360)} = 0.9144$$

$$B_0(720) = \frac{1}{1 + 0.0665(720/360)} = 0.8826$$

The semiannual fixed payment per \$1 of notional principal is calculated as

$$FS(0, n, m) = FS(0,4,180) = \frac{1 - 0.8826}{0.9776 + 0.9499 + 0.9144 + 0.8826} = 0.0315$$

The annualized fixed payment per \$1 of notional principal is 0.0315(360/180) = 0.0630.

B. The new present value factors for 20, 200, 380, and 560 days are as follows:

$$B_{160}(180) = \frac{1}{1 + 0.0544(20/360)} = 0.9970$$

$$B_{160}(360) = \frac{1}{1 + 0.0629(200/360)} = 0.9662$$

$$B_{160}(540) = \frac{1}{1 + 0.0679(380/360)} = 0.9331$$

$$B_{160}(720) = \frac{1}{1 + 0.0697(560/360)} = 0.9022$$

The present value of the remaining fixed payments plus the \$1 notional principal is 0.0315(0.9970 + 0.9662 + 0.9331 + 0.9022) + 1(0.9022) = 1.0219. The value of the equity payment is

$$\left(\frac{1204.10}{1150.89}\right) = 1.0462$$

Based on a notional principal of \$100,000,000, the market value of a swap to pay the fixed and receive the equity return is (1.0462 − 1.0219)100,000,000 = \$2,430,000.

14. A. The asset manager enters into the swap at time t = 0. After moving forward 100 days the next floating payment is due on day 180—that is, 80 days from now. Based on the rate in effect on day 100, the present value factor is

$$B_{100}(180) = \frac{1}{1 + 0.0427(80/360)} = 0.9906$$

The next floating payment, based on the rate in effect on day 90, will be $0.0432(90/360) = 0.0108$. The present value of the next floating payment plus the \$1 market value of the remaining floating payments is $0.9906(1.0108) = 1.0013$. The value of the equity payment is

$$\left(\frac{1595.72}{1561.27}\right) = 1.0221$$

Based on a notional principal of \$50 million, the market value of the swap to the party that pays floating and receives the equity return is $(1.0221 - 1.0013)50,000,000 = \$1,040,000$.

15. The value of the equity payment received on the Russell 2000 is

$$\left(\frac{524.29}{478.19}\right) = 1.0964$$

The value of the equity payment made on the DJIA is

$$\left(\frac{10016}{9867.33}\right) = 1.0151$$

Based on a notional principal of \$15 million, the market value of the swap to the pay the return on the DJIA and receive the return on the Russell 2000 is $(1.0964 - 1.0151)15,000,000 = \$1,219,500$.

16. **A.** The present value factors for 180, 360, 540, and 720 days are as follows:

$$B_0(180) = \frac{1}{1 + 0.042(180/360)} = 0.9794$$

$$B_0(360) = \frac{1}{1 + 0.0474(360/360)} = 0.9547$$

$$B_0(540) = \frac{1}{1 + 0.0554(540/360)} = 0.9246$$

$$B_0(720) = \frac{1}{1 + 0.0661(720/360)} = 0.8832$$

The semiannual fixed payment per \$1 of notional principal is calculated as

$$FS(0, n, m) = FS(0,4,180) = \frac{1 - 0.8832}{0.9794 + 0.9547 + 0.9246 + 0.8832} = 0.0312$$

The annualized fixed payment per \$1 of notional principal is $0.0312(360/180) = 0.0624$. Based on a notional principal of \$50,000,000, the four possible ways to exercise this swaption are

   i. Exercise the swaption, entering into a receive-fixed, pay-floating swap.
   The fixed receipt is (based on the exercise rate of 7 percent) \$50,000,000(0.07 $\times$ 180/360) \$1,750,000.
   The first floating payment is (based on the 180-day rate of 4.20 percent in effect at the time the swap is initiated) \$50,000,000(0.0420 $\times$ 180/360) = \$1,050,000.

   ii. Exercise the swaption, entering into a receive-fixed, pay-floating swap *and* entering into a pay-fixed, receive-floating swap at the market rate.
   The fixed receipt is (based on the exercise rate of 7 percent) \$1,750,000.
   The fixed payment is (based on the rate of 6.24 percent) \$50,000,000 (0.0624 $\times$ 180/360) = \$1,560,000.
   The first floating payment and receipt of \$1,050,000 offset each other.

      iii. Exercise the swaption with offsetting swap netted.
The holder would receive a net payment stream of $1,750,000 − $1,560,000 = $190,000.

      iv. The holder can choose to receive an up-front cash payment now of $190,000 (0.9794 + 0.9547 + 0.9246 + 0.8832) = $710,961.

  B. At expiration, the market value of a bond with face (exercise price) of $1 and annual coupon 7 percent = (0.07 × 180/360)(0.9794 + 0.9547 + 0.9246 + 0.8832) + 1(0.8832) = 1.0142. The payoff on a call option on this bond with exercise price $1 is Max [0,(1.0142 − 1)] = 0.0142. Based on notional principal of $50,000,000, the payoff is $50,000,000(0.0142) = $710,000. This amount is the same as the payoff on the swaption computed in Part A (iv) above (the difference comes from rounding).

17. A. The present value factors for 180, 360, 540, and 720 days are as follows:

$$B_0(180) = \frac{1}{1 + 0.0583(180/360)} = 0.9717$$

$$B_0(360) = \frac{1}{1 + 0.0605(360/360)} = 0.9430$$

$$B_0(540) = \frac{1}{1 + 0.0614(540/360)} = 0.9157$$

$$B_0(720) = \frac{1}{1 + 0.0651(720/360)} = 0.8848$$

The semiannual fixed payment per $1 of notional principal is calculated as

$$FS(0, n, m) = FS(0,4,180) = \frac{1 - 0.8848}{0.9717 + 0.9430 + 0.9157 + 0.8848} = 0.031$$

The annualized fixed payment per $1 of notional principal is 0.031(360/180) = 0.062.

    Based on a notional principal of $10,000,000, the four possible ways to exercise this payer swaption are

      i. Exercise the swaption, entering into pay-fixed and receive-floating swap.
The fixed payment is (based on the exercise rate of 5 percent) $10,000,000 (0.05 × 180/360) = $250,000.
The first floating receipt is (based on the 180-day rate in effect at the time the swap is initiated of 5.83 percent) $10,000,000(0.0583 × 180/360) = $291,500.

      ii. Exercise the swaption, entering into pay-fixed and receive-floating swap, and entering into receive-fixed pay-floating swap at the market rate.
The fixed payment is (based on the exercise rate of 5 percent) $250,000.
The fixed receipt is (based on the rate of 6.2 percent) $10,000,000(0.062 × 180/360) = $310,000.
The first floating payment and receipt of $291,500 offset each other.

      iii. Exercise the swaption with offsetting swap netted.
The holder would receive a net payment stream of $310,000 − $250,000 = $60,000

      iv. The holder can choose to receive an up-front cash payment now of 60,000 (0.9717 + 0.9430 + 0.9157 + 0.8848) = $222,912.

  B. At expiration, the market value of a bond with face (exercise price) of $1 and annual coupon 5 percent = (0.05 × 180/360) (0.9717 + 0.9430 + 0.9157 +

0.8848) + 1(0.8848) = 0.9777. The payoff on a put option on this bond with exercise price $1 is Max [0,(1 − 0.9777)] = 0.0223. The payoff based on a notional principal of $10,000,000 is 0.0223(10,000,000) = $223,000. This amount is the same as the payoff on the swaption as computed in Part A (iv) above (the difference comes from rounding).

18. A. The present value factors for 90, 180, 270, and 360 days are as follows:

$$B_0(180) = \frac{1}{1 + 0.0373(90/360)} = 0.9908$$

$$B_0(360) = \frac{1}{1 + 0.0429(180/360)} = 0.9790$$

$$B_0(540) = \frac{1}{1 + 0.0477(270/360)} = 0.9655$$

$$B_0(720) = \frac{1}{1 + 0.0538(360/360)} = 0.9489$$

The quarterly fixed payment per $1 of notional principal is calculated as

$$FS(0, n, m) = FS(0,4,180) = \frac{1 - 0.9489}{0.9908 + 0.9790 + 0.9655 + 0.9489} = 0.0132$$

The annualized fixed payment per $1 of notional principal is 0.0132(360/90) = 0.0528. The market value at expiration of the receiver swaption is Max {0,[0.065 × (90/360) − 0.0132](0.9908 + 0.9790 + 0.9655 + 0.9489)} = 0.012. Based on notional principal of $100,000,000, the market value is 100,000,000(0.012) = $1,200,000.

B. At expiration, the market value of a bond with face (exercise price) of $1 and annual coupon of 6.5 percent is (0.065 × 90/360)(0.9908 + 0.9790 + 0.9655 + 0.9489) + 1(0.9489) = 1.012. The payoff on a call option on this bond with exercise price $1 is Max [0,(1.012 − 1)] = 0.012. This is the same as the payoff on the swaption.

19. A. The present value factors for 180, 360, 540, and 720 days are as follows:

$$B_0(180) = \frac{1}{1 + 0.0583(180/360)} = 0.9717$$

$$B_0(360) = \frac{1}{1 + 0.0616(360/360)} = 0.9420$$

$$B_0(540) = \frac{1}{1 + 0.0680(540/360)} = 0.9074$$

$$B_0(720) = \frac{1}{1 + 0.0705(720/360)} = 0.8764$$

The semiannual fixed payment per $1 of notional principal is calculated as

$$FS(0, n, m) = FS(0,4,180) = \frac{1 - 0.8764}{0.9717 + 0.9420 + 0.9074 + 0.8764} = 0.0334$$

The annualized fixed payment per $1 of notional principal is calculated as 0.0334(360/180) = 0.0668.

The new present value factors for 180, 360, and 540 days are as follows:

$$B_{180}(180) = \frac{1}{1 + 0.0429(180/360)} = 0.9790$$

$$B_{180}(360) = \frac{1}{1 + 0.0583(360/360)} = 0.9489$$

$$B_{180}(540) = \frac{1}{1 + 0.0618(540/360)} = 0.9152$$

The present value of the remaining fixed payments plus the $1 notional principal is $0.0334(0.9790 + 0.9489 + 0.9152) + 1(0.9152) = 1.0102$.

Because we are on the payment date, the present value of the remaining floating payments plus hypothetical $1 notional principal is automatically 1.0.

The market value of the swap to the pay-floating, receive-fixed party is $(1.0102 - 1) = \$0.0102$. So the market value of the swap to the pay-fixed, receive-floating party is $-\$0.0102$. Because the swap is marked to market, the party that pays floating will now receive $0.0102 per $1 of notional principal from the party that pays fixed. The two parties would then reprice the swap.

B. The new fixed-rate payment per $1 of notional principal is

$$FS(0, n, m) = FS(0,3,180) = \frac{1 - 0.9152}{0.9790 + 0.9489 + 0.9152 + 0.8764} = 0.0298$$

20. A. The present value factors for 90, 180, 270, and 360 days are as follows:

$$B_0(90) = \frac{1}{1 + 0.0252(90/360)} = 0.9937$$

$$B_0(180) = \frac{1}{1 + 0.0305(180/360)} = 0.9850$$

$$B_0(270) = \frac{1}{1 + 0.0373(270/360)} = 0.9728$$

$$B_0(360) = \frac{1}{1 + 0.0406(360/360)} = 0.9610$$

The quarterly fixed payment per $1 of notional principal is calculated as

$$FS(0, n, m) = FS(0,4,90) = \frac{1 - 0.9610}{0.9937 + 0.9850 + 0.9728 + 0.9610} = 0.01$$

The annualized fixed payment per $1 of notional principal is calculated as $0.01(360/90) = 0.04$.

The new present value factors for 90, 180, and 270 days are as follows:

$$B_{90}(90) = \frac{1}{1 + 0.0539(90/360)} = 0.9867$$

$$B_{90}(180) = \frac{1}{1 + 0.0608(180/360)} = 0.9705$$

$$B_{90}(270) = \frac{1}{1 + 0.0653(270/360)} = 0.9533$$

The present value of the remaining fixed payments plus the $1 notional principal is $0.01(0.9867 + 0.9705 + 0.9533) + 1(0.9533) = 0.9824$.

Because we are on the payment date, the present value of the remaining floating payments plus hypothetical $1 notional principal is automatically 1.0.

The market value of the swap to the pay-floating, receive-fixed party is $(0.9824 - 1) = -\$0.0176$. So, the market value of the swap to the pay-fixed, receive-floating party is $0.0176. Because the swap is marked to market, the party that pays floating will now pay $0.0176 per $1 of notional principal to the party that pays fixed. The two parties would then reprice the swap.

B. The new fixed-rate payment per $1 of notional principal is

$$FS(0, n, m) = FS(0,3,90) = \frac{1 - 0.9533}{0.9867 + 0.9705 + 0.9533} = 0.0160$$

RISK MANAGEMENT APPLICATIONS OF FORWARD AND FUTURES STRATEGIES

- ■ Illustrate feasible strategies for managing the risk associated with foreign equity portfolios.
- ■ Discuss the applications in which forward (futures) contracts may be preferred to futures (forward) contracts.
- ■ Explain the advantages and disadvantages of using futures and forwards as a class of derivatives to execute risk management transactions.
- ■ Identify a limitation on the use of futures and forwards for executing risk management transactions.

1   INTRODUCTION

In the preceding chapters, we examined the characteristics and pricing of forwards, futures, options, and swaps. On occasion, we made reference to possible ways in which these instruments could be used. In Chapters 6, 7, and 8, we examine more specifically the strategies and applications that are commonly used with these instruments. Here in Chapter 6, we focus on forward and futures contracts. As we saw in Chapters 2 and 3, these instruments are quite similar. Both involve commitments for one party to buy and the other to sell an underlying instrument at a future date at a price agreed on at the start of the contract. The underlying instrument might be an interest payment, a bond, a stock, or a currency. Forward contracts are customized agreements between two parties: The terms are agreed on by both parties in a formal legal contract that exists in an environment outside of regulatory constraints. Each party is subject to potential default on the part of the other. Futures contracts, on the other hand, are standardized instruments created on a futures exchange, protected against credit losses by the clearinghouse, and subject to federal regulatory oversight.

In this chapter, we examine a number of scenarios in which parties facing risk management problems use forward and futures contracts to alter the risk of their positions. In some situations we use forwards and in others we use futures. For cases in which either would suffice, we pick the instrument that is most commonly used in that type of situation. Although we shall not devote a great deal of space up front to justifying why we picked the instrument we did, we shall provide some discussion of this point in Section 6.

After reading this chapter, you may be surprised to observe that we do not cover an important class of derivative strategies, those that are called *arbitrage*. This omission is not because they are not important enough to cover or that they are not risk management strategies; in fact, we have *already* covered them. When we covered the pricing of forwards, futures, options, and swaps, we explained how these instruments are priced by combining the underlying and risk-free bonds to replicate the derivative or by combining a long position in the underlying and a short position in the derivative to replicate a risk-free position. From there we obtained a formula that gives us the correct price of the derivative. An arbitrage profit is possible if the derivative is not priced according to the formula. We have already looked at how those strategies are executed. We should not expect to encounter arbitrage opportunities very often in practice. They are quickly captured by derivatives trading firms, which themselves cannot expect to be able to *consistently* claim such opportunities before they disappear.[1]

---

[1] Suppose market participants assume that arbitrage opportunities are so infrequent and difficult to capture before they are gone that no one monitors market prices looking for arbitrage opportunities. Then these arbitrage opportunities will begin to occur more frequently. A market in which arbitrage opportunities are rare, and therefore prices are fair and accurate, is ironically a market in which participants believe they can indeed uncover and exploit arbitrage opportunities. Thus, an arbitrage-free market requires disbelievers.

Businesses make products and provide services as they attempt to increase share-holder wealth. In doing so, they face a variety of risks. Managing risk lies at the heart of what companies do. All companies specialize in managing the risk of whatever market their primary business is in: Airlines deal with the risk associated with the demand for air travel, software companies deal with the risk associated with the demand for new computer programs, movie companies deal with the risk associated with the demand for their films. But these companies also deal with other risks, such as the risk of interest rates and exchange rates. Usually these companies take calculated risks in their primary lines of business and avoid risks they do not feel qualified to take, such as interest rate risk and exchange rate risk. Naturally this approach involves a practice called **hedging**.

Hedging involves taking a market position to protect against an undesirable out-come. Suppose a company has a strong belief that interest rates will increase. It engages in a forward rate agreement (FRA) transaction to lock in the rate on a loan it will take out at a later date. This position protects the company from the undesirable outcome of an increase in interest rates, but it also prevents the company from enjoying any decline in rates. In that sense, the position is as much a speculative position as if a speculator had made the following prediction: *We believe that interest rates will rise to an unac-ceptable level, and we intend to trade on that basis to make money.* By engaging in the FRA to hedge this outcome, the company trades to make a profit from its FRA that will help offset any increase in the interest rate on its future loan. But by locking in a rate, it forgoes the possibility of benefiting from a decline in interest rates. The company has made a bet that rates will rise. If they fall, the company has lost the bet and lost money on its FRA that offsets the benefit of the lower interest rate on this loan planned for a later date.

In this book we shall not overindulge in the use of the term hedging. We shall say that companies do more than hedge: *They manage risk.* They carefully consider scenarios and elect to adjust the risk they face to a level they feel is acceptable. In many cases, this adjustment will involve the reduction of risk; in some cases, however, the scenario will jus-tify increasing the company's risk. In all cases, the company is just altering the risk from its current level to the level the company desires. And that is what managing risk is all about.

This chapter is divided into five main parts. Sections 2 and 3 focus on the manage-ment of interest rate and equity market risk, respectively. Section 4 combines interest rate and equity risk management applications by looking at how investors can manage an asset portfolio using futures. Section 5 looks at the management of foreign currency risk. In Sec-tion 6 we examine the general question of whether to use forwards or futures to manage risk, and in Section 7 we look at a few final issues.

2 STRATEGIES AND APPLICATIONS FOR MANAGING INTEREST RATE RISK

Almost every business borrows money from time to time. A company borrowing at a fixed rate may think it is immune to interest rate risk, but that is not the case. Risk arises from the possibility that interest rates can increase from the time the company decides to take the loan to the time it actually takes the loan. Most companies make plans to borrow based on their cash needs at specific future dates. The rates they pay on these loans are impor-tant determinants of their future cash needs, as reflected in their planned interest payments. Exposure to interest rate risk is, therefore, a major concern. Failing to manage interest rate risk can hinder the planning process, as well as result in unexpected demands on cash necessitated by unexpectedly higher interest payments.

2.1 MANAGING THE INTEREST RATE RISK OF A LOAN USING AN FRA

There are several situations in which a company might want to manage the interest rate risk of a loan. The two we look at here involve a company planning to take out a loan at a later date. In one situation, the loan has a single interest rate and a single interest payment. In another situation, a company takes out a floating-rate loan in which the interest rate is reset periodically.

2.1.1 SINGLE-PAYMENT LOAN

Exhibit 6-1 presents the case of Global BioTechnology (GBT), which determines that it will need to borrow money at a later date at a rate of LIBOR plus 200 basis points. Fearing an increase in interest rates between now and the day it takes out the loan, it enters into a long position in an FRA. The FRA has a fixed rate, called the FRA rate, which we learned how to determine in Chapter 2. If the underlying rate at expiration is above the FRA rate, GBT as the holder of the long position will receive a lump sum of cash based on the difference between the FRA rate and the market rate at that time. This payment will help offset the higher rate GBT would be paying on its loan. If the rate in the market falls below the FRA rate, however, GBT will end up paying the counterparty, which will offset the lower rate GBT will be paying on its loan. The end result is that GBT will pay approximately a fixed rate, the FRA rate.

EXHIBIT 6-1   Using an FRA to Lock in the Rate on a Loan

Scenario (15 April)
Global BioTechnology (GBT) is a U.S. corporation that occasionally undertakes short-term borrowings in U.S. dollars with the rate tied to LIBOR. To facilitate its cash flow planning, it uses an FRA to lock in the rate on such loans as soon as it determines that it will need the money.

On 15 April, GBT determines that it will borrow $40 million on 20 August. The loan will be repaid 180 days later on 16 February, and the rate will be at LIBOR plus 200 basis points. Because GBT believes that interest rates will increase, it decides to manage this risk by going long an FRA. An FRA will enable it to receive the difference between LIBOR on 20 August and the FRA rate quoted by the dealer on 15 April. The quoted rate from the dealer is 5.25 percent. GBT wants to lock in a 7.25 percent rate: 5.25 percent plus 200 basis points.

Action
GBT confirms that it will borrow $40 million at LIBOR plus 200 basis points on 20 August. GBT goes long an FRA at a rate of 5.25 percent to expire on 20 August with the underlying being 180-day LIBOR.

Scenario (20 August)
At contract expiration, 180-day LIBOR is 6 percent.

Outcome and Analysis
The FRA payoff is given by our general formula from Chapter 2:

$$
\text{Notional principal} \left[\frac{(\text{Underlying rate at expiration} - \text{Forward contract rate})\left(\dfrac{\text{Days in underlying rate}}{360}\right)}{1 + \text{Underlying rate}\left(\dfrac{\text{Days in underlying rate}}{360}\right)} \right]
$$

or

$$
\$40,000,000\left[\frac{(0.06 - 0.0525)(180/360)}{1 + 0.06(180/360)}\right] = \$145,631
$$

GBT receives this amount in cash. Therefore, to obtain $40 million in cash, it has to borrow $40,000,000 − $145,631 = $39,854,369 at LIBOR plus 200 basis points, 0.06 + 0.02 = 0.08, or 8 percent.

On 16 February GBT pays back $39,854,369[1 + 0.08(180/360)] = $41,448,544. So, it effectively pays a rate of

$$\left(\frac{\$41,448,544}{\$40,000,000} - 1\right)\left(\frac{360}{180}\right) = 0.0724$$

The net effect is that GBT receives $40 million on 20 August and pays back $41,448,544 on 16 February, a rate of 7.24 percent. This rate was effectively locked in on 15 April at the FRA rate of 5.25 percent plus the 200 basis points GBT pays over LIBOR.

Shown below are the results for possible LIBORs on 20 August of 2 percent, 4 percent, . . ., 10 percent.

LIBOR on 20 August	FRA Payoff	Amount Borrowed	LIBOR + 200 bps Loan Rate	Amount Repaid on 16 February	Effective Loan Rate
0.02	−$643,564	$40,643,564	0.04	$41,456,435	0.0728
0.04	−245,098	40,245,098	0.06	41,452,451	0.0726
0.06	145,631	39,854,369	0.08	41,448,544	0.0724
0.08	528,846	39,471,154	0.10	41,444,712	0.0722
0.10	904,762	39,095,238	0.12	41,440,952	0.0720

In this problem, the FRA rate is 5.25 percent. In the exhibit, we described an outcome in which the underlying rate, 180-day LIBOR, is 6 percent. GBT ends up paying 6% + 2% = 8% on the loan, but the FRA pays off an amount sufficient to reduce the effective rate to 7.24 percent. Note the table at the end of the exhibit showing other possible outcomes. In all cases, the rate GBT pays is approximately the FRA rate of 5.25 percent plus 200 basis points. This rate is not precisely 7.25 percent, however, because of the way in which the FRA is constructed to pay off at expiration. When LIBOR on 20 August is above 5.25 percent, the FRA payoff on that day reduces the amount that has to be borrowed at LIBOR plus 200 basis points. This reduction works to the advantage of GBT. Conversely, when rates are below 5.25 percent, the amount that must be borrowed increases but that amount is borrowed at a lower rate. Thus, there is a slight asymmetric effect of a few basis points that prevents the effective loan rate from precisely equaling 7.25 percent.

In a similar manner, a lender could lock in a rate on a loan it plans to make by going short an FRA. Lenders are less inclined to do such transactions, however, because they cannot anticipate the exact future borrowing needs of their customers. In some cases, banks that offer credit lines at floating rates might wish to lock in lending rates using FRAs. But because the choice of whether to borrow is the borrower's and not the lender's, a lender that uses an FRA is taking considerable risk that the loan will not even be made. In that case, the lender would do better to use an option so that, in the worst case, it loses only the option premium.

PRACTICE PROBLEM 1

ABTech plans to borrow $10 million in 30 days at 90-day LIBOR plus 100 basis points. To lock in a borrowing rate of 7 percent, it purchases an FRA at a rate of 6 percent. This contract would be referred to as a 1×4 FRA because it expires in one month (30 days) and the underlying Eurodollar matures four months (120 days) from now. Thirty days later, LIBOR is 7.5 percent. Demonstrate that ABTech's effective borrowing rate is 7 percent if LIBOR in 30 days is 7.5 percent.

SOLUTION

If LIBOR is 7.5 percent at the expiration of the FRA in 30 days, the payoff of the FRA is

$$\text{Notional principal}\left[\frac{(\text{Underlying rate at expiration} - \text{Forward contract rate})\left(\dfrac{\text{Days in underlying rate}}{360}\right)}{1 + \text{Underlying rate}\left(\dfrac{\text{Days in underlying rate}}{360}\right)}\right]$$

which is

$$\$10,000,000\left[\frac{(0.075 - 0.06)(90/360)}{1 + 0.075(90/360)}\right] = \$36,810$$

Because this amount is a cash inflow, ABTech will not need to borrow a full $10,000,000. Instead, it will borrow $10,000,000 − $36,810 = $9,963,190.

The amount it will pay back in 90 days is

$$\$9,963,190[1 + (0.075 + 0.01)(90/360)] = \$10,174,908$$

The effective rate is, therefore,

$$\left(\frac{\$10,174,908}{\$10,000,000} - 1\right)\left(\frac{360}{90}\right) \approx 0.07$$

ABTech borrows at LIBOR plus 100 basis points. Therefore, using an FRA, it should be able to lock in the FRA rate (6 percent) plus 100 basis points, which it does.

2.1.2 FLOATING-RATE LOAN

In the example above, the loan involved only a single payment and, therefore, we had only one setting of an interest rate to worry about. Many loans are floating-rate loans, meaning that their rates are reset several times during the life of the loan. This resetting of the rate poses a series of risks for the borrower.

Suppose a corporation is taking out a two-year loan. The rate for the initial six months is set today. The rate will be reset in 6, 12, and 18 months. Because the current rate is already in place, there is nothing the corporation can do to mitigate that risk.[2] It faces,

---

[2] If a corporation were planning to take out a floating-rate loan at a later date, it would also be concerned about the first interest rate and might attempt to lock in that rate. In the example used here, we placed the company in a situation in which it already knows its initial rate and, therefore, is worried only about the remaining rate resets.

however, the risk of rising interest rates over the remaining life of the loan, which would result in higher interest payments.

One way to control this risk is to enter into a series of FRA transactions with each component FRA tailored to expire on a date on which the rate will be reset. This strategy will not lock in the *same* fixed rate for each semiannual period, but different rates for each period will be locked in. Another alternative would be to use futures. For example, for a LIBOR-based loan, the Eurodollar futures contract would be appropriate. Nonetheless, the use of futures to manage this risk poses significant problems. One problem is that the Eurodollar futures contract has expirations only on specific days during the year. The Chicago Mercantile Exchange offers contract expirations on the current month, the next month, and a sequence of months following the pattern of March, June, September, and December. Thus, it is quite likely that no contracts would exist with expirations that align with the later payment reset dates. The Eurodollar futures contract expires on the second London business day before the third Wednesday of the month. This date might not be the exact day of the month on which the rate is reset. In addition, the Eurodollar futures contract is based only on the 90-day Eurodollar rate, whereas the loan rate is pegged to the 180-day rate. Although many dealer firms use the Eurodollar futures contract to manage the risk associated with their over-the-counter derivatives, they do so using sophisticated techniques that measure and balance the volatility of the futures contract to the volatility of their market positions. Moreover, they adjust their positions rapidly in response to market movements. Without that capability, borrowers who simply need to align their interest rate reset dates with the dates on which their derivatives expire can do so more easily with swaps. We shall cover how this is done in Chapter 8. Nevertheless, an understanding of how FRAs are used will help with an understanding of this application of swaps.

2.2 STRATEGIES AND APPLICATIONS FOR MANAGING BOND PORTFOLIO RISK

In Section 2.1, we dealt with the risk associated with short-term borrowing interest rates, which obviously affects short-term borrowers and lenders. The risk associated with longer-term loans primarily takes the form of bond market risk. Here we shall take a look at a firm managing a government bond portfolio, that is, a lending position. The firm can manage the risk associated with interest rates by using futures on government bonds. In the next three sections, we explore how to measure the risk of a bond portfolio, measure the risk of bond futures, and balance those risks.

2.2.1 MEASURING THE RISK OF A BOND PORTFOLIO

The sensitivity of a bond to a general change in interest rates is usually captured by assuming that the bond price changes in response to a change in its yield, which is driven by the general level of rates. The responsiveness of a bond price to a yield change is captured in two ways: duration and basis point value.[3]

Duration is a measure of the size and timing of the cash flows paid by a bond. It quantifies these factors by summarizing them in the form of a single number, which is interpreted as an average maturity of the bond. To speak in terms of an average maturity of a bond of a given specific maturity sounds somewhat strange, but remember that a coupon bond is really just a combination of zero-coupon bonds.[4] The average maturity of

---

[3] Readers may first wish to review some fixed-income securities material. See especially Chapter 7 of *Fixed Income Analysis for the Chartered Financial Analyst Program*, Frank J. Fabozzi (Frank J. Fabozzi Associates, 2000).

[4] This analogy comes about because the coupons and final principal on a bond can be viewed as zero-coupon bonds, each maturing on the date on which a coupon or the final principal is paid. The value of a coupon or the final principal is analogous to the face value of a zero-coupon bond. In the U.S. Treasury bond market, companies buy coupon bonds and sell claims on the individual coupons and principal, which are referred to as Treasury strips.

these component zero-coupon bonds is the duration. The average is not an ordinary average but a weighted average, with the weights based on the present values of the respective cash payments on the bonds. Hence, the weights are not equal, and the large principal repayment places the greatest emphasis on the final payment.

Suppose the bond price is B, the yield is y_B, and Macaulay duration is DUR_B. Then the relationship between the change in the bond price and its yield is given as

$$\Delta B \approx -DUR_B B \frac{\Delta y_B}{1 + y_B}$$

where the Greek symbol Δ indicates "change in" and where the overall relationship is shown as an approximation ($\approx$). For this relationship to be exact requires that the yield change be very small.[5] The left-hand side, ΔB, is the change in the bond price. The negative sign on the right-hand side is consistent with the inverse relationship between the bond price and its yield.[6]

A somewhat simplified version of the above equation is

$$\Delta B \approx -MDUR_B B \Delta y_B$$

where $MDUR_B = DUR_B/(1 + y_B)$. $MDUR_B$ is called the **modified duration** and is just an adjustment of the duration for the level of the yield. We shall use the relationship as captured by the modified duration.[7]

As an example, suppose the bond price is \$922.50, modified duration is 5.47 years, and the yield increases by 15 basis points. Then the price change should be approximately

$$\Delta B \approx -5.47(\$922.50)(0.0015) = -\$7.57$$

In response to a 15 basis point increase in yield, the bond price should decrease by approximately \$7.57. So the new bond price would be predicted to be \$922.50 − \$7.57 = \$914.93.

The relationship between the bond price and its yield is sometimes stated another way. We often speak in terms of the change in the bond price for a 1 basis point change in yield. This value is sometimes referred to as **basis point value** (or BPV), **present value of a basis point** (or PVBP), or **price value of a basis point** (again PVBP). We refer to this concept as PVBP, defined as

$$PVBP_B \approx MDUR_B B (0.0001)$$

The multiplication by 0.0001 enables PVBP to capture how much the bond price changes for a 1 basis point change. In the example above, the PVBP for our bond is

$$PVBP_B \approx (5.47)(\$922.50)(0.0001) = \$0.5046$$

So for a 1 basis point change, the bond price would change by approximately \$0.5046. Accordingly, a 15 basis point change produces a price change of 15(\$0.5046) = \$7.57. Both duration and PVBP measure the same thing, however, and we shall use only duration.

Duration and PVBP are usually thought of with respect to individual bonds, but in practice, they are typically used at the portfolio level. Hence, we should care more about

---

[5] If the yield change is not sufficiently small, it may be necessary to incorporate second-order effects, which are captured by a bond's convexity.

[6] The above relationship is based on annual coupons. If the coupons are paid semiannually, then $1 + y_B$ should be $1 + y_B/2$. In this case, the duration will be stated as the number of semiannual, rather than annual, periods.

[7] The duration before dividing by $1 + y_B$ is sometimes called the **Macaulay duration**, to distinguish it from the modified duration. It is named for Frederick Macaulay, one of the economists who first derived it.

the duration of a bond portfolio than about the duration of an individual bond. With respect to yield, we do not usually speak in terms of the yield of a bond portfolio, but in this case we must. A given bond portfolio can be thought of as a series of cash flows that can be captured in terms of a representative bond. Thus, we might describe this bond as a bond portfolio with a market value of $922.5 million, a modified duration of 5.47 years, and a portfolio yield that is a complex weighted average of the yields on the component bonds of the portfolio. The portfolio yield can change by a certain number of basis points. That yield change is a weighted average of the yield changes on the component bonds. Given such a yield change, the bond portfolio value will change in an approximate manner according to the duration formula shown above.

The way a bond price changes according to a yield change indicates its responsiveness to interest rates. Given a bond futures contract, we can also measure its sensitivity to interest rate changes.

2.2.2 MEASURING THE RISK OF BOND FUTURES

Having measured the responsiveness of a bond portfolio to an interest rate change, we now need to measure the responsiveness of a futures contract to an interest rate change. Most bond futures contracts are based on a hypothetical benchmark bond. As we described in Chapter 3, the Chicago Board of Trade's U.S. Treasury bond futures contract is based on a 6 percent bond with at least 15 years from the futures expiration to maturity or the first call date. Even though the benchmark bond has a 6 percent coupon, any bond meeting the maturity requirement can be delivered. As we covered in Chapter 3, at any time, a single bond exists that the holder of the short position would find optimal to deliver if current conditions continued. That bond is called the **cheapest to deliver** and can be thought of as the bond on which the futures contract is based. In other words, the cheapest to deliver bond is the underlying. The responsiveness of the futures contract to an interest rate change is equivalent to the responsiveness of that bond on the futures expiration day to an interest rate change.

We can think of this concept as the responsiveness of the underlying bond in a forward context. This responsiveness can be measured as that bond's modified duration on the futures expiration and, as such, we can use the price sensitivity formula to capture the sensitivity of the futures contract to a yield change. Accordingly, we shall, somewhat loosely, refer to this as the implied duration of the futures contract, keeping in mind that what we mean is the duration of the underlying bond calculated as of the futures expiration. Moreover, we also mean that the underlying bond has been identified as the cheapest bond to deliver and that if another bond takes its place, the duration of that bond must be used. We use the term *implied* to emphasize that a futures contract does not itself have a duration but that its duration is implied by the underlying bond. In addition to the duration, we also require an **implied yield** on the futures, which reflects the yield on the underlying bond implied by pricing it as though it were delivered at the futures contract expiration.

Hence, we can express the sensitivity of the futures price to a yield change as

$$\Delta f \approx (MDUR_f) f \, \Delta y_f \tag{6-1}$$

where $MDUR_f$ is the implied modified duration of the futures, f is the futures price, and Δy_f is the basis point change in the implied yield on the futures.

Now that we have a measure of the responsiveness of a bond portfolio and the responsiveness of a bond futures contract to interest rate changes, we should be able to find a way to balance the two to offset the risk.

2.2.3 BALANCING THE RISK OF A BOND PORTFOLIO AGAINST THE RISK OF BOND FUTURES

We now make the simple assumption that a single interest rate exists that drives all interest rates in the market. We assume that a 1 basis point change in this interest rate will cause a

1 basis point change in the yield on the bond portfolio and a 1 basis point change in the implied yield on the futures. We will relax that assumption later. For now, consider a money manager who holds a bond portfolio of a particular market value and will not be adding to it or removing some of it to balance the risk. In other words, the manager will not make any transactions in the actual bonds themselves. The manager can, however, trade any number of futures contracts to adjust the risk. Let N_f be the number of futures contracts traded. To balance the risk, suppose we combine the change in the value of the bond portfolio and the change in the value of N_f futures and set these equal to zero: $\Delta B + N_f \Delta f = 0$. Solving for N_f produces $N_f = -\Delta B / \Delta f$. Substituting our formulas for ΔB and Δf, we obtain

$$N_f = -\left(\frac{MDUR_B}{MDUR_f}\right)\left(\frac{B}{f}\right)\left(\frac{\Delta y_B}{\Delta y_f}\right) = -\left(\frac{MDUR_B}{MDUR_f}\right)\left(\frac{B}{f}\right)$$

where we assume that $\Delta y_B / \Delta y_f = 1$; or in other words, the bond portfolio yield changes one-for-one with the implied yield on the futures.[8]

Now let us go back to the major simplifying assumption we made. We assumed that an interest rate change occurs in the market and drives the yield on the bond and the implied yield on the futures one-for-one. In reality, this assumption is unlikely to hold true. Suppose, for example, the rate driving all rates in the United States is the overnight Fed funds rate.[9] If this rate changes by 1 basis point, not all rates along the term structure are likely to change by 1 basis point. What actually matters, however, is not that all rates change by the same amount but that the yield on the bond portfolio and the implied yield on the futures change by the same amount for a 1 basis point change in this rate. If that is not the case, we need to make an adjustment.

Suppose the yield on the bond portfolio changes by a multiple of the implied yield on the futures in the following manner:

$$\Delta y_B = \beta_y \Delta y_f \tag{6-2}$$

We refer to the symbol β_y as the **yield beta**. It can be more or less than 1, depending on whether the bond yield is more sensitive or less sensitive than the implied futures yield. If we take the formula we previously obtained for ΔB, substitute $\beta_y \Delta y_f$ where we previously had Δy_B, and use this new variation of the formula in the formula $N_f = -\Delta B / \Delta f$, we obtain

$$N_f = -(MDUR_B / MDUR_f)(B/f)\beta_y \tag{6-3}$$

This is the more general formula, because $\beta_y = 1.0$ is just the special case we assumed at the start.

We can modify Equation 6-3 so that it gives us the number of futures contracts needed to change our portfolio's modified duration to meet a target. What we have done so far *completely* balances the risk of the futures position against the risk of the bond portfolio, eliminating the risk. In the practice of risk management, however, we might not always want to eliminate the risk; we might want to adjust it only a little. At some times we might even want to increase it.

The risk of the overall bond portfolio reflects the duration of the bonds and the duration of the futures. Suppose we consider a target overall modified duration of the portfolio, $MDUR_T$. This amount is our desired overall modified duration. Because the portfolio

---

[8] Technically, this equation is the ratio of two approximate formulas, but we remove the approximation symbol from this point onward.

[9] The overnight Fed funds rate is the rate that banks charge each other to borrow and lend excess reserves for one night.

consists of bonds worth B and futures, which have zero value, the overall portfolio value is B.[10] Now we introduce the notion of a dollar duration, which is the duration times the market value. The target dollar duration of our portfolio is set equal to the dollar duration of the bonds we hold and the dollar duration of the futures contracts:

$$B(MDUR_T) = B(MDUR_B) + f(MDUR_f)N_f$$

Solving for N_f, we obtain

$$N_f = \left(\frac{MDUR_T - MDUR_B}{MDUR_f}\right)\left(\frac{B}{f}\right)$$

Observe that if we wish to increase the modified duration from $MDUR_B$ to something higher, then $MDUR_T$ is greater than $MDUR_B$ and the overall sign of N_f will be positive, so we buy futures. This relationship should make sense: Buying futures would add volatility and increase duration. If we wish to reduce the modified duration from $MDUR_B$ to something lower, then $MDUR_T$ will be less than $MDUR_B$ and the sign of N_f will be negative, meaning that we need to sell futures. Selling futures would reduce duration and volatility. In the extreme case in which we want to eliminate risk completely, we want $MDUR_T$ to equal zero. In that case, the above formula reduces to the original one we obtained earlier in this section for the case of completely eliminating risk. In a similar manner, if the bond and futures yields do not change one-for-one, we simply alter the above formula to

$$N_f = \left(\frac{MDUR_T - MDUR_B}{MDUR_f}\right)\left(\frac{B}{f}\right)\beta_y \qquad \text{(6-4)}$$

to incorporate the yield beta.

Now we explore how to use what we have learned in this section.

2.2.4 MANAGING THE RISK OF A GOVERNMENT BOND PORTFOLIO

A money manager can use Equation 6-4 to determine the number of futures contracts to buy or sell to adjust the duration of a portfolio. Such a transaction might be done in anticipation of a strong or weak market in bonds over a temporary period of time. In Exhibit 6-2, we illustrate the case of a pension fund that wants to increase the portfolio duration. We see that the futures transaction was successful in increasing the duration but not as precisely as planned. In fact, even without doing the futures transaction, the portfolio duration was not exactly as the company had believed. Duration is not an exact measure, nor does the bond price change occur precisely according to the duration formula.[11]

EXHIBIT 6-2   Using Bond Futures to Manage the Risk of a Bond Portfolio

Scenario (7 July)
A portion of the pension fund of United Energy Services (UES) is a portfolio of U.S. government bonds. On 7 July, UES obtained a forecast from its economist that over the next month, interest rates are likely to make a significant unexpected decline. Its portfolio manager

---

[10] Recall that futures contracts have value through the accumulation of price changes during a trading day. At the end of the day, all gains and losses are paid out through the marking-to-market process and the value then goes back to zero. We assume we are at one of those points at which the value is zero.

[11] For this reason, we stated that the bond price change, given the duration and yield change, is *approximately* given by the formula in the text.

would like to take a portion of the bond portfolio and increase the duration to take advantage of this forecasted market movement.

Specifically, UES would like to raise the duration on $75 million of bonds from its current level of 6.22 to 7.50. Both of these durations and all durations used in this problem are modified durations. UES has identified an appropriate Treasury bond futures contract that is currently priced at $82,500 and has an implied modified duration of 8.12. UES has estimated that the yield on the bond portfolio is about 5 percent more volatile than the implied yield on the futures. Thus, the yield beta is 1.05.

Action

To increase the duration, UES will need to buy futures contracts. Specifically, the number of futures contracts UES should use is

$$N_f = \left(\frac{MDUR_T - MDUR_B}{MDUR_f} \right) \left(\frac{B}{f} \right) \beta_y = \left(\frac{7.50 - 6.22}{8.12} \right) \left(\frac{\$75,000,000}{\$82,500} \right) 1.05 = 150.47$$

Because fractional contracts cannot be traded, UES will buy 150 contracts.

Scenario (6 August)

The implied yield on the futures has decreased by 35 basis points, and the futures price has now moved to $85,000.[12] The yield on the bond portfolio has decreased by 40 basis points, and the portfolio has increased in value by $1,933,500.

Outcome and Analysis

The profit on the futures transaction is found by multiplying the number of futures contracts by the difference between the new price and the old price:

Profit on futures contract = N_f(New futures price − Old futures price)

In this case, the profit on the futures contract is 150($85,000 − $82,500) = $375,000. Thus, the overall gain is $1,933,500 + $375,000 = $2,308,500.

How effective was the transaction? To answer this question, we compare the *ex post* duration to the planned duration. The purpose was to increase the duration from 6.22 to a planned 7.50. The return on the portfolio was

$$\frac{\$1,933,500}{\$75,000,000} = 0.0258$$

or 2.58 percent without the futures transaction, and

$$\frac{\$2,308,500}{\$75,000,000} = 0.0308$$

or 3.08 percent with the futures transaction. What does this set of calculations imply about the portfolio's *ex post* duration? Recall that duration is a measure of the percentage change in portfolio value with respect to a basis point change in yield. The *ex post* duration[13] of the portfolio can be measured by dividing the percentage change in portfolio value by the 40 basis point change in the portfolio yield:

$$\frac{0.0258}{0.0040} = 6.45$$

---

without the futures transaction and

$$\frac{0.0308}{0.0040} = 7.70$$

with the futures transaction. UES came fairly close to achieving its desired increase in duration using futures.

In the example here, the fund increased its modified duration during a time when interest rates fell and the bond portfolio value increased. It leveraged itself to take advantage of a favorable outlook. Not all such decisions work out so well. Suppose in this example the economist had a different forecast, and as a result, UES wanted to eliminate all interest rate risk. So let us rework the problem under the assumption that the fund put on a full hedge, thereby reducing the modified duration to zero.

With $MDUR_T = 0$, the number of futures contracts would be

$$N_f = \left(\frac{0 - 6.22}{8.12}\right)\left(\frac{\$75,000,000}{\$82,500}\right)1.05 = -731.19$$

Thus, the fund would sell 731 contracts. The profit from the futures transaction[14] would be $-731(\$85,000 - \$82,500) = -\$1,827,500$. The overall transaction earned a profit of $\$1,933,500 - \$1,827,500 = \$106,000$, a gain of

$$\frac{\$106,000}{\$75,000,000} = 0.0014$$

or 0.14 percent. Thus, shorting the futures contracts virtually wiped out all of the gain from the decrease in interest rates. Our *ex ante* objective was to reduce the modified duration to zero. The *ex post* modified duration, however, turned out to be

$$\frac{0.0014}{0.0040} = 0.35$$

Thus, the modified duration was reduced almost to zero.

PRACTICE PROBLEM 2

Debt Management Associates (DMA) offers fixed-income portfolio management services to institutional investors. It would like to execute a duration-changing strategy for a €100 million bond portfolio of a particular client. This portfolio has a modified duration of 7.2. DMA plans to change the modified duration to 5.00 by using a futures contract priced at €120,000, which has an implied modified duration of 6.25. The yield beta is 1.15.

---

[14] Notice that in calculating the profit from a futures transaction, we multiply the number of futures contracts by the futures price at the close of the strategy minus the original futures price. It is important to maintain the correct sign for the number of futures contracts. This formulation always results in a positive number for N_f times the futures selling price and a negative number for N_f times the futures buying price, which should make sense. Of course, as previously noted, we also ignore the marking-to-market feature of futures contracts.

A. Determine how many futures contracts DMA should use and whether it should buy or sell futures.

B. Suppose that the yield on the bond has decreased by 20 basis points at the horizon date. The bond portfolio increases in value by 1.5 percent. The futures price increases to €121,200. Determine the overall gain on the portfolio and the *ex post* modified duration as a result of the futures transaction.

SOLUTIONS

A. The appropriate number of futures contracts is

$$N_f = \left(\frac{5 - 7.2}{6.25}\right)\left(\frac{100,000,000}{120,000}\right)1.15 = -337.33$$

So DMA should sell 337 contracts.

B. The value of the bond portfolio will be €100,000,000(1.015) = €101,500,000. The profit on the futures transaction is −337(€121,200 − 120,000) = −€404,400; a loss of €404,400. Thus, the overall value of the position is €101,500,000 − €404,400 = €101,095,600, a return of approximately 1.1 percent. The bond yield decreases by 20 basis points and the portfolio gains 1.1 percent. The *ex post* modified duration would be 0.0110/0.0020 = 5.50.

Changing the duration—whether increasing it, reducing it partially, or reducing it all the way to zero—is an inexact process. More importantly, however, risk management by adjusting duration is only a means of implementing a strategy in response to an outlook. No one can guarantee that the outlook will not be wrong.

2.2.5 SOME VARIATIONS AND PROBLEMS IN MANAGING BOND PORTFOLIO RISK

In the examples used here, the bond portfolio consisted of government bonds. Of course, corporate and municipal bonds are widely held in bond portfolios. Unfortunately, there is no corporate bond futures contract.[15] A municipal bond futures contract exists in the United States, based on an index of municipal bonds, but its volume is relatively light and the contract may not be sufficiently liquid for a large-size transaction.[16] Government bond futures contracts tend to be relatively liquid. In fact, in the United States, different contracts exist for government securities of different maturity ranges, and most of these contracts are relatively liquid.

If one uses a government bond futures to manage the risk of a corporate or municipal bond portfolio, there are some additional risks to deal with. For instance, the relationship between the yield change that drives the futures contract and the yield change that drives the bond portfolio is not as reliable. The yield on a corporate or municipal bond is driven not only by interest rates but also by the perceived default risk of the bond. We

---

[15] There have been attempts to create futures contracts on corporate bonds, but these contracts have not been successful in generating enough trading volume to survive.

[16] In the Commodity Futures Trading Commission's fiscal year 2001, the Chicago Board of Trade's municipal bond futures contract traded about 1,400 contracts a day. Each contract is worth about $100,000 of municipal bonds. Thus, the average daily volume amounts to about $140 million of municipal bonds—not a very large amount relative to the size of the municipal bond market.

might believe that the yield beta is 1.20, meaning that the yield on a corporate bond portfolio is about 20 percent more volatile than the implied yield that drives the futures contract. But this relationship is usually estimated from a regression of corporate bond yield changes on government bond yield changes. This relationship is less stable than if we were running a regression of government bond yield changes on yield changes of a different government bond, the one underlying the futures.

In addition, corporate and municipal bonds often have call features that can greatly distort the relationship between duration and yield change and also make the measurement of duration more complicated. For example, when a bond's yield decreases, its price should increase. The duration is meant to show approximately how much the bond's price should increase. But when the bond is callable and the yield enters into the region in which a call becomes more likely, its price will increase by far less than predicted by the duration. Moreover, the call feature complicates the measurement of duration itself. Duration is no longer a weighted-average maturity of the bond.

Finally, we should note that corporate and municipal bonds are subject to default risk that is not present in government bonds. As the risk of default changes, the yield spread on the defaultable bond relative to the default-free government bond increases. This effect further destabilizes the relationship between the bond portfolio value and the futures price so that duration-based formulas for the number of futures contracts tend to be unreliable.

It is tempting to think that if one wants to increase (decrease) duration and buys (sells) futures contracts, that at least the transaction was the right type even if the number of futures contracts is not exactly correct. The problem, however, is that changes in the bond portfolio value that are driven by changes in default risk or the effects of call provisions will not be matched by movements in the futures contract. The outcome will not always be what is expected.

Another problem associated with the modified duration approach to measuring and managing bond portfolio risk is that the relationship between duration and yield change used here is an instantaneous one. It captures *approximately* how a bond price changes in response to an immediate and very small yield change. As soon as the yield changes or an instant of time passes, the duration changes. Then the number of futures contracts required would change. Thus, the positions described here would need to be revised, somewhat in the manner we explained when describing delta hedging in Chapter 4 on options. Most bond portfolio managers do not perform these kinds of frequent adjustments, however, and simply accept that the transaction will not work precisely as planned.

We should also consider the alternative that the fund could adjust the duration by making transactions in the bonds themselves. It could sell relatively low-duration bonds and buy relatively high-duration bonds to raise the duration to the desired level. There is still no guarantee, however, that the actual duration will be exactly as desired. Likewise, to reduce the duration to zero, the fund could sell out the entire bond portfolio and place the proceeds in cash securities that have low duration. Reducing the duration to essentially zero would be easier to do than increasing it, because it would not be hard to buy bonds with essentially zero duration. Liquidating the entire portfolio, however, would be quite a drastic thing to do, especially given that the fund would likely remain in that position for only a temporary period.

Raising the duration by purchasing higher-duration bonds would be a great deal of effort to expend if the position is being altered only temporarily. Moreover, the transaction costs of buying and selling actual securities are much greater than those of buying and selling futures.

In this book, we shall consider these adjustments as advanced refinements that one should understand before putting these types of transactions into practice. Although we need to be aware of these technical complications, we shall ignore them in the examples here.

Now let us take a look at managing risk in the equity market.

3 STRATEGIES AND APPLICATIONS FOR MANAGING EQUITY MARKET RISK

Even though interest rates are volatile, the stock market is even more volatile. Hence, the risk associated with stock market volatility is greater than that of bond market volatility. Fortunately, the stock market is generally more liquid than the bond market, at least compared with long-term and corporate and municipal bonds. The risk associated with stock market volatility can be managed relatively well with futures contracts. As we have previously noted, these contracts are based on stock market indices and not individual stocks. Although futures on individual stocks are available, most diversified investors manage risk at the portfolio level, thereby preferring futures on broad-based indices. Accordingly, this will be our focus in this chapter. We look more specifically at the risk of managing individual stocks when we study option strategies in Chapter 7.

3.1 MEASURING AND MANAGING THE RISK OF EQUITIES

Futures provide the best way to manage the risk of diversified equity portfolios. Although the standard deviation, or volatility, is a common measure of stock market risk, we prefer a measure that more accurately reflects the risk of a diversified stock portfolio. One reason for this preference is that we shall use futures that are based on broadly diversified portfolios. The most common risk measure of this type is the **beta**,[17] often denoted with the Greek symbol β. Beta is an important factor in capital market and asset pricing theory and, as we see here, it plays a major role in risk management. Although you may have encountered beta elsewhere, we shall take a quick review of it here.

Beta measures the relationship between a stock portfolio and the market portfolio, which is an abstract hypothetical measure of the portfolio containing *all* risky assets, not just stocks. The market portfolio is the most broadly diversified portfolio of all. We know, however, that it is impossible to identify the composition of the true market portfolio. We tend to use proxies, such as the S&P 500 Index, which do not really capture the true market portfolio. Fortunately, for the purposes of risk management, precision in the market portfolio does not matter all that much. Obviously there are no futures contracts on the true market portfolio; there can be futures contracts only on proxies such as the S&P 500. That being the case, it is appropriate to measure the beta of a portfolio relative to the index on which the futures is based.

Beta is a relative risk measure. The beta of the index we use as a benchmark is 1.0. Ignoring any asset-specific risk, an asset with a beta of 1.10 is 10 percent more volatile than the index. A beta of 0.80 is 20 percent less volatile than the index. Beta is formally measured as

$$\beta = \frac{\text{cov}_{SI}}{\sigma_I^2}$$

where cov_{SI} is the covariance between the stock portfolio and the index and σ_I^2 is the variance of the index. Covariance is a measure of the extent to which two assets, here the portfolio and the index, move together.[18] If the covariance is positive (negative), the portfolio and the index tend to move in the same (opposite) direction. By itself, the magnitude of the covariance is difficult to interpret, but the covariance divided by the product of the standard deviations of the stock and the index produces the familiar measure called the corre-

---

[17] At this point, we must distinguish this beta from the yield beta. When we use the term "yield beta," we mean the relationship of the yield on the instrument being hedged to the implied yield on the futures. When we use the term "beta" without a modifier, we mean the relationship of a stock or portfolio to the market.

[18] More specifically, the covariance measures the extent to which the *returns* on the stock and the index move together.

lation coefficient. For beta, however, we divide the covariance by the variance of the index and obtain a measure of the volatility of the portfolio relative to the market.

It is important to emphasize that beta measures only the portfolio volatility relative to the index. Thus, it is a measure only of the risk that cannot be eliminated by diversifying a portfolio. This risk is called the systematic, nondiversifiable, or market risk. A portfolio that is not well diversified could contain additional risk, which is called the nonsystematic, diversifiable, or asset-specific risk.[19] Systematic risk is the risk associated with broad market movements; nonsystematic risk is the risk unique to a company. An example of the former might be a change in interest rates by the Federal Reserve; an example of the latter might be a labor strike on a particular company. Because it captures only systematic risk, beta may seem to be a limited measure of risk, but the best way to manage nonsystematic risk, other than diversification, is to use options, as we do in Chapter 7. At this point, we focus on managing systematic or market risk.

As a risk measure, beta is similar to duration. Recall that we captured the dollar risk by multiplying the modified duration by the dollar value of the portfolio. For the bond futures contract, we multiplied its implied modified duration by the futures price. We called this the dollar-implied modified duration. In a similar manner, we shall specify a dollar beta by multiplying the beta by the dollar value of the portfolio. For the futures, we shall multiply its beta by the futures price, f. For the futures contract, beta is often assumed to be 1.0, but that is not exactly the case, so we will specify it as β_f. The dollar beta of the futures contract is $\beta_f f$. The dollar beta of the stock portfolio is written as $\beta_S S$, where β_S is the beta of the stock portfolio and S is the market value of the stock portfolio.

If we wish to change the beta, we specify the desired beta as a target beta of β_T. Because the value of the futures starts off each day as zero, the dollar beta of the combination of stock and futures if the target beta is achieved is $\beta_T S$.[20] The number of futures we shall use is N_f, which is the unknown that we are attempting to determine. We set the target dollar beta to the dollar beta of the stock portfolio and the dollar beta of N_f futures:

$$\beta_T S = \beta_S S + N_f \beta_f f$$

We then solve for N_f and obtain

$$N_f = \left(\frac{\beta_T - \beta_S}{\beta_f}\right)\left(\frac{S}{f}\right) \tag{6-5}$$

Observe that if we want to increase the beta, β_T will exceed β_S and the sign of N_f will be positive, which means that we must buy futures. If we want to decrease the beta, β_T will be less than β_S, the sign of N_f will be negative, and we must sell futures. This relationship should make sense: Selling futures will offset some of the risk of holding the stock. Alternatively, buying futures will add risk as $\beta_T > \beta_S$ and $N_f > 0$.

In the special case in which we want to completely eliminate the risk, β_T would be zero and the formula would reduce to

$$N_f = -\left(\frac{\beta_S}{\beta_f}\right)\left(\frac{S}{f}\right)$$

---

[19] We also sometimes use the term "idiosyncratic risk."

[20] Recall that the market value of the portfolio will still be the same as the market value of the stock, because the value of the futures is zero. The futures value becomes zero whenever it is marked to market, which takes place at the end of each day. In other words, the target beta does not appear to be applied to the value of the futures in the above analysis because the value of the futures is zero.

In this case, the sign of N_f will always be negative, which makes sense. To hedge away all of the risk, we definitely need to sell futures.

In the practical implementation of a stock index futures trade, we need to remember that stock index futures prices are quoted on an order of magnitude the same as that of the stock index. The actual futures price is the quoted futures price times a designated multiplier. For example, if the S&P 500 futures price is quoted at 1225, the multiplier of $250 makes the actual futures price 1225($250) = $306,250. This amount would be the value of f in the above formulas. In some situations, the futures price will simply be stated, as for example $306,250. In that case, we can assume the price is quoted as f = $306,250 and the multiplier is 1.

We also need to remember that the futures contract will hedge only the risk associated with the relationship between the portfolio and the index on which the futures contract is based. Thus, for example, a portfolio consisting mostly of small-cap stocks should not be paired with a futures contract on a large-cap index such as the S&P 500. Such a transaction would manage only the risk that large-cap stocks move with small-cap stocks. If any divergence occurs in the relationship between these two sectors, such as large-cap stocks going up and small-cap stocks going down, a transaction designed to increase (decrease) risk could end up decreasing (increasing) risk.

Recall also that dividends can interfere with how this transaction performs. Index futures typically are based only on price indices; they do not reflect the payment and reinvestment of dividends. Therefore, dividends will accrue on the stocks but are not reflected in the index. This is not a major problem, however, because dividends in the short-term period covered by most contracts are not particularly risky.

3.2 MANAGING THE RISK OF AN EQUITY PORTFOLIO

To adjust the beta of an equity portfolio, an investment manager could use Equation 6-5 to calculate the number of futures contracts needed. She can use the formula to either increase or decrease the portfolio's systematic risk. The manager might increase the beta if she expects the market to move up, or decrease the beta if she expects the market to move down. Also, the betas of equity portfolios change constantly by virtue of the market value of the portfolio changing.[21] Therefore, futures can be used to adjust the beta from its actual level to the desired level.

Exhibit 6-3 illustrates the case of a pension fund that wants to increase its equity portfolio beta during a period in which it expects the market to be strong. It increases its beta from 0.90 to 1.10 by purchasing 29 futures contracts. Betas, however, are notoriously difficult to measure. We see after the fact that the beta actually was increased to 1.15. As long as we buy (sell) futures contracts, however, we will increase (decrease) the beta.

EXHIBIT 6-3   Using Stock Index Futures to Manage the Risk of a Stock Portfolio

Scenario (2 September)
BB Holdings (BBH) is a U.S. conglomerate. Its pension fund generates market forecasts internally and receives forecasts from an independent consultant. As a result of these forecasts, BBH expects the market for large-cap stocks to be stronger than it believes everyone else is expecting over the next two months.

---

[21] Consider, for example, a portfolio in which $3 million is invested in stock with a beta of 1.0 and $1 million is invested in cash with a beta of 0.0 and a rate of 5 percent. The equity market weight is, therefore, 0.75, and the overall beta is 1.0(0.75) + 0.0(0.25) = 0.75. Now suppose the following year, the stock increases by 20 percent. Then the stock value will be $3.6 million and the cash balance will be $1.05 million. The overall portfolio value will be $4.65 million, so the equity market weight will be 3.6/4.65 = 0.77. Thus, 77 percent of the portfolio will now have a beta of 1.0(0.77), and the overall beta will have drifted upward to 0.77.

Action

BBH decides to adjust the beta on $38,500,000 of large-cap stocks from its current level of 0.90 to 1.10 for the period of the next two months. It has selected a futures contract deemed to have sufficient liquidity; the futures price is currently $275,000 and the contract has a beta of 0.95. The appropriate number of futures contracts to adjust the beta would be

$$N_f = \left(\frac{\beta_T - \beta_S}{\beta_f}\right)\left(\frac{S}{f}\right) = \left(\frac{1.10 - 0.90}{0.95}\right)\left(\frac{\$38,500,000}{\$275,000}\right) = 29.47$$

So it buys 29 contracts.

Scenario (3 December)

The market as a whole increases by 4.4 percent. The stock portfolio increases to $40,103,000. The stock index futures contract rises to $286,687.50,[22] an increase of 4.25 percent.

Outcome and Analysis

The profit on the futures contract is 29($286,687.50 − $275,000.00) = $338,937.50. The rate of return for the stock portfolio is

$$\frac{\$40,103,000}{\$38,500,000} - 1 = 0.0416$$

or 4.16 percent. Adding the profit from the futures gives a total market value of $40,103,000.00 + $338,937.50 = $40,441,937.50. The rate of return for the stock portfolio is

$$\frac{\$40,441,937.50}{\$38,500,000.00} - 1 = 0.0504$$

or 5.04 percent. Because the market went up by 4.4 percent and the overall gain was 5.04 percent, the effective beta of the portfolio was

$$\frac{0.0504}{0.044} = 1.15$$

Thus, the effective beta is quite close to the target beta of 1.10.

Of course, be aware that increasing the beta increases the risk. Therefore, if the beta is increased and the market falls, the loss on the portfolio will be greater than if beta had not been increased. Decreasing the beta decreases the risk, so if the market rises, the portfolio value will rise less. As an example, consider the outcome described in Exhibit 6-3. Suppose that instead of being optimistic, the fund manager was very pessimistic and

---

[22] In the examples in this chapter, stock futures prices move to a new level in the course of the scenario. These new futures prices come from the cost-of-carry model (assuming there is no mispricing in the market), which was given as Equations 3-13 and 3-14 in Chapter 3.

wanted to decrease the beta to zero. Therefore, the target beta, β_T, is 0.0. Then the number of futures contracts would be

$$N_f = \left(\frac{0.0 - 0.90}{0.95}\right)\frac{\$38,500,000}{\$275,000} = -132.63$$

So the fund sells 133 futures. Given the same outcome as in Exhibit 6-3, the profit on the futures contracts would be

$$-133(\$286,687.50 - \$275,000.00) = -\$1,554,437.50$$

There would be a loss of more than $1.5 million on the futures contracts. The market value of the stock after it moved up was $40,103,000, but with the futures loss, the market value is effectively reduced to $40,103,000.00 − $1,554,437.50 = $38,548,562.50. This is a return of

$$\frac{\$38,548,562.50}{\$38,500,000.00} - 1 = 0.0013$$

Thus, the effective beta is

$$\frac{0.0013}{0.044} = 0.030$$

The beta has been reduced almost to zero. This reduction costs the company virtually all of the upward movement, but such a cost is to be expected if the beta were changed to zero.

PRACTICE PROBLEM 3

Equity Analysts Inc. (EQA) is an equity portfolio management firm. One of its clients has decided to be more aggressive for a short period of time. It would like EQA to move the beta on its $65 million portfolio from 0.85 to 1.05. EQA can use a futures contract priced at $188,500, which has a beta of 0.92, to implement this change in risk.

A. Determine the number of futures contracts EQA should use and whether it should buy or sell futures.

B. At the horizon date, the equity market is down 2 percent. The stock portfolio falls 1.65 percent, and the futures price falls to $185,000. Determine the overall value of the position and the effective beta.

SOLUTIONS

A. The number of futures contracts EQA should use is

$$N_f = \left(\frac{1.05 - 0.85}{0.92}\right)\left(\frac{\$65,000,000}{\$188,500}\right) = 74.96$$

So EQA should buy 75 contracts.

B. The value of the stock portfolio will be $65,000,000(1 − 0.0165) = $63,927,500. The profit on the futures transaction is 75($185,000 − $188,500) = −$262,500. The overall value of the position is $63,927,500 − $262,500 = $63,665,000.

Thus, the overall return is $\dfrac{\$63,665,000}{\$65,000,000} - 1 = -0.0205$

Because the market went down by 2 percent, the effective beta is 0.0205/0.02 = 1.025.

3.3 CREATING EQUITY OUT OF CASH

Stock index futures are an excellent tool for creating synthetic positions in equity, which can result in significant transaction cost savings and preserve liquidity. In this section, we explore how to create a synthetic index fund and how to turn cash into synthetic equity.

In Chapters 2 and 3, we learned that the relationship between a futures or forward contract and the underlying asset is determined by a formula that relates the risk-free interest rate to the dividends on the underlying asset. Entering into a hypothetical arbitrage transaction in which we buy stock and sell futures turns an equity position into a risk-free portfolio. In simple terms, we say that

Long stock + Short futures = Long risk-free bond.

We can turn this equation around to obtain[23]

Long stock = Long risk-free bond + Long futures.

If we buy the risk-free bonds and buy the futures, we replicate a position in which we would be buying the stock. This synthetic replication of the underlying asset can be a very useful transaction when we wish to construct a synthetic stock index fund, or when we wish to convert into equity a cash position that we are required to maintain for liquidity purposes. Both of these situations involve holding cash and obtaining equity market exposure through the use of futures.

3.3.1 CREATING A SYNTHETIC INDEX FUND

A synthetic index fund is an index fund position created by combining risk-free bonds and futures on the desired index. Suppose a U.S. money manager would like to offer a new product, a fund on an index of U.K. stock as represented by the Financial Times Stock Exchange (FTSE) 100 Index. The manager will initiate the fund with an investment of £100 million. In other words, the U.S. money manager would offer clients an opportunity to invest in a position in British stock with the investment made in British pounds.[24] The manager believes the fund is easier to create synthetically using futures contracts.

---

[23] We turn the equation around by noting that to remove a short futures position from the left-hand side, we should buy futures. If we add a long futures position to the left-hand side, we have to add it to the right-hand side.

[24] If you are wondering why U.S. investors would like to invest in a position denominated in British pounds rather than dollars, remember that the currency risk can be a source of diversification. Adding a position in the U.K. equity market provides one tier of diversification, while adding the risk of the dollar/pound exchange rate adds another tier of diversification, especially because the exchange rate is likely to have a low correlation with the U.S. stock market. See Section 5.3 for a discussion of risk management of a foreign asset portfolio.

To create this synthetic index fund, we need to know several more pieces of information. The dividend yield on the U.K. stocks is 2.5 percent, and the FTSE 100 Index futures contract that we shall use expires in three months, has a quoted price of £4,000, and has a multiplier of £10.[25] The U.K. risk-free interest rate is 5 percent.[26] When the futures contract expires, it will be rolled over into a new contract.

To create this synthetic index fund, we must buy a certain number of futures. Let the following be the appropriate values of the inputs:

V = amount of money to be invested, £100 million

f = futures price, £4,000

T = time to expiration of futures, 0.25

δ = dividend yield on the index, 0.025

r = risk-free rate, 0.05

q = multiplier, £10

We would like to replicate owning the stock and reinvesting the dividends. How many futures contracts would we need to buy and add to a long bond position? We designate N_f as the required number of futures contracts and N_f^* as its rounded-off value.

Now observe that the payoff of N_f^* futures contracts will be $N_f^*q(S_T - f)$. This equation is based on the fact that we have N_f^* futures contracts, each of which has a multiplier of q. The futures contracts are established at a price of f. When it expires, the futures price will be the spot price, S_T, reflecting the convergence of the futures price at expiration to the spot price.

The futures payoff can be rewritten as $N_f^*qS_T - N_f^*qf$. The minus sign on the second term means that we shall have to pay N_f^*qf. The (implied) plus sign on the first term means that we shall receive $N_f^*qS_T$. Knowing that we buy N_f^* futures contracts, we also want to know how much to invest in bonds. We shall call this V^* and calculate it based on N_f^*. Below we shall show how to calculate N_f^* and V^*. If we invest enough money in bonds to accumulate a value of N_f^*qf, this investment will cover the amount we agree to pay for the FTSE: $N_f^* \times q \times f$. The present value of this amount is $N_f^*qf/(1 + r)^T$.

Because the amount of money we start with is V, we should have V equal to $N_f^*qf/(1 + r)^T$. From here we can solve for N_f^* to obtain

$$N_f^* = \frac{V(1 + r)^T}{qf} \qquad \text{(rounded to an integer)} \qquad \text{(6-6)}$$

---

[25] Recall that the multiplier is a number multiplied by the quoted futures price to obtain the actual futures price. In this section, accurately pricing the futures contract is important to the success of these strategies. For example, assume the S&P 500 is at 1,000 and the multiplier is $250, so the full price is (1,000)($250) = $250,000. We wish to trade a futures contract priced at f, where f is based on the index value of 1,000 grossed up by the risk-free rate and reduced by the dividends, as described in Chapter 3. If this pricing relationship does not hold, the strategies in Sections 3.2 and 3.3 will not work. It is far easier to think of f in terms of its relationship to S without the multiplier. In one case, however, we shall let the multiplier be 1, so you should be able to handle either situation. In Sections 3.1 and 3.4, we can easily get away with treating the futures price as $250,000 and not worry about the multiplier.

[26] It might be confusing as to why we care about the U.K. interest rate and not the U.S. interest rate. This transaction is completely denominated in pounds, and the futures contract is priced in pounds based on the U.K. dividend yield and interest rate. Hence, the U.K. interest rate plays a role here, and the U.S. interest rate does not.

But once we round off the number of futures, we do not truly have V dollars invested. The amount we actually have invested is

$$V^* = \frac{N_f^* q f}{(1 + r)^T} \qquad (6\text{-}7)$$

We can show that investing V^* in bonds and buying N_f^* futures contracts at a price of f is equivalent to buying $N_f^* q/(1 + \delta)^T$ units of stock.

As noted above, if we have bonds maturing to the value $N_f^* q f$, we have enough cash on hand to pay the obligation of $N_f^* q f$ on our futures contract. The futures contract will pay us the amount $N_f^* q S_T$. If we had actually purchased units of stock, the reinvestment of dividends into new units means that we would end up with the equivalent of $Nf^* q$ units, and means that we implicitly started off with $N_f^* q/(1 + \delta)^T$ units.

In short, this transaction implies that we synthetically start off with $N_f^* q/(1 + \delta)^T$ units of stock, collect and reinvest dividends, and end up with $N_f^* q$ units. We emphasize that all of these transactions are synthetic. We do not actually own the stock or collect and reinvest the dividends. We are attempting only to replicate what would happen if we actually owned the stock and collected and reinvested the dividends.

Exhibit 6-4 illustrates this transaction. The interest plus principal on the bonds is a sufficient amount to buy the stock in settlement of the futures contract, so the fund ends up holding the stock, as it originally wanted.

EXHIBIT 6-4　Constructing a Synthetic Index Fund

Scenario (15 December)
On 15 December, a U.S. money manager for a firm called Strategic Money Management (SMM) wants to construct a synthetic index fund consisting of a position of £100 million invested in U.K. stock. The index will be the FTSE 100, which has a dividend yield of 2.5 percent. A futures contract on the FTSE 100 is priced at £4,000 and has a multiplier of £10. The position will be held until the futures expires in three months, at which time it will be renewed with a new three-month futures. The U.K. risk-free rate is 5 percent. Both the risk-free rate and the dividend yield are stated as annually compounded figures.

Action
The number of futures contracts will be

$$N_f = \frac{V(1 + r)^T}{q f} = \frac{£100,000,000(1.05)^{0.25}}{£10(£4,000)} = 2,530.68$$

Because we cannot buy fractions of futures contracts, we round N_f to $N_f^* = 2,531$. With this rounding, we are actually synthetically investing

$$\frac{2,531(£10)£4,000}{(1.05)^{0.25}} = £100,012,622$$

in stock. So we put this much money in risk-free bonds, which will grow to £100,012,622(1.05)^{0.25} = £101,240,000. The number of units of stock that we have effectively purchased at the start is

$$\frac{N_f^* q}{(1 + \delta)^T} = \frac{2,531(10)}{(1.025)^{0.25}} = 25,154.24$$

If the stock had actually been purchased, dividends would be received and reinvested into additional shares. Thus, the number of shares would grow to $25,154.24(1.025)^{0.25} = 25,310$.

Scenario (15 March)
The index is at S_T when the futures expires.

Outcome and Analysis
The futures contracts will pay off the amount

$$\text{Futures payoff} = 2,531(£10)(S_T - £4,000) = £25,310S_T - £101,240,000$$

This means that the fund will pay £101,240,000 to settle the futures contract and obtain the market value of 25,310 units of the FTSE 100, each worth S_T. Therefore, the fund will need to come up with £101,240,000, but as noted above, the money invested in risk-free bonds grows to a value of £101,240,000.

SMM, therefore, pays this amount to settle the futures contracts and effectively ends up with 25,310 units of the index, the position it wanted in the market.

There are a few other considerations to note. One is that we rounded according to the usual rules of rounding, going up if the fraction is 0.5 or greater. By rounding up, we shall have to invest more than V in bonds. If we rounded down, we shall invest less than V. It does not really matter whether we always round up on 0.5 or greater, but that is the rule we shall use here. It should also be noted that this transaction does not capture the dividends that would be earned if one held the underlying stocks directly. The yield of 2.5 percent is important in the computations here, but the fund does not earn these dividends. All this transaction does is capture the performance of the index. Because the index is a price index only and does not include dividends, this synthetic replication strategy can capture only the index performance without the dividends.[27] Another concern that could be encountered in practice is that the futures contract could expire later than the desired date. If so, the strategy will still be successful if the futures contract is correctly priced when the strategy is completed. Consistent with that point, we should note that any strategy using futures will be effective only to the extent that the futures is correctly priced when the position is opened and also when it is closed. This point underscores the importance of understanding the pricing of futures contracts, as discussed in Chapter 3.

3.3.2 EQUITIZING CASH

The strategy of combining risk-free bonds and futures is used not only to replicate an index; it is also used to take a given amount of cash and turn it into an equity position while maintaining the liquidity provided by the cash. This type of transaction is sometimes called equitizing cash. Consider an investment fund that has a large cash balance. It would like to invest in equity but either is not allowed to do so or cannot afford to take the risk that it might need to liquidate a large amount of stock in a short period of time, which could be difficult to do or might result in significant losses. Nonetheless, the fund is willing to take the risk of equity market exposure provided it can maintain the liquidity. The above transaction can be altered just slightly to show how this is done.

Suppose the fund in Exhibit 6-4 is actually a U.K. insurance company that has about £100 million of cash invested at the risk-free rate. It would like to gain equity market expo-

---

[27] The values of some stock indices, called total return indices, include reinvested dividends. If a futures contract on the total return index is used, then the strategy would capture the dividends. Doing so would, however, require a few changes to the formulas given here.

sure by investing in the FTSE 100 index. By policy, it is allowed to do so, provided that it maintains sufficient liquidity. If it engages in the synthetic index strategy described above, it maintains about £100 million invested in cash in the form of risk-free bonds and yet gains the exposure to about £100 million of U.K. stock. In the event that it must liquidate its position, perhaps to pay out insurance claims, it need only liquidate the U.K. risk-free bonds and close out the futures contracts. Given the liquidity of the futures market and the obvious liquidity of the risk-free bond market, doing so would be relatively easy.

There is one important aspect of this problem, however, over which the fund has no control: the pricing of the futures. Because the fund will take a long position in futures, the futures contract must be correctly priced. If the futures contract is overpriced, the fund will pay too much for the futures. In that case, the risk-free bonds will not be enough to offset the excessively high price effectively paid for the stock. If, however, the futures contract is underpriced, the fund will get a bargain and will come out much better.

Finally, we should note that these strategies can be illustrated with bond futures to gain bond market exposure, but they are more commonly implemented using stock index futures to gain equity market exposure.

PRACTICE PROBLEM 4

Index Advantage (INDEXA) is a money management firm that specializes in turning the idle cash of clients into equity index positions at very low cost. INDEXA has a new client with about $500 million of cash that it would like to invest in the small-cap equity sector. INDEXA will construct the position using a futures contract on a small-cap index. The futures price is 1,500, the multiplier is $100, and the contract expires in six months. The underlying small-cap index has a dividend yield of 1 percent. The risk-free rate is 3 percent per year.

A. Determine exactly how the cash can be equitized using futures contracts.

B. When the futures contract expires, the index is at S_T. Demonstrate how the position produces the same outcome as an actual investment in the index.

SOLUTIONS

A. INDEXA should purchase

$$N_f = \frac{\$500,000,000(1.03)^{0.5}}{\$100(1,500)} = 3,382.96$$

futures contracts. Round this amount to $N_f^* = 3,383$. Then invest

$$\frac{3,383(\$100)(1,500)}{(1.03)^{0.5}} = \$500,005,342$$

in risk-free bonds paying 3 percent interest. Note that this is not exactly an initial investment of $500 million, because one cannot purchase fractions of futures contracts. The bonds will grow to a value of $\$500,005,342(1.03)^{0.5} = \$507,450,000$. The number of units of stock effectively purchased through the use of futures is

$$\frac{N_f^* q}{(1 + \delta)^T} = \frac{3,383(100)}{(1.01)^{0.5}} = 336,621.08$$

> If 336,621.08 shares were actually purchased, the accumulation and reinvestment of dividends would result in there being $336{,}621.08(1.01)^{0.5} = 338{,}300$ shares at the futures expiration.
>
> **B.** At expiration, the payoff on the futures is
>
> $$3{,}383(100)(S_T - 1500) = 338{,}300 S_T - \$507{,}450{,}000$$
>
> In other words, to settle the futures, INDEXA will owe \$507,450,000 and receive the equivalent of 338,300 units of stock worth S_T.

3.4 CREATING CASH OUT OF EQUITY

Because we have the relation Long stock + Short futures = Long risk-free bonds, we should be able to construct a synthetic position in cash by selling futures against a long stock position. Indeed we have already done a similar transaction when we sold futures to reduce the stock portfolio beta to zero. Therefore, if we wish to sell stock, we can do so by converting it to synthetic cash. This move can save transaction costs and avoid the sale of large amounts of stock at a single point in time.

Suppose the market value of our investment in stock is V, and we would like to create synthetic cash roughly equivalent to that amount. We shall sell futures, with the objective that at the horizon date, we shall have $V(1 + r)^T$. Money in the amount of V will have grown in value at the risk-free rate. Each unit of the index is priced at S. The number of units of the index we shall effectively convert to cash would appear to be (V/S), but because of reinvested dividends, we actually end up with $(1 + \delta)^T$ units of stock for every unit we start with. Hence, the number of units we are effectively converting to cash is $(V/S)(1 + \delta)^T$.

As in the example of the synthetic index fund, we shall again have a problem in that the number of futures contracts must be rounded off to an integer. Keeping that in mind, the payoff of the futures contracts will be $qN_f^*(S_T - f) = qN_f^* S_T - qN_f^* f$. If the number of units of stock is $(V/S)(1 + \delta)^T$, then the value of the overall position (long stock plus short futures) will be $(V/S)(1 + \delta)^T S_T + qN_f^* S_T - qN_f^* f$. Because we are trying to convert to risk-free bonds (cash), we need to find a way to eliminate the S_T term. We just solve for the value of N_f^* that will cause the first two terms to offset.[28] We obtain a previous equation, Equation 6-6:

$$N_f^* = -\,\frac{V(1 + r)^T}{qf} \qquad \text{(rounded to an integer)}$$

As usual, the minus sign means that N_f^* is less than zero, which means we are selling futures. Because of rounding, the amount of stock we are actually converting is

$$V^* = \frac{-N_f^* qf}{(1 + r)^T} \tag{6-8}$$

Therefore, if we use N_f^* futures contracts, we have effectively converted stock worth V^* to cash. This will not be the exact amount of stock we own, but it will be close. As in the

---

[28] In order to get this solution, we must take the result that $f = S(1 + r)^T/(1 + \delta)^T$ and turn it around so that $S = f(1 + \delta)^T/(1 + r)^T$ to find the value of S.

case of the synthetic index fund, reinvestment of dividends means that the number of units of stock will be $-N_f*q/(1 + \delta)^T$ at the start and $-N_f*q$ when the futures expires. In Exhibit 6-5, we illustrate the application of this strategy for a pension fund that would like to convert $50 million of stock to synthetic cash.

EXHIBIT 6-5 Creating Synthetic Cash

Scenario (2 June)

The pension fund of Interactive Industrial Systems (IIS) holds a $50 million portion of its portfolio in an indexed position of the Nasdaq 100, which has a dividend yield of 0.75 percent. It would like to convert that position to cash for a two-month period. It can do this using a futures contract on the Nasdaq 100, which is priced at 1484.72, has a multiplier of $100, and expires in two months. The risk-free rate is 4.65 percent.

Action

The fund needs to use

$$N_f = \frac{-V(1 + r)^T}{qf} = -\frac{\$50,000,000(1.0465)^{2/12}}{\$100(1484.72)} = -339.32$$

futures contracts. This amount should be rounded to $N_f* = -339$. Because of rounding, the amount of stock synthetically converted to cash is really

$$\frac{-N_f*q}{(1 + r)^T} = \frac{339(\$100)(1484.72)}{(1.0465)^{2/12}} = \$49,952,173$$

This amount should grow to $49,952,173(1.0465)^{2/12} = \$50,332,008$. The number of units of stock is

$$\frac{-N_f*q}{(1 + \delta)^T} = \frac{339(\$100)}{(1.0075)^{2/12}} = 33,857.81$$

at the start, which grows to $33,857.81(1.0075)^{2/12} = 33,900$ units when the futures expires.

Scenario (4 August)

The stock index is at S_T when the futures expires.

Outcome and Analysis

The payoff of the futures contract is

$$-339(\$100)(S_T - 1484.72) = -\$33,900S_T + \$50,332,008$$

As noted, dividends are reinvested and the number of units of the index grows to 33,900 shares. The overall position of the fund is

Stock worth $33,900S_T$
Futures payoff of $-33,900S_T + \$50,332,008$

or an overall total of $50,332,008. This is exactly the amount we said the fund would have if it invested $49,952,173 at the risk-free rate of 4.65 percent for two months. Thus, the fund has effectively converted a stock position to cash.

PRACTICE PROBLEM 5

Synthetics Inc. (SYNINC) executes a variety of synthetic strategies for pension funds. One such strategy is to enable the client to maintain a liquid balance in cash while retaining exposure to equity market movements. A similar strategy is to enable the client to maintain its position in the market but temporarily convert it to cash. A client with a $100 million equity position wants to convert it to cash for three months. An equity market futures contract is priced at $325,000, expires in three months, and is based on an underlying index with a dividend yield of 2 percent. The risk-free rate is 3.5 percent.

A. Determine the number of futures contracts SYNINC should trade and the effective amount of money it has invested in risk-free bonds to achieve this objective.

B. When the futures contracts expire, the equity index is at S_T. Show how this transaction results in the appropriate outcome.

SOLUTIONS

A. First note that no multiplier is quoted here. The futures price of $325,000 is equivalent to a quoted price of $325,000 and a multiplier of 1.0 The number of futures contracts is

$$N_f = - \frac{\$100,000,000(1.035)^{0.25}}{\$325,000} = -310.35$$

Rounding off, SYNINC should sell 310 contracts. This is equivalent to selling futures contracts on stock worth

$$\frac{310(\$325,000)}{(1.035)^{0.25}} = \$99,887,229$$

and is the equivalent of investing $99,887,229 in risk-free bonds, which will grow to a value of $99,887,229(1.035)^{0.25} = \$100,750,000$. The number of units of stock being effectively converted to cash is (ignoring the minus sign)

$$\frac{N_f^* q}{(1 + \delta)^T} = \frac{310(1)}{(1.02)^{0.25}} = 308.47$$

The accumulation and reinvestment of dividends would make this figure grow to $308.47(1.02)^{0.25} = 310$ units when the futures expires.

B. At expiration, the profit on the futures is $-310(S_T - \$325,000) = -310S_T + \$100,750,000$. That means SYNINC will have to pay $310S_T$ and will receive $100,750,000 to settle the futures contract. Due to reinvestment of dividends, it will end up with the equivalent of 310 units of stock, which can be sold to cover the amount $-310S_T$. This will leave $100,750,000, the equivalent of having invested in risk-free bonds.

You might be wondering about the relationship between the number of futures contracts given here and the number of futures contracts required to adjust the portfolio beta to zero. Here we are selling a given number of futures contracts against stock to effectively convert the stock to a risk-free asset. Does that not mean that the portfolio would then have a beta of zero? In Section 3.2, we gave a different formula to reduce the portfolio beta to zero. These formulas do not appear to be the same. Would they give the same value of N_f? In the example here, we sell the precise number of futures to completely hedge the stock portfolio. The stock portfolio, however, has to be identical to the index. It cannot have a different beta. The other formula, which reduces the beta to zero, is more general and can be used to eliminate the systematic risk on any portfolio. Note, however, that only systematic risk is eliminated. If the portfolio is not fully diversified, some risk will remain, but that risk is diversifiable, and the expected return on that portfolio would still be the risk-free rate. If we apply that formula to a portfolio that is identical to the index on which the futures is based, the two formulas are the same and the number of futures contracts to sell is the same in both cases.[29]

Finally, we should note that we could have changed the beta of the portfolio by making transactions in individual securities. To raise (lower) the beta we could sell (buy) low-beta stocks and buy (sell) high-beta stocks. Alternatively, we could do transactions in the portfolio itself and the risk-free asset. To reduce the beta to zero, for example, we could sell the entire portfolio and invest the money in the risk-free asset. To increase the beta, we could reduce any position we hold in the risk-free asset, even to the point of borrowing by issuing the risk-free asset.[30] In this chapter, we illustrate how these transactions can be better executed using derivatives, which have lower transaction costs and generally greater liquidity. There is no guarantee that either approach will result in the portfolio having the exact beta the investor desired. Betas are notoriously difficult to measure. But executing the transactions in derivatives provides an attractive alternative to having to make a large number of transactions in individual securities. In light of the fact that many of these adjustments are intended to be only temporary, it makes far more sense to do the transactions in derivatives than to make the transactions in the underlying securities, provided that one is willing to keep re-entering positions upon contract expirations.

4 ASSET ALLOCATION WITH FUTURES

It has been widely noted that the most important factor in the performance of an asset portfolio is the allocation of the portfolio among asset classes. In this book, we do not develop techniques for determining the best allocation among asset classes any more than we attempt to determine what beta to set as a target for our stock portfolio or what duration to set as a target for our bond portfolio. We focus instead on how derivative strategies can be used to implement a plan based on a market outlook. As we saw previously in this chapter, we can adjust the beta or duration effectively with lower cost and greater liquidity by using stock index or bond futures. In this section, we look at how to allocate a portfolio among asset classes using futures.

---

[29] A key element in this statement is that the futures beta is the beta of the underlying index, multiplied by the present value interest factor using the risk-free rate. This is a complex and subtle point, however, that we simply state without going into the mathematical proof.

[30] Students of capital market theory will recognize that the transactions we describe in this paragraph are those involving movements up and down the capital market line, which leads to investors finding their optimal portfolios. This kind of trading activity in turn leads to the well-known capital asset pricing model.

4.1 ADJUSTING THE ALLOCATION AMONG ASSET CLASSES

Consider the case of a $300 million portfolio that is allocated 80 percent ($240 million) to stock and 20 percent ($60 million) to bonds. The manager wants to change the allocation to 50 percent ($150 million) stock and 50 percent ($150 million) bonds. Therefore, the manager wants to reduce the allocation to stock by $90 million and increase the allocation to bonds by $90 million. The trick, however, is to use the correct number of futures contracts to set the beta and duration to the desired level. To do this, the manager should sell stock index futures contracts to reduce the beta on the $90 million of stock from its current level to zero. This transaction will effectively convert the stock to cash. She should then buy bond futures contracts to increase the duration on the cash from its current level to the desired level.

Exhibit 6-6 presents this example. The manager sells 516 stock index futures contracts and buys 742 bond futures contracts. Two months later, the position is worth $297,921,622. As we show, had the transactions been done by selling stocks and buying bonds, the portfolio would be worth $297,375,000, a difference of only about 0.2 percent relative to the original market value. Of course, the futures transactions can be executed in a more liquid market and with lower transaction costs.

EXHIBIT 6-6   Adjusting the Allocation between Stocks and Bonds

Scenario (15 November)

Global Asset Advisory Group (GAAG) is a pension fund management firm. One of its funds consists of $300 million allocated 80 percent to stock and 20 percent to bonds. The stock portion has a beta of 1.10 and the bond portion has a duration of 6.5. GAAG would like to temporarily adjust the asset allocation to 50 percent stock and 50 percent bonds. It will use stock index futures and bond futures to achieve this objective. The stock index futures contract has a price of $200,000 (after accounting for the multiplier) and a beta of 0.96. The bond futures contract has an implied modified duration of 7.2 and a price of $105,250. The yield beta is 1. The transaction will be put in place on 15 November, and the horizon date for termination is 10 January.

Action

The market value of the stock is 0.80($300,000,000) = $240,000,000. The market value of the bonds is 0.20($300,000,000) = $60,000,000. Because it wants the portfolio to be temporarily reallocated to half stock and half bonds, GAAG needs to change the allocation to $150 million of each.

Thus, GAAG effectively needs to sell $90 million of stock by converting it to cash using stock index futures and buy $90 million of bonds by using bond futures. This would effectively convert the stock into cash and then convert that cash into bonds. Of course, this entire series of transactions will be synthetic; the actual stock and bonds in the portfolio will stay in place.

Using Equation 6-5, the number of stock index futures, denoted as N_{sf}, will be

$$N_{sf} = \left(\frac{\beta_T - \beta_S}{\beta_f}\right)\frac{S}{f_s}$$

where β_T is the target beta of zero, β_S is the stock beta of 1.10, β_f is the futures beta of 0.96, S is the market value of the stock involved in the transaction of $90 million, and f_s is the price of the stock index futures, $200,000. We obtain

$$N_{sf} = \left(\frac{0. - 1.10}{0.96}\right)\frac{\$90,000,000}{\$200,000} = -515.63$$

Rounding off, GAAG sells 516 contracts.

Using Equation 6-4, the number of bond futures, denoted as N_{bf}, will be

$$N_{bf} = \left(\frac{MDUR_T - MDUR_B}{MDUR_f}\right)\frac{B}{f_b}$$

where $MDUR_T$ is the target modified duration of 6.5, $MDUR_B$ is the modified duration of the existing bonds, $MDUR_f$ is the implied modified duration of the futures (here 7.2), B is the market value of the bonds of $90 million, and f_b is the bond futures price of $105,250. The modified duration of the existing bonds is the modified duration of a cash position. This position would be essentially three-month risk-free bonds with a duration of about 0.25. The existing bonds are considered cash because we are first going to convert $90 million of stock to synthetic cash. Then we convert that synthetic cash into bonds using bond futures. We obtain

$$N_{bf} = \left(\frac{6.5 - 0.25}{7.2}\right)\left(\frac{\$90,000,000}{\$105,250}\right) = 742.28$$

So GAAG buys 742 contracts.

Scenario (10 January)
During this period, the stock portion of the portfolio returns −3 percent and the bond portion returns 1.25 percent. The stock index futures price goes from $200,000 to $193,600, and the bond futures price increases from $105,250 to $106,691.

Outcome and Analysis
The profit on the stock index futures transaction is −516($193,600 − $200,000) = $3,302,400. The profit on the bond futures transaction is 742($106,691 − $105,250) = $1,069,222. The total profit from the futures transactions is, therefore, $3,302,400 + $1,069,222 = $4,371,622. The market value of the stocks and bonds will now be

Stocks: $240,000,000(1 − 0.03) = $232,800,000
Bonds: $60,000,000(1.0125) = $ 60,750,000
Total· $293,550,000

Thus, the total portfolio value, including the futures gains, is $293,550,000 + $4,371,622 = $297,921,622. Had GAAG sold stocks and then converted the proceeds to bonds, the value would have been

Stocks: $150,000,000(1 − 0.03) = $145,500,000
Bonds: $150,000,000(1.0125) = $151,875,000
Total: $297,375,000

This total is a slight difference of about 0.2 percent relative to the market value of the portfolio using derivatives.

Exhibit 6-7 shows a variation of this problem in which a portfolio management firm wants to convert a portion of a bond portfolio to cash to meet a liquidity requirement and another portion to a higher duration. On the portion it wants to convert to cash, it sells 104 futures contracts. This is the correct amount to change the duration to 0.25, the approximate duration of a short-term money market instrument. It then buys 33 futures contracts to raise the duration on the other part of the portfolio. The net is that it executes only one transaction of 71 contracts, and the end result is a portfolio worth $3,030,250 at the end of the period. Had the transactions been done by selling and buying securities, the portfolio would have been worth $3,048,000, or about the same amount. Another question we shall examine is whether this strategy actually meets the liquidity requirement.

EXHIBIT 6-7   Adjusting the Allocation between One Bond Class and Another

Scenario (15 October)
Fixed Income Money Advisors (FIMA) manages bond portfolios for wealthy individual investors. It uses various tactical strategies to alter its mix between long- and short-term bonds to adjust its portfolio to a composition appropriate for its outlook for interest rates. Currently, it would like to alter a $30 million segment of its portfolio that has a modified duration of 6.5. To increase liquidity, it would like to move $10 million into cash but adjust the duration on the remaining $20 million to 7.5. These changes will take place on 15 October and will likely be reversed on 12 December.

Action
The bond futures contract that FIMA will use is priced at $87,500 and has an implied modified duration of 6.85. To convert $10 million of bonds at a duration of 6.5 into cash requires adjusting the duration to that of a cash equivalent. A cash equivalent is a short-term instrument with a duration of less than 1.0. The equivalent instruments that FIMA would use if it did the transactions in cash would be six-month instruments. The average duration of a six-month instrument is three months or 0.25. The interest rate that drives the long-term bond market is assumed to have a yield beta of 1.0 with respect to the interest rate that drives the futures market.

FIMA could solve this problem in either of two ways. It could lower the duration on $10 million of bonds from 6.5 to 0.25. Then it could raise the duration on $20 million from 6.5 to 7.5. If FIMA converts $10 million to a duration of 0.25 and $20 million to a duration of 7.5, the overall duration would be $(10/30)0.25 + (20/30)7.50 = 5.08$. As an alternative, FIMA could just aim for lowering the overall duration to 5.08, but we shall illustrate the approach of adjusting the duration in two steps.

Thus, FIMA needs to lower the duration on $10 million from 6.5 to 0.25. Accordingly, the appropriate number of futures contracts is

$$N_f = \left(\frac{MDUR_T - MDUR_B}{MDUR_f}\right)\left(\frac{B}{f}\right) = \left(\frac{0.25 - 6.50}{6.85}\right)\left(\frac{\$10,000,000}{\$87,50}\right) = -104.28$$

So, FIMA should sell 104 contracts.

To increase the duration on $20 million from 6.5 to 7.5, the appropriate number of futures contracts is

$$N_f = \left(\frac{MDUR_T - MDUR_B}{MDUR_f}\right)\left(\frac{B}{f}\right) = \left(\frac{7.5 - 6.5}{6.85}\right)\left(\frac{\$20,000,000}{\$87,500}\right) = 33.37$$

Thus, FIMA should buy 33 futures contracts.

Because these transactions involve the same futures contract, the net effect is that FIMA should sell 71 contracts. Therefore, FIMA does just one transaction to sell 71 contracts.

Scenario (12 December)
During this period, interest rates rose by 2 percent and the bonds decreased in value by 13 percent (6.5 duration times 2 percent). The futures price fell to $75,250. Thus, the $30 million bond portfolio fell by $30,000,000(0.13) = $3,900,000.

Outcome and Analysis

The profit on the futures contracts is $-71(\$75,250 - \$87,500) = \$869,750$. So the overall loss is $\$3,900,000 - \$869,750 = \$3,030,250$. The change in the portfolio value of 13 percent was based on an assumed yield change of 2 percent (6.5 duration times $0.02 = 0.13$). A portfolio with a modified duration of 5.08 would, therefore, change by approximately $5.08(0.02) = 0.1016$, or 10.16 percent. The portfolio thus would decrease by $\$30,000,000(0.1016) = \$3,048,000$.

The difference in this result and what was actually obtained is $\$17,750$, or about 0.06 percent of the initial $30 million value of the portfolio. Some of this difference is due to rounding and some is due to the fact that bonds do not respond in the precise manner predicted by duration.

We noted in Exhibit 6-7 that the manager wants to convert a portion of the portfolio to cash to increase liquidity. By selling the futures contracts, the manager maintains the securities in long-term bonds but reduces the volatility of those bonds to the equivalent of that of a short-term instrument. We might, however, question whether liquidity has actually been improved. If cash is needed, the fund would have to sell the long-term bonds and buy back the futures. The latter would not present a liquidity problem, but the sale of the long-term bonds could be a problem. Reducing the duration to replicate a short-term instrument does not remove the problem that long-term instruments, which are still held, may have to be liquidated. What it does is convert the volatility of the instrument to that of a short-term instrument. This conversion in no way handles the liquidity problem. It simply means that given an interest rate change, the position will have the sensitivity of a short-term instrument.

In Exhibit 6-8, we illustrate a similar situation involving a pension fund that would like to shift the allocation of its portfolio from large-cap stock to mid-cap stock. With futures contracts available on indices of both the large-cap and mid-cap sectors, the fund can do this by selling futures on the large-cap index and buying futures on the mid-cap index. The results come very close to replicating what would happen if it undertook transactions in the actual stocks. The futures transactions, however, take place in a market with much greater liquidity and lower transaction costs.

EXHIBIT 6-8   Adjusting the Allocation between One Equity Class and Another

Scenario (30 April)

The pension fund of US Integrated Technology (USIT) holds $50 million of large-cap domestic equity. It would like to move $20 million from large-cap stocks to mid-cap stocks. The large-cap stocks have an average beta of 1.03. The desired beta of mid-cap stocks is 1.20. A futures contract on large-cap stocks has a price of $263,750 and a beta of 0.98. A futures contract on mid-cap stocks has a price of $216,500 and a beta of 1.14. The transaction will be initiated on 30 April and terminated on 29 May.

To distinguish the futures contracts, we use N_{Lf} and N_{Mf} as the number of large-cap and mid-cap futures contracts, f_L and f_M as the prices of large-cap and mid-cap futures contracts ($263,750 and $216,500, respectively), β_L and β_M as the betas of large-cap and mid-cap stocks (1.03 and 1.20, respectively), and β_{Lf} and β_{Mf} as the betas of the large-cap and mid-cap futures (0.98 and 1.14, respectively).

Action

USIT first wants to convert $20 million of stock to cash and then convert $20 million of cash into mid-cap stock. It can use large-cap futures to convert the beta from 1.03 to zero and then use mid-cap futures to convert the beta from 0 to 1.20.

To convert the large-cap stock to cash will require

$$N_{Lf} = \left(\frac{\beta_T - \beta_S}{\beta_f}\right)\left(\frac{S}{f}\right) = \left(\frac{0.0 - 1.03}{0.98}\right)\left(\frac{\$20,000,000}{\$263,750}\right) = -79.70$$

So USIT sells 80 large-cap futures contracts. At this point, it has changed the beta to zero. Now it uses mid-cap futures to convert the beta from 0.0 to 1.20:

$$N_{Mf} = \left(\frac{\beta_T - \beta_B}{\beta_f}\right)\left(\frac{B}{f}\right) = \left(\frac{1.20 - 0.0}{1.14}\right)\left(\frac{\$20,000,000}{\$216,500}\right) = 97.24$$

So USIT buys 97 mid-cap futures contracts.

Scenario (29 May)

Large-cap stocks increase by 2.47 percent, and the large-cap futures price increases to $269,948. Mid-cap stocks increase by 2.88 percent, and the mid-cap futures price increases to $222,432. The $50 million large-cap portfolio is now worth $50,000,000(1.0247) = $51,235,000.

Outcome and Analysis

The profit on the large-cap futures contracts is −80($269,948 − $263,750) = −$495,840. The profit on the mid-cap futures contracts is 97($222,432 − $216,500) = $575,404. The total value of the fund is, therefore, $51,235,000 − $495,840 + $575,404 = $51,314,564.

Had the transactions been executed by selling $20 million of large-cap stock and buying $20 million of mid-cap stock, the value of the large-cap stock would be $30,000,000(1.0247) = $30,741,000, and the value of the mid-cap stock would be $20,000,000(1.0288) = $20,576,000, for a total value of $30,741,000 + $20,576,000 = $51,317,000.

This amount produces a difference of $2,436 compared with making the allocation synthetically, an insignificant percentage of the original portfolio value. The difference comes from the fact that stocks do not always respond in the exact manner predicted by their betas and also that the number of futures contracts is rounded off.

PRACTICE PROBLEM 6

Q-Tech Advisors manages a portfolio consisting of $100 million, allocated 70 percent to stock at a beta of 1.05 and 30 percent to bonds at a modified duration of 5.5. As a tactical strategy, it would like to temporarily adjust the allocation to 60 percent stock and 40 percent bonds. Also, it would like to change the beta on the stock position from 1.05 to 1.00 and the modified duration from 5.5 to 5.0. It will use a stock index futures contract, which is priced at $280,000 and has a beta of 0.98, and a bond futures contract, which is priced at $125,000 and has an implied modified duration of 6.50. Assume cash has a duration of 0.25.

A. Determine how many stock index and bond futures contracts it should use and whether to go long or short.

B. At the horizon date, the stock portfolio has fallen by 3 percent and the bonds have risen by 1 percent. The stock index futures price is $272,160, and the bond futures price is $126,500. Determine the market value of the portfolio assuming the transactions specified in Part A are done, and compare it to the market value of the portfolio had the transactions been done in the securities themselves.

SOLUTIONS

A. To reduce the allocation from 70 percent stock ($70 million) and 30 percent bonds ($30 million) to 60 percent stock ($60 million) and 40 percent bonds ($40 million), Q-Tech must synthetically sell $10 million of stock and buy $10 million of bonds. First, assume that Q-Tech will sell $10 million of stock and leave the proceeds in cash. Doing so will require

$$N_{sf} = \left(\frac{0 - 1.05}{0.98}\right)\left(\frac{\$10,000,000}{\$280,000}\right) = -38.27$$

futures contracts. It should sell 38 contracts, which creates synthetic cash of $10 million. To buy $10 million of bonds, Q-Tech should buy

$$N_{bf} = \left(\frac{5.50 - 0.25}{6.50}\right)\left(\frac{\$10,000,000}{\$125,000}\right) = 64.62$$

futures contracts, which rounds to 65. This transaction allows Q-Tech to synthetically borrow $10 million (selling a stock futures contract is equivalent to borrowing cash) and buy $10 million of bonds. Because we have created synthetic cash and a synthetic loan, these amounts offset. Thus, at this point, having sold 38 stock index futures and bought 65 bond futures, Q-Tech has effectively sold $10 million of stock and bought $10 million of bonds. It has produced a synthetically re-allocated portfolio of $60 million of stock and $40 million of bonds.

Now it now needs to adjust the beta on the $60 million of stock to its target of 1.00. The number of futures contracts would, therefore, be

$$N_{sf} = \left(\frac{1.00 - 1.50}{0.98}\right)\left(\frac{\$60,000,000}{\$280,000}\right) = -10.93$$

So it should sell an additional 11 contracts. In total, it should sell 38 + 11 = 49 contracts.

To adjust the modified duration from 5.50 to its target of 5.00 on the $40 million of bonds, the number of futures contracts is

$$N_{bf} = \left(\frac{5 - 5.50}{6.50}\right)\left(\frac{\$40,000,000}{\$125,000}\right) = -24.62$$

So it should sell 25 contracts. In total, therefore, it should buy 65 − 25 = 40 contracts.

B. The value of the stock will be $70,000,000(1 − 0.03) = $67,900,000.
The profit on the stock index futures will be −49($272,160 − $280,000) = $384,160.
The total value of the stock position is therefore $67,900,000 + $384,160 = $68,284,160.
The value of the bonds will be $30,000,000(1.01) = $30,300,000.
The profit on the bond futures will be 40($126,500 − $125,000) = $60,000.
The total value of the bond position is, therefore, $30,300,000 + $60,000 = $30,360,000.
Therefore, the overall position is worth $68,284,160 + $30,360,000 = $98,644,160.
Had the transactions be done in the securities themselves, the stock would be worth $60,000,000(1 − 0.03) = $58,200,000. The bonds would be worth $40,000,000(1.01) = $40,400,000. The overall value of the portfolio would be $58,200,000 + $40,400,000 = $98,600,000, which is a difference of only $44,160 or 0.04 percent of the original value of the portfolio.

So far, we have looked only at allocating funds among different asset classes. In the next section, we place ourselves in the position that funds are not available to invest in any asset classes, but market opportunities are attractive. Futures contracts enable an investor to place itself in the market without yet having the actual cash in place.

4.2 PRE-INVESTING IN AN ASSET CLASS

In all the examples so far, the investor is already in the market and wants to either alter the position to a different asset allocation or get out of the market altogether. Now consider that the investor might not be in the market but wants to get into the market. The investor might not have the cash to invest at a time when opportunities are attractive. Futures contracts do not require a cash outlay but can be used to add exposure. We call this approach *pre-investing*.

An advisor to a mutual fund would like to pre-invest $10 million in cash that it will receive in three months. It would like to allocate this money to a position of 60 percent stock and 40 percent bonds. It can do this by taking long positions in stock index futures and bond futures. The trick is to establish the position at the appropriate beta and duration. This strategy is illustrated in Exhibit 6-9. We see that the result using futures is very close to what it would have been if the fund had actually had the money and invested it in stocks and bonds.

EXHIBIT 6-9 Pre-Investing in Asset Classes

Scenario (28 February)

Quantitative Mutual Funds Advisors (QMFA) uses modern analytical techniques to manage money for a number of mutual funds. QMFA is not necessarily an aggressive investor, but it does not like to be out of the market. QMFA has learned that it will receive an additional $10 million to invest. Although QMFA would like to receive the money now, the money is not available for three months. If it had the money now, QMFA would invest $6 million in stocks at an average beta of 1.08 and $4 million in bonds at a modified duration of 5.25. It believes the market outlook over the next three months is highly attractive. Therefore, QMFA would like to invest now, which it can do by trading stock and bond futures. An appropriate stock index futures contract is selling at $210,500 and has a beta of 0.97. An appropriate bond futures contract is selling for $115,750 and has an implied modified duration of 6.05. The current date is 28 February, and the money will be available on 31 May. The number of stock index futures contracts will be denoted as N_{sf}, and the number of bond futures contracts will be denoted as N_{bf}.

Action

QMFA wants to take a position in $6 million of stock index futures at a beta of 1.08. It currently has no position; hence, its beta is zero. The required number of stock index futures contracts to obtain this position is

$$N_{sf} = \left(\frac{\beta_T - \beta_S}{\beta_f}\right)\left(\frac{S}{f}\right) = \left(\frac{1.08 - 0.0}{0.97}\right)\left(\frac{\$6,000,000}{\$210,500}\right) = 31.74$$

So QMFA buys 32 stock index futures contracts.

To gain exposure at a duration of 5.25 on $4 million of bonds, the number of bond futures contracts is

$$N_{bf} = \left(\frac{MDUR_T - MDUR_B}{MDUR_f}\right)\left(\frac{B}{f}\right) = \left(\frac{5.25 - 0.0}{6.05}\right)\left(\frac{\$4,000,000}{\$115,750}\right) = 29.99$$

Thus, QMFA buys 30 bond futures contracts.

Scenario (31 May)

During this period, the stock increased by 2.2 percent and the bonds increased by 0.75 percent. The stock index futures price increased to $214,500, and the bond futures price increased to $116,734.

Outcome and Analysis

The profit on the stock index futures contracts is 32($214,500 − $210,500) = $128,000. The profit on the bond futures contracts is 30($116,734 − $115,750) = $29,520. The total profit is, therefore, $128,000 + $29,520 = $157,520.

 Had QMFA actually invested the money, the stock would have increased in value by $6,000,000(0.022) = $132,000, and the bonds would have increased in value by $4,000,000(0.0075) − $30,000, for a total increase in value of $132,000 + $30,000 = $162,000, which is relatively close to the futures gain of $157,520. The difference of $4,480 between this approach and the synthetic one is about 0.04 percent of the $10 million invested. This difference is due to the fact that stocks and bonds do not always respond in the manner predicted by their betas and durations and also that the number of futures contracts is rounded off.

 In a transaction like the one just described, the fund is effectively borrowing against the cash it will receive in the future by pre-investing. Recall that

 Long underlying + Short futures = Long risk-free bond

which means that

 Long underlying = Long risk-free bond + Long futures

In this example, however, the investor does not have the long position in the risk-free bond. That would require cash. We can remove the long risk-free bond in the equation above by offsetting it with a loan in which we borrow the cash. Hence, adding a loan to both sides gives[31]

 Long underlying + Loan = Long futures

An outright long position in futures is like a fully leveraged position in the underlying. So in this example, we have effectively borrowed against the cash we will receive in the future and invested in the underlying.

PRACTICE PROBLEM 7

Total Asset Strategies (TAST) specializes in a variety of risk management strategies, one of which is to enable investors to take positions in markets in anticipation of future transactions in securities. One of its popular strategies is to have the client invest when it does not have the money but will be receiving it later. One client interested in this strategy will receive $6 million at a later date but wants to proceed and take a position of $3 million in stock and $3 million in bonds. The desired stock beta is 1.0, and the desired bond duration is 6.2. A stock index futures contract is priced

---

[31] The right-hand side is long a risk-free bond and a loan of the same amount, which offset each other.

at $195,000 and has a beta of 0.97. A bond futures contract is priced at $110,000 and has an implied modified duration of 6.0.

A. Find the number of stock and bond futures contracts TAST should trade and whether it should go long or short.

B. At expiration, the stock has gone down by 5 percent, and the stock index futures price is down to $185,737.50. The bonds are up 2 percent, and the bond futures price is up to $112,090. Determine the value of the portfolio and compare it with what it would have been had the transactions been made in the actual securities.

SOLUTIONS

A. The approximate number of stock index futures is

$$\left(\frac{1.00 - 0.0}{0.97}\right)\left(\frac{\$3,000,000}{\$195,000}\right) = 15.86$$

So TAST should buy 16 contracts. The number of bond futures is

$$\left(\frac{6.2 - 0.0}{6.0}\right)\left(\frac{\$3,000,000}{\$110,000}\right) = 28.18$$

So it should buy 28 contracts.

B. The profit on the stock index futures is $16(\$185,737.50 - \$195,000) = -\$148,200$.

The profit on the bond futures is $28(\$112,090 - \$110,000) = \$58,520$.

The total profit is $-\$148,200 + \$58,520 = -\$89,680$, a loss of $89,680. Suppose TAST had invested directly. The stock would have been worth $\$3,000,000(1 - 0.05) = \$2,850,000$, and the bonds would have been worth $\$3,000,000(1.02) = \$3,060,000$, for a total value of $\$2,850,000 + \$3,060,000 = \$5,910,000$, or a loss of $90,000, which is about the same as the loss using only the futures.

When the cash is eventually received, the investor will close out the futures position and invest the cash. This transaction is equivalent to paying off this implicit loan. The investor will then be long the underlying.

We should remember that this position is certainly a speculative one. By taking a leveraged long position in the market, the investor is speculating that the market will perform well enough to cover the cost of borrowing. If this does not happen, the losses could be significant. But such is the nature of leveraged speculation with a specific horizon.

So far, all of the strategies we have examined have involved domestic transactions. We now take a look at how foreign currency derivatives can be used to handle common transactions faced in global commerce.

5   STRATEGIES AND APPLICATIONS FOR MANAGING FOREIGN CURRENCY RISK

The risk associated with changes in exchange rates between currencies directly affects many companies. Any company that engages in business with companies or customers in other countries is exposed to this risk. The volatility of exchange rates results in considerable uncertainty for companies that sell products in other countries as well as for those companies that buy products in other countries. Companies are affected not only by the exchange rate uncertainty itself but also by its effects on their ability to plan for the future. For example, consider a company with a foreign subsidiary. This subsidiary generates sales in the foreign currency that will eventually be converted back into its domestic currency. To implement a business plan that enables the company to establish a realistic target income, the company must not only predict its foreign sales, but it must also predict the exchange rate at which it will convert its foreign cash flows into domestic cash flows. The company may be an expert on whatever product it makes or service it provides and thus be in a good position to make reasonable forecasts of sales. But predicting foreign exchange rates with much confidence is extremely difficult, even for experts in the foreign exchange business. A company engaged in some other line of work can hardly expect to be able to predict foreign exchange rates very well. Hence, many such businesses choose to manage this kind of risk by locking in the exchange rate on future cash flows with the use of derivatives. This type of exchange rate risk is called *transaction exposure*.

In addition to the risk associated with foreign cash flows, exchange rate volatility also affects a company's accounting statements. When a company combines the balance sheets of foreign subsidiaries into a consolidated balance sheet for the entire company, the numbers from the balance sheets of its foreign subsidiaries must be converted into its domestic currency at an appropriate exchange rate. Hence, exchange rate risk manifests itself in this arena as well. This type of exchange rate risk is called *translation exposure*.

Finally, we should note that exchange rate uncertainty can also affect a company by making its products or services either more or less competitive with those of comparable foreign companies. This type of risk can affect any type of company, even if it does not sell its goods or services in foreign markets. For example, suppose the U.S. dollar is exceptionally strong. This condition makes U.S. products and services more expensive to non-U.S. residents and will lead to a reduction in travel to the United States. Hence, the owner of a hotel in the Disney World area, even though her cash flow is entirely denominated in dollars, will suffer a loss of sales when the dollar is strong because fewer non-U.S. residents will travel to the United States, visit Disney World, and stay in her hotel. Likewise, foreign travel will be cheaper for U.S. citizens, and more of them will visit foreign countries instead of Disney World.[32] This type of risk is called *economic exposure*.

In this book, we shall focus on managing the risk of transaction exposure. The management of translation exposure requires a greater focus on accounting than we can provide here. Managing economic exposure requires the forecasting of demand in light of competitive products and exchange rates, and we shall not address this risk in this book.

The management of a single cash flow that will have to be converted from one currency to another is generally done using forward contracts. Futures contracts tend to be too standardized to meet the needs of most companies. Futures are primarily used by dealers to manage their foreign exchange portfolios.[33] Therefore, in the two examples here, we use forward contracts to manage the risk of a single foreign cash flow.

5.1 MANAGING THE RISK OF A FOREIGN CURRENCY RECEIPT

When due to receive cash flows denominated in a foreign currency, companies can be viewed as being long the currency. They will convert the currency to their domestic currency and, hence, will be selling the foreign currency to obtain the domestic currency. If the domestic currency increases in value while the company is waiting to receive the cash flow, the domestic currency will be more expensive, and the company will receive fewer

---

[32] Even U.S. citizens who would never travel abroad would not increase their trips to Disney World because of the more favorable exchange rate.

[33] In some cases, single cash flows are managed using currency options, which we cover in Chapter 7. A series of foreign cash flows is usually managed using currency swaps, which we cover in Chapter 8.

units of the domestic currency for the given amount of foreign currency. Thus, being long the foreign currency, the company should consider selling the currency in the forward market by going short a currency forward contract.

Exhibit 6-10 illustrates the case of a company that anticipates the receipt of a future cash flow denominated in euros. By selling a forward contract on the amount of euros it expects to receive, the company locks in the exchange rate at which it will convert the euros. We assume the contract calls for actual delivery of the euros, as opposed to a cash settlement, so the company simply transfers the euros to the dealer, which sends the domestic currency to the company. If the transaction were structured to be settled in cash, the company would sell the euros on the market for the exchange rate at that time, S_T, and the forward contract would be cash settled for a payment of $-(S_T - F)$, where F is the rate agreed on at the start of the forward contract—in other words, the forward exchange rate. The net effect is that the company receives F, the forward rate for the euros.

EXHIBIT 6-10   Managing the Risk of a Foreign Currency Receipt

---

Scenario (15 August)
H-Tech Hardware, a U.S. company, sells its products in many countries. It recently received an order for some computer hardware from a major European government. The sale is denominated in euros and is in the amount of €50 million. H-Tech will be paid in euros; hence, it bears exchange rate risk. The current date is 15 August, and the euros will be received on 3 December.

Action
On 15 August, H-Tech decides to lock in the 3 December exchange rate by entering into a forward contract that obligates it to deliver €50 million and receive a rate of $0.877. H-Tech is effectively long the euro in its computer hardware sale, so a short position in the forward market is appropriate.

Scenario (3 December)
The exchange rate on this day is S_T, but as we shall see, this value is irrelevant for H-Tech because it is hedged.

Outcome and Analysis
The company receives its €50 million, delivers it to the dealer, and is paid $0.877 per euro for a total payment of €50,000,000($0.877) = $43,850,000. H-Tech thus pays the €50 million and receives $43.85 million, based on the rate locked in on 15 August.

5.2 MANAGING THE RISK OF A FOREIGN CURRENCY PAYMENT

In Exhibit 6-11, we see the opposite type of problem. A U.S. company is obligated to purchase a foreign currency at a later date. Because an increase in the exchange rate will hurt it, the U.S. company is effectively short the currency. Hence, to lock in the rate now, it needs to go long the forward contract. Regardless of the exchange rate at expiration, the company purchases the designated amount of currency at the forward rate agreed to in the contract now.

EXHIBIT 6-11   Managing the Risk of a Foreign Currency Payment

---

Scenario (2 March)
American Manufacturing Catalyst (AMC) is a U.S. company that occasionally makes steel and copper purchases from non-U.S. companies to meet unexpected demand that cannot be

filled through its domestic suppliers. On 2 March, AMC determines that it will need to buy a large quantity of steel from a Japanese company on 1 April. It has entered into a contract with the Japanese company to pay ¥900 million for the steel. At a current exchange rate of $0.0083 per yen, the purchase will currently cost ¥900,000,000($0.0083) = $7,470,000. AMC faces the risk of the yen strengthening.

Action
In its future steel purchase, AMC is effectively short yen, because it will need to purchase yen at a later date. Thus, a long forward contract is appropriate. AMC decides to lock in the exchange rate for 1 April by entering into a long forward contract on ¥900 million with a dealer. The forward rate is $0.008309. AMC will be obligated to purchase ¥900 million on 1 April and pay a rate of $0.008309.

Scenario (1 April)
The exchange rate for yen is S_T. As we shall see, this value is irrelevant for AMC, because it is hedged.

Outcome and Analysis
The company purchases ¥900 million from the dealer and pays $0.008309, for a total payment of ¥900,000,000($0.008309) = $7,478,100. This amount was known on 2 March. AMC gets the yen it needs and uses it to purchase the steel.

In Exhibit 6-10, a company agreed to accept a fixed amount of the foreign currency for the sale of its computer hardware. In Exhibit 6-11, a company agreed to pay a fixed amount of the foreign currency to acquire the steel. You may be wondering why in both cases the transaction was denominated in the foreign currency. In some cases, a company might be able to lock in the amount of currency in domestic units. It all depends on the relative bargaining power of the buyer and the seller and on how badly each wants to make the sale. Companies with the expertise to manage foreign exchange risk can use that expertise to offer contracts denominated in either currency to their counterparts on the other side of the transaction. For example, in the second case, suppose the Japanese company was willing to lock in the exchange rate using a forward contract with one of its derivatives dealers. Then the Japanese company could offer the U.S. company the contract in U.S. dollars. The ability to manage exchange rate risk and offer customers a price in either currency can be an attractive feature for a seller.

PRACTICE PROBLEM 8

Royal Tech Ltd. is a U.K. technology company that has recently acquired a U.S. subsidiary. The subsidiary has an underfunded pension fund, and Royal Tech has absorbed the subsidiary's employees into its own pension fund, bringing the U.S. subsidiary's defined benefit plan up to an adequate level of funding. Soon Royal Tech will be making its first payments to retired employees in the United States. Royal Tech is obligated to pay about $1.5 million to these retirees. It can easily set aside in risk-free bonds the amount of pounds it will need to make the payment, but it is concerned about the foreign currency risk in making the U.S. dollar payment. To manage this risk, Royal Tech is considering using a forward contract that has a contract rate of £0.60 per dollar.

    A. Determine how Royal Tech would eliminate this risk by identifying an appropriate forward transaction. Be sure to specify the notional principal and state whether to go long or short. What domestic transaction should it undertake?

    B. At expiration of the forward contract, the spot exchange rate is S_T. Explain what happens.

SOLUTIONS

    A. Royal Tech will need to come up with $1,500,000 and is obligated to buy dollars at a later date. It is thus short dollars. To have $1,500,000 secured at the forward contract expiration, Royal Tech would need to go long a forward contract on the dollar. With the forward rate equal to £0.60, the contract will need a notional principal of £900,000. So Royal Tech must set aside funds so that it will have £900,000 available when the forward contract expires. When it delivers the £900,000, it will receive £900,000(1/£0.60) = $1,500,000, where 1/£0.60 ≈ $1.67 is the dollar-per-pound forward rate.

    B. At expiration, it will not matter what the spot exchange rate is. Royal Tech will deliver £900,000 and receive $1,500,000.

5.3 MANAGING THE RISK OF A FOREIGN-MARKET ASSET PORTFOLIO

One of the dominant themes in the world of investments in the last 20 years has been the importance of diversifying internationally. The increasing globalization of commerce has created a greater willingness on the part of investors to think beyond domestic borders and add foreign securities to a portfolio.[34] Thus, more asset managers are holding or considering holding foreign stocks and bonds. An important consideration in making such a decision is the foreign currency risk. Should a manager accept this risk, hedge the foreign market risk and the foreign currency risk, or hedge only the foreign currency risk?

It is tempting to believe that the manager should accept the foreign market risk, using it to further diversify the portfolio, and hedge the foreign currency risk. In fact, many asset managers claim to do so. A closer look, however, reveals that it is virtually impossible to actually do this.

Consider a U.S. asset management firm that owns a portfolio currently invested in euro-denominated stock worth S_0, where S_0 is the current stock price in euros. The exchange rate is FX_0 dollars per euro. Therefore, the portfolio is currently worth $S_0(FX_0)$ in dollars. At a future time, t, the portfolio is worth S_t in euros and the exchange rate is FX_t. So the portfolio would then be worth $S_t(FX_t)$. The firm is long both the stock and the euro.

A forward contract on the euro would require the firm to deliver a certain number of euros and receive the forward rate, F. The number of euros to be delivered, however, would need to be specified in the contract. In this situation, the firm would end up delivering S_t euros. This amount is unknown at the time the forward contract is initiated. Thus, it would not be possible to know how many euros the firm would need to deliver.

Some companies manage this problem by estimating an expected future value of the portfolio. They enter into a hedge based on that expectation and adjust the hedge to accommodate any changes in expectations. Other companies hedge a minimum portfolio value. They estimate that it is unlikely the portfolio value will fall below a certain level and then sell a forward contract for a size based on this minimum value.[35] This approach leaves the

---

[34] Ironically, the increasing globalization of commerce has increased the correlation among the securities markets of various countries. With this higher correlation, the benefits of international diversification are much smaller.

[35] One way to assure a minimum value would be use a put option. We shall take up this strategy in Chapter 7.

companies hedged for a minimum value, but any increase in the value of the portfolio beyond the minimum would not be hedged. Therefore, any such gains could be wiped out by losses in the value of the currency.

So, with the exception of one special and complex case we discuss below, it is not possible to leave the local equity market return exposed and hedge the currency risk.[36] If the local market return is hedged, then it would be possible to hedge the currency risk. The hedge of the local market return would lock in the amount of the foreign currency that would be converted at the hedge termination date. Of course, the company can hedge the local market return and leave the currency risk unhedged. Or it can hedge neither.[37]

In Exhibit 6-12, we examine the two possibilities that can be executed: hedging the local market risk and hedging both the local market risk *and* the foreign currency risk. We first use futures on the foreign equity portfolio as though no currency risk existed. This transaction attempts to lock in the future value of the portfolio. This locked-in return should be close to the foreign risk-free rate. If we also choose to hedge the currency risk, we then know that the future value of the portfolio will tell us the number of units of the foreign currency that we shall have available to convert to domestic currency at the hedge termination date. Then we would know the amount of notional principal to use in a forward contract to hedge the exchange rate risk.

EXHIBIT 6-12   Managing the Risk of a Foreign-Currency-Denominated Asset Portfolio

---

Scenario (31 December)

AZ Asset Management is a U.S. firm that invests money for wealthy individual investors. Concerned that it does not know how to manage foreign currency risk, so far AZ has invested only in U.S. markets. Recently, it began learning about managing currency risk and would like to begin investing in foreign markets with a small position worth €10 million. The proposed portfolio has a beta of 1.10. AZ is considering either hedging the European equity market return and leaving the currency risk unhedged, or hedging the currency risk as well as the European equity market return. If it purchases the €10 million portfolio, it will put this hedge in place on 31 December and plans to leave the position open until 31 December of the following year.

For hedging the European equity market risk, it will use a stock index futures contract on a euro-denominated stock index. This contract is priced at €120,000 and has a beta of 0.95. If it hedges the currency risk, it will use a dollar-denominated forward contract on the euro. That contract has a price of $0.815 and can have any notional principal that the parties agree on at the start. The current spot exchange rate is $0.80. The foreign risk-free rate is 4 percent, which is stated as an annually compounded rate. The domestic risk-free rate is 6 percent.

Action

Hedging the equity market risk only: To eliminate the risk on the portfolio of stock that has a beta of 1.10 would require

$$N_f = \left(\frac{0 - 1.10}{0.95} \right) \left(\frac{10,000,000}{120,000} \right) = -96.49$$

contracts. This amount would be rounded to 96, so AZ would sell 96 contracts.

---

[36] The foreign equity market return is often referred to as the local market return, a term we shall use henceforth.

[37] In fact, some compelling arguments exist for hedging neither. The currency risk can be unrelated to the domestic market risk, thereby offering some further diversifying risk-reduction possibilities.

Hedging the equity market risk and the currency risk: Again, AZ would sell 96 stock index futures contracts. It would enter into a forward contract to lock in the exchange rate on a certain amount of euros on 31 December. The question is, how many euros will it have? If the futures contract hedges the stock portfolio, it should earn the foreign risk-free rate. Thus, the portfolio should be worth €10,000,000(1.04) = €10,400,000. So, AZ expects to have €10,400,000 on the following 31 December and will convert this amount back to dollars. So the notional principal on the forward contract should be €10.4 million. Note that the starting portfolio value in dollars is €10,000,000($0.80) = $8,000,000.

Scenario (31 December of the following year)

During the year, the European stock market went down 4.55 percent. Given the portfolio beta of 1.10, it declines by 4.55(1.10) = 5 percent. The portfolio is now worth €10,000,000(1 − 0.05) = €9,500,000. The exchange rate fell to $0.785, and the futures price fell to €110,600.

Outcome and Analysis

If nothing is hedged: The portfolio is converted to dollars at $0.785 and is worth €9,500,000(0.785) = $7,457,500. This amount represents a loss of 6.8 percent over the initial value of $8,000,000.

If only the European stock market is hedged: The profit on the futures would be −96(€110,600 − €120,000) = €902,400. Adding this amount to the value of the portfolio gives a value of €9,500,000 + €902,400 = €10,402,400, which is an increase in value of 4.02 percent, or approximately the foreign risk-free rate, as it should be. This amount is converted to dollars to obtain €10,402,400($0.785) = $8,165,884, a gain of 2.07 percent.

If the European stock market and the currency risk are both hedged: AZ sold €10.4 million of euros in the forward market at $0.815. The contract will settle in cash and show a profit of €10,400,000($0.785 − $0.815) = $312,000. This leaves the overall portfolio value at $8,165,884 + $312,000 = $8,477,884, a gain of 5.97 percent, or approximately the domestic risk-free rate.

In this case, the foreign stock market went down *and* the foreign currency went down. Without the hedge, the loss was almost 7 percent. With the foreign stock market hedge, the loss turns into a gain of 2 percent. With the currency hedge added, the loss becomes a gain of almost 6 percent. Of course, different outcomes could occur. Gains from a stronger foreign stock market and a stronger currency would be lost if the company had made these same hedges.

Note, however, that once AZ hedges the foreign market return, it can expect to earn only the foreign risk-free rate. If it hedges the foreign market return and the exchange rate, it can expect to earn only its domestic risk-free rate. Therefore, neither strategy makes much sense for the long run. In the short run, however, this strategy can be a good tactic for investors who are already in foreign markets and who wish to temporarily take a more defensive position without liquidating the portfolio and converting it to cash.

PRACTICE PROBLEM 9

FCA Managers (FCAM) is a U.S. asset management firm. Among its asset classes is a portfolio of Swiss stocks worth SF10 million, which has a beta of 1.00. The spot exchange rate is $0.75, the Swiss interest rate is 5 percent, and the U.S. interest rate is 6 percent. Both of these interest rates are compounded in the LIBOR manner: Rate × (Days/360). These rates are consistent with a six-month forward rate of $0.7537. FCAM is considering hedging the local market return on the portfolio and possibly hedging the exchange rate risk for a six-month period. A futures contract on the Swiss market is priced at SF300,000 and has a beta of 0.90.

A. What futures position should FCAM take to hedge the Swiss market return? What return could it expect?

B. Assuming that it hedges the Swiss market return, how could it hedge the exchange rate risk as well, and what return could it expect?

SOLUTIONS

A. To hedge the Swiss local market return, the number of futures contracts is

$$N_f = \left(\frac{0 - 1.00}{0.90}\right)\left(\frac{SF10,000,000}{SF300,000}\right) = -37.04$$

So FCAM should sell 37 contracts. Because the portfolio is perfectly hedged, its return should be the Swiss risk-free rate of 5 percent.

B. If hedged, the Swiss portfolio should grow to a value of SF10,000,000[1 + 0.05(180/360)] = SF10,250,000.

FCAM could hedge this amount with a forward contract with this much notional principal. If the portfolio is hedged, it will convert to a value of SF10,250,000($0.7537) = $7,725,425.

In dollars, the portfolio was originally worth SF10,000,000($0.75) = $7,500,000. Thus, the return is $\dfrac{\$7,725,425}{\$7,500,000} - 1 \approx 0.03$, which is the U.S. risk-free rate for six months.

We see that if only the foreign stock market return is hedged, the portfolio return is the foreign risk-free rate before converting to the domestic currency. If both the foreign stock market and the exchange rate risk are hedged, the return equals the domestic risk-free rate.

As a temporary and tactical strategy, hedging one or both risks can make sense. There are certainly periods when one might be particularly concerned about these risks and might wish to eliminate them. Executing this sort of strategy can be much easier than selling all of the foreign stocks and possibly converting the proceeds into domestic currency. But in the long run, a strategy of investing in foreign markets, hedging that risk, and hedging the exchange rate risk hardly makes much sense.

6 FUTURES OR FORWARDS?

As we have seen, numerous opportunities and strategies exist for managing risk using futures and forwards. We have largely ignored the issue of which instrument—futures or forwards—is better. Some types of hedges are almost always executed using futures, and some are almost always executed using forwards. Why the preference for one over the other? First, let us recall the primary differences between the two:

- Futures contracts are standardized, with all terms except for the price set by the futures exchange. Forward contracts are customized. The two parties set the terms according to their needs.

- Futures contracts are guaranteed by the clearinghouse against default. Forward contracts subject each party to the possibility of default by the other party.

- Futures contracts require margin deposits and the daily settlement of gains and losses. Forward contracts pay off the full value of the contract at expiration. Some participants in forward contracts agree prior to expiration to use margin deposits and occasional settlements to reduce the default risk.

- Futures contracts are regulated by federal authorities. Forward contracts are essentially unregulated.

- Futures contracts are conducted in a public arena, the futures exchange, and are reported to the exchanges and the regulatory authority. Forward contracts are conducted privately, and individual transactions are not generally reported to the public or regulators.

Risks that are associated with very specific dates, such as when interest rates are reset on a loan, usually require forward contracts. Thus, we used an FRA to lock in the rate on a loan. That rate is set on a specific day. A futures contract has specific expirations that may not correspond to the day on which the rate is reset. Although it is possible to use sophisticated models and software to compensate for this problem, typical borrowers do not usually possess the expertise to do so. It is much easier for them to use an FRA.

Oddly enough, however, the risk of most bond portfolios is managed using Treasury bond futures. Those portfolios have horizon dates for which the company is attempting to lock in values. But usually rates are not being reset on that date, and the hedge does not need to be perfect. Often there is flexibility with respect to the horizon date. Treasury bond futures work reasonably well for these investors. Likewise, the risk of equity portfolios tends to be managed with stock index futures. Even though the offsetting of risks is not precise, that is not a necessity. Equity and debt portfolio managers usually need only satisfactory protection against market declines. Nonetheless, in some cases equity and debt portfolio managers use over-the-counter instruments such as forward contracts. In fact, sometimes a portfolio manager will ask a derivatives dealer to write a forward contract on a specific portfolio. This approach is more costly than using futures and provides a better hedge, but, as noted, a perfect hedge is usually not needed. In practice, portfolio managers have traded off the costs of customized hedges with the costs of using standardized futures contracts and have found the latter to be preferable.[38]

Forward contracts are the preferred vehicle for the risk management of foreign currency. This preference partly reflects the deep liquidity in the forward market, which has been around longer than the futures market. Moreover, much of this trading is undertaken by corporations managing the risk of either the issuance of a bond or the inflows and outcomes of specific currency transactions, in which case the precision provided by customized transactions is preferred.

Nevertheless, one might wonder why certain contracts do not die out. Recall that most corporations do not use the Eurodollar futures market to hedge their floating-rate loans. Yet the Eurodollar futures contract is one of the most active of all futures contracts in the world. Where does this volume come from? It is from the dealers in swaps, options, and FRAs. When they enter into transactions with end users in which the underlying rate is LIBOR, they must manage the risk they have assumed, and they must do so very quickly. They cannot afford to leave their positions exposed for long. It is rarely possible for them to simply pick up the phone and find another customer to take the opposite side of the transaction. A corporate client with the exact opposite needs at the exact same time as some other end user would be rare. Therefore, dealers need to execute offsetting trans-

---

[38] Portfolio managers do use swaps on occasion, as we cover in Chapter 8.

actions very quickly. There is no better place to do this than in the Eurodollar futures markets, with its extremely deep liquidity. These dealer companies have sophisticated analysts and software and are able to manage the risk caused by such problems as the futures contract expiring on one day and the payoffs on the FRAs being set on another day. Thus, these risks can be more effectively measured and managed by dealers than by end users.

As we have emphasized, futures contracts require margin deposits and the daily settling of gains and losses. This process causes some administrative problems because money must be deposited into a futures account and cash flows must be managed on a daily basis. When futures brokers call for more money to cover losses, companies using futures contracts must send cash or very liquid securities. Although the brokers may be generating value on the other side of a hedge transaction, that value may not produce actual cash.[39] On the other hand, forward transactions, while not necessarily requiring margin deposits, generate concerns over whether the counterparty will be able to pay at expiration. Of course, those concerns lead some counterparties to require margins and periodic settlements.

Although forward contracts are essentially unregulated while futures contracts are heavily regulated, this factor is not usually a major consideration in deciding which type of contract to use. In some cases, however, regulation prevents use of a specific contract. For example, a country might prohibit foreign futures exchanges from offering their products in its markets. There would probably be no such prohibition on forward contracts.[40] In some cases, regulation prevents or delays usage of certain futures products, making it possible for innovative companies that can create forward products to offer them ahead of the comparable products of futures exchanges. The futures exchanges claim this is unfair by making it more difficult for them to compete with forward markets in providing risk management products.

We also noted that futures contracts are public transactions, whereas forward contracts are private transactions. This privacy characteristic can cause a company to prefer a forward transaction if it does not want others, such as traders on the futures exchange, to know its views.

7 FINAL COMMENTS

A few points are worth repeating. Because they can be somewhat unstable, betas and durations are difficult to measure, even under the best of circumstances. Even when no derivatives transactions are undertaken, the values believed to be the betas and durations may not truly turn out to reflect the sensitivities of stocks and bonds to the underlying sources of risk. Therefore, if derivatives transactions do not work out to provide the exact hedging results expected, users should not necessarily blame derivatives. If, however, speculative long (short) positions are added to an otherwise long position, risk should increase (decrease), although the exact amount of the increase (decrease) cannot be known for sure

---

[39] Consider, for example, a company that sells futures contracts to hedge the value of a bond portfolio. Suppose interest rates fall, the bond portfolio rises, and the futures price also rises. Losses will be incurred on the futures contracts and additional margin deposits will be required. The bond portfolio has increased in value, but it may not be practical to liquidate the portfolio to generate the necessary cash.

[40] In some less developed but highly regulated countries, private financial transactions such as forward contracts can be prohibited.

in advance.[41] Derivatives should not be maligned for their speculative use when there are valuable hedging uses.

We have mentioned that transaction costs are a major consideration in the use of derivatives, and this is clearly the case with futures and forwards. By some reports, transactions costs for stock index derivatives are approximately 95 percent lower than for stock indices.[42] Indeed, one of the major reasons that derivatives exist is that they provide a means of trading at lower transaction costs. To survive as risk management products, derivatives need to be much less expensive than the value of the underlying instruments. There are almost no situations in which transacting in the underlying securities would be preferable to using derivatives on a transaction-cost basis, when taking a position for a specified short horizon.

Transacting in futures and forwards also has a major advantage of being less disruptive to the portfolio and its managers. For example, the asset classes of many portfolios are managed by different persons or firms. If the manager of the overall portfolio wants to change the risk of certain asset classes or alter the allocations between asset classes, he can do so using derivatives. Instead of telling one manager that she must sell securities and another manager that he must buy securities, the portfolio manager can use derivatives to reduce the allocation to one class and increase the allocation to the other. The asset class managers need not even know that the overall asset allocation has been changed. They can concentrate on doing the best they can within their respective areas of responsibility.

In the matter of liquidity, however, futures and forwards do not always offer the advantages often attributed to them. They require less capital to trade than the underlying securities, but they are not immune to liquidity problems. Nowhere is this concern more evident than in using a futures contract that expires a long time from the present. The greatest liquidity in the futures markets is in the shortest expirations. Although there may be futures contracts available with long-term expirations, their liquidity is much lower. Many forward markets are very liquid, but others may not be. High liquidity should not automatically be assumed of all derivatives, although in general, derivatives are more liquid than the underlying securities.

Many organizations are not permitted to use futures or forwards. Futures and forwards are fully leveraged positions, because they essentially require no equity. Some companies might have a policy against fully leveraged positions but might permit options, which are not fully leveraged. Loss potential is much greater on purchased or sold futures or forwards, whereas losses are capped on purchased options. Some organizations, however, permit futures and forwards but prohibit options. Other organizations might prohibit credit-risky instruments, such as forwards and over-the-counter options, but permit credit-risk-free instruments, such as futures and exchange-listed options. These restrictions, although sometimes misguided, are realistic constraints that must be considered when deciding how to manage risk.

In conclusion, futures and forward contracts are both alike and different. On some occasions, one is preferred over the other. Both types of contracts have their niches. The

---

[41] We use the expression "should increase (decrease)" to reflect the fact that some other factors could cause perverse results. We previously mentioned call features and credit risk of such assets as corporate and municipal bonds that could result in a bond price not moving in the same direction as a move in the general level of bond prices. A poorly diversified stock portfolio could move opposite to the market, thereby suggesting a negative beta that is really only diversifiable risk. We assume that these situations are rare or that their likelihood and consequences have been properly assessed by risk managers.

[42] These statements are based on trading all individual stocks that make up an index. Trading through exchange-traded funds would reduce some of these stock trading costs.

most important point they have in common is that they have zero value at the start and offer linear payoffs, meaning that no one "invests" any money in either type of contract at the start, but the cost is paid for by the willingness to give up gains and incur losses resulting from movements in the underlying. As we described in Chapter 5, options, which require a cash investment at the start, allow a party to capture favorable movements in the underlying while avoiding unfavorable movements. This type of payoff is nonlinear. In some cases, options will be preferred to other types of derivatives. We now turn to an examination of option strategies and applications in the next chapter.

KEY POINTS

- A borrower can lock in the rate that will be set at a future date on a single-payment loan by entering into a long position in an FRA. The FRA obligates the borrower to make a fixed interest payment and receive a floating interest payment, thereby protecting the borrower if the loan rate is higher than the fixed rate in the FRA but also eliminating gains if the loan rate is lower than the fixed rate in the FRA.

- The duration of a bond futures contract is determined as the duration of the bond underlying the futures contract as of the futures expiration, based on the yield of the bond underlying the futures contract. The modified duration is obtained by dividing the duration by 1 plus the yield. The duration of a futures contract is implied by these factors and is called the implied (modified) duration.

- The implied yield of a futures contract is the yield implied by the futures price on the bond underlying the futures contract as of the futures expiration.

- The yield beta is the sensitivity of the yield on a bond portfolio relative to the implied yield on the futures contract.

- The number of bond futures contracts required to change the duration of a bond portfolio is based on the ratio of the market value of the bonds to the futures price multiplied by the difference between the target or desired modified duration and the actual modified duration, divided by the implied modified duration of the futures.

- The actual adjusted duration of a bond portfolio may not equal the desired duration for a number of reasons, including that the yield beta may be inaccurate or unstable or the bonds could contain call features or default risk. In addition, duration is a measure of instantaneous risk and may not accurately capture the risk over a long horizon without frequent portfolio adjustments.

- The number of equity futures contracts required to change the beta of an equity portfolio is based on the ratio of the market value of the stock to the futures price times the difference between the target or desired beta and the actual beta, divided by the beta of the futures.

- A long position in stock is equivalent to a long position in futures and a long position in a risk-free bond; therefore, it is possible to synthetically create a long position in stock by buying futures on stock and a risk-free bond. This process is called equitizing cash and can be used to create a synthetic stock index fund.

- A long position in cash is equivalent to a long position in stock and a short position in stock futures. Therefore, it is possible to synthetically create a long position in cash by buying stock and selling futures.

- The allocation of a portfolio between equity and debt can be adjusted using stock index and bond futures. Buy futures to increase the allocation to an asset class, and sell futures to decrease the allocation to an asset class.

- The allocation of a bond portfolio between cash and high-duration bonds can be adjusted by using bond futures. Sell futures to increase the allocation to cash, and buy futures to increase the allocation to long-term bonds.

- The allocation of an equity portfolio among different equity sectors can be adjusted by using stock index futures. Sell futures on an index representing one sector to decrease the allocation to that sector, and buy futures on an index representing another sector to increase the allocation to that sector.

- A portfolio manager can buy bond or stock index futures to take a position in an asset class without having cash to actually invest in the asset class. This type of strategy is sometimes used in anticipation of the receipt of a sum of cash at a later date, which will then be invested in the asset class and the futures position will be closed.

- Transaction exposure is the risk associated with a foreign exchange rate on a specific business transaction such as a purchase or sale. Translation exposure is the risk associated with the conversion of foreign financial statements into domestic currency. Economic exposure is the risk associated with changes in the relative attractiveness of products and services offered for sale, arising out of the competitive effects of changes in exchange rates.

- The risk of a future foreign currency receipt can be eliminated by selling a forward contract on the currency. This transaction locks in the rate at which the foreign currency will be converted to the domestic currency.

- The risk of a future foreign currency payment can be eliminated by buying a forward contract on the currency. This transaction locks in the rate at which the domestic currency will be converted to the foreign currency.

- It is not possible to invest in a foreign equity market and precisely hedge the currency risk only. To hedge the currency risk, one must know the exact amount of foreign currency that will be available at a future date. Without locking in the equity return, it is not possible to know how much foreign currency will be available.

- It is possible to hedge the foreign equity market return and accept the exchange rate risk or hedge the foreign equity market return *and* hedge the exchange rate risk. By hedging the equity market return, one would know the proper amount of currency that would be available at a later date and could use a futures or forward contract to hedge the currency risk. The equity return, however, would equal the risk-free rate.

- Forward contracts are usually preferred over futures contracts when the risk is related to an event on a specific date, such as an interest rate reset. Forward contracts on foreign currency are usually preferred over futures contracts, primarily because of the liquidity of the market. Futures contracts require margins and daily settlements but are guaranteed against credit losses and may be preferred when credit concerns are an issue. Either contract may be preferred or required if there are restrictions on the use of the other. Dealers use both instruments in managing their risk, occasionally preferring one instrument and sometimes preferring the other. Forward contracts are preferred if privacy is important.

- Futures and forwards, as well as virtually all derivatives, have an advantage over transactions in the actual instruments by virtue of their significantly lower transaction costs. They also allow a portfolio manager to make changes in the risk of certain asset classes or the allocation among asset classes without disturbing the asset class or classes themselves. This feature allows the asset class managers to concentrate on their respective asset classes without being concerned about buying and selling to execute risk-altering changes or asset allocation changes.

- Although futures and forwards tend to be more liquid than their underlying assets, they are not always highly liquid. Therefore, it cannot always be assumed that futures and forwards can solve liquidity problems.

PROBLEMS

1. EaseCorp plans to borrow $50,000,000 in 25 days. The loan will have a maturity of 270 days and carry a rate of LIBOR plus 125 basis points. The company is concerned that interest rates will rise, so in order to lock in the borrowing rate, it decides to purchase an FRA at a rate of 6.75 percent. Demonstrate that the effective cost of the loan is approximately 8 percent if 270-day LIBOR in 25 days is 8.25 percent.

2. A bank has committed to lend $25,000,000 to a corporate borrower in 30 days. The loan will mature in 180 days and carries a rate of LIBOR plus 150 basis points. The bank is concerned that interest rates will fall, and in order to lock in the lending rate, it decides to short an FRA with a rate of 5.5 percent. Determine the effective rate on the loan if 180-day LIBOR in 30 days is 3.25 percent.

3. A $500 million bond portfolio currently has a modified duration of 12.5. The portfolio manager wishes to reduce the modified duration of the bond portfolio to 8.0 by using a futures contract priced at $105,250. The futures contract has an implied modified duration of 9.25. The portfolio manager has estimated that the yield on the bond portfolio is about 8 percent more volatile than the implied yield on the futures contract.
   A. Indicate whether the portfolio manager should enter a short or long futures position.
   B. Calculate the number of contracts needed to change the duration of the bond portfolio.
   C. Assume that on the horizon date, the yield on the bond portfolio has declined by 50 basis points and the portfolio value has increased by $31,343,750. The implied yield on futures has decreased by 46 basis points, and the futures contract is priced at $109,742. Calculate the overall gain on the position (bond plus futures). Determine the *ex post* duration with and without the futures transaction.

4. A $200 million bond portfolio currently has a modified duration of 6.53. The portfolio manager wishes to increase the modified duration of the bond portfolio to 9.50 by using a futures contract priced at $95,650. The futures contract has an implied modified duration of 12.65. The portfolio manager has estimated that the yield on the bond portfolio is about 12 percent more volatile than the implied yield on the futures contract.
   A. Indicate whether the portfolio manager should enter a short or long futures position.
   B. Calculate the number of contracts needed to change the duration of the bond portfolio.
   C. Assume that on the horizon date, the yield on the bond portfolio has increased by 30 basis points and the portfolio value has decreased by $3,929,754. The implied yield on futures has increased by 30 basis points, and the futures contract is priced at $92,616. Calculate the overall gain on the position (bond plus futures). Determine the *ex post* duration with and without the futures transaction.

5. An investment management firm wishes to increase the beta for one of its portfolios under management from 0.95 to 1.20 for a three-month period. The portfolio has a market value of $175,000,000. The investment firm plans to use a futures contract priced at $105,790 in order to adjust the portfolio beta. The futures contract has a beta of 0.98.
   A. Calculate the number of futures contracts that should be bought or sold to achieve an increase in the portfolio beta.
   B. At the end of three months, the overall equity market is up 5.5 percent. The stock portfolio under management is up 5.1 percent. The futures contract is priced at

$111,500. Calculate the value of the overall position and the effective beta of the portfolio.

6. A pension fund manager wishes to reduce the beta of the pension portfolio's small-cap component from 0.90 to 0.80 for a period of six months. The small-cap portfolio has a market value of $485,000,000. The pension fund manager plans to use a futures contract priced at $249,000 in order to adjust the portfolio beta. The futures contract has a beta of 0.93.

   A. Calculate the number of futures contracts that should be bought or sold to achieve a change in the portfolio beta.

   B. At the end of six months, the overall equity market is down 8.65 percent. The small-cap portfolio is down 7.75 percent. The futures contract is down 8.05 percent and is priced at $228,956. Calculate the value of the overall position and the effective beta of the portfolio.

7. Consider an asset manager who wishes to create a fund with exposure to the Russell 2000 stock index. The initial amount to be invested is $300,000,000. The fund will be constructed using the Russell 2000 Index futures contract, priced at 498.30 with a $500 multiplier. The contract expires in three months. The underlying index has a dividend yield of 0.75 percent, and the risk-free rate is 2.35 percent per year.

   A. Indicate how the money manager would go about constructing this synthetic index using futures.

   B. Assume that at expiration, the Russell 2000 is at 594.65. Show how the synthetic position produces the same result as investment in the actual stock index.

8. A money manager wishes to create a fund with exposure to the Nikkei 225 stock average. The initial amount to be invested is $650,000,000. The fund will be constructed using the Nikkei 225 futures contract, priced at 11,930 with a $5 multiplier. The contract expires in three months. The underlying index has a dividend yield of 1.25 percent, and the risk-free rate is 3.35 percent per year.

   A. Indicate how the money manager would go about constructing this synthetic index using futures.

   B. Assume that at expiration, the Nikkei 225 is at S_T. Show how the synthetic position produces the same result as investment in the actual stock index.

9. An investment management firm has a client who would like to temporarily reduce his exposure to equities by converting a $25 million equity position to cash for a period of four months. The client would like this reduction to take place without liquidating his equity position. The investment management firm plans to create a synthetic cash position using an equity futures contract. This futures contract is priced at 1170.10, has a multiplier of $250, and expires in four months. The dividend yield on the underlying index is 1.25 percent, and the risk-free rate is 2.75 percent.

   A. Calculate the number of futures contracts required to create synthetic cash.

   B. Determine the effective amount of money committed to this risk-free transaction and the effective number of units of the stock index that are converted to cash.

   C. Assume that the stock index is at 1031 when the futures contract expires. Show how this strategy is equivalent to investing the risk-free asset, cash.

10. An equity portfolio manager currently has a $950 million equity position in the technology sector. He wants to convert this equity position to cash for a period of six months, without liquidating his holdings. An equity futures contract that expires in six months is priced at 1564 and has a multiplier of $100. The dividend yield on the underlying index is 0.45 percent. The risk-free rate is 5.75 percent.

   A. Calculate the number of futures contracts required to create synthetic cash.

    B. Determine the effective amount of money committed to the risk-free asset and the effective number of units of the stock index that are converted to cash.

    C. Assume that the stock index is at 1735 when the futures contract expires. Show how this strategy produces an outcome equivalent to investing in cash at the beginning of the six-month period.

11. Consider a portfolio with a 65 percent allocation to stocks and 35 percent to bonds. The portfolio has a market value of $200 million. The beta of the stock position is 1.15, and the modified duration of the bond position is 6.75. The portfolio manager wishes to increase the stock allocation to 85 percent and reduce the bond allocation to 15 percent for a period of six months. In addition to altering asset allocations, the manager would also like to increase the beta on the stock position to 1.20 and increase the modified duration of the bonds to 8.25. Assume that the modified duration of cash equivalents is 0.25. A stock index futures contract that expires in six months is priced at $157,500 and has a beta of 0.95. A bond futures contract that expires in six months is priced at $109,000 and has an implied modified duration of 5.25. The stock futures contract has a multiplier of one.

    A. Show how the portfolio manager can achieve his goals by using stock index and bond futures. Indicate the number of contracts and whether the manager should go long or short.

    B. After six months, the stock portfolio is up 5 percent and bonds are up 1.35 percent. The stock futures price is $164,005 and the bond futures price is $110,145. Compare the market value of the portfolio in which the allocation is adjusted using futures to the market value of the portfolio in which the allocation is adjusted by directly trading stocks and bonds.

12. A fixed income money manager has a bond portfolio with a 70 percent allocation to long-term bonds and a 30 percent allocation to short-term bonds. The portfolio is currently valued at $75 million. The manager wishes to reduce the long-term bonds allocation to 55 percent and increase the short-term bonds allocation to 45 percent for a period of three months. The modified duration of the long-term bonds is 7.5 and of the short-term bonds is 4.5. A bond futures contract that expires in three months is priced at $95,750 and has a modified duration of 6.25. Assume that the modified duration of cash equivalents is 0.25. Also assume that interest rates that drive long-term and short-term bond prices have a yield beta of 1 with respect to interest rates that drive the bond futures market.

    A. Show how the manager can achieve his goals by using bond futures. Indicate the number of contracts and whether the manager should go long or short.

    B. After three months, the short-term bonds are down 5.63 percent and long-term bonds are down 9.38 percent. The bond futures price is $88,270. Compare the market value of the portfolio using futures to adjust the allocation with the market value of the same portfolio using direct bond trading to adjust the allocation.

13. A portfolio manager has an equity portfolio with a 60 percent allocation to small-cap stocks and a 40 percent allocation to large-cap stocks. The portfolio is currently valued at $150 million. The manager wishes to reduce the small-cap allocation to 45 percent and increase the large-cap allocation to 55 percent for a period of nine months. The large-cap beta is 1.15, and the small-cap beta is 1.25. A small-cap futures contract that expires in nine months is priced at $195,750 and has a beta of 1.12. A large-cap futures contract that expires in nine months is priced at $215,570 and has a beta of 0.92. Assume that both contracts have multipliers of 1.

    A. Show how the manager can achieve the reallocation using stock index futures. Indicate the number of contracts and whether the manager should go long or short.

B. After nine months, the large-cap stocks are up 4.75 percent and small-cap stocks are up 6.25 percent. The large-cap futures price is $223,762, and the small-cap futures price is $206,712. Compare the market value of the portfolio using futures to adjust the allocation with the market value of the same portfolio using direct stock trading to adjust the allocation.

14. Consider a portfolio with a 65 percent allocation to stocks and 35 percent to bonds. The portfolio has a market value of $750 million. The beta of the stock position is 1.20, and the modified duration of the bond position is 7.65. The portfolio manager wishes to decrease the stock allocation to 45 percent and increase the bond allocation to 55 percent for a period of six months. Assume that the modified duration of cash equivalents is 0.25. The portfolio manager intends to use a stock index futures contract, which is priced at $272,500 and has a beta of 0.90, and a bond futures contract, which is priced at $139,120 and has an implied modified duration of 5.35. The stock futures contract has a multiplier of 1.

   A. Show how the portfolio manager can achieve her goals by using stock index and bond futures. Indicate the number of contracts and whether the manager should go long or short.

   B. After six months, the stock portfolio is down 5 percent and bonds are down 1.75 percent. The stock futures price is $262,280, and the bond futures price is $137,420. Compare the market value of the portfolio using futures to adjust the allocation with the market value of the same portfolio using direct stock and bond trading to adjust the allocation.

15. A pension fund manager expects to receive a cash inflow of $50,000,000 in three months and wants to use futures contracts to take a $17,500,000 synthetic position in stocks and $32,500,000 in bonds today. The stock would have a beta of 1.15 and the bonds a modified duration of 7.65. A stock index futures contract with a beta of 0.93 is priced at $175,210. A bond futures contract with a modified duration of 5.65 is priced at $95,750.

   A. Calculate the number of stock and bond futures contracts the fund manager would have to trade in order to synthetically take the desired position in stock and bonds today. Indicate whether the futures positions are long or short.

   B. When the futures contracts expire in three months, stocks have declined by 5.4 percent and bonds have declined by 3.06 percent. Stock index futures are priced at $167,559, and bond futures are priced at $93,586. Show that profits on the futures positions are essentially the same as the change in the value of stocks and bonds during the three-month period.

16. Consider a fund manager who expects to receive a cash inflow of $30,000,000 in two months. The manager wishes to use futures contracts to take a $21,000,000 synthetic position in stocks and $9,000,000 in bonds today. The stock would have a beta of 1.25 and the bonds a modified duration of 6.56. A stock index futures contract with a beta of 0.96 is priced at $225,130. A bond futures contract with a modified duration of 7.25 is priced at $105,120.

   A. Calculate the number of stock and bond futures contracts the fund manager would have to trade in order to synthetically take the desired position in stock and bonds today. Indicate whether the futures positions are long or short.

   B. When the futures contracts expire in two months, stocks have risen by 3.75 percent and bonds have declined by 2.3 percent. Stock index futures are priced at $231,614, and bond futures are priced at $102,453. Show that the profits on the futures positions are essentially the same as the change in the value of stocks and bonds during the two-month period.

17. GEMCO manages fixed-income portfolios. It would like to alter the composition of a $150 million segment of its portfolio for a period of four months. Specifically, the managers wish to convert $60 million into cash and reduce the duration on the remaining $90 million in bonds from 8.75 to 5.25. A bond futures contract that expires in four months is currently priced at $97,250 and has a modified duration of 7.53. Assume that the modified duration of cash equivalents is 0.25. Also assume that interest rates that drive long-term bond prices have a yield beta of 1 with respect to interest rates that drive the bond futures market.

   A. Show how the manager can achieve his goals by using bond futures. Indicate the number of contracts and whether the manager should go long or short.

   B. After four months, interest rates are up by 1.25 percent and long-term bonds are down 10.94 percent. The bond futures price is $88,096. Compare the market value of the portfolio using futures to adjust the allocation with the market value of the same portfolio using direct bond trading to adjust the allocation. To estimate the change in the portfolio value if the transaction is done without derivatives, use the duration approximation.

18. A. Consider a U.S. company, GateCorp, that exports products to the United Kingdom. GateCorp has just closed a sale worth £200,000,000. The amount will be received in two months. Because it will be paid in pounds, the U.S. company bears the exchange risk. In order to hedge this risk, GateCorp intends to use a forward contract that is priced at $1.4272 per pound. Indicate how the company would go about constructing the hedge. Explain what happens when the forward contract expires in two months.

   B. ABCorp is a U.S.-based company that frequently imports raw materials from Australia. It has just entered into a contract to purchase A$175,000,000 worth of raw wool, to be paid in one month. ABCorp fears that the Australian dollar will strengthen, thereby raising the U.S. dollar cost. A forward contract is available and is priced at $0.5249 per Australian dollar. Indicate how ABCorp would go about constructing a hedge. Explain what happens when the forward contract expires in one month.

19. Consider a U.S. asset management firm that wishes to allocate €50,000,000 to the French stock market. This portfolio has a beta of 0.95. The spot exchange rate is $0.8823 per euro. The foreign interest rate is 5.75 percent a year, and the domestic interest rate is 6.45 percent a year. A one-year forward contract on the euro is priced at $0.8881. A stock index futures contract on the CAC 40 (French stock index) is priced at €46,390, with the multiplier taken into account. The stock index futures contract has a beta of 1.05.

   A. Would the asset manager take a long or short position to hedge the equity market risk? Calculate the number of contracts needed.

   B. Suppose the firm also wished to hedge the currency risk using a forward contract on the euro. What should be the notional principal of the forward contract?

   C. Assume that at the end of one year, the French market is up by 8 percent. The exchange rate is $0.8765 per euro, and the futures price is €47,550. Calculate the return if

      i. the portfolio is unhedged.

      ii. only the equity position is hedged.

      iii. both equity and currency risks are hedged.

20. A U.S. asset management firm currently has £150,000,000 allocated to the U.K. stock market. This portfolio has a beta of 1.15. The spot exchange rate is $1.4194 per pound. The U.K. interest rate is 6.75 percent a year, and the U.S. interest rate is 5.25

percent a year. Both rates are quoted in the LIBOR manner of Rate × (Days/360). A three-month forward contract on the pound is priced at $1.4142. A stock index futures contract on the FTSE 100 (U.K. stock index) is priced at £52,665, with the multiplier taken into account. The stock index futures contract has a beta of 0.90.

A. Would the asset manager take a long or short position to hedge equity market risk? Calculate the number of contracts needed.

B. Suppose the firm also wished to hedge the currency risk using a forward contract on the pound. What should be the notional principal of the forward contract?

C. Assume that at the end of three months, the U.K. equity market is down by 3.25 percent. The exchange rate is at $1.4396 per pound, and the futures price is £50,630. Calculate the return if

   i. the portfolio is unhedged.

   ii. only the equity position is hedged.

   iii. both equity and currency risks are hedged.

SOLUTIONS

1. The payoff on the FRA 25 days later, with 270-day LIBOR at 8.25 percent, is

$$\$50,000,000\left[\frac{(0.0825-0.0675)(270/360)}{1+0.0825(270/360)}\right]=\$529,723$$

This payoff reduces the amount that has to be borrowed. The amount borrowed is $50,000,000 − $529,723 = $49,470,277. In 270 days, EaseCorp will repay principal and interest in the amount of

$$\$49,470,277[1+(0.0825+0.0125)(270/360)]=\$52,995,034$$

The effective rate is, therefore, $\left(\dfrac{\$52,995,034}{\$50,000,000}-1\right)\left(\dfrac{360}{270}\right)\approx0.0799$

This rate is approximately the FRA rate plus 125 basis points, or $0.0675 + 0.0125 = 0.08$.

2. The payoff on the short FRA position 30 days later, with 180-day LIBOR at 3.25 percent, is

$$\$25,000,000\left[\frac{(0.0325-0.055)(180/360)}{1+0.0325(180/360)}\right]=-\$276,752$$

Because this position is short, it represents a gain of $276,753 to the bank.

The bank lends $25,000,000. In 180 days, the bank will receive principal and interest in the amount of

$$\$25,000,000[1+(0.0325+0.015)(180/360)]=\$25,593,750$$

Because the bank had a $276,753 gain on the short FRA position, the effective amount loaned by the bank is $25,000,000 − $276,753 = $24,723,247. The effective interest rate on the loan, therefore, is

$$\left(\frac{\$25,593,750}{\$24,723,247}-1\right)\left(\frac{360}{180}\right)=0.0704$$

This rate is approximately the FRA rate plus 150 basis points, or $0.055 + 0.015 = 0.07$.

3. **A.** In order to reduce duration, the portfolio manager will have to sell futures contracts (i.e., a short futures position).

   B. The number of futures contracts that must be traded is

$$N_f=\left(\frac{8-12.5}{9.25}\right)\left(\frac{\$500,000,000}{\$105,250}\right)1.08=-2,495.99$$

   Rounded off, this is −2,496 contracts.

   C. The loss on the short futures position is −2,496($109,742 − $105,250) = −$11,212,032.

   The overall gain on the position is $31,343,750 − $11,212,032 = $20,131,718.

   The return with futures is $20,131,718/$500,000,000 = 4.026 percent.

   The *ex post* duration with futures is 0.04026/0.005 = 8.05, which is close to the target duration of 8.0.

The return without futures is $31,343,750/$500,000,000 = 6.267 percent.
The *ex post* duration without futures is 0.06267/0.005 = 12.54.

4. A. In order to increase duration, the portfolio manager will have to buy futures contracts (i.e., a long futures position).

B. The number of futures contracts that must be bought is

$$N_f = \left(\frac{9.5 - 6.53}{12.65}\right)\left(\frac{\$200,000,000}{\$95,650}\right)1.12 = 549.83$$

Rounded off, this is 550 contracts.

C. The profit on the long futures position is 550($92,616 − $95,650) = −$1,668,700.
The overall profit on the position is −$3,929,754 − $1,668,700 = −$5,598,454.
The return with futures is −$5,598,454/$200,000,000 = −2.799 percent.
The *ex post* duration with futures is −0.02799/0.003 = 9.33, which is close to the target duration of 9.5.
The return without futures is −$3,929,754 /$200,000,000 = −1.965 percent.
The *ex post* duration without futures is −0.01965/0.003 = 6.55.

5. A. The number of futures contracts that must be bought is

$$N_f = \left(\frac{1.2 - 0.95}{0.98}\right)\left(\frac{\$175,000,000}{\$105,790}\right) = 421.99$$

Rounded off, this is 422 contracts.

B. The value of the stock portfolio is $175,000,000(1 + 0.051) = $183,925,000.
The profit on the long futures position is 422($111,500 − $105,790) = $2,409,620.
The overall value of the position (stock plus long futures) is $183,925,000 + $2,409,620 = $186,334,620.
The overall rate of return is $\left(\frac{\$186,334,620}{\$175,000,000}\right) - 1 = 0.0648$
The effective beta is 0.0648/0.055 = 1.18, which is approximately equal to the target beta of 1.2.

6. A. The required number of futures contracts is

$$N_f = \left(\frac{0.8 - 0.9}{093}\right)\left(\frac{\$485,000,000}{\$249,000}\right) = -209.44$$

Rounded off, this is 209 contracts short.

B. The value of the stock portfolio is $485,000,000(1 − 0.0775) = $447,412,500.
The profit on the short futures position is −209($228,956 − $249,000) = $4,189,196.
The overall value of the position (stock plus long futures) is $447,412,500 + $4,189,196 = $451,601,696.
The overall rate of return is $\left(\frac{\$451,601,696}{\$485,000,000}\right) - 1 = -0.0689$
The effective beta is 0.0689/0.0865 = 0.797, which is approximately equal to the target beta of 0.80.

7. A. The number of futures contracts that must be bought is

$$N_f = \frac{\$300,000,000(1.0235)^{0.25}}{\$500(498.30)} = 1,211.11$$

Rounded off, this is 1,211 contracts long.

Now invest the following amount in risk-free bonds, which pay 2.35 percent interest:

$$\frac{1,211(\$500)(498.30)}{(1.0235)^{0.25}} = \$299,973,626$$

This amount will grow to $\$299,973,626(1.0235)^{0.25} = \$301,720,650$. The number of synthetic units of stock is

$$\frac{1211(500)}{(1.0075)^{0.25}} = 604,369.98$$

which would grow to $604,369.98(1.0075)^{0.25} = 605,500$ with the reinvestment of dividends.

B. At expiration in three months, the payoff on the futures is $1,211(\$500)(594.65 - 498.30) = 605,500(594.65) - \$301,720,650$. In order to settle the futures contract, the money manager will owe $301,720,650. This amount can be paid off with the proceeds from the investment in risk-free bonds, leaving the money manager with 605,500 units of the stock index, each worth 594.65. This transaction achieves the desired exposure to the stock index.

8. A. The number of futures contracts that must be bought is

$$N_f = \frac{\$650,000,000(1.0335)^{0.25}}{\$5(11,930)} = 10,987.04$$

Rounded off, this is 10,987 contracts long.

Now invest the following amount in risk-free bonds, which pay 3.35 percent interest:

$$\frac{10,987(\$5)(11,930)}{(1.0225)^{0.25}} = \$649,997,898$$

This amount will grow to $\$649,997,898(1.0335)^{0.25} = \$655,374,550$. The number of synthetic units of stock is

$$\frac{10,987(5)}{(1.0125)^{0.25}} = 54,764.66$$

which would grow to $54,764.66(1.0125)^{0.25} = 54,935$ with reinvestment of dividends.

B. At expiration in three months, the payoff on the futures is $10,987(\$5)(S_T - 11,930) = 54,935(S_T) - \$655,374,550$. In order to settle the futures contract, the money manager will owe $655,374,550. This amount can be paid off with the proceeds from the investment in risk-free bonds, leaving the money manager with

54,935 units of the stock index, each worth S_T. This transaction achieves the desired exposure to the stock index.

9. **A.** In order to create a synthetic cash position, the number of futures contracts to be sold is

$$N_f = \frac{\$25,000,000(1.0275)^{4/12}}{\$250(1170.10)} = 86.24$$

Rounded off, this is 86 contracts short.

B. The effective amount of stock committed to this transaction is actually

$$\frac{86(\$250)(1170.10)}{(1.0275)^{4/12}} = \$24,930,682$$

This amount invested at the risk-free rate should grow to $\$24,930,682(1.0275)^{4/12} = \$25,157,150$, resulting in the following number of shares:

$$\frac{86(\$250)}{(1.0125)^{4/12}} = 21,411.16$$

With reinvestment of dividends, this number would grow to $21,411.16(1.0125)^{4/12} = 21,500$ shares. The short position in futures is equivalent to selling \$24,930,682 of stock.

C. In four months when the futures contract expires, the stock index is at 1031. The payoff of the futures contract is $-86(\$250)(1031 - 1170.10) = -\$21,500(1031) + \$25,157,150 = \$2,990,650$.

Netting the futures payoff against the stock position produces \$25,157,150, equivalent to investing \$24,930,682 at 2.75 percent for four months. The short futures position has thus effectively converted equity to cash.

10. **A.** In order to create synthetic cash, the number of futures contracts to be sold is

$$N_f - \frac{\$950,000,000(1.0575)^{6/12}}{\$100(1564)} = 6,246.36$$

Rounded off, this is 6,246 contracts short.

B. The effective amount of stock committed to this transaction is actually

$$\frac{6246(\$100)(1564)}{(1.0575)^{6/12}} = \$949,945,174$$

Invested at the risk-free rate, this amount should grow to $\$949,945,174(1.0575)^{6/12} = \$976,874,400$, resulting in the following number of shares:

$$\frac{6246(\$100)}{(1.0045)^{6/12}} = 623,199.38$$

With reinvestment of dividends, the number of shares will grow to $623,199.38(1.0045)^{6/12} = 624,600$.

C. In six months when the futures contract expires, the stock index is at 1735. The payoff of the futures contract is $-6,246(\$100)(1735 - 1564) = -\$624,600(1735) + \$976,874,400 = -\$106,806,600$.

Netting the futures payoff against the stock position produces $976,874,400, equivalent to investing $949,945,174 at 5.75 percent for six months. The short futures position has thus effectively converted equity to cash.

11. **A.** The current allocation is as follows: stocks, 0.65($200,000,000) = $130,000,000; bonds, 0.35($200,000,000) = $70,000,000. The new allocation desired is as follows: stocks, 0.85($200,000,000) = $170,000,000; bonds, 0.15($200,000,000) = $30,000,000. So, to achieve the new allocation, the manager must buy stock futures on $170,000,000 − $130,000,000 = $40,000,000. An equivalent amount of bond futures must be sold.

To synthetically sell $40 million in bonds and convert into cash, the manager must sell futures:

$$N_{bf} = \left(\frac{0.25 - 6.75}{5.25}\right)\left(\frac{\$40,000,000}{\$109,000}\right) = -454.35$$

He should sell 454 contracts and create synthetic cash.

To synthetically buy $40 million of stock with synthetic cash, the manager must buy futures:

$$N_{sf} = \left(\frac{1.15 - 0}{0.95}\right)\left(\frac{\$40,000,000}{\$157,500}\right) = 307.44$$

He should buy 307 contracts. Now the manager effectively has $170 million (85 percent) in stocks and $30 million (15 percent) in bonds.

The next step is to increase the beta on the $170 million in stock to 1.20 by purchasing futures. The number of futures contracts would, therefore, be

$$N_{sf} = \left(\frac{1.20 - 1.15}{0.95}\right)\left(\frac{\$170,000,000}{\$157,500}\right) = 56.81$$

An additional 57 stock futures contracts should be purchased. In total, 307 + 57 = 364 contracts are bought.

To increase the modified duration from 6.75 to 8.25 on the $30 million of bonds, the number of futures contracts is

$$N_{bf} = \left(\frac{8.25 - 6.75}{5.25}\right)\left(\frac{\$30,000,000}{\$109,000}\right) = 78.64$$

An additional 79 bond futures contracts should be purchased. In total, 454 −79 = 375 contracts are sold.

B. The value of the stock will be $130,000,000(1 + 0.05) = $136,500,000.
The profit on the stock index futures will be 364($164,005 − $157,500) = $2,367,820.
The value of the bonds will be $70,000,000(1 + 0.0135) = $70,945,000.
The profit on the bond futures will be −375($110,145 − $109,000) = −$429,375.
The total value of the position, therefore, is $136,500,000 + $2,367,820 + $70,945,000 − $429,375 = $209,383,445.

If the reallocation were carried out by trading bonds and stocks:
The stock would be worth $170,000,000(1 + 0.05) = $178,500,000.

The bonds would be worth $30,000,000(1 + 0.0135) = $30,405,000.
The overall value of the portfolio would be $178,500,000 + $30,405,000 = $208,905,000.

The difference between the two approaches is $478,445, only 0.239 percent of the original value of the portfolio.

12. **A.** The current allocation is as follows: long-term bonds, 0.70($75 million) = $52.5 million; short-term bonds, 0.30($75 million) = $22.5 million. The desired allocation is as follows: long-term bonds, 0.55($75 million) = $41.25 million; short-term bonds, 0.45($75 million) = $33.75 million. So to achieve the desired allocation, the manager must use futures to synthetically buy $33.75 million − $22.5 million = $11.25 million of short-term bonds, with proceeds from the synthetic sale of an equal amount of long-term bonds.

To synthetically sell $11.25 million in long-term bonds and convert into cash, the manager must sell futures:

$$N_f = \left(\frac{0.25 - 7.5}{6.25}\right)\left(\frac{\$11,250,000}{\$95,750}\right) = -136.29$$

He should sell 136 contracts and create synthetic cash.

To synthetically buy $11.25 million of short-term bonds with synthetic cash, the manager must buy futures:

$$N_f = \left(\frac{4.5 - 0.25}{6.25}\right)\left(\frac{\$11,250,00}{\$95,750}\right) = 79.89$$

He should buy 80 contracts. This nets out to 136 − 80 = 56 contracts.

Now the manager effectively has $41.25 million (55 percent) in long-term bonds and $33.75 million (45 percent) in short-term bonds.

B. The value of long-term bonds will be $52,500,000(1 − 0.0938) = $47,575,500.
The value of short-term bonds will be $22,500,000(1 − 0.0563) = $21,233,250.
The profit on the bond futures will be (−136 + 80)($88,270 − $95,750) = $418,880.
The total value of the position with futures, therefore, is $47,575,500 + $21,233,250 + $418,880 = $69,227,630.

If the reallocation were carried out by trading long-term and short-term bonds:
The long-term bonds would be worth $41,250,000(1 − 0.0938) = $37,380,750.
The short-term bonds would be worth $33,750,000(1 − 0.0563) = $31,849,875.
The overall value of the portfolio would be $37,380,750 + $31,849,875 = $69,230,625.

The difference between the two approaches is $2,995, only 0.004 percent of the original value of the portfolio.

13. **A.** The current allocation is as follows: small-cap stocks, 0.60($150 million) = $90 million; large-cap stocks, 0.40($150 million) = $60 million. The desired allocation is as follows: small-cap stocks, 0.45($150 million) = $67.5 million; large-cap stocks, 0.55($150 million) = $82.5 million. So, to achieve the desired allocation, the manager must use futures to synthetically buy $82.5 million − $60 million = $22.5 million of large-cap stocks, with proceeds from the synthetic sale of an equal amount of small-cap stocks.

To synthetically sell $22.5 million in small-cap stocks and convert into cash, the manager must sell the following number of futures contracts on small-cap stock:

$$N_{scf} = \left(\frac{0 - 1.25}{1.12}\right)\left(\frac{\$22,500,000}{\$195,750}\right) = -128.28$$

He should sell 128 contracts and create synthetic cash.

To synthetically buy $22.5 million of large-cap stock with synthetic cash, the manager must buy the following number of futures on large-cap stock:

$$N_{lcf} = \left(\frac{1.15 - 0}{0.92}\right)\left(\frac{\$22,500,000}{\$215,570}\right) = 130.47$$

He should buy 130 contracts.

Now the manager effectively has $67.5 million (45 percent) in small-cap stocks and $82.5 million (55 percent) in large-cap stocks.

B. The value of large-cap stocks will be $60,000,000(1 + 0.0475) = $62,850,000.
The value of small-cap stocks will be $90,000,000(1 + 0.0625) = $95,625,000.
The profit on the large-cap futures will be 130($223,762 − $215,570) = $1,064,960.
The profit on the small-cap futures will be −128($206,712 − $195,750) = −$1,403,136.
The total value of the position with futures, therefore, is $62,850,000 + $95,625,000 + $1,064,960 − $1,403,136 = $158,136,824.

If the reallocation were carried out by trading large-cap and small-cap stocks:
The large-cap stocks would be worth $82,500,000(1 + 0.0475) = $86,418,750.
The small-cap stocks would be worth $67,500,000(1 + 0.0625) = $71,718,750.
The overall value of the portfolio would be $86,418,750 + $71,718,750 = $158,137,500.

The difference between the two approaches is $676, or only 0.0005 percent of the original value of the portfolio.

14. A. The current allocation is as follows: stocks, 0.65($750 million) = $487.5 million; bonds, 0.35($750 million) = $262.5 million. The new allocation desired is as follows: stocks, 0.45($750 million) = $337.5 million; bonds, 0.55($750 million) = $412.5 million. So, to achieve the new allocation, the manager must use futures to synthetically buy $412.5 million − $262.5 million = $150 million of bonds with proceeds from the synthetic sale of $150 million of stock.

To synthetically sell $150 million in stock and convert into cash, the manager must sell the following number of futures on stock:

$$N_{sf} = \left(\frac{0 - 1.20}{0.90}\right)\left(\frac{\$150,000,000}{\$272,500}\right) = -733.94$$

She should sell 734 contracts and create synthetic cash.

To synthetically buy $150 million of bonds with synthetic cash, the manager must buy the following number of futures on bonds:

$$N_{bf} = \left(\frac{7.65 - 0.25}{5.35}\right)\left(\frac{\$150,000,000}{\$139,120}\right) = 1,491.35$$

She should buy 1,491 contracts.

Now the manager effectively has $337.5 million (45 percent) in stock and $412.5 million (55 percent) in bonds.

B. The value of the stock will be $487,500,000(1 − 0.05) = $463,125,000.

The profit on the stock index futures will be −734($262,280 − $272,500) = $7,501,480.

The value of the bonds will be $262,500,000(1 − 0.0175) = $257,906,250.

The profit on the bond futures will be 1,491($137,420 − $139,120) = −$2,534,700.

The total value of the position with futures, therefore, is $463,125,000 + $7,501,480 + $257,906,250 − $2,534,700 = $725,998,030.

If the reallocation were carried out by trading bonds and stocks:

The stock would be worth $337,500,000(1 − 0.05) = $320,625,000.

The bonds would be worth $412,500,000(1 − 0.0175) = $405,281,250.

The overall value of the portfolio would be $320,625,000 + $405,281,250 = $725,906,250.

The difference between the two approaches is $91,780, only 0.012 percent of the original value of the portfolio.

15. A. In order to gain effective exposure to stock and bonds today, the manager must use futures to synthetically buy $17,500,000 of stock and $32,500,000 of bonds.

To synthetically buy $17,500,000 in stock, the manager must buy futures:

$$N_{sf} = \left(\frac{1.15 - 0}{0.93}\right)\left(\frac{\$17,500,000}{\$175,210}\right) = 123.51$$

He should buy 124 contracts.

To synthetically buy $32,500,000 of bonds, the manager must buy futures:

$$N_{bf} = \left(\frac{7.65 - 0}{5.65}\right)\left(\frac{\$32,500,000}{\$95,750}\right) = 459.57$$

He should buy 460 contracts.

Now the manager effectively has invested $17,500,000 in stock and $32,500,000 in bonds.

B. The profit on the stock index futures will be 124($167,559 − $175,210) = −$948,724.

The profit on the bond futures will be 460($93,586 − $95,750) = −$995,440.

The total profit with futures = −$948,724 − $995,440 = −$1,944,164.

If bonds and stocks were purchased today, in three months:

The change in value of stock would be $17,500,000(−0.054) = −$945,000.

The change in value of bonds would be $32,500,000(−0.0306) = −$994,500.

The overall change in value of the portfolio would be −$945,000 − $994,500 = −$1,939,500.

The difference between the two approaches is $4,664, only 0.009 percent of the total expected cash inflow.

16. A. In order to gain effective exposure to stock and bonds today, the manager must use futures to synthetically buy $21,000,000 of stock and $9,000,000 of bonds.

To synthetically buy $21,000,000 in stock, the manager must buy futures:

$$N_{sf} = \left(\frac{1.25 - 0}{0.96}\right)\left(\frac{\$21,000,000}{\$225,130}\right) = 121.46$$

He should buy 121 contracts.

To synthetically buy $9,000,000 of bonds, the manager must buy futures:

$$N_{bf} = \left(\frac{6.56 - 0}{7.25}\right)\left(\frac{\$9,000,000}{\$105,120}\right) = 77.47$$

He should buy 77 contracts.

Now the manager effectively has $21,000,000 in stock and $9,000,000 in bonds.

B. The profit on the stock index futures will be 121($231,614 − $225,130) = $784,564.

The profit on the bond futures will be 77($102,453 − $105,120) = −$205,359.
The total profit with futures, therefore, is $784,564 − $205,359= $579,205.

If bonds and stocks were purchased today, in two months:
The change in value of stock would be $21,000,000(0.0375) = $787,500.
The change in value of bonds would be $9,000,000(−0.023) = −$207,000.
The overall change in value of the portfolio would be $787,500 −$207,000 = $580,500.

The difference between the two approaches is $1,295, only 0.004 percent of the total expected cash inflow.

17. A. In order to synthetically convert $60 million in bonds to cash, the manager must sell bond futures. The number of contracts is calculated as

$$N_f = \left(\frac{0.25 - 8.75}{7.53}\right)\left(\frac{\$60,000,000}{\$97,250}\right) = -696.44$$

Rounding off, GEMCO should sell 696 contracts.

To reduce the duration on the remaining $90 million from 8.75 to 5.25, the appropriate number of futures contracts to sell is

$$N_f = \left(\frac{5.25 - 8.75}{7.53}\right)\left(\frac{\$90,000,000}{\$97,250}\right) = -430.16$$

Rounding off, GEMCO should sell 430 futures contracts.

To convert a portion of the portfolio to cash and reduce the duration of the remaining bonds, GEMCO will thus have to sell a total of 1,126 bond futures contracts.

B. Four months later:
The profit on the bond futures is −1,126($88,096 − $97,250) = $10,307,404.
The change in value of the bonds is = $150,000,000(−0.1094) = −$16,410,000.
The total is −$6,102,596.

If the reallocation were carried out by selling bonds instead of using futures, then the weighted duration of cash and bonds would be

$$\left(\frac{\$60,000,000}{\$150,000,000}\right)(0.25) + \left(\frac{\$90,000,000}{\$150,000,000}\right)(5.25) = 3.25$$

This calculation assumes that the duration of the remaining bonds has been reduced to 5.25. Based on an increase of 1.25 percent in interest rates, the bond portfolio would fall by 4.06 percent, which is obtained as $-3.25(0.0125) = 0.0406$.

The change in the value of the bond portfolio would be $150,000,000 $(-0.0406) = -\$6,090,000$.

The difference between the two approaches is $12,596, only 0.008 percent of the portfolio value.

18. **A.** GateCorp will receive £200,000,000 in two months. To hedge the risk that the pound may weaken during this period, the firm should enter into a forward contract to deliver pounds and receive dollars two months from now at a price fixed now. Because it is effectively long the pound, GateCorp will take a short position on the pound in the forward market. GateCorp will thus enter into a two-month short forward contract to deliver £200,000,000 at a rate of $1.4272 per pound.

When the forward contract expires in two months, irrespective of the spot exchange rate, GateCorp will deliver £200,000,000 and receive ($1.4272/£1) (£200,000,000) = $285,440,000.

B. ABCorp will have to pay A$175,000,000 in one month. To hedge the risk that the Australian dollar may strengthen against the U.S. dollar during this period, it should enter into a forward contract to purchase Australian dollars one month from now at a price fixed today. Because it is effectively short the Australian dollar, ABCorp takes a long position in the forward market. ABCorp thus enters into a one-month long forward contract to purchase A$175,000,000 at a rate of US$0.5249 per Australian dollar.

When the forward contract expires in one month, irrespective of the spot exchange rate, ABCorp will pay ($0.5249/A$)(A$175,000,000) = $91,857,500 to purchase A$175,000,000. This amount is used to purchase the raw material needed.

19. **A.** In order to hedge against a decline in the French equity market, the manager must take a short position in the equity futures contract. The number of contracts to be sold is

$$N_f = \left(\frac{0 - 0.95}{1.05}\right)\left(\frac{50,000,000}{46,390}\right) = -975.17$$

Rounded, 975 contracts would be sold.

B. In order to hedge the currency risk, the manager would have to enter into a forward contract to sell euros one year from now. If the equity position were fully hedged, then the portfolio would earn the foreign risk-free rate of 5.75 percent. The portfolio would be worth €50,000,000(1.0575) = €52,875,000. Therefore, the notional principal on the forward contract should be €52,875,000.

C. The French equity market went up by 8 percent during the year. The portfolio is thus worth €50,000,000(1 + 0.08) = €54,000,000.

Because the exchange rate at the end of one year is $0.8765 per euro, the dollar value of the portfolio is €54,000,000($0.8765/€) = $47,331,000.

The initial dollar value of the portfolio was €50,000,000($0.8823/€) = $44,115,000.

i. The return on the unhedged portfolio is $\left(\dfrac{\$47,331,000}{\$44,115,000}\right) - 1 = 0.0729$

ii. If only equity market risk is hedged, the return is calculated as follows:
Foreign currency (euro) value of the portfolio = €54,000,000.
Profit on stock index futures = −975(€47,550 − €46,390) = −€1,131,000.
Total value of position = €54,000,000 − €1,131,000 = €52,869,000.

The dollar value of the position is €52,869,000($0.8765/€) = $46,339,679.

The return is $\left(\dfrac{\$46,339,679}{\$44,115,000}\right) - 1 = 0.0504$

iii. If both currency risk and equity risk are hedged, the return is calculated as follows:

The value of the equity portfolio and the stock index futures one year later is €52,869,000, which is $46,339,679.

The amount of foreign currency shorted is €52,875,000.

The profit on the currency forward is −€52,875,000($0.8765/€ − $0.8881/€) = $613,350.

So the total value of the position is $613,350 + $46,339,679 = $46,953,029.

The return is $\left(\dfrac{\$46,953,029}{\$44,115,000}\right) - 1 = 0.0643$

Therefore, if both equity and currency risk are hedged, the return is approximately the same as the domestic risk-free rate of 6.45 percent.

20. A. In order to hedge against a decline in the U.K. equity market, the manager would have to short the stock index futures contract. The number of contracts sold would be

$$N_f = \left(\frac{0 - 1.15}{0.90}\right)\left(\frac{150,000,000}{52,665}\right) = -3,639.36$$

Rounded, 3,639 contracts would be sold.

B. In order to hedge currency risk, the manager would have to enter into a forward contract to sell pounds three months from now. If the equity position were fully hedged, then the portfolio would earn the foreign risk-free rate of 0.0675(90/360) = 0.016875. The portfolio would be worth £150,000,000(1.016875) = £152,531,250. The notional principal on the forward contract should thus be £152,531,250.

C. The U.K. equity market fell by 3.25 percent during the three-month period. The portfolio is thus worth £150,000,000(1 − 0.0325) = £145,125,000.

The exchange rate at the end of one year is $1.4396 per pound, so the dollar value of the portfolio is £145,125,000 ($1.4396/£) = $208,921,950.

The initial dollar value of the portfolio was £150,000,000($1.4194/£) = $212,910,000.

i. The return on the unhedged portfolio is $\left(\dfrac{\$208,921,950}{\$212,910,000}\right) - 1 = -0.0187$

This rate reflects an annualized return of −0.0187(360/90) = −0.0748.

ii. If only equity market risk is hedged, the return is calculated as follows:

Foreign currency value of the portfolio = £145,125,000.

Profit on stock index futures = −3,639(£50,630 − £52,665) = £7,405,365.

Total value of position = £145,125,000 + £7,405,365 = £152,530,365.

The dollar value of the position is £152,530,365($1.4396/£) = $219,582,713.

The return is $\left(\dfrac{\$219,582,713}{\$212,910,000}\right) - 1 = 0.0313$

The annualized return is 0.0313(360/90) = 0.1252.

iii. If both currency risk and equity risk are hedged, the return is calculated as follows:

The value of the equity portfolio and the stock index futures one year later is £152,530,365, which is $219,582,713.

The amount of foreign currency shorted is £152,531,250.

The profit on the currency forward is −£152,531,250($1.4396/£ − $1.4142/£) = −$3,874,294.

The total value of the position is \$219,582,713 − \$3,874,294 = \$215,708,419.

The return is $\left(\dfrac{\$215,708,419}{\$212,910,000}\right) - 1 = 0.0131$

The annualized return is 0.0131(360/90) = 0.0524. Therefore, if both equity and currency risk are hedged, the return is approximately the same as the domestic risk-free rate of 5.25 percent.

RISK MANAGEMENT APPLICATIONS OF OPTION STRATEGIES

LEARNING OUTCOMES

After completing this chapter, you will be able to do the following:

- Determine the value at expiration, profit, maximum profit, maximum loss, breakeven underlying price at expiration, and general shape of the graph of the strategies for buying and selling calls, and explain each strategy's characteristics.

- Determine the value at expiration, profit, maximum profit, maximum loss, breakeven underlying price at expiration, and general shape of the graph of the strategies for buying and selling puts, and explain each strategy's characteristics.

- Determine the value at expiration, profit, maximum profit, maximum loss, breakeven underlying price at expiration, and general shape of the graph of the covered call strategy, and explain the strategy's characteristics.

- Determine the value at expiration, profit, maximum profit, maximum loss, breakeven underlying price at expiration, and general shape of the graph of the protective put strategy, and explain the strategy's characteristics.

- Determine the value at expiration, profit, maximum profit, maximum loss, breakeven underlying price at expiration, and general shape of the graph of the bull spread strategy, and explain the strategy's characteristics.

- Determine the value at expiration, profit, maximum profit, maximum loss, breakeven underlying price at expiration, and general shape of the graph of the bear spread strategy, and explain the strategy's characteristics.

- Determine the value at expiration, profit, maximum profit, maximum loss, breakeven underlying price at expiration, and general shape of the graph of the butterfly spread strategy, and explain the strategy's characteristics.

- Determine the value at expiration, profit, maximum profit, maximum loss, breakeven underlying price at expiration, and general shape of the graph of the collar strategy, and explain the strategy's characteristics.

- Determine the value at expiration, profit, maximum profit, maximum loss, breakeven underlying price at expiration, and general shape of the graph of the straddle strategy, and explain the strategy's characteristics.

- Determine the value at expiration and profit of the box spread strategy, and explain the strategy's characteristics.

- Determine the effective annual rate for a given interest rate outcome when a borrower manages the risk of an anticipated loan using an interest rate call option.

- Determine the effective annual rate for a given interest rate outcome when a lender manages the risk of an anticipated loan using an interest rate put option.

- Determine the payoffs for a series of interest rate outcomes when a floating-rate loan is combined with an interest rate cap.

- Determine the payoffs for a series of interest rate outcomes when a floating-rate loan is combined with an interest rate floor.

- Determine the payoffs for a series of interest rate outcomes when a floating-rate loan is combined with an interest rate collar.

- Explain why and how a dealer delta hedges an option portfolio, how the portfolio delta changes, and how the dealer adjusts the position to maintain the hedge.

- Identify the conditions under which a delta-hedged portfolio is influenced by the second-order gamma effect.

- Explain how vega and volatility risk can affect a delta-hedged portfolio.

1 INTRODUCTION

In the previous chapter, we examined strategies that employ forward and futures contracts. Recall that forward and futures contracts have linear payoffs and do not require an initial outlay. Options, on the other hand, have nonlinear payoffs and require the payment of cash up front. By having nonlinear payoffs, options permit their users to benefit from movements in the underlying in one direction and to not be harmed by movements in the other direction. In many respects, they offer the best of all worlds, a chance to profit if expectations are realized with minimal harm if expectations turn out to be wrong. The price for this opportunity is the cash outlay required to establish the position. From the standpoint of the holder of the short position, options can lead to extremely large losses. Hence, sellers of options must be well compensated in the form of an adequate up-front premium and must skillfully manage the risk they assume.

In this chapter we examine the most widely used option strategies. The chapter is divided into three parts. In the first part, we look at option strategies that are typically used in equity investing, which include standard strategies involving single options and strategies that combine options with the underlying. In the second part, we look at the specific strategies that are commonly used in managing interest rate risk. In the third part, we examine option strategies that are used primarily by dealers and sophisticated traders to manage the risk of option positions.

Let us begin by reviewing the necessary notation. These symbols are the same ones we have previously used. First recall that time 0 is the time at which the strategy is initiated and time T is the time the option expires, stated as a fraction of a year. Accordingly, the amount of time until expiration is simply $T - 0 = T$, which is (Days to expiration)/365. The other symbols are

c_0, c_T = price of the call option at time 0 and time T

p_0, p_T = price of the put option at time 0 and time T[1]

X = exercise price

S_0, S_T = price of the underlying at time 0 and time T

V_0, V_T = value of the position at time 0 and time T

Π = profit from the transaction: $V_T - V_0$

r = risk-free rate

Some additional notation will be introduced when necessary.

Note that we are going to measure the profit from an option transaction, which is simply the final value of the transaction minus the initial value of the transaction. Profit does not take into account the time value of money or the risk. Although a focus on profit is not completely satisfactory from a theoretical point of view, it is nonetheless instructive, simple, and a common approach to examining options. Our primary objective here is to obtain a general picture of the manner in which option strategies perform. With that in mind, discussing profit offers probably the best trade-off in terms of gaining the necessary knowledge with a minimum of complexity.

In this chapter, we assume that the option user has a view regarding potential movements of the underlying. In most cases that view is a prediction of the direction of the underlying, but in some cases it is a prediction of the volatility of the underlying. In all cases, we assume this view is specified over a horizon that corresponds to the option's life or that the option expiration can be tailored to the horizon date. Hence, for the most part, these options should be considered customized, over-the-counter options.[2] Every interest rate option is a customized option.

Because the option expiration corresponds to the horizon date for which a particular view is held, there is no reason to use American options. Accordingly, all options in this chapter are European options. Moreover, we shall not consider terminating the strategy early. Putting an option in place and closing the position prior to expiration is certainly a legitimate strategy. It could reflect the arrival of new information over the holding period, but it requires an understanding of more complex issues, such as valuation of the option and the rate at which the option loses its time value. Thus, we shall examine the outcome of a particular strategy over a range of possible values of the underlying only on the expiration day.

Section 2 of this chapter focuses on option strategies that relate to equity investments. Section 3 concentrates on strategies using interest rate options. In Section 4, we focus on managing an option portfolio.

2 OPTION STRATEGIES FOR EQUITY PORTFOLIOS

Many typical illustrations of option strategies use individual stocks, but we shall use options on a stock index, the Nasdaq 100, referred to simply as the Nasdaq. We shall assume that in addition to buying and selling options on the Nasdaq, we can also buy the index, either through construction of the portfolio itself, through an index mutual fund, or

---

[1] As in Chapter 4, lower case indicates European options, and upper case indicates American options. In this chapter, all options are European.

[2] If the options discussed were exchange-listed options, it would not significantly alter the material in this chapter.

an exchange-traded fund.[3] We shall simply refer to this instrument as a stock. We are given the following numerical data:

S_0 = 2000, value of the Nasdaq 100 when the strategy is initiated

T = 0.0833, the time to expiration (one month = 1/12)

The options available will be the following:[4]

Exercise Price	Call Price	Put Price
1950	108.43	56.01
2000	81.75	79.25
2050	59.98	107.39

Let us start by examining an initial strategy that is the simplest of all: to buy or sell short the underlying. Panel A of Exhibit 7-1 illustrates the profit from the transaction of buying a share of stock. We see the obvious result that if you buy the stock and it goes up, you

EXHIBIT 7-1   Simple Stock Strategies

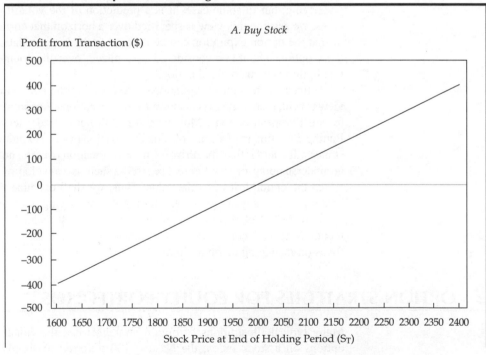

---

[3] Exchange-traded shares on the Nasdaq 100 are called Nasdaq 100 Trust Shares and QQQs, for their ticker symbol. They are commonly referred to as Qubes, trade on the Amex, and are the most active exchange-traded fund and often the most actively traded of all securities. Options on the Nasdaq 100 are among the most actively traded as well.

[4] These values were obtained using the Black–Scholes–Merton model. By using this model, we know we are working with reasonable values that do not permit arbitrage opportunities.

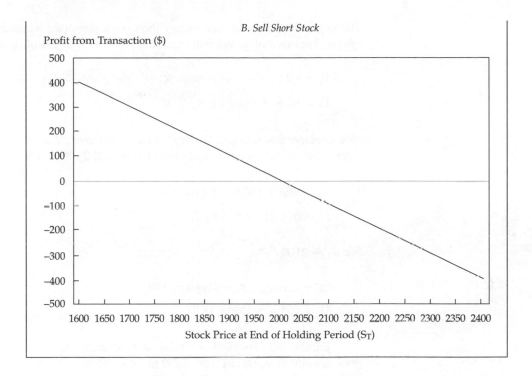

B. Sell Short Stock

make a profit; if it goes down, you incur a loss. Panel B shows the case of selling short the stock. Recall that this strategy involves borrowing the shares from a broker, selling them at the current price, and then buying them back at a later date. In this case, if you sell short the stock and it goes down, you make a profit. Conversely, if it goes up, you incur a loss. Now we shall move on to strategies involving options, but we shall use the stock strategies again when we combine options with stock.

In this section we examine option strategies in the context of their use in equity portfolios. Although these strategies are perfectly applicable for fixed-income portfolios, corporate borrowing scenarios, or even commodity risk management situations, they are generally more easily explained and understood in the context of investing in equities or equity indices.

To analyze an equity option strategy, we first assume that we establish the position at the current price. We then determine the value of the option at expiration for a specific value of the index at expiration. We calculate the profit as the value at expiration minus the current price. We then generate a graph to illustrate the value at expiration and profit for a range of index values at expiration. Although the underlying is a stock index, we shall just refer to it as the underlying to keep things as general as possible. We begin by examining the most fundamental option transactions, long and short positions in calls and puts.

2.1 STANDARD LONG AND SHORT POSITIONS

2.1.1 CALLS

Consider the purchase of a call option at the price c_0. The value at expiration, c_T, is $c_T = \max(0, S_T - X)$. Broken down into parts,

$$c_T = 0 \qquad \text{if } S_T \le X$$

$$c_T = S_T - X \qquad \text{if } S_T > X$$

The profit is obtained by subtracting the option premium, which is paid to purchase the option, from the option value at expiration, $\Pi = c_T - c_0$. Broken down into parts,

$$\Pi = -c_0 \qquad\qquad \text{if } S_T \le X$$

$$\Pi = S_T - X - c_0 \quad \text{if } S_T > X$$

Now consider this example. We buy the call with the exercise price of 2000 for 81.75. Consider values of the index at expiration of 1900 and 2100. For $S_T = 1900$,

$$c_T = \max(0, 1900 - 2000) = 0$$

$$\Pi = 0 - 81.75 = -81.75$$

For $S_T = 2100$,

$$c_T = \max(0, 2100 - 2000) = 100$$

$$\Pi = 100 - 81.75 = 18.25$$

Exhibit 7-2 illustrates the value at expiration and profit when S_T, the underlying price at expiration, ranges from 1600 to 2400. We see that buying a call results in a limited loss of the premium, 81.75. For an index value at expiration greater than the exercise price of 2000, the value and profit move up one-for-one with the index value, and there is no upper limit.

It is important to identify the breakeven index value at expiration. Recall that the formula for the profit is $\Pi = \max(0, S_T - X) - c_0$. We would like to know the value of S_T for which $\Pi = 0$. We shall call that value S_T^*. It would be nice to be able to solve $\Pi = \max(0, S_T^* - X) - c_0 = 0$ for S_T^*, but that is not directly possible. Instead, we observe that there are two ranges of outcomes, one in which $\Pi = S_T^* - X - c_0$ for $S_T^* > X$, the case of the option expiring in-the-money, and the other in which $\Pi = -c_0$ for $S_T \le X$, the case of the option expiring out-of-the-money. It is obvious from the equation and by observing Exhibit 7-2 that in the latter case, there is no possibility of breaking even. In the former case, we see that we can solve for S_T^*. Setting $\Pi = S_T^* - X - c_0 = 0$, we obtain $S_T^* = X + c_0$.

Thus, the breakeven is the exercise price plus the option premium. This result should be intuitive: The value of the underlying at expiration must exceed the exercise price by the amount of the premium to recover the cost of the premium. In this problem, the breakeven is $S_T^* = 2000 + 81.75 = 2081.75$. Observe in Exhibit 7-2 that the profit line crosses the axis at this value.

In summarizing the strategy, we have the following results for the option buyer:

$c_T = \max(0, S_T - X)$

Value at expiration $= c_T$

Profit: $\Pi = c_T - c_0$

Maximum profit $= \infty$

Maximum loss $= c_0$

Breakeven: $S_T^* = X + c_0$

EXHIBIT 7-2   Buy Call

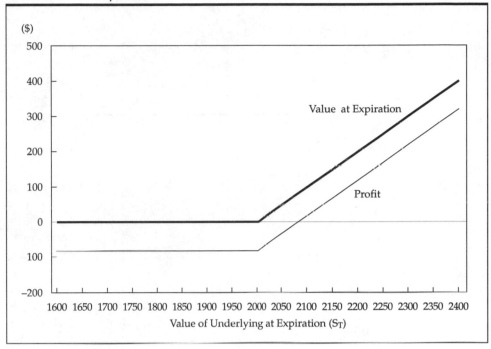

Call options entice naive speculators, but it is important to consider the *likely* gains and losses more than the *potential* gains and losses. For example, in this case, the underlying must go up by about 4.1 percent in one month to cover the cost of the call. This increase equates to an annual rate of almost 50 percent and is an unreasonable expectation by almost any standard. If the underlying does not move at all, the loss is 100 percent of the premium.

For the seller of the call, the results are just the opposite. The sum of the positions of the seller and buyer is zero. Hence, we can take the value and profit results for the buyer and change the signs. The results for the maximum profit and maximum loss are changed accordingly, and the breakeven is the same. Hence, for the option seller,

$c_T = \max(0, S_T - X)$

Value at expiration $= -c_T$

Profit: $\Pi = -c_T + c_0$

Maximum profit $= c_0$

Maximum loss $= \infty$

Breakeven: $S_T^* = X + c_0$

Exhibit 7-3 shows the results for the seller of the call. Note that the value and profit have a fixed maximum. The worst case is an infinite loss. Just as there is no upper limit to the buyer's potential gain, there is no upper limit to how much the seller can lose.

Call options are purchased by investors who are bullish. We now turn to put options, which are purchased by investors who are bearish.

EXHIBIT 7-3   Sell Call

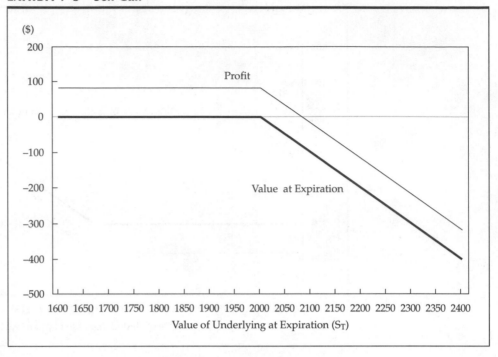

PRACTICE PROBLEM 1

Consider a call option selling for $7 in which the exercise price is $100 and the price of the underlying is $98.

A. Determine the value at expiration and the profit for a buyer under the following outcomes:
   i. The price of the underlying at expiration is $102.
   ii. The price of the underlying at expiration is $94.

B. Determine the value at expiration and the profit for a seller under the following outcomes:
   i. The price of the underlying at expiration is $91.
   ii. The price of the underlying at expiration is $101.

C. Determine the following:
   i. The maximum profit to the buyer (maximum loss to the seller)
   ii. The maximum loss to the buyer (maximum profit to the seller)

D. Determine the breakeven price of the underlying at expiration.

SOLUTIONS

A. Call buyer
   i. Value at expiration = $c_T = \max(0, S_T - X) = \max(0, 102 - 100) = 2$
      $\Pi = c_T - c_0 = 2 - 7 = -5$
   ii. Value at expiration = $c_T = \max(0, S_T - X) = \max(0, 94 - 100) = 0$
      $\Pi = c_T - c_0 = 0 - 7 = -7$

B. Call seller

    i. Value at expiration $= -c_T = -\max(0, S_T - X) = -\max(0, 91 - 100) = 0$
        $\Pi = -c_T + c_0 = -0 + 7 = 7$

    ii. Value at expiration $= -c_T = -\max(0, S_T - X) = -\max(0, 101 - 100) = -1$
        $\Pi = -c_T + c_0 = -1 + 7 = 6$

C. Maximum and minimum

    i. Maximum profit to buyer (loss to seller) $= \infty$
    ii. Maximum loss to buyer (profit to seller) $= c_0 = 7$

D. $S_T^* = X + c_0 = 100 + 7 = 107$

2.1.2 PUTS

The value of a put at expiration is $p_T = \max(0, X - S_T)$. Broken down into parts,

$$p_T = X - S_T \quad \text{if } S_T < X$$

$$p_T = 0 \qquad\quad \text{if } S_T \geq X$$

The profit is obtained by subtracting the premium on the put from the value at expiration:

$$\Pi = p_T - p_0$$

Broken down into parts,

$$\Pi = X - S_T - p_0 \quad \text{if } S_T < X$$

$$\Pi = -p_0 \qquad\qquad \text{if } S_T \geq X$$

For our example and outcomes of $S_T = 1900$ and 2100, the results are as follows:

$S_T = 1900$:

$$p_T = \max(0, 2000 - 1900) = 100$$

$$\Pi = 100 - 79.25 = 20.75$$

$S_T = 2100$:

$$p_T = \max(0, 2000 - 2100) = 0$$

$$\Pi - 0 - 79.25 = -79.25$$

These results are shown in Exhibit 7-4. We see that the put has a maximum value and profit and a limited loss, the latter of which is the premium. The maximum value is obtained when the underlying goes to zero.[5] In that case, $p_T = X$. So the maximum profit is $X - p_0$. Here that will be $2000 - 79.25 = 1920.75$.

---

[5] The maximum value and profit are not visible on the graph because we do not show S_T all the way down to zero.

EXHIBIT 7-4   Buy Put

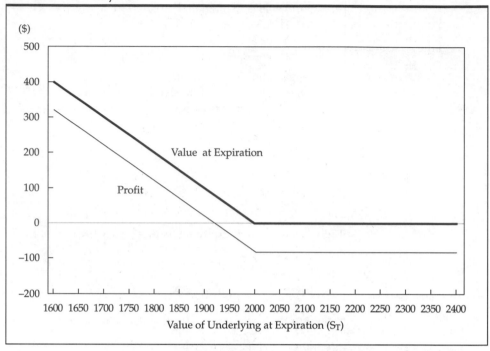

The breakeven is found by breaking up the profit equation into its parts, $\Pi = X - S_T - p_0$ for $S_T < X$ and $\Pi = -p_0$ for $S_T \geq X$. In the latter case, there is no possibility of breaking even. It refers to the range over which the entire premium is lost. In the former case, we denote the breakeven index value as S_T^*, set the equation to zero, and solve for S_T^* to obtain $S_T^* = X - p_0$. In our example, the breakeven is $S_T^* = 2000 - 79.25 = 1920.75$.

In summary, for the strategy of buying a put we have

$p_T = \max(0, X - S_T)$

Value at expiration $= p_T$

Profit: $\Pi = p_T - p_0$

Maximum profit $= X - p_0$

Maximum loss $= p_0$

Breakeven: $S_T^* = X - p_0$

Now consider the *likely* outcomes for the holder of the put. In this case, the underlying must move down by almost 4 percent in one month to cover the premium. One would hardly ever expect the underlying to move down at an annual rate of almost 50 percent. Moreover, if the underlying does not move downward at all (a likely outcome given the positive expected return on most assets), the loss is 100 percent of the premium.

For the sale of a put, we simply change the sign on the value at expiration and profit. The maximum profit for the buyer becomes the maximum loss for the seller and the maximum loss for the buyer becomes the maximum profit for the seller. The breakeven for the seller is the same as for the buyer. So, for the seller,

$$p_T = max(0, X - S_T)$$

Value at expiration $= -p_T$

Profit: $\Pi = -p_T + p_0$

Maximum profit $= p_0$

Maximum loss $= X - p_0$

Breakeven: $S_T{}^* = X - p_0$

Exhibit 7-5 graphs the value at expiration and the profit for this transaction.

EXHIBIT 7-5 Sell Put

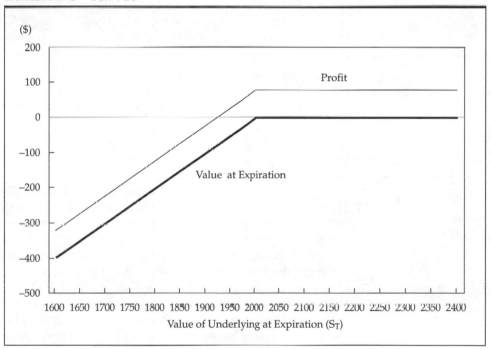

PRACTICE PROBLEM 2

Consider a put option selling for $4 in which the exercise price is $60 and the price of the underlying is $62.

A. Determine the value at expiration and the profit for a buyer under the following outcomes:
   i. The price of the underlying at expiration is $62.
   ii. The price of the underlying at expiration is $55.

B. Determine the value at expiration and the profit for a seller under the following outcomes:
   i. The price of the underlying at expiration is $51.
   ii. The price of the underlying at expiration is $68.

C. Determine the following:
   i. The maximum profit to the buyer (maximum loss to the seller)
   ii. The maximum loss to the buyer (maximum profit to the seller)
D. Determine the breakeven price of the underlying at expiration.

SOLUTIONS

A. Put buyer
   i. Value at expiration $= p_T = \max(0, X - S_T) = \max(0, 60 - 62) = 0$
      $\Pi = p_T - p_0 = 0 - 4 = -4$
   ii. Value at expiration $= p_T = \max(0, X - S_T) = \max(0, 60 - 55) = 5$
      $\Pi = p_T - p_0 = 5 - 4 = 1$
B. Put seller
   i. Value at expiration $= -p_T = -\max(0, X - S_T) = -\max(0, 60 - 51) = -9$
      $\Pi = -p_T + p_0 = -9 + 4 = -5$
   ii. Value at expiration $= -p_T = -\max(0, X - S_T) = -\max(0, 60 - 68) = 0$
      $\Pi = -p_T + p_0 = 0 + 4 = 4$
C. Maximum and minimum
   i. Maximum profit to buyer (loss to seller) $= X - p_0 = 60 - 4 = 56$
   ii. Maximum loss to buyer (profit to seller) $= p_0 = 4$
D. $S_T^* = X - p_0 = 60 - 4 = 56$

It may be surprising to find that we have now covered all of the information we need to examine all of the other option strategies. We need to learn only a few basic facts. We must know the formula for the value at expiration of a call and a put. Then we need to know how to calculate the profit for the purchase of a call and a put, but that calculation is simple: the value at expiration minus the initial value. If we know these results, we can calculate the value at expiration of the option and the profit for any value of the underlying at expiration. If we can do that, we can graph the results for a range of possible values of the underlying at expiration. Because graphing can take a long time, however, it is probably helpful to learn the basic shapes of the value and profit graphs for calls and puts. Knowing the profit equation and the shapes of the graphs, it is easy to determine the maximum profit and maximum loss. The breakeven can be determined by setting the profit equation to zero for the case in which the profit equation contains S_T. Once we have these results for the long call and put, it is an easy matter to turn them around and obtain the results for the short call and put. Therefore, little if any memorization is required. From there, we can go on to strategies that combine an option with another option and combine options with the underlying.

2.2 RISK MANAGEMENT STRATEGIES WITH OPTIONS AND THE UNDERLYING

In this section, we examine two of the most widely used option strategies, particularly for holders of the underlying. One way to reduce exposure without selling the underlying is to sell a call on the underlying; the other way is to buy a put.

2.2.1 COVERED CALLS

A **covered call** is a relatively conservative strategy, but it is also one of the most misunderstood strategies. A covered call is a position in which you own the underlying and sell a call. The value of the position at expiration is easily found as the value of the underlying plus the value of the short call:

$$V_T = S_T - \max(0, S_T - X)$$

Therefore,

$$V_T = S_T \qquad\qquad \text{if } S_T \leq X$$
$$V_T = S_T - (S_T - X) = X \quad \text{if } S_T > X$$

We obtain the profit for the covered call by computing the change in the value of the position, $V_T - V_0$. First recognize that V_0, the value of the position at the start of the contract, is the initial value of the underlying minus the call premium. We are long the underlying and short the call, so we must subtract the call premium that was received from the sale of the call. The initial investment in the position is what we pay for the underlying less what we receive for the call. Hence, $V_0 = S_0 - c_0$. The profit is thus

$$\Pi = S_T - \max(0, S_T - X) - (S_0 - c_0)$$
$$= S_T - S_0 - \max(0, S_T - X) + c_0$$

With the equation written in this manner, we see that the profit for the covered call is simply the profit from buying the underlying, $S_T - S_0$, plus the profit from selling the call, $-\max(0, S_T - X) + c_0$. Breaking it down into ranges,

$$\Pi = S_T - S_0 + c_0 \qquad\qquad\qquad \text{if } S_T \leq X$$
$$\Pi = S_T - S_0 - (S_T - X) + c_0 = X - S_0 + c_0 \quad \text{if } S_T > X$$

In our example, $S_0 = 2000$. In this section we shall use a call option with the exercise price of 2050. Thus $X = 2050$, and the premium, c_0, is 59.98. Let us now examine two outcomes: $S_T = 2100$ and $S_T = 1900$. The value at expiration when $S_T = 2100$ is $V_T = 2100 - (2100 - 2050) = 2050$, and when $S_T = 1900$, the value of the position is $V_T = 1900$.

In the first case, we hold the underlying worth 2100 but are short a call worth 50. Thus, the net value is 2050. In the second case, we hold the underlying worth 1900 and the option expires out-of-the-money.

In the first case, $S_T = 2100$, the profit is $\Pi = 2050 - 2000 + 59.98 = 109.98$. In the second case, $S_T = 1900$, the profit is $\Pi = 1900 - 2000 + 59.98 = -40.02$. These results are graphed for a range of values of S_T in Exhibit 7-6. Note that for all values of S_T greater than 2050, the value and profit are maximized. Thus, 2050 is the maximum value and 109.98 is the maximum profit.[6]

As evident in Exhibit 7-6 and the profit equations, the maximum loss would occur when S_T is zero. Hence, the profit would be $S_T - S_0 + c_0$. The profit is $-S_0 + c_0$ when $S_T = 0$. This means that the maximum loss is $S_0 - c_0$. In this example, $-S_0 + c_0$ is $-2000 + 59.98 = -1940.02$. Intuitively, this would mean that you purchased the underlying for 2000 and sold the call for 59.98. The underlying value went to zero, resulting in a loss of 2000, but the call expired with no value, so the gain from the option is the option premium. The total loss is 1940.02.

---

[6] Note in Exhibit 7-6 that there is large gap between the value at expiration and profit, especially compared with the graphs of buying and selling calls and puts. This difference occurs because a covered call is mostly a position in the underlying asset. The initial value of the asset, S_0, accounts for most of the difference in the two lines. Note also that because of the put–call parity relationship we covered in Chapter 4, a covered call looks very similar to a short put.

EXHIBIT 7-6   Covered Call (Buy Underlying, Sell Call)

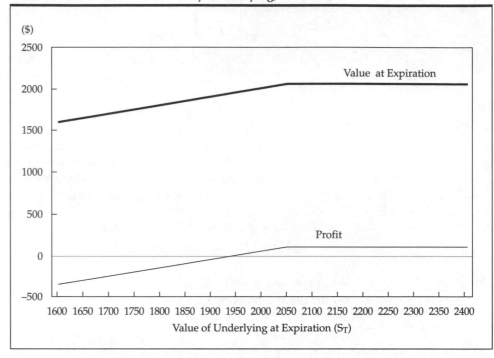

The breakeven underlying price is found by examining the profit equations and focusing on the equation that contains S_T. In equation form, $\Pi = S_T - S_0 + c_0$ when $S_T \leq X$. We let $S_T{}^*$ denote the breakeven value of S_T, set the equation to zero, and solve for $S_T{}^*$ to obtain $S_T{}^* = S_0 - c_0$. The breakeven and the maximum loss are identical. In this example, the breakeven is $S_T{}^* = 2000 - 59.98 = 1940.02$, which is seen in Exhibit 7-6.

To summarize the covered call, we have the following:

Value at expiration: $V_T = S_T - \max(0, S_T - X)$

Profit: $\Pi = V_T - S_0 + c_0$

Maximum profit $= X - S_0 + c_0$

Maximum loss $= S_0 - c_0$

Breakeven: $S_T{}^* = S_0 - c_0$

Because of the importance and widespread use of covered calls, it is worthwhile to discuss this strategy briefly to dispel some misunderstandings. First of all, some investors who do not believe in using options fail to see that selling a call on a position in the underlying reduces the risk of that position. Options do not automatically increase risk. The option part of this strategy alone, viewed in isolation, seems an extremely risky strategy. We noted in Section 2.1.1 that selling a call without owning the stock exposes the investor to unlimited loss potential. But selling a covered call—adding a short call to a long position in a stock—reduces the overall risk. Thus, any investor who holds a stock cannot say he is too conservative to use options.

Following on that theme, however, one should also view selling a covered call as a strategy that reduces not only the risk but also the expected return compared with simply holding the underlying. Hence, one should not expect to make a lot of money writing calls on the underlying. It should be apparent that in fact the covered call writer could miss out on significant gains in a strong bull market. The compensation for this willingness to give up potential upside gains, however, is that in a bear market the losses on the underlying will be cushioned by the option premium.

It may be disconcerting to some investors to look at the profit profile of a covered call. The immediate response is to think that no one in their right mind would invest in a strategy that has significant downside risk but a limited upside. Just owning the underlying has significant downside risk, but at least there is an upside. But it is important to note that the visual depiction of the strategy, as in Exhibit 7-6, does not tell the whole story. It says nothing about the likelihood of certain outcomes occurring.

For example, consider the covered call example we looked at here. The underlying starts off at 2000. The maximum profit occurs when the option expires with the underlying at 2050 or above, an increase of 2.5 percent over the life of the option. We noted that this option has a one-month life. Thus, the underlying would have to increase at an approximate annual rate of at least $2.5\%(12) = 30\%$ for the covered call writer to forgo all of the upside gain. There are not many stocks, indices, or other assets in which an investor would expect the equivalent of an annual move of at least 30 percent. Such movements obviously do occur from time to time, but they are not common. Thus, covered call writers do not often give up large gains.

But suppose the underlying did move to 2050 or higher. As we previously showed, the value of the position would be 2050. Because the initial value of the position is $2000 - 59.98 = 1940.02$, the rate of return would be 5.7 percent for one month. Hence, the maximum return is still outstanding by almost anyone's standards.[7]

Many investors believe that the initial value of a covered call should not include the value of the underlying if the underlying had been previously purchased. Suppose, for example, that this asset, currently worth 2000, had been bought several months ago at 1900. It is tempting to ignore the current value of the underlying; there is no current outlay. This view, however, misses the notion of opportunity cost. If an investor currently holding an asset chooses to write a call on it, she has made a conscious decision not to sell the asset. Hence, the current value of the asset should be viewed as an opportunity cost that is just as real as the cost to an investor buying the underlying at this time.

Sellers of covered calls must make a decision about the chosen exercise price. For example, one could sell the call with an exercise price of 1950 for 108.43, or sell the call with exercise price of 2000 for 81.75, or sell the call with exercise price of 2050 for 59.98. The higher the exercise price, the less one receives for the call but the more room for gain on the upside. There is no clear-cut solution to deciding which call is best; the choice depends on the risk preferences of the investor.

Finally, we should note that anecdotal evidence suggests that writers of call options make small amounts of money, but make it often. The reason for this phenomenon is generally thought to be that buyers of calls tend to be overly optimistic, but that argument is fallacious. The real reason is that the expected profits come from rare but large payoffs. For example, consider the call with exercise price of 2000 and a premium of 81.75. As we learned in Section 2.1, the breakeven underlying price is 2081.75—a gain of about 4.1 percent in a one-month period, which would be an exceptional return for almost any asset. These prices were obtained using the Black–Scholes–Merton model, so they are fair

---

[7] Of course, we are not saying that the performance reflects a positive alpha. We are saying only that the upside performance given up reflects improbably high returns, and therefore the limits on the upside potential are not too restrictive.

prices. Yet the required underlying price movement to profit on the call is exceptional. Obviously someone buys calls, and naturally, someone must be on the other side of the transaction. Sellers of calls tend to be holders of the underlying or other calls, which reduces the enormous risk they would assume if they sold calls without any other position.[8] Hence, it is reasonable to expect that sellers of calls would make money often, because large underlying price movements occur only rarely. Following this line of reasoning, however, it would appear that sellers of calls can consistently take advantage of buyers of calls. That cannot possibly be the case. What happens is that buyers of calls make money less often than sellers, but when they do make money, the leverage inherent in call options amplifies their returns. Therefore, when call writers lose money, they tend to lose big, but most call writers own the underlying or are long other calls to offset the risk.

PRACTICE PROBLEM 3

Consider a bond selling for $98 per $100 face value. A call option selling for $8 has an exercise price of $105. Answer the following questions about a covered call.

A. Determine the value of the position at expiration and the profit under the following outcomes:
    i. The price of the bond at expiration is $110.
    ii. The price of the bond at expiration is $88.

B. Determine the following:
    i. The maximum profit
    ii. The maximum loss

C. Determine the breakeven bond price at expiration.

SOLUTIONS

A. **i.** $V_T = S_T - \max(0, S_T - X) = 110 - \max(0, 110 - 105)$
        $= 110 - 110 + 105 = 105$
        $\Pi = V_T - V_0 = 105 - (S_0 - c_0) = 105 - (98 - 8) = 15$
  ii. $V_T = S_T - \max(0, S_T - X) = 88 - \max(0, 88 - 105) = 88 - 0 = 88$
        $\Pi = V_T - V_0 = 88 - (S_0 - c_0) = 88 - (98 - 8) = -2$

B. **i.** Maximum profit $= X - S_0 + c_0 = 105 - 98 + 8 = 15$
  ii. Maximum loss $= S_0 - c_0 = 98 - 8 = 90$

C. $S_T^* = S_0 - c_0 = 98 - 8 = 90$

Covered calls represent one widely used way to protect a position in the underlying. Another popular means of providing protection is to buy a put.

2.2.2 PROTECTIVE PUTS

Because selling a call provides some protection to the holder of the underlying against a fall in the price of the underlying, buying a put should also provide protection. A put, after all, is designed to pay off when the price of the underlying moves down. In some ways,

---

[8] Sellers of calls who hold other calls are engaged in transactions called spreads. We discuss several types of spreads in Section 2.3.

buying a put to add to a long stock position is much better than selling a call. As we shall see here, it provides downside protection while retaining the upside potential, but it does so at the expense of requiring the payment of cash up front. In contrast, a covered call generates cash up front but removes some of the upside potential.

Holding an asset and a put on the asset is a strategy known as a **protective put**. The value at expiration and the profit of this strategy are found by combining the value and profit of the two strategies of buying the asset and buying the put. The value is $V_T = S_T + \max(0, X - S_T)$. Thus, the results can be expressed as

$$V_T = S_T + (X - S_T) = X \quad \text{if } S_T \leq X$$

$$V_T = S_T \qquad\qquad\qquad \text{if } S_T > X$$

When the underlying price at expiration exceeds the exercise price, the put expires with no value. The position is then worth only the value of the underlying. When the underlying price at expiration is less than the exercise price, the put expires in-the-money and is worth $X - S_T$, while the underlying is worth S_T. The combined value of the two instruments is X. When the underlying is worth less than the exercise price at expiration, the put can be used to sell the underlying for the exercise price.

The initial value of the position is the initial price of the underlying, S_0, plus the premium on the put, p_0. Hence, the profit is $\Pi = S_T + \max(0, X - S_T) - (S_0 + p_0)$. The profit can be broken down as follows:

$$\Pi = X - (S_0 + p_0) \quad \text{if } S_T \leq X$$

$$\Pi = S_T - (S_0 + p_0) \quad \text{if } S_T > X$$

In this example, we are going to use the put with an exercise price of 1950. Its premium is 56.01. Recalling that the initial price of the underlying is 2000, the value at expiration and profit for the case of $S_T = 2100$ are

$$V_T = 2100$$

$$\Pi = 2100 - (2000 + 56.01) = 43.99$$

For the case of $S_T = 1900$, the value at expiration and profit are

$$V_T = 1950$$

$$\Pi = 1950 - (2000 + 56.01) = -106.01$$

The results for a range of outcomes are shown in Exhibit 7-7. Note how the protective put provides a limit on the downside with no limit on the upside.[9] Therefore, we can say that the upper limit is infinite. The lower limit is a loss of 106.01. In the worst possible case, we can sell the underlying for the exercise price, but the up-front cost of the underlying and put are 2056.01, for a maximum loss of 106.01.

Now let us find the breakeven price of the underlying at expiration. Note that the two profit equations are $\Pi = S_T - (S_0 + p_0)$ if $S_T > X$ and $\Pi = X - (S_0 + p_0)$ if $S_T \leq X$. In the latter case, there is no value of the underlying that will allow us to break even. In the

---

[9] Note that the graph for a protective put looks like the graph for a call. This result is due to put–call parity, as covered in Chapter 4.

EXHIBIT 7-7   Protective Put (Buy Underlying, Buy Put)

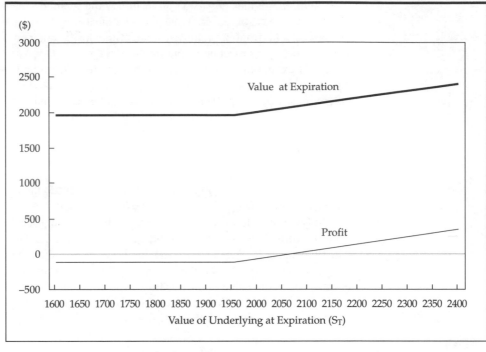

former case, $S_T > X$, we change the notation on S_T to S_T^* to denote the breakeven value, set this expression equal to zero, and solve for S_T^*:

$$S_T^* = S_0 + p_0$$

To break even, the underlying must be at least as high as the amount expended up front to establish the position. In this problem, this amount is $2000 + 56.01 = 2056.01$.

To summarize the protective put, we have the following:

Value at expiration: $V_T = S_T + \max(0, X - S_T)$

Profit: $\Pi = V_T - S_0 - p_0$

Maximum profit $= \infty$

Maximum loss $= S_0 + p_0 - X$

Breakeven: $S_T^* = S_0 + p_0$

A protective put can appear to be a great transaction with no drawbacks. It provides downside protection with upside potential, but let us take a closer look. First recall that this is a one-month transaction and keep in mind that the option has been priced by the Black–Scholes–Merton model and is, therefore, a fair price. The maximum loss of 106.01 is a loss of $106.01/2056.01 = 5.2\%$. The breakeven of 2056.01 requires an upward move of 2.8 percent, which is an annual rate of about 34 percent. From this angle, the protective put strategy does not look quite as good, but in fact, these figures simply confirm that protection against downside loss is expensive. When the protective put is fairly priced, the protection buyer must give up considerable upside potential that may not be particularly evident from just looking at a graph.

The purchase of a protective put also presents the buyer with some choices. In this example, the buyer bought the put with exercise price of 1950 for 56.01. Had he bought the put with exercise price of 2000, he would have paid 79.25. The put with exercise price of 2050 would have cost 107.39. The higher the price for which the investor wants to be able to sell the underlying, the more expensive the put will be.

The protective put is often viewed as a classic example of insurance. The investor holds a risky asset and wants protection against a loss in value. He then buys insurance in the form of the put, paying a premium to the seller of the insurance, the put writer. The exercise price of the put is like the insurance deductible because the magnitude of the exercise price reflects the risk assumed by the party holding the underlying. The higher the exercise price, the less risk assumed by the holder of the underlying and the more risk assumed by the put seller. The lower the exercise price, the more risk assumed by the holder of the underlying and the less risk assumed by the put seller. In insurance, the higher the deductible, the more risk assumed by the insured party and the less risk assumed by the insurer. Thus, a higher exercise price is analogous to a lower insurance deductible.

Like traditional insurance, this form of insurance provides coverage for a period of time. At the end of the period of time, the insurance expires and either pays off or not. The buyer of the insurance may or may not choose to renew the insurance by buying another put.

PRACTICE PROBLEM 4

Consider a currency selling for $0.875. A put option selling for $0.075 has an exercise price of $0.90. Answer the following questions about a protective put.

A. Determine the value at expiration and the profit under the following outcomes:
  i. The price of the currency at expiration is $0.96.
  ii. The price of the currency at expiration is $0.75.

B. Determine the following:
  i. The maximum profit
  ii. The maximum loss

C. Determine the breakeven price of the currency at expiration.

SOLUTIONS

A. **i.** $V_T = S_T + \max(0, X - S_T) = 0.96 + \max(0, 0.90 - 0.96) = 0.96$
       $\Pi = V_T - V_0 = 0.96 - (S_0 + p_0) = 0.96 - (0.875 + 0.075) = 0.01$
    ii. $V_T = S_T + \max(0, X - S_T) = 0.75 + \max(0, 0.90 - 0.75) = 0.90$
       $\Pi = V_T - V_0 = 0.90 - (S_0 + p_0) = 0.90 - (0.875 + 0.075) = -0.05$

B. **i.** Maximum profit $= \infty$
    ii. Maximum loss $= S_0 + p_0 - X = 0.875 + 0.075 - 0.90 = 0.05$

C. $S_T^* = S_0 + p_0 = 0.875 + 0.075 = 0.95$

Finally, we note that a protective put can be modified in a number of ways. One in particular is to sell a call to generate premium income to pay for the purchase of the put. This strategy is known as a collar. We shall cover collars in detail in Section 2.4.1 when we look at combining puts and calls. For now, however, let us proceed with strategies that combine calls with calls and puts with puts. These strategies are called spreads.

2.3 MONEY SPREADS

A spread is a strategy in which you buy one option and sell another option that is identical to the first in all respects except either exercise price or time to expiration. If the options differ by time to expiration, the spread is called a time spread. Time spreads are strategies designed to exploit differences in perceptions of volatility of the underlying. They are among the more specialized strategies, and we do not cover them here. Our focus is on money spreads, which are spreads in which the two options differ only by exercise price. The investor buys an option with a given expiration and exercise price and sells an option with the same expiration but a different exercise price. Of course, the options are on the same underlying asset. The term *spread* is used here because the payoff is based on the difference, or spread, between option exercise prices.

2.3.1 BULL SPREADS

A **bull spread** is designed to make money when the market goes up. In this strategy we combine a long position in a call with one exercise price and a short position in a call with a higher exercise price. Let us use X_1 as the lower of the two exercise prices and X_2 as the higher. Following the notation we introduced in Chapter 4, the European call prices would be denoted as $c(X_1)$ and $c(X_2)$, but we shall simplify this notation somewhat in this chapter by using the symbols c_1 and c_2, respectively. We found that the value of a call at expiration is $c_T = \max(0, S_T - X)$. So, the value of the spread at expiration is

$$V_T = \max(0, S_T - X_1) - \max(0, S_T - X_2)$$

Therefore,

$$
\begin{aligned}
V_T &= 0 - 0 = 0 & &\text{if } S_T \leq X_1 \\
V_T &= S_T - X_1 - 0 = S_T - X_1 & &\text{if } X_1 < S_T < X_2 \\
V_T &= S_T - X_1 - (S_T - X_2) = X_2 - X_1 & &\text{if } S_T \geq X_2
\end{aligned}
$$

The profit is obtained by subtracting the initial outlay for the spread from the above value of the spread at expiration. To determine the initial outlay, recall that a call option with a lower exercise price will be more expensive than a call option with a higher exercise price. Because we are buying the call with the lower exercise price and selling the call with the higher exercise price, the call we buy will cost more than the call we sell. Hence, the spread will require a net outlay of funds. This net outlay is the initial value of the position of $V_0 = c_1 - c_2$, which we call the net premium. The profit is $V_T - V_0$. Therefore,

$$\Pi = \max(0, S_T - X_1) - \max(0, S_T - X_2) - (c_1 - c_2)$$

In this manner, we see that the profit is the profit from the long call, $\max(0, S_T - X_1) - c_1$, plus the profit from the short call, $-\max(0, S_T - X_2) + c_2$. Broken down into ranges, the profit is

$$
\begin{aligned}
\Pi &= -c_1 + c_2 & &\text{if } S_T \leq X_1 \\
\Pi &= S_T - X_1 - c_1 + c_2 & &\text{if } X_1 < S_T < X_2 \\
\Pi &= X_2 - X_1 - c_1 + c_2 & &\text{if } S_T \geq X_2
\end{aligned}
$$

If S_T is below X_1, the strategy will lose a limited amount of money. The profit on the upside, if S_T is at least X_2, is also limited. When both options expire out-of-the-money, the investor loses the net premium, $c_1 - c_2$.

In this example, we use exercise prices of 1950 and 2050. Thus $X_1 = 1950$, $c_1 = 108.43$, $X_2 = 2050$, and $c_2 = 59.98$. Let us examine the outcomes in which the asset price at expiration is 2100, 2000, and 1900. In one outcome, the underlying is above the upper exercise price at expiration, and in one, the underlying is below the lower exercise price at expiration. Let us also examine one case between the exercise prices with S_T equal to 2000.

When $S_T = 2100$, the value at expiration is $V_T = 2050 - 1950 = 100$.

When $S_T = 2000$, the value at expiration is $V_T = 2000 - 1950 = 50$.

When $S_T = 1900$, the value at expiration is $V_T = 0$.

To calculate the profit, we simply subtract the initial value for the call with exercise price X_1 and add the initial value for the call with exercise price X_2.

When $S_T = 2100$, the profit is $\Pi = 100 - 108.43 + 59.98 = 51.55$.

When $S_T = 2000$, the profit is $\Pi = 50 - 108.43 + 59.98 = 1.55$.

When $S_T = 1900$, the profit is $\Pi = -108.43 + 59.98 = -48.45$.

When S_T is greater than 2100, we would obtain the same outcome as when S_T equals 2100. When S_T is less than 1900, we would obtain the same outcome as when S_T equals 1900.

Exhibit 7-8 depicts these results graphically. Note how the bull spread provides a limited gain as well as a limited loss. Of course, just purchasing a call provides a limited loss. But when selling the call in addition to buying the call, the investor gives up the upside in order to reduce the downside. In the bull spread, the investor sells gains from the call beyond

EXHIBIT 7-8 **Bull Spread (Buy Call with Exercise Price X_1, Sell Call with Exercise Price X_2)**

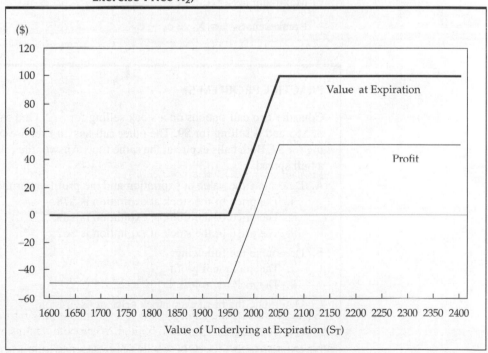

the higher exercise price. Thus, a bull spread has some similarities to the covered call. With a covered call, the long position in the underlying "covers" the short position in the call. In a bull spread, the long position in the call with the lower exercise price "covers" the short position in the call with the higher exercise price. For both strategies, the short call can be viewed as giving up the gains beyond its exercise price. The upside gain can also be viewed as paying a premium of $c_1 - c_2$ to buy the underlying for X_1 and sell it for X_2. Accordingly, the maximum gain is $X_2 - X_1 - c_1 + c_2 = 2050 - 1950 - 108.43 + 59.98 = 51.55$, as computed above. This amount represents a maximum return of about 106 percent.[10] The maximum loss is the net premium, 48.45, which is a 100 percent loss.

As can be seen from the graph and the profit equations, there is a breakeven asset price at expiration that falls between the two exercise prices. We let S_T^* be the breakeven asset price at expiration and set the profit for the case of $X_1 < S_T < X_2$ to zero:

$$S_T^* = X_1 + c_1 - c_2$$

To achieve a profit of zero or more, the asset price at expiration must exceed the lower exercise price by at least the net premium paid for the options. The long option must expire in-the-money by enough to cover the net premium. In our example,

$$S_T^* = 1950 + 108.43 - 59.98 = 1,998.45$$

What this result means is that the underlying must not move down by more than 0.08 percent.

To summarize the bull spread, we have

Value at expiration: $V_T = \max(0,S_T - X_1) - \max(0,S_T - X_2)$

Profit: $\Pi = V_T - c_1 + c_2$

Maximum profit $= X_2 - X_1 - c_1 + c_2$

Maximum loss $= c_1 - c_2$

Breakeven: $S_T^* = X_1 + c_1 - c_2$

PRACTICE PROBLEM 5

Consider two call options on a stock selling for $72. One call has an exercise price of $65 and is selling for $9. The other call has an exercise price of $75 and is selling for $4. Both calls expire at the same time. Answer the following questions about a bull spread:

A. Determine the value at expiration and the profit under the following outcomes:
   i. The price of the stock at expiration is $78.
   ii. The price of the stock at expiration is $69.
   iii. The price of the stock at expiration is $62.

B. Determine the following:
   i. The maximum profit
   ii. The maximum loss

C. Determine the breakeven stock price at expiration.

---

[10] This calculation is based on the fact that the initial value of the position is $108.43 - 59.98 = 48.45$ and the maximum value is 100, which is a gain of 106.4 percent.

SOLUTIONS

A. **i.** $V_T = \max(0, S_T - X_1) - \max(0, S_T - X_2) = \max(0, 78 - 65) - \max(0, 78 - 75) = 13 - 3 = 10$
$\Pi = V_T - V_0 = V_T - (c_1 - c_2) = 10 - (9 - 4) = 5$

   ii. $V_T = \max(0, S_T - X_1) - \max(0, S_T - X_2) = \max(0, 69 - 65) - \max(0, 69 - 75) = 4 - 0 = 4$
$\Pi = V_T - V_0 = V_T - (c_1 - c_2) = 4 - (9 - 4) = -1$

   iii. $V_T = \max(0, S_T - X_1) - \max(0, S_T - X_2) = \max(0, 62 - 65) - \max(0, 62 - 75) = 0 - 0 = 0$
$\Pi = V_T - V_0 = 0 - (c_1 - c_2) = 0 - (9 - 4) = -5$

B. **i.** Maximum profit $= X_2 - X_1 - (c_1 - c_2) = 75 - 65 - (9 - 4) = 5$

   ii. Maximum loss $= c_1 - c_2 = 9 - 4 = 5$

C. $S_T^* = X_1 + c_1 - c_2 = 65 + 9 - 4 = 70$

Bull spreads are used by investors who think the underlying price is going up. There are also bear spreads, which are used by investors who think the underlying price is going down.

2.3.2 BEAR SPREADS

If one uses the opposite strategy, selling a call with the lower exercise price and buying a call with the higher exercise price, the opposite results occur. The graph is completely reversed: The gain is on the downside and the loss is on the upside. This strategy is called a **bear spread**. The more intuitive way of executing a bear spread, however, is to use puts. Specifically, we would buy the put with the higher exercise price and sell the put with the lower exercise price.

The value of this position at expiration would be $V_T = \max(0, X_2 - S_T) - \max(0, X_1 - S_T)$. Broken down into ranges, we have the following relations:

$$V_T = X_2 - S_T - (X_1 - S_T) = X_2 - X_1 \quad \text{if } S_T \leq X_1$$
$$V_T = X_2 - S_T - 0 = X_2 - S_T \quad \text{if } X_1 < S_T < X_2$$
$$V_T = 0 - 0 = 0 \quad \text{if } S_T \geq X_2$$

To obtain the profit, we subtract the initial outlay. Because we are buying the put with the higher exercise price and selling the put with the lower exercise price, the put we are buying is more expensive than the put we are selling. The initial value of the bear spread is $V_0 = p_2 - p_1$. The profit is, therefore, $V_T - V_0$, which is

$$\Pi = \max(0, X_2 - S_T) - \max(0, X_1 - S_T) - p_2 + p_1$$

We see that the profit is the profit from the long put, $\max(0, X_2 - S_T) - p_2$, plus the profit from the short put, $-\max(0, X_1 - S_T) + p_1$. Broken down into ranges, the profit is

$$\Pi = X_2 - X_1 - p_2 + p_1 \quad \text{if } S_T \leq X_1$$
$$\Pi = X_2 - S_T - p_2 + p_1 \quad \text{if } X_1 < S_T < X_2$$
$$\Pi = -p_2 + p_1 \quad \text{if } S_T \geq X_2$$

In contrast to the profit in a bull spread, the bear spread profit occurs on the downside; the maximum profit occurs when $S_T \leq X_1$. This profit reflects the purchase of the underlying at X_1, which occurs when the short put is exercised, and the sale of the underlying at X_2, which occurs when the long put is exercised. The worst outcome occurs when $S_T > X_2$, in which case both puts expire out-of-the-money and the net premium is lost.

In the example, we again use options with exercise prices of 1950 and 2050. Their premiums are $p_1 = 56.01$ and $p_2 = 107.39$. We examine the three outcomes we did with the bull spread: S_T is 1900, 2000, or 2100.

With $S_T = 1900$, the value at expiration is $V_T = 2050 - 1950 = 100$.

With $S_T = 2000$, the value at expiration is $V_T = 2050 - 2000 = 50$.

With $S_T = 2100$, the value at expiration is $V_T = 0$.

The profit is obtained by taking the value at expiration, subtracting the premium of the put with the higher exercise price, and adding the premium of the put with the lower exercise price:

When $S_T = 1900$, the profit is $\Pi = 100 - 107.39 + 56.01 = 48.62$.

When $S_T = 2000$, the profit is $\Pi = 50 - 107.39 + 56.01 = -1.38$.

When $S_T = 2100$, the profit is $\Pi = -107.39 + 56.01 = -51.38$.

When S_T is less than 1900, the outcome is the same as when S_T equals 1900. When S_T is greater than 2100, the outcome is the same as when S_T equals 2100.

The results are graphed in Exhibit 7-9. Note how this strategy is similar to a bull spread but with opposite outcomes. The gains are on the downside underlying moves and the losses

EXHIBIT 7-9   Bear Spread (Buy Put with Exercise Price X_2, Sell Put with Exercise Price X_1)

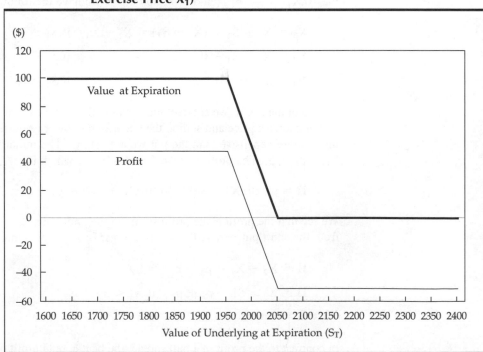

are on the upside underlying. The maximum profit occurs when both puts expire in-the-money. You end up using the short put to buy the asset and the long put to sell the asset. The maximum profit is $X_2 - X_1 - p_2 + p_1$, which in this example is $100 - 107.39 + 56.01 = 48.62$, a return of 94 percent.[11] The maximum loss of $p_2 - p_1$ occurs when both puts expire out-of-the-money, and in this case is $107.39 - 56.01 = 51.38$, a loss of 100 percent.

The breakeven asset price occurs between the two exercise prices. Let $S_T{}^*$ be the breakeven asset price at expiration, set the profit equation for the middle case to zero, and solve for $S_T{}^*$ to obtain $S_T{}^* = X_2 - p_2 + p_1$. In this case, the breakeven is $S_T{}^* = 2050 - 107.39 + 56.01 = 1,998.62$. The underlying need move down only as little as 0.07 percent to make a profit.

To summarize the bear spread, we have

Value at expiration: $V_T = \max(0, X_2 - S_T) - \max(0, X_1 - S_T)$

Profit: $\Pi = V_T - p_2 + p_1$

Maximum profit $= X_2 - X_1 - p_2 + p_1$

Maximum loss $= p_2 - p_1$

Breakeven: $S_T{}^* = X_2 - p_2 + p_1$

PRACTICE PROBLEM 6

Consider two put options on a bond selling for $92 per $100 par. One put has an exercise price of $85 and is selling for $3. The other put has an exercise price of $95 and is selling for $11. Both puts expire at the same time. Answer the following questions about a bear spread:

A. Determine the value at expiration and the profit under the following outcomes:
   i. The price of the bond at expiration is $98.
   ii. The price of the bond at expiration is $91.
   iii. The price of the bond at expiration is $82.

B. Determine the following:
   i. The maximum profit
   ii. The maximum loss

C. Determine the breakeven bond price at expiration.

SOLUTIONS

A. **i.** $V_T = \max(0, X_2 - S_T) - \max(0, X_1 - S_T) = \max(0, 95 - 98) - \max(0, 85 - 98) = 0 - 0 = 0$
$\Pi = V_T - V_0 = V_T - (p_2 - p_1) = 0 - (11 - 3) = -8$
   ii. $V_T = \max(0, X_2 - S_T) - \max(0, X_1 - S_T) = \max(0, 95 - 91) - \max(0, 85 - 91) = 4 - 0 = 4$
$\Pi = V_T - V_0 = V_T - (p_2 - p_1) = 4 - (11 - 3) = -4$
   iii. $V_T = \max(0, X_2 - S_T) - \max(0, X_1 - S_T) = \max(0, 95 - 82) - \max(0, 85 - 82) = 13 - 3 = 10$
$\Pi = V_T - V_0 = 10 - (p_2 - p_1) = 10 - (11 - 3) = 2$

---

[11] The net premium is $107.39 - 56.01 = 51.38$, so the maximum value of 100 is a return of about 94 percent.

B.   **i.** Maximum profit = $X_2 - X_1 - (p_2 - p_1) = 95 - 85 - (11 - 3) = 2$
      ii. Maximum loss = $p_2 - p_1 = 11 - 3 = 8$
C. $S_T^* = X_2 - p_2 + p_1 = 95 - 11 + 3 = 87$

The bear spread with calls involves selling the call with the lower exercise price and buying the one with the higher exercise price. Because the call with the lower exercise price will be more expensive, there will be a cash inflow at initiation of the position and hence a profit if the calls expire worthless.

Bull and bear spreads are but two types of spread strategies. We now take a look at another strategy, which combines bull and bear spreads.

2.3.3 Butterfly Spreads

In both the bull and bear spread, we used options with two different exercise prices. There is no limit to how many different options one can use in a strategy. As an example, the **butterfly spread** combines a bull and bear spread. Consider three different exercise prices, X_1, X_2, and X_3. Suppose we first construct a bull spread, buying the call with exercise price of X_1 and selling the call with exercise price of X_2. Recall that we could construct a bear spread using calls instead of puts. In that case, we would buy the call with the higher exercise price and sell the call with the lower exercise price. This bear spread is identical to the sale of a bull spread.

Suppose we sell a bull spread by buying the call with exercise price X_3 and selling the call with exercise price X_2. We have now combined a long bull spread and a short bull spread (or a bear spread). We own the calls with exercise price X_1 and X_3 and have sold two calls with exercise price X_2. Combining these results, we obtain a value at expiration of

$$V_T = \max(0, S_T - X_1) - 2\max(0, S_T - X_2) + \max(0, S_T - X_3)$$

This can be broken down into ranges of

$$V_T = 0 - 2(0) + 0 = 0 \qquad\qquad\qquad\qquad\qquad \text{if } S_T \leq X_1$$
$$V_T = S_T - X_1 - 2(0) + 0 = S_T - X_1 \qquad\qquad \text{if } X_1 < S_T < X_2$$
$$V_T = S_T - X_1 - 2(S_T - X_2) + 0 = -S_T + 2X_2 - X_1 \quad \text{if } X_2 \leq S_T < X_3$$
$$V_T = S_T - X_1 - 2(S_T - X_2) + S_T - X_3 = 2X_2 - X_1 - X_3 \quad \text{if } S_T \geq X_3$$

If the exercise prices are equally spaced, $2X_2 - X_1 - X_3$ would equal zero.[12] In virtually all cases in practice, the exercise prices are indeed equally spaced, and we shall make that assumption. Therefore,

$$V_T = 2X_2 - X_1 - X_3 = 0 \quad \text{if } S_T \geq X_3$$

To obtain the profit, we must subtract the initial value of the position, which is $V_0 = c_1 - 2c_2 + c_3$. Is this value positive or negative? It turns out that it will always be positive. The bull spread we buy is more expensive than the bull spread we sell, because the lower exer-

---

[12] For example, suppose the exercise prices are equally spaced with $X_1 = 30$, $X_2 = 40$, and $X_3 = 50$. Then $2X_2 - X_3 - X_1 = 2(40) - 50 - 30 = 0$.

cise price on the bull spread we buy (X_1) is lower than the lower exercise price on the bull spread we sell (X_2). Because the underlying is more likely to move higher than X_1 than to move higher than X_2, the bull spread we buy is more expensive than the bull spread we sell.

The profit is thus $V_T - V_0$, which is

$$\Pi = \max(0, S_T - X_1) - 2\max(0, S_T - X_2) + \max(0, S_T - X_3) - c_1 + 2c_2 - c_3$$

Broken down into ranges,

$$\Pi = -c_1 + 2c_2 - c_3 \qquad \text{if } S_T \leq X_1$$
$$\Pi = S_T - X_1 - c_1 + 2c_2 - c_3 \qquad \text{if } X_1 < S_T < X_2$$
$$\Pi = -S_T + 2X_2 - X_1 - c_1 + 2c_2 - c_3 \quad \text{if } X_2 \leq S_T < X_3$$
$$\Pi = -c_1 + 2c_2 - c_3 \qquad \text{if } S_T \geq X_3$$

Note that in the lowest and highest ranges, the profit is negative; a loss. It is not immediately obvious what happens in the middle two ranges. Let us look at our example. In this example, we buy the calls with exercise prices of 1950 and 2050 and sell two calls with exercise price of 2000. So, $X_1 = 1950$, $X_2 = 2000$, and $X_3 = 2050$. Their premiums are $c_1 = 108.43$, $c_2 = 81.75$, and $c_3 = 59.98$. Let us examine the outcomes in which $S_T = 1900$, 1975, 2025, and 2100. These outcomes fit into each of the four relevant ranges.

When $S_T = 1900$, the value at expiration is $V_T = 0 - 2(0) + 0 = 0$.

When $S_T = 1975$, the value at expiration is $V_T = 1975 - 1950 = 25$.

When $S_T = 2025$, the value at expiration is $V_T = -2025 + 2(2000) - 1950 = 25$.

When $S_T = 2100$, the value at expiration is $V_T = 0$.

Now, turning to the profit,

When $S_T = 1900$, the profit will be $\Pi = 0 - 108.43 + 2(81.75) - 59.98 = -4.91$.

When $S_T = 1975$, the profit will be $\Pi = 25 - 108.43 + 2(81.75) - 59.98 = 20.09$.

When $S_T = 2025$, the profit will be $\Pi = 25 - 108.43 + 2(81.75) - 59.98 = 20.09$.

When $S_T = 2100$, the profit will be $\Pi = 0 - 108.43 + 2(81.75) - 59.98 = -4.91$.

Exhibit 7-10 depicts these results graphically. Note that the strategy is based on the expectation that the volatility of the underlying will be relatively low. The expectation must be that the underlying will trade near the middle exercise price. The maximum loss of 4.91 occurs if the underlying ends up below the lower strike, 1950, or above the upper strike, 2050. The maximum profit occurs if the underlying ends up precisely at the middle exercise price. This maximum profit is found by examining either of the middle two ranges with S_T set equal to X_2:

$$\Pi \text{ (maximum)} = S_T - X_1 - c_1 + 2c_2 - c_3$$
$$= X_2 - X_1 - c_1 + 2c_2 - c_3 \qquad \text{if } S_T = X_2$$
$$\Pi \text{ (maximum)} = -S_T + 2X_2 - X_1 - c_1 + 2c_2 - c_3$$
$$= X_2 - X_1 - c_1 + 2c_2 - c_3 \qquad \text{if } S_T = X_2$$

In this case, the maximum profit is Π (maximum) $= 2000 - 1950 - 108.43 + 2(81.75) - 59.98 = 45.09$, which is a return of 918 percent.[13]

EXHIBIT 7-10   Butterfly Spread (Buy Calls with Exercise Price X_1 and X_3, Sell Two Calls with Exercise Price X_2)

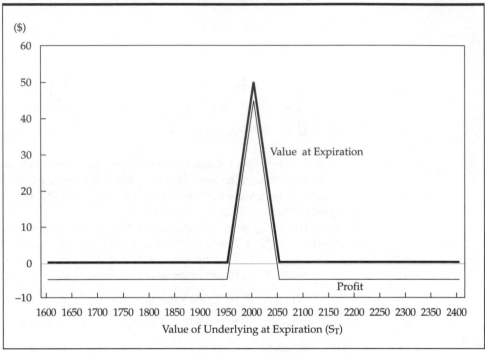

There are two breakeven prices, and they lie within the two middle profit ranges. We find them as follows:

For $X_1 < S_T < X_2$:

$$\Pi = S_T^* - X_1 - c_1 + 2c_2 - c_3 = 0$$

$$S_T^* = X_1 + c_1 - 2c_2 + c_3$$

For $X_2 \leq S_T < X_3$:

$$\Pi = -S_T^* + 2X_2 - X_1 - c_1 + 2c_2 - c_3 = 0$$

$$S_T^* = 2X_2 - X_1 - c_1 + 2c_2 - c_3$$

In this example, therefore, the breakeven prices are

$$S_T^* = X_1 + c_1 - 2c_2 + c_3$$

$$= 1950 + 108.43 - 2(81.75) + 59.98 = 1954.91$$

---

[13] This return is based on a maximum value of $2000 - 1950 = 50$ versus the initial value of 4.91, a return of 918 percent.

$$S_T^* = 2X_2 - X_1 - c_1 + 2c_2 - c_3$$
$$= 2(2000) - 1950 - 108.43 + 2(81.75) - 59.98 = 2045.09$$

These movements represent a range of roughly ± 2.3 percent from the starting value of 2000. Therefore, if the underlying stays within this range, the strategy will be profitable.
In summary, for the butterfly spread

Value at expiration: $V_T = \max(0, S_T - X_1) - 2\max(0, S_T - X_2) + \max(0, S_T - X_3)$

Profit: $\Pi = V_T - c_1 + 2c_2 - c_3$

Maximum profit $= X_2 - X_1 - c_1 + 2c_2 - c_3$

Maximum loss $= c_1 - 2c_2 + c_3$

Breakeven: $S_T^* = X_1 + c_1 - 2c_2 + c_3$ and $S_T^* = 2X_2 - X_1 - c_1 + 2c_2 - c_3$

As we noted, a butterfly spread is a strategy based on the expectation of low volatility in the underlying. Of course, for a butterfly spread to be an appropriate strategy, the user must believe that the underlying will be less volatile than the market expects. If the investor buys into the strategy and the market is more volatile than expected, the strategy is likely to result in a loss. If the investor expects the market to be more volatile than he believes the market expects, the appropriate strategy could be to sell the butterfly spread. Doing so would involve selling the calls with exercise prices of X_1 and X_3 and buying two calls with exercise prices of X_2.[14]

Alternatively, a butterfly spread can be executed using puts. Note that the initial value of the spread using calls is $V_0 = c_1 - 2c_2 + c_3$. Recall that from put–call parity, $c = p + S - X/(1 + r)^T$. If we use the appropriate subscripts and substitute $p_i + S - X_i/(1 + r)^T$ for c_i where $i = 1, 2$, and 3, we obtain $V_0 = p_1 - 2p_2 + p_3$. The positive signs on p_1 and p_3 and the negative sign on $2p_2$ mean that we could buy the puts with exercise prices X_1 and X_3 and sell two puts with exercise price of X_2 to obtain the same result. We would, in effect, be buying a bear spread with puts consisting of buying the put with exercise price of X_3 and selling the put with exercise price of X_2, and also selling a bear spread by selling the put with exercise price of X_2 and buying the put with exercise price of X_1. If the options are priced correctly, it does not really matter whether we use puts or calls.[15]

PRACTICE PROBLEM 7

Consider three put options on a currency that is currently selling for $1.45. The exercise prices are $1.30, $1.40, and $1.50. The put prices are $0.08, $0.125, and $0.18, respectively. The puts all expire at the same time. Answer the following questions about a butterfly spread.

A. Determine the value at expiration and the profit under the following outcomes:
    i. The price of the currency at expiration is $1.26.
    ii. The price of the currency at expiration is $1.35.

---

[14] A short butterfly spread is sometimes called a **sandwich spread**.

[15] If puts were underpriced, it would be better to buy the butterfly spread using puts. If calls were underpriced, it would be better to buy the butterfly spread using calls. Of course, other strategies could also be used to take advantage of any mispricing.

    iii. The price of the currency at expiration is \$1.47.

    iv. The price of the currency at expiration is \$1.59.

B. Determine the following:

    i. The maximum profit

    ii. The maximum loss

C. Determine the breakeven currency price at expiration.

SOLUTIONS

A.   **i.** $V_T = \max(0,X_1 - S_T) - 2\max(0,X_2 - S_T) + \max(0,X_3 - S_T) = \max(0,1.30 - 1.26) - 2\max(0,1.40 - 1.26) + \max(0,1.50 - 1.26) = 0.04 - 2(0.14) + 0.24 = 0.0$

      $\Pi = V_T - V_0 = V_T - (p_1 - 2p_2 + p_3) = 0.0 - [0.08 - 2(0.125) + 0.18] = -0.01$

  ii. $V_T = \max(0,X_1 - S_T) - 2\max(0,X_2 - S_T) + \max(0,X_3 - S_T) = \max(0,1.30 - 1.35) - 2\max(0,1.40 - 1.35) + \max(0,1.50 - 1.35) = 0.0 - 2(0.05) + 0.15 = 0.05$

      $\Pi = V_T - V_0 = V_T - (p_1 - 2p_2 + p_3) = 0.05 - [0.08 - 2(0.125) + 0.18] = 0.04$

 iii. $V_T = \max(0,X_1 - S_T) - 2\max(0,X_2 - S_T) + \max(0,X_3 - S_T) = \max(0,1.30 - 1.47) - 2\max(0,1.40 - 1.47) + \max(0,1.50 - 1.47) = 0.0 - 2(0) + 0.03 = 0.03$

      $\Pi = V_T - V_0 = V_T - (p_1 - 2p_2 + p_3) = 0.03 - [0.08 - 2(0.125) + 0.18] = 0.02$

  iv. $V_T = \max(0,X_1 - S_T) - 2\max(0,X_2 - S_T) + \max(0,X_3 - S_T) = \max(0,1.30 - 1.59) - 2\max(0,1.40 - 1.59) + \max(0,1.50 - 1.59) = 0.0 - 2(0) + 0.0 = 0.0$

      $\Pi = V_T - V_0 = V_T - (p_1 - 2p_2 + p_3) = 0.0 - [0.08 - 2(0.125) + 0.18] = -0.01$

B.   **i.** Maximum profit $= X_2 - X_1 - (p_1 - 2p_2 + p_3) = 1.40 - 1.30 - [0.08 - 2(0.125) + 0.18] = 0.09$

  ii. Maximum loss $= p_1 - 2p_2 + p_3 = 0.08 - 2(0.125) + 0.18 = 0.01$

C. $S_T{}^* = X_1 + p_1 - 2p_2 + p_3 = 1.30 + 0.08 - 2(0.125) + 0.18 = 1.31$

    $S_T{}^* = 2X_2 - X_1 - p_1 + 2p_2 - p_3 = 2(1.40) - 1.30 - 0.08 + 2(0.125) - 0.18 = 1.49$

So far, we have restricted ourselves to the use of either calls or puts, but not both. We now look at strategies that involve positions in calls *and* puts.

2.4   COMBINATIONS OF CALLS AND PUTS

2.4.1   COLLARS

Recall that in Section 2.2 we examined the protective put. In that strategy, the holder of the underlying asset buys a put to provide protection against downside loss. Purchasing the put requires the payment of the put premium. One way to get around paying the put premium is to sell another option with a premium equal to the put premium, which can be done by selling a call with an exercise price above the current price of the underlying.

Although it is not necessary that the call premium offset the put premium, and the call premium can even be more than the put premium, the typical collar has the call and put premiums offset. When this offsetting occurs, no net premium is required up front. In effect, the holder of the asset gains protection below a certain level, the exercise price of the put, and pays for it by giving up gains above a certain level, the exercise price of the call. This strategy is called a **collar**. When the premiums offset, it is sometimes called a **zero-cost collar**. This term is a little misleading, however, as it suggests that there is no "cost" to this transaction. The cost takes the form of forgoing upside gains. The term "zero-cost" refers only to the fact that no cash is paid up front.

A collar is a modified version of a protective put and a covered call and requires different exercise prices for each. Let the put exercise price be X_1 and the call exercise price be X_2. With X_1 given, it is important to see that X_2 is not arbitrary. If we want the call premium to offset the put premium, the exercise price on the call must be set such that the price of the call equals the price of the put. We thus can select any exercise price of the put. Then the call exercise price is selected by determining which exercise price will produce a call premium equal to the put premium. Although the put can have any exercise price, typically the put exercise price is lower than the current value of the underlying. The call exercise price then must be above the current value of the underlying.[16]

So let X_1 be set. The put with this exercise price has a premium of p_1. We now need to set X_2 such that the premium on the call, c_2, equals the premium on the put, p_1. To do so, we need to use an option valuation model, such as Black–Scholes–Merton, to find the exercise price of the call that will make $c_2 = p_1$. Recall that the Black–Scholes–Merton formula is

$$c = S_0 N(d_1) - X e^{-r^c T} N(d_2)$$

where

$$d_1 = \frac{\ln(S_0/X) + (r^c + \sigma^2/2)T}{\sigma\sqrt{T}}$$

$$d_2 = d_1 - \sigma\sqrt{T}$$

and where r^c is the continuously compounded risk-free rate and $N(d_1)$ and $N(d_2)$ are normal probabilities associated with the values d_1 and d_2. Ideally we would turn the equation around and solve for X in terms of c, but the equation is too complex to be able to isolate X on one side. So, we must solve for X by trial and error. We substitute in values of X until the option price equals c, where c is the call premium that we want to equal the put premium.

Consider the Nasdaq example. Suppose we use the put with exercise price of 1950. Its premium is 56.01. So now we need a call with a premium of 56.01. The call with exercise price of 2000 is worth 81.75. So to get a lower call premium, we need a call with an exercise price higher than 2000. By trial and error, we insert higher and higher exercise prices until the call premium falls to 56.01, which occurs at an exercise price of about 2060.[17] So now we have it. We buy the put with an exercise price of 1950 for 56.01 and sell the call with exercise price of 2060 for 56.01. This transaction requires no cash up front.

---

[16] It can be proven in general that the call exercise price would have to be above the current value of the underlying. Intuitively, it can be shown through put–call parity that if the call and put exercise prices were equal to the current value of the underlying, the call would be worth more than the put. If we lower the put exercise price below the price of the underlying, the put price would decrease. Then the gap between the call and put prices would widen further. We would then need to raise the call exercise price above the current price of the underlying to make its premium come down.

[17] The other necessary information to obtain the exercise price of the call are that the volatility is 0.35, the risk-free rate is 0.02, and the dividend yield is 0.005. The actual call price at a stock price of 2060 is 56.18. At 2061, the call price is 55.82. Thus, the correct exercise price lies between 2060 and 2061; we simply round to 2060.

The value of the position at expiration is the sum of the value of the underlying asset, the value of the put, and the value of the short call:

$$V_T = S_T + max(0, X_1 - S_T) - max(0, S_T - X_2)$$

Broken down into ranges, we have

$$V_T = S_T + X_1 - S_T - 0 = X_1 \quad \text{if } S_T \leq X_1$$
$$V_T = S_T + 0 - 0 = S_T \quad\quad\quad \text{if } X_1 < S_T < X_2$$
$$V_T = S_T + 0 - (S_T - X_2) = X_2 \quad \text{if } S_T \geq X_2$$

The initial value of the position is simply the value of the underlying asset, S_0. The profit is $V_T - V_0$:

$$\Pi = S_T + max(0, X_1 - S_T) - max(0, S_T - X_2) - S_0$$

Broken down into ranges, we have

$$\Pi = X_1 - S_0 \quad \text{if } S_T \leq X_1$$
$$\Pi = S_T - S_0 \quad \text{if } X_1 < S_T < X_2$$
$$\Pi = X_2 - S_0 \quad \text{if } S_T \geq X_2$$

Using our example where $X_1 = 1950$, $p_1 = 56.01$, $X_2 = 2060$, $c_2 = 56.01$, and $S_0 = 2000$, we obtain the following values at expiration:

If $S_T = 1900$, $V_T = 1950$

If $S_T = 2000$, $V_T = 2000$

If $S_T = 2100$, $V_T = 2060$

The profit for $S_T = 1900$ is $\Pi = 1950 - 2000 = -50$.

If $S_T = 2000$, $\Pi = 2000 - 2000 = 0$

If $S_T = 2100$, $\Pi = 2060 - 2000 = 60$

A graph of this strategy is shown in Exhibit 7-11. Note that the lines are flat over the range of S_T up to the put exercise price of 1950 and in the range beyond the call exercise price of 2060. Below 1950, the put provides protection against loss. Above 2060, the short call forces a relinquishment of the gains, which are earned by the buyer of the call. In between these ranges, neither the put nor the call has value. The profit is strictly determined by the underlying and moves directly with the value of the underlying. The maximum profit is $X_2 - S_0$, which here is $2060 - 2000 = 60$, a return of 3 percent. The maximum loss is $S_0 - X_1$, which here is $2000 - 1950 = 50$, a loss of 2.5 percent. Keep in mind that these options have lives of one month, so those numbers represent one-month returns. The breakeven is simply the original underlying price of 2000.

In summary, for the collar

Value at expiration: $V_T = S_T + max(0, X_1 - S_T) - max(0, S_T - X_2)$

Profit: $\Pi = V_T - S_0$

EXHIBIT 7-11 Zero-Cost Collar (Buy Put with Exercise Price X_1, Sell Call with Exercise Price X_2, Put and Call Premiums Offset)

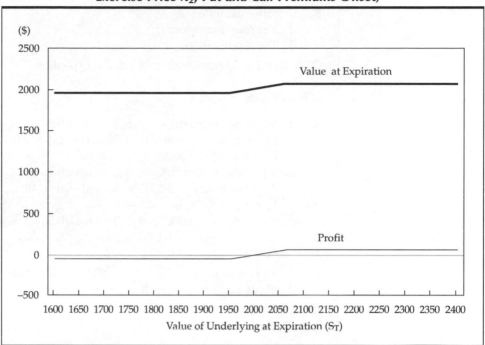

Maximum profit $= X_2 - S_0$

Maximum loss $= S_0 - X_1$

Breakeven: $S_T^* = S_0$

Collars are also known as range forwards and risk reversals.[18] Asset managers often use them to guard against losses without having to pay cash up front for the protection. Clearly, however, they are virtually the same as bull spreads. The latter has a cap on the gain and a floor on the loss but does not involve actually holding the underlying. In Section 3.0, we shall encounter this strategy again in the form of an interest rate collar, which protects floating-rate borrowers against high interest rates.

PRACTICE PROBLEM 8

The holder of a stock worth $42 is considering placing a collar on it. A put with an exercise price of $40 costs $5.32. A call with the same premium would require an exercise price of $50.59.

A. Determine the value at expiration and the profit under the following outcomes:
  i. The price of the stock at expiration is $55.

---

[18] It is not clear why a collar is sometimes called a risk reversal. It is clear, however, why a collar is sometimes called a range forward. Like a forward contract, it requires no initial outlay other than for the underlying. Unlike a forward contract, which has a strictly linear payoff profile, the collar payoff breaks at the two exercise prices, thus creating a range.

ii. The price of the stock at expiration is $48.

iii. The price of the stock at expiration is $35.

B. Determine the following:

   i. The maximum profit

   ii. The maximum loss

C. Determine the breakeven stock price at expiration.

SOLUTIONS

A. i. $V_T = S_T + max(0, X_1 - S_T) - max(0, S_T - X_2) = 55 + max(0, 40 - 55) - max(0, 55 - 50.59) = 55 + 0 - (55 - 50.59) = 50.59$
$\Pi = V_T - S_0 = 50.59 - 42 = 8.59$

  ii. $V_T = S_T + max(0, X_1 - S_T) - max(0, S_T - X_2) = 48 + max(0, 40 - 48) - max(0, 48 - 50.59) = 48 + 0 - 0 = 48$
$\Pi = V_T - S_0 = 48 - 42 = 6$

  iii. $V_T = S_T + max(0, X_1 - S_T) - max(0, S_T - X_2) = 35 + max(0, 40 - 35) - max(0, 35 - 50.59) = 35 + 5 - 0 = 40$
$\Pi = V_T - S_0 = 40 - 42 = -2$

B. i. Maximum profit $= X_2 - S_0 = 50.59 - 42 = 8.59$

  ii. Maximum loss $= S_0 - X_1 = 42 - 40 = 2$

C. $S_T^* = S_0 = 42$

Collars are one of the many directional strategies, meaning that they perform based on the direction of the movement in the underlying. Of course, butterfly spreads perform based on the volatility of the underlying. Another strategy in which performance is based on the volatility of the underlying is the straddle.

2.4.2 STRADDLE

To justify the purchase of a call, an investor must be bullish. To justify the purchase of a put, an investor must be bearish. What should an investor do if he believes the market will be volatile but does not feel particularly strongly about the direction? We discussed earlier that a short butterfly spread is one strategy. It benefits from extreme movements, but its gains are limited. There are other, more-complex strategies, such as time spreads, that can benefit from high volatility; however, one simple strategy, the **straddle**, also benefits from high volatility.

Suppose the investor buys both a call and a put with the same exercise price on the same underlying with the same expiration. This strategy enables the investor to profit from upside or downside moves. Its cost, however, can be quite heavy. In fact, a straddle is a wager on a large movement in the underlying.

The value of a straddle at expiration is the value of the call and the value of the put: $V_T = max(0, S_T - X) + max(0, X - S_T)$. Broken down into ranges,

$$V_T = X - S_T \quad \text{if } S_T < X$$

$$V_T = S_T - X \quad \text{if } S_T \geq X$$

The initial value of the straddle is simply $V_0 = c_0 + p_0$. The profit is $V_T - V_0$ or $\Pi = max(0, S_T - X) + max(0, X - S_T) - c_0 - p_0$. Broken down into ranges,

$$\Pi = X - S_T - c_0 - p_0 \quad \text{if } S_T < X$$
$$\Pi = S_T - X - c_0 - p_0 \quad \text{if } S_T \geq X$$

In our example, let $X = 2000$. Then $c_0 = 81.75$ and $p_0 = 79.25$.

If $S_T = 2100$, the value of the position at expiration is $V_T = 2100 - 2000 = 100$.

If $S_T = 1900$, the value of the position at expiration is $V_T = 2000 - 1900 = 100$.

If $S_T = 2100$, the profit is $\Pi = 100 - 81.75 - 79.25 = -61$.

If $S_T = 1900$, the profit is $\Pi = 100 - 81.75 - 79.25 = -61$.

Note the symmetry, whereby a move of 100 in either direction results in a change in value of 61. The put and call payoffs are obviously symmetric. It is also apparent that these outcomes are below breakeven.

Observe the results in Exhibit 7-12. Note that the value and profit are V-shaped, thereby benefiting from large moves in the underlying in either direction. Like the call option the straddle contains, the gain on the upside is unlimited. Like the put, the downside gain is not unlimited, but it is quite large. The underlying can go down no further than zero. Hence, on the downside the maximum profit is $X - c_0 - p_0$, which in this case is $2000 - 81.75 - 79.25 = 1839$. The maximum loss occurs if the underlying ends up precisely at the exercise price. In that case, neither the call nor the put expires with value and the premiums are lost on both. Therefore, the maximum loss is $c_0 + p_0$, which is $81.75 + 79.25 = 161$.

EXHIBIT 7-12   Straddle (Buy Call and Put with Exercise Price X)

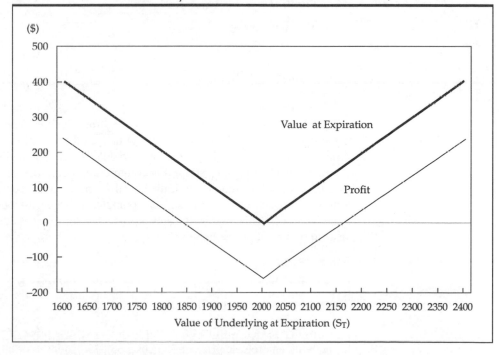

There are two breakevens. Using S_T^* to denote the breakevens, we set each profit equation to zero and solve for S_T^*:

If $S_T \geq X$,

$$\Pi = S_T^* - X - c_0 - p_0 = 0$$

$$S_T^* = X + c_0 + p_0$$

If $S_T < X$,

$$\Pi = X - S_T^* - c_0 - p_0 = 0$$

$$S_T^* = X - c_0 - p_0$$

The breakevens thus equal the exercise price plus or minus the premiums. So in this case, the breakevens are $2000 \pm 161 = 2161$ and 1839. A move of 161 is a percentage move of 8.1 percent over a one-month period. Hence, in this example, the purchase of a straddle is a bet that the underlying will move at nearly a 100 percent annual rate over a one-month period, quite a risky bet. An investor would make such a bet only when he felt that the underlying would be exceptionally volatile. An obvious time to use a straddle would be around major events such as earnings announcements. But because earnings announcements are known and anticipated events, the greater uncertainty surrounding them should already be reflected in the options' prices. Recall that the greater the volatility, the higher the prices of both puts and calls. Therefore, using a straddle in anticipation of an event that everyone knows is coming is not necessarily a good idea. Only when the investor believes the market will be more volatile than everyone else believes would a straddle be advised.

In summary, for a straddle

Value at expiration: $V_T = \max(0, S_T - X) + \max(0, X - S_T)$

Profit: $\Pi = V_T - (c_0 + p_0)$

Maximum profit $= \infty$

Maximum loss $= c_0 + p_0$

Breakeven: $S_T^* = X \pm (c_0 + p_0)$

As we have noted, a straddle would tend to be used by an investor who is expecting the market to be volatile but does not have strong feelings one way or the other on the direction. An investor who leans one way or the other might considering adding a call or a put to the straddle. Adding a call to a straddle is a strategy called a **strap**, and adding a put to a straddle is called a **strip**. It is even more difficult to make a gain from these strategies than it is for a straddle, but if the hoped-for move does occur, the gains are leveraged. Another variation of the straddle is a **strangle**, in which the put and call have different exercise prices. This strategy creates a graph similar to a straddle but with a flat section instead of a point on the bottom.

PRACTICE PROBLEM 9

Consider a stock worth $49. A call with an exercise price of $50 costs $6.25 and a put with an exercise price of $50 costs $5.875. An investor buys a straddle.

A. Determine the value at expiration and the profit under the following outcomes:
   i. The price of the stock at expiration is $61.
   ii. The price of the stock at expiration is $37.

B. Determine the following:
    i. The maximum profit
    ii. The maximum loss
C. Determine the breakeven stock price at expiration.

SOLUTIONS

A. **i.** $V_T = \max(0, S_T - X) + \max(0, X - S_T) = \max(0, 61 - 50) + \max(0, 50 - 61) = 11 - 0 = 11$
      $\Pi = V_T - (c_0 + p_0) = 11 - (6.25 + 5.875) = -1.125$
  ii. $V_T = \max(0, S_T - X) + \max(0, X - S_T) = \max(0, 37 - 50) + \max(0, 50 - 37) = 0 + 13 = 13$
      $\Pi = V_T - S_0 = 13 - (6.25 + 5.875) = 0.875$

B. **i.** Maximum profit $= \infty$
  ii. Maximum loss $= c_0 + p_0 = 6.25 + 5.875 = 12.125$

C. $S_T{}^* = X \pm (c_0 + p_0) = 50 \pm (6.25 + 5.875) = 62.125, 37.875$

Now we turn to a strategy that combines more than one call and more than one put. It should not be surprising that we shall recognize this strategy as just a combination of something we have already learned.

2.4.3 BOX SPREADS

In Chapter 4 we exploited an arbitrage opportunity with a neutral position three alternative ways: using put–call parity, using the binomial model, or using the Black–Scholes–Merton model. Exploiting put–call parity requires a position in the underlying. Using the binomial or Black–Scholes–Merton model requires that the model holds in the market. In addition, both models require a position in the underlying and an estimate of the volatility.

A **box spread** can also be used to exploit an arbitrage opportunity but it requires that neither the binomial nor Black–Scholes–Merton model holds, it needs no estimate of the volatility, and all of the transactions can be executed within the options market, making implementation of the strategy simpler, faster, and with lower transaction costs.

In basic terms, a box spread is a combination of a bull spread and a bear spread. Suppose we buy the call with exercise price X_1 and sell the call with exercise price X_2. This set of transactions is a bull spread. Then we buy the put with exercise price X_2 and sell the put with exercise price X_1. This is a bear spread. Intuitively, it should sound like a combination of a bull spread and a bear spread would leave the investor with a fairly neutral position, and indeed, that is the case.

The value of the box spread at expiration is

$$V_T = \max(0, S_T - X_1) - \max(0, S_T - X_2) + \max(0, X_2 - S_T) - \max(0, X_1 - S_T)$$

Broken down into ranges, we have

$$V_T = 0 - 0 + X_2 - S_T - (X_1 - S_T) = X_2 - X_1 \quad \text{if } S_T \le X_1$$

$$V_T = S_T - X_1 - 0 + X_2 - S_T - 0 = X_2 - X_1 \quad \text{if } X_1 < S_T < X_2$$

$$V_T = S_T - X_1 - (S_T - X_2) + 0 - 0 = X_2 - X_1 \quad \text{if } S_T \ge X_2$$

These outcomes are all the same. In each case, two of the four options expire in-the-money, and the other two expire out-of-the-money. In each case, the holder of the box spread ends up buying the underlying with one option, using either the long call at X_1 or the short put at X_1, and selling the underlying with another option, using either the long put at X_2 or the short call at X_2. The box spread thus results in buying the underlying at X_1 and selling it at X_2. This outcome is known at the start.

The initial value of the transaction is the value of the long call, short call, long put, and short put, $V_0 = c_1 - c_2 + p_2 - p_1$. The profit is, therefore, $\Pi = X_2 - X_1 - c_1 + c_2 - p_2 + p_1$.

In contrast to all of the other strategies, the outcome is simple. In all cases, we end up with the same result. Using the options with exercise prices of 1950 and 2050, which have premiums of $c_1 = 108.43$, $c_2 = 59.98$, $p_1 = 56.01$, and $p_2 = 107.39$, the value at expiration is always $2050 - 1950 = 100$ and the profit is always $\Pi = 100 - 108.43 + 59.98 - 107.39 + 56.01 = 0.17$. This value may seem remarkably low. We shall see why momentarily.

The initial value of the box spread is $c_1 - c_2 + p_2 - p_1$. The payoff at expiration is $X_2 - X_1$. Because the transaction is risk free, the present value of the payoff, discounted using the risk-free rate, should equal the initial outlay. Hence, we should have

$$(X_2 - X_1)/(1 + r)^T = c_1 - c_2 + p_2 - p_1$$

If the present value of the payoff exceeds the initial value, the box spread is underpriced and should be purchased.

In this example, the initial outlay is $V_0 = 108.43 - 59.98 + 107.39 - 56.01 = 99.83$. To obtain the present value of the payoff, we need an interest rate and time to expiration. The prices of these options were obtained using a time to expiration of one month and a risk-free rate of 2.02 percent. The present value of the payoff is

$$(X_2 - X_1)/(1 + r)^r = (2050 - 1950)/(1.0202)^{1/12} = 99.83$$

In other words, this box spread is correctly priced. This result should not be surprising, because we noted that we used the Black–Scholes–Merton model to price these options. The model should not allow arbitrage opportunities of any form.

Recall that the profit from this transaction is 0.17, a very low value. This profit reflects the fact that the box spread is purchased at 99.83 and matures to a value of 100, a profit of 0.17, which is a return of the risk-free rate for one month.[19] The reason the profit seems so low is that it is just the risk-free rate.

Let us assume that one of the long options, say the put with exercise price of 2050, is underpriced. Let its premium be 105 instead of 107.39. Then the net premium would be $108.43 - 59.98 + 105 - 56.01 = 97.44$. Again, the present value of the payoff is 99.83. Hence, the box spread would generate a gain in value clearly in excess of the risk-free rate. If some combination of the options was such that the net premium is more than the present value of the payoff, then the box spread would be overpriced. Then we should sell the X_1 call and X_2 put and buy the X_2 call and X_1 put. Doing so would generate an outlay at expiration with a present value less than the initial value.

So to summarize the box spread, we say that

Value at expiration: $V_T = X_2 - X_1$

---

[19] That is, $99.83(1.0202)^{1/12} \approx 100$. Hence, the profit of 0.17 is about 2.02 percent, for one month.

Profit: $\Pi = X_2 - X_1 - (c_1 - c_2 + p_2 - p_1)$

Maximum profit = (same as profit)

Maximum loss = (no loss is possible, given fair option prices)

Breakeven: no breakeven; the transaction always earns the risk-free rate, given fair option prices.

PRACTICE PROBLEM 10

Consider a box spread consisting of options with exercise prices of 75 and 85. The call prices are 16.02 and 12.28 for exercise prices of 75 and 85, respectively. The put prices are 9.72 and 15.18 for exercise prices of 75 and 85, respectively. The options expire in six months and the discrete risk-free rate is 5.13 percent.

A. Determine the value of the box spread and the profit for any value of the underlying at expiration.

B. Show that this box spread is priced such that an attractive opportunity is available.

SOLUTIONS

A. The box spread always has a value at expiration of $X_2 - X_1 = 85 - 75 = 10$
$\Pi = V_T - (c_1 - c_2 + p_2 - p_1) = 10 - (16.02 - 12.28 + 15.18 - 9.72) = 0.80$

B. The box spread should be worth $(X_2 - X_1)/(1 + r)^T$, or

$(85 - 75)/(1.0513)^{0.5} = 9.75$

The cost of the box spread is $16.02 - 12.28 + 15.18 - 9.72 = 9.20$. The box spread is thus underpriced. At least one of the long options is priced too low or at least one of the short options is priced too high; we cannot tell which. Nonetheless, we can execute this box spread, buying the call with exercise price $X_1 = 75$ and put with exercise price $X_2 = 85$ and selling the call with exercise price $X_2 = 85$ and put with exercise price $X_1 = 75$. This would cost 9.20. The present value of the payoff is 9.75. Therefore, the box spread would generate an immediate increase in value of 0.55.

We have now completed our discussion of equity option strategies. Although the strategies are applicable, with minor changes, to fixed-income securities, we shall not explore that area here. We shall, however, look at interest rate option strategies, which require some significant differences in presentation and understanding compared with equity option strategies.

3 INTEREST RATE OPTION STRATEGIES

In Chapter 4 we examined options, which included a group of options in which the underlying is an interest rate and the exercise price is expressed in terms of a rate. Recall that this group of options consists of calls, which pay off if the option expires with the underlying interest rate above the exercise rate, and puts, which pay off if the option expires with the underlying interest rate below the exercise rate. Interest rate call and put options are usually purchased to protect against changes in interest rates. For dollar-based interest rate derivatives, the underlying is usually LIBOR but is always a specific rate, such as the rate on a 90- or 180-day underlying instrument. An interest rate option is based on a specific notional principal, which determines the payoff when the option is exercised. Traditionally, the payoff does not occur immediately upon exercise but is delayed by a period corresponding to the life of the underlying instrument from which the interest rate is taken, an issue we review below.

Recall from Chapter 4 that the payoff of an interest rate call option (Equation 4-1) is

$$\text{(Notional principal) max}\left(0, \text{Underlying rate at expiration} - \text{Exercise rate}\right)\left(\frac{\text{Days in underlying rate}}{360}\right)$$

where "days in underlying" refers to the maturity of the instrument from which the underlying rate is taken. In some cases, "days in underlying" may be the exact day count during a period. For example, if an interest rate option is used to hedge the interest paid over an m-day period, then "days in underlying" would be m. Even though LIBOR of 30, 60, 90, 180 days, etc., whichever is closest to m, might be used as the underlying rate, the actual day count would be m, the exact number of days. In such cases, the payment date is usually set at 30, 60, 90, 180, etc. days after the option expiration date. So, for example, 180-day LIBOR might be used as the underlying rate, and "days in underlying" could be 180 or perhaps 182, 183, etc. The most important point, however, is that the rate is determined on one day, the option expiration, and payment is made m days later. This practice is standard in floating-rate loans and thus is used with interest rate options, which are designed to manage the risk of floating-rate loans.

Likewise, the payoff of an interest rate put (Equation 4-2) is

$$\text{(Notional principal) max}\left(0, \text{Exercise rate} - \text{Underlying rate at expiration}\right)\left(\frac{\text{Days in underlying rate}}{360}\right)$$

Now let us take a look at some applications of interest rate options.

3.1 USING INTEREST RATE CALLS WITH BORROWING

Let us examine an application of an interest rate call to establish a maximum interest rate for a loan to be taken out in the future. In brief, a company can buy an interest rate call that pays off from increases in the underlying interest rate beyond a chosen level. The call payoff then compensates for the higher interest rate the company has to pay on the loan.

Consider the case of a company called Global Computer Technology (GCT), which occasionally takes out short-term loans in U.S. dollars with the rate tied to LIBOR. Anticipating that it will take out a loan at a later date, GCT recognizes the potential for an interest rate increase by that time. In this example, today is 14 April, and GCT expects to borrow $40 million on 20 August at LIBOR plus 200 basis points. The loan will involve the receipt of the money on 20 August with full repayment of principal and interest 180 days later on 16 February. GCT would like protection against higher interest rates, so it purchases an interest rate call on 180-day LIBOR to expire on 20 August. GCT chooses an exercise rate of 5 percent. This option gives it the right to receive an interest payment of the difference between the 20 August LIBOR and 5 percent. If GCT exercises the option on 20 August, the payment will occur 180 days later on 16 February when the loan is paid off. The cost of the call is $100,000, which is paid on 14 April. LIBOR on 14 April is 5.5 percent.

The transaction is designed such that if LIBOR is above 5 percent on 20 August, GCT will benefit and be protected against increases in interest rates. To determine how the transaction works, we need to know the effective rate on the loan. Note that the sequence of events is as follows:

14 April $\longrightarrow$ 20 August $\longrightarrow$ 16 February
GCT buys call   Call expires; loan starts   Loan repaid and call payoff made

So cash is paid for the call on 14 April. Cash proceeds from the loan are received on 20 August. On 16 February, the loan is repaid and the call payoff (if any) is made.

To evaluate the effectiveness of the overall transaction, we need to determine how the call affects the loan. Therefore, we need to incorporate the payment of the call premium on 14 April into the cash flow on the loan. So, it would be appropriate to compound the call premium from 14 April to 20 August. In effect, we need to know what the call, purchased on 14 April, effectively costs on 20 August. We compound its premium for the 128 days from 14 April to 20 August at the rate at which GCT would have to borrow on 14 April. This rate would be LIBOR on 14 April plus 200 basis points, or 7.5 percent. The call premium thus effectively costs

$$\$100,000\left[1 + 0.075\left(\frac{128}{360}\right)\right] = \$102,667$$

on 20 August.[20] On that date, GCT takes out the loan, thereby receiving $40 million. We should, however, reduce this amount by $102,667, because GCT effectively receives less money because it must buy the call. So, the loan proceeds are effectively $40,000,000 − $102,667 = $39,897,333.

Next we must calculate the amount of interest paid on the loan and the amount of any call payoff. Let us assume that LIBOR on 20 August is 8 percent. In that case, the loan rate will be 10 percent. The interest on the loan will be

$$\$40,000,000(0.10)\left(\frac{180}{360}\right) = \$2,000,000$$

This amount, plus $40 million principal, is repaid on 16 February. With LIBOR assumed to be 8 percent on 20 August, the option payoff is

$$\$40,000,000 \max(0,0.08 - 0.05)\left(\frac{180}{360}\right) = \$40,000,000(0.03)\left(\frac{180}{360}\right) = \$600,000$$

This amount is paid on 16 February. The effective interest paid on 16 February is thus $2,000,000 − $600,000 = $1,400,000. So, GCT effectively receives $39,897,333 on 20 August and pays back $40,000,000 plus $1,400,000 or $41,400,000 on 16 February. The effective annual rate is

$$\left(\frac{\$41,400,000}{\$39,897,333}\right)^{365/180} - 1 = 0.0779$$

Exhibit 7-13 presents a complete description of the transaction and the results for a range of possible LIBORs on 20 August. Exhibit 7-14 illustrates the effective loan rate

---

[20] The interpretation of this calculation is that GCT's cost of funds is 7.5 percent, making the option premium effectively $102,667 by the time the loan is taken out.

compared with LIBOR on 20 August. We see that the strategy places an effective ceiling on the rate on the loan of about 7.79 percent while enabling GCT to benefit from decreases in LIBOR. Of course, a part of this maximum rate is the 200 basis point spread over LIBOR that GCT must pay.[21] In effect, the company's maximum rate without the spread is 5.79 percent. This reflects the exercise rate of 5.5 percent plus the effect of the option premium.

EXHIBIT 7-13   Outcomes for an Anticipated Loan Protected with an Interest Rate Call

Scenario (14 April)
Global Computer Technology (GCT) is a U.S. corporation that occasionally undertakes short-term borrowings in U.S. dollars with the rate tied to LIBOR. To facilitate its cash flow planning, it buys an interest rate call to put a ceiling on the rate it pays while enabling it to benefit if rates fall. A call gives GCT the right to receive the difference between LIBOR on the expiration date and the exercise rate it chooses when it purchases the option. The payoff of the call is determined on the expiration date, but the payment is not received until a certain number of days later, corresponding to the maturity of the underlying LIBOR. This feature matches the timing of the interest payment on the loan.

Action
GCT determines that it will borrow $40 million at LIBOR plus 200 basis points on 20 August. The loan will be repaid with a single payment of principal and interest 180 days later on 16 February.

To protect against increases in LIBOR between 14 April and 20 August, GCT buys a call option on LIBOR with an exercise rate of 5 percent to expire on 20 August with the underlying being 180-day LIBOR. The call premium is $100,000. We summarize the information as follows:

Loan amount:	$40,000,000
Underlying:	180-day LIBOR
Spread:	200 basis points over LIBOR
Current LIBOR:	5.5 percent
Expiration:	20 August (128 days later)
Exercise rate:	5 percent
Call premium:	$100,000

Scenario (20 August)
LIBOR on 20 August is 8 percent.

Outcome and Analysis
For any LIBOR, the call payoff at expiration is given below and will be received 180 days later:

$$\$40,000,000 \max(0, \text{LIBOR} - 0.05)\left(\frac{180}{360}\right)$$

For LIBOR of 8 percent, the payoff is

$$\$40,000,000 \max(0, 0.08 - 0.05)\left(\frac{180}{360}\right) = \$600,000$$

---

[21] It should be noted that the effective annual rate is actually more than 200 basis points. For example, if someone borrows $100 at 2 percent for 180 days, the amount repaid would be $100[1 + 0.02(180/360)] = $101. The effective annual rate would be ($101/$100)$^{365/180} - 1 = 0.0204$.

The premium compounded from 14 April to 20 August at the original LIBOR of 5.5 percent plus 200 basis points is

$$\$100,000\left[1 + (0.055 + 0.02)\left(\frac{128}{360}\right)\right] - \$102,667$$

So the call costs $100,000 on 14 April, which is equivalent to $102,667 on 20 August. The effective loan proceeds are $40,000,000 − $102,667 = $39,897,333. The loan interest is

$$\$40,000,000(\text{LIBOR on 20 August} + 200 \text{ basis points})\left(\frac{180}{360}\right)$$

For LIBOR of 8 percent, the loan interest is

$$\$40,000,000(0.08 + 0.02)\left(\frac{180}{360}\right) = \$2,000,000$$

The call payoff was given above. The loan interest minus the call payoff is the effective interest. The effective rate on the loan is

$$\left(\frac{\$40,000,000 \text{ plus effective interest}}{\$39,897,333}\right)^{365/180} - 1$$

$$= \left(\frac{\$40,000,000 + \$2,000,000 - \$600,000}{\$39,897,333}\right)^{365/180} - 1 = 0.0779$$

or 7.79 percent.

The results are shown below for a range of LIBORs on 20 August.

LIBOR on 20 August	Loan Rate	Loan Interest Paid on 16 February	Call Payoff	Effective Interest	Effective Loan Rate
0.010	0.030	$600,000	$0	$600,000	0.0360
0.015	0.035	700,000	0	700,000	0.0412
0.020	0.040	800,000	0	800,000	0.0464
0.025	0.045	900,000	0	900,000	0.0516
0.030	0.050	1,000,000	0	1,000,000	0.0568
0.035	0.055	1,100,000	0	1,100,000	0.0621
0.040	0.060	1,200,000	0	1,200,000	0.0673
0.045	0.065	1,300,000	0	1,300,000	0.0726
0.050	0.070	1,400,000	0	1,400,000	0.0779
0.055	0.075	1,500,000	100,000	1,400,000	0.0779
0.060	0.080	1,600,000	200,000	1,400,000	0.0779
0.065	0.085	1,700,000	300,000	1,400,000	0.0779
0.070	0.090	1,800,000	400,000	1,400,000	0.0779
0.075	0.095	1,900,000	500,000	1,400,000	0.0779
0.080	0.100	2,000,000	600,000	1,400,000	0.0779
0.085	0.105	2,100,000	700,000	1,400,000	0.0779
0.090	0.110	2,200,000	800,000	1,400,000	0.0779

EXHIBIT 7-14   The Effective Rate on an Anticipated Future Loan Protected with an Interest Rate Call Option

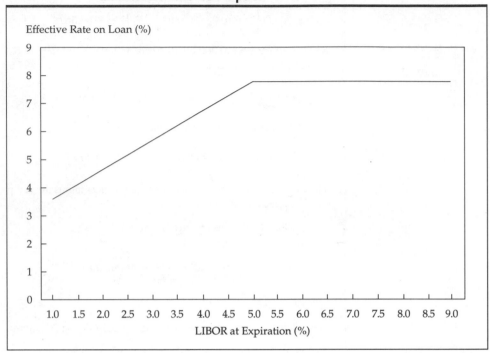

PRACTICE PROBLEM 11

On 10 January, ResTex Ltd. determines that it will need to borrow $5 million on 15 February at 90-day LIBOR plus 300 basis points. The loan will be an add-on interest loan in which ResTex will receive $5 million and pay it back plus interest on 16 May. To manage the risk associated with the interest rate on 15 February, ResTex buys an interest rate call that expires on 15 February and pays off on 16 May. The exercise rate is 5 percent, and the option premium is $10,000. The current 90-day LIBOR is 5.25 percent. Assume that this rate, plus 300 basis points, is the rate it would borrow at for any period of up to 90 days if the loan were taken out today. Interest is computed on the exact number of days divided by 360.

Determine the effective annual rate on the loan for each of the following outcomes:
 i. 90-day LIBOR on 15 February is 6 percent.
ii. 90-day LIBOR on 15 February is 4 percent.

SOLUTION

First we need to compound the premium from 10 January to 15 February, which is 36 days. This calculation tells us the effective cost of the call as of the time the loan is taken out:

$$\$10,000\left[1 + (0.0525 + 0.03)\left(\frac{36}{360}\right)\right] = \$10,083$$

The loan proceeds will therefore be $5,000,000 − $10,083 = $4,989,917.

i. LIBOR is 6 percent. The loan rate will be 9 percent.

The interest on the loan will be $5,000,000(0.06 + 0.03)(90/360) = $112,500.

The option payoff will be $5,000,000 max(0,0.06 − 0.05)(90/360) = $12,500.

Therefore, the effective interest will be $112,500 − $12,500 = $100,000.

The effective rate on the loan will be $\left(\dfrac{\$5,000,000 + \$100,000}{\$4,989,917}\right)^{365/90} - 1 =$ 0.0925.

Of course, a little more than 300 basis points of this amount is the spread.

ii. LIBOR is 4 percent. The loan rate will be 7 percent.

The interest on the loan will be $5,000,000(0.04 + 0.03)(90/360) = $87,500.

The option payoff will be $5,000,000 max(0,0.04 − 0.05)(90/360) = $0.00.

The effective interest will, therefore, be $87,500.

The effective rate on the loan will be $\left(\dfrac{\$5,000,000 + \$87,500}{\$4,989,917}\right)^{365/90} - 1 =$ 0.0817.

Of course, a little more than 300 basis points of this amount is the spread.

Whereas interest rate call options are appropriate for borrowers, lenders also face the risk of interest rates changing. As you may have guessed, they make use of interest rate puts.

3.2 USING INTEREST RATE PUTS WITH LENDING

Now consider an application of an interest rate put to establish a minimum interest rate for a commitment to give a loan in the future. A lender can buy a put that pays off if the interest rate falls below a chosen level. The put payoff then compensates the bank for the lower interest rate on the loan.

For example, consider Arbitrage Bank Inc. (ABInc) which makes loan commitments to corporations. It stands ready to make a loan at LIBOR at a future date. To protect itself against decreases in interest rates between the time of the commitment and the time the loan is taken out, it buys interest rate puts. These options pay off if LIBOR is below the exercise rate at expiration. If LIBOR is above the exercise rate at expiration, the option expires unexercised and the lender benefits from the higher rate on the loan.

In this example, ABInc makes a commitment on 15 March to lend $50 million at 90-day LIBOR plus 2.5 percent on 1 May, which is 47 days later. Current LIBOR is 7.25 percent. It buys a put with an exercise rate of 7 percent for $62,500. Assume that the opportunity cost of lending in the LIBOR market is LIBOR plus a spread of 2.5 percent. Therefore, the effective cost of the premium compounded to the option's expiration is[22]

$$\$62,500\left[1 + (0.0725 + 0.025)\left(\frac{47}{360}\right)\right] = \$63,296$$

When it lends $50 million on 1 May, it effectively has an outlay of $50,000,000 + $63,296 = $50,063,296. The loan rate is set on 1 May and the interest, paid 90 days later on 30 July, is

$$\$50,000,000\left[\text{LIBOR on 1 May plus 250 basis points}\left(\frac{90}{360}\right)\right]$$

---

[22] The interpretation of this calculation is that the bank could have otherwise made a loan of $62,500, which would have paid back $63,296 on 1 May.

The put payoff is

$$\$50,000,000 \max(0, 0.07 - \text{LIBOR on 1 May})\left(\frac{90}{360}\right)$$

The loan interest plus the put payoff make up the effective interest. The effective rate on the loan is

$$\left(\frac{\text{Principal plus effective interest}}{\$50,063,296}\right)^{365/90} - 1$$

Suppose LIBOR on 1 May is 6 percent. In that case, the loan rate will be 8.5 percent, and the interest on the loan will be

$$\$50,000,000\left[(0.06 + 0.025)\left(\frac{90}{360}\right)\right] = \$1,062,500$$

The put payoff is

$$\$50,000,000 \max(0, 0.07 - 0.06)\left(\frac{90}{360}\right) = \$125,000$$

This amount is paid on 30 July. The put cost of \$62,500 on 15 March is equivalent to paying \$63,296 on 1 May. Thus, on 1 May the bank effectively commits \$50,000,000 + \$63,296 = \$50,063,296. The effective interest it receives is the loan interest of \$1,062,500 plus the put payoff of \$125,000, or \$1,187,500. The effective annual rate is

$$\left(\frac{\$50,000,000 + \$1,187,500}{\$50,063,296}\right)^{365/90} - 1 = 0.0942$$

Exhibit 7-15 presents the results for a range of possible LIBORs at expiration, and Exhibit 7-16 graphs the effective loan rate against LIBOR on 1 May. Note how there is a minimum effective loan rate of 9.42 percent. Of this rate, 250 basis points is automatically built in as the loan spread.[23] The remaining amount reflects the exercise rate on the put of 7 percent minus the cost of the put premium.

EXHIBIT 7-15   Outcomes for an Anticipated Loan Protected with an Interest Rate Put

Scenario (15 March)
Arbitrage Bank Inc. (ABInc) is a U.S. bank that makes loan commitments to corporations. When ABInc makes these commitments, it recognizes the risk that LIBOR will fall by the date the loan is taken out. ABInc protects itself against interest rate decreases by purchasing interest rate puts, which give it the right to receive the difference between the exercise rate it chooses and LIBOR at expiration. LIBOR is currently 7.25 percent.

Action
ABInc commits to lending \$50 million to a company at 90-day LIBOR plus 250 basis points. The loan will be a single-payment loan, meaning that it will be made on 1 May and the principal and interest will be repaid 90 days later on 30 July.

---

[23] As in the case of the borrower, the spread is effectively more than 250 basis points when the effective annual rate is determined. For this 90-day loan, this effectively amounts to 256 basis points.

To protect against decreases in LIBOR between 15 March and 1 May, ABInc buys a put option with an exercise rate of 7 percent to expire on 1 May with the underlying being 90-day LIBOR. The put premium is $62,500. We summarize the information as follows:

Loan amount: $50,000,000
Underlying: 90-day LIBOR
Spread: 250 basis points over LIBOR
Current LIBOR: 7.25 percent
Expiration: 1 May
Exercise rate: 7 percent
Put premium: $62,500

Scenario (1 May)
LIBOR is now 6 percent.

Outcome and Analysis
For any LIBOR, the payoff at expiration is given below and will be received 90 days later:

$$\$50,000,000 \max(0, 0.07 - \text{LIBOR})\left(\frac{90}{360}\right)$$

For LIBOR of 6 percent, the payoff is

$$\$50,000,000 \max(0, 0.07 - 0.060)\left(\frac{90}{360}\right) = \$125,000$$

The premium compounded from 15 March to 1 May at current LIBOR plus 250 basis points is

$$\$62,500\left[1 + (0.0725 + 0.025)\left(\frac{47}{360}\right)\right] = \$63,296$$

So the put costs $62,500 on 15 March, which is equivalent to $63,296 on 1 May. The effective amount loaned is $50,000,000 + $63,296 = $50,063,296. For any LIBOR, the loan interest is

$$\$50,000,000\left[\text{LIBOR on 1 May plus 250 basis points}\left(\frac{90}{360}\right)\right]$$

With LIBOR at 6 percent, the interest is

$$\$50,000,000\left[(0.06 + 0.025)\left(\frac{90}{360}\right)\right] = \$1,062,500$$

The loan interest plus the put payoff is the effective interest on the loan. The effective rate on the loan is

$$\left(\frac{\text{Principal plus effective interest}}{\$50,063,296}\right)^{365/90} - 1$$

$$= \left(\frac{\$50,000,000 + \$1,062,500 + \$125,000}{\$50,063,296}\right)^{365/90} - 1 = 0.0942$$

or 9.42 percent. The results are shown below for a range of LIBORs on 1 May.

LIBOR on 1 May	Loan Rate	Loan Interest Paid on 30 July	Put Payoff	Effective Interest	Effective Loan Rate
0.030	0.055	$687,500	$500,000	$1,187,500	0.0942
0.035	0.060	750,000	437,500	1,187,500	0.0942
0.040	0.065	812,500	375,000	1,187,500	0.0942
0.045	0.070	875,000	312,500	1,187,500	0.0942
0.050	0.075	937,500	250,000	1,187,500	0.0942
0.055	0.080	1,000,000	187,500	1,187,500	0.0942
0.060	0.085	1,062,500	125,000	1,187,500	0.0942
0.065	0.090	1,125,000	62,500	1,187,500	0.0942
0.070	0.095	1,187,500	0	1,187,500	0.0942
0.075	0.100	1,250,000	0	1,250,000	0.0997
0.080	0.105	1,312,500	0	1,312,500	0.1051
0.085	0.110	1,375,000	0	1,375,000	0.1106
0.090	0.115	1,437,500	0	1,437,500	0.1161
0.095	0.120	1,500,000	0	1,500,000	0.1216
0.100	0.125	1,562,500	0	1,562,500	0.1271
0.105	0.130	1,625,000	0	1,625,000	0.1327
0.110	0.135	1,687,500	0	1,687,500	0.1382

EXHIBIT 7-16   The Effective Rate on an Anticipated Loan with an Interest Rate Put Option

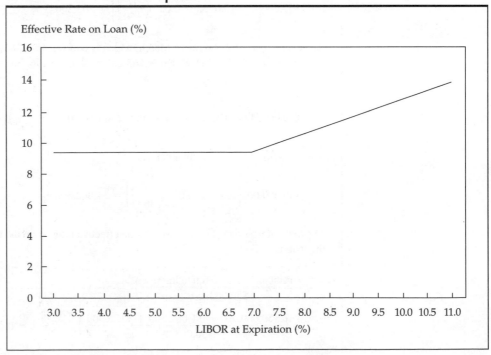

PRACTICE PROBLEM 12

State Bank and Trust (SBT) is a lender in the floating-rate instrument market, but it has been hurt by recent interest rate decreases. SBT often makes loan commitments for its customers and then accepts the rate in effect on the day the loan is taken out. SBT has avoided floating-rate financing in the past. It takes out a certain amount of fixed-rate financing in advance to cover its loan commitments. One particularly large upcoming loan has it worried. This is a $100 million loan to be made in 65 days at 180-day LIBOR plus 100 basis points. The loan will be paid back 182 days after being taken out, and interest will be based on an exact day count and 360 days in a year. Current LIBOR is 7.125 percent, which is the rate it could borrow at now for any period less than 180 days. SBT considers the purchase of an interest rate put to protect it against an interest rate decrease over the next 65 days. The put will have an exercise price of 7 percent and a premium of $475,000.

Determine the effective annual rate on the loan for the following outcomes:
  i. 180-day LIBOR at the option expiration is 9 percent.
 ii. 180-day LIBOR at the option expiration is 5 percent.

SOLUTION

First we need to compound the premium for 65 days. This calculation tells us the effective cost of the put as of the time the loan is made:

$$\$475,000\left[1 + (0.07125 + 0.01)\left(\frac{65}{360}\right)\right] = \$481,968$$

The outlay will effectively be $100,000,000 + $481,968 = $100,481,968.
  i. LIBOR is 9 percent. The loan rate will be 10 percent.
     The interest on the loan will be $100,000,000(0.09 + 0.01)(182/360) = $5,055,556.
     The option payoff will be $100,000,000 max(0,0.07 − 0.09)(182/360) = $0.0.
     Because there is no option payoff, the effective interest will be $5,055,556.
     The effective rate on the loan will be $\left(\dfrac{\$100,000,000 + \$5,055,556}{\$100,481,968}\right)^{365/182} - 1 = 0.0934.$
     Of course, a little more than 100 basis points of this amount is the spread.
 ii. LIBOR is 5 percent. The loan will be 6 percent.
     The interest on the loan will be $100,000,000(0.05 + 0.01)(182/360) = $3,033,333.
     The option payoff will be $100,000,000 max(0,0.07 − 0.05)(182/360) = $1,011,111.
     The effective interest will, therefore, be $3,033,333 + $1,011,111 = $4,044,444.
     The effective rate on the loan will be $\left(\dfrac{\$100,000,000 + \$4,044,444}{\$100,481,968}\right)^{365/182} - 1 = 0.0724.$
     Of course, a little more than 100 basis points of this amount is the spread.

Interest rate calls and puts can be combined into packages of multiple options, which are widely used to manage the risk of floating-rate loans.

3.3 USING AN INTEREST RATE CAP WITH A FLOATING-RATE LOAN

As we have described previously in this book, many corporate loans are floating-rate loans. They require periodic interest payments in which the rate is reset on a regularly scheduled basis. Because there is more than one interest payment, there is effectively more than one distinct risk. If a borrower wanted to use an interest rate call to place a ceiling on the effective borrowing rate, it would require more than one call. In effect, it would require a distinct call option expiring on each interest rate reset date. As described in Chapter 4, a combination of interest rate call options designed to align with the rates on a loan is called a **cap**. The component options are called **caplets**. Each caplet is distinct in having its own expiration date, but typically the exercise rate on each caplet is the same.

To illustrate the use of a cap, consider a company called Measure Technology (MesTech), which borrows in the floating-rate loan market. It usually takes out a loan for several years at a spread over LIBOR, paying the interest semiannually and the full principal at the end. On 15 April, MesTech takes out a $10 million three-year loan at 100 basis points over 180-day LIBOR from a bank called SenBank. Current 180-day LIBOR is 9 percent, which sets the rate for the first six-month period at 10 percent. Interest payments will be on the 15th of October and April for three years. This means that the day counts for the six payments will be 183, 182, 183, 182, 183, and 182.

To protect against increases in interest rates, MesTech purchases an interest rate cap with an exercise rate of 8 percent. The component caplets expire on 15 October, the following 15 April, and so forth until the last caplet expires on a subsequent 15 October. The loan has six interest payments, but because the first rate is already set, there are only five risky payments so the cap will contain five caplets. The payoff of each caplet will be determined on its expiration date, but the caplet payoff, if any, will actually be made on the next payment date. This enables the caplet payoff to line up with the date on which the loan interest is paid. The cap premium, paid up front on 15 April, is $75,000.

In the example of a single interest rate call, we looked at a range of outcomes several hundred basis points around the exercise rate. In a cap, however, many more outcomes are possible. Ideally we would examine a range of outcomes for each caplet. In the example of a single cap, we looked at the exercise rate and 8 rates above and below for a total of 17 rates. For five distinct rate resets, this same procedure would require 5^{17} or more than 762 billion different possibilities. So, we shall just look at one possible combination of rates.

We shall examine a set of outcomes in which LIBOR is

8.50 percent on 15 October

7.25 percent on 15 April the following year

7.00 percent on the following 15 October

6.90 percent on the following 15 April

8.75 percent on the following 15 October

The loan interest is computed as

$$\$10,000,000(\text{LIBOR on previous reset date} + 100 \text{ basis points})\left(\frac{\text{Days in settlement period}}{360}\right)$$

Thus, the first interest payment is

$$\$10,000,000(0.10)\left(\frac{183}{360}\right) = \$508,333$$

which is based on 183 days between 15 April and 15 October. This amount is certain, because the first interest rate has already been set. The remaining interest payments are based on the assumption we made above about the course of LIBOR over the life of the loan.

    The results for these assumed rates are shown in the table at the end of Exhibit 7-17. Note several things about the effective interest, displayed in the last column. First, the initial interest payment is much higher than the other interest payments because the initial rate is somewhat higher than the remaining rates that prevailed over the life of the loan. Also, recall that the initial rate is already set, and it would make no sense to add a caplet to cover the initial rate, because the caplet would have to expire immediately in order to pay off on the first 15 October. If the caplet expired immediately, the amount MesTech would have to pay for it would be the amount of the caplet payoff, discounted for the defer ral of the payoff. In other words, it would make no sense to have an option, or any derivative for that matter, that is purchased and expires immediately. Note also the variation in the effective interest payments, which occurs for two reasons. One is that, in contrast to previous examples, interest is computed over the exact number of days in the period. Thus, even if the rate were the same, the interest could vary by the effect of one or two days of interest. The other reason is that in some cases the caplets do expire with value, thereby reducing the effective interest paid.

EXHIBIT 7-17   Interest Rate Cap

Scenario (15 April)

Measure Technology (MesTech) is a corporation that borrows in the floating-rate instrument market. It typically takes out a loan for several years at a spread over LIBOR. MesTech pays the interest semiannually and the full principal at the end.

    To protect against rising interest rates over the life of the loan, MesTech usually buys an interest rate cap in which the component caplets expire on the dates on which the loan rate is reset. The cap seller is a derivatives dealer.

Action

MesTech takes out a $10 million three-year loan at 100 basis points over LIBOR. The payments will be made semiannually. The lender is SenBank. Current LIBOR is 9 percent, which means that the first rate will be at 10 percent. Interest will be based on 1/360 of the exact number of days in the six-month period. MesTech selects an exercise rate of 8 percent. The caplets will expire on 15 October, 15 April of the following year, and so on for three years, but the caplet payoffs will occur on the next payment date to correspond with the interest payment based on LIBOR that determines the cap payoff. The cap premium is $75,000. We thus have the following information:

Loan amount:	$10,000,000
Underlying:	180-day LIBOR
Spread:	100 basis points over LIBOR
Current LIBOR:	9 percent
Interest based on:	actual days/360
Component caplets:	five caplets expiring 15 October, 15 April, etc.
Exercise rate:	8 percent
Cap premium:	$75,000

Scenario (various dates throughout the loan)
Shown below is one particular set of outcomes for LIBOR:

  8.50 percent on 15 October
  7.25 percent on 15 April the following year
  7.00 percent on the following 15 October
  6.90 percent on the following 15 April
  8.75 percent on the following 15 October

Outcome and Analysis
The loan interest due is computed as

$$\$10,000,000(\text{LIBOR on previous reset date} + 100 \text{ basis points})\left(\frac{\text{Days in settlement period}}{360}\right)$$

The caplet payoff is

$$\$10,000,000 \max(0, \text{LIBOR on previous reset date} - 0.08)\left(\frac{\text{Days in settlement period}}{360}\right)$$

The previous reset date is the expiration date of the caplet. The effective interest is the interest due minus the caplet payoff.

The first caplet expires on the first 15 October and pays off the following April, because LIBOR on 15 October was 8.5 percent. The payoff is computed as

$$\$10,000,000 \max(0, 0.085 - 0.08)\left(\frac{182}{360}\right) = \$10,000,000(0.005)\left(\frac{182}{360}\right) = \$25,278$$

which is based on 182 days between 15 October and 15 April. The following table shows the payments on the loan and cap:

Date	LIBOR	Loan Rate	Days in Period	Interest Due	Caplet Payoffs	Effective Interest
15 April	0.0900	0.1000				
15 October	0.0850	0.0950	183	$508,333		$508,333
15 April	0.0725	0.0825	182	480,278	$25,278	455,000
15 October	0.0700	0.0800	183	419,375	0	419,375
15 April	0.0690	0.0790	182	404,444	0	404,444
15 October	0.0875	0.0975	183	401,583	0	401,583
15 April			182	492,917	37,917	455,000

Note that on the following three dates, the caplets are out-of-the-money, because the LIBORs are all lower than 8 percent. On the final 15 October, however, LIBOR is 8.75 percent, which leads to a final caplet payoff of $37,917 on the following 15 April, at which time the loan principal is repaid.

We do not show the effective rate on the loan. Because the loan has multiple payments, the effective rate would be analogous to the internal rate of return on a capital investment project or the yield-to-maturity on a bond. This rate would have to be found with a financial calculator or spreadsheet, and we would have to account for the principal received up front and paid back at maturity, as well as the cap premium. It is sufficient for us to see that the cap protects the borrower any time the rate rises above the exercise rate and allows the borrower to benefit from rates lower than the exercise rate.

Finally, there is one circumstance under which this cap might contain a sixth caplet, one expiring on the date on which the loan is taken out. If the borrower purchased the cap in advance of taking out the loan, the first loan rate would not be set until the day the loan is actually taken out. The borrower would thus have an incentive to include a caplet that would protect the first rate setting.

PRACTICE PROBLEM 13

Healthy Biosystems (HBIO) is a typical floating-rate borrower, taking out loans at LIBOR plus a spread. On 15 January 2002, it takes out a loan of $25 million for one year with quarterly payments on 12 April, 14 July, 16 October, and the following 14 January. The underlying rate is 90-day LIBOR, and HBIO will pay a spread of 250 basis points. Interest is based on the exact number of days in the period. Current 90-day LIBOR is 6.5 percent. HBIO purchases an interest rate cap for $20,000 that has an exercise rate of 7 percent and has caplets expiring on the rate reset dates.

Determine the effective interest payments if LIBOR on the following dates is as given:

12 April:	7.250 percent
14 July:	6.875 percent
16 October:	7.125 percent

SOLUTION

The interest due for each period is computed as $25,000,000(LIBOR on previous reset date + 0.0250)(Days in period/360). For example, the first interest payment is calculated as $25,000,000(0.065 + 0.025)(87/360) = $543,750, based on the fact that there are 87 days between 15 January and 12 April. Each caplet payoff is computed as $25,000,000 max(0,LIBOR on previous reset date − 0.07)(Days in period/360), where the "previous reset date" is the caplet expiration. Payment is deferred until the date on which the interest is paid at the given LIBOR. For example, the caplet expiring on 12 April is worth $25,000,000 max(0,0.0725 − 0.07)(93/360) = $16,145, which is paid on 14 July and is based on the fact that there are 93 days between 12 April and 14 July.

The effective interest is the actual interest minus the caplet payoff. The payments are shown in the table below:

Date	LIBOR	Loan Rate	Days in Period	Interest Due	Caplet Payoff	Effective Interest
15 January	0.065	0.09				
12 April	0.0725	0.0975	87	$543,750		$543,750
14 July	0.06875	0.09375	93	629,688	$16,146	613,542
16 October	0.07125	0.09625	94	611,979	0	611,979
14 January			90	601,563	7,813	593,750

Lenders who use floating-rate loans face the same risk as borrowers. As such they can make use of combinations of interest rate puts.

3.4 USING AN INTEREST RATE FLOOR WITH A FLOATING-RATE LOAN

Let us now consider the same problem from the point of view of the lender, which is Sen-Bank in this example. It would be concerned about falling interest rates. It could, therefore, buy a combination of interest rate put options that expire on the various interest rate reset dates. This combination of puts is called a **floor**, and the component options are called **floorlets**. Specifically, let SenBank buy a floor with floorlets expiring on the interest rate reset dates and with an exercise rate of 8 percent. The premium is $72,500.[24] Exhibit 7-18 illustrates the results using the same outcomes we looked at when examining the interest rate cap. Note that the floorlet expires in-the-money on three dates when LIBOR is less than 8 percent, and out-of-the-money on two dates when LIBOR is greater than 8 percent. In those cases in which the floorlet expires in-the-money, the actual payoff does not occur until the next settlement period. This structure aligns the floorlet payoffs with the interest payments they are designed to protect. We see that the floor protects the lender against falling interest rates. Any time the rate is below 8 percent, the floor compensates the bank for any difference between the rate and 8 percent. When the rate is above 8 percent, the floorlets simply expire unused.

EXHIBIT 7-18   Interest Rate Floor

Scenario (15 April)

SenBank lends in the floating-rate instrument market. Often it uses floating-rate financing, thereby protecting itself against decreases in the floating rates on its loans. Sometimes, however, it finds it can get a better rate with fixed-rate financing, but it then leaves itself exposed to interest rate decreases on its floating-rate loans. Its loans are typically for several years at a spread over LIBOR with interest paid semiannually and the full principal paid at the end.

To protect against falling interest rates over the life of the loan, SenBank buys an interest rate floor in which the component floorlets expire on the dates on which the loan rate is reset. The floor seller is a derivatives dealer.

Action

SenBank makes a $10 million three-year loan at 100 basis points over LIBOR to MesTech (see cap example). The payments will be made semiannually. Current LIBOR is 9 percent, which means that the first interest payment will be at 10 percent. Interest will be based on the exact number of days in the six-month period divided by 360. SenBank selects an exercise rate of 8 percent. The floorlets will expire on 15 October, 15 April of the following year, and so on for three years, but the floorlet payoffs will occur on the next payment date so as to correspond with the interest payment based on LIBOR that determines the floorlet payoff. The floor premium is $72,500. We thus have the following information:

Loan amount:	$10,000,000
Underlying:	180-day LIBOR
Spread:	100 basis points over LIBOR
Current LIBOR:	9 percent
Interest based on:	actual days/360
Component floorlets:	five floorlets expiring 15 October, 15 April, etc.
Exercise rate:	8 percent
Floor premium:	$72,500

---

[24] Note that the premiums for the cap and floor are not the same. This difference occurs because the premiums for a call and a put with the same exercise price are not the same, as can be seen by examining put–call parity.

Outcomes (various dates throughout the loan)
Shown below is one particular set of outcomes for LIBOR:

8.50 percent on 15 October

7.25 percent on 15 April the following year

7.00 percent on the following 15 October

6.90 percent on the following 15 April

8.75 percent on the following 15 October

Outcome and Analysis
The loan interest is computed as

$$\$10,000,000(\text{LIBOR on previous reset date} + 100 \text{ basis points})\left(\frac{\text{Days in settlement period}}{360}\right)$$

The floorlet payoff is

$$\$10,000,000 \max(0, 0.08 - \text{LIBOR on previous reset date})\left(\frac{\text{Days in settlement period}}{360}\right)$$

The effective interest is the interest due plus the floorlet payoff. The following table shows the payments on the loan and floor:

Date	LIBOR	Loan Rate	Days in Period	Interest Due	Floorlet Payoffs	Effective Interest
15 April	0.0900	0.1000				
15 October	0.0850	0.0950	183	$508,333		$508,333
15 April	0.0725	0.0825	182	480,278	$0	480,278
15 October	0.0700	0.0800	183	419,375	38,125	457,500
15 April	0.0690	0.0790	182	404,444	50,556	455,000
15 October	0.0875	0.0975	183	401,583	55,917	457,500
15 April			182	492,917	0	492,917

PRACTICE PROBLEM 14

Capitalized Bank (CAPBANK) is a lender in the floating-rate loan market. It uses fixed-rate financing on its floating-rate loans and buys floors to hedge the rate. On 1 May 2002, it makes a loan of $40 million at 180-day LIBOR plus 150 basis points. Interest will be paid on 1 November, the following 5 May, the following 1 November, and the following 2 May, at which time the principal will be repaid. The exercise rate is 4.5 percent, the floorlets expire on the rate reset dates, and the premium will be $120,000. Interest will be calculated based on the actual number of days in the period over 360. The current 180-day LIBOR is 5 percent.

Determine the effective interest payments CAPBANK will receive if LIBOR on the following dates is as given:

1 November: 4.875 percent

5 May: 4.25 percent

1 November: 5.125 percent

SOLUTION

The interest due for each period is computed as $40,000,000(LIBOR on previous reset date + 0.0150)(Days in period/360). For example, the first interest payment is $40,000,000(0.05 + 0.0150)(184/360) = $1,328,889, based on the fact that there are 184 days between 1 May and 1 November. Each floorlet payoff is computed as $40,000,000 max(0,0.045 − LIBOR on previous reset date)(Days in period/360), where the "previous reset date" is the floorlet expiration. Payment is deferred until the date on which the interest is paid at the given LIBOR. For example, the floorlet expiring on 5 May is worth $40,000,000 max(0,0.045 − 0.0425)(180/360) = $50,000, which is paid on 1 November and is based on the fact that there are 180 days between 5 May and 1 November.

The effective interest is the actual interest plus the floorlet payoff. The payments are shown in the table below:

Date	LIBOR	Loan Rate	Days in Period	Interest Due	Caplet Payoff	Effective Interest
1 May	0.05	0.065				
1 November	0.04875	0.06375	184	$1,328,889		$1,328,889
5 May	0.0425	0.0575	185	1,310,417	$0	1,310,417
1 November	0.05125	0.06625	180	1,150,000	50,000	1,200,000
2 May			182	1,339,722	0	1,339,722

When studying equity option strategies, we combined puts and calls into a single transaction called a collar. In a similar manner, we now combine caps and floors into a single transaction, also called a collar.

3.5 USING AN INTEREST RATE COLLAR WITH A FLOATING-RATE LOAN

As we showed above, borrowers are attracted to caps because they protect against rising interest rates. They do so, however, at the cost of having to pay a premium in cash up front. A collar combines a long position in a cap with a short position in a floor. The sale of the floor generates a premium that can be used to offset the premium on the cap. Although it is not necessary that the floor premium completely offset the cap premium, this arrangement is common.[25] The exercise rate on the floor is selected such that the floor premium is precisely the cap premium. As with equity options, this type of strategy is called a zero-cost collar. Recall, however, that this term is a bit misleading because it suggests that this transaction has no true "cost." The cost is simply not up front in cash. The sale of the floor results in the borrower giving up any gains from interest rates below the exercise rate on the floor. Therefore, the borrower pays for the cap by giving away some of the gains from the possibility of falling rates.

Recall that for equity investors, the collar typically entails ownership of the underlying asset and the purchase of a put, which is financed with the sale of a call. In contrast, an interest rate collar is more commonly seen from the borrower's point of view: a position as a borrower and the purchase of a cap, which is financed by the sale of a floor. It is quite possible, however, that a lender would want a collar. The lender is holding an asset, the loan, and wants protection against falling interest rates, which can be obtained by buy-

---

[25] It is even possible for the floor premium to be greater than the cap premium, thereby *generating cash* up front.

ing a floor, which itself can be financed by selling a cap. Most interest rate collars, however, are initiated by borrowers.

In the example we used previously, MesTech borrows $10 million at LIBOR plus 100 basis points. The cap exercise rate is 8 percent, and the premium is $75,000. We now change the numbers a little and let MesTech set the exercise rate at 8.625 percent. To sell a floor that will generate the same premium as the cap, the exercise rate is set at 7.5 percent. It is not necessary for us to know the amounts of the cap and floor premiums; it is sufficient to know that they offset.

Exhibit 7-19 shows the collar results for the same set of interest rate outcomes we have been previously using. Note that on the first 15 October, LIBOR is between the cap and floor exercise rates, so neither the caplet nor the floorlet expires in the money. On the following 15 April, 15 October, and the next 15 April, the rate is below the floor exercise rate, so MesTech has to pay up on the expiring floorlets. On the final 15 October, LIBOR is above the cap exercise rate, so MesTech gets paid on its cap.

EXHIBIT 7-19 Interest Rate Collar

Scenario (15 April)

Consider the Measure Technology (MesTech) scenario described in the cap and floor example in Exhibits 7-17 and 7-18. MesTech is a corporation that borrows in the floating-rate instrument market. It typically takes out a loan for several years at a spread over LIBOR. MesTech pays the interest semiannually and the full principal at the end.

To protect against rising interest rates over the life of the loan, MesTech usually buys an interest rate cap in which the component caplets expire on the dates on which the loan rate is reset. To pay for the cost of the interest rate cap, MesTech can sell a floor at an exercise rate lower than the cap exercise rate.

Action

Consider the $10 million three-year loan at 100 basis points over LIBOR. The payments are made semiannually. Current LIBOR is 9 percent, which means that the first rate will be at 10 percent. Interest is based on the exact number of days in the six-month period divided by 360. MesTech selects an exercise rate of 8.625 percent for the cap. Generating a floor premium sufficient to offset the cap premium requires a floor exercise rate of 7.5 percent. The caplets and floorlets will expire on 15 October, 15 April of the following year, and so on for three years, but the payoffs will occur on the following payment date to correspond with the interest payment based on LIBOR that determines the caplet and floorlet payoffs. Thus, we have the following information:

Loan amount:	$10,000,000
Underlying:	180-day LIBOR
Spread:	100 basis points over LIBOR
Current LIBOR:	9 percent
Interest based on:	actual days/360
Component options:	five caplets and floorlets expiring 15 October, 15 April, etc.
Exercise rate:	8.625 percent on cap, 7.5 percent on floor
Premium:	no net premium

Scenario (various dates throughout the loan)

Shown below is one particular set of outcomes for LIBOR:

8.50 percent on 15 October

7.25 percent on 15 April the following year

7.00 percent on the following 15 October

6.90 percent on the following 15 April

8.75 percent on the following 15 October

Outcome and Analysis

The loan interest is computed as

$$\$10{,}000{,}000(\text{LIBOR on previous reset date} + 100 \text{ basis points})\left(\frac{\text{Days in settlement period}}{360}\right)$$

The caplet payoff is

$$\$10{,}000{,}000 \max(0, \text{LIBOR on previous reset date} - 0.08625)\left(\frac{\text{Days in settlement period}}{360}\right)$$

The floorlet payoff is

$$(\$10{,}000{,}000 \max(0, 0.075 - \text{LIBOR on previous reset date})\left(\frac{\text{Days in settlement period}}{360}\right)$$

The effective interest is the interest due minus the caplet payoff minus the floorlet payoff. Note that because the floorlet was sold, the floorlet payoff is either negative (so we would subtract a negative number, thereby adding an amount to obtain the total interest due) or zero.

The following table shows the payments on the loan and collar:

Date	LIBOR	Loan Rate	Days in Period	Interest Due	Caplet Payoffs	Floorlet Payoffs	Effective Interest
15 April	0.0900	0.1000					
15 October	0.0850	0.0950	183	$508,333			$508,333
15 April	0.0725	0.0825	182	480,278	$0	$0	480,278
15 October	0.0700	0.0800	183	419,375	0	−12,708	432,083
15 April	0.0690	0.0790	182	404,444	0	−25,278	429,722
15 October	0.0875	0.0975	183	401,583	0	−30,500	432,083
15 April			182	492,917	6,319	0	486,598

A collar establishes a range, the cap exercise rate minus the floor exercise rate, within which there is interest rate risk. The borrower will benefit from falling rates and be hurt by rising rates within that range. Any rate increases above the cap exercise rate will have no net effect, and any rate decreases below the floor exercise rate will have no net effect. The net cost of this position is zero, provided that the floor exercise rate is set such that the floor premium offsets the cap premium.[26] It is probably easy to see that collars are popular among borrowers.

---

[26] It is certainly possible that the floor exercise rate would be set first, and the cap exercise rate would then be set to have the cap premium offset the floor premium. This would likely be the case if a lender were doing the collar. We assume, however, the case of a borrower who wants protection above a certain level and then decides to give up gains below a particular level necessary to offset the cost of the protection.

PRACTICE PROBLEM 15

Exegesis Systems (EXSYS) is a floating-rate borrower that manages its interest rate risk with collars, purchasing a cap and selling a floor in which the cost of the cap and floor are equivalent. EXSYS takes out a $35 million one-year loan at 90-day LIBOR plus 200 basis points. It establishes a collar with a cap exercise rate of 7 percent and a floor exercise rate of 6 percent. Current 180-day LIBOR is 6.5 percent. The interest payments will be based on the exact day count over 360. The caplets and floorlets expire on the rate reset dates. The rates will be set on the current date (5 March), 4 June, 5 September, and 3 December, and the loan will be paid off on the following 3 March.

Determine the effective interest payments if LIBOR on the following dates is as given:

4 June:	7.25 percent
5 September:	6.5 percent
3 December:	5.875 percent

SOLUTION

The interest due for each period is computed as $35,000,000(LIBOR on previous reset date $+$ 0.02)(Days in period/360). For example, the first interest payment is $35,000,000(0.065 $+$ 0.02)(91/360) $=$ $752,014, based on the fact that there are 91 days between 5 March and 4 June. Each caplet payoff is computed as $35,000,000 max(0,LIBOR on previous reset date $-$ 0.07)(Days in period/360), where the "previous reset date" is the caplet expiration. Payment is deferred until the date on which the interest is paid at the given LIBOR. For example, the caplet expiring on 4 June is worth $35,000,000 max(0,0.0725 $-$ 0.07)(93/360) $=$ $22,604, which is paid on 5 September and is based on the fact that there are 93 days between 4 June and 5 September. Each floorlet payoff is computed as $35,000,000 max(0,0.06 $-$ LIBOR on previous reset date)(Days in period/360). For example, the floorlet expiring on 3 December is worth $35,000,000 max(0,0.06 $-$ 0.05875)(90/360) $=$ $10,938, based on the fact that there are 90 days between 3 December and 3 March. The effective interest is the actual interest minus the caplet payoff plus the floorlet payoff. The payments are shown in the table below:

Date	LIBOR	Loan Rate	Days in Period	Interest Due	Caplet Payoff	Floorlet Payoff	Effective Interest
5 March	0.065	0.085					
4 June	0.0725	0.0925	91	$752,014			$752,014
5 September	0.065	0.085	93	836,354	$22,604	$0	813,750
3 December	0.05875	0.07875	89	735,486	0	0	735,486
3 March			90	689,063	0	−10,938	700,001

Of course, caps, floors, and collars are not the only forms of protection against interest rate risk. We have previously covered FRAs and interest rate futures. The most widely used protection, however, is the interest rate swap. We cover swap strategies in the next chapter.

In the final section of this chapter, we examine the strategies used to manage the risk of an option portfolio.

4 OPTION PORTFOLIO RISK MANAGEMENT STRATEGIES

So far we have looked at examples of how companies and investors use options. As we have described previously, many options are traded by dealers who make markets in these options, providing liquidity by first taking on risk and then hedging their positions in order to earn the bid–ask spread without taking the risk. In this section, we shall take a look at the strategies dealers use to hedge their positions.[27]

Let us assume that a customer contacts a dealer with an interest in purchasing a call option. The dealer, ready to take either side of the transaction, quotes an acceptable ask price and the customer buys the option. Recall from earlier in this chapter that a short position in a call option is a very dangerous strategy, because the potential loss on an upside underlying move is open ended. The dealer would not want to hold a short call position for long. The ideal way to lay off the risk is to find someone else who would take the exact opposite position, but in most cases, the dealer will not be so lucky.[28] Another ideal possibility is for the dealer to lay off the risk using put–call parity. Recall that put–call parity says that $c = p + S - X/(1 + r)^T$. The dealer that has sold a call needs to buy a call to hedge the position. The put–call parity equation means that a long call is equivalent to a long put, a long position in the asset, and issuing a zero-coupon bond with a face value equal to the option exercise price and maturing on the option expiration date. Therefore, if the dealer could buy a put with the same exercise price and expiration, buy the asset, and sell a bond or take out a loan with face value equal to the exercise price and maturity equal to that of the option's expiration, it would have the position hedged. Other than buying an identical call, as described above, this hedge would be the best because it is static: No change to the position is required as time passes.

Unfortunately, neither of these transactions can be commonly employed. The necessary options may not be available or may not be favorably priced. As the next best alternative, dealers **delta hedge** their positions using an available and attractively priced instrument. The dealer is short the call and will need an offsetting position in another instrument. An obvious offsetting instrument would be a long position of a certain number of units of the underlying. The size of that long position will be related to the option's delta. In Chapter 4, we discussed the concept of an option's delta. Let us briefly review delta here. By definition,

$$\text{Delta} = \frac{\text{Change in option price}}{\text{Change in underlying price}}$$

Delta expresses how the option price changes relative to the price of the underlying. Technically, we should use an approximation sign ($\approx$) in the above equation, but for now we shall assume the approximation is exact. Let ΔS be the change in the underlying price and

---

[27] For over-the-counter options, these dealers are usually the financial institutions that make markets in these options. For exchange-traded options, these dealers are the traders at the options exchanges, who may trade for their own accounts or could represent firms.

[28] Even luckier would be the dealer's original customer who might stumble across a party who wanted to sell the call option. The two parties could then bypass the dealer and negotiate a transaction directly between each other, which would save each party half of the bid–ask spread.

Δc be the change in the option price. Then Delta = $\Delta c/\Delta S$. Recall from Chapter 4 that the delta usually lies between 0.0 and 1.0.[29] Delta will be 1.0 only at expiration and only if the option expires in-the-money. Delta will be 0.0 only at expiration and only if the option expires out-of-the-money. So most of the time, the delta will be between 0.0 and 1.0. Hence, 0.5 is often given as an "average" delta, but one must be careful because even before expiration the delta will tend to be higher than 0.5 if the option is in-the-money.

Now, let us assume that we construct a portfolio consisting of N_S units of the underlying and N_c call options. The value of the portfolio is, therefore,

$$V = N_S S + N_c c$$

The change in the value of the portfolio is

$$\Delta V = N_S \Delta S + N_c \Delta c$$

If we want to hedge the portfolio, then we want the change in V, given a change in S, to be zero. Dividing by ΔS, we obtain

$$\frac{\Delta V}{\Delta S} = N_S \frac{\Delta S}{\Delta S} + N_c \frac{\Delta c}{\Delta S}$$

$$= N_S + N_c \frac{\Delta c}{\Delta S}$$

Setting this result equal to zero and solving for N_c/N_S, we obtain

$$\frac{N_c}{N_S} = -\frac{1}{\Delta c/\Delta S}$$

The ratio of calls to shares has to be the negative of 1 over the delta. Thus, if the dealer sells a given number of calls, say 100, it will need to own 100(Delta) shares.

How does delta hedging work? Let us say that we sell call options on 200 shares (this quantity is 2 standardized call contracts on an options exchange) and the delta is 0.5. We would, therefore, need to hold 200(0.5) = 100 shares. Say the underlying falls by $1. Then we lose $100 on our position in the underlying. If the delta is accurate, the option should decline by $0.50. By having 200 options, the loss in value of the options collectively is $100. Because we are short the options, the loss in value of the options is actually a gain. Hence, the loss on the underlying is offset by the gain on the options. If the dealer were long the option, it would need to sell short the shares.

This illustration may make delta hedging sound simple: Buy (sell) delta shares for each option short (long). But there are three complicating issues. One is that delta is only an approximation of the change in the call price for a change in the underlying. A second issue is that the delta changes if anything else changes. Two factors that change are the price of the underlying and time. When the price of the underlying changes, delta changes, which affects the number of options required to hedge the underlying. Delta also changes

---

[29] In the following text, we always make reference to the delta lying between 0.0 and 1.0, which is true for calls. For puts, the delta is between -1.0 and 0.0. It is common, however, to refer to a put delta of -1.0 as just 1.0, in effect using its absolute value and ignoring the negative. In all discussions in this chapter, we shall refer to delta as ranging between 1.0 and 0.0, recalling that a put delta would range from -1.0 to 0.0.

as time changes; because time changes continuously, delta also changes continuously. Although a dealer can establish a delta-hedged position, as soon as anything happens—the underlying price changes or time elapses—the position is no longer delta hedged. In some cases, the position may not be terribly out of line with a delta hedge, but the more the underlying changes, the further the position moves away from being delta hedged. The third issue is that the number of units of the underlying per option must be rounded off, which leads to a small amount of imprecision in the balancing of the two opposing positions.

In Chapter 4, we took a basic look at the concept of delta hedging. In the following section, we examine how a dealer delta hedges an option position, carrying the analysis through several days with the additional feature that excess cash will be invested in bonds and any additional cash needed will be borrowed.

4.1 DELTA HEDGING AN OPTION OVER TIME

In the previous section, we showed how to set up a delta hedge. As we noted, a delta-hedged position will not remain delta hedged over time. The delta will change as the underlying changes and as time elapses. The dealer must account for these effects.

Let us first examine how actual option prices are sensitive to the underlying and what the delta tells us about that sensitivity. Consider a call option in which the underlying is worth 1210, the exercise price is 1200, the continuously compounded risk-free rate is 2.75 percent, the volatility of the underlying is 20 percent, and the expiration is 120 days. There are no dividends or cash flows on the underlying. Substituting these inputs into the Black–Scholes–Merton model, the option is worth 65.88. Recall from our study of the Black–Scholes–Merton model that delta is the term "$N(d_1)$" in the formula and represents a normal probability associated with the value d_1, which is provided as part of the Black–Scholes–Merton formula. In this example, the delta is 0.5826.[30]

Suppose that the underlying price instantaneously changes to 1200, a decline of 10. Using the delta, we would estimate that the option price would be

$$65.88 + (1200 - 1210)(0.5826) = 60.05$$

If, however, we plugged into the Black–Scholes–Merton model the same parameters but with a price of the underlying of 1200, we would obtain a new option price of 60.19—not much different from the previous result. But observe in Exhibit 7-20 what we obtain for various other values of the underlying. Two patterns become apparent: (1) The further away we move from the current price, the worse the delta-based approximation, and (2) the effects are asymmetric. A given move in one direction does not have the same effect on the option as the same move in the other direction. Specifically, for calls, the delta underestimates the effects of increases in the underlying and overestimates the effects of decreases in the underlying.[31] Because of this characteristic, the delta hedge will not be perfect. The larger the move in the underlying, the worse the hedge. Moreover, whenever the underlying price changes, the delta changes, which requires a rehedging or adjustment to the position. Observe in the last column of the table in Exhibit 7-20 we have recomputed the delta using the new price of the underlying. A dealer must adjust the position according to this new delta.

---

[30] All calculations were done on a computer for best precision.

[31] For puts, delta underestimates the effects of price decreases and overestimates the effects of price increases.

EXHIBIT 7-20   Delta and Option Price Sensitivity

S = 1210
X = 1200
r^c = 0.0275 (continuously compounded)
σ = 0.20
T = 0.328767 (based on 120 days/365)
No dividends
c = 65.88 (from the Black–Scholes–Merton model)

New Price of Underlying	Delta-Estimated Call Price[a]	Actual Call Price[b]	Difference (Actual − Estimated)	New Delta
1180	48.40	49.69	1.29	0.4959
1190	54.22	54.79	0.57	0.5252
1200	60.05	60.19	0.14	0.5542
1210	65.88	65.88	0.00	0.5826
1220	71.70	71.84	0.14	0.6104
1230	77.53	78.08	0.55	0.6374
1240	83.35	84.59	1.24	0.6635

[a]Delta-estimated call price = Original call price + (New price of underlying − Original price of underlying)Delta.
[b]Actual call price obtained from Black–Scholes–Merton model using new price of underlying; all other inputs are the same.

Now let us consider the effect of time on the delta. Exhibit 7-21 shows the delta and the number of units of underlying required to hedge 1,000 short options when the option has 120 days, 119, etc. on down to 108. A critical assumption is that we are holding the underlying price constant. Of course, this constancy would not occur in practice, but to focus on understanding the effect of time on the delta, we must hold the underlying price constant. Observe that the delta changes slowly and the number of units of the underlying required changes gradually over this 12-day period. Another not-so-obvious effect is also present: When we round up, we have more units of the underlying than needed, which has a negative effect that hurts when the underlying goes down. When we round down, we have fewer units of the underlying than needed, which hurts when the underlying goes up.

EXHIBIT 7-21   The Effect of Time on the Delta

S = 1210
X = 1200
r^c = 0.0275 (continuously compounded)
σ = 0.20
T = 0.328767 (based on 120 days/365)
No dividends
c = 65.88 (from the Black–Scholes–Merton model)
Delta = 0.5826

Delta hedge 1,000 short options by holding 1,000(0.5826) = 582.6 units of the underlying.

Time to Expiration (days)	Delta	Number of Units of Underlying Required
120	0.5826	582.6
119	0.5825	582.5
118	0.5824	582.4
117	0.5823	582.3
116	0.5822	582.2
115	0.5821	582.1
114	0.5820	582.0
113	0.5819	581.9
112	0.5818	581.8
111	0.5817	581.7
110	0.5816	581.6
109	0.5815	581.5
108	0.5814	581.4

The combined effects of the underlying price changing and the time to expiration changing interact to present great challenges for delta hedgers. Let us set up a delta hedge and work through a few days of it. Recall that for the option we have been working with, the underlying price is $1,200, the option price is $65.88, and the delta is 0.5826. Suppose a customer comes to us and asks to buy calls on 1,000 shares. We need to buy a sufficient number of shares to offset the sale of the 1,000 calls. Because we are short 1,000 calls, and this number is fixed, we need 0.5826 shares per call or about 583 shares. So we buy 583 shares to balance the 1,000 short calls. The value of this portfolio is

$$583(\$1,210) - 1,000(\$65.88) = \$639,550$$

So, to initiate this delta hedge, we would need to invest $639,550. To determine if this hedge is effective, we should see this value grow at the risk-free rate. Because the Black–Scholes–Merton model uses continuously compounded interest, the formula for compounding a value at the risk-free rate for one day is $\exp(r^c/365)$, where r^c is the continuously compounded risk-free rate. One day later, this value should be $639,550 $\exp(0.0275/365)$ = $639,598. This value becomes our benchmark.

Now, let us move forward one day and have the underlying go to $1,215. We need a new value of the call option, which now has one less day until expiration and is based on an underlying with a price of $1,215. The market would tell us the option price, but we do not have the luxury here of asking the market for the price. Instead, we have to appeal to a model that would tell us an appropriate price. Naturally, we turn to the Black–Scholes–Merton model. We recalculate the value of the call option using Black–Scholes–Merton, with the price of the underlying at $1,215 and the time to expiration at 119/365 = 0.3260. The option value is $68.55, and the new delta is 0.5966. The portfolio is now worth

$$583(\$1,215) - 1,000(\$68.55) = \$639,795$$

This value differs from the benchmark by a small amount: $639,795 − $639,598 = $197. Although the hedge is not perfect, it is off by only about 0.03 percent.

Now, to move forward and still be delta hedged, we need to revise the position. The new delta is 0.5966. So now we need 1,000(0.5966) = 597 units of the underlying and must buy 14 units of the underlying. This purchase will cost 14($1,215) = $17,010. We obtain this money by borrowing it at the risk-free rate. So we issue bonds in the amount of $17,010. Now our position is 597 units of the underlying, 1,000 short calls, and a loan of $17,010. The value of this position is still

$$597(\$1,215) - 1,000(\$68.55) - \$17,010 = \$639,795$$

Of course, this is the same value we had before adjusting the position. We could not expect to generate or lose money just by rearranging our position. As we move forward to the next day, we should see this value grow by one day's interest to $639,795 exp(0.0275/365) = $639,843. This amount is the benchmark for the next day.

Suppose the next day the underlying goes to $1,198, the option goes to 58.54, and its delta goes to 0.5479. Our loan of $17,010 will grow to $17,010 exp(0.0275/365) = $17,011. The new value of the portfolio is

$$597(\$1,198) - 1,000(\$58.54) - \$17,011 = \$639,655$$

This amount differs from the benchmark by $639,655 − $639,843 = −$188, an error of about 0.03 percent.

With the new delta at 0.5479, we now need 548 shares. Because we have 597 shares, we now must sell 597 − 548 = 49 shares. Doing so would generate 49($1,198) = $58,702. Because the value of our debt was $17,011 and we now have $58,702 in cash, we can pay back the loan, leaving $58,702 − $17,011 = $41,691 to be invested at the risk-free rate. So now we have 548 units of the underlying, 1,000 short calls, and bonds of $41,691. The value of this position is

$$548(\$1,198) - 1,000(\$58.54) + \$41,691 = \$639,655$$

Of course, this is the same value we had before buying the underlying. Indeed, we cannot create or destroy any wealth by just rearranging the position.

Exhibit 7-22 illustrates the delta hedge, carrying it through one more day. After the third day, the value of the position should be $639,655 exp(0.0275/365) = $639,703. The actual value is $639,870, a difference of $639,870 − $639,703 = $167.

EXHIBIT 7-22   Delta Hedge of a Short Options Position

S = $1,210
X = $1,200
r^c = 0.0275 (continuously compounded)
σ = 0.20
T = 0.328767 (based on 120 days/365)
No dividends
c = $65.88 (from the Black–Scholes–Merton model)
Delta = 0.5826

Units of option constant at 1,000
Units of underlying required = 1000 × Delta

Units of underlying purchased = (Units of underlying required one day) − (Units of underlying required previous day)

Bonds purchased = −S(Units of underlying purchased)

Bond balance = (Previous balance) exp(r^c/365) + Bonds purchased

Value of portfolio = (Units of underlying)S + (Units of options)c + Bond balance

Day	S	c	Delta	Options Sold	Units of Underlying Required	Units of Underlying Purchased	Value of Bonds Purchased	Bond Balance	Value of Portfolio
0	$1,210	$65.88	0.5826	1,000	583	583	$0	$0	$639,550
1	1,215	68.55	0.5965	1,000	597	14	−17,010	−17,010	639,795
2	1,198	58.54	0.5479	1,000	548	−49	58,702	41,691	639,655
3	1,192	55.04	0.5300	1,000	530	−18	21,456	63,150	639,870

As we can see, the delta hedge is not perfect, but it is pretty good. After three days, we are off by $167, only about 0.03 percent of the benchmark.

In our example and the discussions here, we have noted that the dealer would typically hold a position in the underlying to delta-hedge a position in the option. Trading in the underlying would not, however, always be the preferred hedge vehicle. In fact, we have stated quite strongly that trading in derivatives is often easier and more cost effective than trading in the underlying. As noted previously, ideally a short position in a particular option would be hedged by holding a long position in that same option, but such a hedge requires that the dealer find another customer or dealer who wants to sell that same option. It is possible, however, that the dealer might be able to more easily buy a different option on the same underlying and use that option as the hedging instrument.

For example, suppose one option has a delta of Δ_1 and the other has a delta of Δ_2. These two options are on the same underlying but are not identical. They differ by exercise price, expiration, or both. Using c_1 and c_2 to represent their prices and N_1 and N_2 to represent the quantity of each option in a portfolio that hedges the value of one of the options, the value of the position is

$$V = N_1 c_1 + N_2 c_2$$

Dividing by ΔS, we obtain

$$\frac{\Delta V}{\Delta S} = N_1 \frac{\Delta c_1}{\Delta S} + N_2 \frac{\Delta c_2}{\Delta S}$$

To delta hedge, we set this amount to zero and solve for N_1/N_2 to obtain

$$\frac{N_1}{N_2} = -\frac{\Delta c_2}{\Delta c_1}$$

The negative sign simply means that a long position in one option will require a short position in the other. The desired quantity of Option 1 relative to the quantity of Option 2 is the ratio of the delta of Option 2 to the delta of Option 1. As in the standard delta-hedge example, however, these deltas will change and will require monitoring and modification of the position.[32]

---

[32] Because the position is long one option and short another, whenever the options differ by exercise price, expiration, or both, the position has the characteristics of a spread. In fact, it is commonly called a **ratio spread**.

PRACTICE PROBLEM 16

DynaTrade is an options trading company that makes markets in a variety of derivative instruments. DynaTrade has just sold 500 call options on a stock currently priced at $125.75. Suppose the trade date is 18 November. The call has an exercise price of $125, 60 days until expiration, a price of $10.89, and a delta of 0.5649. DynaTrade will delta-hedge this transaction by purchasing an appropriate number of shares. Any additional transactions required to adjust the delta hedge will be executed by borrowing or lending at the continuously compounded risk-free rate of 4 percent.

DynaTrade has begun delta hedging the option. Two days later, 20 November, the following information applies:

Stock price:	$122.75
Option price:	$9.09
Delta:	0.5176
Number of options:	500
Number of shares:	328
Bond balance:	−$6,072
Market value:	$29,645

A. At the end of 19 November, the delta was 0.6564. Based on this number, show how 328 shares of stock is used to delta hedge 500 call options.

B. Show the allocation of the $29,645 market value of DynaTrade's total position among stock, options, and bonds on 20 November.

C. Show what transactions must be done to adjust the portfolio to be delta hedged for the following day (21 November).

D. On 21 November, the stock is worth $120.50 and the call is worth $7.88. Calculate the market value of the delta-hedged portfolio and compare it with a benchmark, based on the market value on 20 November.

SOLUTIONS

A. If the stock moves up (down) $1, the 328 shares should change by $328. The 500 calls should change by 500(0.6564) = $328.20, rounded off to $328. The calls are short, so any change in the value of the stock position is an opposite change in the value of the options.

B. Stock worth 328($122.75) = $40,262

Options worth −500($9.09) = −$4,545

Bonds worth −$6,072

   Total of $29,645

C. The new required number of shares is 500(0.5176) = 258.80. Round this number to 259. So we need to have 259 shares instead of 328 shares and must sell 69 shares, generating 69($122.75) = $8,470. We invest this amount in risk-free bonds. We had a bond balance of −$6,072, so the proceeds from the sale will pay off all of this debt, leaving a balance of $8,470 − $6,072 = $2,398 going into the next day. The composition of the portfolio would then be as follows:

Shares worth 259($122.75) = $31,792

Options worth −500($9.09) = −$4,545

Bonds worth $2,398

   Total of $29,645

D. The benchmark is $29,645 exp(0.04/365) = $29,648. Also, the value of the bond one day later will be $2,398 exp(0.04/365) = $2,398. (This is less than a half-dollar's interest, so it essentially leaves the balance unchanged.) Now we have

Shares worth 259($120.50) = $31,210

Options worth −500($7.88) = −$3,940

Bonds worth $2,398

   Total of $29,668

This is about $20 more than the benchmark.

As previously noted, the delta is a fairly good approximation of the change in the option price for a very small and rapid change in the price of the underlying. But the underlying does not always change in such a convenient manner, and this possibility introduces a risk into the process of delta hedging.

Note Exhibit 7-23, a graph of the actual option price and the delta-estimated option price from the perspective of day 0 in Exhibit 7-20. At the underlying price of $1,210, the option price is $65.88. The curved line shows the exact option price, calculated with the

EXHIBIT 7-23   Actual Option Price (——) and Delta-Estimated Option Price (——)

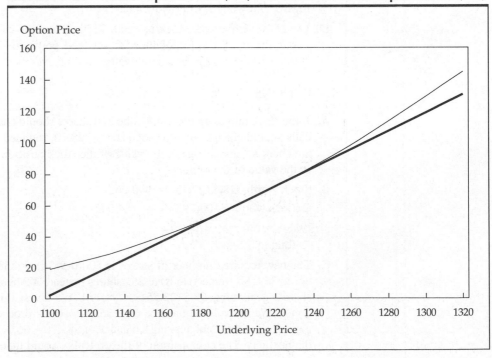

Black–Scholes–Merton model, for a range of underlying prices. The heavy line shows the option price estimated using the delta as we did in Exhibit 7-20. In that exhibit, we did not stray too far from the current underlying price. In Exhibit 7-23, we let the underlying move a little further. Note that the further we move from the current price of the underlying of $1,210, the further the heavy line deviates from the solid line. As noted earlier, the actual call price moves up more than the delta approximation and moves down less than the delta approximation. This effect occurs because the option price is convex with respect to the underlying price, a point we discussed in Section 7.3.1 of Chapter 4. This convexity, which is quite similar to the convexity of a bond price with respect to its yield, means that a first-order price sensitivity measure like delta, or its duration analog for bonds, is accurate only if the underlying moves by a small amount. With duration, a second-order measure called convexity reflects the extent of the deviation of the actual pricing curve from the approximation curve. With options, the second-order measure is called **gamma**.

4.2 GAMMA AND THE RISK OF DELTA

As noted, in Chapter 4 we introduced the concept of the gamma, which is a measure of several effects. We already mentioned that it reflects the deviation of the exact option price change from the price change as approximated by the delta. It also measures the sensitivity of delta to a change in the underlying. In effect, it is the delta of the delta. Specifically,

$$\text{Gamma} = \frac{\text{Change in delta}}{\text{Change in underlying price}}$$

Like delta, gamma is actually an approximation, but we shall treat it as exact. Although a formula exists for gamma, we need to understand only the concept.

If a delta-hedged position were risk free, its gamma would be zero. The larger the gamma, the more the delta-hedged position deviates from being risk free. Because gamma reflects movements in the delta, let us first think about how delta moves. Focusing on call options, recall that the delta is between 0.0 and 1.0. At expiration, the delta is 1.0 if the option expires in-the-money and 0.0 if it expires out-of-the-money. During its life, the delta will tend to be above 0.5 if the option is in-the-money and below 0.5 if the option is out-of-the-money. As expiration approaches, the deltas of in-the-money options will move toward 1.0 and the deltas of out-of-the-money options will move toward 0.0.[33] They will, however, move slowly in their respective directions. The largest moves occur near expiration, when the deltas of at-the-money options move quickly toward 1.0 or 0.0. These rapid movements are the ones that cause the most problems for delta hedgers. Options that are deep in-the-money or deep out-of-the-money tend to have their deltas move closer to 1.0 or 0.0 well before expiration. Their movements are slow and pose fewer problems for delta hedgers. Thus, it is the rapid movements in delta that concern delta hedgers. These rapid movements are more likely to occur on options that are at-the-money and/or near expiration. Under these conditions, the gammas tend to be largest and delta hedges are hardest to maintain.

When gammas are large, some delta hedgers choose to also gamma hedge. This somewhat advanced strategy requires adding a position in another option, combining the underlying and the two options in such a manner that the delta is zero and the gamma is zero. Because it is a somewhat advanced and specialized topic, we do not cover the details of how this is done.

The delta is not the only important factor that changes in the course of managing an option position. The volatility of the underlying can also change.

---

[33] The deltas of options that are very slightly in-the-money will temporarily move down as expiration approaches. Exhibit 7-21 illustrates this effect. But they will eventually move up toward 1.0.

4.3 VEGA AND VOLATILITY RISK

As we covered in Chapter 4, the sensitivity of the option price to the volatility is called the vega and is defined as

$$\text{Vega} = \frac{\text{Change in option price}}{\text{Change in volatility}}$$

As with delta and gamma, the relationship above is an approximation, but we shall treat it as exact. As we noted in Chapter 4, an option price is very sensitive to the volatility of the underlying. Moreover, the volatility is the only unobservable variable required to value an option. Hence, volatility is the most critical variable. When we examined option-pricing models, we studied the Black–Scholes–Merton and binomial models. In neither of these models is the volatility allowed to change. Yet no one believes that volatility is constant; on some days the stock market is clearly more volatile than on other days. This risk of changing volatility can greatly affect a dealer's position in options. A delta-hedged position with a zero or insignificant gamma can greatly change in value if the volatility changes. If, for example, the dealer holds the underlying and sells options to delta hedge, an increase in volatility will raise the value of the options, generating a potentially large loss for the dealer.

Measuring the sensitivity of the option price to the volatility is difficult. The vega from the Black–Scholes–Merton or binomial models is a somewhat artificial construction. It represents how much the model price changes if one changes the volatility by a small amount. But in fact, the model itself is based on the assumption that volatility does not change. Forcing the volatility to change in a model that does not acknowledge that volatility can change has unclear implications.[34] It is clear, however, that an option price is more sensitive to the volatility when it is at-the-money.

Dealers try to measure the vega, monitor it, and in some cases hedge it by taking on a position in another option, using that option's vega to offset the vega on the original option. Managing vega risk, however, cannot be done independently of managing delta and gamma risk. Thus, the dealer is required to jointly monitor and manage the risk associated with the delta, gamma, and vega. We should be aware of the concepts behind managing these risks.

5 FINAL COMMENTS

In Chapter 6, we examined forward and futures strategies. These types of contracts provide gains from movements of the underlying in one direction but result in losses from movements of the underlying in the other direction. The advantage of a willingness to incur losses is that no cash is paid at the start. Options offer the advantage of having one-directional effects: The buyer of an option gains from a movement in one direction and loses only the premium from movements in the other direction. The cost of this advantage is that options require the payment of cash at the start. Some market participants choose forwards and

---

[34] If this point seems confusing, consider this analogy. In the famous Einstein equation $E = mc^2$, E is energy, m is mass, and c is the constant representing the speed of light. For a given mass, we could change c, which would change E. The equation allows this change, but in fact the speed of light is constant at 186,000 miles per second. So far as scientists know, it is a universal constant and can never change. In the case of option valuation, the model assumes that volatility of a given stock is like a universal constant. We can change it, however, and the equation would give us a new option price. But are we allowed to do so? Unlike the speed of light, volatility does indeed change, even though our model says that it does not. What happens when we change volatility in our model? We do not know.

futures because they do not have to pay cash at the start. They can justify taking positions without having to come up with the cash to do so. Others, however, prefer the flexibility to benefit when their predictions are right and suffer only a limited loss when wrong. The trade-off between the willingness to pay cash at the start versus incurring losses, given one's risk preferences, is the deciding factor in whether to use options or forwards/futures.

All option strategies are essentially rooted in the transactions of buying a call or a put. Understanding a short position in either type of option means understanding the corresponding long position in the option. All remaining strategies are just combinations of options, the underlying, and risk-free bonds. We looked at a number of option strategies associated with equities, which can apply about equally to index options or options on individual stocks. The applicability of these strategies to bonds is also fairly straightforward. The options must expire before the bonds mature, but the general concepts associated with equity option strategies apply similarly to bond option strategies.

Likewise, strategies that apply to equity options apply in nearly the same manner to interest rate options. Nonetheless, significant differences exist between interest rate options and equity or bond options. If nothing else, the notion of bullishness is quite opposite. Bullish (bearish) equity investors buy calls (puts). In interest rate markets, bullish (bearish) investors buy puts (calls) on interest rates, because being bullish (bearish) on interest rates means that one thinks rates are going down (up). Interest rate options pay off as though they were interest payments. Equity or bond options pay off as though the holder were selling or buying stocks or bonds. Finally, interest rate options are very often combined into portfolios in the form of caps and floors for the purpose of hedging floating-rate loans. Standard option strategies such as straddles and spreads are just as applicable to interest rate options.

Recall that in Chapter 4, we examined one other slightly different type of option, one in which the underlying is a futures contract. Despite some subtle differences between the option strategies examined in this chapter and comparable strategies using options on futures, the differences are relatively minor and do not warrant separate coverage here. If you have a good grasp of the basics of the option strategies presented in this chapter, you can easily adapt those strategies to ones in which the underlying is a futures contract.

In Chapter 8, we take up strategies using swaps. As we have so often mentioned, interest rate swaps are the most widely used financial derivative. They are less widely used with currencies and equities than are forwards, futures, and options. Nonetheless, there are many applications of swaps to currencies and equities, and we shall certainly look at them. To examine swaps, however, we must return to the types of instruments with two-directional payoffs and no cash payments at the start. Indeed, as we showed in Chapter 5, swaps are a lot like forward contracts, which themselves are a lot like futures.

KEY POINTS

- The profit from buying a call is the value at expiration, $\max(0, S_T - X)$, minus c_0, the option premium. The maximum profit is infinite, and the maximum loss is the option premium. The breakeven underlying price at expiration is the exercise price plus the option premium. When one sells a call, these results are reversed.

- The profit from buying a put is the value at expiration, $\max(0, X - S_T)$, minus p_0, the option premium. The maximum profit is the exercise price minus the option premium, and the maximum loss is the option premium. The breakeven underlying price at expiration is the exercise price minus the option premium. When one sells a put, these results are reversed.

- The profit from a covered call—the purchase of the underlying and sale of a call—is the value at expiration, $S_T - \max(0,S_T - X)$, minus $S_0 - c_0$, the cost of the underlying minus the option premium. The maximum profit is the exercise price minus the original underlying price plus the option premium, and the maximum loss is the cost of the underlying less the option premium. The breakeven underlying price at expiration is the original price of the underlying minus the option premium.

- The profit from a protective put—the purchase of the underlying and a put—is the value at expiration, $S_T + \max(0,X - S_T)$, minus the cost of the underlying plus the option premium, $S_0 + p_0$. The maximum profit is infinite, and the maximum loss is the cost of the underlying plus the option premium minus the exercise price. The breakeven underlying price at expiration is the original price of the underlying plus the option premium.

- The profit from a bull spread—the purchase of a call at one exercise price and the sale of a call with the same expiration but a higher exercise price—is the value at expiration, $\max(0,S_T - X_1) - \max(0,S_T - X_2)$, minus the net premium, $c_1 - c_2$, which is the premium of the long option minus the premium of the short option. The maximum profit is $X_2 - X_1$ minus the net premium, and the maximum loss is the net premium. The breakeven underlying price at expiration is the lower exercise price plus the net premium.

- The profit from a bear spread—the purchase of a put at one exercise price and the sale of a put with the same expiration but a lower exercise price—is the value at expiration, $\max(0,X_2 - S_T) - \max(0,X_1 - S_T)$, minus the net premium, $p_2 - p_1$, which is the premium of the long option minus the premium of the short option. The maximum profit is $X_2 - X_1$ minus the net premium, and the maximum loss is the net premium. The breakeven underlying price at expiration is the higher exercise price minus the net premium.

- The profit from a butterfly spread—the purchase of a call at one exercise price, X_1, sale of two calls at a higher exercise price, X_2, and the purchase of a call at a higher exercise price, X_3—is the value at expiration, $\max(0,S_T - X_1) - 2\max(0,S_T - X_2)$, $+ \max(0,S_T - X_3)$, minus the net premium, $c_1 - 2c_2 + c_3$. The maximum profit is $X_2 - X_1$ minus the net premium, and the maximum loss is the net premium. The breakeven underlying prices at expiration are $2X_2 - X_1$ minus the net premium and X_1 plus the net premium. A butterfly spread can also be constructed by trading the corresponding put options.

- The profit from a collar—the holding of the underlying, the purchase of a put at one exercise price, X_1, and the sale of a call with the same expiration and a higher exercise price, X_2, and in which the premium on the put equals the premium on the call—is the value at expiration, $S_T + \max(0,X_1 - S_T) - \max(0,S_T - X_2)$, minus S_0, the original price of the underlying. The maximum profit is $X_2 - S_0$, and the maximum loss is $S_0 - X_1$. The breakeven underlying price at expiration is the initial price of the underlying.

- The profit from a straddle—a long position in a call and a put with the same exercise price and expiration—is the value at expiration, $\max(0,S_T - X) + \max(0,X - S_T)$, minus the premiums on the call and put, $c_0 + p_0$. The maximum profit is infinite, and the maximum loss is the sum of the premiums on the call and put, $c_0 + p_0$. The breakeven prices at expiration are the exercise price plus and minus the premiums on the call and put.

- A box spread is a combination of a bull spread using calls and a bear spread using puts, with one call and put at an exercise price of X_1 and another call and put at an exercise price of X_2. The profit is the value at expiration, $X_2 - X_1$, minus the net premiums, $c_1 - c_2 + p_2 - p_1$. The transaction is risk free, and the net premium paid should be the present value of this risk-free payoff.

- A long position in an interest rate call can be used to place a ceiling on the rate on an anticipated loan from the perspective of the borrower. The call provides a payoff if the interest rate at expiration exceeds the exercise rate, thereby compensating the borrower when the rate is higher than the exercise rate. The effective interest paid on the loan is the actual interest paid minus the call payoff. The call premium must be taken into account by compounding it to the date on which the loan is taken out and deducting it from the initial proceeds received from the loan.

- A long position in an interest rate put can be used to lock in the rate on an anticipated loan from the perspective of the lender. The put provides a payoff if the interest rate at expiration is less than the exercise rate, thereby compensating the lender when the rate is lower than the exercise rate. The effective interest paid on the loan is the actual interest received plus the put payoff. The put premium must be taken into account by compounding it to the date on which the loan is taken out and adding it to initial proceeds paid out on the loan.

- An interest rate cap can be used to place an upper limit on the interest paid on a floating rate loan from the perspective of the borrower. A cap is a series of interest rate calls, each of which is referred to as a caplet. Each caplet provides a payoff if the interest rate on the loan reset date exceeds the exercise rate, thereby compensating the borrower when the rate is higher than the exercise rate. The effective interest paid is the actual interest paid minus the caplet payoff. The premium is paid at the start and is the sum of the premiums on the component caplets.

- An interest rate floor can be used to place a lower limit on the interest received on a floating-rate loan from the perspective of the lender. A floor is a series of interest rate puts, each of which is called a floorlet. Each floorlet provides a payoff if the interest rate at the loan reset date is less than the exercise rate, thereby compensating the lender when the rate is lower than the exercise rate. The effective interest received is the actual interest plus the floorlet payoff. The premium is paid at the start and is the sum of the premiums on the component floorlets.

- An interest rate collar, which consists of a long interest rate cap at one exercise rate and a short interest rate floor at a lower exercise rate, can be used to place an upper limit on the interest paid on a floating-rate loan. The floor, however, places a lower limit on the interest paid on the floating-rate loan. Typically the floor exercise rate is set such that the premium on the floor equals the premium on the cap, so that no cash outlay is required to initiate the transaction. The effective interest is the actual interest paid minus any payoff from the long caplet plus any payoff from the short floorlet.

- Dealers offer to take positions in options and typically hedge their positions by establishing delta-neutral combinations of options and the underlying or other options. These positions require that the sensitivity of the option position with respect to the underlying be offset by a quantity of the underlying or another option. The delta will change, moving toward 1.0 for in-the-money calls (-1.0 for puts) and 0.0 for out-of-the-money options as expiration approaches. Any change in the underlying price will also change the delta. These changes in the delta necessitate buying and selling options or the underlying to maintain the delta-hedged position. Any additional funds required to buy the underlying or other options are obtained by issuing risk-free bonds. Any additional funds released from selling the underlying or other options are invested in risk-free bonds.

- The delta of an option changes as the underlying changes and as time elapses. The delta will change more rapidly with large movements in the underlying and when the option is approximately at-the-money and near expiration. These large changes in the delta will prevent a delta-hedged position from being truly risk free. Dealers usually monitor their gammas and in some cases hedge their gammas by adding other options to their positions such that the gammas offset.

- The sensitivity of an option to volatility is called the vega. An option's volatility can change, resulting in a potentially large change in the value of the option. Dealers monitor and sometimes hedge their vegas so that this risk does not impact a delta-hedged portfolio.

PROBLEMS

1. Consider a call option selling for $4 in which the exercise price is $50.
   A. Determine the value at expiration and the profit for a buyer under the following outcomes:
      i. The price of the underlying at expiration is $55.
      ii. The price of the underlying at expiration is $51.
      iii. The price of the underlying at expiration is $48.
   B. Determine the value at expiration and the profit for a seller under the following outcomes:
      i. The price of the underlying at expiration is $49.
      ii. The price of the underlying at expiration is $52.
      iii. The price of the underlying at expiration is $55.
   C. Determine the following:
      i. The maximum profit to the buyer (maximum loss to the seller)
      ii. The maximum loss to the buyer (maximum profit to the seller)
   D. Determine the breakeven price of the underlying at expiration.

2. Suppose you believe that the price of a particular underlying, currently selling at $99, is going to increase substantially in the next six months. You decide to purchase a call option expiring in six months on this underlying. The call option has an exercise price of $105 and sells for $7.
   A. Determine the profit under the following outcomes for the price of the underlying six months from now.
      i. $99
      ii. $104
      iii. $105
      iv. $109
      v. $112
      vi. $115
   B. Determine the breakeven price of the underlying at expiration. Check that your answer is consistent with the solution to Part A of this problem.

3. Consider a put option on the Nasdaq 100 selling for $106.25 in which the exercise price is 2100.
   A. Determine the value at expiration and the profit for a buyer under the following outcomes:
      i. The price of the underlying at expiration is 2125.
      ii. The price of the underlying at expiration is 2050.
      iii. The price of the underlying at expiration is 1950.
   B. Determine the value at expiration and the profit for a seller under the following outcomes:
      i. The price of the underlying at expiration is 1975.
      ii. The price of the underlying at expiration is 2150.
   C. Determine the following:
      i. The maximum profit to the buyer (maximum loss to the seller)
      ii. The maximum loss to the buyer (maximum profit to the seller)
   D. Determine the breakeven price of the underlying at expiration.

4. Suppose you believe that the price of a particular underlying, currently selling at $99, will decrease considerably in the next six months. You decide to purchase a put option expiring in six months on this underlying. The put option has an exercise price of $95 and sells for $5.

    A. Determine the profit for you under the following outcomes for the price of the underlying six months from now:
- **i.** $100
- **ii.** $95
- **iii.** $93
- **iv.** $90
- **v.** $85

    B. Determine the breakeven price of the underlying at expiration. Check that your answer is consistent with the solution to Part A of this problem.

    C. **i.** What is the maximum profit that you can have?

       ii. At what expiration price of the underlying would this profit be realized?

5. You simultaneously purchase an underlying priced at $77 and write a call option on it with an exercise price of $80 and selling at $6.

    A. What is the term commonly used for the position that you have taken?

    B. Determine the value at expiration and the profit for your strategy under the following outcomes:
- **i.** The price of the underlying at expiration is $70.
- **ii.** The price of the underlying at expiration is $75.
- **iii.** The price of the underlying at expiration is $80.
- **iv.** The price of the underlying at expiration is $85.

    C. Determine the following:
- **i.** The maximum profit
- **ii.** The maximum loss
- **iii.** The expiration price of the underlying at which you would realize the maximum profit
- **iv.** The expiration price of the underlying at which you would incur the maximum loss

    D. Determine the breakeven price at expiration.

6. Suppose you simultaneously purchase an underlying priced at $77 and a put option on it, with an exercise price of $75 and selling at $3.

    A. What is the term commonly used for the position that you have taken?

    B. Determine the value at expiration and the profit for your strategy under the following outcomes:
- **i.** The price of the underlying at expiration is $70.
- **ii.** The price of the underlying at expiration is $75.
- **iii.** The price of the underlying at expiration is $80.
- **iv.** The price of the underlying at expiration is $85.
- **v.** The price of the underlying at expiration is $90.

    C. Determine the following:
- **i.** The maximum profit
- **ii.** The maximum loss
- **iii.** The expiration price of the underlying at which you would incur the maximum loss

    D. Determine the breakeven price at expiration.

7. You are bullish about an underlying that is currently trading at a price of $80. You choose to go long one call option on the underlying with an exercise price of $75 and selling at $10, and go short one call option on the underlying with an exercise price of $85 and selling at $2. Both the calls expire in three months.

    A. What is the term commonly used for the position that you have taken?

    B. Determine the value at expiration and the profit for your strategy under the following outcomes:

      i. The price of the underlying at expiration is $89.

      ii. The price of the underlying at expiration is $78.

      iii. The price of the underlying at expiration is $70.

  C. Determine the following:

      i. The maximum profit

      ii. The maximum loss

  D. Determine the breakeven underlying price at expiration of the call options.

  E. Verify that your answer to Part D above is correct.

8. You expect a currency to depreciate with respect to the U.S. dollar. The currency is currently trading at a price of $0.75. You decide to go long one put option on the currency with an exercise price of $0.85 and selling at $0.15, and go short one put option on the currency with an exercise price of $0.70 and selling at $0.03. Both the puts expire in three months.

  A. What is the term commonly used for the position that you have taken?

  B. Determine the value at expiration and the profit for your strategy under the following outcomes:

      i. The price of the currency at expiration is $0.87.

      ii. The price of the currency at expiration is $0.78.

      iii. The price of the currency at expiration is $0.68.

  C. Determine the following:

      i. The maximum profit

      ii. The maximum loss

  D. Determine the breakeven underlying price at the expiration of the put options.

  E. Verify that your answer to Part D above is correct.

9. A stock is currently trading at a price of $114. You construct a butterfly spread using calls of three different strike prices on this stock, with the calls expiring at the same time. You go long one call with an exercise price of $110 and selling at $8, go short two calls with an exercise price of $115 and selling at $5, and go long one call with an exercise price of $120 and selling at $3.

  A. Determine the value at expiration and the profit for your strategy under the following outcomes:

      i. The price of the stock at the expiration of the calls is $106.

      ii. The price of the stock at the expiration of the calls is $110.

      iii. The price of the stock at the expiration of the calls is $115.

      iv. The price of the stock at the expiration of the calls is $120.

      v. The price of the stock at the expiration of the calls is $123.

  B. Determine the following:

      i. The maximum profit

      ii. The maximum loss

      iii. The stock price at which you would realize the maximum profit

      iv. The stock price at which you would incur the maximum loss

  C. Determine the breakeven underlying price at expiration of the call options.

10. A stock is currently trading at a price of $114. You construct a butterfly spread using puts of three different strike prices on this stock, with the puts expiring at the same time. You go long one put with an exercise price of $110 and selling at $3.50, go short two puts with an exercise price of $115 and selling at $6, and go long one put with an exercise price of $120 and selling at $9.

  A. Determine the value at expiration and the profit for your strategy under the following outcomes:

      i. The price of the stock at the expiration of the puts is $106.

      ii. The price of the stock at the expiration of the puts is $110.
      iii. The price of the stock at the expiration of the puts is $115.
      iv. The price of the stock at the expiration of the puts is $120.
      v. The price of the stock at the expiration of the puts is $123.
  B. Determine the following:
      i. The maximum profit
      ii. The maximum loss
      iii. The stock price at which you would realize the maximum profit
      iv. The stock price at which you would incur the maximum loss
  C. Determine the breakeven underlying price at expiration of the put options.
  D. Verify that your answer to Part C above is correct.

11. A stock is currently trading at a price of $80. You decide to place a collar on this stock. You purchase a put option on the stock, with an exercise price of $75 and a premium of $3.50. You simultaneously sell a call option on the stock with the same maturity and the same premium as the put option. This call option has an exercise price of $90.
  A. Determine the value at expiration and the profit for your strategy under the following outcomes:
      i. The price of the stock at expiration of the options is $92.
      ii. The price of the stock at expiration of the options is $90.
      iii. The price of the stock at expiration of the options is $82.
      iv. The price of the stock at expiration of the options is $75.
      v. The price of the stock at expiration of the options is $70.
  B. Determine the following:
      i. The maximum profit
      ii. The maximum loss
      iii. The stock price at which you would realize the maximum profit
      iv. The stock price at which you would incur the maximum loss
  C. Determine the breakeven underlying price at expiration of the put options.

12. You believe that the market will be volatile in the near future, but you do not feel particularly strongly about the direction of the movement. With this expectation, you decide to buy both a call and a put with the same exercise price and the same expiration on the same underlying stock trading at $28. You buy one call option and one put option on this stock, both with an exercise price of $25. The premium on the call is $4 and the premium on the put is $1.
  A. What is the term commonly used for the position that you have taken?
  B. Determine the value at expiration and the profit for your strategy under the following outcomes:
      i. The price of the stock at expiration is $35.
      ii. The price of the stock at expiration is $29.
      iii. The price of the stock at expiration is $25.
      iv. The price of the stock at expiration is $20.
      v. The price of the stock at expiration is $15.
  C. Determine the following:
      i. The maximum profit
      ii. The maximum loss
  D. Determine the breakeven stock price at expiration of the options.

13. Consider a box spread consisting of options on a stock trading at $27.95. The options have exercise prices of $25 and $30, and they mature in six months. The call options for the exercise prices of $25 and $30 have a premium of $5.30 and $2.75, respectively. The put options for these exercise prices have a premium of $2.00 and $4.30, respectively. What should the discrete risk-free rate be if these options are correctly priced?

14. World Scanners, Inc. is a U.S. corporation that occasionally undertakes short-term borrowings in U.S. dollars with the rate tied to LIBOR. The 90-day LIBOR on 18 May is 6 percent. The company determines on this day that it will borrow $10 million at LIBOR plus 200 basis points on 15 July. The loan will be a pure discount loan to be repaid with a single payment of principal and interest 90 days later. To protect against increases in LIBOR between 18 May and 15 July, the company buys a call option on LIBOR with an exercise rate of 5.5 percent to expire on 15 July with the underlying being 90-day LIBOR. The call premium is $25,000. Complete the table below for a range of possible LIBORs on 15 July.

LIBOR on 15 July	Loan Rate	Loan Interest Paid 13 October	Call Payoff	Effective Interest	Effective Loan Rate
0.015					
0.030					
0.045					
0.060					
0.075					
0.090					

15. On 15 March, Techies, Inc. determines that it will need to borrow $3,000,000 at LIBOR plus 3 percent on 1 May. The 180-day LIBOR on 15 March is 5.5 percent. The loan will be a pure discount loan to be repaid with a single payment of principal and interest 180 days later. To protect against increases in LIBOR between 15 March and 1 May, the company buys a call option on LIBOR with an exercise rate of 5.25 percent to expire on 1 May with the underlying being 180-day LIBOR. The call premium is $8,000. What is the effective ceiling on the rate on the loan as a result of the strategy adopted by Techies, Inc.?

16. Lenders, Inc. makes loan commitments to corporations. On 16 April, it makes a commitment to lend $100 million at 180-day LIBOR plus 250 basis points on 1 June, which is 46 days later. Current LIBOR is 6.5 percent. The loan will be a single-payment loan made on 1 June; the principal and interest will be repaid 180 days later on 28 November. To protect itself against the risk that LIBOR will fall by the date the loan is taken out, Lenders, Inc. protects itself by purchasing an interest rate put, with an exercise rate of 6.25 percent to expire on 1 June with the underlying being 180-day LIBOR. The put premium is $120,000.

Complete the table below for a range of possible LIBORs on 1 June.

LIBOR on 1 June	Loan Rate	Loan Interest Paid 28 Nov	Put Payoff	Effective Interest	Effective Loan Rate
0.030					
0.045					
0.060					
0.075					
0.090					
0.105					

17. Consider a company that borrows in the floating-rate instrument market. It takes out a $10 million one-year loan on 1 March. The loan is an interest-only loan, requiring quarterly interest payments on the first day of each corresponding month: 1 June, 1 September, 1 December, and 1 March of the following year, with the full principal payment at the end. The interest rate is 90-day LIBOR plus 200 basis points. Current 90-day LIBOR is 7 percent, which sets the rate for the first three-month period at 9 percent. The rates are reset every three months. To protect itself against the risk of increases in interest rates when the rates are reset, the company purchases an interest rate cap with an exercise rate of 7.25 percent. The component caplets expire on the rate reset dates. The cap premium, paid up front on 1 March, is $25,000.

    Determine the effective interest payments if LIBOR on the following dates is as given:

1 June:	7.25 percent
1 September:	7.50 percent
1 December:	8.00 percent

18. Careful Bank is a lender in the floating-rate instrument market. It uses fixed-rate financing on its floating-rate loans and buys floors to hedge the rate. It makes a $20 million one-year loan on 16 July. The loan is an interest-only loan, requiring quarterly interest payments on the 16th day of each corresponding month: 16 October, and 16 January, 16 April, and 16 July of the following year, with the full principal payment at the end on 16 July of the following year. The interest rate is 90-day LIBOR plus 250 basis points. Current 90-day LIBOR is 6 percent, which sets the rate for the first three-month period at 8.5 percent. The rates are reset every three months. To protect itself against the risk of decreases in interest rates when the rates are reset, the company purchases an interest rate floor. The component floorlets expire on the rate reset dates. LIBOR on the following dates turn out to be as given:

16 October:	5.25 percent
16 January:	5.50 percent
16 April:	5.75 percent

   A. Determine the effective interest payments if the bank had purchased a floor with an exercise rate of 5.75 percent, with a premium of $50,000 paid up front on 16 July.

   B. Determine the effective interest payments if the bank had purchased a floor with an exercise rate of 6.00 percent, with a higher premium paid up front on 16 July.

   C. Determine the effective interest payments if the bank had purchased a floor with an exercise rate of 5.50 percent, with a lower premium paid up front on 16 July.

19. Technocrats, Inc. is a floating-rate borrower. It takes out a $20 million one-year loan on 1 March. The loan is an interest-only loan, requiring quarterly interest payments on the first day of each corresponding month: 1 June, 1 September, 1 December, and 1 March of the following year, and the full principal payment at the end. The interest rate is 90-day LIBOR plus 1.5 percent. Current 90-day LIBOR is 6 percent, which sets the rate for the first three-month period at 7.5 percent. The rates are reset every three months. Technocrats manages the risk of rising interest rates over the life of the loan by purchasing an interest rate cap and offsetting the cost of the cap by selling an interest rate floor. It chooses an interest rate cap with an exercise rate of 6.25 percent. The component caplets expire on the rate reset dates. To generate a floor premium suf-

ficient to offset the cap premium, Technocrats sells a floor with an exercise rate of 5.25 percent.

Determine the effective interest payments if LIBOR on the following dates is as given:

1 June:	6.50 percent
1 September:	5.50 percent
1 December:	5.00 percent

20. Consider the following information:
    * Stock price: $46
    * Exercise price of call options: $45
    * Call premium: $5
    * Delta: 0.5420
    * Number of calls sold: 1,000
    * Delta at the end of the previous day: 0.64
    * Continuously compounded risk-free rate: 4.5 percent.
    A. How many shares of stock are needed to delta hedge the call position at the end of the previous day?
    B. Suppose that at the end of the previous day, we had a loan balance of $3,000. What is the market value of the portfolio today using the new information given above?
    C. Show what transactions would need to be done to adjust the portfolio to be delta hedged for the following day.
    D. On the following day, the stock is worth $45.50 and the call is worth $4.71. Calculate the market value of the delta-hedged portfolio and compare it with a benchmark, based on the market value computed in Part B above.

SOLUTIONS

1. **A.** Call buyer

    i. $c_T = \max(0, S_T - X) = \max(0, 55 - 50) = 5$
    $\Pi = c_T - c_0 = 5 - 4 = 1$
    ii. $c_T = \max(0, S_T - X) = \max(0, 51 - 50) = 1$
    $\Pi = c_T - c_0 = 1 - 4 = -3$
    iii. $c_T = \max(0, S_T - X) = \max(0, 48 - 50) = 0$
    $\Pi = c_T - c_0 = 0 - 4 = -4$

  B. Call seller

    i. Value $= -c_T = -\max(0, S_T - X) = -\max(0, 49 - 50) = 0$
    $\Pi = -c_T + c_0 = -0 + 4 = 4$
    ii. Value $= -c_T = -\max(0, S_T - X) = -\max(0, 52 - 50) = -2$
    $\Pi = -c_T + c_0 = -2 + 4 = 2$
    iii. Value $= -c_T = -\max(0, S_T - X) = -\max(0, 55 - 50) = -5$
    $\Pi = -c_T + c_0 = -5 + 4 = -1$

  C. Maximum and minimum

    i. Maximum profit to buyer (loss to seller) $= \infty$
    ii. Maximum loss to buyer (profit to seller) $= c_0 = 4$

  D. $S_T^* = X + c_0 = 50 + 4 = 54$

2. **A.** **i.** $c_T = \max(0, S_T - X) = \max(0, 99 - 105) = 0$
    $\Pi = c_T - c_0 = 0 - 7 = -7$
    ii. $c_T = \max(0, S_T - X) = \max(0, 104 - 105) = 0$
    $\Pi = c_T - c_0 = 0 - 7 = -7$
    iii. $c_T = \max(0, S_T - X) = \max(0, 105 - 105) = 0$
    $\Pi = c_T - c_0 = 0 - 7 = -7$
    iv. $c_T = \max(0, S_T - X) = \max(0, 109 - 105) = 4$
    $\Pi = c_T - c_0 = 4 - 7 = -3$
    v. $c_T = \max(0, S_T - X) = \max(0, 112 - 105) = 7$
    $\Pi = c_T - c_0 = 7 - 7 = 0$
    vi. $c_T = \max(0, S_T - X) = \max(0, 115 - 105) = 10$
    $\Pi = c_T - c_0 = 10 - 7 = 3$

  B. $S_T^* = X + c_0 = 105 + 7 = 112$

    Clearly, this result is consistent with our solution above, where the profit is exactly zero in Part A(v), in which the price at expiration is 112.

3. **A.** Put buyer

    i. $p_T = \max(0, X - S_T) = \max(0, 2100 - 2125) = 0$
    $\Pi = p_T - p_0 = 0 - 106.25 = -106.25$
    ii. $p_T = \max(0, X - S_T) = \max(0, 2100 - 2050) = 50$
    $\Pi = p_T - p_0 = 50 - 106.25 = -56.25$
    iii. $p_T = \max(0, X - S_T) = \max(0, 2100 - 1950) = 150$
    $\Pi = p_T - p_0 = 150 - 106.25 = 43.75$

  B. Put seller

    i. Value $= -p_T = -\max(0, X - S_T) = -\max(0, 2100 - 1975) = -125$
    $\Pi = -p_T + p_0 = -125 + 106.25 = -18.75$
    ii. Value $= -p_T = -\max(0, X - S_T) = -\max(0, 2100 - 2150) = 0$
    $\Pi = -p_T + p_0 = -0 + 106.25 = 106.25$

  C. Maximum and minimum

    i. Maximum profit to buyer (loss to seller) $= X - p_0 = 2100 - 106.25 = 1993.75$

      ii. Maximum loss to buyer (profit to seller) $= p_0 = 106.25$

  D. $S_T^* = X - p_0 = 2100 - 106.25 = 1993.75$

4. A.   **i.** $p_T = \max(0,X - S_T) = \max(0,95 - 100) = 0$

        $\Pi = p_T - p_0 = 0 - 5 = -5$

    ii. $p_T = \max(0,X - S_T) = \max(0,95 - 95) = 0$

        $\Pi = p_T - p_0 = 0 - 5 = -5$

   iii. $p_T = \max(0,X - S_T) = \max(0,95 - 93) = 2$

        $\Pi = p_T - p_0 = 2 - 5 = -3$

    iv. $p_T = \max(0,X - S_T) = \max(0,95 - 90) = 5$

        $\Pi = p_T - p_0 = 5 - 5 = 0$

     v. $p_T = \max(0,X - S_T) = \max(0,95 - 85) = 10$

        $\Pi = p_T - p_0 = 10 - 5 = 5$

  B. $S_T^* = X - p_0 = 95 - 5 = 90$

  Clearly, this result is consistent with our solution above, where the profit is exactly zero in Part A(iv), in which the price at expiration is 90.

  C.   **i.** Maximum profit (to put buyer) $= X - p_0 = 95 - 5 = 90$.

    ii. This profit would be realized in the unlikely scenario of the price of the underlying falling all the way down to zero.

5. A. This position is commonly called a covered call.

  B.   **i.** $V_T = S_T - \max(0,S_T - X) = 70 - \max(0,70 - 80) = 70 - 0 = 70$

        $\Pi = V_T - V_0 = 70 - (S_0 - c_0) = 70 - (77 - 6) = 70 - 71 = -1$

    ii. $V_T = S_T - \max(0,S_T - X) = 75 - \max(0,75 - 80) = 75 - 0 = 75$

        $\Pi = V_T - V_0 = 75 - (S_0 - c_0) = 75 - (77 - 6) = 4$

   iii. $V_T = S_T - \max(0,S_T - X) = 80 - \max(0,80 - 80) = 80 - 0 = 80$

        $\Pi = V_T - V_0 = 80 - (S_0 - c_0) = 80 - (77 - 6) = 9$

    iv. $V_T - S_T - \max(0,S_T - X) = 85 \quad \max(0,85 - 80) = 85 - 5 - 80$

        $\Pi = V_T - V_0 = 80 - (S_0 - c_0) = 80 - (77 - 6) = 9$

  C.   **i.** Maximum profit $= X - S_0 + c_0 = 80 - 77 + 6 = 9$

    ii. Maximum loss $= S_0 - c_0 = 77 - 6 - 71$

   iii. The maximum profit would be realized if the expiration price of the underlying is at or above the exercise price of \$80.

    iv. The maximum loss would be incurred if the underlying price drops to zero.

  D. $S_T^* = S_0 - c_0 = 77 - 6 = 71$

6. A. This position is commonly called a protective put.

  B.   **i.** $V_T = S_T + \max(0,X - S_T) = 70 + \max(0,75 - 70) = 70 + 5 = 75$

        $\Pi = V_T - V_0 = 75 - (S_0 + p_0) = 75 - (77 + 3) = 75 - 80 = -5$

    ii. $V_T = S_T + \max(0,X - S_T) = 75 + \max(0,75 - 75) = 75 + 0 = 75$

        $\Pi = V_T - V_0 = 75 - (S_0 + p_0) = 75 - (77 + 3) = 75 - 80 = -5$

   iii. $V_T = S_T + \max(0,X - S_T) = 80 + \max(0,75 - 80) = 80 + 0 = 80$

        $\Pi = V_T - V_0 = 80 - (S_0 + p_0) = 80 - (77 + 3) = 80 - 80 = 0$

    iv. $V_T = S_T + \max(0,X - S_T) = 85 + \max(0,75 - 85) = 85 + 0 = 85$

        $\Pi = V_T - V_0 = 85 - (S_0 + p_0) = 85 - (77 + 3) = 85 - 80 = 5$

     v. $V_T = S_T + \max(0,X - S_T) = 90 + \max(0,75 - 90) = 90 + 0 = 90$

        $\Pi = V_T - V_0 = 90 - (S_0 + p_0) = 90 - (77 + 3) = 90 - 80 = 10$

  C.   **i.** Maximum profit $= \infty$

    ii. Maximum loss $= -(X - S_0 - p_0) = -(75 - 77 - 3) = 5$

   iii. The maximum loss would be incurred if the expiration price of the underlying were at or below the exercise price of \$75.

  D. $S_T^* = S_0 + p_0 = 77 + 3 = 80$

7. **A.** This position is commonly called a bull spread.
   B. Let X_1 be the lower of the two strike prices and X_2 be the higher of the two strike prices.
      i. $V_T = \max(0, S_T - X_1) - \max(0, S_T - X_2) = \max(0, 89 - 75) - \max(0, 89 - 85) = 14 - 4 = 10$
          $\Pi = V_T - V_0 = V_T - (c_1 - c_2) = 10 - (10 - 2) = 2$
      ii. $V_T = \max(0, S_T - X_1) - \max(0, S_T - X_2) = \max(0, 78 - 75) - \max(0, 70 - 85) = 3 - 0 = 3$
          $\Pi = V_T - V_0 = V_T - (c_1 - c_2) = 3 - (10 - 2) = -5$
      iii. $V_T = \max(0, S_T - X_1) - \max(0, S_T - X_2) = \max(0, 70 - 75) - \max(0, 70 - 85) = 0 - 0 = 0$
          $\Pi = V_T - V_0 = V_T - (c_1 - c_2) = 0 - (10 - 2) = -8$
   C. **i.** Maximum profit $= X_2 - X_1 - (c_1 - c_2) = 85 - 75 - (10 - 2) = 2$
      ii. Maximum loss $= c_1 - c_2 = 10 - 2 = 8$
   D. $S_T{}^* = X_1 + (c_1 - c_2) = 75 + (10 - 2) = 83$
   E. $V_T = \max(0, S_T - X_1) - \max(0, S_T - X_2) = \max(0, 83 - 75) - \max(0, 83 - 85) = 8 - 0 = 8$
      $\Pi = V_T - V_0 = V_T - (c_1 - c_2) = 8 - (10 - 2) = 0$
   Therefore, the profit or loss if the price of the underlying increases to 83 at expiration is indeed zero.

8. **A.** This position is commonly called a bear spread.
   B. Let X_1 be the lower of the two strike prices and X_2 be the higher of the two strike prices.
      i. $V_T = \max(0, X_2 - S_T) - \max(0, X_1 - S_T) = \max(0, 0.85 - 0.87) - \max(0, 0.70 - 0.87) = 0 - 0 = 0$
          $\Pi = V_T - V_0 = V_T - (p_2 - p_1) = 0 - (0.15 - 0.03) = -0.12$
      ii. $V_T = \max(0, X_2 - S_T) - \max(0, X_1 - S_T) = \max(0, 0.85 - 0.78) - \max(0, 0.70 - 0.78) = 0.07 - 0 = 0.07$
          $\Pi = V_T - V_0 = V_T - (p_2 - p_1) = 0.07 - (0.15 - 0.03) = -0.05$
      iii. $V_T = \max(0, X_2 - S_T) - \max(0, X_1 - S_T) = \max(0, 0.85 - 0.68) - \max(0, 0.70 - 0.68) = 0.17 - 0.02 = 0.15$
          $\Pi = V_T - V_0 = V_T - (p_2 - p_1) = 0.15 - (0.15 - 0.03) = 0.03$
   C. **i.** Maximum profit $= X_2 - X_1 - (p_2 - p_1) = 0.85 - 0.70 - (0.15 - 0.03) = 0.03$
      ii. Maximum loss $= p_2 - p_1 = 0.15 - 0.03 = 0.12$
   D. Breakeven point $= X_2 - (p_2 - p_1) = 0.85 - (0.15 - 0.03) = 0.73$
   E. $V_T = \max(0, X_2 - S_T) - \max(0, X_1 - S_T) = \max(0, 0.85 - 0.73) - \max(0, 0.70 - 0.73) = 0.12 - 0 = 0.12$
      $\Pi = V_T - V_0 = V_T - (p_2 - p_1) = 0.12 - (0.15 - 0.03) = 0$
   Therefore, the profit or loss if the price of the currency decreases to \$0.73 at expiration of the puts is indeed zero.

9. **A.** Let X_1 be 110, X_2 be 115, and X_3 be 120.
      $V_0 = c_1 - 2c_2 + c_3 = 8 - 2(5) + 3 = 1$
      i. $V_T = \max(0, S_T - X_1) - 2\max(0, S_T - X_2) + \max(0, S_T - X_3)$
          $V_T = \max(0, 106 - 110) - 2\max(0, 106 - 115) + \max(0, 106 - 120) = 0$
          $\Pi = V_T - V_0 = 0 - 1 = -1$
      ii. $V_T = \max(0, S_T - X_1) - 2\max(0, S_T - X_2) + \max(0, S_T - X_3)$
          $V_T = \max(0, 110 - 110) - 2\max(0, 110 - 115) + \max(0, 110 - 120) = 0$
          $\Pi = V_T - V_0 = 0 - 1 = -1$

iii. $V_T = max(0, S_T - X_1) - 2max(0, S_T - X_2) + max(0, S_T - X_3)$
$V_T = max(0, 115 - 110) - 2max(0, 115 - 115) + max(0, 115 - 120) = 5$
$\Pi = V_T - V_0 = 5 - 1 = 4$

iv. $V_T = max(0, S_T - X_1) - 2max(0, S_T - X_2) + max(0, S_T - X_3)$
$V_T = max(0, 120 - 110) - 2max(0, 120 - 115) + max(0, 120 - 120) = 10$
$- 10 + 0 = 0$
$\Pi = V_T - V_0 = 0 - 1 = -1$

v. $V_T = max(0, S_T - X_1) - 2max(0, S_T - X_2) + max(0, S_T - X_3)$
$V_T = max(0, 123 - 110) - 2max(0, 123 - 115) + max(0, 123 - 120) = 13 -$
$16 + 3 = 0$
$\Pi = V_T - V_0 = 0 - 1 = -1$

B. **i.** Maximum profit $= X_2 - X_1 - (c_1 - 2c_2 + c_3) = 115 - 110 - 1 = 4$

ii. Maximum loss $= c_1 - 2c_2 + c_3 = 1$

iii. The maximum profit would be realized if the price of the stock at expiration of the options is at the exercise price of $115.

iv. The maximum loss would be incurred if the price of the stock is at or below the exercise price of $110, or if the price of the stock is at or above the exercise price of $120.

C. Breakeven: $S_T^* = X_1 + (c_1 - 2c_2 + c_3)$ and $S_T^* = 2X_2 - X_1 - (c_1 - 2c_2 + c_3)$. So, $S_T^* = 110 + 1 = 111$ and $S_T^* = 2(115) - 110 - 1 = 119$.

10. A. Let X_1 be 110, X_2 be 115, and X_3 be 120.
$V_0 = p_1 - 2p_2 + p_3 = 3.50 - 2(6) + 9 = 0.50$

i. $V_T = max(0, X_1 - S_T) - 2max(0, X_2 - S_T) + max(0, X_3 - S_T)$
$V_T = max(0, 110 - 106) - 2max(0, 115 - 106) + max(0, 120 - 106) =$
$4 - 2(9) + 14 = 0$
$\Pi = V_T - V_0 = 0 - 0.50 = -0.50$

ii. $V_T = max(0, X_1 - S_T) - 2max(0, X_2 - S_T) + max(0, X_3 - S_T)$
$V_T = max(0, 110 - 110) - 2max(0, 115 - 110) + max(0, 120 - 110) =$
$0 - 2(5) + 10 = 0$
$\Pi = V_T - V_0 = 0 - 0.50 = 0.50$

iii. $V_T = max(0, X_1 - S_T) - 2max(0, X_2 - S_T) + max(0, X_3 - S_T)$
$V_T = max(0, 110 - 115) - 2max(0, 115 - 115) + max(0, 120 - 115) =$
$0 - 2(0) + 5 = 5$
$\Pi = V_T - V_0 = 5 - 0.50 = 4.50$

iv. $V_T = max(0, X_1 - S_T) - 2max(0, X_2 - S_T) + max(0, X_3 - S_T)$
$V_T = max(0, 110 - 120) - 2max(0, 115 - 120) + max(0, 120 - 120) = 0$
$\Pi = V_T - V_0 = 0 - 0.50 = -0.50$

v. $V_T = max(0, X_1 - S_T) - 2max(0, X_2 - S_T) + max(0, X_3 - S_T)$
$V_T = max(0, 110 - 123) - 2max(0, 115 - 123) + max(0, 120 - 123) = 0$
$\Pi = V_T - V_0 = 0 - 0.50 = -0.50$

B. **i.** Maximum profit $= X_2 - X_1 - (p_1 - 2p_2 + p_3) = 115 - 110 - 0.50 = 4.50$

ii. Maximum loss $= p_1 - 2p_2 + p_3 = 0.50$

iii. The maximum profit would be realized if the expiration price of the stock is at the exercise price of $115.

iv. The maximum loss would be incurred if the expiration price of the stock is at or below the exercise price of $110, or if the expiration price of the stock is at or above the exercise price of $120.

C. Breakeven: $S_T^* = X_1 + (p_1 - 2p_2 + p_3)$ and $S_T^* = 2X_2 - X_1 - (p_1 - 2p_2 + p_3)$. So, $S_T^* = 110 + 0.50 = 110.50$ and $S_T^* = 2(115) - 110 - 0.50 = 119.50$

D. For $S_T = 110.50$:

$V_T = \max(0, X_1 - S_T) - 2\max(0, X_2 - S_T) + \max(0, X_3 - S_T)$

$V_T = \max(0, 110 - 110.50) - 2\max(0, 115 - 110.50) + \max(0, 120 - 110.50) = -2(4.50) + 9.50 = 0.50$

$\Pi = V_T - V_0 = 0.50 - 0.50 = 0$

For $S_T = 119.50$:

$V_T = \max(0, X_1 - S_T) - 2\max(0, X_2 - S_T) + \max(0, X_3 - S_T)$

$V_T = \max(0, 110 - 119.50) - 2\max(0, 115 - 119.50) + \max(0, 120 - 119.50) = 0.50$

$\Pi = V_T - V_0 = 0.50 - 0.50 = 0$

Therefore, we see that the profit or loss at the breakeven points computed in Part D above is indeed zero.

11. A.   **i.** $V_T = S_T + \max(0, X_1 - S_T) - \max(0, S_T - X_2) =$

$92 + \max(0, 75 - 92) - \max(0, 92 - 90) = 92 + 0 - 2 = 90$

$\Pi = V_T - S_0 = 90 - 80 = 10$

      ii. $V_T = S_T + \max(0, X_1 - S_T) - \max(0, S_T - X_2) =$

$90 + \max(0, 75 - 90) - \max(0, 90 - 90) = 90 + 0 - 0 = 90$

$\Pi = V_T - S_0 = 90 - 80 = 10$

      iii. $V_T = S_T + \max(0, X_1 - S_T) - \max(0, S_T - X_2) =$

$82 + \max(0, 75 - 82) - \max(0, 82 - 90) = 82 + 0 - 0 = 82$

$\Pi = V_T - S_0 = 82 - 80 = 2$

      iv. $V_T = S_T + \max(0, X_1 - S_T) - \max(0, S_T - X_2) =$

$75 + \max(0, 75 - 75) - \max(0, 75 - 90) = 75 + 0 - 0 = 75$

$\Pi = V_T - S_0 = 75 - 80 = -5$

      v. $V_T = S_T + \max(0, X_1 - S_T) - \max(0, S_T - X_2) =$

$70 + \max(0, 75 - 70) - \max(0, 70 - 90) = 70 + 5 - 0 = 75$

$\Pi = V_T - S_0 = 75 - 80 = -5$

B.   **i.** Maximum profit $= X_2 - S_0 = 90 - 80 = 10$

      ii. Maximum loss $= -(X_1 - S_0) = -(75 - 80) = 5$

      iii. The maximum profit would be realized if the price of the stock at the expiration of options is at or above the exercise price of \$90.

      iv. The maximum loss would be incurred if the price of the stock at the expiration of options were at or below the exercise price of \$75.

C. Breakeven: $S_T^* = S_0 = 80$

12. A. This position is commonly called a straddle.

B.   **i.** $V_T = \max(0, S_T - X) + \max(0, X - S_T) = \max(0, 35 - 25) + \max(0, 25 - 35) = 10 + 0 = 10$

$\Pi = V_T - (c_0 + p_0) = 10 - (4 + 1) = 5$

      ii. $V_T = \max(0, S_T - X) + \max(0, X - S_T) = \max(0, 29 - 25) + \max(0, 25 - 29) = 4 + 0 = 4$

$\Pi = V_T - (c_0 + p_0) = 4 - (4 + 1) = -1$

      iii. $V_T = \max(0, S_T - X) + \max(0, X - S_T) = \max(0, 25 - 25) + \max(0, 25 - 25) = 0 + 0 = 0$

$\Pi = V_T - (c_0 + p_0) = 0 - (4 + 1) = -5$

      iv. $V_T = \max(0, S_T - X) + \max(0, X - S_T) = \max(0, 20 - 25) + \max(0, 25 - 20) = 0 + 5 = 5$

$\Pi = V_T - (c_0 + p_0) = 5 - (4 + 1) = 0$

      v. $V_T = \max(0, S_T - X) + \max(0, X - S_T) = \max(0, 15 - 25) + \max(0, 25 - 15) = 0 + 10 = 10$

$\Pi = V_T - (c_0 + p_0) = 10 - (4 + 1) = 5$

   C. i. Maximum profit $= \infty$
   ii. Maximum loss $= c_0 + p_0 = 4 + 1 = 5$
   D. $S_T^* = X \pm (c_0 + p_0) = 25 \pm (4 + 1) = 30, 20$

13. Regardless of the stock price at the expiration of the options, the box spread always has a value at expiration of $X_2 - X_1 = 30 - 25 = 5$. So,

$$\Pi = V_T - V_0 = V_T - (c_1 - c_2 + p_2 - p_1)$$
$$= 5 - (5.30 - 2.75 + 4.30 - 2.00)$$
$$= 5 - 4.85 = 0.15$$

Because the transaction is risk free, the present value of the payoff, discounted using the risk-free rate, should equal the initial outlay if the options are correctly priced. Hence, we should have

$$(X_2 - X_1)/(1 + r)^T = c_1 - c_2 + p_2 - p_1$$

Because $X_2 - X_1 = 5$, $T = 6/12 = 0.50$, and initial outlay $= c_1 - c_2 + p_2 - p_1 = 4.85$, we have

$$5/(1 + r)^{0.50} = 4.85$$

Solving for r, we have $r = 0.0628$ or 6.28 percent.

14. The payoff from the call at expiration on 15 July is given below and will be received 90 days later on 13 October:

$$\$10,000,000 \max(0, \text{LIBOR} - 0.055)\left(\frac{90}{360}\right)$$

The premium on the call is paid on 18 May. So, we need to compute its value compounded from 18 May to 15 July. Because there are 58 days between 18 May and 15 July, the compounded value of the call premium of \$25,000, based on the current LIBOR plus 200 basis points is

$$\$25,000\left[1 + (0.06 + 0.02)\left(\frac{58}{360}\right)\right] = \$25,322$$

So the call costs \$25,000 on 18 May, which is equivalent to \$25,322 on 15 July. The effective loan proceeds are

$$\$10,000,000 - \$25,322 = \$9,974,678$$

The loan interest is

$$\$10,000,000 \ (\text{LIBOR on 15 July} + 200 \text{ basis points})\left(\frac{90}{360}\right)$$

The call payoff was given above. The loan interest minus the call payoff is the effective interest. The effective rate on the loan is

$$\left(\frac{\$10{,}000{,}000 \text{ plus effective interest}}{\$9{,}974{,}678}\right)^{365/90} - 1$$

The results are shown below for a range of LIBORs on 15 July.

LIBOR on 15 July	Loan Rate	Loan Interest Paid 13 October	Call Payoff	Effective Interest	Effective Loan Rate
0.015	0.035	$87,500	$0	$87,500	0.0467
0.030	0.050	125,000	0	125,000	0.0625
0.045	0.065	162,500	0	162,500	0.0786
0.060	0.080	200,000	12,500	187,500	0.0894
0.075	0.095	237,500	50,000	187,500	0.0894
0.090	0.110	275,000	87,500	187,000	0.0894

15. The payoff from the call at expiration on 1 May is given below and will be received 180 days later on 28 October:

$$\$3{,}000{,}000 \max(0, \text{LIBOR} - 0.0525)\left(\frac{180}{360}\right)$$

The premium on the call is paid on 15 March. So, we need to compute its value compounded from 15 March to 1 May. Because there are 47 days between 15 March and 1 May, the compounded value of the call premium of $8,000, based on the current LIBOR plus 3 percent is

$$\$8{,}000\left[1 + (0.055 + 0.03)\left(\frac{47}{360}\right)\right] = \$8{,}089$$

So the call costs $8,000 on 15 March, which is equivalent to $8,089 on 1 May. The effective loan proceeds are

$$\$3{,}000{,}000 - \$8{,}089 = \$2{,}991{,}911$$

The loan interest is

$$\$3{,}000{,}000(\text{LIBOR on 1 May} + 0.03)\left(\frac{180}{360}\right)$$

The call payoff was given above. The loan interest minus the call payoff is the effective interest. The effective rate on the loan is

$$\left(\frac{\$3{,}000{,}000 \text{ plus effective interest}}{\$2{,}991{,}911}\right)^{365/180} - 1$$

The effective interest rate for the company will continue to increase until LIBOR reaches the strike rate. Beyond this point, the effective interest rate will remain the same regardless of the increase in LIBOR. So, to get the effective ceiling on the rate, we could compute the effective rate when LIBOR on 1 May equals the strike rate, or 5.25 percent. Then the loan interest is

$$\$3{,}000{,}000(0.0525 + 0.03)\left(\frac{180}{360}\right) = \$123{,}750$$

The call payoff is zero. So, the effective interest is $123,750.
The effective rate on the loan is

$$\left(\frac{\$3{,}000{,}000 + \$123{,}750}{\$2{,}991{,}911}\right)^{365/180} - 1 = 0.0914, \text{ or } 9.14\%$$

This is the effective ceiling on the rate.

16. The payoff at expiration is given below and will be received 180 days later.

$$\$100{,}000{,}000 \max(0, 0.0625 - \text{LIBOR})\left(\frac{180}{360}\right)$$

The option premium compounded from 16 April to 1 June is

$$\$120{,}000\left[1 + (0.065 + 0.025)\left(\frac{46}{360}\right)\right] = \$121{,}380$$

So the put costs $120,000 on 16 April, which is equivalent to $121,380 on 1 June. The effective amount lent is

$$\$100{,}000{,}000 + \$121{,}380 = \$100{,}121{,}380$$

The loan interest is

$$\$100{,}000{,}000\left[\text{LIBOR on 1 June plus 250 basis points}\left(\frac{180}{360}\right)\right]$$

The put payoff was given above. The loan interest plus the put payoff is the effective interest on the loan. The effective rate on the loan is

$$\left(\frac{\$100{,}000{,}000 \text{ plus effective interest}}{\$100{,}121{,}380}\right)^{365/180} - 1$$

The results are shown below for a range of LIBORs on 1 June.

LIBOR on 1 June	Loan Rate	Loan Interest Paid on 28 Nov	Put Payoff	Effective Interest	Effective Loan Rate
0.030	0.055	$2,750,000	$1,625,000	$4,375,000	0.0880
0.045	0.070	3,500,000	875,000	4,375,000	0.0880
0.060	0.085	4,250,000	125,000	4,375,000	0.0880
0.075	0.100	5,000,000	0	5,000,000	0.1013
0.090	0.115	5,750,000	0	5,750,000	0.1173
0.105	0.130	6,500,000	0	6,500,000	0.1334

17. The number of days in each period is as follows:

1 March − 1 June:	92 days
1 June − 1 September:	92 days
1 September − 1 December:	91 days
1 December − 1 March:	90 days

The interest due for each period is computed as

$$\$10,000,000(\text{LIBOR on previous reset date} + 200 \text{ basis points})\left(\frac{\text{Days in period}}{360}\right)$$

For example, the first interest payment is calculated as

$$\$10,000,000(0.07 + 0.02)\left(\frac{92}{360}\right) = \$230,000$$

Each caplet payoff is computed as:

$$\$10,000,000 \max\left(0,\text{LIBOR on previous reset date} - 0.0725\right)\left(\frac{\text{Days in period}}{360}\right)$$

where the "previous reset date" is the caplet expiration, and 0.0725 corresponds to the strike rate. Payment is deferred until the date on which the interest is paid at the given LIBOR. For example, the caplet expiring on 1 September is worth $10,000,000 max (0,0.0750 − 0.0725)(91/360) = $6,319, which is paid on 1 December. The effective interest is the actual interest minus the caplet payoff. The payments are shown in the table below:

Date	LIBOR	Loan Rate	Days in Period	Interest Due	Caplet Payoff	Effective Interest
1 March	0.0700	0.0900				
1 June	0.0725	0.0925	92	$230,000		$230,000
1 September	0.0750	0.0950	92	236,389	$0	236,389
1 December	0.0800	0.1000	91	240,139	6,319	233,819
1 March			90	250,000	18,750	231,250

18. The number of days in each period is as follows:

16 July − 16 October:	92 days
16 October − 16 January:	92 days
16 January − 16 April:	90 days
16 April − 16 July:	91 days

The interest due for each period is computed as

$$\$20,000,000(\text{LIBOR on previous reset date} + 0.0250)\left(\frac{\text{Days in period}}{360}\right)$$

For example, the first interest payment is

$$\$20{,}000{,}000(0.06 + 0.0250)\left(\frac{92}{360}\right) = \$434{,}444$$

A. Each floorlet payoff is computed as

$$\$20{,}000{,}000 \; \max(0, 0.0575 - \text{LIBOR on previous reset date})\left(\frac{\text{Days in period}}{360}\right)$$

where the "previous reset date" is the floorlet expiration. Payment is deferred until the date on which the interest is paid at the given LIBOR. For example, the floorlet expiring on 16 October is worth $\$20{,}000{,}000 \max(0, 0.0575 - 0.0525)(92/360) = \$25{,}556$, which is paid on 16 January. Similarly, the floorlet expiring on 16 January is worth $\$20{,}000{,}000 \max(0, 0.0575 - 0.055)(90/360) = 12{,}500$, which is paid on 16 April. The effective interest is the actual interest plus the floorlet payoff. The payments are shown in the table below:

Date	LIBOR	Loan Rate	Days in Period	Interest Due	Floorlet Payoff	Effective Interest
16 July	0.0600	0.0850				
16 October	0.0525	0.0775	92	$434,444		$434,444
16 January	0.0550	0.0800	92	396,111	$25,556	370,556
16 April	0.0575	0.0825	90	400,000	12,500	387,500
16 July			91	417,083	0	417,083

B. Each floorlet payoff is computed as

$$\$20{,}000{,}000 \; \max(0, 0.0600 - \text{LIBOR on previous reset date})\left(\frac{\text{Days in period}}{360}\right)$$

where the "previous reset date" is the floorlet expiration. The payments are shown in the table below. Note that there is no change in the first four columns. Because of the higher strike price of the call, the floorlet payoff is higher than in Part A above and the effective interest is lower.

Date	LIBOR	Loan Rate	Days in Period	Interest Due	Floorlet Payoff	Effective Interest
16 July	0.0600	0.0850				
16 October	0.0525	0.0775	92	$434,444		$434,444
16 January	0.0550	0.0800	92	396,111	$38,333	357,778
16 April	0.0575	0.0825	90	400,000	25,000	375,000
16 July			91	417,083	12,639	404,444

C. Each floorlet payoff is computed as

$$\$20{,}000{,}000 \; \max(0, 0.0550 - \text{LIBOR on previous reset date})\left(\frac{\text{Days in period}}{360}\right)$$

where the "previous reset date" is the floorlet expiration. The payments are shown in the table below. Note that there is no change in the first four columns. Because of the lower strike price of the call, the floorlet payoff is lower than in Part A above and the effective interest is higher.

Date	LIBOR	Loan Rate	Days in Period	Interest Due	Floorlet Payoff	Effective Interest
16 July	0.0600	0.0850				
16 October	0.0525	0.0775	92	$434,444		$434,444
16 January	0.0550	0.0800	92	396,111	$12,778	383,333
16 April	0.0575	0.0825	90	400,000	0	400,000
16 July			91	417,083	0	417,083

19. The loan interest is computed as

$$\$20,000,000(\text{LIBOR on previous reset date} + 0.015)\left(\frac{\text{Days in settlement period}}{360}\right)$$

The caplet payoff is

$$\$20,000,000\max(0,\text{LIBOR on previous reset date} - 0.0625)\left(\frac{\text{Days in settlement period}}{360}\right)$$

The floorlet payoff is

$$-\$20,000,000\max(0,0.0525 - \text{LIBOR on previous reset date})\left(\frac{\text{Days in settlement period}}{360}\right)$$

The effective interest is the interest due plus the caplet payoff plus the floorlet payoff (note that the floorlet payoff is negative).

The following table shows the payments on the loan and collar:

Date	LIBOR	Loan Rate	Days in Period	Interest Due	Caplet Payoffs	Floorlet Payoffs	Effective Interest
1 March	0.0600	0.075					
1 June	0.0650	0.080	92	$383,333			$383,333
1 September	0.0550	0.070	92	408,889	$12,778	$0	396,111
1 December	0.0500	0.065	91	353,889	0	0	353,889
1 March			90	325,000	0	−12,500	337,500

20. A. If the stock moves up (down) by $1, 1,000 calls should change by 1,000(0.64) = $640. Thus, 640 shares are needed.

B. Shares worth 640($46) = $29,440
Options worth −1,000($5) = −$5,000
Bonds worth −$3,000
   Total = 29,440 − 5,000 − 3,000 = $21,440

C. The new required number of shares is 1,000(0.5420) = 542. So we need to have 542 shares instead of 640 shares. That means we would sell 640 − 542 = 98 shares, generating 98($46) = $4,508. We would invest this amount in risk-free bonds. We had a bond balance of −$3,000, so this amount pays off all of this debt, leaving a balance of $4,508 −$3,000 = $1,508 going into the next day.

The composition of the portfolio will then be as follows:

    Shares worth 542($46) = $24,932

    Options worth −1,000($5) = −$5,000

    Bonds worth $1,508

      Total = 24,932 − 5,000 + 1,508 = $21,440

D. Shares worth 542($45.50) = $24,661

Options worth −1,000($4.71) = −$4,710

Bonds worth 1,508 exp(0.045/365) − $1,508

    Total = 24,661 − 4,710 + 1,508 = $21,459

The benchmark is $21,440 exp(0.045/365) = $21,442, which is about $17 less than the market value computed above.

RISK MANAGEMENT APPLICATIONS OF SWAP STRATEGIES

LEARNING OUTCOMES

After reading this chapter, you will be able to do the following:

- Demonstrate and explain how an interest rate swap can be used to convert a floating-rate (fixed-rate) loan to a fixed-rate (floating-rate) loan.

- Explain how to obtain the duration of an interest rate swap.

- Use duration to explain why the conversion of a floating-rate loan to a fixed-rate loan reduces the risk of the cash flows but increases the risk of the market value for a borrower.

- Determine the notional principal on an interest rate swap necessary to change the duration of a fixed-income portfolio to a desired level.

- Demonstrate and explain how an interest rate swap can be used to manage the risk of a leveraged floating-rate note.

- Demonstrate and explain how an interest rate swap can be used to manage the risk of an inverse floating-rate note.

- Demonstrate and explain how a currency swap can be used to convert a loan in one currency into a loan in another currency.

- Explain how a party can issue a loan or bond in its own currency and use a currency swap to convert it to another currency for the purpose of generating savings.

- Explain why a party to a currency swap would prefer fixed (floating) payments over floating (fixed) payments.

- Demonstrate and explain how a party can use a currency swap with no notional principal to convert a series of foreign cash receipts into domestic cash flows.

- Define a dual-currency bond and explain and illustrate how currency swaps can be used to manage such a bond's exchange rate risk.

- Demonstrate and explain how an equity swap can be used to add diversification to a concentrated portfolio without the sale of any stock.

- Demonstrate and explain how an equity swap can be used to provide international diversification to a domestic portfolio without the sale of any stock.

- Demonstrate and explain how an equity swap can be used to alter the allocation between stock and bond asset classes.

- Demonstrate and explain the use of an equity swap by a corporate insider.
- Explain the investor implications of the possible use of equity swaps by corporate insiders.
- Discuss how cash flow and tracking error considerations differentiate equity swaps from interest rate and currency swaps.
- Demonstrate and explain how a party that anticipates taking out a loan at a future date can use an interest rate swaption.
- Demonstrate and explain how to use an interest rate swaption to terminate a swap.
- Demonstrate and explain how to use an interest rate receiver swaption to synthetically remove the call feature on a callable bond.
- Demonstrate and explain how to use an interest rate receiver swaption to synthetically add a call feature to a noncallable bond.

1 INTRODUCTION

This chapter is the final in a series of three in which we examine strategies and applications of various derivative instruments. Chapter 6 covered forwards and futures, and Chapter 7 covered options. We now turn to swaps. Recall from Chapter 5 that a swap is a transaction in which two parties agree to exchange a series of cash flows over a specific period of time. At least one set of cash flows must be variable—that is, not known at the beginning of the transaction and determined over the life of the swap by the course of an underlying source of uncertainty. The other set of cash flows can be fixed or variable. Typically, no net exchange of money occurs between the two parties at the start of the contract.[1]

Because at least one set of swap payments is random, it must be driven by an underlying source of uncertainty. This observation provides a means for classifying swaps. The four types of swaps are interest rate, currency, equity, and commodity swaps. Interest rate swaps typically involve one side paying at a floating interest rate and the other paying at a fixed interest rate. In some cases both sides pay at a floating rate, but the floating rates are different. Currency swaps are essentially interest rate swaps in which one set of payments is in one currency and the other is in another currency. The payments are in the form of interest payments; either set of payments can be fixed or floating, or both can be fixed or floating. With currency swaps, a source of uncertainty is the exchange rate so the payments can be fixed and still have uncertain value. In equity swaps, at least one set of payments is determined by the course of a stock price or stock index. In commodity swaps at least one set of payments is determined by the course of a commodity price, such as the price of oil or gold. In this book we focus exclusively on financial derivatives and, hence, do not cover commodity swaps.

In Chapter 5, we examined the characteristics and pricing of swaps. We found that swaps can be viewed as combinations of forward contracts. A forward contract is an agreement between two parties in which one party agrees to buy from another an underlying asset

---

[1] Currency swaps can be structured to have an exchange of the notional principals in the two currencies at the start, but because these amounts are equivalent after adjusting for the exchange rate, no *net* exchange of money takes place. At expiration of the swap, the two parties reverse the original exchange, which does result in a net flow of money if the exchange rate has changed, as will probably be the case. Also as we discussed in Chapter 5, a few swaps, called *off-market swaps*, involve an exchange of money at the start, but they are the exception, not the rule.

at a future date at a price agreed on at the start. This agreed-upon price is a fixed payment, but the value received for the asset at the future date is a variable payment because it is subject to risk. A swap extends this notion of an exchange of variable and fixed payments to more than one payment. Hence, a swap is like a series of forward contracts.[2] We also saw that a swap is like a combination of options. We showed that pricing a swap involves determining the terms that the two parties agree to at the start, which usually involves the amount of any fixed payment. Because no net flow of money changes hands at the start, a swap is a transaction that starts off with zero market value. Pricing the swap is done by finding the terms that result in equivalence of the present values of the two streams of payments.

After a swap begins, market conditions change and the present values of the two streams of payments are no longer equivalent. The swap then has a nonzero market value. To one party, the swap has a positive market value; to the other, its market value is negative. The process of valuation involves determining this market value. For the most part, valuation and pricing is a process that requires only the determination of present values using current interest rates and, as necessary, stock prices or exchange rates.

In Chapter 5, we also examined the swaption, an instrument that combines swaps and options. Specifically, a swaption is an option to enter into a swap. There are two kinds of swaptions: those to make a fixed payment, called payer swaptions, and those to receive a fixed payment, called receiver swaptions. Like options, swaptions require the payment of a premium at the start and grant the right, but not the obligation, to enter into a swap.[3]

In this chapter, we shall examine ways in which swaps can be used to achieve risk management objectives. We already examined certain risk management strategies when we introduced the subject of swaps in Chapter 5. Here, we go into more detail on these strategies and, of course, introduce quite a few more. We shall also discuss how swaptions are used to achieve risk management objectives.

2 STRATEGIES AND APPLICATIONS FOR MANAGING INTEREST RATE RISK

In previous chapters, we examined the use of forwards, futures, and options to manage interest rate risk. The interest rate swap, however, is unquestionably the most widely used instrument to manage interest rate risk.[4] In Chapters 6 and 7, we examined two primary forms of interest rate risk. One is the risk associated with borrowing and lending in short-term markets. This risk itself has two dimensions: the risk of rates changing from the time a loan is anticipated until it is actually taken out, and the risk associated with changes in interest rates once the loan is taken out. Swaps are not normally used to manage the risk of an anticipated loan; rather, they are designed to manage the risk on a series of cash flows on loans already taken out or in the process of being taken out.[5]

---

[2] As we noted in Chapter 5, there are some technical distinctions between a series of forward contracts and a swap, but the essential elements of equivalence are there.

[3] Forward swaps, on the other hand, are obligations to enter into a swap.

[4] The Bank for International Settlements, in its June 2002 survey of derivative positions of global banks published on 8 November 2002, indicates that swaps make up more than 75 percent of the total notional principal of all interest rate derivative contracts (see www.bis.org).

[5] It is technically possible to use a swap to manage the risk faced in anticipation of taking out a loan, but it would not be easy and would require a great deal of analytical skill to match the volatility of the swap to the volatility of the gain or loss in value associated with changes in interest rates prior to the date on which a loan is taken out. Other instruments are better suited for managing this type of risk.

The other form of interest rate risk that concerns us is the risk associated with managing a portfolio of bonds. As we saw in Chapter 6, managing this risk generally involves controlling the portfolio duration. Although futures are commonly used to make duration changes, swaps can also be used, and we shall see how in this chapter.

In this section, we look at one more situation in which swaps can be used to manage interest rate risk. This situation involves the use of a relatively new financial instrument called a **structured note**, which is a variation of a floating-rate note that has some type of unusual characteristic. We cover structured notes in Section 2.3.

2.1 Using
Interest Rate
Swaps to Convert
a Floating-Rate
Loan to a
Fixed-Rate Loan
(and Vice Versa)

In previous chapters, we have discussed corporations taking out floating-rate loans. Because much of the funding banks receive is at a floating rate, most banks prefer to make floating-rate loans. By lending at a floating rate, banks pass on the interest rate risk to borrowers. As we previously saw, borrowers can use forwards, futures, and options to manage their exposure to rising interest rates, but swaps are the preferred instrument for managing this risk.[6] A typical situation involves a corporation agreeing to borrow at a floating rate even though it would prefer to borrow at a fixed rate. The corporation will use a swap to convert its floating-rate loan to a fixed-rate loan. We examined this type of scenario in Chapter 5 when introducing swaps, but we shall look at another situation here.

Internet Book Publishers (IBP) is a corporation that typically borrows at a floating rate from a lender called Prime Lending Bank (PLB). In this case, it takes out a one-year $25 million loan at 90-day LIBOR plus 300 basis points. The payments will be made at specific dates about 91 days apart. The rate is initially set today, the day the loan is taken out, and is reset on each payment date: On the first payment date, the rate is reset for the second interest period. With four loan payments, the first rate is already set, but IBP is exposed to risk on the other three reset dates. Interest is calculated based on the actual day count since the last payment date, divided by 360. The loan begins on 2 March and the interest payment dates are 2 June, 2 September, 1 December, and the following 1 March.

IBP manages this interest rate risk by using a swap. It contacts a swap dealer, Swaps Provider Inc. (SPI), which is the derivatives subsidiary of a major investment banking firm. Under the terms of the swap, SPI will make payment to IBP at a rate of LIBOR, and IBP will pay SPI a fixed rate of 6.27 percent, with payments to be made on the dates on which the loan interest payments are made.

Recall that in Chapter 5, we learned how the fixed rate on a swap is determined. The dealer prices this rate into the swap such that the present values of the two payment streams are equal. The floating rates on the swap will be set today and on the first, second, and third loan interest payment dates, thereby corresponding to the dates on which the loan interest rate is reset. The notional principal on the swap is $25 million, the face value of the loan. The swap interest payments are structured so that the actual day count is used, as is done on the loan.

So, IBP borrows $25 million at a floating rate and arranges for the swap, which involves no cash flows at the origination date. The flow of money on each loan/swap pay-

---

[6] It is not clear why swaps are preferred over other instruments to manage the exposure to rising interest rates, but one possible reason is that when swaps were first invented, they were marketed as equivalent to a pair of loans. By being long one loan and short another, a corporation could alter its exposure without having to respond to claims that it was using such instruments as futures or options, which might be against corporate policy. In other words, while swaps are derivatives, their equivalence to a pair of loans meant that no policy existed to prevent their use. Moreover, because of the netting of payments and no exchange of notional principal, interest rate swaps were loans with considerably less credit risk than ordinary loans. Hence, the corporate world easily and widely embraced them.

ment date is illustrated in Exhibit 8-1. We see that IBP makes its loan payments at LIBOR plus 0.03.[7] The actual calculation of the loan interest is as follows:

$$(\$25 \text{ million})(\text{LIBOR} + 0.03)(\text{Days}/360)$$

The swap payments are calculated in the same way but are based on either LIBOR or the fixed rate of 6.27 percent. The interest owed on the loan based on LIBOR is thus offset by the interest received on the swap payment based on LIBOR.[8] Consequently, IBP does not *appear to be exposed* to the uncertainty of changing LIBOR, but we shall see that it is indeed exposed. The net effect is that IBP pays interest at the swap fixed rate of 6.27 percent plus the 3 percent spread on the loan for a total of 9.27 percent.

EXHIBIT 8-1   Converting a Floating-Rate Loan to a Fixed-Rate Loan Using an Interest Rate Swap

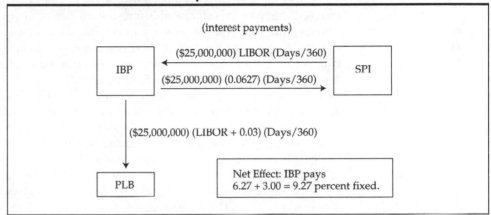

IBP's swap transaction appears to remove its exposure to LIBOR. Indeed, having done this transaction, most corporations would consider themselves hedged against rising interest rates, which is usually the justification corporations give for doing swap transactions. It is important to note, however, that IBP is also speculating on rising interest rates. If rates fall, IBP will not be able to take advantage, as it is locked in to a synthetic fixed-rate loan at 9.27 percent. There can be a substantial opportunity cost to taking this position and being wrong. To understand this point, let us reintroduce the concept of duration.

We need to measure the sensitivity of the market value of the overall position compared to what it would have been had the loan been left in place as a floating-rate loan. For that we turn to duration, a measure of sensitivity to interest rates. If a default-free bond is a floating-rate bond, its duration is nearly zero because interest sensitivity reflects how much the market value of an asset changes for a given change in interest rates. A floating-rate bond is designed with the idea that its market value will not drift far from par. Because

---

[7] Remember that when we refer to the payment at a rate of LIBOR, that rate was established at the previous settlement date or at the beginning of the swap if this is the first settlement period.

[8] Of course in practice, the swap payments are netted and only a single payment flows from one party to the other. Netting reduces the credit risk but does not prevent the LIBOR component of the net swap payment from offsetting the floating loan interest payment, which is the objective of the swap.

the coupon will catch up with the market rate periodically, only during the period between interest payment dates can the market value stray from par value. Moreover, during this period, it would take a substantial interest rate change to have much effect on the market value of the floating-rate bond. Without showing the details, we shall simply state the result that a floating-rate bond's duration is approximately the amount of time remaining until the next coupon payment. For a bond with quarterly payments, the maximum duration is 0.25 years and the minimum duration is zero. Consequently, the average duration is about 0.125 years. From the perspective of the *issuer* rather than the holder, the duration of the position is −0.125.

The duration of IBP's floating-rate loan position in this example is an average of −0.125, which is fairly low compared with most financial instruments. Therefore, the market value of the loan is not very interest-rate sensitive. If interest rates fall, the loan rate will fall in three months, and IBP will not have much of a loss from the market value of the loan. If interest rates rise, IBP will not have much of a gain from the market value of the loan.

Now let us discuss the duration of a swap. Remember that entering a pay-fixed, receive-floating swap is similar to issuing a fixed-rate bond and using the proceeds to buy a floating-rate bond. The duration of a swap is thus equivalent to the duration of a long position in a floating-rate bond and a short position in a fixed-rate bond. The duration of the long position in the floating-rate bond would, again, be about 0.125. What would be the duration of the short position in the fixed-rate bond? A one-year fixed-rate bond with quarterly payments would probably have a duration of between 0.6 and 1.0. Let us assume this duration is about 0.75 (nine months) or 75 percent of the maturity, an assumption we shall make from here out. So the duration of the swap would be roughly 0.125 − 0.75 = −0.625.

Combining the swap with the loan means that the duration of IBP's overall position will be −0.125 − 0.625 = −0.75. The swap was designed to convert the floating-rate loan to a fixed-rate loan. Hence, the position should be equivalent to that of taking out a fixed-rate loan. As we assumed for a one-year fixed-rate bond with quarterly payments, the duration would be 0.75. The duration of a borrower's position in a fixed-rate loan would be −0.75, the same as the duration of borrowing with the floating-rate loan and engaging in the swap. The negative duration means that a fixed-rate borrower will be helped by rising rates and a falling market value.[9]

Although the duration of the one-year fixed-rate loan is not large, at least relative to that of bonds and longer-term loans, it is nonetheless six times that of the floating-rate loan. Consequently, the sensitivity of the market value of the overall position is six times what it would have been had the loan been left in place as a floating-rate loan. From this angle, it is hard to see how such a transaction could be called a hedge because declining rates and increasing market values will hurt the fixed-rate borrower. The actual risk increases sixfold with this transaction![10]

So, can this transaction be viewed as a hedge? If not, why is it so widely used? From a cash flow perspective, the transaction does indeed function as a hedge. IBP knows that its interest payments will all be $25,000,000(0.0927)(Days/360). Except for the slight variation in days per quarter, this amount is fixed and can be easily built into plans and budgets. So from a planning and accounting perspective, the transaction serves well as a hedge. From a market value perspective, however, it is tremendously speculative. But does

---

[9] Remember from Chapter 6 that the percentage change in the market value of an asset or portfolio is −1 times the duration times the change in yield over 1 plus the yield. So, if the duration is negative, the double minus results in the position benefiting from rising interest rates.

[10] In the example here, the company is a corporation. A bank might have assets that would be interest sensitive and could be used to balance the duration. A corporation's primary assets have varying, inconsistent, and difficult-to-measure degrees of interest sensitivity.

market value matter? Indeed it does. From the perspective of finance theory, maximizing the market value of shareholders' equity is the objective of a corporation. Moreover, under recently enacted accounting rules, companies must mark derivative and asset positions to market values, which has improved transparency.

So, in summary, using a swap to convert a floating-rate loan to a fixed-rate loan is a common transaction, one ostensibly structured as a hedge. Such a transaction, despite stabilizing a company's cash outflows, however, increases the risk of the company's market value. Whether this issue is of concern to most companies is not clear. This situation remains one of the most widely encountered scenarios and the one for which interest rate swaps are most commonly employed.

PRACTICE PROBLEM 1

Consider a bank that holds a $5 million loan at a fixed rate of 6 percent for three years, with quarterly payments. The bank had originally funded this loan at a fixed rate, but because of changing interest rate expectations, it has now decided to fund it at a floating rate. Although it cannot change the terms of the loan to the borrower, it can effectively convert the loan to a floating-rate loan by using a swap. The fixed rate on three-year swaps with quarterly payments at LIBOR is 7 percent. We assume the number of days in each quarter to be 90 and the number of days in a year to be 360.

A. Explain how the bank could convert the fixed-rate loan to a floating-rate loan using a swap.

B. Explain why the effective floating rate on the loan will be less than LIBOR.

SOLUTIONS

A. The interest payments it will receive on the loan are $5,000,000(0.06)(90/360) = $75,000. The bank could do a swap to pay a fixed rate of 7 percent and receive a floating rate of LIBOR. Its fixed payment would be $5,000,000(0.07)(90/360) = $87,500. The floating payment it would receive is $5,000,000L(90/360), where L is LIBOR established at the previous reset date. The overall cash flow is thus $5,000,000(L − 0.01)(90/360), LIBOR minus 100 basis points.

B. The bank will effectively receive less than LIBOR because when the loan was initiated, the rate was 6 percent. Then when the swap was executed, the rate was 7 percent. This increase in interest rates hurts the fixed-rate lender. The bank cannot implicitly change the loan from fixed rate to floating rate without paying the price of this increase in interest rates. It pays this price by accepting a lower rate than LIBOR when the loan is effectively converted to floating. Another factor that could contribute to this rate being lower than LIBOR is that the borrower's credit risk at the time the loan was established is different from the bank's credit risk as reflected in the swap fixed rate, established in the LIBOR market when the swap is initiated.

Equipped with our introductory treatment of the duration of a swap, we are now in a position to move on to understanding how to use swaps to manage the risk of a longer-term position that is also exposed to interest rate risk.

2.2 USING SWAPS TO ADJUST THE DURATION OF A FIXED-INCOME PORTFOLIO

We saw in the previous section that the duration of a swap is the net of the durations of the equivalent positions in fixed- and floating-rate bonds. Thus, the position of the pay-fixed party in a pay-fixed, receive-floating swap has the duration of a floating-rate bond minus the duration of a fixed-rate bond, where the floating- and fixed-rate bonds have cash flows equivalent to the corresponding cash flows of the swap.[11] The pay-fixed, receive-floating swap has a negative duration, because the duration of a fixed-rate bond is positive and larger than the duration of a floating-rate bond, which is near zero. Moreover, the negative duration of this position makes sense in that the position would be expected to benefit from rising interest rates.

Consider the following transaction. Quality Asset Management (QAM) controls a $500 million fixed-income portfolio that has a duration of 6.75. It is considering reducing the portfolio duration to 3.50 by using interest rate swaps. QAM has determined that the interest sensitivity of the bond portfolio is adequately captured by its relationship with LIBOR; hence, a swap using LIBOR as the underlying rate would be appropriate. But first there are several questions to ask:

- Should the swap involve paying fixed, receiving floating or paying floating, receiving fixed?
- What should be the terms of the swap (maturity, payment frequency)?
- What should be the notional principal?

As for whether the swap should involve paying fixed or receiving fixed, the value of the bond portfolio is inversely related to interest rates. To reduce the duration, it would be necessary to hold a position that moves directly with interest rates. To do this we must add a negative-duration position. Hence, the swap should be a pay-fixed swap to receive floating.

The terms of the swap will affect the need to renew it as well as its duration and the notional principal required. It would probably be best for the swap to have a maturity at least as long as the period during which the duration adjustment applies. Otherwise, the swap would expire before the bond matures, and QAM would have to initiate another swap. The maturity and payment frequency of the swap affect the duration. Continuing with the assumption (for convenience) that the duration of the fixed-rate bond is approximated as 75 percent of its maturity, we find, for example, that a one-year swap with semiannual payments would have a duration of $0.25 - 0.75 = -0.50$. A one-year swap with quarterly payments would have a duration of $0.125 - 0.75 = -0.625$. A two-year swap with semiannual payments would have a duration of $0.25 - 1.50 = -1.25$. A two-year swap with quarterly payments would have a duration of $0.125 - 1.50 = -1.375$.

These different durations affect the notional principal required, which leads us to the third question. Prior to the duration adjustment, the portfolio consists of $500 million at a duration of 6.75. QAM then adds a position in a swap with a notional principal of NP and a modified duration of $MDUR_S$.[12] The swap will have zero market value. The bonds and the swap will then combine to make up a portfolio with a market value of $500 million and a duration of 3.50. This relationship can be expressed as follows:

$$\$500,000,000(6.75) + NP(MDUR_S) = \$500,000,000(3.50)$$

---

[11] Recall, however, that an interest rate swap does not involve a notional principal payment up front or at expiration. But because a swap is equivalent to being long a fixed- (or floating-) rate bond and short a floating- (or fixed-) rate bond, the principals on the bonds offset, leaving their cash flows identical to that of a swap.

[12] Recall that the market value of a swap is zero at the start. This market value can obviously vary over time from zero, and such deviations should be taken into account, but to start, the market value will be zero.

The solution for NP is

$$NP = \$500{,}000{,}000\left(\frac{3.50 - 6.75}{\text{MDUR}_S}\right)$$

The duration of the swap is determined once QAM decides which swap to use. Suppose it uses a one-year swap with semiannual payments. Then, as shown above, the duration would be -0.50. The amount of notional principal required would, therefore, be

$$NP = \$500{,}000{,}000\left(\frac{3.50 - 6.75}{-0.50}\right) = \$3{,}250{,}000{,}000$$

In other words, this portfolio adjustment would require a swap with a notional principal of more than \$3 billion! This would be a very large swap, probably too large to execute. Consider the use of a five-year swap with semiannual payments. Its duration would be $0.25 - 3.75 = -3.50$. Then the notional principal would be

$$NP = \$500{,}000{,}000\left(\frac{3.50 - 6.75}{-3.50}\right) = \$464{,}290{,}000$$

With this longer duration, the notional principal would be about \$464 million, a much more reasonable amount, although still a fairly large swap.

So, in general, the notional principal of a swap necessary to change the duration of a bond portfolio worth B from MDUR_B to a target duration, MDUR_T, is

$$NP = B\left(\frac{\text{MDUR}_T - \text{MDUR}_B}{\text{MDUR}_S}\right)$$

PRACTICE PROBLEM 2

A \$250 million bond portfolio has a duration of 5.50. The portfolio manager wants to reduce the duration to 4.50 by using a swap. Consider the possibility of using a one-year swap with monthly payments or a two-year swap with semiannual payments.

A. Determine the durations of the two swaps under the assumption of paying fixed and receiving floating. Assume that the duration of a fixed-rate bond is 75 percent of its maturity.

B. Choose the swap with the longer absolute duration and determine the notional principal of the swap necessary to change the duration as desired. Explain your results.

SOLUTIONS

A. The duration of a one-year pay-fixed, receive-floating swap with monthly payments is the duration of a one-year floating-rate bond with monthly payments minus the duration of a one-year fixed-rate bond with monthly payments. The duration of the former is about one-half of the length of the payment interval. That is 1/24 of a year, or 0.042. Because the duration of the one-year fixed-rate bond is 0.75 (75 percent of one year), the duration of the swap is $0.042 - 0.75 = -0.708$.

The duration of a two-year swap with semiannual payments is the duration of a two-year floating-rate bond with semiannual payments minus the duration of a two-year fixed-rate bond. The duration of the former is about one-quarter of a year, or 0.25. The duration of the latter is 1.50 (75 percent of two years). The duration of the swap is thus $0.25 - 1.50 = -1.25$.

B. The longer- (more negative) duration swap is the two-year swap with semiannual payments. The current duration of the $250 million portfolio is 5.50 and the target duration is 4.50. Thus, the required notional principal is

$$\text{NP} = \text{B}\left(\frac{\text{MDUR}_T - \text{MDUR}_B}{\text{MDUR}_S}\right)$$

$$= \$250,000,000\left(\frac{4.50 - 5.50}{-1.25}\right) = \$200,000,000$$

So, to lower the duration requires the addition of an instrument with a duration lower than that of the portfolio. The duration of a receive-floating, pay-fixed swap is negative and, therefore, lower than that of the existing portfolio.

2.3 USING SWAPS TO CREATE AND MANAGE THE RISK OF STRUCTURED NOTES

Structured notes are short- or intermediate-term floating-rate securities that have some type of unusual feature that distinguishes them from ordinary floating-rate notes. This unusual feature can be in the form of leverage, which results in the interest rate on the note moving at a multiple of market rates, or can be an inverse feature, meaning that the interest rate on the note moves opposite to market rates. Structured notes are designed to be sold to specific investors, who are often motivated by constraints that restrict their ability to hold derivatives or use leverage. For example, many insurance companies and pension funds are attracted to structured notes, because the instruments qualify as fixed-income securities but have features that are similar to options, swaps, and margin transactions. Issuers typically create the notes, sell them to these investors, and then manage the risk, earning a profit by replicating the opposite position at a cost lower than what they could sell the notes for.

In this section, we shall use the notation FP as the principal/face value of the note, ci as the fixed interest rate on a bond, and FS as the fixed interest rate on the swap.

2.3.1 USING SWAPS TO CREATE AND MANAGE THE RISK OF LEVERAGED FLOATING-RATE NOTES

Kappa Alpha Traders (KAT) engages in a variety of arbitrage-related transactions designed to make small risk-free or low-risk profits. One such transaction involves the issuance of structured notes, which it sells to insurance companies. KAT plans to issue a leveraged structured note with a principal of FP that pays an interest rate of 1.5 times LIBOR. This type of instrument is usually called a **leveraged floating-rate note**, or **leveraged floater**. The reference to *leverage* is to the fact that the coupon is a multiple of a specific market rate of interest such as LIBOR. The note will be purchased by an insurance company called LifeCo. KAT will use the proceeds to buy a fixed-rate bond that pays an interest rate of ci. It will then combine the position with a plain vanilla swap with dealer Omega Swaps. Exhibit 8-2 illustrates how this works.

KAT issues the leveraged floater, selling it to LifeCo Insurance with the intent of financing it with a fixed-rate bond and swapping the fixed rate for a floating rate to match the leveraged floater. The periodic interest payment on the leveraged floater will be 1.5L,

EXHIBIT 8-2   Proceeds from a Leveraged Floater Used to Buy a Fixed-Rate Bond, with Risk Managed with a Plain Vanilla Swap

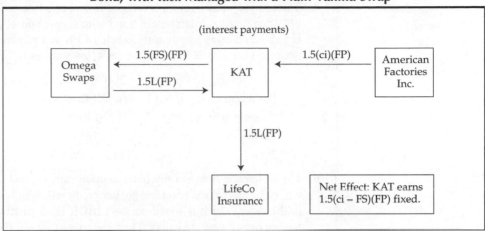

where L is LIBOR, times FP.[13] It then takes the proceeds and buys a fixed-rate bond issued by a company called American Factories Inc. This bond will have face value of 1.5(FP) and pay a coupon of ci. KAT is then in a position of receiving a fixed coupon of ci on principal of 1.5(FP) and paying a floating coupon of 1.5L on a principal of FP. It then enters into a swap with dealer Omega Swaps on notional principal of 1.5FP. KAT will pay a fixed rate of FS and receive a floating rate of LIBOR (L). Note the net effect: KAT's obligation on the leveraged floater of 1.5L(FP) is matched by its receipt on the swap. KAT receives 1.5(ci)(FP) on the fixed-rate bond and pays out 1.5(FS)(FP) on the swap, netting 1.5(FP) (ci − FS). Is this amount an inflow or outflow? It depends. If the interest rate on American Factories' debt reflects greater credit risk than that implied by the fixed rate on the swap, then KAT receives a net payment. Generally that would be the case. Thus, KAT identifies an attractively priced fixed-rate note and captures its return over the swap rate, offsetting the floating rate on the swap with the structured note. Of course, KAT is assuming some credit risk, the risk of default by American Factories, as well as the risk of default by Omega Swaps. On the other hand, KAT put up no capital to engage in this transaction. The cost of the American Factories bond was financed by issuing the structured note.

PRACTICE PROBLEM 3

A company issues a floating-rate note that pays a rate of twice LIBOR on notional principal FP. It uses the proceeds to buy a bond paying a rate of ci. It also enters into a swap with a fixed rate of FS to manage the risk of the LIBOR payment on the leveraged floater.

A. Demonstrate how the company can engage in these transactions, leaving it with a net cash flow of 2(FP)(ci − FS).

B. Explain under what condition the amount (ci − FS) is positive.

---

[13] These payments could be made semiannually, in which case they would be half of 1.5L(FP).

SOLUTIONS

A. The company has issued a leveraged floater at a rate of 2L on notional principal FP. Then it should purchase a bond with face value of 2(FP) and coupon ci. It enters into a swap to pay a fixed rate of FS and receive a floating rate of L on notional principal 2(FP). The net cash flows are as follows:

From leveraged floater:	$-2L(FP)$
From bond:	$+(ci)2(FP)$
Floating side of swap:	$+(L)2(FP)$
Fixed side of swap:	$-(FS)2(FP)$
Total	$2FP(ci - FS)$

B. The difference between the bond coupon rate, ci, and the swap fixed rate, FS, will be positive if the bond has greater credit risk than is implied by the fixed rate in the swap, which is based on the LIBOR term structure and reflects the borrowing rate of London banks. Thus, the gain of $2(ci - FS)(FP)$ is likely to reflect a credit risk premium.

2.3.2   USING SWAPS TO CREATE AND MANAGE THE RISK OF INVERSE FLOATERS

Another type of structured note is the **inverse floater**. Consider a company called Vega Analytics that, like KAT, engages in a variety of arbitrage trades using structured notes. Vega wants to issue an inverse floater paying a rate of b minus LIBOR, $b - L$, on notional principal FP. Vega sets the value of b in negotiation with the buyer of the note, taking into account a number of factors. The rate on the note moves inversely with LIBOR, but if LIBOR is at the level b, the rate on the note goes to zero. If LIBOR rises above b, the rate on the note is negative! We shall address this point later in this section.

The pattern will be the same as the pattern used for the leveraged floater: Finance the structured note by a fixed-rate note and then swap the fixed rate for a floating rate to match the structured note. Exhibit 8-3 shows how Vega issues the note to a company called Metrics Finance and uses the proceeds to purchase a fixed-rate note issued by a company called Telltale Systems, Inc., which pays a rate of (ci)(FP). Vega then enters into an interest rate swap with notional principal FP with a counterparty called Denman Dealer Holdings. In this swap, Vega receives a fixed rate of FS and pays L. Observe that the net effect is that Vega's overall cash flow is $FP[-(b - L) + ci + FS - L] = FP(FS + ci - b)$.

Clearly if b is set below $FS + ci$, then the overall cash flow is positive. Vega can potentially do this because of the credit risk it assumes. Vega sets b but cannot set FS, and ci is based on both the level of market interest rates and the credit risk of Telltale. The lower Vega sets b, the larger its cash flow from the overall transactions. But one major consideration forces Vega to limit how low it sets b: The lower it sets b, the less attractive the note will be to potential investors.

Remember that the inverse floater pays $b - L$. When L reaches the level of b, the interest rate on the inverse floater is zero. If L rises above b, then the interest rate on the inverse floater becomes negative. A negative interest rate would imply that the lender (Metrics) pays interest to the borrower (Vega). Most lenders would find this result unacceptable, but the lower b is set, the more likely this outcome will occur. Thus, Vega will want to set b at a reasonably high level but below $FS + ci$.

Regardless of where Vega sets b, the possibility remains that L will exceed b. Metrics may have Vega guarantee that the interest rate on the floater will go no lower than

EXHIBIT 8-3   Proceeds from an Inverse Floater Used to Buy a Fixed-Rate Bond, with Risk Managed with a Plain Vanilla Swap

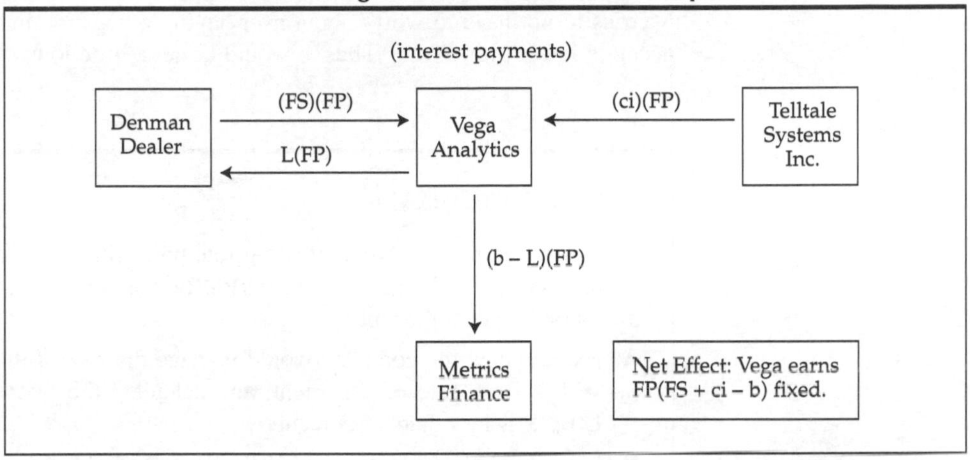

0 percent. To manage the risk associated with this guarantee, Vega will buy an interest rate cap. Let us see how all of this works with a numerical example.

Suppose the swap fixed rate, FS, is 6 percent, and ci, the rate on Telltale's note, is 7 percent. Vega sets b at 12 percent and guarantees to Metrics that the interest rate will go no lower than zero. Then the inverse floater pays 12 percent − L. As long as LIBOR is below 12 percent, Vega's cash flow is $6 + 7 − 12 = 1$ percent. Suppose L is 14 percent. Then Vega's cash flows are

+7 percent from the Telltale note

0 percent to Metrics

+6 percent from Denman

14 percent to Denman

Net: outflow of 1 percent

Vega's net cash flow is negative. To avoid this problem, Vega would buy an interest rate cap in which the underlying is LIBOR and the exercise rate is b. The cap would have a notional principal of FP and consist of individual caplets expiring on the dates on which the inverse floater rates are set. Thus, on a payment date, when L exceeds b, the inverse floater does not pay interest, but the caplet expires in-the-money and pays L − b. Then the cash flows would be

+7 percent from the Telltale note

0 percent to Metrics

+6 percent from Denman

14 percent to Denman

$(14\% − 12\%) = 2$ percent from the caplet

Net: inflow of 1 percent

Thus, Vega has restored its guaranteed cash inflow of 1 percent.

Of course, the premium on the cap would be an additional cost that Vega would pass on in the form of a lower rate paid to Metrics on the inverse floater. In other words, for Metrics to not have to worry about ever having a negative interest rate, it would have to accept a lower overall rate. Thus, b would be set a little lower.

PRACTICE PROBLEM 4

A company issues an inverse floating-rate note with a face value of $30 million and a coupon rate of 14 percent minus LIBOR. It uses the proceeds to buy a bond with a coupon rate of 8 percent.

A. Explain how the company would manage the risk of this position using a swap with a fixed rate of 7 percent, and calculate the overall cash flow given that LIBOR is less than 14 percent.

B. Explain what would happen if LIBOR exceeds 14 percent. What could the company do to offset this problem?

SOLUTIONS

A. The company would enter into a swap in which it pays LIBOR and receives a fixed rate of 7 percent on notional principal of $30 million. The overall cash flows are as follows:

From the inverse floater:	$-(0.14 - L)\$30,000,000$
From the bond it buys:	$+(0.08)\$30,000,000$
From the swap:	
Fixed payment	$+(0.07)\$30,000,000$
Floating payment	$-(L)\$30,000,000$
Overall total	$+(0.01)\$30,000,000$

B. If LIBOR is more than 14 percent, then the inverse floater payment of $(0.14 - L)$ would be negative. The lender would then have to pay interest to the borrower. For this reason, in most cases, an inverse floater has a floor at zero. In such a case, the total cash flow to this company would be $(0 + 0.08 + 0.07 - L)\$30,000,000$. There would be zero total cash flow at $L = 15$ percent. But at an L higher than 15 percent, the otherwise positive cash flow to the lender becomes negative.

To offset this effect, the lender would typically buy an interest rate cap with an exercise rate of 14 percent. The cap would have caplets that expire on the interest rate reset dates of the swap/loan and have a notional principal of $30 million. Then when $L > 0.14$, the caplet would pay off $L - 0.14$ times the $30 million. This payoff would make up the difference. The price paid for the cap would be an additional cost.

In Chapter 5, we illustrated how interest rate swaps are special cases of currency swaps—cases in which the payments are made in different currencies. We now take a look at ways in which currency swaps are used.

3 STRATEGIES AND APPLICATIONS FOR MANAGING EXCHANGE RATE RISK

Currency swaps are designed for the purpose of managing exchange rate risk. They also play a role in managing interest rate risk, but only in cases in which exchange rate risk is present. In this section, we look at three situations in which exchange rate risk can be managed using currency swaps.

3.1 CONVERTING A LOAN IN ONE CURRENCY INTO A LOAN IN ANOTHER CURRENCY

Royal Technology Ltd. (ROTECH) is a British high-tech company that is currently planning an expansion of about £30 million into Europe. To implement this expansion, it requires funding in euros. The current exchange rate is €1.62/£, so the expansion will cost €48.6 million. ROTECH could issue a euro-denominated bond, but it is not as well known in the euro market as it is in the United Kingdom where, although not a top credit, its debt is rated investment grade. As an alternative, ROTECH could issue a pound-denominated bond and convert it to a euro-denominated bond using a currency swap. Exhibit 8-4 on page 520 illustrates how it could do this.

The transaction begins on 1 June. ROTECH will borrow for three years. It issues a bond for £30 million, receiving the proceeds from its bondholders. The bond carries an interest rate of 5 percent and will require annual interest payments each 1 June. ROTECH then enters into a currency swap with a dealer called Starling Bank (SB). It pays SB £30 million and receives from SB €48.6 million. The terms of the swap call for ROTECH to pay interest to SB at a rate of 3.25 percent in euros and receive interest from SB at a rate of 4.5 percent in pounds. With the exchange of principals up front, ROTECH then has the euros it needs to proceed with its expansion. Panel A of Exhibit 8-4 illustrates the flow of funds at the start of the transaction.

The interest payments and swap payments, illustrated in Panel B, occur each year on 1 June. The interest payments on the pound-denominated bond will be £30,000,000(0.05) = £1,500,000. The interest due to ROTECH from SB is £30,000,000(0.045) = £1,350,000. The interest ROTECH owes SB is €48,600,000(0.0325) = €1,579,500. The net effect is that ROTECH pays interest in euros. The interest received from the dealer, however, does not completely offset the interest it owes on its bond. ROTECH cannot borrow in pounds at the swap market fixed rate, because its credit rating is not as good as the rating implied in the LIBOR market term structure.[14] The net effect is that ROTECH will pay additional interest of (0.05 − 0.045)£30,000,000 = £150,000.

Panel C of Exhibit 8-4 shows the cash flows that occur at the end of the life of the swap and the maturity date of the bond. ROTECH receives the principal of £30 million from SB and pays it to its bondholders, discharging its liability. It then pays €48.6 million to SB to make the final principal payment on the swap.

This type of transaction is an extremely common use of currency swaps. The advantage of borrowing this way rather than directly in another currency lies in the fact that the borrower can issue a bond or loan in the currency in which it is better known as a creditor. Then, by engaging in a swap with a bank with which it is familiar and probably already doing business, it can borrow in the foreign currency indirectly. For example, in this case, SB is probably a large multinational bank and is well known in foreign markets. But SB also has

---

[14] Remember that swap fixed rates are determined in the LIBOR market. This market consists of high-quality London banks, which borrow at an excellent rate. Hence, it is unlikely that ROTECH can borrow at as favorable a rate as these London banks.

EXHIBIT 8-4 **Issuing a Pound-Denominated Bond and Using a Currency Swap to Convert to a Euro-Denominated Bond**

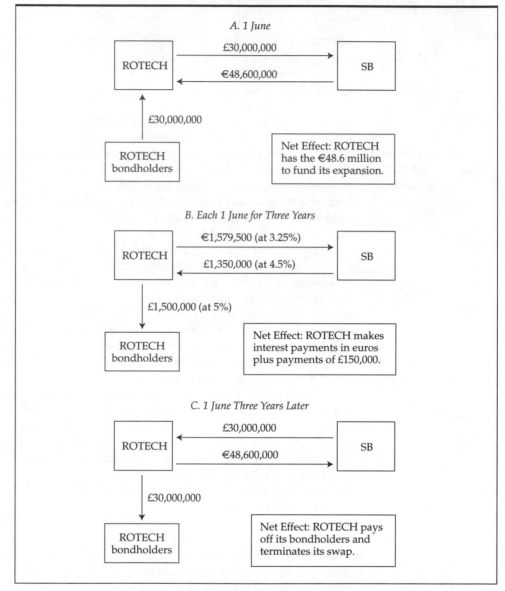

a longstanding banking relationship with ROTECH. Consequently, SB can operate in foreign exchange markets, using its advantage, and pass that advantage on to ROTECH.[15]

Another reason this transaction is attractive for borrowers like ROTECH is that the company can lower its borrowing cost by assuming some credit risk. If ROTECH had issued debt in euros directly, it would face no credit risk.[16] By engaging in the swap, how-

---

[15] SB accepts the foreign exchange risk in the swap from ROTECH and almost surely passes on that risk by hedging its position with some other type of foreign exchange transaction.

[16] Of course, ROTECH's bondholders would face the credit risk that ROTECH could default.

ever, ROTECH assumes the credit risk that SB will default on its swap payments. If SB defaults, ROTECH would still have to make its interest and principal payments to its bondholders. In exchange for accepting this risk, it is likely that ROTECH would get a better overall deal. Of course, the desired result would not be achieved if SB defaults. But ROTECH would not engage in the transaction if it thought there was much chance of default. Therefore, ROTECH acknowledges and accepts some credit risk in return for expecting a better overall rate than if it issues euro-denominated debt.

Because it cannot borrow at the same rate as the fixed rate on the swap, ROTECH must pay £150,000 more in interest annually. Recall that the fixed rate on the swap is the rate that would be paid if a London bank issued a par bond. ROTECH, like most companies, would not be able to borrow at a rate that attractive. The £150,000 in interest that ROTECH pays can be viewed as a credit risk premium, which it would have to pay regardless of whether it borrowed directly in the euro market or indirectly through a swap.

In this transaction, the interest payments were made at a fixed rate. As we previously learned, a currency swap can be structured to have both sides pay fixed, both pay floating, or one pay fixed and the other floating. If ROTECH wanted to issue debt in euros at a floating rate, it could issue the bond at a fixed rate and structure the swap so that the dealer pays it pounds at a fixed rate and it pays the dealer euros at a floating rate. Alternatively, it could issue the pound-denominated bond at a floating rate and structure the swap so that the dealer pays it pounds at a floating rate and ROTECH pays euros at a floating rate.[17] A currency swap party's choice to pay a fixed or floating rate depends on its views about the direction of interest rate movements. Companies typically choose floating rates when they think interest rates are likely to fall. They choose fixed rates when they think interest rates are likely to rise.

It should also be noted that companies often choose a particular type of financing (fixed or floating) and then change their minds later by executing another swap. For example, suppose ROTECH proceeds with this transaction as we illustrated it: paying a fixed rate on its pound-denominated bonds, receiving a fixed rate on the pound payments on its swap, and paying a fixed rate on its euro payments on the swap. Suppose that part of the way through the life of the swap, ROTECH thinks that euro interest rates are going down. If it wants to take action based on this view, it could enter into a plain vanilla interest rate swap in euros with SB or some other dealer. It would promise to pay the counterparty interest in euros at a floating rate and receive interest in euros at a fixed rate. This transaction would shift the euro interest obligation to floating.

Exhibit 8-5 illustrates this example. Of course, this transaction is speculative, based as it is on a perception of likely interest rate movements. Moreover, the fixed payments would not offset due to different interest rates.

When we introduced currency swaps in Chapter 5, we noted that one important way in which they differ from interest rate swaps is that currency swaps involve the payment of notional principal. We did note, however, that not all currency swaps involve the payment of notional principal. In transactions such as the ROTECH swap with SB described here, the payment of notional principal is important. The notional principal payment is required, because it offsets the principal on the bond that ROTECH issued in pounds. In the next section, we look at a currency swap in which the notional principal is not paid.

---

[17] It would not matter how ROTECH structured the payments on the pound-denominated bond. Either type of payment would be passed through with the currency swap, which would be structured to match that type of payment.

EXHIBIT 8-5   Reversing a Prior Swap to Change from a Fixed-Rate to an Overall Floating-Rate Status

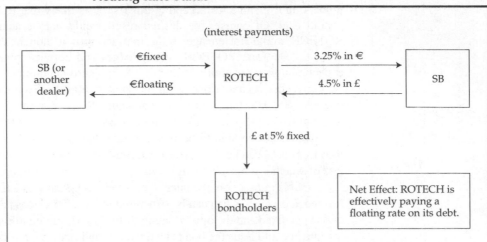

PRACTICE PROBLEM 5

A Japanese company issues a bond with face value of ¥1.2 billion and a coupon rate of 5.25 percent. It decides to use a swap to convert this bond into a euro-denominated bond. The current exchange rate is ¥120/€. The fixed rate on euro-denominated swaps is 6 percent, and the fixed rate on yen-denominated swaps is 5 percent. All payments will be made annually, so there is no adjustment such as Days/360.

A. Describe the terms of the swap and identify the cash flows at the start.

B. Identify all interest cash flows at each interest payment date.

C. Identify all principal cash flows at the maturity of the bond.

SOLUTIONS

A. The company will enter into a swap with notional principal of ¥1,200,000,000/(¥120/€1) = €10,000,000. The swap will involve an exchange of notional principals at the beginning and end. The annual cash flows will involve paying euros and receiving yen. The following cash flows occur at the start:

From issuance of yen bond:	+ ¥1,200,000,000
From swap:	− ¥1,200,000,000
	+ €10,000,000
Net	+ €10,000,000

B. The following cash flows occur at the annual interest payment dates:

Interest payments on bond: (¥1,200,000,000)(0.0525) = − ¥63,000,000

Swap payments:

Yen	+(¥1,200,000,000)(0.05) = + ¥60,000,000
Euro	−(€10,000,000)(0.06) = −€600,000
Net	− ¥3,000,000 − €600,000

C. The following cash flows occur at the end of the life of the swap:

Principal repayment on bond:	− ¥1,200,000,000
Swap principal payments:	
Yen	+ ¥1,200,000,000
Euro	− €10,000,000
Net	− €10,000,000

3.2 CONVERTING FOREIGN CASH RECEIPTS INTO DOMESTIC CURRENCY

Companies with foreign subsidiaries regularly generate cash in foreign currencies. Some companies repatriate that cash back into their domestic currency on a regular basis. If these cash flows are predictable in quantity, the rate at which they are converted can be locked in using a currency swap.

Colorama Software (COLS) is a U.S. company that writes software for digital imaging. So far it has expanded internationally only into the Japanese market, where it generates a net cash flow of about ¥1.2 billion a year. It converts this cash flow into U.S. dollars four times a year, with conversions taking place on the last day of March, June, September, and December. The amounts converted are equal to ¥300 million at each conversion.

COLS would like to lock in its conversion rate for several years, but it does not feel confident in predicting the amount it will convert beyond one year. Thus, it feels it can commit to only a one-year transaction to lock in the conversion rate. It engages in a currency swap with a dealer bank called U.S. Multinational Bank (USMULT) in which COLS will make fixed payments in Japanese yen and receive fixed payments in U.S. dollars. The current spot exchange rate is ¥132/$, which is $0.00757576/¥, or $0.757576 per 100 yen.

The fixed rate on plain vanilla swaps in Japan is 6 percent, and the fixed rate on plain vanilla swaps in the United States is 6.8 percent. To create a swap that will involve the exchange of ¥300 million per quarter into U.S. dollars would require a Japanese notional principal of ¥300,000,000/(0.06/4) = ¥20,000,000,000, which is equivalent to a U.S. dollar notional principal of ¥20,000,000,000/¥132 = $151,515,152.[18]

Thus, COLS engages in a swap for ¥20 billion in which it will pay 6 percent on a quarterly basis, or 1.5 percent per quarter in Japanese yen, and receive 6.8 percent on a quarterly basis, or 1.7 percent on $151,515,152. There is no initial or final exchange of notional principals. The cash flows in the swap are illustrated in Exhibit 8-6.

COLS pays USMULT ¥20,000,000,000(0.06/4) = ¥300,000,000 quarterly on the swap. This amount corresponds to the cash flow it generates on its Japanese operations. It then receives 6.8 percent on a dollar notional principal of $151,515,152 for a total of $151,515,152(0.068/4) = $2,575,758. So the swap effectively locks in the conversion of its quarterly yen cash flows for one year.

COLS does face some risk in this transaction. Besides the credit risk of the swap counterparty defaulting, COLS faces the risk that its operations will not generate at least ¥300 million. Of course, COLS' operations could generate more than ¥300 million, but that would mean only that some of its cash flows would not convert at a locked-in rate. If its operations do not generate at least ¥300 million, COLS still must pay ¥300 million to the swap counterparty.

Currency swaps can be used for purposes other than managing conversion risks. These swaps are also used by dealers to create synthetic strategies that allow them to offer new instruments or hedge existing instruments. In the next section, we look at how currency swaps can be used to synthesize an instrument called a dual-currency bond.

---

[18] A currency swap at 6 percent with quarterly payments and a notional principal of ¥20 billion would require payments of (¥20,000,000,000)(0.06/4) = ¥300,000,000 per quarter.

EXHIBIT 8-6 Converting a Series of Foreign Cash Flows into Domestic Currency Using a Currency Swap

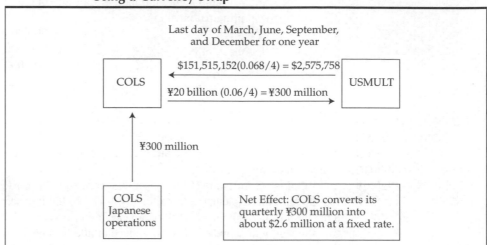

PRACTICE PROBLEM 6

A Canadian corporation with a French subsidiary generates cash flows of €10 million a year. It wants to use a currency swap to lock in the rate at which it converts to Canadian dollars. The current exchange rate is C$0.825/€. The fixed rate on a currency swap in euros is 4 percent, and the fixed rate on a currency swap in Canadian dollars is 5 percent.

A. Determine the notional principals in euros and Canadian dollars for a swap with annual payments that will achieve the corporation's objective.

B. Determine the overall periodic cash flow from the subsidiary operations and the swap.

SOLUTIONS

A. With the euro fixed rate at 4 percent, the euro notional principal should be

$$\frac{€10,000,000}{0.04} = €250,000,000$$

The equivalent Canadian dollar notional principal would be €250,000,000 × C$0.825 = C$206,250,000.

B. The cash flows will be as follows:

From subsidiary operations:	€10,000,000
Swap euro payment:	−0.04(€250,000,000) = −€10,000,000
Swap Canadian dollar payment:	0.05(C$206,250,000) = C$10,312,500

The net effect is that the €10 million converts to C$10,312,500.

3.3 USING CURRENCY SWAPS TO CREATE AND MANAGE THE RISK OF A DUAL-CURRENCY BOND

A financial innovation in recent years is the dual-currency bond, on which the interest is paid in one currency and the principal is paid in another. Such a bond can be useful to a multinational company that might generate sufficient cash in a foreign currency to pay interest but not enough to pay the principal, which it thus might want to pay in its home currency. Dual-currency bonds can be shown to be equivalent to issuing an ordinary bond in one currency and combining it with a currency swap that has no principal payments. Consider the following transactions:

- Issue a bond in dollars.
- Engage in a currency swap with no principal payments. The swap will require the company to pay interest in the foreign currency and receive interest in dollars.

Because the company issued the bond in dollars, it will make interest payments in dollars. The currency swap, however, will result in the company receiving interest in dollars to offset the interest paid on the dollar-denominated bond and making interest payments on the currency swap in the foreign currency.[19] Effectively, the company will make interest payments in the foreign currency. At the maturity date of the bond and swap, the company will pay off the dollar-denominated bond, and there will be no payments on the swap.

Of course, this example illustrates the synthetic creation of a dual-currency bond. Alternatively, a company can create the dual-currency bond directly by issuing a bond in which it promises to pay the principal in one currency and the interest in another. Then, it might consider offsetting the dual-currency bond by synthetically creating the opposite position. The company is short a dual-currency bond. A synthetic dual-currency bond can be created through the purchase of a domestic bond and a currency swap. If the synthetic dual-currency bond is cheaper than the actual dual-currency bond, the company can profit by offsetting the short position in the actual bond by a long position in the synthetic bond. Let us see how this strategy can be implemented using a trading firm that finds an opportunity to earn an arbitrage profit doing so.

Trans Mutual Arbitrage (TMARB) is such a firm. It has a major client, Omega Construction (OGCONS), that would like to purchase a five-year dual-currency bond. The bond will have a face value of $10 million and an equivalent face value in euros of €12.5 million.[20] The bond will pay interest in euros at a rate of 4.5 percent. TMARB sees an opportunity to issue the bond, take the proceeds, and buy a 5.25 percent (coupon rate) U.S. dollar-denominated bond issued by an insurance company called Kappa Insurance Co. (KINSCO). TMARB will also engage in a currency swap with dealer American Trading Bank (ATB) in which TMARB will receive interest payments in euros at a rate of 4.5 percent on notional principal of €12.5 million and pay interest at a rate of 5.0 percent on notional principal of $10 million.[21] The swap does not involve the payment of notional principals. The swap and bond begin on 15 May and involve annual payments every 15 May for five years.

Exhibit 8-7 illustrates the structure of this swap. In Panel A, we see the initial cash flows. TMARB receives $10 million from OGCONS for the issuance of the dual-currency bond. It then takes the $10 million and buys a $10 million dollar-denominated bond issued by KINSCO. There are no initial cash flows on the currency swap.

---

[19] It does not matter if the dollar bond has fixed- or floating-rate interest. The currency swap would be structured to have the same type of interest to offset.

[20] The current exchange rate must, therefore, be $0.80/€.

[21] We have made the fixed rate on the bond the same as the euro fixed rate on the swap for convenience. In practice, there probably would be a spread between the two rates, but the size of the spread would be fixed.

EXHIBIT 8-7   Issuing a Dual-Currency Bond and Managing the Risk with an Ordinary Bond and a Currency Swap

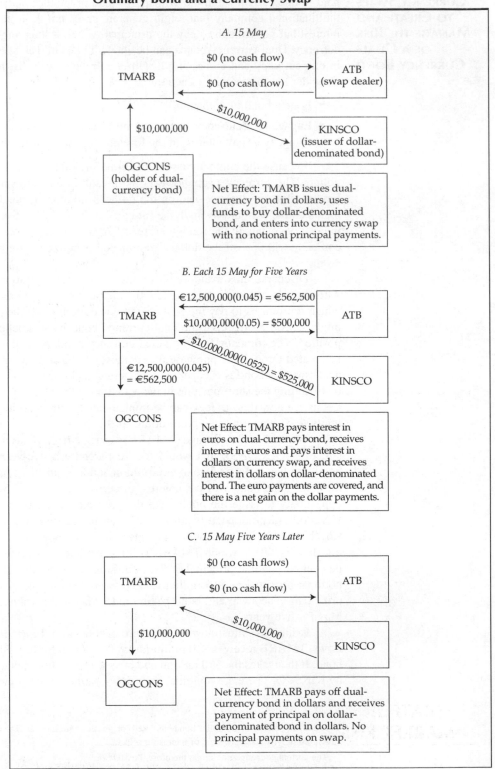

Panel B shows the annual cash flows, which occur on 15 May for five years. TMARB pays interest of €12,500,000(0.045) = €562,500 to OGCONS on the dual-currency bond. It receives interest of an equivalent amount from ATB on the currency swap. It pays interest of $10,000,000(0.05) = $500,000 on the currency swap and receives interest of $10,000,000 × 0.0525 = $525,000 from KINSCO on the dollar-denominated bond. TMARB's euro interest payments are fully covered, and it nets a gain from its dollar interest payments. This opportunity resulted because TMARB found a synthetic way to issue a bond at 5.00 percent and buy one paying 5.25 percent. Of course, TMARB will be accepting some credit risk, from both the swap dealer and KINSCO, and its gain may reflect only this credit risk.

Panel C provides the final payments. TMARB pays off OGCONS its $10 million obligation on the dual-currency bond and receives $10 million from KINSCO on the dollar-denominated bond. There are no payments on the swap.

The end result is that TMARB issued a dual-currency bond and offset it with an ordinary dollar-denominated bond and a currency swap with no principal payments. TMARB earned a profit, which may be compensation for the credit risk taken.

PRACTICE PROBLEM 7

From the perspective of the issuer, construct a synthetic dual-currency bond in which the principal is paid in U.S. dollars and the interest is paid in Swiss francs. The face value will be $20 million, and the interest rate will be 5 percent in Swiss francs. The exchange rate is $0.80/SF. Assume that the appropriate interest rate for a $20 million bond in dollars is 5.5 percent. The appropriate fixed rates on a currency swap are 5.5 percent in dollars and 5.0 percent in Swiss francs.

SOLUTION

Issue a $20 million bond in dollars, paying interest at 5.5 percent. Enter into a currency swap on $20 million, equivalent to SF25 million. The currency swap will involve the receipt of dollar interest at 5.5 percent and payment of Swiss franc interest at 5.0 percent. You will receive $20 million at the start and pay back $20 million at maturity. The annual cash flows will be as follows:

On dollar bond issued: −0.055($20,000,000) = −$1,100,000

On swap:

     Dollars   +0.055($20,000,000) = +$1,100,000

     Swiss francs   −0.05(SF25,000,000) = −SF1,250,000

Net   −SF1,250,000

In the next section, we look at swap strategies in the management of equity market risk.

4 STRATEGIES AND APPLICATIONS FOR MANAGING EQUITY MARKET RISK

Equity portfolio managers often want to realign the risk of their portfolios. In previous chapters, we have learned how to do so using other instruments. Swaps can also be used for this purpose. In Chapter 6, we covered equity swaps, which are swaps in which at least one set of payments is tied to the price of a stock or stock index. Equity swaps are ideal for use by equity managers to make changes to portfolios by synthetically buying and selling stock without making any trades in the actual stock. Of course, equity swaps have a defined expiration date and thus achieve their results only temporarily. To continue managing equity market risk, a swap would need to be renewed periodically and would be subject to whatever new conditions exist in the market on the renewal date.

4.1   DIVERSIFYING A CONCENTRATED PORTFOLIO

Diversification is one of the most important principles of sound investing. Some portfolios, however, are not very diversified. A failure to diversify can be due to investor ignorance or inattention, or it can arise through no fault of the investor. For example, a single large donation to a charitable organization can result in a high degree of concentration of an endowment portfolio. The recipient could be constrained or at least feel constrained from selling the stock. Equity swaps can be used to achieve diversification without selling the stock, as we shall see in the following example.

Commonwealth Foundation (CWF) is a charitable organization with an endowment of $50 million invested in diversified stock. Recently, Samuel Zykes, a wealthy member of the community, died and left CWF a large donation of stock in a company he founded called Zykes Technology (ZYKT). The stock is currently worth $30 million. The overall endowment value is now at $80 million, but the portfolio is highly undiversified, with more than a third of its value concentrated in one stock. CWF has considered selling the stock, but its development director believes that the Zykes family will possibly give more money to the foundation at a later date. If CWF sells the stock, the Zykes family may get the impression that the foundation does not want or appreciate the gift. Therefore, the foundation has concluded that it must hold onto the stock. The prospects for very limited growth in the portfolio through other sources, combined with the desire to attract further donations from the Zykes family, lead CWF to conclude that it cannot diversify the portfolio by traditional means anytime soon.

CWF's bank suggests that it consult with a swap dealer called Capital Swaps (CAPS). CAPS recommends an equity swap in which CWF would pay CAPS the return on the $30 million of ZYKT stock, while CAPS would pay CWF the return on $30 million of the S&P 500 Index, considered by all parties to be an acceptable proxy for a diversified portfolio. The payments will be made quarterly. CAPS mentions that technically the transaction would need an ending date. Anticipating the possibility of another transaction of this sort pending further

EXHIBIT 8-8   Diversifying a Concentrated Portfolio

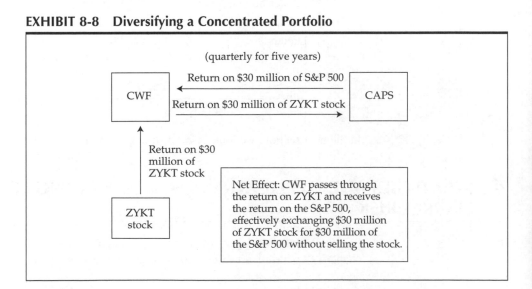

donations by the Zykes family in about five years, the parties agree to set the maturity date of the swap at five years. The transaction entails no exchange of notional principal at the start or at the end of the life of the swap. Thus, CWF will maintain possession of the stock, including the voting rights. Exhibit 8-8 illustrates the structure of the transaction.

So, CWF passes through the return on $30 million of ZYKT stock and receives the return on the S&P 500. Both parties, however, must keep in mind a number of considerations. One is that a cash flow problem could arise for CWF, which must make cash payments each quarter equal to the return on the ZYKT stock. Though CWF will receive cash payments equal to the return on the S&P 500, CWF will have a net cash outflow if ZYKT outperforms the S&P 500. In fact, it is quite possible that in some quarters, ZYKT will have a positive total return, necessitating a cash obligation, and the S&P 500 will have a negative total return. In that case, the cash payment that CAPS would ordinarily make to CWF for the S&P 500 return would actually be reversed: CWF would owe CAPS for the S&P 500. In short, CWF would owe on both legs of the swap. This possibility could pose a significant cash flow problem and might necessitate the actual sale of some ZYKT stock. The position would then be imbalanced because CWF would own less than $30 million of ZYKT stock but still owe payments on $30 million of ZYKT stock. Cash flow management can be a major difficulty in equity swaps.

PRACTICE PROBLEM 8

The manager of a charitable foundation's $50 million stock portfolio is concerned about the portfolio's heavy concentration in one stock, Noble Petroleum (NBP). Specifically, the fund has $20 million of this stock as a result of a recent donation to the fund. She is considering using an equity swap to reduce the exposure to NBP and allow the fund to invest indirectly in the Wilshire 5000 Index. The stock is currently selling for $20 a share, and the fund owns 1 million shares. The manager is not quite ready to reduce all of the fund's exposure to NBP, so she decides to synthetically sell off one-quarter of the position. Explain how she would do this and identify some problems she might encounter.

SOLUTION

To reduce her exposure on one quarter of her NBP holdings, the manager would have the fund enter into a swap to sell the total return on $5 million of NBP stock, which is 250,000 shares. The fund will receive from the swap dealer the return on $5 million invested in the Wilshire 5000.

The swap may result in cash flow problems, however, because the fund must pay out the return on 250,000 shares of NBP stock but does not want to sell that stock. If the return received on $5 million invested in the Wilshire 5000 is significantly less than the return the fund pays, or if the return on the Wilshire is negative, the fund could have insufficient cash to make its payment. Then it might be forced to sell the stock, something it was trying to avoid in the first place.

Continuing with the example of ZYKT stock, what is the position of the dealer CAPS? It agrees to accept the return on ZYKT stock and pay the return on the S&P 500. This means it is long ZYKT and short the S&P 500. It is likely to hedge its position by buying the equivalent of the S&P 500 through either an index fund or an exchange-traded fund, and selling short ZYKT stock.[22] In fact, its short sale of the ZYKT stock is analogous to

---

[22] Instead of buying or selling short stock, it could use any of a variety of derivative strategies in which it would benefit from a decrease in the price of ZYKT relative to the S&P 500.

CWF selling the stock. CAPS effectively sells the stock for CWF. Also, CAPS is not likely to be able to sell all of the ZYKT stock at one time so it will probably do so over a period of a few days. CAPS may also have a cash flow problem on occasion. If it owes more on the S&P 500 payment than is due it on the ZYKT payment, CAPS may have to liquidate some S&P 500 stock.[23]

In addition, to make a profit CAPS would probably either not pay quite the full return on the S&P 500 stock or require that CWF pay slightly more than the full return on the ZYKT stock.

We see that equity swaps can be used to diversify a concentrated portfolio. Next we turn to a situation in which equity swaps can be used to achieve diversification on an international scale.

4.2 ACHIEVING INTERNATIONAL DIVERSIFICATION

The benefits of international diversification are well documented. The correlations between foreign markets and domestic markets generally lead to greater diversification and more efficient investing. Nonetheless, many investors have not taken the step of diversifying their portfolios across international boundaries. Here we shall take a look at a situation in which equity swaps can facilitate the transition from domestic to global diversification.

In this example, Underscore Retirement Management (USRM) is responsible for a $500 million fund of retirement accounts in the United States. It has never diversified internationally, investing all of its funds in U.S. stock. Representing U.S. large-, medium- and small-cap stocks, the Russell 3000 Index is the portfolio's benchmark. USRM has decided that it needs to add non-U.S. stocks to its portfolio. It would like to start by selling 10 percent of its U.S. stock and putting the funds in non-U.S. stock. Its advisor, American Global Bank (AGB), has suggested that an equity swap would be a better way to do this than to transact in the stock directly. AGB often deals in non-U.S. stock and has subsidiaries and correspondent relationships in many countries to facilitate the transactions. It is capable of transacting in all stock at lower costs than its clients, and can pass on those savings through derivative transactions.

AGB suggests an equity swap with quarterly payments in which USRM would pay it the return on $50 million of the Russell 3000 Index. USRM would presumably generate this return from the portfolio it holds. AGB would, in turn, pay USRM the return on $50 million invested in the Morgan Stanley Capital International (MSCI) EAFE Index, which provides broad coverage of equity markets in Europe, Australasia, and the Far East. This transaction would result in USRM giving up some diversified domestic stock performance and receiving diversified international stock performance. Exhibit 8-9 illustrates the structure of the transaction.

USRM must also consider a number of additional factors. The points made in Section 4.1 regarding the possibility of negative cash flow are highly relevant here as well, and we shall not repeat them. In addition, USRM's domestic stock holding generates a return that will not match perfectly the return on the Russell 3000. This difference in returns, in which the performance of an index does not match the performance of a portfolio that is similar to the index, is called the **tracking error**. In an extreme case, the domestic stock may go down while the Russell index goes up, which could pose a serious cash flow problem for USRM. USRM may be able to quantify this problem and find that it can effectively manage it. Otherwise, this concern could be an important one for USRM to weigh against the benefits of doing this transaction, which are primarily the savings in transaction costs on the domestic side and on the foreign side. In addition, AGB has currency risk and market risk and passes on to USRM its costs of hedging that risk.

---

[23] To make matters worse, if the S&P goes up and ZYKT goes down, it will owe both sets of payments.

EXHIBIT 8-9   Achieving International Diversification

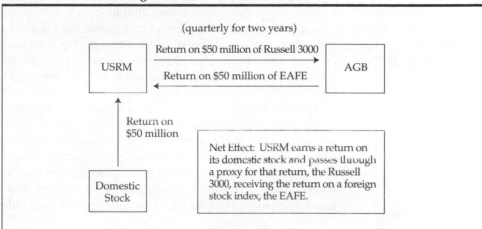

PRACTICE PROBLEM 9

A Canadian trust fund holds a portfolio of C$300 million of Canadian domestic stock. The manager would like to sell off C$100 million and invest the funds in a pan-European portfolio. The manager arranges to do so using an equity swap in which the domestic stock is represented by the Toronto 300 Composite and the European portfolio is represented by the Dow Jones Euro STOXX 50, an index of leading stocks in the eurozone. Explain how to structure such a swap, and describe how tracking error could potentially interfere with the success of the transaction.

SOLUTION

The swap would specify the following transactions on a periodic basis for a specific number of years:

- Receive return on DJ Euro STOXX 50.
- Pay return on Toronto 300.

Tracking error here is the failure of the derivative cash flow to match precisely the cash flow from the underlying portfolio. In this case, tracking error means that the return actually earned on the domestic portfolio is not likely to perfectly match the Toronto 300 return. These returns are supposed to offset, but they are not likely to do so, certainly not with perfection. The return received on the DJ Euro STOXX 50 does not give rise to tracking error concerns. The index will simply represent the return on the investment in European stocks. If an actual investment in European stocks were made, it would likely differ from this return.

We see in this example that a company can use an equity swap to change its asset allocation. Indeed, an asset allocation change is the major use of equity swaps. In the next section, we shall see a company use equity swaps, combined with a similar swap based on a fixed-income instrument, to implement an asset allocation change. This fixed-income swap will be a slightly new and different instrument from what we have already seen.

4.3 CHANGING
AN ASSET
ALLOCATION
BETWEEN STOCKS
AND BONDS

Consider an investment management firm called Tactical Money Management (TMM). It is interested in changing the asset allocation on a $200 million segment of its portfolio. This money is invested 75 percent in domestic stock and 25 percent in U.S. government and corporate bonds. Within the stock sector, the funds are invested 60 percent in large cap, 30 percent in mid cap, and 10 percent in small cap. Within the bond sector, the funds are invested 80 percent in U.S. government and 20 percent in investment-grade corporate bonds. TMM would like to change the overall allocation to 90 percent stock and 10 percent bonds. Within each class, TMM would also like to make some changes. Specifically, TMM would like to change the stock allocation to 65 percent large cap and 25 percent mid cap, leaving the small-cap allocation at 10 percent. It would like to change the bond allocation to 75 percent U.S. government and 25 percent investment-grade corporate. TMM knows that these changes would entail a considerable amount of trading in stocks and bonds. Below we show the current position, the desired new position, and the necessary transactions to get from the current position to the new position:

Stock	Current ($150 million, 75%)	New ($180 million, 90%)	Transaction
Large cap	$90 million (60%)	$117 million (65%)	Buy $27 million
Mid cap	$45 million (30%)	$45 million (25%)	None
Small cap	$15 million (10%)	$18 million (10%)	Buy $3 million

Bonds	Current ($50 million, 25%)	New ($20 million, 10%)	Transaction
Government	$40 million (80%)	$15 million (75%)	Sell $25 million
Corporate	$10 million (20%)	$5 million (25%)	Sell $5 million

TMM decides it can execute a series of swaps that would enable it to change its position temporarily, but more easily and less expensively than by executing the transactions in stock and bonds. It engages a dealer, Dynamic Derivatives Inc. (DYDINC), to perform the swaps. The return on the large-cap sector is represented by the return on $27 million invested in the S&P 500 (SP500) Index. Note that the mid-cap exposure of $45 million does not change, so we do not need to incorporate a mid-cap index into the swap. The return on the small-cap sector is represented by the return on $3 million invested in the S&P Small Cap 600 Index (SPSC). The return on the government bond sector is represented by the return on $25 million invested in the Lehman Long Treasury Bond index (LLTB), and the return on the corporate bond sector is represented by the return on $5 million invested in the Merrill Lynch Corporate Bond index (MLCB). Note that for the overall fixed-income sector, TMM will be reducing its exposure.

TMM must decide the frequency of payments and the length of the swap. Equity swap payments tend to be set at quarterly intervals. Fixed-income payments in the form of coupon interest tend to occur semiannually. TMM could arrange for quarterly equity swap payments and semiannual fixed-income swap payments. It decides, however, to structure the swap to have all payments occur on the same dates six months apart. The length of the swap should correspond to the period during which the firm wants this new allocation to hold. TMM decides on one year. Should it wish to extend this period, TMM would need to renegotiate the swap at expiration. Likewise, TMM could decide to unwind the position prior to one year, which it could do by executing a new swap with opposite payments for the remainder of the life of the original swap.

The equity swaps in this example involve receiving payments tied to the SP500 and the SPSC and making either fixed payments or floating payments tied to LIBOR. Let us start by assuming that the equity swap payments will be paired with LIBOR-based floating payments. For the fixed-income payments, however, TMM needs a slightly different type of swap—specifically, a fixed-income swap. This instrument is exactly like an equity swap, but instead of the payment being tied to a stock or stock index, it is tied to a bond or bond index. This type of swap is not the same as an interest rate swap, which involves payments tied to a floating rate such as LIBOR. Fixed-income swaps, like equity swaps, require the payment of the total return on a bond or bond index against some other index, such as LIBOR. They are very similar to equity swaps in many respects: The total return is not known until the end of the settlement period, and because the capital gain can be negative, it is possible for the overall payment to be negative. In contrast to equity swaps, however, fixed-income swaps are more dominated by the fixed payment of interest. For equities, the dividends are small, not fixed, and do not tend to dominate capital gains. Other than the amounts paid, however, fixed-income swaps are conceptually the same as equity swaps.[24]

The swaps are initially structured as follows:

Equity swaps
> Receive return on SP500 on $27 million
>> Pay LIBOR on $27 million
> Receive return on SPSC on $3 million
>> Pay LIBOR on $3 million

Fixed-income swaps
> Receive LIBOR on $25 million
>> Pay return on LLTB on $25 million
> Receive LIBOR on $5 million
>> Pay return on MLCB on $5 million

Note that the overall position involves no LIBOR payments. TMM pays LIBOR on $27 million and on $3 million from its equity swaps, and it receives LIBOR on $25 million and on $5 million from the fixed-income swaps. Therefore, the LIBOR payments can be eliminated. Furthermore, the equity and fixed-income swaps can be combined into a single swap with the following payments:

> Receive return on SP500 on $27 million
> Receive return on SPSC on $3 million
>> Pay return on LLTB on $25 million
>> Pay return on MLCB on $5 million

This combined equity/fixed-income swap is a single transaction that accomplishes TMM's objective. Exhibit 8-10 illustrates the overall transaction.

Of course, this transaction will not completely achieve TMM's goals. The performance of the various sectors of its equity and fixed-income portfolios are not likely to match perfectly the indices on which the swap payments are based. This problem is what we referred to previously as tracking error. In addition, TMM could encounter a cash flow

---

[24] Fixed-income swaps, when referred to as total return swaps, are a form of a credit derivative, an instrument we shall cover in Chapter 9.

EXHIBIT 8-10   Changing an Asset Allocation

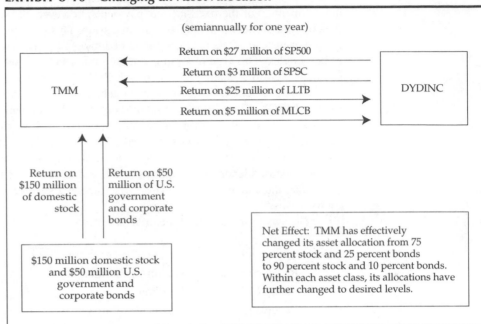

problem if its fixed-income payments exceed its equity receipts and its portfolio does not generate enough cash to fund its net obligation. The actual stock and bond portfolio will generate cash only from dividends and interest. The capital gains on the stock and bond portfolio will not be received in cash unless a portion of the portfolio is liquidated. But avoiding liquidation of the portfolio is the very reason that TMM wants to use swaps.[25]

PRACTICE PROBLEM 10

A $30 million investment account of a bank trust fund is allocated one-third to stocks and two-thirds to bonds. The portfolio manager wants to change the overall allocation to 50 percent stock and 50 percent bonds, and the allocation within the stock fund from 70 percent domestic stock and 30 percent foreign stock to 60 percent domestic and 40 percent foreign. The bond allocation will remain entirely invested in domestic corporate issues. Explain how an equity swap could be used to implement this adjustment. You do not need to refer to specific stock indices.

SOLUTION

Currently the allocation is $10 million stock and $20 million bonds. Within the stock category, the current allocation is $7 million domestic and $3 million foreign. The desired allocation is $15 million stock and $15 million bonds. Thus, the allocation must change by moving $5 million into stock and out of bonds. The desired stock allocation is $9 million domestic and $6 million foreign. The desired bond allocation is $15 million, all domestic corporate.

---

[25] Even worse would be if its fixed-income payments were positive and its equity receipts were negative.

> To make the change with a swap, the manager must enter into a swap to receive the return on $5 million based on a domestic equity index and pay the return on $5 million based on a domestic corporate bond index. The $5 million return based on a domestic equity index should be allocated such that $2 million is based on domestic stock and $3 million is based on foreign stock.

So far we have seen that an equity swap can be used to reduce or increase exposure to a stock or stock index. One type of investor that is highly exposed to the performance of a single stock is a corporate insider. In the following section, we examine a swap strategy that has been increasingly used in recent years to reduce such exposure.

4.4 REDUCING INSIDER EXPOSURE

Michael Spelling is the founder and sole owner of a U.S.-based company called Spelling Software and Technology (SPST). After founding the company about 10 years ago, Spelling took it public 2 years ago and retains significant ownership in the form of 10,200,000 shares, currently valued at $35 a share, for a total value of $357 million, which represents about 10 percent of the company. Spelling wants to retain this degree of control of the company, so he does not wish to sell any of his shares. He is concerned, however, that his personal wealth is nearly 100 percent exposed to the fortunes of a single company.

A swap dealer called Swap Solutions Inc. (SSI) approaches Spelling about a strategy that it has been using lately with much success. This transaction involves an equity swap whereby Spelling would pay the dealer the return on some of his shares in SPST and receive a diversified portfolio return. Spelling finds the idea intriguing and begins thinking about how he would like to structure the arrangement. He decides to initially base the transaction on 500,000 shares of stock, about 4.9 percent of his ownership. If he is satisfied with how the strategy works, he may later increase his commitment to the swap. At $35 a share, this transaction has an exposure of $17.5 million. Specifically, Spelling will pay the total return on 500,000 shares of SPST stock and receive a diversified portfolio return on $17.5 million. He decides to split the diversified return into 80 percent stock and 20 percent bonds. The former will be represented by the return on $14.0 million invested in the Russell 3000, and the latter will be represented by the return on $3.5 million invested in the Lehman Brothers Government Bond Index (LGB). The payments will occur quarterly for two years, at which time Spelling will re-evaluate his position and may choose to extend the swap, terminate it, or change the allocation or other terms.

Exhibit 8-11 illustrates the structure of the swap. Spelling achieves his objectives, but he must consider some important issues in addition to the cash flow problem we have already mentioned. One is that under U.S. law, this transaction is considered an insider sale and must be reported to the regulatory authorities Thus, there is some additional paperwork. Shareholders and potential investors may consider the sale a signal of bad prospects for the company. U.S. tax laws also require that the synthetic sale of securities through equity swaps forces a termination of the holding period on the stock. Hence, this transaction has no tax advantages. Spelling will also want to consider the fact that he has sold off some of his exposure but retains control. Shareholders will surely resent the fact that Spelling controls 500,000 votes but does not have any exposure to this stock.[26] Of course, he still retains exposure to 9.7 million shares.

---

[26] An interesting question in this regard is whether the shareholders would actually know that the executive had done such a transaction. Careful research is required to identify that executives have made these transactions.

EXHIBIT 8-11   Reducing Insider Exposure

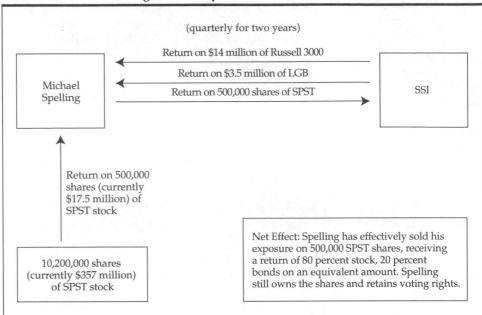

PRACTICE PROBLEM 11

The CEO of a corporation owns 100 million shares of his company's stock, which is currently priced at €30 a share. Given the tremendous exposure of his personal wealth to this one company, he has decided to sell 10 percent of his position and invest the funds in a floating interest rate instrument. A derivatives dealer suggests that he do so using an equity swap. Explain how to structure such a swap.

SOLUTION

The swap is structured so that the executive pays the return on 10 million shares, which is 10 percent of his holdings, of the company's stock and receives the return based on a floating interest rate, such as LIBOR, on a notional principal of €300 million.

Equity swaps of this sort can be a significant concern for financial analysts. Their possible use makes it difficult to determine if executives have the full exposure represented by the number of shares they own.

Equity swaps involving executives can also have significant agency cost implications. A company incurs agency costs when an executive does not act on behalf of shareholders. Consider the extreme case of an executive who owns more than 50 percent of a company but who reduces her equity exposure to zero with equity swaps. The executive retains full control of the company, although she has eliminated her equity exposure. This action could entail significant costs to outside shareholders, as the executive does not bear any of the costs of actions or expenditures that increase her personal welfare at the expense of the company. Of course, executives are unlikely to sell off all of their exposure, but the elimination of any exposure on shares still retained for control purposes raises significant questions about whether an executive would act in the best interests of the shareholders. The executive's incentive to perform well would certainly be reduced.

In Sections 2, 3, and 4, we examined the use of interest rate swaps, currency swaps, and equity swaps for managing risk. When we first covered swaps in Chapter 5, we also introduced a related instrument, the swaption, which is an option on a swap. In the following section, we examine strategies involving the use of swaptions to manage risk.

5   STRATEGIES AND APPLICATIONS USING SWAPTIONS

A swaption is an option to enter into a swap. Although there are swaptions to enter into equity, currency, and commodity swaps, we will focus exclusively on swaptions to enter into interest rate swaps, which is by far the largest swaptions market. Let us briefly review swaptions.

First, recall that there are two types of swaptions, payer swaptions and receiver swaptions, which are analogous to puts and calls. A payer swaption is an option that allows the holder to enter into a swap as the fixed-rate payer, floating-rate receiver. A receiver swaption is an option that allows the holder to enter into a swap as the fixed-rate receiver, floating-rate payer. In both cases, the fixed rate is specified when the option starts. The buyer of a swaption pays a premium at the start of the contract and receives the right to enter into a swap. The counterparty is the seller of the swaption. The seller receives the premium at the start and grants the right to enter into the swap at the specified fixed rate to the buyer of the swaption. A swaption can be European style or American style, meaning that it can be exercised only at expiration (European) or at any time prior to expiration (American). We shall illustrate applications of both.

A swaption is based on an underlying swap. The underlying swap has a specific set of terms: the notional principal, the underlying interest rate, the time it expires, the specific dates on which the payments will be made, and how the interest is calculated. *All* of the terms of the underlying swap must be specified. Although an ordinary option on an asset has an exercise *price*, a swaption is more like an interest rate option in that it has an exercise *rate*. The exercise rate is the fixed rate at which the holder can enter into the swap as either a fixed-rate payer or fixed-rate receiver. When a swaption expires, the holder decides whether to exercise it based on the relationship of the then-current market rate on the underlying swap to the exercise rate on the swaption. A swaption can be exercised either by actually entering into the swap or by having the seller pay the buyer an equivalent amount of cash. The method used is determined by the parties when the contract is created.

For example, suppose the underlying swap is a three-year swap with semiannual payments with LIBOR as the underlying floating rate. Consider a payer swaption, which allows entry into this swap as the fixed-rate payer, with an exercise rate of 7 percent. At expiration, let us say that three-year, semiannual-pay LIBOR swaps have a fixed rate of 7.25 percent. If the holder exercises the swaption, it enters a swap, agreeing to pay a fixed rate of 7 percent and receive a floating rate of LIBOR. If the holder has another position for which it might want to maintain the swap, it might simply hold the swap in place. If the holder does not want to maintain the swap, it can enter into a swap in the market, specifying the opposite set of payments—it can pay LIBOR and receive the market fixed rate of 7.25 percent. If this swap is done with a different counterparty than the swaption seller, then the two sets of LIBOR payments are made but are equivalent in amount. Then the payer swaption holder finds itself with a stream of cash flows consisting of 7 percent payments and 7.25 percent receipts, for a net overall position of an annuity of 0.25 percent, split into 0.125 percent twice a year, for three years. If this swap at the market rate of 7.25 percent is done with the swaption seller, the two parties are likely to agree to offset the LIBOR payments and have the swaption seller pay the holder the stream of payments of 0.125 percent twice a year. If the parties settle the contract in cash, the swaption seller pays the swaption holder the present value of a series of six semiannual payments of 0.125 percent.

As we saw in Chapter 5, a swaption can also be viewed as an option on a coupon bond. Specifically, a payer swaption with exercise rate x in which the underlying is a swap with notional principal P and maturity of N years at the swaption expiration is equivalent to an at-the-money put option in which the underlying is an N-year bond at expiration with a coupon of x percent. Likewise, a receiver swaption is analogous to an at-the-money call option on a bond. These identities will be useful in understanding swaption strategies.

5.1 **USING AN INTEREST RATE SWAPTION IN ANTICIPATION OF A FUTURE BORROWING**	We have illustrated extensively the use of swaps to convert fixed-rate loans to floating-rate loans and vice versa. We now consider a situation in which a company anticipates taking out a loan at a future date. The company expects that the bank will require the loan to be at a floating rate, but the company would prefer a fixed rate. It will use a swap to convert the payment pattern of the loan. A swaption will give it the flexibility to enter into the swap at an attractive rate.

In Chapter 5, we used the notation FS(0,n,m) to represent the fixed rate established at time 0 for a swap of n payments in which the underlying is m-day LIBOR. In this section, we can simplify this notation somewhat. For example, we will use the notation FS(1,3) for the fixed rate on a swap established at time 1 and ending at time 3.

Benelux Chemicals (BCHEM) is a Brussels-based industrial company that often takes out floating-rate loans. In the course of planning, BCHEM finds that it must borrow €10 million in one year at the floating rate of Euribor, the rate on euros in Frankfurt, from the Antwerp National Bank (ANB). The loan will require semiannual payments for two years. BCHEM knows that it will swap the loan into a fixed-rate loan, using the going rate for two-year Euribor-based swaps at the time the loan is taken out. BCHEM is concerned that interest rates will rise before it takes out the loan. DTD, a Rotterdam derivatives dealer, approaches BCHEM with the idea of doing a European-style swaption. Specifically, for a cash payment up front of €127,500, BCHEM can obtain the right to enter into the swap in one year as a fixed-rate payer at a rate of 7 percent. BCHEM decides to go ahead with the deal; that is, it buys a 7 percent payer swaption.

Exhibit 8-12 illustrates this transaction. In Panel A, BCHEM pays DTD €127,500 in cash and receives the payer swaption. In Panel B, we examine what happens starting when the swaption expires one year later. Note first that regardless of the outcome of the swaption, BCHEM will make floating interest payments of Euribor(180/360)€10 million on its loan.[27] In Part (i) of Panel B, we assume that at expiration of the swaption, the rate in the market on the underlying swap, FS(1,3), is greater than the swaption exercise rate of 7 percent. In this case, the swaption is worth exercising.[28] BCHEM enters into the swap with DTD, thereby making payments of 0.07(180/360)€10 million and receiving payments of Euribor(180/360)€10 million.[29] Both streams of floating payments at Euribor are made, but the payment from DTD exactly offsets the payment to ANB. BCHEM is left paying 7 percent fixed.

---

[27]　Again, recall that being a floating rate, Euribor is set at the beginning of the settlement period, and the payment is made at the end of that period.

[28]　To review, remember that at the swaption expiration in one year, which we denote as time 1, the underlying swap is a two-year swap. If the fixed rate on a two-year swap is higher than the rate at which the swaption holder can pay to enter a two-year swap, the swaption is in-the-money. As we showed in Chapter 5 and in Section 5 of this chapter, its value at that point is the present value of a stream of payments equal to the difference between the market fixed rate and the exercise rate on the swaption.

[29]　The swap payments would, of course, be netted, but that fact does not affect the point we are making here.

EXHIBIT 8-12 Using a Swaption in Anticipation of a Future Borrowing

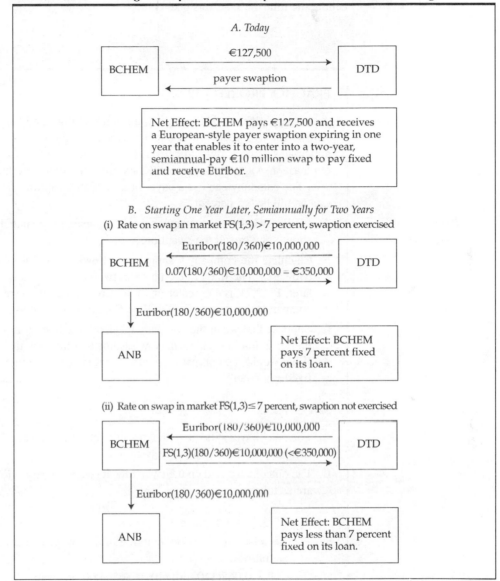

A. Today

Net Effect: BCHEM pays €127,500 and receives a European-style payer swaption expiring in one year that enables it to enter into a two-year, semiannual-pay €10 million swap to pay fixed and receive Euribor.

B. Starting One Year Later, Semiannually for Two Years
(i) Rate on swap in market FS(1,3) > 7 percent, swaption exercised

Euribor(180/360)€10,000,000

0.07(180/360)€10,000,000 – €350,000

Euribor(180/360)€10,000,000

Net Effect: BCHEM pays 7 percent fixed on its loan.

(ii) Rate on swap in market FS(1,3) ≤ 7 percent, swaption not exercised

Euribor(180/360)€10,000,000

FS(1,3)(180/360)€10,000,000 (<€350,000)

Euribor(180/360)€10,000,000

Net Effect: BCHEM pays less than 7 percent fixed on its loan.

In Part (ii) of Panel B, at expiration of the swaption, the rate in the market on the underlying swap, FS(1,3), is less than or equal to the swaption exercise rate of 7 percent. The swaption, therefore, expires out-of-the-money. BCHEM still enters into a swap with DTD but does so at the market rate of FS(1,3), which is less than 7 percent and the payments are less than €350,000. Of course, both sets of Euribor payments must be made on the loan.

Thus, BCHEM obtained the advantage of flexibility, the right to pay a fixed rate of 7 percent or less. Of course, this right does not come without a cost. BCHEM had to pay a premium of €127,500 for that right. Therefore, when the loan was taken out one year after the swaption was purchased, the €10 million received was effectively reduced by the €127,500 paid one year earlier plus one year's interest. Whether this premium would be worth paying depends on whether the swaption is correctly priced.[30] Whether this

---

[30] We did not take up swaption pricing in Chapter 5, but the basic idea is that a model would be used to obtain a fair price for the swaption, to which the market price of €127,500 would be compared.

premium was worth it after the fact depends on how far the market rate ended above 7 percent at the time the loan was taken out.

PRACTICE PROBLEM 12

A company plans to take out a $10 million floating-rate loan in two years. The loan will be for five years with annual payments at the rate of LIBOR. The company anticipates using a swap to convert the loan into a fixed-rate loan. It would like to purchase a swaption to give it the flexibility to enter into the swap at an attractive rate. The company can use a payer or a receiver swaption. Assume that the exercise rate would be 6.5 percent.

A. Identify what type of swaption would achieve this goal and whether the company should buy or sell the swaption.

B. Calculate the company's annual cash flows beginning two years from now for two cases: The fixed rate on a swap two years from now to terminate five years later, FS(2,7), is 1) greater or 2) not greater than the exercise rate. Assume the company takes out the $10 million floating-rate loan as planned.

C. Suppose that when the company takes out the loan, it has changed its mind and prefers a floating-rate loan. Now assume that the swaption expires in-the-money. What would the company do, given that it now no longer wants to convert to a fixed-rate loan?

SOLUTIONS

A. The company wants the option to enter into the swap as a fixed-rate payer, so the company would buy a payer swaption.

B. The outcomes based on the swap rate at swaption expiration, denoted as FS(2,7), are as follows:

FS(2,7) > 6.5 percent

Exercise the swaption, entering into a swap. The annual cash flows will be as follows:

Pay 0.065($10 million) = $650,000 on swap

Receive L($10 million) on swap

Pay L($10 million) on loan

Net, pay $650,000

FS(2,7) ≤ 6.5 percent

Do not exercise swaption; enter into swap at market rate. The annual cash flows will be as follows:

Pay FS(2,7)($10 million) on swap

Receive L($10 million) on swap

Pay L($10 million) on loan

Net, pay FS(2,7)($10 million)

(Note: This is less than $650,000)

C. In this situation, the company has changed its mind about converting the floating-rate loan to a fixed-rate loan. If the swaption expires out-of-the-money, the company will simply take out the floating-rate loan. If the swaption expires in-the-money, it has value and the company should not fail to exercise it. But exercising the swaption will initiate a swap to pay fixed and receive floating, which would leave the company in the net position of paying a fixed rate of 6.5 percent when it wants a floating-rate loan. The company would exercise the swaption and then enter into the opposite swap in the market, receiving a fixed rate of FS(2,7) and paying L. The net effect is that the company will pay 6.5 percent, receive FS(2,7), which is more than 6.5 percent, and pay L. So in effect it will pay a floating-rate loan of less than LIBOR.

In this example, we showed how a swaption is used to create a swap. Similarly, a swaption can be used to terminate a swap.

5.2 Using an Interest Rate Swaption to Terminate a Swap

When a company enters a swap, it knows it may need to terminate the swap before the expiration day. It can do so by either entering an offsetting swap or buying a swaption.

As with any over-the-counter option, the holder of a swap can terminate the swap by entering into an identical swap from the opposite perspective at whatever rate exists in the market. Consider, for example, a Japanese company that enters into a five-year ¥800 million notional principal swap in which it pays a fixed rate and receives a floating rate; that is, it enters a pay-fixed swap. Two years later, the company wants to terminate the swap. It can do so by entering into a new swap with a notional principal of ¥800 million, a remaining life of three years, and with the company paying the floating rate and receiving the fixed rate. If it engages in this swap with a different counterparty than the counterparty of the original swap, then both swaps would remain in place, but the floating payments would be equivalent. The net effect would be that the company would make a stream of fixed payments at one rate and receive a stream of fixed payments at another rate. The rate that is greater depends on the course of interest rates since the time the original swap was put into place. If the new swap is done with the same counterparty as in the original swap, the two parties would likely agree to offset and eliminate both swaps. Then one party would be paying the other a lump sum of the present value of the difference between the two streams of fixed payments. If the company offsets the swap with a new swap in this manner, it must accept the conditions in the market at the time it offsets the swap.

The second way of terminating a swap is for a company to buy a swaption before it wants to offset the swap. Suppose that when this Japanese company enters into a pay-fixed, receive-floating swap, it also purchases a receiver swaption that allows it to enter into an ¥800 million swap to receive fixed and pay floating with the same terms as the original swap. The swaption exercise rate is 8 percent. The company must pay cash up front for the swaption, but it then has the right to enter into a new swap to receive a fixed rate of 8 percent and pay the floating rate. We assume for maximum flexibility that the swaption is structured as an American-style option, allowing the company to exercise it at any time. We also assume that the swaption counterparty is the counterparty to the swap, so that if the swaption is exercised, the payments can be canceled and replaced by a lump sum payment.

Consider this example. Internet Marketing Solutions (IMS) takes out a $20 million one-year loan with quarterly floating payments at LIBOR from a lender called Financial Solutions (FINSOLS). Fearing an increase in interest rates, IMS engages in a pay-fixed, receive-floating swap that converts the loan into a fixed-rate loan at 8 percent. IMS believes, however, that the interest rate outlook could change, and it would like the flexibility to terminate the swap, thereby returning to the status of a floating-rate payer. To give it this flexibility, IMS purchases an American-style receiver swaption for $515,000. The swaption allows it to enter into a receive-fixed, pay-floating swap at a fixed rate of 8 percent at the swaption expiration. The swap and swaption counterparty is Wheatstone Dealer (WHD).

Exhibit 8-13 illustrates this transaction. In Panel A, IMS takes out the loan from FINSOLS, receiving $20 million. It engages in the swap with WHD, thereby committing to pay fixed and receive LIBOR. There are no cash flows at the start of the swap contract, but IMS pays WHD $515,000 for the swaption. Now let us move to the expiration of the swaption, at which time we shall assume that IMS is no longer concerned about rising interest rates and would like to return to the status of a floating-rate borrower. In Panel B(i), at the expiration of the swaption, the market swap rate is greater than or equal to 8 percent. This panel shows the cash flows if the loan plus swap (note that the loan is floating rate) is converted to a fixed rate using the market fixed rate because the swaption is out-of-the-money. IMS makes interest payments of LIBOR(90/360)$20 million to FINSOLS. IMS makes a swap payment of 8 percent, which is $400,000, to WHD, which pays LIBOR.[31] Thus, to offset the effect of the pay-fixed swap, IMS is better off entering a new swap rather than exercising its swaption. IMS then enters into a swap to receive the market fixed rate, FS, which is greater than or equal to 8 percent, and pay LIBOR. IMS is, in effect, paying a floating rate less than LIBOR (or equal to LIBOR if the market swap rate is exactly 8 percent).[32]

In Panel B(ii), the market swap rate is less than 8 percent and the loan is converted back to a floating-rate loan by exercising the swaption. IMS makes loan interest payments at LIBOR to FINSOLS and swap payment of 8 percent or $400,000 to WHD, which pays LIBOR. Exercise of the swaption results in IMS entering into a swap to receive a fixed rate of 8 percent and pay a floating rate of LIBOR. The swap and swaption would probably be structured to offset and terminate both swaps. At the end of the transaction, the loan is paid off and there are no payments on the swap or swaption. If IMS wants to continue as a fixed-rate payer, the swaption would still be exercised if it is in-the-money but not if it is out-of-the-money.

We see that the swaption offers the holder the opportunity to terminate the swap at the exercise rate or better. Because the swaption is American style, a variety of complex issues are involved in the exercise decision, but let us focus on the moneyness and the holder's view of market conditions. If a borrower feels that rates will fall, it would then want to convert its pay-fixed position to a pay-floating position. If the market rate is more than the exercise rate, the borrower can do so by entering into a swap at the market rate. It can then receive more than the exercise rate, which more than offsets the rate it pays on the swap. The borrower would then effectively be paying less than LIBOR. If the rate in the market is less than the exercise rate, the borrower can exercise the swaption, thereby receiving the exercise rate to offset the rate it pays on the swap. Alternatively, it can choose to continue paying a floating rate but can still exercise the swaption if doing so is optimal.

As we previously described, swaptions are equivalent to options on bonds. A payer swaption is equivalent to a put option on a bond, and a receiver swaption is equivalent to a call option on a bond. The interest rate swaptions market is a very liquid one, and many companies use swaptions as substitutes for options on bonds. Any strategy that one might apply with options on bonds can be applied with swaptions. We shall not go over the myriad of such strategies, as they have been covered extensively in other literature. We shall, however, look at a particular one, in which a swaption can be used to substitute for a callable bond.

---

[31] In practice, the two parties would net the difference and have one party pay the other.

[32] In practice, IMS might choose to not enter into the swap at the market fixed rate and just carry the old swap to reduce the cost of the loan.

EXHIBIT 8-13   Using an American-Style Swaption to Terminate a Swap

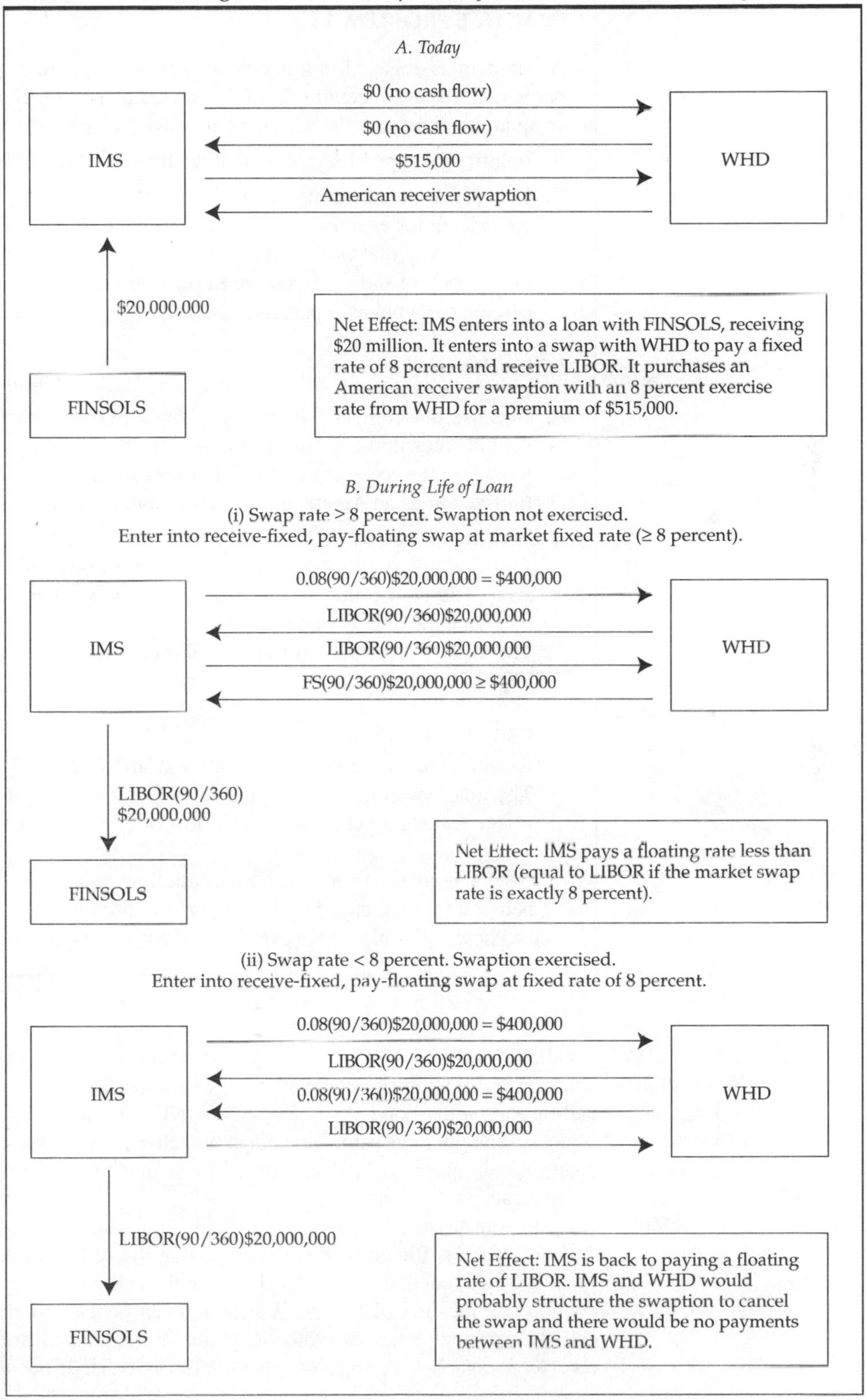

A. Today

IMS → WHD: $0 (no cash flow)

WHD → IMS: $0 (no cash flow)

IMS → WHD: $515,000

WHD → IMS: American receiver swaption

FINSOLS → IMS: $20,000,000

> Net Effect: IMS enters into a loan with FINSOLS, receiving $20 million. It enters into a swap with WHD to pay a fixed rate of 8 percent and receive LIBOR. It purchases an American receiver swaption with an 8 percent exercise rate from WHD for a premium of $515,000.

B. During Life of Loan

(i) Swap rate > 8 percent. Swaption not exercised.
Enter into receive-fixed, pay-floating swap at market fixed rate (≥ 8 percent).

IMS → WHD: $0.08(90/360)\$20,000,000 = \$400,000$

WHD → IMS: LIBOR(90/360)$20,000,000

IMS → WHD: LIBOR(90/360)$20,000,000

WHD → IMS: FS(90/360)$20,000,000 ≥ $400,000

IMS → FINSOLS: LIBOR(90/360) $20,000,000

> Net Effect: IMS pays a floating rate less than LIBOR (equal to LIBOR if the market swap rate is exactly 8 percent).

(ii) Swap rate < 8 percent. Swaption exercised.
Enter into receive-fixed, pay-floating swap at fixed rate of 8 percent.

IMS → WHD: $0.08(90/360)\$20,000,000 = \$400,000$

WHD → IMS: LIBOR(90/360)$20,000,000

WHD → IMS: $0.08(90/360)\$20,000,000 = \$400,000$

IMS → WHD: LIBOR(90/360)$20,000,000

IMS → FINSOLS: LIBOR(90/360)$20,000,000

> Net Effect: IMS is back to paying a floating rate of LIBOR. IMS and WHD would probably structure the swaption to cancel the swap and there would be no payments between IMS and WHD.

PRACTICE PROBLEM 13

A company is engaged in a two-year swap with quarterly payments. It is paying 6 percent fixed and receiving LIBOR. It would like the flexibility to terminate the swap at any time prior to the end of the two-year period.

A. Identify the type of swaption that would achieve this objective.

B. Consider a time t during this two-year life of the swaption in which it is being considered for exercise. Use a 7 percent exercise rate. The fixed rate in the market on a swap that would offset the existing swap is denoted as $FS(t,2)$. Examine the payoffs of the swaption based on whether $FS(t,2)$ is 1) equal to or above 7 percent or 2) below 7 percent.

SOLUTIONS

A. Because the company is paying a fixed rate and receiving a floating rate, it should enter into a swap to receive a fixed rate and pay a floating rate. It thus would want a receiver swaption. For maximum flexibility, it should structure the transaction as an American-style swaption.

B. $FS(t,2) \geq 7$ percent
   The swaption is out-of-the-money and is not exercised. To terminate the existing swap, one would enter into a swap at the market rate. This swap would involve receiving the market rate $FS(t,2)$, which is at least 7 percent, and paying LIBOR. The LIBOR payments offset, and the net effect is a net positive cash flow of $FS(t,2) - 6$ percent.

   $FS(t,2) < 7$ percent
   Exercise the swaption, entering into a swap to receive 7 percent and pay LIBOR. The other swap involves paying 6 percent and receiving LIBOR. The LIBORs offset, leaving a net positive cash flow of $7 - 6 = 1$ percent.

   Note: It is not necessary that the net cash flow be positive. The positive net cash flow here is a result of choosing a 7 percent exercise rate, but a lower exercise rate could be chosen. The higher the exercise rate, the more expensive the receiver swaption.

5.3 SYNTHETICALLY REMOVING (ADDING) A CALL FEATURE IN CALLABLE (NONCALLABLE) DEBT

A callable bond is a bond in which the issuer has the right to retire it early. The issuer has considerable flexibility to take advantage of declining interest rates. This feature is like a call option on the bond. As interest rates fall, bond prices rise. By calling the bond, the issuer essentially buys back the bond at predetermined terms, making it equivalent to exercising a call option to buy the bond. The issuer pays for this right by paying a higher coupon rate on the bond.

In some cases, the issuer of a callable bond may find that it no longer expects interest rates to fall sufficiently over the remaining life of the bond to justify calling the bond. Then it would feel that it is not likely to use the call feature, but it is still paying the higher coupon rate for the call feature. A swaption can be used to effectively sell the embedded call. This strategy involves synthetically removing the call from callable debt by selling a receiver swaption.[33] A receiver swaption (receive fixed) becomes more valuable as rates

---

[33] This strategy is sometimes referred to as *monetizing* a call.

decline, thus balancing the short call. In effect, the call feature is sold for cash. Recall that a receiver swaption is like a call option on a bond. Because the issuer of the callable bond holds a call on the bond, it would need to sell a call to offset the call embedded in the debt. It can effectively do so by selling a receiver swaption. This swaption will not cancel the bond's call feature. Both options will be in force, but both options should behave identically. If the call feature is worth exercising, so should the swaption. Let us see how this strategy works.

5.3.1   SYNTHETICALLY REMOVING THE CALL FROM CALLABLE DEBT

Several years ago, Chemical Industries (CHEMIND) issued a callable $20 million face value bond that pays a fixed rate of 8 percent interest semiannually. The bond now has five years until maturity. CHEMIND does not believe it is likely to call the bond for the next two years and would like to effectively eliminate the call feature during that time. To simplify the problem somewhat, we shall assume that the bond would be called only in exactly two years and not any time sooner. Thus, CHEMIND can manage this problem by selling a European swaption that would expire in two years.[34] Because the bond would have a three-year life when it is called, the swap underlying the swaption would be a three-year swap. It would also be a swap to receive fixed and pay floating, with payment dates aligned with the interest payment dates on the bond.

Let us suppose that the 8 percent rate CHEMIND is paying on the bond includes a credit spread of 2.5 percent, which should be viewed as a credit premium paid over the LIBOR par rate. CHEMIND is paying 2.5 percent for the credit risk it poses for the holder of the bond. On the receiver swaption it wants to sell, CHEMIND must set the exercise rate at $8 - 2.5 = 5.5$ percent. Note that the credit spread is not part of the exercise rate. The swaption can be used to manage only the risk of interest rate changes driven by the term structure and not credit. We are assuming no change in CHEMIND's credit risk. Hence, it will continue to pay the credit spread in the rate on the new bond that it issues if it calls the old bond.

The swaption dealer, Top Swaps (TSWAPS), prices the swaption at $425,000. The strategy is illustrated in Exhibit 8-14.

Panel A shows that CHEMIND receives $425,000 from selling the receiver swaption to dealer TSWAPS. This cash effectively reduces its remaining interest payments on the bond. In Panel B, we see what happens at the swaption expiration in two years. Remember that the swaption is identical to a call option on the bond, so if the swaption is exercised, the call on the bond will be exercised at the same time. Let FS(2,5) be the fixed rate at the swaption expiration on a three-year swap. We first assume that FS(2,5) is greater than or equal to the exercise rate on the swaption of 5.5 percent. Because interest rates have not fallen below 5.5 percent, it is unprofitable to exercise the swaption or call the bond. CHEMIND continues making interest payments of 8 percent on $20 million, which is $800,000 semiannually for three more years. Panel B(i) illustrates this outcome.

In Panel B(ii), we let FS(2,5) be less than 5.5 percent. Then the swaption will be exercised and the bond will be called. To fund the bond call, a new bond will be issued at a rate of FS(2,5) plus the credit spread of 2.5 percent, which we assume has not changed. The swaption is exercised, so CHEMIND is obligated to enter into a swap to pay 5.5 percent and receive LIBOR. Now, however, CHEMIND is receiving LIBOR and making fixed payments to its bondholders and to TSWAPS. It can reverse the LIBOR flow by entering into a swap at the market rate of FS(2,5). In other words, it enters into a new swap to receive FS(2,5) and pay LIBOR. Note from the figure that it receives LIBOR and pays

---

[34] CHEMIND might prefer an American swaption to give it the flexibility to exercise at any time, but we simplify the problem a little and use a European swaption.

EXHIBIT 8-14   Selling a Receiver Swaption to Offset the Call Feature on a Bond

A. Today; During Life of the Bond

$425,000

| CHEMIND | ← European receiver swaption → | TSWAPS |

Net Effect: CHEMIND currently making interest payments of $20,000,000(0.08/2) = $800,000 semiannually on a bond with five years remaining. This rate includes a credit spread of 2.5 percent. CHEMIND sells two-year receiver swaption with exercise rate of 5.5 percent to dealer TSWAPS for $425,000 with underlying being a three-year swap. Swaption premium effectively reduces rate on bond, making it equivalent to rate on noncallable bond instead of callable bond.

B. At Expiration of the Swaption

(i) If FS(2,5) (Market rate on underlying swap) ≥ 5.5 percent

| CHEMIND | (Swaption expires out of the money; no cash flows) | TSWAPS |

Interest payments of
$20,000,000(0.08/2)
= $800,000 semiannually
for three more years
↓

| Bondholders |

Net Effect: CHEMIND continues paying fixed rate of 8 percent.

(ii) If FS(2,5) (Market rate on underlying swap) < 5.5 percent

$20,000,000(0.055)(180/360) = $550,000 →
LIBOR
| CHEMIND | ← $20,000,000[FS(2,5)](180/360) | TSWAPS |
LIBOR →

Bond called and new bond issued.
Interest payments of $20,000,000
(FS(2,5) + 0.025)/2 semiannually
for three years.
↓

| Bondholders |

Net Effect: CHEMIND calls bond and issues new bond at FS(2,5) + credit spread of 2.5 percent. Swaption exercised so CHEMIND forced to enter into swap to pay 5.5 percent and receive LIBOR. CHEMIND enters into swap in market to pay LIBOR and receive FS(2,5). CHEMIND effectively pays 5.5 + 2.5 = 8 percent, equivalent to noncallable bond.

LIBOR. These two flows would likely be canceled. CHEMIND makes fixed swap payments at a rate of 5.5 percent and receives fixed swap payments at a rate of FS(2,5), which is 250 basis points (the credit spread) less than the rate on the new fixed rate bond it has issued. These payments at the rate FS(2,5) offset all but the credit spread portion of the interest payments on its loan. CHEMIND then effectively pays a fixed rate of 5.5 percent, the swaption exercise rate, plus 2.5 percent, the credit spread. So, CHEMIND ends up paying 8 percent, the same as the rate on the original debt. The swaption has effectively converted the callable bond into a noncallable bond by removing the call feature from the bond. It hopes that this outcome, in which the bond is called and the swaption is exercised, does not occur, or it will regret having removed the call feature. Nonetheless, it received cash up front for the swaption and is paying a lower effective interest rate as it would had the bond been noncallable in the first place, so it must accept this risk.

5.3.2 SYNTHETICALLY ADDING A CALL TO NONCALLABLE DEBT

If a swaption can undo a call feature, it can also add a call feature. Market Solutions, Inc. (MSI) has a $40 million noncallable bond outstanding at a rate of 9 percent paid semiannually with three more years remaining. Anticipating the possibility of declining interest rates in about one year, MSI wishes this bond were callable. It can synthetically add the call feature by purchasing a receiver swaption. A receiver swaption is equivalent to a call option on a bond because the option to receive a fixed rate increases in value as rates decline. By purchasing the receiver swaption, it has in effect purchased an option on the bond.

To structure the receiver swaption properly, MSI notes that the interest rate it is paying on the bond includes a credit spread of 3 percent over the par bond rate from the LIBOR term structure. It should set the exercise rate on the swaption at $9 - 3 = 6$ percent. The swaption will be on a two-year swap with payment dates coinciding with the interest payment dates on the bond. The notional principal will be the $40 million face value on the bond. To simplify the problem, we assume a European swaption, meaning that the only time MSI will consider exercising the swaption or calling the bond will be in exactly one year, with the bond having two years to maturity at that time. The swaption will cost $625,000, and the counterparty dealer will be Swap Shop (SWSHP). Exhibit 8-15 illustrates the transaction.

In Panel A, we see MSI paying $625,000 for the swaption. This cost effectively raises the interest rate MSI pays on the bond to that of a callable bond. Panel B(i) illustrates the case in which the fixed rate on the underlying swap, FS(1,3), is greater than or equal to the exercise rate on the swaption at the swaption expiration. Remember that if market conditions are such that the swaption would be exercised, then the bond would be called. In this case, however, interest rates are not low enough to justify exercise of the swaption or calling of the bond. MSI will continue making its 9 percent interest payments on the bond.

In Panel B(ii), we let FS(1,3) be less than 6 percent. Then MSI will exercise the swaption, thereby entering into a swap to pay LIBOR and receive 6 percent. Note, however, that it is receiving a fixed rate of 6 percent, paying a fixed rate of 9 percent, and paying LIBOR. Here, this transaction is not equivalent to it having called the bond, because MSI makes floating payments. To offset the floating payments, it enters into a new swap in the market at the market rate of FS(1,3). Specifically, it pays FS(1,3) and receives LIBOR. The two streams of LIBOR payments would offset and would probably be canceled, leaving an inflow of 6 percent and an outflow of FS(1,3) on the swaps and an outflow of 9 percent on the bond. The net effect would be an outflow of FS(1,3) plus 3 percent. Because FS(1,3) is below 6 percent, the overall rate paid is below 9 percent, thereby making this position similar to that of a bond that has been called, with a new bond issued in its place at a lower rate.

So we see that a swaption can be used to replicate the call feature on a callable bond. A swaption can synthetically add a call feature when it does not exist or offset a call feature that does exist. The cash paid or received from the swaption occurs all at once, but if allocated appropriately over time, it would be equivalent to the additional amount of interest that a borrower pays for the call feature. Of course, there are some tricky elements to making this strategy work. We have ignored taxes and transaction costs, which can affect exercise and call decisions. Also, when the swaption is held by another party, there is no guarantee that exercise will occur at the optimal time.

EXHIBIT 8-15   Buying a Receiver Swaption to Add a Call Feature to a Bond

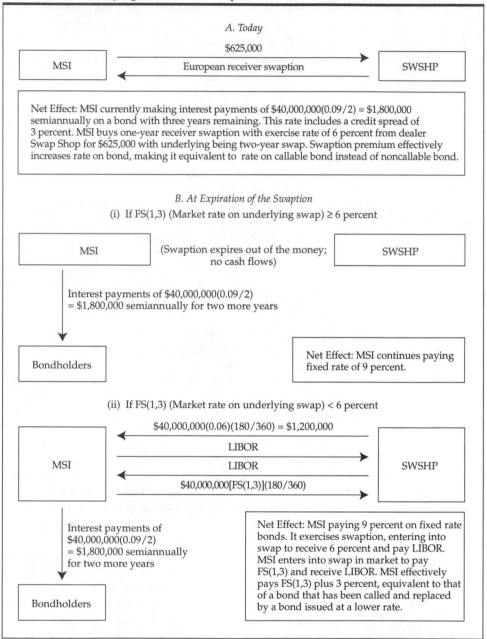

A. Today

$625,000

MSI ────────────────────────→ SWSHP
     European receiver swaption

Net Effect: MSI currently making interest payments of $40,000,000(0.09/2) = $1,800,000 semiannually on a bond with three years remaining. This rate includes a credit spread of 3 percent. MSI buys one-year receiver swaption with exercise rate of 6 percent from dealer Swap Shop for $625,000 with underlying being two-year swap. Swaption premium effectively increases rate on bond, making it equivalent to rate on callable bond instead of noncallable bond.

B. At Expiration of the Swaption

(i) If FS(1,3) (Market rate on underlying swap) ≥ 6 percent

MSI   (Swaption expires out of the money;   SWSHP
          no cash flows)

Interest payments of $40,000,000(0.09/2)
= $1,800,000 semiannually for two more years

Bondholders

Net Effect: MSI continues paying fixed rate of 9 percent.

(ii) If FS(1,3) (Market rate on underlying swap) < 6 percent

$40,000,000(0.06)(180/360) = $1,200,000

MSI   LIBOR   SWSHP
          LIBOR
     $40,000,000[FS(1,3)](180/360)

Interest payments of $40,000,000(0.09/2) = $1,800,000 semiannually for two more years

Bondholders

Net Effect: MSI paying 9 percent on fixed rate bonds. It exercises swaption, entering into swap to receive 6 percent and pay LIBOR. MSI enters into swap in market to pay FS(1,3) and receive LIBOR. MSI effectively pays FS(1,3) plus 3 percent, equivalent to that of a bond that has been called and replaced by a bond issued at a lower rate.

PRACTICE PROBLEM 14

A German company issues a five-year noncallable bond with a face value of €40 million. The bond pays a coupon annually of 10 percent, of which 3 percent is estimated to be a credit premium.

A. The company would like to make the bond callable in exactly two years. Design a strategy using a European swaption that will achieve this goal. When the swaption expires, the fixed rate on the underlying swap will be denoted as FS(2,5).

Evaluate what happens when this rate is at least the exercise rate and also when it is less than the exercise rate.

B. Reconsider the bond described above and assume it was actually issued as a callable bond with a 10 percent coupon. Construct a swaption strategy that will synthetically remove the call feature. As in Part A, let the swaption expire in two years and evaluate the outcomes.

SOLUTIONS

A. To synthetically add the call feature to this bond, the company should purchase a receiver swaption. The exercise rate should be the coupon rate on the bond minus the credit premium: $10 - 3 - 7$ percent. At the swaption expiration, we have the following outcomes:

> $FS(2,5) \geq 7$ percent
>
> The swaption will not be exercised, and the bond will not be called. The company continues to pay 10 percent on its bond.

> $FS(2,5) < 7$ percent
>
> The swaption is exercised.
>> Enter into swap
>> Receive 7 percent
>> Pay LIBOR
>
> Enter into a new swap at the market rate.
>> Receive LIBOR
>> Pay $FS(2,5)$
>> Company continues to pay 10 percent on its bond
>
> Net effect: Pay $FS(2,5) + 10\% - 7\% =$ Pay $FS(2,5) + 3\% < 10\%$

The company has thus effectively issued a new bond at a lower rate. The option premium, however, effectively raised the coupon rate on the old bond to that of a callable bond.

B. To synthetically remove the call feature on this bond, the company should sell a receiver swaption. The exercise rate should be the coupon rate on the bond minus the credit premium: $10 - 3 = 7$ percent. At the swaption expiration, we have the following outcomes:

> $FS(2,5) \geq 7$ percent
>
> The swaption will not be exercised. The company continues to pay 10 percent on its bond.

> $FS(2,5) < 7$ percent
>
> The swaption is exercised.
>> Enter into swap
>> Receive LIBOR
>> Pay 7 percent
>
> Enter into a new swap at the market rate.
>> Receive $FS(2,5)$

> Pay LIBOR
>
> Bond called. Issue new bond at FS(2,5) + 3%
>
> Net effect: Pay FS(2,5) + 3% + 7% − FS(2,5) = 10%
>
> Therefore, if the company sells the receiver swaption, the bond's call option is offset and effectively removed. The option premium, received up front, effectively reduces the coupon rate on the outstanding bond to make it equivalent to that of a noncallable bond.

Finally, you may be wondering why a receiver swaption was used in these strategies. Why not a payer swaption? Remember that a call feature on a bond is a call option. To add or offset a call feature, we need to use an instrument equivalent to a call option. A receiver swaption is equivalent to a call option. A payer swaption is equivalent to a put option. Payer swaptions would be useful in situations involving put features. Putable bonds do exist but are not particularly common. A putable bond allows the bondholder to sell the bond back, usually at par, to the issuer. Therefore, the option, which is a put, is held by the bondholder and sold by the bond issuer. If a bond is putable, the coupon rate on the bond would be lower. If the issuer of the bond wanted to synthetically add a put to an otherwise nonputable bond, it would sell a payer swaption. The premium received would effectively lower the coupon rate on the bond. If the issuer of a putable bond wanted to eliminate the put, it would buy a payer swaption. This would give it the right to exercise the swaption, which is a put on the bond, at the same time as the put feature would be exercised by the holder of the bond. Again, we note that put features are not common, and we shall not pursue this strategy here.

5.4   A Note on Forward Swaps

In Chapter 5 we briefly mentioned that there are also forward contracts on swaps. Called forward swaps, these instruments are commitments to enter into swaps. They do not require a cash payment at the start but force the parties to enter into a swap at a later date at terms, including the fixed rate, set at the start. Although we shall not examine forward swap strategies, note that the same strategies examined in this section can all be used with forward swaps.

6   CONCLUSIONS

In concluding this chapter, we have now examined all of the derivatives strategies introduced in this book. In Chapters 2 though 5, we looked at four types of instruments (forwards, futures, options, and swaps) and learned how to price them. In Chapters 6 through 8, we saw how to use them in strategies. These instruments are designed to manage risk. Managing risk involves the buying and selling of risk, perhaps to increase the overall level of one's risk or perhaps to offset an existing risk. As we have seen, these instruments are highly leveraged. As you can imagine, proper use of derivatives requires a significant amount of expertise. More importantly, however, monitoring and control are essential ingredients for the proper use of derivatives. Managing risk is the primary justification for the use of derivatives. So far, we have focused on markets, instruments, and strategies. We have not said much about the *process* of risk management and to that end, we move into our final chapter. In it, we shall look at risk management; what it is, and why and how companies practice it. In the course of doing so, we shall encounter some new techniques and strategies that do not fall neatly into the categories we have covered so far.

KEY POINTS

- A floating-rate loan can be converted to a fixed-rate loan by entering into an interest rate swap to pay a fixed rate and receive a floating rate. The floating cash flows offset, leaving the borrower with a net fixed payment. Likewise, a fixed-rate loan can be converted to a floating-rate loan by entering into an interest rate swap to pay a floating rate and receive a fixed rate. The fixed cash flows offset, leaving the party paying a floating rate.

- To obtain the duration of an interest rate swap, consider the difference between the duration of a fixed-rate bond and the duration of a floating-rate bond. The latter is close to zero, leaving the duration of an interest rate swap close to that of a fixed-rate bond. If the party pays a fixed rate and receives a floating rate, the duration of the position is that of the equivalent floating-rate bond minus that of the equivalent fixed-rate bond.

- When a floating-rate loan is converted to a fixed-rate loan, the resulting duration is that of a fixed-rate loan. The duration of a fixed-rate loan is normally much higher than that of a floating-rate loan, which has a duration relatively close to zero. Compared with a floating-rate loan, however, a fixed-rate loan has stable cash flows, which reduce cash flow risk, but has a much greater duration, which increases market value risk.

- The notional principal on an interest rate swap added to a position to adjust its overall duration is determined by the existing duration of the portfolio, the duration of the swap, the desired duration, and the market value of the portfolio. A swap can be used to change the duration of the position without changing the market value.

- An interest rate swap can be used to manage the risk related to a structured note with a coupon at a multiple of a floating rate by adjusting the notional principal on the swap to reflect the coupon multiple for the structured note. The swap should be a receive-floating, pay-fixed swap.

- An interest rate swap can be used to manage the risk of the issuance of an inverse floating-rate note by paying the floating rate to the swap dealer. When interest rates rise (fall), the inverse floater payments decrease (increase), and this effect is passed on to the dealer, which in turn pays a fixed rate.

- A loan in one currency can be converted into a loan in another currency by entering into a currency swap in which it pays interest in one currency and receives interest in the currency in which it makes its loan interest payments. This strategy leaves the borrower paying interest in a different currency than the one in which the loan interest is paid. To offset the principal payment, the currency swap should provide for payment of the notional principal as well.

- Converting a loan in one currency into a loan in another using a currency swap can offer savings because a borrower can normally issue debt at a more attractive rate in its own currency. By entering into a swap with a dealer that can operate more efficiently in global markets, the borrower can effectively convert its domestic debt into foreign debt. In addition, by engaging in the currency swap rather than borrowing in the desired currency in the first place, the borrower takes on a small amount of credit risk that can generate savings if no default takes place.

- The party to a currency swap would make the payments be fixed or floating depending on whether a loan paired with the currency swap is made at a fixed or floating rate and whether the party wants to make payments at a fixed or floating rate. This decision is usually made based on the expected direction of interest rates.

- A series of foreign cash receipts can be combined with a currency swap with no notional principal payments to convert the receipts into domestic currency cash flows. The foreign interest payments on the currency swap must equal the amounts of the foreign cash flows.

- In a dual-currency bond, the interest is paid in one currency and the principal is paid in another. A borrower issuing a dual-currency bond can use the proceeds to buy a bond denominated in the currency of the principal repayment on the dual-currency bond. It can then enter into a currency swap with no notional principal payment, enabling it to fund the interest payments from the dual-currency bond in one currency and make interest payments in another currency.

- An equity swap can be used to provide diversification to a concentrated portfolio by having the party pay the return on the stock that makes up too large a portion of the portfolio and receive the return on a diversified market proxy.

- An equity swap can add international diversification to a domestic portfolio by having the party pay the return on a domestic market benchmark and receive the return on an international market benchmark.

- An equity swap can be used to change the allocation between stock and bond asset classes by having the party pay the return on the asset class in which it wants to reduce its exposure and receive the return on the asset class in which it wants to increase its exposure.

- A corporate insider can use an equity swap to reduce exposure to his company by paying the return on the company's stock and receiving the return on a diversified portfolio benchmark or a fixed- or floating-rate interest payment.

- There can be important implications if corporate insiders use equity swaps. Insiders can reduce their exposure without giving up their voting rights, which can lead to significant agency costs. Although it is clearly necessary for investors and analysts to gauge the exposure of corporate insiders, equity swaps can make this task more difficult.

- Equity swaps pose some difficulties not faced in interest rate and currency swaps. In particular, equity swaps can generate significant cash flow problems, resulting from the fact that equity returns can be negative, meaning that one party can be required to make both sides of payments. In addition, equity swaps can involve tracking error, in which the swap returns, which are pegged to an index, do not match the returns on the actual equity portfolio that is combined with the swap.

- A party would use an interest rate swaption if it anticipates taking out a loan at a future date and entering into a swap to convert the loan from floating rate to fixed rate or vice versa. The swaption gives the party the right to enter into the swap at a specific fixed rate or better. The cost of this flexibility is the swaption premium paid up front.

- An interest rate swaption can be used to provide a means of terminating a swap at a favorable rate. A party engaged in a swap can use a swap with the opposite cash flows to effectively terminate the position. By purchasing a swaption, the party can enter into this swap at a specific rate, established in advance, or take a better rate as given in the market.

- An interest rate receiver swaption is equivalent to a call option on a bond. A party that has issued a callable bond and believes it will not call the bond can sell an interest rate receiver swaption to offset the call feature. The swaption premium received at the start offsets the higher coupon paid for the call feature on the bond. If interest rates fall enough to trigger the bond being called, the swaption will also be exercised. The party must enter into the underlying swap and can enter into an opposite swap at the market rate. The net effect is that the party ends up paying the same rate it would have paid if it had not called the bond.

• A party that has issued a noncallable bond can synthetically add a call feature by purchasing an interest rate receiver swaption. The premium paid for the swaption effectively raises the coupon rate on the bond. If rates fall sufficiently, the receiver swaption is exercised and the party enters into the underlying swap. The party then enters into a swap in the market at the market rate. The net effect is that the party pays a lower fixed rate, as though the bond had been called.

PROBLEMS

1. A company has issued floating-rate notes with a maturity of one year, an interest rate of LIBOR plus 125 basis points, and total face value of $50 million. The company now believes that interest rates will rise and wishes to protect itself by entering into an interest rate swap. A dealer provides a quote on a swap in which the company will pay a fixed rate 6.5 percent and receive LIBOR. Interest is paid quarterly, and the current LIBOR is 5 percent. Indicate how the company can use a swap to convert the debt to a fixed rate. Calculate the overall net payment (including the loan) by the company. Assume that all payments will be made on the basis of 90/360.

2. A bank is currently lending $10 million at an interest rate of LIBOR plus 50 basis points. The loan maturity is two years, and the loan calls for quarterly payments. The bank expects interest rates to fall and wishes to hedge against this by entering into an interest rate swap. A dealer provides a quote on a swap in which the bank will receive a fixed payment of 5 percent and pay a floating rate of LIBOR. Calculate the overall net payment by the bank if it enters the swap. Assume that all payments will be made on the basis of 90/360.

3. **A.** Calculate the duration of a five-year pay-fixed, receive-floating swap with quarterly payments. Assume the duration of a fixed-rate bond is 75 percent of its maturity.
   B. Calculate the duration of a three-year pay-floating, receive-fixed swap with semi-annual payments.

4. Assume that you manage a $100 million bond portfolio with a duration of 1.5 years. You wish to increase the duration of the bond portfolio to 3.5 years by using a swap. Assume the duration of a fixed-rate bond is 75 percent of its maturity.
   A. Discuss whether the swap you enter into should involve paying fixed, receiving floating or paying floating, receiving fixed.
   B. Would you prefer a four-year swap with quarterly payments or a three-year swap with semiannual payments?
   C. Determine the notional principal of the swap you would prefer.

5. A company issues a leveraged floating-rate note with a face value of $5,000,000 that pays a coupon of 2.5 times LIBOR. The company plans to generate a profit by selling the notes, using the proceeds to purchase a bond with a fixed coupon rate of 7 percent a year, and hedging the risk by entering into an appropriate swap. A swap dealer provides a quote with a fixed rate of 6 percent and a floating rate of LIBOR. Discuss whether the company should enter into a swap involving paying fixed, receiving floating or paying floating, receiving fixed. Calculate the amount of the arbitrage profit the company can earn by entering into the appropriate swap. In your answer, indicate the cash flows generated at each step. Also explain what additional risk the company is taking on by doing the swap.

6. A company issues an inverse floater with a face value of $20,000,000 that pays a coupon of 13 percent minus LIBOR. The company plans to earn a profit by selling the notes, using the proceeds to purchase a bond with a fixed coupon rate of 7.5 percent a year, and hedging the risk by entering into an appropriate swap. A swap dealer provides a quote with a fixed rate of 6.5 percent and a floating rate of LIBOR. Discuss whether the company should enter into a swap involving paying fixed, receiving floating or paying floating, receiving fixed. Calculate the amount of the arbitrage profit the company can earn by entering into the appropriate swap. In your answer, indicate the cash flows generated at each step. Also explain what additional risk the company is taking on.

7. A German corporation needs to raise $115,000,000 to expand production facilities in the United States. Because the company is not well known in the United States, it is hesitant to issue dollar-denominated bonds there. If the company issues euro denominated bonds in Germany, it can get a coupon rate of 6.25 percent. The fixed rate on euro-denominated swaps is 5.5 percent, and the fixed rate on dollar-denominated swaps is 2.5 percent. Indicate how the German company can use a currency swap to achieve its objective of raising $115,000,000. Indicate the cash flows that take place at the inception of the swap, during the tenure of the swap, and at the end of the life of the swap. The exchange rate is $1.15/€. Assume annual payments.

8. A U.S. company needs to raise €100,000,000. It plans to raise this money by issuing dollar-denominated bonds and using a currency swap to convert the dollars to euros. The company expects interest rates in both the United States and the eurozone to fall.
   A. Should the swap be structured with interest paid at a fixed or a floating rate?
   B. Should the swap be structured with interest received at a fixed or a floating rate?

9. A company based in the United Kingdom has a German subsidiary. The subsidiary generates €15,000,000 a year, received in equivalent semiannual installments of €7,500,000. The British company wishes to convert the euro cash flows to pounds twice a year. It plans to engage in a currency swap in order to lock in the exchange rate at which it can convert the euros to pounds. The current exchange rate is €1.5/£. The fixed rate on a plain vanilla currency swap in pounds is 7.5 percent per year, and the fixed rate on a plain vanilla currency swap in euros is 6.5 percent per year.
   A. Determine the notional principals in euros and pounds for a swap with semiannual payments that will help achieve the objective.
   B. Determine the semiannual cash flows from this swap.

10. Consider a company that issues a dual-currency bond with a face value of €45,000,000, which pays an interest rate of 3.5 percent a year in dollars. Indicate how the company can manage the risk on this bond issue, and calculate the net cash flows associated with the transactions. You also have the following additional information: A bond with a face value of €45,000,000 that pays 5 percent annual interest in euros is available for purchase; the fixed rates on a currency swap are 4 percent in dollars and 4.75 percent in euros; and the exchange rate is €1.15/$.

11. You wish to synthetically construct a dual-currency bond with a face value of £25,000,000 that pays interest annually in euros. You can issue a domestic bond with a face value of £25,000,000 that pays interest of 5 percent a year in pounds. The fixed rates on a currency swap are 5.25 percent in pounds and 4.25 percent in euros. The exchange rate is £0.65/€. Indicate how you would go about constructing the synthetic dual-currency bond, and calculate the net cash flows associated with the transactions.

12. A portfolio has a total market value of £100,000,000. The portfolio is allocated as follows: Sixty percent is invested in a broadly diversified portfolio of domestic stocks, and 40 percent is invested in the stock of the INV Corporation, which is currently selling for £30 per share. The portfolio manager wishes to reduce exposure to the INV stock to 25 percent of the overall portfolio. He plans to achieve this objective by entering into a two-year equity swap, which will use the FTSE 100 Index. Assume that settlement is made at the end of each year. Also assume that after one year, the return on the INV stock is 5 percent and the return on the FTSE 100 market index is 6 percent.
   A. Explain the structure of the equity swap.
   B. Calculate the net cash flow for the swap at the end of one year.
   C. Discuss some problems the manager might encounter with the swap.

13. A portfolio has a total market value of $105,000,000. The portfolio is allocated as follows: $65,000,000 is invested in a broadly diversified portfolio of domestic stocks, and

$40,000,000 is invested in the stock of the JK Corporation. The portfolio manager wishes to reduce exposure to JK stock by $30,000,000. The manager plans to achieve this objective by entering into a three-year equity swap using the S&P 500. Assume that settlement is made at the end of each year. Also assume that after one year the return on JK stock is 4 percent and the return on the S&P 500 market index is −3 percent.

A. Explain the structure of the equity swap.

B. Calculate the net cash flow for the swap at the end of one year.

14. The LKS Company is a U.S.-based mutual fund company that manages a global portfolio 80 percent invested in domestic stocks and 20 percent invested in international stocks. The international component mimics the MSCI EAFE index. The total market value of the portfolio is $750,000,000. The fund manager wishes to reduce the allocation to domestic stocks to 70 percent and increase the international allocation to 30 percent. The manager plans to achieve this objective by entering into a two-year equity swap using the Russell 3000 and the EAFE index. Assume that settlement is made at the end of the first year. Also assume that after one year, the return on the Russell 3000 market index is 5 percent and the return on the EAFE index is 6 percent.

A. Explain the structure of the equity swap.

B. Calculate the net cash flow for the swap at the end of one year.

15. A U.S.-based mutual fund company manages a global portfolio that is 80 percent invested in domestic stocks and 20 percent invested in international stocks. The international component mimics the MSCI EAFE index. The total market value of the portfolio is $500,000,000. The fund manager wishes to increase the allocation to domestic stocks to 90 percent and reduce the international allocation to 10 percent. The manager plans to achieve this objective by entering into a two-year equity swap using the Russell 3000 and the EAFE. Assume that settlement is made at the end of the year. Also assume that after one year, the return on the Russell 3000 market index is 5 percent and the return on the EAFE index is 7 percent.

A. Explain the structure of the equity swap.

B. Calculate the net cash flow for the swap at the end of one year.

16. A diversified portfolio with a market value of $800,000,000 currently has the following allocations:

Equity	80 percent	$640,000,000
Bonds	20 percent	$160,000,000

The equity portion of the portfolio is allocated as follows:

U.S. large-cap stocks	70 percent	$448,000,000
International stocks	30 percent	$192,000,000

The bond portion of the portfolio is allocated as follows:

U.S. government bonds	80 percent	$128,000,000
U.S corporate bonds	20 percent	$32,000,000

The portfolio manager wishes to change the overall allocation of the portfolio to 75 percent equity and 25 percent bonds. Within the equity category, the new allocation is to be 75 percent U.S. large cap and 25 percent international stocks. In the bond category, the new allocation is to be 75 percent U.S. government bonds and 25 percent U.S. corporate bonds. The manager wants to use four-year swaps to achieve the desired allocations, with settlements at the end of each year. Assume that the counterparty payments or receipts are tied to LIBOR. Use generic stock or bond indices where appropriate. Indicate how the manager can use swaps to achieve the desired allocations. Construct the most efficient overall swap, in which all equivalent but opposite LIBOR payments are consolidated.

17. An entrepreneur has all of her wealth tied up in a public company she formed five years ago. The total value of her holdings is $750,000,000. She wishes to reallocate her portfolio so that 75 percent remains invested in the company while 25 percent is invested in a diversified portfolio. The diversified portfolio will invest 60 percent in stocks and 40 percent in U.S. Treasury bonds. She has been advised to carry out the restructuring using four-year swaps. The payments will be made annually. Assume that at the end of one year, the return on the Russell 3000 is 7.5 percent, the return on the Lehman Brothers Long Treasury Bond index (LLTB) is 5 percent, and the return on the company's stock is 6.5 percent. Indicate how the swaps should be structured, and calculate the net cash flow on the swap after one year.

18. A company plans to borrow $20,000,000 in two years. The loan will be for three years and pay a floating interest rate of LIBOR with interest payments made every quarter. The company expects interest rates to rise in future years and thus is certain to swap the loan into a fixed-rate loan. In order to ensure that it can lock in an attractive rate, the company plans to purchase a payer swaption expiring in two years, with an exercise rate of 5 percent a year. The cost of the swaption is $250,000, and the settlement dates coincide with the interest payment dates for the original loan. Assume LIBOR at the beginning of the settlement period is 6.5 percent a year.
    A. Calculate the net cash flows on the first settlement date if FS(2,5) is above the exercise rate.
    B. Calculate the net cash flows on the first settlement date if FS(2,5) is below the exercise rate.

19. A company has an outstanding $50,000,000 loan that matures in three years. The interest rate on the loan is LIBOR payable at the end of each year. In order to hedge against an increase in interest rates, the company enters a swap to pay a fixed rate of 8 percent and receive LIBOR. In order to gain added flexibility in case rates fall, the company plans to purchase a swaption with an exercise rate of 8.5 percent. Assume that the company will consider unwinding the swap at the first settlement date and that the swaption is European style, meaning it can be exercised only at its expiration on the first settlement date and not before. Also assume that if the company exercises the swaption, it will do so by actually entering into the swap.
    A. Should the company buy a receiver or a payer swaption?
    B. Calculate the net cash flows on the first settlement date if the fixed rate on the underlying swap is 9 percent.
    C. Calculate the net cash flows on the first settlement date assuming LIBOR if the fixed rate on the underlying swap is 7.5 percent.

20. A U.S. company named USFIRM has a callable bond outstanding that has a face value of $50,000,000, pays an annual coupon of 9 percent (3 percent credit premium), and matures in eight years. USFIRM does not believe it is likely to call the bond for the next three years. Assume that the call feature on the bond is applicable only at exactly three years and not anytime sooner. To effectively eliminate this call feature applicable at exactly three years, the company decides to use a swaption.

A. Discuss whether the swaption should be a European or an American swaption. Also discuss whether USFIRM should buy or sell a swaption and whether it should be a receiver or a payer swaption. Finally, indicate what should be the expiration of the swaption, the maturity of the underlying swap, and the exercise rate on the swaption.

B. Calculate the net cash flows at the expiration of the swaption if the relevant fixed rate at the swaption expiration is 7 percent.

C. Calculate the net cash flows at the expiration of the swaption if the relevant fixed rate at the swaption expiration is 4 percent.

SOLUTIONS

1. The company can enter into a swap to pay a fixed rate of 6.5 percent and receive a floating rate. The first floating payment will be at 5 percent.

   Interest payment on the floating rate note = $50,000,000(0.05 + 0.0125)(90/360) = $781,250

   Swap fixed payment = $50,000,000(0.065)(90/360) = $812,500

   Swap floating receipts = $50,000,000(0.05)(90/360) = $625,000

   The overall cash payment made by the company is $812,500 + $781,250 − $625,000 = $968,750.

2. By entering into a swap to receive a fixed rate of 5 percent and pay a floating rate of LIBOR, the bank converts the floating rate to a fixed rate. Let L be the LIBOR established at the previous settlement date.

   Interest received on the loan = $10,000,000(L + 0.005)(90/360)

   Swap floating payment = $10,000,000(L)(90/360)

   Swap fixed receipt = $10,000,000(0.05)(90/360)

   The overall cash payment is $10,000,000[L − (L + 0.005) − (0.05)](90/360) = $10,000,000(−0.055)(90/360) = −$137,500. So an amount of $137,500 will be paid to the bank.

3. **A.** First note that a pay-fixed, receive-floating swap is equivalent to being short a fixed-rate bond and long a floating-rate bond.

   Therefore, the duration of this swap is equal to the duration of a short position in a five-year fixed-rate bond with quarterly payments, plus the duration of a long position in a five-year floating-rate bond with quarterly payments. The duration of a fixed-rate bond is approximated as 75 percent of the number of years to maturity. The duration of the floating-rate bond is approximated as the average of the minimum possible duration, 0, and the maximum possible duration, 0.25 year for a bond with quarterly payments.

   Duration of short fixed bond   = −(0.75)(5) = −3.75 years
   Duration of long floating bond   = (0 + 0.25)/2 = 0.125 years
   Duration of swap   = −3.625 years

   B. Note that a pay-floating, receive-fixed swap is equivalent to being short a floating-rate bond and long a fixed-rate bond.

   Therefore, the duration of this swap is equal to the duration of a short position in a three-year floating-rate bond with semiannual payments, plus the duration of a long position in a three-year fixed-rate bond with semiannual payments. The duration of a fixed-rate bond is approximated as 75 percent of the number of years to maturity. The duration of the floating-rate bond is approximated as the average of the minimum possible duration, 0, and the maximum possible duration, 0.5 years for a bond with semiannual payments.

   Duration of long fixed bond   = (0.75)(3) = 2.25 years

Duration of short floating bond $= -(0 + 0.5)/2 = -0.25$ years

Duration of swap $= 2$ years

4. A. The value of the bond portfolio is inversely related to interest rates. To increase the duration, it would be necessary to hold a position that moves inversely with the interest rates. Hence the swap should be pay floating, receive fixed.

B. Duration of a four-year pay-floating, receive-fixed swap with quarterly payments $= (0.75)(4) - 0.125 = 2.875$

Duration of a three-year pay-floating, receive-fixed swap with semiannual payments $= (0.75)(3) - 0.25 = 2.0$

Because the objective is to increase the duration of the bond portfolio, the four-year pay-floating, receive-fixed swap is the better choice.

C. The notional principal is

$$NP = B\left(\frac{MDUR_T - MDUR_B}{MDUR_S}\right)$$

$$NP = \$100,000,000\left(\frac{3.5 - 1.5}{2.875}\right) = \$69,565,217$$

5. Because the company has a floating-rate obligation on the floating-rate note, it should enter into a swap involving receiving a floating rate. Accordingly, the appropriate swap to hedge the risk and earn a profit would be a pay-fixed, receive-floating swap. Let LIBOR be L. Cash flows generated at each step are as follows:

1. Issue leveraged floating-rate notes and pay coupon $= L(2.5)(\$5,000,000) = \$12,500,000L$

2. Buy bonds with a face value $= (2.5)(\$5,000,000) = \$12,500,000$
   Receive a coupon $= (0.07)(\$12,500,000) = \$875,000$

3. Enter into a pay-fixed, receive-floating swap:
   Pay $= (0.06)(2.5)(\$5,000,000) = \$750,000$
   Receive $= L(2.5)(\$5,000,000) = \$12,500,000L$

4. Net cash flow $= -\$12,500,000L + \$875,000 - \$750,000 + \$12,500,000L = \$125,000$

In addition to the risk of default by the bond issuer, the company is taking the credit risk of the dealer by entering into a swap. The profit of $125,000 may be compensation for taking on this additional risk.

6. Let L be the LIBOR. The company has a floating outflow of $(0.13 - L)(FP)$ and a fixed inflow of $(0.075)(FP)$, where $FP = \$20,000,000$. On the outflow, $-$LIBOR is effectively an inflow, so the appropriate swap would be a pay-floating, receive-fixed swap.

Cash flows generated at each step are as follows:

1. Issue inverse floating-rate notes and pay coupon $= (0.13 - L)(20,000,000) = \$2,600,000 - \$20,000,000L$

2. Buy bonds with a face value $= \$20,000,000$
   Receive a coupon $= (0.075)(20,000,000) = \$1,500,000$

3. Enter into a pay-floating, receive-fixed swap:
   Pay $= (L)(20,000,000)$
   Receive $= (0.065)(20,000,000) = \$1,300,000$

4. Net cash flow = $-(2{,}600{,}000 - 20{,}000{,}000L) + 1{,}500{,}000 - 20{,}000{,}000L + 1{,}300{,}000 = \$200{,}000$

The company is taking on additional risk because of the credit risk of the swap dealer. The profit of $200,000 may be compensation for this additional risk.

7. The German company can initially issue domestic bonds with a face value of €100,000,000 = $115,000,000/\$1.15 per euro. The company can then enter into a swap to pay a fixed rate in dollars and receive a fixed rate in euros, in which the fixed rate on euro-denominated swaps would be 5.5 percent and the fixed rate on dollar-denominated swaps would be 2.5 percent.

1. At the inception of the currency swap, the company

   - receives €100,000,000 from the domestic bond issue
   - receives $115,000,000 and pays €100,000,000 on the swap

2. During the life of the swap, the company

   - pays interest on the bond = €100,000,000(0.0625) = €6,250,000
   - receives interest on the swap = €100,000,000(0.055) = €5,500,000
   - pays interest on the swap = $115,000,000(0.025) = \$2,875,000

   The net interest payment will be $2,875,000 + €750,000

3. At the end of the swap, the company

   - repays the bond principal = €100,000,000
   - repays dollar swap principal = $115,000,000
   - receives euro swap principal = €100,000,000

8. **A.** The U.S. company would pay the interest rate in euros. Because it expects that the interest rate in the eurozone will fall in the future, it should choose a swap with a floating rate on the interest paid in euros to let the interest rate on its debt float down.
   B. The U.S. company would receive the interest rate in dollars. Because it expects that the interest rate in the United States will fall in the future, it should choose a swap with a fixed rate on the interest received in dollars to prevent the interest rate it receives from going down.

9. **A.** The semiannual cash flow that must be converted into pounds is €15,000,000/2 = €7,500,000. In order to create a swap to convert €7,500,000, the equivalent notional principals are

   - Euro notional principal = €7,500,000/(0.065/2) = €230,769,231
   - Pound notional principal = €230,769,231/€1.5/£ = £153,846,154

   B. The cash flows from the swap will now be

   - Company makes swap payment = €230,769,231(0.065/2) = €7,500,000
   - Company receives swap payment = £153,846,154(0.075/2) = £5,769,231

   The company has effectively converted euro cash receipts to pounds.

10. The company first issues the dual-currency bond with a face value of €45,000,000 that pays interest of 3.5 percent a year in dollars. The dollar value of a bond with a face value of €45,000,000 = €45,000,000/(€1.15/\$) = \$39,130,435. The dollar interest

paid on this bond is $39,130,435(0.035) = $1,369,565. The company will do the following:

1. Purchase a bond with a face value of €45,000,000 that pays interest of 5 percent in euros.

$$\text{Annual interest received} = €45,000,000(0.05) = €2,250,000$$

2. Enter into a currency swap with no exchange of notional principal to

   - receive a fixed rate of 4 percent on notional principal of $39,130,435 = $39,130,435(0.04) = $1,565,217
   - pay a fixed rate of 4.75 percent on notional principal of €45,000,000 = €45,000,000(0.0475) = €2,137,500

   with all payments made annually. The annual net cash flow to the company is −$1,369,565 + $1,565,217 = $195,652 and €2,250,000 − €2,137,500 = €112,500.

11. The notional principal of £25,000,000 is £25,000,000/(£0.65/€1) = €38,461,538. In order to construct a synthetic dual-currency bond with principal in pounds and interest paid in euros, you must do the following:

    1. Issue a domestic currency bond with a face value of £25,000,000 that pays interest of 5 percent in pounds. Annual interest paid = (0.05)(£25,000,000) = £1,250,000.

    2. Enter into a currency swap with no exchange of notional principal to

       - receive a fixed rate of 5.25 percent on notional principal of £25,000,000 = £25,000,000(0.0525) = £1,312,500
       - pay a fixed rate of 4.25 percent on notional principal of €38,461,538 = €38,461,538(0.0425) = €1,634,615

       with all payments made annually. The net cash flow after all the transactions are as follows:

       $$\text{Pounds: } −£1,250,000 + £1,312,500 = £62,500$$
       $$\text{Euros: } −€1,634,615$$

    You have thus effectively converted the interest payment on the original bond issue from pounds to euros. The principal on the bond issue remains unchanged. Some cash flows remain in pounds because the rate on the swap will not usually equal the rate on the domestic bond.

12. **A.** The portfolio currently has (0.40)(£100,000,000) = £40,000,000 allocated to the INV stock. The desired allocation to the INV stock is (0.25)(£100,000,000) = £25,000,000. So, the desired reduction in the exposure to the INV stock is £40,000,000 − £25,000,000 = £15,000,000. The portfolio manager can achieve this reduction by entering into an equity swap in which the manager

    - pays or sells the return on £15,000,000 of INV stock, which is 500,000 shares.
    - receives or buys the return on £15,000,000 worth of the FTSE 100 index.

    B. At the end of the first year, the manager will

    $$\text{Pay } (0.05)(£15,000,000) = £750,000$$
    $$\text{Receive } (0.06)(£15,000,000) = £900,000$$

    $$\text{Net cash flow} = −£750,000 + £900,000 = £150,000$$

C. The manager may encounter some cash flow problems because he will have to pay out the return on 500,000 shares of INV stock but will not sell the stock. If the return received on the £15,000,000 invested in the FTSE 100 is significantly less than the return the portfolio pays, or if the return on the FTSE 100 is negative, the portfolio could have insufficient cash to make the payment, and the manager may have to liquidate some of the INV stock to cover the shortfall.

13. A. The portfolio manager can reduce exposure to JK stock by entering into an equity swap in which the manager

- pays or sells the return on $30,000,000 of JK stock.
- receives or buys the return on $30,000,000 worth of the S&P 500.

B. On the equity swap, at the end of each year, the manager will

Pay (0.04)($30,000,000) = $1,200,000

Receive (−0.03)($30,000,000) = −$900,000

(Note: Receiving a negative value means paying.)

Net cash flow = −$1,200,000 − $900,000 = −$2,100,000

Notice here that because the return on the index is significantly lower than the return on the stock, the swap has created a large cash flow problem.

14. A. The manager needs to reduce the allocation to domestic stocks by 10 percent and increase the allocation to international stocks by 10 percent. So the manager needs to reduce the allocation to domestic stocks by (0.10)($750,000,000) = $75,000,000 and increase the allocation to international stocks by $75,000,000. This can be done by entering into an equity swap in which the manager

- pays or sells the return on the Russell 3000 on notional principal of $75,000,000.
- receives or buys the return on the MSCI EAFE index on notional principal of $75,000,000.

B. On the equity swap, at the end of the first year, the manager will

Pay (0.05)($75,000,000) = $3,750,000

Receive (0.06)($75,000,000) = $4,500,000

Net cash flow = −$3,750,000 + $4,500,000 = $750,000

15. A. The manager needs to increase the allocation to domestic stocks from 80 percent to 90 percent (by 10 percent) and correspondingly decrease the allocation to international stocks by 10 percent. So the manager needs to increase the allocation to domestic stocks by (0.10)($500,000,000) = $50,000,000, and reduce the allocation to international stocks by $50,000,000. This can be done by entering into an equity swap in which the manager

- pays or sells the return on the EAFE on notional principal of $50,000,000.
- receives or buys the return on the Russell 3000 on notional principal of $50,000,000.

B. On the equity swap, at the end of the first year, the manager will

Pay (0.07)($50,000,000) = $3,500,000

Receive (0.05)($50,000,000) = $2,500,000

Net cash flow = −$3,500,000 + $2,500,000 = −$1,000,000

16. The following are the current allocations, the desired new allocations, and the transactions needed to go from the current positions to the new positions.

Stock	Current ($640 million, 80%)	New ($600 million, 75%)	Transaction
Large cap	$448 million (70%)	$450 million (75%)	Buy $2 million
International	$192 million (30%)	$150 million (25%)	Sell $42 million

Bonds	Current ($160 million, 20%)	New ($200 million, 25%)	Transaction
Government	$128 million (80%)	$150 million (75%)	Buy $22 million
Corporate	$32 million (20%)	$50 million (25%)	Buy $18 million

The following swap transactions would achieve the desired allocations:

<u>Equity Swaps</u>

Receive return on U.S. large-cap index on $2,000,000

Pay LIBOR on $2,000,000

Pay return on international stock index on $42,000,000

Receive LIBOR on $42,000,000

<u>Fixed-Income Swaps</u>

Receive return on U.S. government bond index on $22,000,000

Pay LIBOR on $22,000,000

Receive return on U.S. corporate bond index on $18,000,000

Pay LIBOR on $18,000,000

The overall position involves no LIBOR payments or receipts. The portfolio receives LIBOR on $42 million on equity swaps. It pays LIBOR on $2 million on equity swaps, and $22 million and $18 million on fixed-income swaps, for a total payment of LIBOR on $42 million. Thus, overall, there are no LIBOR payments or receipts.

17. The total value of the portfolio is $750,000,000. The entrepreneur needs to decrease the allocation to her company stock by $(0.25)(\$750,000,000) = \$187,500,000$ and create a diversified asset class of $187,500,000. She can do so by entering into a series of swaps in which she

- pays or sells the return on the company's stock on notional principal of $187,500,000. This is a first-year return of $(0.065)(\$187,500,000) = \$12,187,500$.

- receives or buys the return on the Russell 3000 index on notional principal of $187,500,000. This is a first-year return of $(0.075)(\$187,500,000) = \$14,062,500$.

- receives or buys the return on the LLTB index on notional principal of $187,500,000. This is a first-year return of $(0.05)(\$187,500,000) = \$9,375,000$.

Net cash flow after the first year $= -\$12,187,500 + \$14,062,500 + \$9,375,000 = \$11,250,000$.

18. A. If FS(2,5) is above the exercise rate, it will be worth exercising the swaption to enter a three-year swap to pay a fixed rate of 5 percent and receive LIBOR of 6.5 percent.

Swap payments on first quarterly settlement date:
   Pay $20,000,000(90/360)(0.05) = $250,000
   Receive $20,000,000(90/360)(0.065) = $325,000
   Loan payment = $20,000,000(90/360)(0.065) = $325,000
Net cash flow = −$250,000

B. If FS(2,5) is below the exercise rate, it will not be worth exercising the swaption. However, the company can enter a three-year swap to pay a fixed rate of 4 percent, for example, and receive LIBOR of 6.5 percent.

Swap payments on first quarterly settlement date:
   Pay $20,000,000(90/360)(0.04) = $200,000
   Receive $20,000,000(90/360)(0.065) = $325,000
   Loan payment = $20,000,000(90/360)(0.065) = $325,000
Net cash flow = −$200,000

19. A. Because the original swap is a pay-fixed, receive-floating swap, the company should buy a swaption that allows it to enter a receive-fixed, pay-floating swap—it should buy a receiver swaption.
   B. If the fixed rate on the underlying swap is 9 percent, it will not be worth exercising the swaption because the fixed rate on the underlying swap of 9 percent exceeds the exercise rate of 8.5 percent. Let L be the LIBOR.

Swap payments on first settlement date:
   Pay $50,000,000(0.08) − $4,000,000
   Receive $50,000,000(L)
   Loan payment = $50,000,000(L)
Net cash flow = −$4,000,000

C. If the fixed rate on the underlying swap is 7.5 percent, it will be worth exercising the swaption, because the fixed rate on the underlying swap of 7.5 percent is less than the exercise rate of 8.5 percent. Let L be the LIBOR.

Payments on the original swap on first settlement date:
   Pay $50,000,000(0.08) = $4,000,000
   Receive $50,000,000(L)
   Loan payment = $50,000,000(L)

The company exercises the swaption and has the following cash flows on the underlying swap (Fixed rate = Exercise rate = 8.5 percent).

Pay $50,000,000(L)
Receive $50,000,000(0.085) = $4,250,000

Because the fixed rate in the market on the underlying swap is 7.5 percent, the company enters into a swap in the market, specifying the opposite set of payments.

It pays the market fixed rate of 7.5 percent and receives LIBOR. The cash flows are as follows:

Pay $50,000,000(0.075) = $3,750,000

Receive $50,000,000(L)

Overall, the LIBOR payments and receipts offset. The net cash flow is −$4,000,000 + $4,250,000 − $3,750,000 = −$3,500,000.

20. **A.** Because the call feature on the bond is available only at exactly three years and not anytime sooner, the swaption must be a European swaption and not an American swaption. To offset the call option on the bonds that USFIRM holds, it needs to sell a call. It can do so by selling a receiver swaption, as the receiver swaption is like a call option on a bond. Because the company does not believe it is likely to call the bond for the next three years, the expiration of the swaption would be three years. Because the bond would have a five-year life when it is called, the swap underlying the swaption would be a five-year swap. The exercise rate on the swaption should be $9 - 3 = 6$ percent.

B. Let FS(3,8) be the fixed rate at the swaption expiration on a five-year swap. If FS(3,8) = 7 percent, the buyer of the receiver swaption will not exercise the swaption.

Loan interest payment by USFIRM = $50,000,000(0.09) = $4,500,000

Net cash flow = −$4,500,000

C. If FS(3,8) = 4 percent, the buyer will exercise the swaption and USFIRM will have to enter into a swap to pay a fixed rate of 6 percent and receive LIBOR. The company will call the original bond and issue a new bond with a coupon interest rate of 7 percent [FS(3,8) of 4% + credit premium of 3%]. The company will also enter into a swap to pay LIBOR and receive FS(3,8) of 4 percent.

The cash flows are as follows:

Pay $50,000,000(0.06) = $3,000,000 on the swap

Receive $50,000,000(L) on the swap

New bond interest payments = $50,000,000(0.07) = $3,500,000

Pay $50,000,000(L) on the swap entered into at the market rate

Receive $50,000,000(0.04) = $2,000,000 on the swap entered into at the market rate

Net cash flow = −$3,000,000 + $50,000,000(L) − $3,500,000 − $50,000,000(L) + $2,000,000 = −$4,500,000

Thus, USFIRM effectively pays $6 + 3 = 9$ percent, equivalent to a noncallable bond.

RISK MANAGEMENT

LEARNING OUTCOMES

After completing this chapter, you will be able to do the following:

- Discuss risk management.
- Distinguish between financial and nonfinancial risks.
- Discuss the sources of financial risk.
- Explain why risk should be managed.
- Describe the general process of risk management.
- Discuss market risk.
- Discuss the traditional measures of market risk that reflect sensitivity to the underlying, volatility, and the correlation among assets.
- Discuss Value at Risk (VAR), noting the relationship between VAR as a maximum loss and VAR as a minimum loss.
- Discuss the two important parameter choices in deciding how to use VAR.
- Explain how to use the analytical or variance–covariance method to estimate VAR, and discuss the advantages and disadvantages of this technique.
- Explain how to use the historical method to estimate VAR, and discuss the advantages and disadvantages of this technique.
- Explain how to use Monte Carlo simulation to estimate VAR, and discuss the advantages and disadvantages of this technique.
- Discuss some limitations and attractions of VAR in general.
- Discuss two dimensions of credit risk.
- Discuss two time elements of credit risk: current and potential credit risk.
- Explain the nature of credit risk in forward contracts.
- Explain the nature of credit risk in swaps.
- Explain the nature of credit risk in options.
- Identify and briefly explain how limiting exposure, marking to market, collateral, netting, and enhanced derivative products are used to control credit risk.
- Explain how VAR is used in managing credit risk and how this application differs from the standard VAR used to manage market risk.
- Define credit derivatives and explain in general the principle behind how they work.

- Illustrate four main types of credit derivatives.
- Explain how liquidity is a source of financial risk.
- Identify sources of nonfinancial risk.
- Discuss the two sets of standards on best practices in risk management.
- Describe risk governance.
- Describe risk budgeting.
- Explain how risk management relates to performance evaluation.
- Identify some of the key rules for effective risk management.

1   INTRODUCTION

As we move into the last chapter of this book, let us quickly review what we have covered. Following the introductory chapter, we explored forward contracts, futures, options, and swaps in Chapters 2 through 5, respectively. After describing the characteristics of these instruments, we then looked at their pricing. In Chapters 6 through 8, we examined trading strategies using these instruments. Some of these strategies are speculative. Many are *hedging strategies*. We typically think of hedging as a form of risk reduction. In Chapter 6 we stated that hedging is taking a market position to protect against an undesirable outcome. Companies and individuals that use hedging strategies are often viewed as engaging in solid and conservative business practices. But if a little hedging is good, is not more hedging even better? And if more hedging is better, is not hedging everything best? In other words, why should a company not hedge all of its risks?

If a company hedges all of its risks, it ends up taking no risk. In that case, however, the company would not be operating a business. A company takes risks for the purpose of generating cash flows that increase its owners' wealth. The owners of corporations, the shareholders, risk their capital with the objective of increasing their wealth. Without risk taking, there would be little economic growth and development. Although companies are naturally concerned about their own risk-taking activities, they should also be concerned about the risk-taking activities of their competitors. A competitor that does a better job of managing risk is as formidable an opponent as one that produces a better product or service.

Risk-taking activity is not confined to businesses. Nonprofit organizations engage in activities that require risk taking. In fact, nonprofits tend to rely heavily on their endowments, which are usually invested in financial markets.

Governments also take risks. They engage in a variety of activities that compete with the private sector. For example, governments provide transportation and postal services. Not only do they take risks in these activities, but they also compete with private companies that take risks. Even government activities that do not compete with the private sector involve elements of risk taking. For example, when a federal government creates a new regulatory agency, it invests a vast amount of public resources in organizing and operating the agency. Yet that agency may ultimately fail to achieve its objective, thereby wasting taxpayer resources. Governments purchase assets such as oil, borrow money, and engage in activities that require payment in foreign currencies. All of these activities are characterized by risk.

Individuals engage in numerous risky activities in the conduct of their personal and professional lives. In addition, through participation in retirement and pension funds, they may be engaged in risky commercial activities in an indirect manner.

Risk taking is an innate characteristic of human activity and as old as humankind itself. Without risk, there is little possibility of reward. But without the measurement and control of risk, the perils are like sailing on an open sea with no idea what lies ahead. Therein lies the obvious reason for managing risk.

2 THE CONCEPT OF RISK MANAGEMENT

Businesses, nonprofits, governments, and individuals engage in risk-taking activities. Although they may hedge their risks on occasion, they should not restrict their activities to those that are risk free. The fact that these entities engage in risky activities raises a number of important questions:

- How is risk defined?
- How does one recognize and measure risk?
- Which risks are worth taking on a regular basis, which are worth taking on occasion, and which should never be taken?
- How are risks reduced or eliminated? What strategies should be used?
- How are the processes of risk taking and risk elimination monitored?

These questions and many others collectively define the process of *risk management*. In short, how is risk managed? To understand this concept, we start with a formal definition of risk management:

> *Risk management is the process of identifying the level of risk that an entity wants, measuring the level of risk that an entity currently has, taking actions that bring the actual level of risk to the desired level of risk, and monitoring the new actual level of risk so that it continues to be aligned with the desired level of risk. The process is continuous and may require alterations in any of these activities to reflect new policies, preferences, and information.*

What we have done here is shift the focus from simply hedging (i.e., reducing risk) to a more comprehensive view of managing risk. Risk management is a proactive, anticipative, and reactive process that continuously monitors and controls risk. Although hedging is strictly reducing risk, risk can sometimes be reduced by too much and should be increased. Risk management is a general practice that can entail reducing or increasing risk.

As noted above, businesses, governments, and individuals face a variety of risks. An industrial corporation faces the risk of accidents occurring in one of its factories. A government faces the risk that an employee might sue it for discrimination. An individual faces the risk of contracting a fatal disease. Many of these risks are managed using insurance. Indeed, insurance is an important tool for managing risk, and the profession of insurance is sometimes referred to as "risk management." Although these risks are certainly important, they are not the focus of this book. Consistent with our previous coverage, we concentrate on those risks arising from commercial transactions that are affected by interest rates, stock prices, and exchange rates.[1] We shall, however, identify some of the other risks, because they play a prominent contemporary role in understanding the process of risk management. Moreover, the management of these other risks has benefited greatly from advances learned from the management of interest rate, stock price, and exchange rate risks.

---

[1] As previously noted, a fourth source of risk is commodity prices, but they will not be our concern in this book.

2.1   SOURCES OF RISK
A company faces a variety of risks in its everyday activities. In this book, we have identified four types of risks: the risks arising from interest rates, exchange rates, equity prices, and commodity prices.[2] These risks can be characterized as *financial risks*. We have not yet discussed two other types of financial risks: credit risk and liquidity risk. These six sources of risk make up the spectrum of financial risk. A company faces many other types of risks as well; we collectively call these nonfinancial risks. Exhibit 9-1 illustrates all of these risks, financial and nonfinancial.

EXHIBIT 9-1   The Sources of Risk

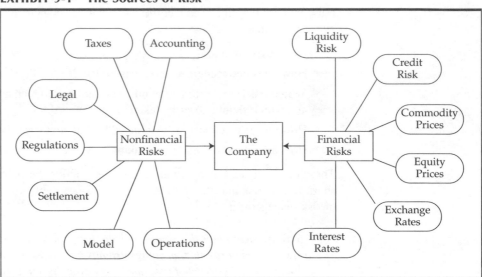

In this chapter we explore the topic of credit, which is another major source of risk. We shall define and briefly discuss the other types of risks in a later section.

2.2   WHY MANAGE RISK?
During the 1980s, derivatives began to be used to a significant degree to manage risk. In the 1990s, the derivatives industry grew explosively. These changes occurred during a period of frequently high volatility in interest rates, stock prices, exchange rates, and commodity prices. Increasingly, companies began to fear the power of these markets to harm their performance. A company operates in the markets for the products it manufactures and the services it provides. The risks in these markets are inherent in the nature of their lines of business. When, for instance, a multinational company experiences outstanding sales growth and excellent cost control in its foreign markets but has those gains wiped out by a strong domestic exchange rate, significant value is destroyed. Companies that succeed in doing the activities they should be able to do well cannot afford to fail overall because of activities in which they have no expertise. Accordingly, many companies adopted the policy of hedging risks that arise from areas in which they have no expertise or comparative advantage. In areas in which they do have an edge (i.e., their primary line of business), they tend to hedge only tactically. They hedge when they feel they have sufficient information to suggest a lower risk position. They manage risk, increasing it when they feel a compet-

---

[2] As noted, in this book we focus only on interest rate, exchange rate, and equity price risk.

itive advantage and decreasing it when they feel a competitive disadvantage. But practicing risk management makes good economic sense for many other reasons.

In a perfect world in which investors have access to all information, no taxes or transaction costs exist, and the market is efficient, there are no shareholder benefits to a company's practice of risk management, at least so far as financing is concerned. The celebrated Modigliani–Miller (MM) propositions of corporate finance mean that risk management on the right-hand side of the balance sheet offers no advantages to shareholders. Risk management of liabilities, such as the capital structure decision of how much debt to issue and the decision about whether to pay dividends, should not affect a company's value. If shareholders wanted their companies to hedge the risk of interest rate changes on their loans, they could take positions in their own personal portfolios to offset that risk. The shareholders could do the hedging themselves, instead of having the company hedge.[3]

But shareholders cannot easily engage in these types of activities. They do not have access to all of the necessary information, such as when and how much to hedge, nor can they obtain the best prices on derivative transactions in the market. A company like IBM can better hedge its liabilities using swaps than can a shareholder hedge his or her small portion of IBM's liability by engaging in some type of derivative transaction. On the asset side, a company can have a competitive advantage in the product and commodity markets and might increase or decrease its risk based on its expertise and informational advantage.

By stabilizing an organization's cash flows and income, the practice of risk management can lead to several other important benefits. One advantage results from the progressive tax structure found in most countries. If corporate tax rates increase with higher taxable incomes, which is referred to as a progressive or convex tax schedule, companies with highly volatile taxable incomes find that the additional taxes they pay in high-income years are not offset by the lower taxes they pay in low-income years. Without the ability to average income over time, high tax years will dominate low tax years. Hedging can stabilize income, resulting in a lower level of taxes over time.

Bankruptcy or a significant possibility of bankruptcy results in a company incurring a number of costs not otherwise encountered in its ordinary business operations. For example, suppliers cut off credit, employees quit, and customers lose confidence in the company. Perhaps the largest of these costs are those associated with the role of the legal system in the bankruptcy process. Because of the event or prospect of bankruptcy, additional parties that did not assume risk have a claim on the company's assets. By reducing the expected value of these costs, a company can increase its value. Managing risk can reduce the probability of bankruptcy, thereby reducing the expected value of these costs and, consequently, increasing the value of a company.

Practicing risk management can increase a company's debt capacity and lower its cost of debt. Companies that practice risk management send a signal to creditors that they are serious about protecting the interests of creditors as well as shareholders. For such companies, creditors will be more favorably inclined to not only lend money but also charge an attractive interest rate. Having reliable and inexpensive sources of credit gives companies considerable flexibility for future financing needs.

By managing risk, a company can avoid getting into a condition in which it has no incentive to undertake profitable projects. Society as a whole thus benefits from risk

---

[3] As noted above, the MM propositions deal with only the right-hand side of the balance sheet—that is, the financing decision. Decisions related to the left-hand side of the balance sheet (asset or investment decisions) are not addressed. The MM propositions are consistent with the idea that hedging can be valuable in asset markets, in which companies can have strategic advantages. On the financing side, however, companies operate in competitive capital markets and have no advantages in the issuance of debt or equity, the distribution of dividends, share repurchases, and other related financing decisions.

management. Companies that are in a near-bankrupt state may find that they have an incentive to pass up attractive investment projects simply because the profits from such projects benefit only creditors. There is no incentive for shareholders to engage in these projects if they will not receive any benefits. As a result, the company should pass up such projects. From society's point of view, this is suboptimal.

One of the most important reasons for practicing risk management is to stabilize cash flows in order to ensure an adequate amount of funds for capital investment. Most companies look first to internally generated funds to meet their financing needs. They are reluctant to go to the debt or equity markets because additional debt usually comes with costly restrictions and extensive monitoring by creditors. Additional equity dilutes the claims of existing shareholders. Hence, companies tend to prefer internally generated funds. The level of these funds fluctuates, however, with the fortunes of the company. By practicing risk management, companies can stabilize their cash flows, ensuring that adequate funds are available for investment.

Finally, we note that risk management is sometimes required in some heavily regulated industries, such as banking. Other industries are finding increased pressure from shareholders, creditors, and the financial analyst community to practice risk management.

2.3 HOW RISK IS MANAGED

Risk management should be a *process*, not just an activity. A process is continuous and subject to evaluation and revision. Constant monitoring and adjustments are required.

EXHIBIT 9-2   Risk Management Process: The Practice of Risk Management

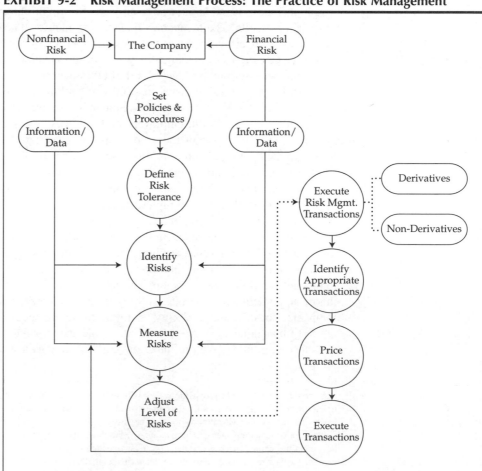

Exhibit 9-2 illustrates the process of risk management as it applies to the practice of risk management. We see at the top that the company faces financial and nonfinancial risks. Moving down the figure, we see that the company establishes risk management policies and procedures. It defines its risk tolerance, which is the level of risk it is willing and able to bear. It then identifies the risks, drawing on all sources of information, and attempts to measure these risks using information or data related to all of its identified exposures. Measuring risk can be an activity as simple as estimating the volatility of an exchange rate. More often than not, however, a more sophisticated and detailed analysis of risk is required. The company then adjusts the level of risk so that the desired level of risk equals the actual level of risk. The company accomplishes necessary risk adjustments by executing risk management transactions, which can take the form of derivatives or nonderivatives transactions. The execution of risk management transactions is itself a distinct process consisting of identifying the appropriate transactions, pricing them, and then executing the transactions. The process then loops around to the measurement of risk and continues in that manner, constantly monitoring and adjusting the risk to make the actual level of risk equal the desired level of risk.

We have discussed many aspects of this process of risk management in this book. One in particular that we have focused on involves the pricing of transactions. A considerable amount of detail goes into the pricing of a transaction. Exhibit 9-3 illustrates this process of pricing and measuring risk. We see at the top that in pricing the transaction, we first identify the source(s) of uncertainty. Then we select the appropriate pricing model.

EXHIBIT 9-3   Risk Management Process: Pricing and Measuring Risk

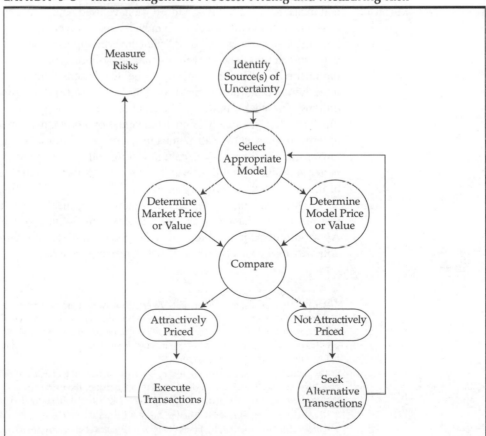

From there, we determine the market price or value of the transaction.[4] This is the price at which a transaction can be executed and might come from a dealer's quote. We simultaneously determine the transaction's model price or value. We compare the two. If we are buying and the market price exceeds the model price, the transaction is unattractively priced and we would seek an alternative transaction. If we are selling, however, the transaction would be attractively priced and we would execute the transaction. After executing the transaction, we would then return to the process of measuring the risk.

In spite of everything we have covered in this book, we have not yet covered all we need to know to obtain a solid overview of the process of risk management. In this chapter, we shall fill in some of those gaps, tie together much of what we have already done, and provide a framework for understanding why the use of derivatives is so inextricably tied to the practice of risk management. In the next two sections, we examine the management of the two primary forms of risk: market risk and credit risk.

3   MANAGING MARKET RISK

Market risk refers to the risk associated with interest rates, exchange rates, and equity prices.[5] In previous chapters, we have focused primarily on hedging market risk and in doing so, we have touched on concepts related to market risk management in a broader sense.

3.1   TRADITIONAL NOTIONS OF MARKET RISK

A general notion of market risk is the sensitivity of the price of an asset or derivative to a change in the underlying source of uncertainty. For a stock or stock portfolio, beta is a typical measure of market risk. Indeed we have used beta to measure the sensitivity of a stock or stock portfolio to market-wide movements. For a bond, duration and convexity are common measures of market risk.[6] When covering options, we also discussed the concepts of delta and gamma. The former measures the option's sensitivity to a change in the value of the underlying. The latter measures the delta's sensitivity to a change in the value of the underlying. Delta and gamma are legitimate concepts for stocks and bonds as well as options. For stocks, however, the delta is one and the gamma is zero, so they do not add much to what we already know from beta. For a bond, delta measures the bond's response to term structure shifts and gamma measures the response of the bond's delta to term structure shifts. For the most accurate modeling and management of risk, delta and gamma are better and more general measures for bonds than are duration and convexity, although all of these measures are widely used.

Duration, convexity, delta, and gamma are measures of the response of a financial instrument to a change in the source of risk. But we must consider some other risk factors. As we discussed in Chapter 4, a major factor in determining the price of an option is the volatility of the underlying. This risk is reflected in a measure we referred to as vega. Vega

---

[4] Recall from our chapters on forwards, futures, and swaps that we discussed the difference between pricing and valuation. In that context, pricing means to find the rate on the contract at the start and valuation means to find the market value. We contrasted this use of the terms *pricing* and *valuation* to their typical use in the process of analyzing assets, wherein an asset trades at a price, though its value might be different. It is the latter context to which we refer here.

[5] The definition of market risk given here is the one used in the practice of risk management. The term *market risk*, however, is often used elsewhere to refer to the risk of the market as a whole, which is usually known as systematic risk. In this chapter, we define market risk as it is defined by risk management professionals.

[6] Convexity is covered in some detail in Level I, Chapter 7, of *Fixed Income Analysis for the Chartered Financial Analyst Program*, by Frank J. Fabozzi (Frank J. Fabozzi Associates, 2000).

is the change in the price of an option for a change in the volatility of the underlying. Most pricing models assume that volatility does not change, but in fact volatility does change. This change is sometimes easy to observe in markets: Some days are far more volatile than others. Options are typically very responsive to a change in volatility. Swaps, futures, and forwards are not responsive to volatility.

Correlation is a source of risk for financial derivatives that have unusual or exotic features. For example, some derivatives have more than one underlying. Consider a type of index call option in which the underlyings are both the S&P 500 Index and the S&P MidCap 400 Index. The option permits the holder to buy either the S&P 500 or the S&P MidCap 400 at a fixed price. The choice is made by which of the two had the better performance over the life of the option. Because the S&P 500 and the S&P MidCap 400 Index levels are on different orders of magnitude, the indices are typically normalized to a value of 1.0. When the option expires, the expiration value of the index is divided by its original value and multiplied by 100. Suppose the S&P 500 rose 10 percent and the MidCap 400 Index rose 4 percent during the option's life. Then the S&P 500 would be considered to expire with a value of 110, and the MidCap 400 would be considered to expire with a value of 104. If the exercise price is 105, the option would be exercised using the S&P 500 and would be in-the-money by 5. The value of such an option is greatly influenced not only by the volatilities of the S&P 500 and the MidCap 400 but also by the correlation between the two indices. Similarly, some interest rate derivatives are affected by the correlations among interest rates across the term structure. Thus, correlation is a source of risk for some types of options.

Although there are a few other less important sources of market risk, the primary ones for derivatives are the first- and second-order effects of the underlying, the effect of the volatility, and the effect of the correlations among assets, if applicable. These risks are particularly important for dealers, which engage in a large volume of transactions. As we have frequently noted, dealers make markets on either side of a transaction to meet the needs of their customers. They then typically lay off their risks by hedging them with other transactions. Ultimately, they hope to profit from the bid–ask spread. To properly manage these risks, dealers must invest in risk-management technology and personnel. They must accurately measure their deltas, gammas, and vegas and identify transactions that will add just the right amount of delta, gamma, and vega to offset their existing positions.

Solving such problems is complex. For example, when a company sells an option, it takes on delta, gamma, and vega risk. If it hedges the delta with a futures contract, it has reduced its delta to zero but has done nothing to its gamma and vega. If it then adds an option to hedge its gamma, it will not have hedged the vega. Moreover, the delta-hedged position it had before adding this option will no longer be delta-hedged. Thus, the company must solve the problem of delta, gamma, and vega hedging simultaneously.

Not all dealers hedge their gammas and vegas, but all of them monitor their gammas and vegas with an objective of hedging them when the risk has increased. As we discussed in Chapter 4, gamma risk is highest when options are at-the-money and close to expiration. Vega risk is highest when options are at-the-money. Dealers pay particular attention to these risks under these circumstances.

We have talked a lot about dealers, but what about end users? Most end users employ derivatives to manage a particular risk. They identify a risk, such as having a stock portfolio with a beta that is too high. An end user might sell the appropriate number of futures contracts to reduce that beta to its desired level. Compared to dealers, end users do not typically invest as much capital in technology and personnel to continuously monitor their risks. Nonetheless, end users should make serious efforts to measure and monitor risk as effectively as possible, given their constraints. In practice, most end users do an effective job.

Market risk measurement and management require a considerable amount of data. Many sources of data are available, particularly on the Internet. J.P. Morgan (now J.P. Morgan Chase) developed the original concept of publishing data and information on managing risk on its website called RiskMetrics (www.riskmetrics.com).[7] This site is an excellent data source for risk management information, and many other good sources and services for such information are available.

In this section, we have briefly reviewed traditional notions of risk measurement. In the following section, we introduce a new topic, one that took the industry by storm: Value at Risk.

3.2 VALUE AT RISK

During the 1990s, Value at Risk—or VAR, as it is commonly known—emerged as the premier risk management technique.[8] Probably no other risk management topic has generated as much attention and controversy. In this section we take an introductory look at VAR, examine an application, and look at VAR's strengths and limitations.

VAR is a probability-based measure of loss potential for a company, a fund, a portfolio, a transaction, or a strategy. Any position that exposes one to loss is potentially a candidate for VAR measurement. VAR is most widely and easily used to measure the loss from market risk, but it can also be used—subject to much greater complexity—to measure the loss from credit risk and other types of risks.

We have noted that VAR is a probability-based measure of loss potential. This definition is very general, however, and we need something more specific. More formally, *VAR is the loss that would be exceeded with a given probability over a specific time period.* This definition has three important elements.

First, we see that *VAR is a loss that would be exceeded.* Hence, it is a measure of a minimum loss. Second, we see that *VAR is associated with a given probability.* It is the loss that would be exceeded with a given probability. Thus we would state that there is a certain percent chance that a particular loss would be exceeded. Finally, *VAR is defined for a specific period of time.* Therefore, the loss that would be exceeded with a given probability is a loss that would be expected to occur over a specific time period. There is a big difference among potential losses that are incurred daily, weekly, monthly, quarterly, or annually. Potential losses over longer periods should be larger than those over shorter periods.

Consider the following example of VAR for an investment portfolio: *The VAR for a portfolio is $1.5 million for one day with a probability of 0.05.* Consider what this statement says: *There is a 5 percent chance that the portfolio will lose at least $1.5 million in a single day.* The emphasis here should be on the fact that *the loss is a minimum, not a maximum.* There has been considerable misunderstanding of the concept of VAR, with some referring to it as a maximum loss. It is possible to describe VAR in the form of a maximum, but one must be careful. To state the VAR as a maximum, we would say that the probability is 0.95, or that we are 95 percent confident, that the portfolio will lose no more than $1.5 million.

It is not possible to state with certainty what the maximum possible loss will be, other than to say that the maximum possible loss is the entire value of the portfolio. Our preference is to express VAR in the form of a minimum loss with a given probability. This approach is a bit more conservative, as it reminds us that the loss could be worse.

---

[7] RiskMetrics Group has now spun off from J.P. Morgan and is an independent company.

[8] The terminology "Value-at-Risk" is expressed in different ways. For example, sometimes hyphens are used and sometimes it is just written as "Value at Risk." Sometimes it is abbreviated as VAR and sometimes as VaR. Those who have studied econometrics should be alert to the fact that the letters VAR also refer to an estimation technique called Vector Autoregression, which has nothing to do with Value at Risk. We shall use the abbreviation "VAR."

3.2.1 ELEMENTS OF MEASURING VALUE AT RISK

Establishing a VAR measure involves a number of decisions. Two important ones are the choice of probability and the choice of the time period over which the VAR will be measured.

The probability chosen is typically either 0.05 or 0.01. The use of 0.01 leads to a more conservative VAR. It allows for only a 1 percent chance that the VAR value will be exceeded. The trade-off, however, is that the VAR number will be much larger than with a 0.05 probability. In the above example, we might have to state that the VAR is $2.1 million for one day with a probability of 0.01. The risk manager selects 0.01 or 0.05; there is no definitive rule to prefer one probability to the other.

The second important decision is the choice of time period. VAR is often measured over a day, but other time periods are common. Banking regulators prefer a two-week period. Many companies state their quarterly and annual VARs because quarterly and annual numbers are more consistent with their performance reporting cycles. Derivatives dealers seem to prefer daily VAR, perhaps because of the high turnover at their positions. Regardless of the choice of time period, the longer the time period, the greater will be the VAR number, because the magnitude of potential losses increases when measuring risk over a longer period of time. The choice of time period is also a decision made by an individual or the individuals responsible for risk management.

Once these primary parameters are chosen, one can proceed to actually obtain the VAR estimate. This procedure involves another decision, the choice of technique. The basic idea behind estimating VAR is to identify the characteristics of the probability distribution of the returns on a portfolio. Consider the information in Exhibit 9-4, which is a simple probability distribution for the return on a portfolio over a specified time period. Suppose we were interested in the VAR at a probability of 0.05. We add up the probabilities for the class intervals until we get a cumulative probability of 0.05. Observe that the probability is 0.01 that the portfolio will lose at least 40 percent, 0.01 that the portfolio will lose between 30 percent and 40 percent, and 0.03 that the portfolio will lose between 20 percent and 30 percent. Thus, the probability is 0.05 that the portfolio will lose at least 20 percent. Because we want to express our risk measure in units of money, we would then multiply 20 percent by the market value of the portfolio and obtain the VAR. The VAR for

EXHIBIT 9-4   Sample Probability Distribution of Returns on a Portfolio

Return on Portfolio	Probability
Less than −40%	0.01
−40% to −30%	0.01
−30% to −20%	0.03
−20% to −10%	0.05
−10% to −5%	0.10
−5% to −2.5%	0.125
−2.5% to 0%	0.175
0% to 2.5%	0.175
2.5% to 5%	0.125
5% to 10%	0.10
10% to 20%	0.05
20% to 30%	0.03
30% to 40%	0.01
Greater than 40%	0.01
	1.000

a probability of 0.01 would be 40 percent multiplied by the market value. We can interpret this to mean that we estimate with 99 percent confidence that our portfolio will lose less than 40 percent of its value over the specified time period.

Exhibit 9-4 is a simplified representation of the information necessary to estimate the VAR. This information is not easy to obtain. In practice, we must resort to one of three methods for estimating VAR: the analytical or variance–covariance method, the historical method, or the Monte Carlo simulation method. We shall illustrate each of these in turn.

3.2.2   THE ANALYTICAL OR VARIANCE–COVARIANCE METHOD

The analytical or variance–covariance method begins with the assumption that portfolio returns are normally distributed. Recall that we briefly studied the normal distribution when we introduced the Black–Scholes–Merton model. Also, recall from your study of portfolio management that a normal distribution can be completely described by its expected value and standard deviation.

Consider the *standard normal distribution*, a special case of the normal distribution that is centered on an expected value of zero and has a standard deviation of 1.0. Any outcome drawn from a nonstandard normal distribution can be converted to a standard normal value by taking the outcome of interest, subtracting its mean, and dividing the result by its standard deviation. The resulting value then conforms to the standard normal distribution.[9] With the standard normal distribution, 5 percent of possible outcomes are likely to be smaller than -1.65. Thus, to calculate a 5 percent VAR for a portfolio, we would estimate its expected return and subtract 1.65 times its estimated standard deviation of returns. So the key to using the analytical or variance–covariance method is to estimate the portfolio's expected return and standard deviation of returns. To do this at the portfolio level requires a brief review of the principles of portfolio theory and diversification.

Suppose the portfolio contains two asset classes, with 75 percent of the money invested in an asset class represented by the S&P 500 and 25 percent invested in an asset class represented by the Nasdaq Composite Index.[10] Recall that the expected return of a portfolio is a weighted average of the expected returns of its component stocks or asset classes. The variance of a portfolio is a weighted average of the variances and covariances of the component stocks or asset classes. Assume that μ_S and μ_N are the expected returns of the S&P 500 and Nasdaq, respectively, σ_S and σ_N are their standard deviations, and ρ is the correlation between the two asset classes. The expected return, μ_p, and variance, σ_p^2, of the combined positions are given as

$$\mu_p = w_S\mu_S + w_N\mu_N$$

$$\sigma_p^2 = w_S^2\sigma_S^2 + w_N^2\sigma_N^2 + 2w_Sw_N\sigma_S\sigma_N\rho$$

where the w's indicate the percentage allocated to the respective classes. The standard deviation of the portfolio is just the square root of its variance. The expected value and standard deviation of the portfolio using actual numbers are estimated in Exhibit 9-5, where we obtain μ_p of 0.135 and σ_p of 0.244.

---

[9] For example, suppose you were interested in knowing the probability of obtaining a return of 15 percent or less when the expected return is 12 percent and the standard deviation is 20 percent. The standard normal value, called a "z," is obtained as $(0.15 - 0.12)/0.20 = 0.15$. Then you look up this value in a table or use a spreadsheet function, such as Microsoft Excel's "=normsdist()" function. In this case, the probability is 0.5596.

[10] The extension to three or more classes is relatively straightforward once one knows how to calculate the variance of a portfolio of more than two assets. We shall focus here on the two-asset class case.

EXHIBIT 9-5   Estimating the Expected Return and Standard Deviation of a Portfolio Combining Two Asset Classes

	S&P 500	Nasdaq	Combined Portfolio
Percentage invested (w)	0.75	0.25	1.00
Expected return (μ)	0.12	0.18	0.135*
Standard deviation (σ)	0.20	0.40	0.244**
Correlation		0.90	

*Expected return of portfolio: $\mu_p = w_S\mu_S + w_N\mu_N = 0.75(0.12) + 0.25(0.18) = 0.135$
**Standard deviation of portfolio:
$\sigma^2 = w_S^2\sigma_S^2 + w_N^2\sigma_N^2 + 2w_Sw_N\sigma_S\sigma_N\rho = (0.75)^2 (0.20)^2$
$+ (0.25)^2 (0.40)^2 + 2(0.75)(0.25)(0.20)(0.40)(0.90) = 0.0595$
$\sigma = \sqrt{\sigma^2} = \sqrt{0.0595} = 0.244$

Assuming we are comfortable with the assumption of a normal distribution and the accuracy of our estimates of the expected returns, variances, and the correlation, we can be satisfied that the properties of the distribution of the returns on this portfolio are well captured by these estimates of the portfolio's expected return and standard deviation of return. Thus, we can proceed to calculate the portfolio's VAR in a straightforward manner, illustrated graphically in Exhibit 9-6.

EXHIBIT 9-6   Annual VAR for a Portfolio with Expected Return of 0.135 and Standard Deviation of 0.244

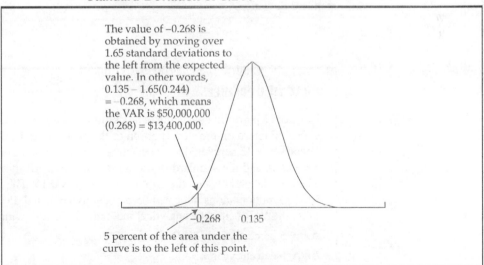

The value of −0.268 is obtained by moving over 1.65 standard deviations to the left from the expected value. In other words, 0.135 − 1.65(0.244) = −0.268, which means the VAR is $50,000,000 (0.268) = $13,400,000.

−0.268   0.135

5 percent of the area under the curve is to the left of this point.

The VAR is first obtained in terms of the return on the portfolio. With an expected return of 0.135, we move over 1.65 standard deviations in the direction of lower returns. Each standard deviation is 0.244. Thus, we would obtain $0.135 - 1.65(0.244) = -0.268$. At this point, the VAR could be expressed as a loss of 26.8 percent. We could say that there is a 5 percent chance that the portfolio will lose at least 26.8 percent in a year. It is customary, however, to express the VAR in terms of the currency unit of the portfolio. Thus, if the portfolio is worth \$50 million, the VAR would be expressed as \$50,000,000(0.268) = \$13.4 million.

This figure is an annual VAR. If we prefer a daily VAR, we would adjust the expected return to its daily average of approximately 0.135/250 = 0.00054 and the standard deviation to its daily value of $0.244/\sqrt{250}$ = 0.01543, which are based on the assumption of 250 trading days in a year and statistical independence between days. Then the daily VAR would be 0.00054 − 1.65(0.01543) = −0.0249. On a dollar basis, the daily VAR would be \$50,000,000(0.0249) = \$1.245 million.

For a 1 percent VAR, we would move over 2.33 standard deviations in the direction of lower returns. Thus, the annual VAR would be 0.135 − 2.33(0.244) = −0.434 or \$50,000,000(0.434) = \$21.7 million. The daily VAR would be 0.00054 − 2.33(0.01543) = −0.035 or \$50,000,000(0.035) = \$1.75 million.

Some approaches to estimating VAR using the analytical method assume an expected return of zero. This assumption is generally thought to be acceptable for a daily VAR in which the expected return will indeed tend to be very close to zero. Because expected returns are typically positive, shifting the distribution by assuming a zero expected return will result in a larger loss, so the VAR will be greater. Therefore, this small adjustment is slightly more conservative and avoids the problem of having to estimate the expected return, which is typically much harder to estimate than the volatility. Another advantage of this adjustment is that it is easier to adjust the VAR for a different time period. For example, if the daily VAR is estimated at \$100,000, the annual VAR would be $100,000\sqrt{250}$ = \$1,581,139. This result could also be obtained by adjusting the standard deviation as indicated above or in this more direct manner. This simple conversion of a shorter-term VAR to a longer-term VAR (or vice versa) does not work, however, if the average return is not zero. Then one would have to convert the average return and standard deviation to the different time period and compute the VAR from the adjusted average and standard deviation.

PRACTICE PROBLEM 1

Consider a portfolio consisting of stocks as one asset class and bonds as another. The expected return on the stock portion of the portfolio is 12 percent, and the standard deviation is 22 percent. The expected return on the bond portion of the portfolio is 5 percent, and the standard deviation is 7 percent. All of these figures are annual. The correlation between the two asset classes is 0.15. The portfolio's market value is \$150 million and is allocated 65 percent to stock and 35 percent to bonds. Determine the VAR using the analytical method for the following cases:

A. A 5 percent yearly VAR

B. A 1 percent yearly VAR

C. A 5 percent weekly VAR

D. A 1 percent weekly VAR

SOLUTIONS

First we must calculate the annual portfolio expected return and standard deviation. Using "S" to indicate stocks and "B" to indicate bonds, we have

$$\mu_p = w_S\mu_S + w_B\mu_B = 0.65(0.12) + 0.35(0.05) = 0.0955$$

$$\sigma_p^2 = w_S^2\sigma_S^2 + w_B^2\sigma_B^2 + 2w_Sw_B\sigma_S\sigma_B\rho$$

$$= (0.65)^2(0.22)^2 + (0.35)^2(0.07)^2 + 2(0.65)(0.35)(0.22)(0.07)(0.15) = 0.0221$$

$$\sigma_p = \sqrt{0.0221} = 0.1487$$

A. For a 5 percent yearly VAR, we have $\mu_p - 1.65\sigma = 0.0955 - 1.65(0.1487) = -0.1499$. Then the VAR would be $150,000,000(0.1499) = $22.485 million.

B. For a 1 percent yearly VAR, we have $\mu_p - 2.33\sigma = 0.0955 - 2.33(0.1487) = -0.251$. Then the VAR would be $150,000,000(0.251) = $37.65 million.

C. For weekly VAR, we adjust the expected return to $0.0955/52 = 0.00184$ and the standard deviation to $0.1487/\sqrt{52} = 0.02062$. The 5 percent weekly VAR would then be $\mu_p - 1.65\sigma = 0.00184 - 1.65(0.02062) = -0.03218$. Then the VAR would be $150,000,000(0.03218) = $4.827 million.

D. The 1 percent weekly VAR would be $\mu_p - 2.33\sigma = 0.00184 - 2.33(0.02062) = -0.0462$. Then the VAR would be $150,000,000(0.0462) = $6.93 million.

The primary advantage of the analytical or variance–covariance method is its simplicity. Its primary disadvantage lies in the fact that it relies on the assumption of a normal distribution. In principle, there is no reason why a normal distribution is required, but if any other distribution is assumed, the calculation becomes somewhat more difficult because risk measures other than variance must be taken into account. For example, the normal distribution is symmetric, but many distributions have skewness, making it impossible to estimate the VAR from the expected value and variance alone.

Many observed distributions of returns have an abnormally large number of extreme events. This quality is called the property of fat tails. Equity markets in particular tend to have more frequent large market declines than a normal distribution would predict. Thus, using a normal distribution to estimate the VAR would severely understate the actual magnitude and frequency of large losses. VAR would then fail at precisely what it is supposed to do: measure the risk associated with large losses.

A related problem that surfaces with the analytical or variance–covariance method is that the assumption of a normal distribution is inappropriate when the portfolio contains options. The return distributions of options are far from normal. Remember that a normal distribution has an unlimited upside and an unlimited downside. Call options have unlimited upside potential, as in a normal distribution, but the downside is a fixed value, the call's premium, and the distribution of call returns is highly skewed. Similarly, put options have a limited upside and a large but fixed downside, and the distribution of put returns is also highly skewed. Likewise, covered calls and protective puts have return distributions that are sharply skewed in one direction or the other.

Thus, when portfolios contain options, the assumption of a normal distribution to estimate VAR presents a significant problem. One common solution to this problem is to estimate the option's price sensitivity using its delta. Recall that delta expresses a linear relationship between an option's price and the price of the underlying (i.e., Delta = Percent Δ option price/Percent Δ underlying). A linear relationship lends itself more easily to treatment with a normal distribution. That is, a normally distributed random variable remains normally distributed when multiplied by a constant. In this case, the constant is the delta. The change in the option price is assumed to equal the change in the underlying price multiplied by the delta. This trick converts the normal distribution for the return on the underlying into a normal distribution for the option return. As such, the use of delta to estimate the option's price sensitivity for VAR purposes has led some to also call the technique the **delta-normal method**. So, the analytical method is also called the variance–covariance method and the delta-normal method. As we saw in Chapter 4, however, the use of delta is appropriate only for small changes in the underlying. Yet it is the large changes in the underlying that are the very reason for using VAR. As an alternative, some users of the delta-normal method add the second-order effect, which, as we saw in Chapters 4 and 7, is captured by the gamma. Unfortunately, as these higher-order effects are added, the relationship between the option price and the price of the underlying begins to approximate the true nonlinear relationship. At that point, using a normal distribution becomes completely inappropriate. Therefore, the use of the analytical method could cause problems if a portfolio has options.

3.2.3 THE HISTORICAL METHOD

Another method used to estimate VAR is the historical method. This approach simply uses data from the returns of the portfolio over a recent past period. It compiles these data in the form of a histogram. From there, it becomes easy to identify the level of return that is exceeded with a probability of 5 percent (or 1 percent, if preferred).

Consider the portfolio we have been examining, consisting of 75 percent invested in the S&P 500 and 25 percent invested in the Nasdaq Composite Index. Exhibit 9-7 is a histogram showing the daily returns on this portfolio for a recent calendar year. First, we note that the distribution bears a similarity to a normal distribution but also differs from it somewhat. There seem to be a few more returns slightly lower than the midpoint of the distribution than would be the case for a normal distribution. With the historical method, however, we are not constrained to using the normal distribution. We simply collect the historical data and identify the return below which 5 (or 1) percent of returns fall. Although we could attempt to read this number from the histogram, it is much easier to simply rank order the returns and determine the VAR figure from the sorted returns and the dollar value of the portfolio.

The year examined here contains 248 returns. To have 5 percent of the returns in the lower tail of the distribution would mean that about 12 returns should be less than the VAR return. Thus, the approximate VAR return would be indicated by the 12th worst return. A rank ordering of the data reveals that the 12th worst return is −0.0294. For a $50,000,000 portfolio, the VAR would thus be 0.0294($50,000,000) = $1.47 million.[11]

The historical method has the advantage of avoiding any assumptions about the type of probability distribution that generates returns. The disadvantage, however, is that this method relies completely on events of the past, and whatever distribution prevailed in the past might not hold in the future. In particular, periods of unusually large negative returns, such as the 23 percent one-day decline in the Dow Jones Industrial Average on 19 October 1987, might be questionable as an assumption for the future.

The historical method is also sometimes called the **historical simulation method**. This term is somewhat misleading because the approach does not involve a *simulation* of the past but rather what *actually happened* in the past. In this context, it is important to note that a portfolio that an investor might have held in the past might not even be the same as the one it will have in the future. When using the historical method, one must reflect any

---

[11] Technically, the VAR would fall between the 12th and 13th worst returns. Using the 13th worst return gives a more conservative VAR. Alternatively, we might average the 12th and 13th worst returns.

EXHIBIT 9-7 Historical Daily Returns on a Portfolio Invested 75 Percent in S&P 500 and 25 Percent in Nasdaq

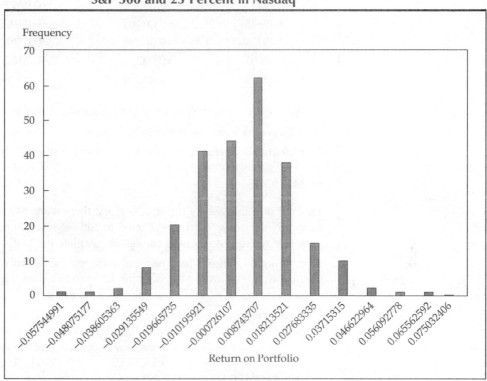

known changes such as portfolio composition.[12] In addition, instruments such as bonds and most derivatives behave differently at different times in their lives, so their behavior in the past must be adjusted if they remain in the portfolio going forward. When a company uses a different portfolio composition to calculate its historical VAR than the one it actually had in the past, it may be more appropriate to call the method a historical simulation. Nonetheless, to fully appreciate the concept of simulation, one must become familiar with the third method of estimating VAR, Monte Carlo simulation.

PRACTICE PROBLEM 2

For simplicity, we shall use a one-stock portfolio. Shown below are the 40 worst monthly returns on IBM stock during the last 20 years:

−0.17867	−0.07237	−0.05031	−0.03372
−0.17505	−0.07234	−0.04889	−0.02951
−0.17296	−0.07220	−0.04697	−0.02905
−0.16440	−0.07126	−0.04439	−0.02840

---

[12] For example, in the two-asset portfolio we illustrated here, the weights were 75 percent S&P 500 and 25 percent Nasdaq. If the company were going forward with a different set of weights, it would obviously need to use the weights it planned to use in the future when calculating the VAR by the historical method.

−0.10655	−0.07064	−0.04420	−0.02584
−0.09535	−0.06966	−0.04173	−0.02508
−0.09348	−0.06465	−0.04096	−0.02270
−0.08236	−0.06266	−0.03633	−0.02163
−0.08065	−0.06204	−0.03626	−0.02115
−0.07779	−0.05304	−0.03464	−0.01976

For both calculations below, assume the portfolio value is $100,000.

A. Calculate a 5 percent monthly VAR using the historical method.

B. Calculate a 1 percent monthly VAR using the historical method.

SOLUTIONS

First we note that during the last 20 years, there were 240 monthly returns. We see here only the worst 40 returns. Therefore, although we do not have the entire distribution of returns, we do have enough to calculate the VAR.

A. Out of 240 returns, the 5 percent worst are the 12 worst returns. Therefore, the historical VAR would be about the 12th worst return. From the table of data, we see that this is −0.07234. So, the VAR would be 0.07234($100,000) = $7,234.

B. The 1 percent worst returns are 2.4 returns. We would probably use the second worst return, which is −0.17505. The VAR would be 0.17505($100,000) = $17,505. Alternatively, we might average the second and third worst returns to obtain (−0.17505 + −0.17296)/2 = −0.17401. Then the VAR would be 0.17401($100,000) = $17,401.

3.2.4   THE MONTE CARLO SIMULATION METHOD

The third approach to estimating VAR is Monte Carlo simulation. In general, it is a technique for producing random outcomes to examine what might happen given a particular set of risks. Monte Carlo simulation is widely used in the sciences as well as in business to study a variety of problems. In the financial world in recent years, it has become an extremely important technique for measuring risk. Monte Carlo simulation generates random outcomes according to an assumed probability distribution and a set of input parameters. These outcomes are then analyzed to gauge the risk associated with the events in question. When estimating VAR, Monte Carlo simulation is used to produce random portfolio returns. These returns are then assembled into a summary distribution from which one can determine at which level the lower 5 percent (or 1 percent, if preferred) of return outcomes occur. This figure is then applied to the portfolio value to obtain the VAR.

Monte Carlo simulation uses a probability distribution for each variable of interest and a mechanism to randomly generate outcomes according to each distribution. Our goal here is to gain a basic understanding of the technique and how to use it. Therefore, we illustrate it without explaining the full details of how to generate the random values.

Suppose we return to the example of our $50 million portfolio invested 75 percent in the S&P 500 and 25 percent in the Nasdaq Composite Index. We assume, as previously, that this portfolio should have an annual expected return of 13.5 percent and a standard deviation of 24.4 percent. We shall now conduct a Monte Carlo simulation using the normal distribution with these parameters. Keep in mind that in practice, one of the advantages of Monte Carlo simulation is that it does not require a normal distribution, but the normal distribution is often used and we shall stay with it for illustrative purposes.

A random number generator is used to produce a random value, which is then converted into a normally distributed value representing a rate of return for this portfolio over a period of one year. Suppose the first value it produces is a return of −21.87 percent. This rate would correspond to an end-of-year portfolio value of $39.07 million. The second random return it produces is −4.79 percent, which takes the portfolio value to $47.61 million.[13] The third random return it produces is 31.38 percent, which makes the portfolio value $65.69 million. We continue this process a large number of times, perhaps several thousand or even several million. To keep the simulation to a manageable size for illustrative purposes, we generate only 300 outcomes.

Exhibit 9-8 shows the histogram of portfolio outcomes. Notice that even though we used a normal distribution to generate the outcomes, the resulting distribution does not look much like the normal distribution. Of course, we should be surprised if it did, because we used only 300 random outcomes, which is a relatively small sample.

To obtain the point that is exceeded in the lower tail by 5 percent of the outcomes, we rank-order the data and find the 15th lowest outcome, which is a portfolio value of $34.25 million, corresponding to a loss of $15.75 million. This value is higher than the annual VAR estimated using the analytical method ($13.4 million). These two values would be the same if we had employed a sufficiently large sample size in the Monte Carlo simulation so that the sample VAR would converge to the true population VAR.

EXHIBIT 9-8   Simulated Values after One Year for a Portfolio Invested 75 Percent in S&P 500 and 25 Percent in Nasdaq

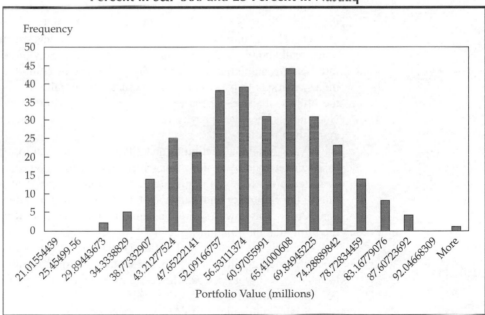

Although the normal distribution is widely used in Monte Carlo simulation, one of the advantages of this technique is that it can be used with virtually any type of probability distribution. In most practical applications, a non-normal distribution is more appropriate. For many derivatives dealers, the problems of managing the risk of these

---

[13] The random outcomes are independent, not sequential. Each outcome thus represents a return relative to the full initial value of the portfolio of $50 million.

instruments is compounded by the fact that there may be hundreds if not thousands of random variables affecting the value of their overall position. Most of the probability distributions are non-normal, and many of them interact in complex ways. Monte Carlo simulation is often the only practical means of generating the information necessary to manage the risk. With tens of thousands of transactions on the books of most dealers, Monte Carlo simulation can require extensive commitments of computer resources.

3.2.5   FURTHER COMMENTS ON VALUE AT RISK

Value at Risk is now a widely used but imperfect technique for quantifying risk. VAR can be difficult to estimate, and different estimation methods can give quite different values. VAR can also lull one into a false sense of security by giving the impression that the risk is properly measured and under control. VAR often underestimates the frequency of the worst returns, although this problem primarily results from wrong assumptions and models. Also, VAR puts no emphasis on the best possible outcomes. As such, VAR does not give a total risk picture. It shows only the risk of bad outcomes, and not the good. A certain amount of bad risk can be tolerated if matched with good risk, but VAR does not take the good risk into account.

Users of VAR should test to determine if their VAR estimates prove to be accurate after time passes. For example, if the daily VAR at 0.05 is estimated at $1 million, then over a reasonable period of time, such as a year, a loss of at least $1 million should be exceeded about $250(0.05) = 12.5$ or so days. If this is not the case, then the VAR estimate could be a bad one.

In addition, VAR can be extremely difficult to obtain for complex organizations. In the simple example we used here, VAR was driven solely by the large- and small-cap stock markets. This assumption might be acceptable for an investment fund. For a large international bank, however, the exposures might be to a variety of domestic and foreign interest rate markets, numerous exchange rates, perhaps some equity markets, and even some commodity markets. A bank could have exposure to literally thousands of risks. Consolidating the effects of these exposures into a single risk measure can be extremely difficult.[14] Nonetheless, most large banks manage to do so and, generally, do an excellent job of managing their risk.

VAR has the attraction of quantifying the potential loss in simple terms and can be easily understood by senior management. Regulatory bodies have taken note of VAR as a risk measure, and some require that institutions supply it in their reports. In the United States, the Securities and Exchange Commission now requires that publicly traded companies report on how they are managing financial risk. VAR is one acceptable method of reporting that information.

Exhibit 9-9 shows how The Coca-Cola Company reports its VAR. We see that Coca-Cola provides a quarterly VAR based on the historical simulation method, with data collected over a 10-year period. The company expresses its 5 percent VAR in the form of a 95 percent confidence level.

Many companies use VAR as a measure of their capital at risk. They will estimate the VAR associated with a particular activity, such as a line of business, an asset manager, a subsidiary, or a division. Then they evaluate performance, taking into account the VAR associated with this risky activity. In some cases, companies allocate capital on the basis

---

[14] Most banks with sophisticated systems measure these numerous risks by identifying a set of unnamed factors that reflect common risks. This approach is somewhat similar to identifying the stock market as a whole as a primary factor that affects stock prices and various industries as factors that affect stock prices in a secondary manner.

EXHIBIT 9-9   Value at Risk at The Coca-Cola Company

Our company monitors our exposure to financial market risks using several objective measurement systems, including value-at-risk models. Our value-at-risk calculations use a historical simulation model to estimate potential future losses in the fair value of our derivatives and
other financial instruments that could occur as a result of adverse movements in foreign currency and interest rates. We have not considered the potential impact of favorable movements
in foreign currency and interest rates on our calculations. We examined historical weekly
returns over the previous 10 years to calculate our value at risk. The average value at risk represents the simple average of quarterly amounts over the past year. As a result of our foreign
currency value-at-risk calculations, we estimate with 95 percent confidence that the fair values of our foreign currency derivatives and other financial instruments, over a one-week
period, would decline by less than $34 million, $43 million and $37 million, respectively,
using 2002, 2001 or 2000 average fair values and by less than $31 million and $37 million,
respectively, using December 31, 2002 and 2001 fair values. According to our interest rate
value-at-risk calculations, we estimate with 95 percent confidence that any increase in our net
interest expense due to an adverse move in our 2002 average or in our December 31, 2002 interest rates over a one-week period would not have a material impact on our financial statements.
Our December 31, 2001 and 2000 estimates also were not material to our financial statements.

Source: Coca-Cola Company, *2002 Annual Report*, p. 52.

of VAR. For example, a pension fund might determine its overall acceptable VAR and then
inform each asset class manager that it can operate subject to its VAR not exceeding a certain amount. The manager's goal is to earn the highest return possible given its VAR. This
activity is known as risk budgeting and is covered more in a later section. VAR can also be
used to make decisions about the addition of an asset to a portfolio or company. A company with an overall VAR will sometimes evaluate a proposed asset's or portfolio's mar-
ginal contribution to the company's VAR. Although this approach gives an extremely
limited picture of the asset's or portfolio's contribution to risk, it nonetheless provides useful information on the effect that adding the asset or portfolio will have on the company's
overall risk as reflected in its VAR.

　　VAR is, nonetheless, controversial and has even been criticized by some as being worse
than not measuring risk at all. If a risk manager uses VAR with an awareness of its limitations,
however, she will definitely have a better picture of the risk than with no risk measure at all.
Even if VAR gives an incorrect measure of the loss potential, the risk manager can take this
risk measurement error into account when making the key overall decisions.[15]

　　Probably no subject has claimed as much attention in the literature on risk management as VAR. Researchers have devoted significant resources to improving the estimation
of VAR. The controversy remains, but VAR as a risk measure is unlikely to ever be completely rejected. It conveys in a single number a great deal of information on the magnitude of risk. It should not, however, be used in isolation.

---

[15] A well-known critic of VAR has likened its use to flying an aircraft with a potentially flawed altimeter. With
an altimeter, a pilot may think he knows the correct altitude. Without an altimeter, the pilot will look out the
window. Of course, this argument presumes that there are no clouds below. The probability of hitting trees or a
mountain is the joint probability that the aircraft is too low *and* the altimeter gives a false signal, which is less
than the simple probability that the aircraft is too low. Aware of the potential for the altimeter to be flawed, the
pilot will also seek information from other sources, which themselves are less than 100 percent accurate. So
will the risk manager. Both will gauge the risk against their tolerance for risk and take appropriate action. We
look at some of these other sources of risk information in the next section.

3.3 **IMPROVEMENTS**
AND SUPPLEMENTS
TO VAR

There are several other ways to improve upon and supplement VAR as a risk measure. One method, borrowed from engineering, is **stress testing**. In stress testing, the risk manager examines the performance of the portfolio under certain high-risk scenarios. These scenarios will often be situations in which many markets incur large losses simultaneously and, therefore, involve high correlations across markets. Some scenarios might even include unusual world events that amplify financial market reactions. This approach is also sometimes called **scenario analysis**.

Some variations of VAR are **cash flow at risk** (CFAR) and **earnings at risk** (EAR). CFAR measures the risk of a company's cash flow instead of its market value and is more appropriately used when the portfolio of assets generates cash flows but cannot be valued in a publicly traded market. Therefore, it is used most often by corporations whose assets are more physical than financial. Some companies take a broader picture and focus on EAR, which is the same concept as VAR except that the underlying is profit or earnings per share.

Another useful tool to supplement VAR is the expected loss in excess of VAR. What loss would be expected, given that a loss in excess of VAR is incurred?

VAR developed initially as a measure for market risk, which is the risk associated with the primary market forces of interest rates, exchange rates, stock prices, and commodity prices. With some difficulty, VAR can be extended to handle credit risk, the risk that a counterparty will not pay what it owes.

4 MANAGING CREDIT RISK

In Section 3, we examined market risk. The other primary type of risk is credit risk, sometimes called default risk, which is the risk of loss due to nonpayment by a counterparty. Until the era of over-the-counter derivatives, credit risk was exclusively a concern in bond and loan markets. Exchange-traded derivatives are guaranteed against credit loss. Over-the-counter derivatives, however, contain no explicit credit guaranty and, therefore, are subject to loss when the counterparty fails to pay.

Before over-the-counter derivatives were widely used, bond portfolio managers and bank loan officers were the primary credit risk managers. They assessed credit risk in a number of ways.[16] The quality of a company would be evaluated by examining financial statements, calculating credit scores, and relying on the opinions of others. In fact, rating agencies and credit bureaus were, and to some extent still are, the primary sources of information on credit quality. With the growth in the over-the-counter derivatives market, however, the proliferation and complexity of financial instruments has placed new demands on the understanding of credit risk. Fortunately, concerns about credit risk in the over-the-counter derivatives market have led to significant progress in understanding and managing this risk.

4.1 **TRADITIONAL**
NOTIONS OF
CREDIT RISK

The idea behind credit as a source of risk is that one party owing money to the other could default. If the defaulting party has insufficient resources to cover the loss or the creditor cannot impose a claim on the debtor's assets that are unrelated to the line of business in which the credit was extended, the creditor can suffer a loss.[17] A creditor might be able to recover some of the loss, perhaps by having the debtor sell assets and pay the creditors a

---

[16] Credit risk in the more general context of fixed-income securities is discussed in more detail in Level II, Chapter 9, of *Fixed Income Analysis for the Chartered Financial Analyst Program* (Fabozzi, 2000). Many of the principles of credit risk analysis for fixed-income securities also apply to derivatives.

[17] The personal assets of the owners of a corporation are shielded from creditors by the principle of limited liability, which can also apply to certain partnerships. The law supporting limited liability is a fundamental one in most societies and supports the notion that default is a right. Indeed, option-pricing theory has been used to value this right as the option that it actually is.

portion of their claim. Ultimately in a bankruptcy situation, the creditor's claim simply goes in a pool in the order specified by bankruptcy law. Equity claimants are supposed to be paid last and not until all creditors are paid; in reality, however, that does not always happen. Bankruptcy laws often work against creditors, seemingly to attempt to keep the company alive. To do that, however, equityholders and potential suppliers of new equity capital must have an incentive. This effect works to the disadvantage of creditors.

Credit losses have two dimensions, the event of loss and the amount lost (which reflects the recovery rate). The event of loss is a probabilistic occurrence: A given probability exists that the debtor will default. Given that default occurs, however, it is then necessary to assess the recovery rate. In relation to data on losses from market movements, the amount of data on credit losses is much smaller. Credit losses do not occur often in derivatives markets and the infrequency of loss means that there is not much data from which to assess the magnitude of losses. Although some statistical data are available, historical recovery rates can be unreliable. It can be hard to predict what an asset could be sold for in bankruptcy proceedings, and claims are not always paid in the order specified by bankruptcy law.

In the risk management business, risk is often viewed as having two time elements. One is the risk associated with events happening now, and the other is the risk associated with events to happen in the future. With respect to credit risk, the risk of events happening now is called *current* credit risk. It relates to the risk that amounts due at the present will not be paid. For example, a loan interest payment or swap payment could be due immediately. There is clearly some risk that this payment will not be made. Assuming, however, that the counterparty is solvent and the payment will be made with certainty, there remains the risk that the counterparty will default at a later date. This risk is called *potential* credit risk. It can differ quite significantly from current credit risk and may seem to be much greater than current credit risk, but that is not always so. A company experiencing financial difficulties at the present could, with sufficient time, be able to work out its problems and be in better financial condition at a later date. Regardless of which is greater, however, a creditor must assess credit risk at different points in time. In doing so, it is important to understand how different financial instruments have different patterns of credit risk both across instruments and across time within a given instrument. This point will be discussed later in this section.

Another element of credit risk blends current and potential credit risk. This is the possibility that a counterparty will default on a current payment to one party bearing its current credit risk, and thus indirectly default on another party bearing only its potential credit risk. For example, suppose Party A owes Party B, but no payments are due for some time. Party A, however, currently owes a payment to Party C and is unable to pay. A is, therefore, in default to C. Depending on what actions C takes, A may be forced into bankruptcy. If so, then B's claim simply goes into the pool of other claims on A. In that case, A has technically defaulted to B without actually having a payment due.

4.1.1 OPTION PRICING THEORY AND CREDIT RISK

In this book we have devoted a great deal of effort to understanding options, but our primary goal has been to learn how options can be used in financial strategies. There are, however, some added benefits to understanding options. One in particular is that options enable us to better understand the nature of credit risk. In this section we will see that the stock of a company with leverage can be viewed as a call option on the assets. This approach will lead to the result that a bond with credit risk can be viewed as a default-free bond plus an implicit short put option written by the bondholders for the stockholders.

Consider a company with assets with a market value of A_0 and debt with a face value of F. The debt is in the form of a single zero-coupon bond due at time T. The market value of the bond is B_0. Thus, the market value of the stock is

$$S_0 = A_0 - B_0$$

At time T, the assets will be worth A_T, and the company will owe F. If $A_T \geq F$, the company will pay off its debt, leaving the amount $A_T - F$ for the stockholders. Thus, S_T would be worth $A_T - F$. If the value of the assets is not sufficient to pay off the debt ($A_T < F$), the stockholders will discharge their obligation by turning over the assets to the bondholders. Thus, the bondholders will receive A_T, which is less than their claim of F, and the stockholders will receive nothing. The company is, therefore, bankrupt. These results are illustrated below by showing the payoffs to the two suppliers of capital.

Payoffs to the Suppliers of Capital to the Company

Source of Capital	Market Value at Time 0	Payoffs at Time T	
		$A_T < F$	$A_T \geq F$
Bondholders	B_0	A_T	F
Stockholders	S_0	0	$A_T - F$
Total	$B_0 + S_0 = A_0$	A_T	A_T

Notice that the payoffs to the stockholders resemble those of a call option in which the underlying is the assets, the exercise price is F, and the option expires at time T, the maturity date of the bond. Indeed, the stock of a company with a single zero-coupon bond issue is a call option on the assets.

To better understand the nature of stock as an option, let us recall the concept of put–call parity from Chapter 4. In the notation of that chapter, $p_0 + S_0 = c_0 + X/(1 + r)^T$. The put price plus the underlying price equals the call price plus the present value of the exercise price. The following correspondence between the traditional framework of Chapter 4 and the current framework applies:

Variable	Traditional Framework	Current Framework
Underlying	S_0 (stock)	A_0 (value of assets)
Exercise price	X	F (face value of bond)
Time to expiration	T	T (maturity of bond)
Risk-free rate	r	r
Call price	c_0	S_0 (value of stock)
Put price	p_0	p_0

Note the last line. We see that in the traditional framework, there is a put option, which we know is an option to sell the underlying at a fixed price. In fact, we know from put–call parity that $p_0 = c_0 - S_0 + X/(1 + r)^T$. The put is equivalent to a long call, a short position in the underlying stock, and a long position in a risk-free bond with face value equal to the exercise price. In the current framework, the standard expression of put–call parity would be $p_0 + A_0$ (put plus underlying) $= S_0 + F/(1 + r)^T$ (stock plus present value of bond principal). Turning this expression around and reversing the order of the put and bond, we obtain

$$A_0 = S_0 + F/(1 + r)^T - p_0$$

Noting, however, that by definition the asset value, A_0, equals the market value of the stock, S_0, plus the market value of the bond, B_0,

$$A_0 = S_0 + B_0$$

we see that the market value of the bond must be equivalent to

$$B_0 = F/(1 + r)^T - p_0$$

The first term on the right-hand side is equivalent to a default-free zero-coupon bond paying F at maturity. The second term is a short put. The claim of the bondholders, which is subject to default, can thus be viewed as a default-free bond and a short put on the assets. In other words, the bondholders have implicitly written the stockholders a put on the assets. From the stockholders' perspective, this put is their right to fully discharge their liability by turning over the assets to the bondholders, even though those assets could be worth less than the bondholders' claim. In legal circles, this put option is known as the stockholders' right of limited liability.

The existence of this implicit put option is the difference between a default-free bond and a bond subject to default. This approach to understanding credit risk forms the basis for models that use option pricing theory to explain credit risk premiums, probabilities of default, and the valuation of companies that use leverage. In practice, the capital structures of most companies are more complex than the one used here, but practical applications of variations of the model are found in the financial industry.

4.1.2 THE CREDIT RISK OF FORWARD CONTRACTS

When we covered the different types of derivative instruments in previous chapters, we briefly described the credit risk associated with them. We shall now discuss those points in a little more detail. First we consider forward contracts.

Recall that forward contracts involve commitments on the part of each party. No cash is due at the start, and no cash is paid until expiration, at which time one party owes the greater amount to the other. The party that owes the larger amount could default, leaving the other with a claim of the defaulted amount.[18] Each party assumes the credit risk of the other. Prior to expiration, there is no current credit risk, as no current payments are owed, but there is potential credit risk in connection with the payments to be made at expiration.[19] Current credit risk arises when the contract is at its expiration. In what follows, we will examine how potential credit risk changes over the life of the contract as the value of the underlying changes.

As we showed in Chapter 2, from the perspective of a given party, the market value of a forward contract can be easily calculated as the present value of the amount owed to it minus the present value of the amount it owes. So, the market value at a given time reflects the potential credit risk. This is another reason the calculation of market value is important: It indicates the amount of a claim that would be subject to loss in the event of a default.

In Chapter 2, we examined a forward contract that expires in one year. The underlying asset price is $100 and the risk-free interest rate is 5 percent. We determined that the forward price is $100(1.05) = $105. We then assumed that three months later the asset price is $102. We determined that the value of the long forward contract at that time is $102 - $105/(1.05)^{0.75} = $0.7728. This is the value to the long, because the contract is a claim on the asset, which is currently worth $102, and an obligation to pay $105 for it in

---

[18] The description here is more like that of a cash-settled forward contract, rather than one in which the short delivers the underlying asset to the long. The credit risk is about the same, however, as either the short could fail to deliver the asset or the long could fail to pay for the delivered asset.

[19] We should also remember that, as described earlier, a company can default on an obligation to another party, thereby triggering bankruptcy, even though there is no obligation on the forward contract until later.

nine months. To the holder of the long position, this contract is worth $0.7728, and to the holder of the short position, it is worth $-$0.7728.

Which party bears the potential credit risk? The claim of the long is positive. The claim of the short is negative. Therefore, the long currently bears the credit risk. As it stands right now, the value of the long's claim is $0.7728. No payment is currently due and hence there is no current credit risk, but the payments that are due later have a present value of $0.7728. Actual default may or may not occur at expiration. Moreover, at expiration, the amount owed is not likely to be this same amount. In fact, if the spot price falls enough, the situation will have turned around and the long could owe the short the greater amount. Nonetheless, in assessing the credit risk three months into the contract, the long's claim is $0.7728. This claim has a probability of not being paid and the potential for recovery of a portion of the loss in the event of default. If the counterparty declares bankruptcy before the contract expires, the claim of the nondefaulting counterparty is the market value of the forward contract at the time of the bankruptcy, assuming this value is positive. So if the short declares bankruptcy at this time, the long has a claim worth $0.7728. If the long declares bankruptcy, the long holds an asset worth $0.7728.

4.1.3 THE CREDIT RISK OF SWAPS

As we previously described, a swap is similar to a series of forward contracts. The periodic payments associated with a swap imply, however, that there are a series of points during the life of the contract at which there is current credit risk. As with forward contracts, the market value of the swap can be calculated at any time and reflects the present value of the amount at risk for a credit loss (i.e., the potential credit risk).

For example, in Chapter 5 we gave an example of a plain vanilla interest rate swap with a one-year life and quarterly payments at LIBOR. Using the term structure, we determined that the swap has a fixed rate of 3.68 percent, leading to quarterly fixed payments of $0.0092 per $1 notional principal. We then moved forward 60 days into the life of the swap and, with a new term structure, we determined that the market value of the swap is $0.0047 per $1 notional principal. To the party that is long (i.e., paying fixed and receiving floating), the swap has a positive market value. To the counterparty, which pays floating and receives fixed, the claim has a market value of $-$0.0047.

As with a forward contract, the market value indicates the present value of the payments owed to the party minus the present value of the payments the party owes. Only 60 days into the life of a swap with quarterly payments, a payment is not due for 30 more days. Thus, there is no current credit risk. There is, however, potential credit risk. The market value of $0.0047 represents the amount that is at risk of loss for default. Of course, if default occurs, it will be at a later date when the amount will probably be different. Moreover, the market value could reverse its sign. At this time, the amount owed by the short to the long is greater, but at a later date, the amount owed by the long to the short could be greater. As with forward contracts, if the party to which the value is negative defaults, the counterparty has a claim of that value. If the party to which the value is positive defaults, the defaulting party holds an asset with the positive market value. Also, the counterparty could default to someone else, thereby being forced to declare bankruptcy before a payment on this swap is due. In that case, the market value of the swap at that time is either the claim of the creditor or the asset held by the bankrupt party in bankruptcy proceedings.

The credit risk of swaps can vary greatly among types of swaps and during the life of a swap. For interest rate and equity swaps, the potential credit risk is largest during the middle period of the life of the swap. During the beginning of the life of the swap, we would typically assume that the credit risk is not very great. Otherwise, the counterparty would not engage in the swap. At the end of the life of the swap, the credit risk is not very great because the amount at risk is smaller. There are fewer payments at the end of a swap than at any other time during its life; hence, the amount that can be lost due to a default is smaller. This leaves the greatest exposure during the middle period of the life of the swap. Many currency swaps, however, provide for the payment of the notional principal at the beginning and at the end of the life of the swap. Because the notional principal tends to be a large amount relative to the payments, the potential for loss due to the counterparty defaulting on the final notional principal payment is great. Thus, whereas interest rate swaps have their greatest credit risk midway during the life of the swap, currency swaps have their greatest credit risk between the midpoint and the end of the life of the swap.

4.1.4 THE CREDIT RISK OF OPTIONS

Forward contracts and swaps have bilateral default risk. Though only one party will end up making a given payment, each party could potentially be the party owing the net amount. Options, on the other hand, have unilateral credit risk. The buyer of an option pays a cash premium at the start and owes nothing more. The buyer is not required to exercise the option.[20] Thus, the seller assumes no credit risk from the buyer. The buyer assumes credit risk from the seller, which could be quite significant. If the buyer exercises the option, the seller is obligated to do something. If the option is a call, the seller must deliver the underlying or pay an equivalent cash settlement. If the option is a put, the seller must accept delivery of the underlying and pay for it or pay an equivalent cash settlement. If the seller fails to fulfill her end of the obligation, she is in default. Like forward contracts, European options have no payments due until expiration. Hence, there is no current credit risk until expiration, although there is significant potential credit risk.

Consider an option we looked at in Chapter 4. The underlying price is 52.75, and its standard deviation is 0.35. The exercise price is 50, the risk-free rate is 4.88 percent continuously compounded, and the option expires in nine months. Using the Black–Scholes–Merton model, we found that the price of a European call option is 8.5580. The holder of this call option thus has potential credit risk represented by a present claim of 8.5580. This amount can be thought of as the amount that is at risk, even though at expiration the option will probably be worth something else. In fact, the option might even expire out-of-the-money, in which case it would not matter if the short were bankrupt. If the short declares bankruptcy before expiration, the long has a claim on the value of the option under bankruptcy law.

If the option were American, the value could be greater. Moreover, with American options, the current credit risk could arise if the option holder decides to exercise the option early. This alternative creates the possibility of the short defaulting before expiration.

PRACTICE PROBLEM 3

Calculate the amount at risk of a credit loss in the following examples. You may wish to refer back to previous chapters to determine how to do these calculations.

A. A party goes long a forward contract on one euro denominated in dollars in which the underlying is the euro. The original term of the contract was two years, and the forward rate was \$0.90. The contract now has 18 months to go. The spot rate is \$0.862. The U.S. interest rate is 6 percent, and the euro interest rate is 5 percent. The interest rates are based on discrete compounding/discounting. Determine the amount at risk of a credit loss and which party currently bears the risk.

---

[20] Even if the option is in-the-money, the buyer is under no obligation to exercise it. The seller would certainly be pleased if that happened, but such an event would be extremely rare.

B. Consider a plain vanilla interest rate swap with two months to go before the next payment. Six months after that, the swap will have its final payment. The swap fixed rate is 7 percent, and the upcoming floating payment is 6.9 percent. All payments are based on 30 days in a month and 360 days in a year. Two-month LIBOR is 7.250 percent, and eight-month LIBOR is 7.375 percent. Determine the amount at risk of a credit loss and which party currently bears the risk. Assume a $1 notional principal.

C. A party has sold an option on a stock for $35. The option is currently worth $46, as quoted in the market. Determine the amount at risk of a credit loss and which party currently bears the risk.

SOLUTIONS

A. The contract has 1.5 years remaining. We find the value of the contract to the long, which is

$$\frac{\$0.862}{(1.05)^{1.5}} - \frac{\$0.90}{(1.06)^{1.5}} = -\$0.0235$$

per $1 notional principal. The position has a negative value to the long, so the credit risk is currently borne by the short. From the short's point of view, the contract has a value of $0.0235 per $1 notional principal. No payments are due for 18 months, but the short's claim on the long is worth $0.0235 more than the long's claim on the short. Therefore, this amount is the current value of the amount at risk for a credit loss. Of course, the amount could, and probably will, change over the life of the contract. The credit risk exposure might even shift to the other party.

B. First we find the present value factors for two and eight months:

$$\frac{1}{1 + 0.0725(60/360)} = 0.9881$$

$$\frac{1}{1 + 0.07375(240/360)} = 0.9531$$

The next floating payment will be 0.069(180/360) = 0.0345. The present value of the floating payments (plus hypothetical notional principal) is 1.0345(0.9881) = 1.0222.

Given an annual rate of 7 percent, the fixed payments will be 0.07 × 180/360 = 0.035. The present value of the fixed payments (plus hypothetical notional principal) is, therefore, 0.035(0.9881) + 1.035(0.9531) = 1.0210.

Therefore, the market value of the swap to the party paying fixed and receiving floating is 1.0222 − 1.0210 = 0.0012. This value is positive to the party paying fixed and receiving floating; thus, this party currently assumes the credit risk. Of course, the value will change over the life of the swap and may turn negative, meaning that the credit risk is then assumed by the party paying floating and receiving fixed.

C. All of the credit risk is borne by the owner, because he will look to the seller for the payoff if the owner exercises the option. The current value of the amount at risk is the market price of $46.

The credit risk of derivatives can be quite substantial, but this risk is considerably less than the risk faced by most lenders. When a lender makes a loan, the interest and principal are at risk. The loan principal corresponds closely to the notional principal of most derivative contracts. With the exception of currency swaps, the notional principal is never exchanged in a swap. Even with currency swaps, however, the risk is much smaller than on a loan. If a counterparty defaults on a currency swap, the amount owed to the defaulting counterparty serves as a type of collateral because the creditor is not required to pay it to the defaulting party.[21] Therefore, the credit risk on derivatives transactions tends to be quite small relative to that on loans. On forward and swap transactions, the netting of payments makes the risk extremely small relative to the notional principal and to the credit risk on a bond or loan of equivalent principal.

4.2 TECHNIQUES FOR MANAGING CREDIT RISK

Throughout history, society has developed a variety of means of managing credit risk, some not altogether honorable. Fortunately, debtors' prisons and the proverbial leg-breaking and worse of gangsters are illegal today. Modern society has taken the appropriate view that failing to pay amounts owed is not normally a result of dishonesty but usually follows a period of financial misfortune. Although financial misfortune could come from poor financial management, society does not punish for such deeds, providing that there were no violations of the law. If fraud is not involved, bankruptcy laws tend to be supportive and often encourage a debtor to remain in operation effectively with negative equity. During the process, creditors often are convinced to give up some of their claims as an inducement for new parties to supply equity capital.

With these points in mind, it is important that creditors do a good job of measuring and controlling credit risk. The infrequency of credit losses means that not much history is available for study. Moreover, credit losses are considerably different from losses from market moves. Credit is a one-sided risk. If Party B owes Party A the amount of $1,000, B will end up paying A either $1,000 or some amount ranging from zero to $1,000. A's rate of return is certainly not normally distributed and not even symmetric. All of the risk is downside. Thus, credit risk is not easily analyzed and controlled using such measures as standard deviation and VAR.

4.2.1 REDUCING CREDIT RISK BY LIMITING EXPOSURE

Limiting the amount of exposure to a given party is the primary means of managing credit risk. Just as a bank will not lend too much money to one party, neither will a party engage in too many derivatives transactions with one counterparty. Exactly how much exposure to a given counterparty is too much is still not easy to quantify. Risk managers typically have a good sense of when to limit their exposure, and they make extensive use of quantitative measures of credit exposure. Banks have regulatory constraints on the amount of credit risk they can assume, which are specified in terms of formulas.

4.2.2 REDUCING CREDIT RISK BY MARKING TO MARKET

As we learned in Chapter 3, one device used by the futures market to control credit risk is marking to market. The over-the-counter derivatives market also uses marking to market to deal with credit risk. Over-the-counter contracts are not marked to market every day, but some are marked to market periodically during their lives. Recall that a forward contract or swap has a market value that is positive to one party and negative to another. When a

---

[21] This rule is the case in most modern countries whose courts recognize the principle of netting, a topic we take up in a later section.

contract calls for marking to market, the party to which the value is negative pays the market value to the party to which the value is positive. Then the fixed rate on the contract is recalculated, taking into account the new spot price, interest rate, and time to expiration. We briefly covered the marking to market of forward contracts in Chapter 2 when we discussed valuation.

From Chapter 2 and Section 4.1.2 of this chapter, recall that we examined a one-year forward contract with an initial forward price of $105. Three months later when the asset price was $102, its value was $0.7728 to the long. If the contract were marked to market, the short would pay the long $0.7728. Then the two parties would enter into a new contract expiring in nine months with a new forward price, which would be $102(1.05)^{0.75} = $105.80.

PRACTICE PROBLEM 4

Consider a one-year forward contract established at a rate of $105. The contract is four months into its life. The spot price is $108, the risk-free rate is 4.25 percent, and the underlying makes no cash payments. The two parties decided at the start that they will mark the contract to market every four months. Determine what would happen at this point.

SOLUTION

We find the market value of the contract as $108 − $105/(1.0425)^{8/12} = $5.873. This is positive to the long, so the short pays the long $5.873. The parties then reprice the contract. The new price is $108(1.0425)^{8/12} = $111.04.

At this point, the forward price is reset to $111.04. The parties will then mark to market again at the eight-month point and reset the forward price. This price will then stay in force until expiration.

An option is usually not marked to market because its value is always positive to one side of the transaction. Of course, there is certainly credit risk to one party of an option, but marking to market is usually done only with contracts with two-way credit risk.[22] Option credit risk is normally handled by collateral.

4.2.3 REDUCING CREDIT RISK WITH COLLATERAL

Collateral is often used in bank lending and is common in derivatives transactions as well. In fact, the margin deposits required in futures markets are similar to collateral. Some over-the-counter derivative markets use collateral, which is usually in the form of cash or highly liquid, low-risk securities. A typical collateral specification states an amount that must be maintained in a special account. Often, collateral is required only of the party that owes the greater amount. If a contract has a positive value to Party A and a negative value to Party B, then Party B owes more than Party A, and Party B would be required to put some

---

[22] Options are not typically marked to market because if they were, it could create credit risk for the holder of the short position, where none otherwise existed. Suppose the price first changes such that the long receives mark-to-market gains. Then suppose the price changes such that the short gains. The short then has to collect from the long, exposing the short to credit risk.

collateral into an account. As the market value changes, the amount of collateral that would need to be maintained would vary, increasing as the market value increases and decreasing as the market value decreases. At some point, if the market value goes from positive to negative, the party that would be required to post collateral could change, which would allow the release of collateral for the party that had originally posted it. Collateral is sometimes determined using a formula that specifies that it must be posted based on the level of the market value of the contract or sometimes determined based on a party's credit rating. A change in credit rating could require the posting of more or less collateral.

4.2.4 REDUCING CREDIT RISK WITH NETTING

One of the most common features used in two-way credit risk contracts such as forwards and swaps is netting, which we have already briefly discussed here and in more detail in Chapter 5 on swaps. If a payment is due and Party A owes more to Party B than B owes to A, the difference in the amounts owed is calculated and Party A pays the net amount owed. This procedure, called **payment netting**, reduces the credit risk by reducing the amount of money that must be paid. If Party A owes $100,000 to Party B, which owes $40,000 to A, then the net amount owed is $60,000, which A owes to B. Without netting, B would need to send $40,000 to A, which would send $100,000 to B. Suppose B was in the process of sending its $40,000 to A but was unaware that A was in default and unable to send the $100,000 to B. If the $40,000 gets in A's hands, B might not be able to get it back until the bankruptcy court decides what to do, which could take years. If netting is used, only the $60,000 owed by A to B is at risk.

In the examples we have seen so far, netting is applied on the payment date. The concept of netting can be extended to what happens when a bankruptcy occurs. Suppose A and B are counterparties to a number of derivative contracts with each other. On some of the contracts, the market value to A is positive, and on other contracts, the market value to B is positive. If A declares bankruptcy, netting can be used to solve a number of problems. If A and B agree to do so before the bankruptcy, they can net the market values of *all* of their derivative contracts to determine one overall value owed by one party to another. It could well be the case that, even though A is bankrupt, B might owe more to A than A owes to B. Then B is not a creditor of A in the bankruptcy proceedings. In fact, A's claim on B becomes one of A's remaining assets. This process is referred to as **closeout netting**.[23]

During this bankruptcy process, netting plays an important role in reducing the practice of cherry-picking. Cherry-picking occurs when a bankrupt company is allowed to enforce contracts that are favorable to it while walking away from contracts that are unfavorable to it. In our example, without netting, A could default on the contracts in which it owes more to B than B owes to A, but B could be forced to pay up on those contracts in which it owes more to A than A owes to it.

To be supported through the bankruptcy process, however, netting must be recognized by the legal system. The legal systems of most, but not all, countries recognize netting.

4.2.5 REDUCING CREDIT RISK WITH MINIMUM CREDIT STANDARDS AND ENHANCED DERIVATIVE PRODUCT COMPANIES

As noted above, the first line of defense against credit risk is limiting the amount of business one party engages in with another. Carrying this strategy one step further, an organization might choose to do business only with parties of at least a minimum level of credit

---

[23] If A and B agree, they can even choose to net *all* contracts, not just derivatives, between them. Therefore, if one of these parties is a bank, they might include any loans in determining the overall net amount owed by one party to the other. This approach is referred to as **cross-product netting**.

quality. Normally this credit quality is measured by the company's rating from a rating agency, such as Moody's Investors Service or Standard & Poor's. Some companies will not do business with a company unless its rating from these agencies is at least as good as some specified rating. This practice can pose a problem for some derivatives dealers. Most derivatives dealers are engaged in other lines of work that put them at a variety of other risks. For example, banks are the most common derivatives dealers. Investment banking and brokerage firms deal in derivatives in addition to their main lines of business. To an end user considering engaging in a derivative contract with a dealer, the potential for the dealer's other business to cause the dealer to default is a serious concern. Banks, in particular, are involved in consumer and commercial lending, which can be quite risky. In the United States, for example, we have seen banking crises involving bad loans to the real estate industry and underdeveloped countries.

The possibility that bad loans will result in a bank defaulting on its derivatives transactions is quite real. The dealers themselves have this concern because of the potential it has for reducing the amount of business they can do. Hence, many derivatives dealers have taken action to control this risk. One device used is to form a type of subsidiary that is separate from the dealer's other activities. These subsidiaries are referred to as **enhanced derivatives products companies** (EDPCs), sometimes known as **special purpose vehicles** (SPVs). These companies are usually completely separate from the parent organization and are not liable for the parent's debts. They tend to be very heavily capitalized and are committed to hedging all of their derivatives positions. As a result of these features, these subsidiaries almost always receive the highest credit quality rating by the rating agencies. In the event that the parent goes bankrupt, the EDPC is not liable for the parent company's debts; but if the EDPC goes under, the parent is liable for an amount up to its equity investment and may find it necessary to provide even more protection.[24] Hence, an EDPC would typically have a higher credit rating than its parent.

In the previous section, we discussed how value at risk is used to measure market risk. VAR is also used, albeit with greater difficulty, to measure credit risk. This measure is sometimes called **Credit VAR**, default VAR, or credit at risk. Like ordinary VAR, it reflects the minimum loss with a given probability over a period of time. A company might, for example, quote a Credit VAR of $10 million for one year at 5 percent. This statement means that there is a 5 percent chance the company will incur losses due to default of at least $10 million in one year. Note that Credit VAR cannot be separated from market VAR, because credit risk arises from gains on market positions held. Thus, to accurately measure Credit VAR, a risk manager would focus on the upper tail of the distribution of market returns, where the return to the position is positive, in contrast to market risk VAR, which focuses on the lower tail.[25] Suppose the 5 percent upper tail of the market risk distribution is $5 million. The Credit VAR can be roughly thought of as $5 million, but this thinking assumes that the probability of loss is 100 percent and the net amount recovered in the event of a loss is 0 percent. Further refinements incorporating more-accurate measures of the default probability and recovery rate should lead to a lower and more accurate Credit VAR. Thus, estimating Credit VAR is more complicated than estimating market VAR. As noted above, credit events are rare and do not provide much historical experience.

---

[24] Many EDPCs carry the name of the parent company as part of their name. Hence, the parent company cannot afford to have the subsidiary go under. To date no EDPCs have gone bankrupt, but it is generally believed that a parent company would support its EDPC to probably a greater extent than its equity investment.

[25] In the case of a party with a short position, one would first look at the lower tail of the distribution of market returns.

Recovery rates can be hard to estimate. The interaction between credit risk and market risk is complex. Are markets in which trading gains are earned also markets in which credit losses would be higher? This scenario can be true for some companies but not others, leading to another complication: that credit risk is less easily aggregated than market risk. The correlations between the credit risk of counterparties must be considered.

In spite of these problems, credit risk measurement, whether through Credit VAR or other ways, is not a new problem. Banks have been in the lending business since ancient times. Managing the complexities of lending is certainly not a new practice. The growth and widespread acceptance of derivatives have simply brought more focus on the problem of credit risk management. Fortunately, the vast amount of resources dedicated by derivatives dealers to risk management has led to significant improvements in credit risk management techniques.

4.3 INSURANCE AND CREDIT DERIVATIVES

Insurance is one of the oldest forms of risk management. In an insurance contract, one party (the insured) pays a fixed amount of money (the premium) to another party (the insurer) and receives a guarantee that the latter will compensate the former for a specified portion of any loss incurred due to a particular event or group of events over a defined period of time. When we covered put options in Chapter 4, we explained how they can serve as a form of insurance against financial loss: The option premium corresponds to the insurance premium, and the option's life corresponds to the term of the insurance contract.

Although insurance is traditionally used to provide protection against nonfinancial risk, such as losses due to liability and losses of property, life, and health, it has been used to provide protection against credit risk as well. One area in which insurance has been applied is with mortgage-backed securities. These securities, which are claims on portfolios of mortgages, are sold to investors who wish to earn returns from investing in mortgages.[26] As a practical matter, these investors typically cannot assess the credit risk of all of the ordinary homeowner borrowers represented in the portfolio of mortgages. Therefore, the issuer of the mortgage-backed security usually obtains credit protection in the form of insurance. A third party guarantees that if any homeowners default on their mortgages, the amounts owed will be paid. Hence, in most cases a party buying a guaranteed mortgage-backed security can be assured that the credit risk is essentially zero.[27]

Other forms of insurance against credit loss exist in the financial markets, but generally insurance has not developed as a widespread source of credit loss protection. In recent years, however, new financial instruments in the form of derivatives have developed to protect specifically against credit risk. These instruments are called **credit derivatives**. A credit derivative is a financial contract in which one party has the right to claim a payment from another in the event that a specific credit event occurs during the life of the contract. A credit event is defined in precise terms in the contract and usually refers to such events as failure to make a required payment, bankruptcy, repudiation of debts, a significant

---

[26] For more information on mortgage-backed securities, see Level II, Chapters 3 and 4, of *Fixed Income Analysis for the Chartered Financial Analysis Program* (Fabozzi, 2000).

[27] There are two important points to add here. One is that the assumption of no credit risk is based on the condition that the insurer does not default. Another is that the insurer guarantees only that the principal and interest payments *will* be made, not *when* these payments will be made. Because nearly all mortgages permit homeowners to prepay, homeowners who do so curtail the stream of promised interest payments, thereby forcing a loss on holders of the mortgage-backed securities. Because of the credit guarantee, mortgage-backed securities have often been advertised as "guaranteed" when the guarantee is really just a credit guarantee. Moreover, because one of the guarantors is sometimes a government agency, mortgage-backed securities have been sold in a misleading way as "government guaranteed." The credit guarantee of mortgage-backed securities has often been used by aggressive sales personnel to mislead investors.

restructuring of debt, and a few other specific events that materially affect the likelihood of default on future payments. A credit event can even be defined as a change in the credit rating, as determined by an outside credit rating company.

In many respects, credit derivatives are like insurance, but they have developed more rapidly in the 1990s and with considerably more innovation than ordinary insurance. Although insurance primarily serves to protect against nonfinancial risks, credit derivatives have developed to protect exclusively against credit risk. Although insurance companies have entered the business of selling credit derivatives, credit derivatives have been primarily developed by the same types of financial firms that make markets in other financial derivatives.

Credit derivatives are an important innovation in the market for financial risk management services. They permit parties to separate market risk from credit risk, selling each to parties that want to accept that risk. There are four primary forms of credit derivatives: credit swaps, total return swaps, credit spread options, and credit-linked notes.

4.3.1 Credit Swaps

A credit swap is very similar to an insurance contract. Consider a party holding a debt asset that generates a return but is subject to the possibility that the counterparty will default and be unable to pay the promised return. The asset could be a loan, a bond, or a derivative. The party owning the asset wants to buy protection against credit loss. It pays to the seller of the credit derivative an annual premium of a certain number of basis points relative to the face value of the underlying asset. The asset holder receives a payment if the credit event occurs. For example, if the protection buyer fails to receive payment on the asset, it receives compensation from the protection seller. This compensation can take the form of cash or the protection buyer can deliver the defaulted asset to the protection seller and receive a fixed amount that compensates for the loss.

Exhibit 9-10 illustrates the structure of a credit swap. Note that the protection buyer holds an asset or derivative, which is called a reference asset and which is specifically identified in the contract. The asset generates a total return, meaning that it produces interest and principal payments or capital gains and is subject to the possibility of default. The buyer pays an annual premium to the seller and receives a payment from the seller only if the credit event occurs.

EXHIBIT 9-10   Credit Swap

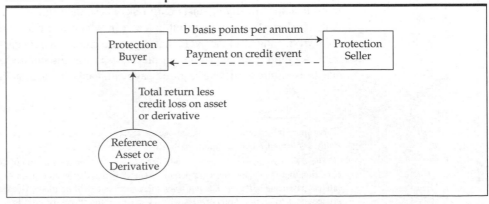

Note, however, that even with a credit derivative, some credit risk remains. The seller of the credit derivative could default. Hence, sellers of credit derivatives must have excellent credit ratings and must do a good job of managing the credit risk they assume.

In most respects, this transaction is not really a swap. Recalling that a swap is a transaction in which two parties exchange a series of payments, we see that one party makes a payment only if a credit event occurs. The other party makes a series of equal annual payments in the amount of a certain number of basis points, which we denote as b. Because the payments of the protection seller are contingent on the occurrence of an event, a credit swap is much more like an option than like a swap.[28] Although credit swaps are not really swaps and more like options, it is possible to use a swap as a type of credit derivative.

4.3.2 TOTAL RETURN SWAP

A total return swap, illustrated in Exhibit 9-11, is one of the most widely used and simplest credit derivatives. Again, the protection buyer holds a reference debt asset or derivative on which it is receiving the total return (interest plus principal or capital gains or a derivative payment). It enters into a swap with a protection seller, agreeing to pay the total return on the reference asset or derivative to the protection seller and receive an underlying floating rate such as LIBOR plus a spread of a given number of basis points. This instrument is a true swap. Each party makes a series of payments to the other. The protection buyer has swapped the total return on the reference asset or derivative for LIBOR plus b basis points. If there is a credit event, the total return on the asset will fall, through either capital losses or default. In fact, the total return could even be negative. Regardless of what happens, the protection buyer passes on the total return to the protection seller. Thus, if the total return is negative, the protection seller pays the protection buyer. Of course, the protection seller always pays the protection buyer LIBOR plus the spread. The protection buyer has simply purchased a floating-rate asset paying LIBOR plus a spread. It has converted the credit-risky asset into a LIBOR-based asset, thereby eliminating the credit risk of the reference asset. As with credit swaps, however, there is still credit risk in the form of the liability of the protection seller.

EXHIBIT 9-11   Total Return Swap

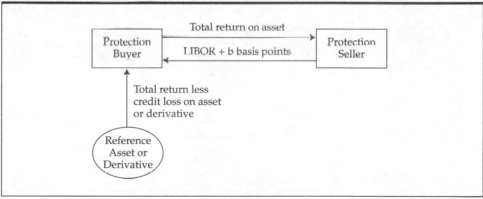

Total return swaps resemble some other swaps we have already examined. Equity swaps involve the payment of the total return on a stock or index to a counterparty, which pays either a fixed rate, a floating rate, or the rate on another stock or index. In a total return swap credit derivative, the underlying is a bond instead of a stock. When covering applications of swaps in Chapter 8, we looked at fixed-income swaps, which were total

---

[28] Technically, it is an option that allows payment of the premium on a periodic basis. Such options are called installment options and are considered among the more exotic financial derivatives.

return swaps in which the underlying is a bond. In that case, we were effectively looking at the same type of instrument that is used as a credit derivative.

Although total return swaps are widely used as credit derivatives, there are some limits to their use. The reference asset must be one that trades actively in a liquid market. Otherwise, it is not easy to determine the total return. It must be possible to obtain good price quotes, ones that are not easily biased or manipulated. Hence, total return swaps are not practical for standard commercial loans and tend to be created on bonds that are issued by well-known companies.[29]

4.3.3   CREDIT SPREAD OPTION

Another type of credit derivative is a credit spread option. This is an option on the yield spread on a bond. The yield spread is the difference between a bond's yield and the yield on a default-free security, usually a government note, of the same maturity. The yield spread is primarily determined by the market's perception of a bond's credit risk. When the market believes the credit risk has increased (decreased), the spread increases (decreases). Because this spread is a random variable determined in a relatively competitive marketplace and reflects the market's perception of the credit risk, it can be used as the underlying in a derivative contract. Credit spread options are options on this spread and have an exercise price expressed in terms of a yield spread.

For example, let us say a typical yield spread on the reference bond is 100 basis points and is the current spread. Assume that the holder of the bond would like a credit spread option struck at 100 basis points.[30] The buyer of a credit spread call option then pays the seller the premium and receives the right to a payment based on the credit spread on the bond minus 100 basis points. A credit spread put option gives the holder the right to receive 100 basis points minus the credit spread. Exhibit 9-12 illustrates the credit spread option.

EXHIBIT 9-12   Credit Spread Option

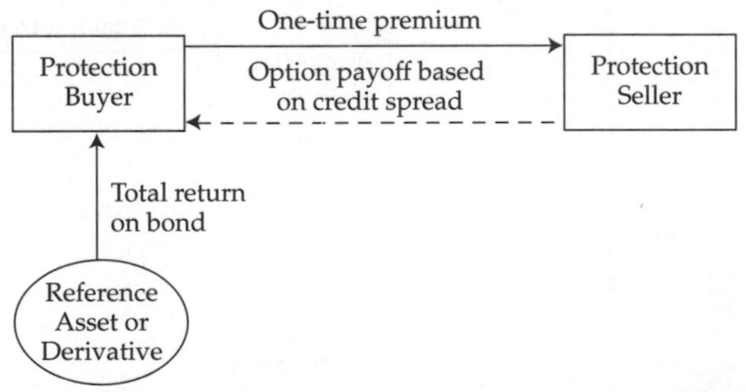

Like the underlying in a total return swap, the underlying in a credit spread option must be an actively traded instrument so that the credit spread can be determined in a liq-

---

[29] One of the consequences of this fact is that bonds issued by well-known companies tend to be bonds of relatively high credit quality. These bonds are not those most in need of credit protection. Lower-quality bonds do not trade as actively and do not make good underlyings for total return swaps.

[30] As with any option, there is no requirement that it be at-the-money at the start, as in this example. The option buyer can specify any desired exercise rate.

uid market that is not subject to bias or manipulation. Hence, credit spread options tend to exist only for bonds issued by well-known companies.[31]

A variation of a credit spread option is a credit put option. This is essentially an option to sell a bond at its current market price as represented by the exercise price, which is struck to reflect the credit spread. The exercise price is expressed as a price obtained by discounting the bond at its normal yield, which includes a yield spread. The option is then just a put option on the market value of the bond, but the purpose of the put option is different from what we have seen in earlier chapters. If the market value falls due to a widening of the credit spread, then its value will fall below the exercise price and the put will gain in value.[32] Of course, this instrument also protects the holder against market risk.

4.3.4 CREDIT-LINKED NOTES

Credit-linked notes are fixed-income securities in which the issuer has the right to withhold payment to the holder if a credit event on another financial instrument occurs. Exhibit 9-13 illustrates how this structure works. The seller of the credit-linked note holds an underlying reference asset, which typically pays principal and interest. The buyer of the credit-linked note pays cash at the start and receives principal and interest from the seller of the credit-linked note. If the reference security defaults, the seller of the credit-linked note reduces the amount of principal owed to the buyer of the credit-linked note. The seller of the credit-linked note is protected against default loss on the reference instrument, with the risk assumed by the buyer of the credit-linked note.

EXHIBIT 9-13   Credit-Linked Note

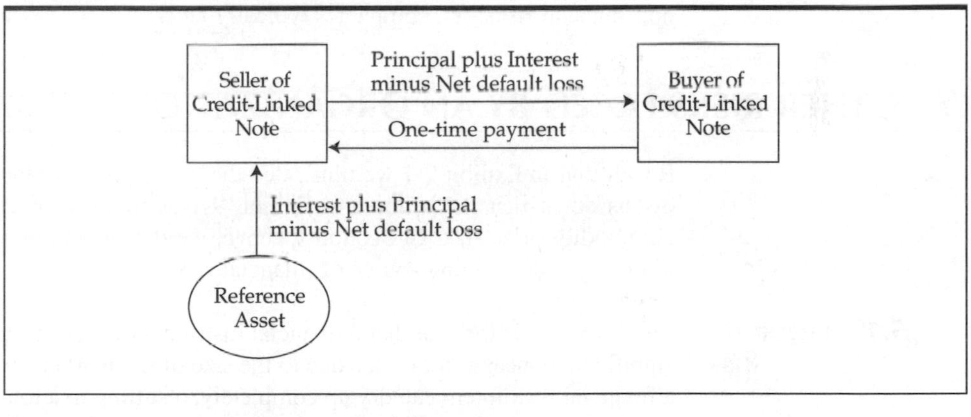

4.3.5 SOME FINAL COMMENTS ON CREDIT DERIVATIVES

There are some other variations of credit derivatives. As an example, in some cases the underlying is a portfolio of credit-sensitive securities. Then the derivative is often structured to pay off on the first security to default. Credit derivatives of this sort are often combined with asset-backed securities, so that the holder of an asset-backed security can be compensated when one of the underlying securities defaults.

---

[31] As with total return swaps, credit spread options are less practical for low-liquidity bonds. Therefore, lower-quality bonds, which tend to have lower liquidity, would not be good candidates for credit spread options. Yet these are the types of bonds for which credit protection would often be sought.

[32] This instrument itself has a number of variations, including the combination of it and a swap.

Credit derivatives work by separating market risk from credit risk and allowing each of these risks to be priced and traded in separate markets. A party with a high concentration of credit risk can strip off the risk and sell it to someone else. Consider, for example, a bank that is currently assuming all of the credit risk it can afford to bear from a given counterparty. Yet it would like to continue to service the counterparty by engaging in loan and derivative transactions. It can do so by using credit derivatives to pass on the credit risk to another party. A bank with too much credit risk concentrated in one industry might also consider using credit derivatives to pass on some of the risk to another party. In general, banks and other lenders can use credit derivatives to restructure their balance sheets to assume an acceptable level of credit risk.

We have spoken of credit derivatives as though they are motivated only by the party wishing to eliminate the credit risk. Obviously a demand to purchase credit risk must also exist. Credit derivatives allow a party to purchase a risk that is often uncorrelated with the party's current risk, thus providing diversification. They allow parties to take risks to which they might not otherwise have access. As compensation for assuming this risk comes the expectation of higher returns.

The size of the credit derivatives market is not well known. The Bank for International Settlements (BIS) conducts an extensive triennial survey that includes questions on the use of credit derivatives. The BIS estimated that as of June 2001, the global credit derivatives market was $698 billion of notional principal with a market value of about $21 billion.[33] In June 1998, the notional principal and market value were estimated at $118 billion and $4 billion, respectively. Clearly there has been phenomenal growth in the use of credit derivatives in recent years, and this trend is unlikely to abate in the near future.

We have now covered market risk and credit risk, which are the primary financial risks faced by a company. There is, however, one other financial risk and numerous other nonfinancial risks that companies typically face.

5   OTHER RISKS FACED BY AN ORGANIZATION

Recall that in Exhibit 9-1 we illustrated the variety of risks faced by a company. We have discussed market risk, shown in Exhibit 9-1 as interest rate, exchange rate, equity, and commodity price risk. In Section 4 above, we discussed credit risk. We now turn to liquidity as the remaining source of financial risk.

5.1   LIQUIDITY RISK

Liquidity risk is the risk that a financial instrument cannot be purchased or sold without a significant concession in price due to the size of the market. In some cases, the market for a financial instrument can dry up completely, resulting in a total inability to trade an asset. This risk manifests itself much more on the sell side of a transaction than on the buy side. Parties that wish to purchase a security in an illiquid market can often choose not to buy it if the price is unacceptable. In many cases, a substitute security can be found. But parties that need to sell a security often have little choice but to sell it in an illiquid market. As we discussed in previous chapters, derivatives can be used as substitutes for the sale of an asset, but derivatives will not typically help in managing liquidity risk. If the underlying is illiquid, there is a good possibility that the derivative on the underlying is also illiquid.

Liquidity risk is usually observed in the size of the spread between the bid and ask prices. When markets are illiquid, dealers expect to sell at relatively high prices and buy at relatively low prices to justify their assumption of this risk.

Liquidity risk is a serious and frequently latent risk. It is not always apparent that certain securities are illiquid. Some securities that are liquid when purchased can be illiq-

---

[33] See www.bis.org/publ/regpubl.htm and choose the latest *Central Bank Survey of Foreign Exchange and Derivatives Market Activity*.

uid by the time they are sold. Complete liquidity is usually assumed in valuation models and is a difficult risk to incorporate into models. Liquidity requires trading, but illiquidity discourages trading. Like the proverbial chicken and the egg, it is not clear which comes first, liquidity or the willingness to trade, but each requires the other.

Companies also face an array of nonfinancial risks. Let us briefly define each of them, starting at the bottom of Exhibit 9-1 and working upward.

5.2 OPERATIONS RISK

Operations risk, sometimes called operational risk, is the risk of loss from failures in a company's systems and procedures. These risks can arise due to computer failures (including bugs, viruses, and hardware problems), human failures, and events completely outside of the control of companies, which include "acts of God" and terrorist actions.

Computer failures are quite common but usually manageable with backup systems. Computer bugs and viruses are potentially quite risky but have become largely manageable with the proper personnel, software, and systems. Even the smallest business has learned to back up files and take them off of the premises. Larger businesses have much more extensive computer risk management practices.

Human failures include unintentional errors that, although potentially significant, are usually manageable. The more critical human issues in risk management are those of the so-called rogue trader. A rogue trader is an individual in an organization who has entered into either high-risk unauthorized transactions or high-risk authorized transactions that are not being monitored. In some cases, such as occurred in the Singapore office of Barings Bank, a rogue trader can destroy the entire organization. The number of stories of rogue traders has multiplied since the early 1990s, but in nearly all cases, the company involved had inadequate controls and oversight, or even none at all. In some cases, the trader got away with violating simple rules that would have stopped him had there been only a modest amount of oversight.

Fires and floods are typically covered by insurance, but insurance provides only cash compensation for losses. If a flood destroys the trading room of a bank, money will not come close to paying for the loss of customers who take their trading elsewhere. Hence, most companies have backup facilities they can activate in such cases. The 1993 bombing of the World Trade Center in New York City led many companies to establish backup systems in the event of another terrorist attack, which sadly took place on a greater scale eight years later.

In some cases, companies manage operational risk by using insurance contracts. There are even a few types of derivative contracts that pay off for operational losses, but the market for these has not developed very well. These instruments are essentially insurance contracts. Most companies manage operational risk, however, by monitoring their systems, taking preventive actions, and having a plan in place to respond if such events occur.

5.3 MODEL RISK

In this book, we have introduced how to use models to price derivatives. There are, in fact, many more models to choose from than those we have seen here. For many derivatives contracts, it is not always clear which model to use. This problem introduces another type of risk, one associated with the choice and use of a model. This is called model risk, which refers to the use of a wrong model or the improper use of the right model. The latter problem usually occurs from use of wrong inputs to the model or misapplication of a model.

A simple example of this problem occurs when valuing American options using the Black–Scholes–Merton model. The Black–Scholes–Merton model strictly holds for European options. If it is used to price American options, it can undervalue the option.[34] The potential for use of a bad estimate of volatility in the right model also introduces an element of risk. For some complex options, it is unclear what type of model to use. These problems of misapplying a model can be a significant source of risk. The best defense

---

[34] An exception is that an American call on an asset in which there are no underlying cash flows such as dividends or interest will not be exercised and can thus be valued as a European call. This point is covered in Chapter 4.

against them is knowledge of the right way to value derivatives. If uncertainty exists about the appropriateness of a model, then the model's results should be used with a prudent awareness that there may be errors arising from model risk.

Model risk in some form is almost always present. Few real-world situations perfectly match the assumptions of a model. If other market participants are just as uncertain about the appropriate model or appropriate use of an agreed-upon model, then model risk will be even greater because prices will fluctuate with no consistent association with a particular model.

Model risk is especially acute with options, if for no other reason than the fact that volatility must be estimated. Forward contracts and swaps are valued unambiguously using simple present value calculations with known inputs and are less prone to model risk.

5.4 SETTLEMENT (HERSTAATT) RISK

The payments involved in swaps, forward contracts, and options are referred to as settlements. The process of settling a contract involves one or both parties making payments to the other. With swaps and forward contracts, the settlements are two-way, meaning that each party pays the other. This situation creates the problem that one party could be in the process of paying the other while the other is declaring bankruptcy. Netting reduces this problem for interest rate derivatives, but currency derivatives are not netted. Because currency swaps often involve two parties in different countries, the potential may be high for one party to be unaware that the other party is declaring bankruptcy. The derivatives industry is working toward solutions to this problem, primarily through the use of a clearinghouse, but the problem has not yet been solved.

Fortunately, bankruptcy does not occur often, so this risk is much more a threat than a reality. One famous incident of settlement risk did occur in 1974, when a German bank called the Herstaatt Bank failed at a time when counterparties were sending money to it. For that reason, settlement risk has come to be known as Herstaatt risk.

5.5 REGULATORY RISK

Futures markets and exchange-traded options markets are regulated at the federal level, whereas over-the-counter markets are essentially unregulated. Federal authorities in most countries take the position that over-the-counter derivatives transactions are private transactions between sophisticated parties and should be relatively free of regulations. There is some degree of regulation in that companies are not allowed to break any laws such as those dealing with fraud. Moreover, standard contract law always applies, and companies that are regulated in other ways have their derivatives business indirectly regulated. For example, banks are heavily regulated by federal and state banking authorities, which results in indirect regulation of their derivatives. For the most part, however, there is no specific governmental regulation of the over-the-counter derivatives business.

Regulation, whether it exists or not, is a source of uncertainty. Markets that are regulated are always subject to the risk that existing regulations will be changed such that new regulations are more onerous, more restrictive, or more costly. Unregulated markets are subject to the risk that they will become regulated, thereby imposing greater costs and more restrictions. Regulatory risk is difficult to predict in that regulations are written by politicians, occasionally imposed and enforced by bureaucratic fiat, and often change with changes in political parties and regulatory personnel. They often reflect attitudes and philosophies. Regulatory risk and the degree of regulation varies widely from country to country.

Regulatory risk often arises from the arbitrage nature of derivatives transactions. For example, a long position in stock accompanied by borrowing can replicate a forward contract or a futures contract. Stocks are regulated by securities regulators, and loans are typically regulated by banking regulators. Forward contracts are essentially unregulated. Futures contracts are regulated at the federal level in most countries, but not always by the same agency that regulates the stock market. Hence, equivalent combinations are not always regulated in the same way or by the same regulator.

The derivatives business has faced major periods of regulatory uncertainty. The misunderstanding of derivatives by politicians and the general public has led to much doubt and suspicion of the industry. Whenever companies announce significant derivatives losses, there is usually a wave of calls for new regulations. The derivatives industry has lobbied hard for lighter regulation and has been largely successful. Indeed, attempting to influence politicians and regulators is about the only technique for the management of regulatory risk.

5.6 LEGAL RISK

Derivatives are contracts and, as such, are subject to contract law. In any contract, there are two parties, with each obligated to do something for the other. If one of the parties fails to perform or one party believes that the other has engaged in a fraudulent practice, the contract can be abrogated. A dispute would then likely arise and could involve litigation, especially if there are large losses. In a number of cases, a party that lost money on a derivative contract has repudiated the loss, thereby transferring the loss to the counterparty. In some cases, the losing party on the derivative has claimed that the counterparty acted fraudulently or that the contract was not legal in the first place and, therefore, should be declared null and void. The possibility of such a claim being upheld in court creates a form of legal risk, the risk that the legal system will not enforce the contract.

Legal risk is more often faced by a dealer. Dealers in derivatives are typically large financial institutions, and lawsuits are not uncommon for them. If the dealer's counterparty suffers a loss, it may attempt to repudiate the contract, trying a variety of strategic legal claims. In some cases, it might claim that the dealer acted fraudulently. In other cases, it could argue that it viewed the dealer as an advisor and that the dealer should have informed it that the contract was extremely risky and not in the counterparty's best interests. In still other cases, the counterparty has been able to argue that the dealer should have known that the counterparty had no legal authority to even enter into the contract.

The legal system has upheld many of these claims. This is not to say that the dealer has always been in the wrong, but simply that dealers have sometimes put themselves into precarious situations. Dealers are indeed often advisors to their counterparties, giving the impression that if the dealer and counterparty enter into a contract, the counterparty expects nothing to go wrong. Dealers are now going to great lengths to make clear that they are the opposite party, not an advisor. Dealers are also writing contracts more carefully to cover the various contingencies that have been used against them in litigation.

5.7 TAX RISK

Tax risk is the uncertainty associated with tax laws. The taxation of derivatives transactions is an area of much confusion and uncertainty. On occasion, tax rulings clarify these matters, but on other occasions, they confuse them further. In addition, new derivative instruments are frequently created. When tax laws do not already cover the new instruments, considerable uncertainty can exist about how such instruments will be taxed. This uncertainty can materialize in the form of treating the transactions incorrectly for tax purposes, possibly leading to back taxes due at a later date. In some cases, transactions could appear to not require tax payments, but later it is found that taxes are owed.

We noted in discussing regulatory risk that equivalent combinations of financial instruments are not always regulated the same way. Likewise, equivalent combinations are not always taxed the same way. This fact creates a tremendous burden of inconsistency and confusion, but on occasion the opportunity arises for arbitrage gains, although the tax authorities often quickly close such opportunities.

Like regulatory risk, tax risk is often related to how politicians and bureaucrats behave. Companies invest considerable resources in lobbying as well as hiring tax experts and consultants to control tax risk.

5.8 ACCOUNTING RISK

Accounting statements are a key, if not *the* primary, source of information on publicly traded companies. In the United States, accounting standards are established primarily by the Financial Accounting Standards Board (FASB). Legal requirements in the area of accounting are enforced for publicly traded companies by federal securities regulators and by the stock exchanges if the stock is traded thereon. Non-U.S. domiciled companies that raise capital in the United States are also subject to these standards and laws. Laws require accurate accounting statements, and inaccurate statements can be the subject of civil and criminal litigation for fraud. In addition, the market punishes companies that do not provide accurate accounting statements, as was the case for Enron and its auditor Arthur Andersen.

The International Accounting Standards Board (IASB) attempts to set global standards for accounting, sometimes leading or following the FASB. Nonetheless, accounting standards vary from country to country, with some countries requiring a high level of disclosure and others only a low level. It is unlikely that accounting standards can ever be internationalized, any more than we could expect taxes and regulations to be standardized around the world.

Considerable confusion has arisen concerning proper accounting for derivative contracts. When confusion occurs, there is a risk that transactions accounted for one way could later need to be adjusted, which can lead to a restatement of earnings. Restating earnings is almost always embarrassing for a company, because it suggests that either the company was trying to hide something or it did not fully understand what it was doing. This confusion over the proper accounting for derivatives gives rise to accounting as a source of risk. As with regulatory and tax risk, it is also sometimes the case that equivalent combinations of derivatives are not accounted for in the same way. The accounting profession typically moves to close such loopholes, but it does not move quickly, so problems nearly always remain.

At one time, most derivative contracts were considered off-balance-sheet items. The large contract sizes and exposure that many companies have to derivatives led the FASB and the International Accounting Standards Committee (predecessor of the IASB) to mandate new rules requiring the inclusion of derivatives and their associated gains and losses on financial statements. These rulings, called SFAS 133 (Statement of Financial Accounting Standard No. 133) and IAS 39 (International Accounting Standard No. 39), have cleared up much of the confusion, but some uncertainty remains. These rulings contain some confusion and inconsistency themselves, with considerable room for interpretation.[35]

Most companies deal with accounting risk by having personnel with the latest accounting knowledge on their staffs. In addition, companies lobby and communicate actively with the accounting regulatory bodies and federal regulators in efforts to shift accounting rules in a favorable manner and to add lucidity. Companies have tended to fight rules requiring more disclosure, arguing that disclosure per se is not always beneficial. A trade-off exists between being forced to disclose practices that would be best if kept from competitors and providing investors and the public with adequate information. This controversy is not likely to go away, suggesting that accounting risk will continue to be present.

6   BEST PRACTICES IN RISK MANAGEMENT

The practice of risk management has a great deal of variation. Broad policies and procedures and detailed practices can vary acceptably from company to company, but there is considerable room for misapplication in the practice of risk management. To improve the practice of risk management, the profession has identified a set of procedures it considers to be the appropriate way to practice risk management. These procedures, informally referred to as "best practices," provide suggestions and guidance but are not mandatory. Working from different perspectives, two primary groups have established these guide-

---

[35] An excellent source of information on the accounting for derivatives is *Risk Management, Derivatives, and Financial Analysis under SFAS No. 133* by Gary L. Gastineau, Donald J. Smith, and Rebecca Todd, Charlottesville, VA: The Research Foundation of AIMR (2001).

lines. The first is the Group of 30 (G–30), a global organization of economic and financial experts, which published a well-known report in 1993. This report detailed 24 recommendations primarily for derivatives dealers, though still somewhat applicable to end users. The second report comes from the Risk Standards Working Group, an informal committee of institutional investors and consultants, whose standards are designed to improve the practice of risk management in the investment management industry. In the next sections, we shall take an overview of these two sets of recommendations.

6.1 The G–30 Report: Best Practices for Derivatives Dealers and General End Users

Appendix 9A provides a summary statement of the G–30 recommendations. These recommendations place considerable emphasis on the responsibility of senior management for understanding what a company's derivatives and risk management practices are and for ensuring that adequate personnel and systems are in place. Risk management must start at the top of the organization. Note how many of the recommendations cover policies and procedures, guidelines, oversight, and organization structure, which are issues typically addressed by senior management. Some of the recommendations go into considerable detail regarding the measurement of risk. Note Recommendation 5, which mentions VAR, delta, gamma, and other risk measures we have studied. Recommendations 11–14 cover credit risk, and Recommendation 16 mentions operational risk. Accounting and disclosure issues are also covered in Recommendations 19 and 20, although these recommendations are somewhat superseded by new accounting rules mentioned above. The G–30 report also makes recommendations to legal and regulatory bodies that would improve the practice of risk management. The G–30 report is primarily aimed at derivatives dealers, but Recommendation 9 (shown here as Exhibit 9-14) does refer to end users.

EXHIBIT 9-14 G-30 Recommendation 9: Practices by End-Users

> As appropriate to the nature, size, and complexity of their derivatives activities, end-users should adopt the same valuation and market-risk management practices that are recommended for dealers. Specifically they should consider regularly marking to market their derivatives transactions for risk-management purposes; periodically forecasting the cash investing and funding requirements arising from their derivatives transactions; and establishing a clearly independent and authoritative function to design and assure adherence to prudent risk limits.

6.2 The Risk Standards Working Group Report: Best Practices for Investment Management Organizations

Our interest in this book is more in the area of end-user risk management. In particular, what are the appropriate practices for investment risk management end users? The Risk Standards Working Group Recommendations on Derivatives and Risk Management Practices addressed this question for institutional investors, and Appendix 9B summarizes the group's recommendations. The recommendations are divided into three primary areas: management, measurement, and oversight. Many of the recommendations resemble those of the G–30 Report, which is not surprising. Much of the process of risk management is common business sense, such as responsibility, policies, and control. The report also addresses the importance of accurate valuation of financial instruments, *ex post* risk-adjusted performance measurement, stress testing, and back testing. It also emphasizes the importance of reviewing the entire risk management process.

The practice of risk management has not reached the stage of the practice of accounting, in which an industrywide organization such as the FASB makes recommendations for how the profession should be practiced. Those recommendations carry no legal weight but are widely regarded as the only acceptable standards for accounting in the United States, where auditors cannot certify financial statements that have not met FASB standards. Risk management, however, is not like accounting and is unlikely ever to evolve into a practice with specific standards, such as what model should be used or how volatility should be estimated. This lack of standardization is probably appropriate, because risk management is a dynamic practice that must adapt quickly to the tremendous pace at which financial markets evolve. The accounting profession, by contrast, requires years of studying a problem before implementing a new ruling.[36] Risk management is best practiced in light of general guidelines, such as those in the G–30 and Risk Standards reports, and the evolving state of knowledge of the profession. There is also a healthy respect for the ability of the market to punish those that fail to practice good risk management.

Risk management activities can be summarized under three areas: risk governance, which refers to the responsibility of management for the practice of risk management; risk budgeting, which refers to the setting of risk practices and limits; and performance measurement. We briefly address these topics here.

6.3 RISK GOVERNANCE

As can be seen from the reports of the G–30 and the Risk Standards Working Group, the responsibility of senior management for risk management is a critical element of a quality risk management system. There are now far too many stories of senior executives who were either ignorant of what was going on, thought they knew what was going on but did not, or knew they did not know what was going on but trusted those under them too much. It should be obvious that senior management is ultimately responsible for *everything* that goes on in an organization. This liability of senior management has clearly been seen in litigation. Although corporations usually provide legal support to their executives, many individual executives face personal lawsuits for their actions. It is imperative that senior management ensure that a company has established policies and procedures and is staffed with knowledgeable personnel.

Organizations engage in hundreds of activities that can expose them to losses. Companies manufacture products that, in some rare occasions, have been dangerous or have been exposed to tampering. Some companies provide services that, on occasion, have been dangerous, such as air transportation. Most companies have learned to manage these risks very effectively and rarely are companies forced into bankruptcy over risks associated with their daily operations. When companies determine that their risks need to be managed using derivatives, however, the act of managing their risks becomes itself a risky activity. We have seen that derivatives are highly leveraged instruments. When used improperly, they can lead to greater risks.

The setting of overall policies and standards in risk management is referred to as **risk governance**. Risk governance begins with organizational structure. Risk management can be centralized or decentralized. A centralized risk management system means that a company has a single risk management group that monitors and controls all of the risk-taking activities of the organization. A decentralized system allows individual units to manage risk. Decentralization results in duplication of efforts but has the advantage of allowing people closer to the risk to be more directly involved in its management. Centralization permits economies of scale and allows a company to use some of its risks to offset other risks. For example, suppose one subsidiary of a company buys from a company in Japan and another sells to a company in Japan, with both engaged in yen-denominated transactions. Each subsidiary would perceive some foreign exchange exposure. From a centralized point of view, however, these risks can be seen to have offsetting effects, thereby reducing the need to

---

[36] For example, it was well known in the early 1990s that accounting for derivatives was an area of much confusion when the FASB began to formally study the problem. Its proposal, SFAS 133, was initially released in 1998 and went into effect in June 2000.

hedge. In addition, centralized risk management puts the responsibility on a level closer to senior management. It gives an overall picture of the company's risk position, and ultimately the overall picture is what counts. This centralized type of risk management is now called **enterprise risk management**, or sometimes firmwide risk management.

Regardless of the system chosen, it is critical that the trading function be separated from the risk management function. The positions taken by the traders or risk-takers must be monitored by an individual or group that operates independently of the trading function. The risk manager has the responsibility for monitoring the risky positions taken and executing any strategies necessary to control the level of risk. To do this, the risk manager must have fast and accurate information, authority, and independence from the trading function.

One of the important components of a risk management system is the back office. Typically a back office encompasses clerical personnel and their activities. Quite often this function is viewed as somewhat less important than the work of the executives, traders, and other risk takers of an organization. Yet in organizations that engage in derivatives transactions, it has become increasingly important that back-office personnel have a high level of knowledge and competence. Errors and oversights of back-office personnel can lead to significant losses that, through leverage, can be even more damaging than they might initially appear. Companies are beginning to invest significant resources in the education and training of back-office personnel. Back-office personnel are, in many ways, the front line of defense against operational risk and are an important part of the independent monitoring and control system essential to effective risk management.

6.4 RISK BUDGETING AND PERFORMANCE EVALUATION

In recent years, companies have begun to implement a new approach to risk management called **risk budgeting**. Risk budgeting involves the establishment of objectives for individuals, groups, or divisions of an organization that take into account the allocation of an acceptable level of risk. As an example, the foreign exchange trading desk could be allocated capital of $100 million and permitted a daily VAR of $5 million. In other words, the foreign exchange trading desk is granted a budget, expressed in terms of allocated capital and an acceptable level of risk. There are other variations that might specify limits on the amount of capital that can be allocated to a transaction or the size of positions that can be taken. In any case, the innovation here is that risk levels are specified before the fact to provide guidance on the acceptable degree of activities that can be undertaken.

After the fact, performance must be measured and evaluated against the risk assumed and budgeted. A considerable body of knowledge covers the evaluation of investment performance. Traditional approaches take into account return against a risk penalty. These approaches are now being used in other areas of business activity besides portfolio management. In addition, other measures of risk such as VAR are being used.[37] Some banks have developed sophisticated performance evaluation systems that account for risk and have marketed these successfully to clients.

The process of performance evaluation is covered better in investments books and in the portfolio management component of the CFA curriculum, so we have not devoted much attention to it here. What we learn about performance evaluation from the study of derivatives is the critical nature of risk-adjusted performance evaluation. Derivatives provide a powerful means of buying and selling risk, leading potentially to much greater or much lower risk. All business activities should be evaluated against the risk taken, and the use of derivatives has brought that requirement to greater light.

---

[37] For example, the Sharpe ratio, which is defined as the return minus the risk-free rate over the volatility (sometimes modified to just the return over the volatility) is often changed to the return minus the risk-free rate (or just the return) over the VAR. This modified Sharpe ratio gives the risk premium (or return) earned over the VAR.

7 CONCLUDING COMMENTS

A recent advertisement for the RiskMetrics Group (www.riskmetrics.com) identified the following nine rules for effective risk management:

- *There is no return without risk. Rewards go to those who take risks.*
- *Be transparent. Risk should be fully understood.*
- *Seek experience. Risk is measured and managed by people, not mathematical models.*
- *Know what you don't know. Question the assumptions you make.*
- *Communicate. Risk should be discussed openly.*
- *Diversify. Multiple risks will produce more consistent rewards.*
- *Show discipline. A consistent and rigorous approach will beat a constantly changing strategy.*
- *Use common sense. It is better to be approximately right, than to be precisely wrong.*
- *Return is only half the equation. Decisions should be made only by considering the risk and return of the possibilities.*

Risk management is in so many ways just good common business sense. It is quite remarkable, however, that common rules are violated so easily and so often. But that problem is not unique to risk management.

Currently, two professional organizations are devoted to risk management. The Global Association of Risk Professionals (GARP) and the Professional Risk Managers' International Association (PRMIA) are actively involved in promoting knowledge in the field of risk management. You may wish to visit their Web sites at www.garp.com and www.prmia.org.

We have now come to the end of this book on derivatives. We have seen that derivative instruments are powerful tools that can be used effectively in the management of risk. But with their power comes danger. Derivatives, like fire and chemicals, can bring great advances when used properly, but they must be used carefully and with the necessary knowledge and controls in order to avoid disaster. Financial markets are a powerful force in punishing the ignorant and incompetent, and derivatives can be a fast way to earn punishment. But in contrast, financial markets also reward competence and knowledge, and used properly, derivatives can be the ideal instruments for successful risk management.

KEY POINTS

- Risk management is the process of identifying the level of risk that an entity wants, measuring the level of risk that an entity currently has, taking actions that bring the actual level of risk to the desired level of risk, and monitoring the new actual level of risk so that it continues to be aligned with the desired level of risk.

- Financial risk refers to the risk associated with financial markets as well as credit risk and liquidity risk. Nonfinancial risk refers to any other types of risks, such as operations risk or legal risk.

- The six sources of financial risk are interest rates, exchange rates, stock prices, commodity prices, credit, and liquidity.

- Typically, risks should be hedged when companies do not have comparative advantages in the associated markets, activities, or lines of business. Risk management can also be justified to reduce taxes, reduce the costs associated with bankruptcy, stabilize a company's cash flows for investment purposes, increase debt capacity, and lower the cost of debt. Risk should also be managed simply because regulators and investors expect it.

- The process of managing risk involves setting policies and procedures, defining the level of risk tolerance, identifying the risk, measuring the risk, and adjusting the level of risk.

- Market risk is the risk associated with interest rates, exchange rates, stock prices, and commodity prices.

- Traditional measures of market risk include beta for stocks, duration and convexity for bonds, and more generally delta and gamma, which reflect the price sensitivity of the derivative to movements in the underlying asset. In addition, vega reflects a derivative's sensitivity to movements in volatility. The sensitivity to movements in the correlation among assets is relevant for certain types of instruments.

- Value at Risk (VAR) gives the minimum loss that a party would expect to experience over a period of time with a given probability. Using the complementary probability, VAR can be expressed as a maximum loss. There is no absolute maximum, however, other than the entire value of the portfolio.

- A decision to use VAR requires the determination of the acceptable probability level and the time period over which VAR will apply.

- The analytical or variance–covariance method can be used to determine VAR under the assumption that returns are normally distributed. Subtract the standard deviation times a factor reflecting the normal probability distribution (1.65 for a 5 percent VAR, 2.33 for a 1 percent VAR) from the expected return. The result is the return that is exceeded (in a negative sense) 5 percent or 1 percent (depending on the user's choice) of the time. The advantage of the method is its simplicity. The disadvantages are that returns are rarely normally distributed and that the method does not work well when portfolios contain options.

- The historical method provides an estimate of the VAR from data on the performance of the portfolio over a historical period. The returns are ranked, and the VAR is obtained by determining the return that is exceeded in a negative sense 5 percent or 1 percent (depending on the user's choice) of the time. The historical method has the advantage of being simple and not requiring the assumption of a normal distribution. It has the disadvantage that the past distribution of returns may not accurately reflect the future distribution of returns.

- Monte Carlo simulation is used to estimate VAR by generating random returns and determining the 5 percent or 1 percent (depending on the user's choice) worst outcomes. It has the advantage that it does not require a normal distribution and it can handle complex relationships among risks. The disadvantage is that it can be very time consuming and costly to conduct the large number of simulations required for accuracy. It also requires the estimation of input values, which can be difficult to do.

- VAR can be difficult to estimate, can give a wide range of values, and can lead to a false sense of security that risk is accurately measured and under control. VAR also puts all emphasis on the negative outcomes, ignoring the positive outcomes. Moreover, it places no real emphasis on the truly worst possible outcomes, often underestimating the likelihood of extremely bad returns. It can be difficult to obtain VAR in a large complex organization with many exposures. On the other hand, VAR is a simple and easy-to-understand risk measure that is widely accepted, in spite of its shortcomings.

- Credit risk has two dimensions, the probability of default and the amount of loss, which reflects the possibility of recovery of a portion of the loss.

- Current credit risk is the risk that a party will not pay an amount currently due. Potential credit risk is the risk that a party will not pay an amount due in the future. In addition, a counterparty might owe nothing now but could declare bankruptcy because of liabilities currently due to other parties.

- Credit risk in a forward contract is assumed by the party to which the market value is positive. The market value represents the current value of the claim that one party has on the other. The actual payoff at expiration could differ, but the market value reflects the current value of that future claim.

- Credit risk in swaps is similar to credit risk in forward contracts. The market value represents the current value of the claim on the future payments. The party holding the positive market value assumes the credit risk at that time. For interest rate and equity swaps, credit risk is greatest near the middle of the life of the swap. For currency swaps with payment of notional principal, credit risk is greatest near the end of the life of the swap.

- Credit risk in options is one-directional. Because the buyer of the option does not have to do anything, the seller faces no credit risk. The buyer faces the risk that the seller will not pay if the buyer exercises the option. The market value of the option is the current value of the future claim the buyer has on the seller.

- One means of controlling credit risk is by limiting the amount of exposure to a given party. Another means is marking a derivative contract to market, which results in one party paying the other the market value before it expires and the contract being repriced. Another method is to use collateral. Netting reduces credit risk by specifying that offsetting amounts owed from each party are reduced to the net difference, wherein one party pays the other only a single amount. Netting reduces the risk associated with one party paying while the other is defaulting. Another method of credit reduction is to use minimum credit standards. For dealers, establishing a sufficiently high credit rating is often done by enhanced derivatives product companies, which are subsidiaries of derivatives dealers that are not liable for the debts of the parent company.

- VAR can be used to measure credit risk. The interpretation is the same as with standard VAR, but a credit-based VAR is more complex because it must interact with VAR based on market risk. Credit risk arises only when market risk results in gains to trading. Credit VAR must take into account the complex interaction of market movements, the possibility of default, and recovery rates. Credit VAR is also difficult to aggregate across markets and counterparties.

- Credit derivatives are financial instruments, similar to insurance, that pay off when credit events occur. Credit derivatives allow the separation of market risk from credit risk and permit parties to buy and sell credit risk. Parties wanting to reduce credit risk can do so by passing it on to other parties that want to increase credit risk. For some parties, credit risk can be a desirable risk to take on because it is a risk that is often uncorrelated with their existing risks.

- The four main types of credit derivatives are credit swaps, which are similar to insurance contracts; total return swaps, which are similar to equity and fixed-income swaps; credit spread options, which are options on the yield spread of a bond; and credit-linked notes, which are notes that permit a party to not pay the full principal in the event that a third party defaults.

- Liquidity is a significant source of risk in financial markets. Sellers in particular can find that the instruments they need to sell have very thin markets or high bid–ask spreads. Markets can even shut down completely. Financial models usually do not reflect liquidity risk, partially because it is such a difficult risk to measure.

- The primary sources of nonfinancial risk are operations risk, model risk, settlement risk, regulatory risk, legal risk, tax risk, and accounting risk.

- The two sets of standards on best practices in risk management are the G–30 report and the Risk Standards Working Group report. Both studies focus on the importance of senior management in the establishment of policies, procedures, control and evaluation systems, and staffing with qualified personnel.

- Risk governance refers to the process of setting risk management policies and standards in an organization. Risk governance is done at the senior level of management, which is ultimately responsible for all organizational activities.

- Risk budgeting is the establishment of objectives that take into account the allocation of an acceptable level of risk.

- Risk management plays an important role in performance evaluation and should be incorporated into the process of evaluating performance. In some cases, risk management techniques such as VAR are used as risk measures in performance evaluation.

- Some of the key rules for risk management are that risk goes with return, risk should be transparent (disclosed), risk management requires experienced personnel who are aware of limitations of models, risk should be openly discussed, diversification reduces risk, risk management requires discipline and common sense, and return is only part of the process.

Appendix 9A The Group of 30 Recommendations on Derivatives and Risk Management Practices

GENERAL POLICIES

Recommendation 1: The Role of Senior Management

Dealers and end-users should use derivatives in a manner consistent with the overall management and capital policies approved by their boards of directors. These policies should be reviewed as business and market circumstances change. Policies governing derivatives use should be clearly defined, including the purposes for which these transactions are to be undertaken. Senior management should approve procedures and controls to implement these policies, and management at all levels should enforce them.

VALUATION AND MARKET RISK MANAGEMENT

Recommendation 2: Marking to Market

Dealers should mark their derivatives positions to market, on at least a daily basis, for risk management purposes.

Recommendation 3: Market Valuation Methods

Derivatives portfolios of dealers should be valued based on mid-market levels less specific adjustments, or on appropriate bid or offer levels. Mid-market valuation adjustments should allow for expected future costs, such as unearned credit spread, closeout costs, investing and funding costs, and administrative costs.

Recommendation 4: Identifying Revenue Sources

Dealers should measure the components of revenue regularly and in sufficient detail to understand the sources of risk.

Recommendation 5: Measuring Market Risk

Dealers should use a consistent measure to calculate daily the market risk of their derivatives positions and compare it to market risk limits.

- Market risk is best measured as "value at risk" using probability analysis based upon a common confidence interval (e.g., two standard deviations) and time horizon (e.g., a one-day exposure).

- Components of market risk that should be considered across the term structure include: absolute price or rate change (delta); convexity (gamma); volatility (vega); time decay (theta); basis or correlation; and discount rate (rho).

Recommendation 6: Stress Simulation

Dealers should periodically perform simulations to determine how their portfolios would perform under stress conditions.

Recommendation 7: Investing and Funding Forecasts

Dealers should periodically forecast the cash investing and funding requirements arising from their derivatives portfolios.

Recommendation 8: Independent Market Risk Management

Dealers should have a market risk management function, with clear independence and authority, to ensure that the following responsibilities are carried out:

- The development of risk limit policies and the monitoring of transactions and positions for adherence to these policies. (See Recommendation 5.)

- The design of stress scenarios to measure the impact of market conditions, however improbable, that might cause market gaps, volatility swings, or disruptions of major relationships, or might reduce liquidity in the face of unfavorable market linkages, concentrated market making, or credit exhaustion. (See Recommendation 6.)

- The design of revenue reports quantifying the contribution of various risk components, and of market risk measures such as value at risk. (See Recommendations 4 and 5.)

- The monitoring of variance between the actual volatility of portfolio value and that predicted by the measure of market risk.

- The review and approval of pricing models and valuation systems used by front- and back-office personnel, and the development of reconciliation procedures if different systems are used.

Recommendation 9: Practices by End-Users

As appropriate to the nature, size, and complexity of their derivatives activities, end-users should adopt the same valuation and market-risk management practices that are recommended for dealers. Specifically they should consider: regularly marking to market their derivatives transactions for risk management purposes; periodically forecasting the cash investing and funding requirements arising from their derivatives transactions; and establishing a clearly independent and authoritative function to design and assure adherence to prudent risk limits.

CREDIT RISK MEASUREMENT AND MANAGEMENT

Recommendation 10: Measuring Credit Exposure

Dealers and end-users should measure credit exposure on derivatives in two ways:

- Current exposure, which is the replacement cost of derivatives transactions, that is, their market value, and

- Potential exposure, which is an estimate of the future replacement cost of derivatives transactions. It should be calculated using probability analysis based upon broad confidence intervals (e.g., two standard deviations) over the remaining terms of the transactions.

Recommendation 11: Aggregating Credit Exposures

Credit exposures on derivatives, and all other credit exposures to a counterparty, should be aggregated taking into consideration enforceable netting arrangements. Credit exposures should be calculated regularly and compared to credit limits.

Recommendation 12: Independent Credit Risk Management

Dealers and end-users should have a credit risk management function with clear independence and authority, and with analytical capabilities in derivatives, responsible for

- Approving credit exposure measurement demands.

- Setting credit limits and monitoring their use.

- Reviewing credits and concentrations of credit risk.

- Reviewing and monitoring risk-reduction arrangements.

Recommendation 13: Master Agreements

Dealers and end-users are encouraged to use one master agreement as widely as possible with each counterparty to document existing and future derivatives transactions, including foreign-exchange forwards and options. Master agreements should provide for payments netting and close-out netting, using a full two-way payments approach.

Recommendation 14: Credit Enhancement

Dealers and end-users should assess both the benefits and costs of credit enhancement and risk-reduction arrangements. Where it is proposed that credit downgrades would trigger early termination or collateral requirements, participants should carefully consider their own capacity and that of their counterparties to meet the potentially substantial funding needs that might result.

ENFORCEABILITY

Recommendation 15: Promoting Enforceability

Dealers and end-users should work together on a continuing basis to identify and recommend solutions for issues of legal enforceability, both within and across jurisdictions, as activities evolve and new types of securities are developed.

SYSTEMS, OPERATIONS, AND CONTROLS

Recommendation 16: Professional Expertise

Dealers and end-users must ensure that their derivatives activities are undertaken by professionals in sufficient number and with the appropriate experience, skill levels, and degrees of specialization. These professionals include specialists who transact and manage the risks involved, their supervisors, and those responsible for processing, reporting, controlling, and auditing the activities.

Recommendation 17: Systems

Dealers and end-users must ensure that adequate systems for data capture, processing, settlement, and management reporting are in place so that derivatives transactions are conducted in an orderly and efficient manner in compliance with management policies. Dealers should have risk management systems that measure the risks incurred in their derivatives activities including market and credit risks. End-users should have risk management systems that measure the risks incurred in their derivatives activities based upon their nature, size, and complexity.

Recommendation 18: Authority

Management of dealers and end-users should delegate who is authorized to commit their institutions to derivatives transactions.

ACCOUNTING AND DISCLOSURE

Recommendation 19: Accounting Policies

International harmonization of accounting standards for derivatives is desirable. Pending the adoption of harmonized standards, the following accounting practices are recommended:

- Dealers should account for derivatives transactions by marking them to market, taking changes in value to income each period.
- End-users should account for derivatives used to manage risks so as to achieve a consistency of income recognition treatment between those instruments and the risks being managed. Thus, if the risk being managed is accounted for at cost (or, in the case of an anticipatory hedge, not yet recognized), changes in the value of a qualify-

ing risk management instrument should be deferred until a gain or loss is recognized on the risk being managed. Or, if the risk being managed is marked to market with changes in value being taken to income, a qualifying risk-management instrument should be treated in a comparable fashion.

- End-users should account for derivatives not qualifying for risk management treatment on a mark-to-market basis.

- Amounts due to and from counterparties should only be offset when there is a legal right to set off or when enforceable netting arrangements are in place.

Where local regulations prevent adoption of these practices, disclosure along these lines is nevertheless recommended.

Recommendation 20: Disclosures

Financial statements of dealers and end-users should contain sufficient information about their use of derivatives to provide an understanding of the purposes for which transactions are undertaken, the extent of the transactions, the degree of risk involved, and how the transactions have been accounted for. Pending the adoption of harmonized accounting standards, the following disclosures are recommended:

- Information about management's attitude to financial risk, how instruments are used, and how risks are monitored and controlled.

- Accounting policies.

- Analysis of position at the balance sheet date.

- Analysis of the credit risk inherent in those positions.

- For dealers only, additional information about the extent of their activities in financial instruments.

RECOMMENDATIONS FOR LEGISLATORS, REGULATORS, AND SUPERVISORS

Recommendation 21: Recognizing Netting

Regulators and supervisors should recognize the benefits of netting arrangements where and to the full extent that they are enforceable, and encourage their use by reflecting these arrangements in capital adequacy standards. Specifically, they should promptly implement the recognition of the effectiveness of bilateral close-out netting in bank capital regulations.

Recommendation 22: Legal and Regulatory Uncertainties

Legislators, regulators, and supervisors, including central banks, should work in concert with dealers and end-users to identify and remove any remaining legal and regulatory uncertainties with respect to:

- The form of documentation required to create legally enforceable agreements (statute of frauds).

- The capacity of parties, such as governmental entities, insurance companies, pension funds, and building societies, to enter into transactions (ultra vires).

- The enforceability of bilateral close-out netting and collateral arrangements in bankruptcy.

- The enforceability of multibranch netting arrangements in bankruptcy.

- The legality/enforceability of derivatives transactions.

Recommendation 23: Tax Treatment

Legislators and tax authorities are encouraged to review and, where appropriate, amend tax laws and regulations that disadvantage the use of derivatives in risk management strategies. Tax impediments include the inconsistent or uncertain tax treatment of gains and losses on the derivatives, in comparison with the gains and losses that arise from the risks being managed.

Recommendation 24: Accounting Standards

Accounting standards-setting bodies in each country should, as a matter of priority, provide comprehensive guidance on accounting and reporting of transactions in financial instruments, including derivatives, and should work toward harmonization of standards on this subject. Also, the International Accounting Standards Committee should finalize its accounting standard on financial instruments.

Source: The Group of Thirty, *Derivatives: Practices and Principles* (1993).

Appendix 9B Risk Standards Working Group Recommendations on Derivatives and Risk Management Practices for Institutional Investors

I. Management

Risk Standard 1: Acknowledgement of fiduciary responsibility
Fiduciary responsibilities should be defined in writing and acknowledged in writing by the parties responsible.

Risk Standard 2: Approved written policies, definitions, guidelines and investment documentation
The Primary and Manager Fiduciaries should approve formal written policies which reflect their overall risk management objectives. The Primary and Manager Fiduciaries also should approve investment guidelines, management agreements and all other contracts that govern investments. Technical terms should be defined. All policies, definitions, guidelines and investment documentation should be reviewed and updated as appropriate and more often if significant market events or changes in strategy occur.

Risk Standard 3: Independent risk oversight, checks and balances, written procedures and controls
Oversight of compliance with risk policies should be independent of line investment activities and conducted according to up-to-date written policies and procedures. Front, middle, and back office activities should be separate wherever possible and sufficient checks and balances and appropriate controls should exist. When separation is not possible due to limited staff, alternative checks, balances and controls should be established.

Risk Standard 4: Clearly defined organizational structure and key roles
Organizational structure and reporting lines should be defined clearly and distributed to all parties. Key personnel and their roles in all front, middle and back office areas should be identified. Changes in key personnel should be communicated immediately to all relevant parties.

Risk Standard 5: Consistent application of risk policies
The Primary Fiduciary's risk policies should apply both to internal and external managers and should be consistent across similar asset classes and strategies.

Risk Standard 6: Adequate education, systems and resources, backup and disaster recovery plans
The Primary and Manager Fiduciaries should ensure that adequate education, systems and resources are available to implement and administer their risk policies. They should also establish and test back-up procedures and disaster recovery plans.

Risk Standard 7: Identification and understanding of key risks
Risks should be analyzed to determine relevancy. This entails understanding strategies and their vulnerabilities, as well as assumptions built into an instrument, system, process, model or strategy. Key risks should be reviewed periodically as well as when significant events occur.

Risk Standard 8: Setting risk limits
Risk limits should be set for the aggregate portfolio and all individual portfolios. These may include limits on asset classes, individual instruments and specific types of risk.

Risk Standard 9: Routine reporting, exception reporting and escalation procedures
The Primary and Manager Fiduciaries should specify what positions, risks and other information must be reported and to whom. This policy also should define what constitutes required reporting or an exception to guidelines, to whom the exception should be reported, what action must be taken for different levels of violation and what procedures must be followed for ongoing or increased violations.

II. Measurement

Risk Standard 10: Valuation procedures
All readily priced instruments should be valued daily, less-readily priced instruments at least weekly and non-readily priced instruments as often as feasible and whenever a material event occurs. The pricing mechanism and methodologies must be known, understood, follow written policies and be applied consistently by the Primary and Manager Fiduciaries, Managers, custodian and other subcontractors.

Risk Standard 11: Valuation reconciliation, bid/offer adjustments and overrides
Material discrepancies in valuations from different sources should be reconciled following established procedures. A procedure for bid/offer adjustments and overrides to valuations should be established in writing and monitored independently.

Risk Standard 12: Risk measurement and risk/return attribution analysis
The Primary and Manager Fiduciaries should regularly measure relevant risks and quantify the key drivers of risk and return.

Risk Standard 13: Risk-adjusted return measures
Risk-adjusted returns should be measured at the aggregate and individual portfolio level to gain a true measure of relative performance.

Risk Standard 14: Stress testing
Simulation or other stress tests should be performed to ascertain how the aggregate portfolio and individual portfolios would behave under various conditions. These include changes in key risk factors, correlations or other key assumptions and unusual events such as large market moves.

Risk Standard 15: Back testing
Risk and return forecasts and models should be back tested at least quarterly and whenever material events occur to assess their reliability.

Risk Standard 16: Assessing model risk
Dependence on models and assumptions for valuation, risk measurement and risk management should be evaluated and monitored.

III. Oversight

Risk Standard 17: Due diligence, policy compliance and guideline monitoring
The Primary and Manager Fiduciaries should perform frequent, independent reviews of all Managers' risk policies and controls. Where policies and controls fall short of the requirements set forth by the Primary or Manager Fiduciaries, plans for future compliance or corrective action should be documented and communicated. Managers should ensure continuing compliance with their clients' risk policies and guidelines.

Risk Standard 18: Comparison of Manager strategies to compensation and investment activity

The Primary Fiduciary should require each Manager to submit a statement of strategy and ensure that the Manager's activities and compensation are consistent with that strategy. Key risk and return factors should be documented and reviewed at least annually and updated whenever the strategy changes.

Risk Standard 19: Independent review of methodologies, models and systems

All methodologies, models and related systems should be independently reviewed or audited prior to use as well as annually. Significant market moves or changes in market practice should trigger interim reviews.

Risk Standard 20: Review process for new activities

The Primary and Manager Fiduciaries should document the review process for permitting the use of new instruments, strategies or asset classes. Policies for initiating new activities should be consistent with the Primary and Manager Fiduciaries' risk and return goals as well as the Manager's strategy and expertise.

Source: Capital Market Risk Advisors, www.cmra.com/html/the_risk_standards.html

PROBLEMS   1. An organization's risk management function has computed that a portfolio held by the trading function has a 1 percent weekly Value at Risk (VAR) of $4.25 million. Describe what is meant in terms of a minimum loss.

2. An organization's risk management function has computed that a portfolio held by the trading function has a 99 percent weekly VAR of $4.25 million. Describe what is meant in terms of a maximum loss.

3. Suppose you are given the following sample probability distribution of annual returns on a portfolio whose market value is $10 million.

Return on Portfolio	Probability
Less than −50%	0.005
−40% to −50%	0.005
−30% to −40%	0.010
−20% to −30%	0.015
−10% to −20%	0.015
−5% to −10%	0.165
0% to −5%	0.250
0% to 5%	0.250
5% to 10%	0.145
10% to 20%	0.075
20% to 30%	0.025
30% to 40%	0.020
40% to 50%	0.015
Greater than 50%	0.005
	1.000

Based on this probability distribution, determine the following.
   A. 1 percent yearly VAR
   B. 5 percent yearly VAR

4. A portfolio manager is interested in computing the VAR for a portfolio consisting of two classes of assets. The first consists of a group of securities that mimics an equally weighted portfolio of stocks traded on the NYSE. On an annual basis, the expected return on this asset class is 14.59 percent and the standard deviation is 14.51 percent. The second asset class consists of a group of securities that mimics an equally weighted portfolio of stocks traded on Nasdaq. The expected annual return on this asset class is 15.58 percent, and the standard deviation is 23.35 percent. The correlation between the annual returns of the two asset classes is 0.71. The market value of the portfolio is $10 million, and the portfolio is invested 70 percent and 30 percent in the two asset classes, respectively. Based on the analytical or variance–covariance method, compute the following.
   A. 5 percent yearly VAR
   B. 1 percent yearly VAR
   C. 5 percent daily VAR
   D. 1 percent daily VAR

5. An analyst would like to know the VAR for a portfolio consisting of two asset classes: long-term government bonds issued in the United States, and long-term government bonds issued in the United Kingdom. The expected monthly return on U.S. bonds is 0.85 percent, and the standard deviation is 3.20 percent. The expected monthly return on U.K. bonds, in U.S. dollars, is 0.95 percent, and the standard deviation is 5.26 percent. The correlation between the U.S. dollar returns of U.K. and U.S. bonds is 0.35. The portfolio market value is $100 million and is equally weighted between the two asset classes. Using the analytical or variance–covariance method, compute the following.
   A. 5 percent monthly VAR
   B. 1 percent monthly VAR
   C. 5 percent weekly VAR
   D. 1 percent weekly VAR

6. You invested $25,000 in the stock of Dell Computer Corporation in early 2002. You have compiled the monthly returns on Dell's stock during the 1997–2001 period, as given below.

1997	1998	1999	2000	2001
0.2447	0.1838	0.3664	−0.2463	0.4982
0.0756	0.4067	−0.1988	0.0618	−0.1627
−0.0492	−0.0313	0.0203	0.3216	0.1743
0.2375	0.1919	0.0077	−0.0707	0.0215
0.3443	0.0205	−0.1639	−0.1397	−0.0717
0.0439	0.1263	0.0744	0.1435	0.0735
0.4561	0.1700	0.1047	−0.1090	0.0298
−0.0402	−0.0791	0.1942	−0.0071	−0.2061
0.1805	0.3150	−0.1434	−0.2937	−0.1333
−0.1729	−0.0038	−0.0404	−0.0426	0.2941
0.0507	−0.0716	0.0717	−0.3475	0.1647
−0.0022	0.2035	0.1861	−0.0942	−0.0269

Using the historical method, compute the following.
   A. 5 percent monthly VAR
   B. 1 percent monthly VAR

7. Each of the following statements about VAR is true *except*:
   A. VAR is the loss that would be exceeded with a given probability over a specific time period.
   B. Establishing a VAR involves several decisions, such as the probability and time period over which the VAR will be measured and the technique to be used.
   C. VAR will be larger when it is measured at 5 percent probability than when it is measured at 1 percent probability.
   D. VAR will be larger when it is measured over a month than when it is measured over a day.

8. Consider a $10 million portfolio of stocks. You perform a Monte Carlo simulation to estimate the VAR for this portfolio. You choose to perform this simulation using a normal distribution of returns for the portfolio, with an expected annual return of 14.8 percent and a standard deviation of 20.5 percent. You generate 700 random

outcomes of annual return for this portfolio, of which the worst 40 outcomes are given below.

−0.400	−0.320	−0.295	−0.247
−0.398	−0.316	−0.282	−0.233
−0.397	−0.314	−0.277	−0.229
−0.390	−0.310	−0.273	−0.226
−0.355	−0.303	−0.273	−0.223
−0.350	−0.301	−0.261	−0.222
−0.347	−0.301	−0.259	−0.218
−0.344	−0.300	−0.253	−0.216
−0.343	−0.298	−0.251	−0.215
−0.333	−0.296	−0.248	−0.211

Using the above information, compute the following.
A. 5 percent annual VAR
B. 1 percent annual VAR

9. Consider an investment portfolio consisting of stocks as well as options on stocks. You would like to determine the VAR for this portfolio and are thinking about the technique to be used. Discuss the problem with using the analytical or variance–covariance method for determining the VAR of this portfolio.

10. Indicate which of the following statements about credit risk is (are) false, and explain why:
    A. Because credit losses occur often, it is easy to assess the probability of a credit loss.
    B. One element of credit risk is the possibility that the counterparty to a contract will default on an obligation to another party.
    C. Like the buyer of a European-style option, the buyer of an American-style option does not face any current credit risk until the expiration of the option.

11. Consider an asset priced at $50. A new forward contract on this asset expires in six months. The risk-free rate, with discrete compounding, is 4 percent.
    A. Two months after the contract is initiated, the price of the asset has increased to $50.85. What is the amount of credit risk at this time? Which party bears this risk, the long or the short?
    B. Suppose instead that two months after the contract is initiated, the price of the asset has decreased to $49.55. How much is the credit risk then? Which party bears this risk, the long or the short?

12. The spot exchange rate for the British pound is $1.4486. The annual U.S. interest rate is 6.1 percent, and the annual British interest rate is 5.8 percent. The interest rates are based on discrete compounding/discounting. A party goes long a forward contract on one pound, with a maturity of one year, at a forward price of $1.4527. Suppose that three months have elapsed since then, and the spot exchange rate for the British pound has changed to $1.4484. Determine the amount currently at risk of a credit loss and which party bears this risk.

13. Two parties entered into a six-month forward contract on €10 million. The contract is denominated in U.S. dollars and the forward rate agreed on is $0.9971/€. Now, two months into the contract, the current spot rate is $0.9935/€. The annual interest rates, based on discrete compounding/discounting, are 5.5 percent in the United States and 4 percent on the euro.

    A. Determine the value of the contract to the long and short parties.

    B. How much is the current credit risk, and which party bears this risk?

14. Consider a two-year forward contract established six months ago at a rate of $55. The underlying asset makes no cash payments. The risk-free rate is 5 percent. The two parties to the contract have decided that they will mark the contract to market every six months. We are now six months into the contract. Determine what would happen at this point in the following alternative situations:

    A. The spot price now of the underlying asset is $54.

    B. The spot price now of the underlying asset is $51.

15. Indicate which of the following statements about credit risk derivatives is (are) false and explain why:

    A. The buyer of a credit derivative still faces some credit risk, because the seller of the credit derivative could default.

    B. A credit swap is a particular type of credit derivative that is more like a swap and less like an option.

    C. Credit derivatives work by separating market risk from credit risk and allowing each of these risks to be priced and traded in different markets.

    D. Credit derivatives are motivated not only by the parties wishing to eliminate credit risk but also by parties wishing to purchase credit risk.

16. Tony Smith believes that the price of a particular underlying, which is currently selling at $96, will increase substantially in the next six months, so he purchases a European call option expiring in six months on this underlying. The call option has an exercise price of $101 and is selling for $6.

    A. How much is the current credit risk, if any?

    B. How much is the current value of the potential credit risk, if any?

    C. Which party bears the credit risk(s), Tony Smith or the seller?

17. Consider a plain vanilla one-year interest rate swap with semiannual payments. The underlying is six-month LIBOR. Both the floating-rate and fixed payments are on the basis of 180/360. The fixed rate, on an annualized basis, is 6.60 percent. The six-month LIBOR at the beginning of the swap is 6.0 percent. Suppose that now, three months into the life of the swap, the three-month and nine-month LIBORs are 5.90 percent and 6.35 percent, respectively. Assume a notional principal of $1. Determine the amount at risk of a credit loss and which party bears the risk.

18. Consider a one-year plain vanilla interest rate swap with quarterly payments. The underlying is three-month LIBOR. Both the floating and fixed payments are on the basis of 90/360. The fixed rate, on an annualized basis, is 4.50 percent. Three-month LIBOR at the beginning of the swap is 4.33 percent. Suppose we have now moved two months into the life of the swap. Now, the 1-month, 4-month, 7-month, and 10-month LIBORs are 5.00 percent, 5.08 percent, 5.15 percent, and 5.22 percent, respectively. The notional principal is $10 million. Determine the amount at risk of a credit loss and state which party bears the risk.

19. Indicate which of the following statements about liquidity risk is (are) false and explain why:

    A. Liquidity risk is more of a concern for the sellers of a security than for the buyers.

    B. In general, derivatives can be used to substantially reduce the liquidity risk of a security.

    C. Liquidity risk is usually observed in the size of the spread between the bid and ask prices of a security; the less liquid the security, the higher the bid–ask spread.

20. Indicate which of the following statements about the practice of risk management is (are) true and explain why:
    A. Risk management is a more general practice than hedging, and the purpose of risk management is to reduce risk.
    B. In both centralized and decentralized risk management systems, the trading function should be separated from the risk management function.
    C. Risk budgeting is the establishment of expectations for performance standards that take into account allocated capital and an allowable level of risk.

SOLUTIONS

1. There is a 1 percent chance that the portfolio will lose at least $4.25 million in one week.

2. There is a 99 percent chance that the portfolio will lose no more than $4.25 million in one week.

3. **A.** The probability is 0.005 that the portfolio will lose at least 50 percent in a year. The probability is 0.005 that the portfolio will lose between 40 percent and 50 percent in a year. Cumulating these two probabilities implies that the probability is 0.01 that the portfolio will lose at least 40 percent in a year. So, the 1 percent yearly VAR is 40 percent of the market value of $10 million, which is $4 million.

   B. The probability is 0.005 that the portfolio will lose at least 50 percent in a year, 0.005 that it will lose between 40 and 50 percent, 0.010 that it will lose between 30 and 40 percent, 0.015 that it will lose between 20 and 30 percent, and 0.015 that it will lose between 10 and 20 percent. Cumulating these probabilities indicates that the probability is 0.05 that the portfolio will lose at least 10 percent in a year. So, the 5 percent yearly VAR is 10 percent of the market value of $10 million, which is $1 million.

4. First we calculate the annual portfolio expected return and standard deviation. Using "1" to indicate the first asset class and "2" to indicate the second asset class, we have

$$\mu_p = w_1\mu_1 + w_2\mu_2 = 0.70(0.1459) + 0.30(0.1558) = 0.1489$$

$$\sigma_p^2 = w_1^2\sigma_1^2 + w_2^2\sigma_2^2 + 2w_1w_2\sigma_1\sigma_2\rho$$

$$= (0.70)^2(0.1451)^2 + (0.30)^2(0.2335)^2 + 2(0.70)(0.30)(0.1451)(0.2335)(0.71)$$

$$= 0.0253$$

$$\sigma_p = \sqrt{0.0253} = 0.1591$$

   A. For a 5 percent yearly VAR, we have $\mu_p - 1.65\sigma_p = 0.1489 - 1.65(0.1591) = -0.1136$. Then the VAR would be $10,000,000(0.1136) = $1.136 million.

   B. For a 1 percent yearly VAR, we have $\mu_p - 2.33\sigma_p = 0.1489 - 2.33(0.1591) = -0.2218$. Then the VAR would be $10,000,000(0.2218) = $2.218 million.

   C. Assuming 250 trading days per year, for daily VAR, we adjust the expected return to $0.1489/250 = 0.0005956$ and the standard deviation to $0.1591/\sqrt{250} = 0.01006$. The 5 percent daily VAR would then be $\mu_p - 1.65\sigma_p = 0.0005956 - 1.65(0.01006) = -0.0160$. Then the VAR would be $10,000,000(0.0160) = $160,000.

   D. The 1 percent daily VAR would be $\mu_p - 2.33\sigma_p = 0.0005956 - 2.33(0.01006) = -0.02284$. Then the VAR would be $10,000,000(0.02284) = $228,400.

5. First we must calculate the monthly portfolio expected return and standard deviation. Using "1" to indicate the U.S. government bonds and "2" to indicate the U.K. government bonds, we have

$$\mu_p = w_1\mu_1 + w_2\mu_2 = 0.50(0.0085) + 0.50(0.0095) = 0.0090$$

$$\sigma_p^2 = w_1^2\sigma_1^2 + w_2^2\sigma_2^2 + 2w_1w_2\sigma_1\sigma_2\rho$$

$$= (0.50)^2(0.0320)^2 + (0.50)^2(0.0526)^2 + 2(0.50)(0.50)(0.0320)(0.0526)(0.35)$$

$$= 0.001242$$

$$\sigma_p = \sqrt{0.001242} = 0.0352$$

A. For a 5 percent monthly VAR, we have $\mu_p - 1.65\sigma_p = 0.0090 - 1.65(0.0352) = -0.0491$. Then the VAR would be $\$100,000,000(0.0491) = \$4.91$ million.

B. For a 1 percent monthly VAR, we have $\mu_p - 2.33\sigma_p = 0.0090 - 2.33(0.0352) = -0.0730$. Then the VAR would be $\$100,000,000(0.0730) = \$7.30$ million.

C. There are 12 months or 52 weeks in a year. So, to convert the monthly return of 0.0090 to weekly return, we first multiply the monthly return with 12 to convert it to an annual return, and then divide the annual return with 52 to convert it to a weekly return. So, the expected weekly return is $0.0090(12/52) = 0.0021$. Similarly, we adjust the standard deviation to $0.0352(\sqrt{12}/\sqrt{52}) = 0.01691$. The 5 percent weekly VAR would then be $\mu_p - 1.65\sigma_p = 0.0021 - 1.65(0.01691) = -0.0258$. Then the VAR in dollars would be $\$100,000,000(0.0258) = \$2.58$ million.

D. The 1 percent weekly VAR would be $\mu_p - 2.33\sigma_p = 0.0021 - 2.33(0.01691) = -0.0373$. Then the VAR would be $\$100,000,000(0.0373) = \$3.73$ million.

6. A. For the five-year period, there are 60 monthly returns. Of the 60 returns, the 5 percent worst are the 3 worst returns. Therefore, based on the historical method, the 5 percent VAR would be the third worst return. From the returns given, the third worst return is -0.2463. So, the VAR in dollars would be $0.2463(\$25,000) = \$6,157.50$.

B. Of the 60 returns, the 1 percent worst are the 0.6 worst returns. Therefore, we would use the single worst return. From the returns given, the worst return is -0.3475. So, the VAR in dollars would be $0.3475(\$25,000) = \$8,687.50$.

7. Statement A, which is the definition of VAR, is clearly correct. Statement B is also correct, because these are the important decisions involved in measuring VAR. Statement D is correct: The longer the time period, the larger the possible losses. Statement C, however, is not correct. The VAR number would be larger for a 1 percent probability than for a 5 percent probability. Accordingly, the correct answer is C.

8. A. Of the 700 outcomes, the worst 5 percent are the 35 worst returns. Therefore, the 5 percent VAR would be the 35th worst return. From the data given, the 35th worst return is -0.223. So, the 5 percent annual VAR in dollars $= 0.223(\$10,000,000) = \$2,230,000$.

B. Of the 700 outcomes, the worst 1 percent are the 7 worst returns. Therefore, the 1 percent VAR would be the seventh worst return. From the data given, the seventh worst return is -0.347. So, the 1 percent annual VAR in dollars $= 0.347(\$10,000,000) = \$3,470,000$.

9. The analytical or variance–covariance method begins with the assumption that portfolio returns are normally distributed. A normal distribution has an unlimited upside and an unlimited downside. The assumption of a normal distribution is inappropriate when the portfolio contains options, because the return distributions of options are far from normal. Call options have unlimited upside potential, as in a normal distribution, but the downside return is truncated at a loss of 100 percent. Similarly, put options have a limited upside and a large but limited downside. Likewise, covered calls and protective puts have limits in one direction or the other. Therefore, for the portfolio that has options, the assumption of a normal distribution to estimate VAR has a number of problems.

10. The fact that credit losses do not occur often makes Statement A incorrect. Unlike a European-style option, which cannot be exercised prior to expiration and thus has no

current credit risk, an American-style option does have the potential for current credit risk. Therefore, Statement C is not correct. Statement B, however, is correct.

11. **A.** The forward price when the contract was initiated was $50(1.04)^{0.5} = \$50.99$. Now, two months later, to the holder of the long position, the contract is worth $50.85 - 50.99/(1.04)^{4/12} = \$0.52$. This is the amount of credit risk. Because the value of the contract is positive to the long party, this party bears the credit risk.

    B. To the holder of the long position, the contract is worth $49.55 - 50.99/(1.04)^{4/12} = -\$0.78$. Therefore, the value of the contract is negative to the long party. The contract is worth \$0.78 to the short party. This is the amount of credit risk, which is borne by the short party.

12. The value of the contract to the long is $\dfrac{\$1.4484}{(1.058)^{9/12}} - \dfrac{\$1.4527}{(1.061)^{9/12}} = -\$0.0012$

per £1. Therefore, the position has a negative value to the long and a positive value to the short. So, the credit risk is currently borne by the short. No payments are due for nine months, but the short's claim on the long is worth \$0.0012 more than the long's claim on the short. This amount is the current value of the amount at risk for a credit loss. Of course, this amount could, and probably will, change over the life of the contract. The credit risk exposure might even shift to the other party.

13. **A.** The value of the contract to the long is $\dfrac{\$0.9935}{(1.04)^{4/6}} - \dfrac{\$0.9971}{(1.055)^{4/6}} = \$0.00572$

    per €1. So, for a contract of €10 million, the value of the contract to the long is €10,000,000(0.00572) = \$57,200. The value of the contract to the short is −\$57,200.

    B. The current credit risk is \$57,200 and is borne by the long. Of course, this amount could, and probably will, change over the life of the contract. The credit risk exposure might even shift to the other party.

14. Because we are 6 months into a two-year forward contract, 18 months or 1.5 years remain until expiration. The long party has an obligation to pay \$55 in 1.5 years. The present value of that amount is $\$55/(1.05)^{1.5} = \$51.12$.

    A. The market value of the contract is $\$54.00 - \$51.12 = \$2.88$. This amount is positive to the long party; so the short party pays the long \$2.88 per \$1 notional principal. The parties then reprice the contract. The new price would be $\$54(1.05)^{1.5} = \$58.10$. Thus, at this point, the forward contract would be set to \$58.10. The parties will then mark to market again at the 12-month point (6 months from now) and reset the price. They will then mark to market again at the 18-month point and reset the price. This price will then stay in force until expiration.

    B. The market value of the contract is $\$51.00 - \$51.12 = -\$0.12$. This amount is negative to the long party; so the long party pays the short \$0.12 per \$1 notional principal. The parties then reprice the contract. The new price would be $\$51(1.05)^{1.5} = \$54.87$. Thus, at this point, the forward contract would be set to \$54.87. The parties will then mark to market again at the 12-month point (6 months from now) and reset the price. They will then mark to market again at the 18-month point and reset the price. This price will then stay in force until expiration.

15. Statements A and C about credit risk derivatives are clearly true. Statement D is also true. There is a demand to purchase credit risk. Credit derivatives provide an opportunity to their buyers to take risks they may not otherwise have access to and thus diversify their current risk. Statement B, however, is not correct. Even though it is referred to as a swap, a credit swap is more like an option than like a swap because one party makes a payment only if a credit event occurs.

16. **A.** Because the option is a European-style option, it cannot be exercised prior to expiration. Therefore, there is no current credit risk.

    B. The current value of the potential credit risk is the current market value of the option, which is $6. Of course, at expiration, the option is likely to be worth a different amount and could even expire out of the money.

    C. Options have unilateral credit risk. The risk is borne by the buyer of the option, Tony Smith, as he will look to the seller for the payoff at expiration if the option expires in the money.

17. Because we have moved three months into the life of the swap, and the payments are semiannual, the next payment will be in three months from now. We need to compute the present value factors for three and nine months, respectively. They are given below.

$$\frac{1}{1 + 0.059(90/360)} = 0.9855$$

$$\frac{1}{1 + 0.0635(270/360)} = 0.9545$$

Given an annual fixed rate of 6.60 percent, the semiannual fixed payments will be $0.066(180/360) = 0.033$ per $1 of notional principal. The present value of the remaining fixed payments of $0.033, including the hypothetical $1 notional principal, is $0.033(0.9855 + 0.9545) + $1.0(0.9545) = 1.0185. Six-month LIBOR at the start was 6 percent, so the first floating payment would be $0.06(180/360) = 0.03$. The present value of the floating payments plus hypothetical $1 notional principal will be $1.03 (0.9855) = 1.0151.

Therefore, the present value of the remaining floating payments and the hypothetical notional principal of $1 is $1.0151, and the present value of the remaining fixed payments and the hypothetical notional principal of $1 is $1.0185. Therefore, the value of the swap for the party paying fixed and receiving floating is $1.0151 − $1.0185 = −$0.0034$ per $1 notional principal. The value of the swap for the party paying floating and receiving fixed is $0.0034 per $1 notional principal. So, the party paying floating and receiving fixed is the one assuming a credit risk of $0.0034 per $1 notional principal. Of course, the amount at risk could, and probably will, change over the life of the swap. The credit risk exposure might even shift to the party paying fixed and receiving floating.

18. Because we have moved two months into the life of the swap and the payments are quarterly, the next payment will be in one month. We need to compute the present value factors for 1, 4, 7, and 10 months, respectively, given below.

$$\frac{1}{1 + 0.0500(30/360)} = 0.9959$$

$$\frac{1}{1 + 0.0508(120/360)} = 0.9833$$

$$\frac{1}{1 + 0.0515(210/360)} = 0.9708$$

$$\frac{1}{1 + 0.0522(300/360)} = 0.9583$$

Let us first look at a notional principal of $1. Given an annual fixed rate of 4.50 percent, the quarterly fixed payments will be $0.045(90/360) = 0.01125$. The present value of the remaining fixed payments of $0.01125, including the hypothetical $1 in notional principal, is $0.01125(0.9959 + 0.9833 + 0.9708 + 0.9583) + $1.0(0.9583) = 1.0023. To find the present value of the floating payments, recall that at the start of the swap, the three-month LIBOR was 4.33 percent. So, the first floating payment will be $0.0433(90/360) = 0.0108$. The present value of the floating payments plus hypothetical $1 notional principal will be $1.0108(0.9959) = 1.0067.

Hence, the value of the swap for the party paying fixed and receiving floating is $1.0067 − $1.0023 = 0.0044 per $1 notional principal. Because the actual swap was for a notional principal of $10 million, the value would be $10,000,000(0.0044) = $44,000$. Because the positive value is for the party paying fixed and receiving floating, this is the party assuming the credit risk of $44,000. Of course, this value could, and probably would, change over the life of the swap. The credit risk exposure might even shift to the party paying floating and receiving fixed.

19. Statement A is true. Liquidity risk manifests much more on the sell side of a transaction than on the buy side. Parties that wish to buy a security in an illiquid market can often choose not to buy it if the price is unacceptable. They may also find a substitute security. Statement B is not true. Derivatives usually do not help in managing liquidity risk, because the illiquidity in the spot market typically passes right through to the derivatives market. Statement C is true. When markets are illiquid, dealers expect to sell at relatively higher prices and buy at relatively lower prices.

20. Unlike hedging, which is always aimed at reducing risk, risk management can entail reducing *or increasing* risk. Therefore, Statement A is false. Statement B is true because regardless of centralization or decentralization of risk management, the trading function should always be separated from the risk management function. Statement C, a definition of risk budgeting, is also true.

GLOSSARY

Accounting risk The risk associated with accounting standards that vary from country to country or with any uncertainty about how certain transactions should be recorded.

Add-on interest A procedure for determining the interest on a bond or loan in which the interest is added onto the face value of a contract.

American option An option that can be exercised on any day through the expiration day. Also referred to as *American-style exercise.*

Amortizing and accreting swaps A swap in which the notional principal changes according to a formula related to changes in the underlying.

Arbitrage The condition in a financial market in which equivalent assets or combinations of assets sell for two different prices, creating an opportunity to profit at no risk with no commitment of money. In a well-functioning financial market, few arbitrage opportunities are possible. Equivalent to the *law of one price.*

Arrears swap A type of interest rate swap in which the floating payment is set at the end of the period and the interest is paid at that same time.

At the money An option in which the underlying value equals the exercise price.

Backwardation A condition in the futures markets in which the benefits of holding an asset exceed the costs, leaving the futures price less than the spot price.

Basis point value (BPV) Also called *present value of a basis point* or *price value of a basis point* (PVBP), the change in the bond price for a 1 basis point change in yield.

Basis swap A swap in which both parties pay a floating rate.

Bear spread An option strategy that involves selling a put with a lower exercise price and buying a put with a higher exercise price. It can also be executed with calls.

Beta A measure of the relationship between the return on a stock portfolio and the return on the market portfolio, which is a portfolio containing *all* risky assets in the market.

Binomial model A model for pricing options in which the underlying price can move to only one of two possible new prices.

Binomial tree A diagram representing price movements of the underlying in a binomial model.

Bond option An option in which the underlying is a bond; primarily traded in over-the-counter markets.

Box spread An option strategy that combines a bull spread and a bear spread having two different exercise prices, which produces a risk-free payoff of the difference in the exercise prices.

Brokers See *futures commission merchants.*

Bull spread An option strategy that involves buying a call with a lower exercise price and selling a call with a higher exercise price. It can also be executed with puts.

Butterfly spread An option strategy that combines two bull or bear spreads and has three exercise prices.

Call An option that gives the holder the right to buy an underlying asset from another party at a fixed price over a specific period of time.

Cap A combination of interest rate call options designed to hedge a borrower against rate increases on a floating-rate loan.

Caplet Each component call option in a cap.

Capped swap A swap in which the floating payments have an upper limit.

Cash flow at risk (CFAR) A variation of VAR that reflects the risk of a company's cash flow instead of its market value.

Cash price or spot price The price for immediate purchase of the underlying asset.

Cash settlement A procedure used in certain derivative transactions that specifies that the long and short parties engage in the equivalent cash value of a delivery transaction.

Centralized risk management or companywide risk management When a company has a single risk

635

management group that monitors and controls all of the risk-taking activities of the organization. Centralization permits economies of scale and allows a company to use some of its risks to offset other risks. See also *enterprise risk management.*

Cheapest to deliver A bond in which the amount received for delivering the bond is largest compared with the amount paid in the market for the bond.

Cherry-picking When a bankrupt company is allowed to enforce contracts that are favorable to it while walking away from contracts that are unfavorable to it.

Clearinghouse An entity associated with a futures market that acts as middleman between the contracting parties and guarantees to each party the performance of the other.

Closeout netting Netting the market values of *all* derivative contracts between two parties to determine one overall value owed by one party to another in the event of bankruptcy.

Collar An option strategy involving the purchase of a put and sale of a call in which the holder of an asset gains protection below a certain level, the exercise price of the put, and pays for it by giving up gains above a certain level, the exercise price of the call. Collars also can be used to provide protection against rising interest rates on a floating-rate loan by giving up gains from lower interest rates.

Commodity forward A contract in which the underlying asset is oil, a precious metal, or some other commodity.

Commodity futures Futures contracts in which the underlying is a traditional agricultural, metal, or petroleum product.

Commodity option An option in which the asset underlying the futures is a commodity, such as oil, gold, wheat, or soybeans.

Commodity swap A swap in which the underlying is a commodity such as oil, gold, or an agricultural product.

Constant maturity swap or CMT swap A swap in which the floating rate is the rate on a security known as a constant maturity treasury or CMT security.

Constant maturity treasury or CMT A hypothetical U.S. Treasury note with a constant maturity. A CMT exists for various years in the range of 2 to 10.

Contango A condition in the futures markets in which the costs of holding an asset exceed the benefits, leaving the futures price more than the spot price.

Contingent claims Derivatives in which the payoffs occur if a specific event occurs; generally referred to as options.

Continuous time Time thought of as advancing in extremely small increments.

Convenience yield The nonmonetary return offered by an asset when the asset is in short supply, often associated with assets with seasonal production processes.

Conversion factor An adjustment used to facilitate delivery on bond futures contracts in which any of a number of bonds with different characteristics are eligible for delivery.

Cost of carry The costs of holding an asset.

Cost of carry model A model for pricing futures contracts in which the futures price is determined by adding the cost of carry to the spot price.

Covariance A measure of the extent to which the returns on two assets move together.

Covered call An option strategy involving the holding of an asset and sale of a call on the asset.

Covered interest arbitrage A transaction executed in the foreign exchange market in which a currency is purchased (sold) and a forward contract is sold (purchased) to lock in the exchange rate for future delivery of the currency. This transaction should earn the risk-free rate of the investor's home country.

Credit derivatives A contract in which one party has the right to claim a payment from another party in the event that a specific credit event occurs over the life of the contract.

Credit risk or default risk The risk of loss due to nonpayment by a counterparty.

Credit spread option An option on the yield spread on a bond.

Credit swap A type of swap transaction used as a credit derivative in which one party makes periodic payments to the other and receives the promise of a payoff if a third party defaults.

Credit VAR, Default VAR, or Credit at Risk A variation of VAR that reflects credit risk.

Credit-linked notes Fixed-income securities in which the holder of the security has the right to withhold payment of the full amount due at maturity if a credit event occurs.

Cross-product netting Netting the market values of all contracts, not just derivatives, between parties.

Currency forward A forward contract in which the underlying is a foreign currency.

Currency option An option that allows the holder to buy (if a call) or sell (if a put) an underlying currency at a fixed exercise rate, expressed as an exchange rate.

Currency swap A swap in which each party makes interest payments to the other in different currencies.

Current credit risk The risk associated with the possibility that a payment currently due will not be made.

Daily settlement See *marking to market*.

Day trader A trader holding a position open somewhat longer than a scalper but closing all positions at the end of the day.

Decentralized risk management A system that allows individual units within an organization to manage risk. Decentralization results in duplication of effort but has the advantage of having people closer to the risk be more directly involved in its management.

Deep in the money Options that are far in-the-money.

Deep out of the money Options that are far out-of-the-money.

Delivery A process used in a deliverable forward contract in which the long pays the agreed-upon price to the short, which in turn delivers the underlying asset to the long.

Delivery option The feature of a futures contract giving the short the right to make decisions about what, when, and where to deliver.

Delta The relationship between the option price and the underlying price, which reflects the sensitivity of the price of the option to changes in the price of the underlying.

Delta hedge An option strategy in which a position in an asset is converted to a risk-free position with a position in a specific number of options. The number of options per unit of the underlying changes through time, and the position must be revised to maintain the hedge.

Delta-normal method A measure of VAR equivalent to the analytical method but that refers to the use of delta to estimate the option's price sensitivity.

Derivative A financial instrument that offers a return based on the return of some other underlying asset.

Derivatives dealers The commercial and investment banks that make markets in derivatives. Also referred to as market makers.

Diff swaps A swap in which the payments are based on the difference between interest rates in two countries but payments are made in only a single currency.

Discount interest A procedure for determining the interest on a loan or bond in which the interest is deducted from the face value in advance.

Discrete time Time thought of as advancing in distinct finite increments.

Duration A measure of the size and timing of the cash flows paid by a bond. It quantifies these factors by summarizing them in the form of a single number. For bonds without option features attached, duration is interpreted as a weighted average maturity of the bond.

Dynamic hedging A strategy in which a position is hedged by making frequent adjustments to the quantity of the instrument used for hedging in relation to the instrument being hedged.

Earnings at risk (EAR) A variation of VAR that reflects the risk of a company's earnings instead of its market value.

Economic exposure The risk associated with changes in the relative attractiveness of products and services offered for sale, arising out of the competitive effects of changes in exchange rates.

Enhanced derivatives products companies (EDPC) or special purpose vehicles (SPVs) A type of subsidiary engaged in derivatives transactions that is separated from the parent company in order to have a higher credit rating than the parent company.

Enterprise risk management A form of *centralized risk management* that typically encompasses the management of a broad variety of risks, including insurance risk.

Equitizing cash A strategy used to replicate an index. It is also used to take a given amount of cash and turn it into an equity position while maintaining the liquidity provided by the cash.

Equity forward A contract calling for the purchase of an individual stock, a stock portfolio, or a stock index at a later date at an agreed-upon price.

Equity options Options on individual stocks; also known as stock options.

Equity swap A swap in which the rate is the return on a stock or stock index.

Eurodollar A dollar deposited outside the United States.

European option An option that can be exercised only at expiration. Also referred to as *European-style exercise*.

Exchange for physicals (EFP) A permissible delivery procedure used by futures market participants, in which the long and short arrange a delivery procedure other than the normal procedures stipulated by the futures exchange.

Exercise or exercising the option The process of using an option to buy or sell the underlying.

Exercise price, strike price, striking price, or strike The fixed price at which an option holder can buy or sell the underlying.

Exercise rate or strike rate The fixed rate at which the holder of an interest rate option can buy or sell the underlying.

Expiration date The date on which a derivative contract expires.

Fiduciary call A combination of a European call and a risk-free bond that matures on the option expiration day and has a face value equal to the exercise price of the call.

Financial futures Futures contracts in which the underlying is a stock, bond, or currency.

Fixed-income forward A forward contract in which the underlying is a bond.

Floating-rate loan A loan in which the interest rate is reset at least once after the starting date.

Floor A combination of interest rate put options designed to hedge a lender against lower rates on a floating-rate loan.

Floor traders or locals Market makers that buy and sell by quoting a bid and an ask price. They are the primary providers of liquidity to the market.

Floored swap A swap in which the floating payments have a lower limit.

Floorlet Each component put option in a floor.

Forward contract An agreement between two parties in which one party, the buyer, agrees to buy from the other party, the seller, an underlying asset at a later date for a price established at the start of the contract.

Forward price or forward rate The fixed price or rate at which the transaction scheduled to occur at the expiration of a forward contract will take place. This price is agreed on at the initiation date of the contract.

Forward rate agreement (FRA) A forward contract calling for one party to make a fixed interest payment and the other to make an interest payment at a rate to be determined at the contract expiration.

Forward swap A forward contract to enter into a swap.

Futures commission merchants (FCMs) Individuals or companies that execute futures transactions for other parties off the exchange.

Futures contract A variation of a forward contract that has essentially the same basic definition but with some additional features, such as a clearinghouse guarantee against credit losses, a daily settlement of gains and losses, and an organized electronic or floor trading facility.

Futures exchange A legal corporate entity whose shareholders are its members. The members of the exchange have the privilege of executing transactions directly on the exchange.

Gamma A numerical measure of how sensitive an option's delta is to a change in the underlying.

Hedge ratio The relationship of the quantity of an asset being hedged to the quantity of the derivative used for hedging.

Hedging A general strategy usually thought of as reducing, if not eliminating, risk.

Historical method A method of estimating VAR that uses data from the returns of the portfolio over a recent past period and compiles this data in the form of a histogram.

Historical simulation method Another term for the historical method of estimating VAR. This term is somewhat misleading in that the method involves not a *simulation* of the past but rather what *actually happened* in the past, sometimes adjusted to reflect the fact that a different portfolio may have existed in the past than is planned for the future.

Homogenization Creating a contract with standard and generally accepted terms, which makes it more acceptable to a broader group of participants.

Implied repo rate The rate of return from a cash-and-carry transaction implied by the futures price relative to the spot price.

Implied volatility The volatility that option traders use to price an option, implied by the price of the option and a particular option-pricing model.

Implied yield A measure of the yield on the underlying bond of a futures contract implied by pricing it as though the underlying will be delivered at the futures expiration.

Index amortizing swap An interest rate swap in which the notional principal is indexed to the level of interest rates and declines with the level of interest rates according to a predefined scheduled. This type of swap is frequently used to hedge securities that are prepaid as interest rates decline, such as mortgage-backed securities.

Index option An option in which the underlying is a stock index.

Initial margin requirement The margin requirement on the first day of a transaction as well as on any day in which additional margin funds must be deposited.

Interest rate call An option in which the holder has the right to make a known interest payment and receive an unknown interest payment.

Interest rate cap or cap A series of call options on an interest rate, with each option expiring at the date on which the floating loan rate will be reset, and with each option having the same exercise rate. A cap in general can have an underlying other than an interest rate.

Interest rate collar A combination of a long cap and a short floor, or a short cap and a long floor. A collar in general can have an underlying other than an interest rate.

Interest rate floor or floor A series of put options on an interest rate, with each option expiring at the date on which the floating loan rate will be reset, and with each option having the same exercise rate. A floor in general can have an underlying other than the interest rate.

Interest rate forward (See *forward rate agreement*)

Interest rate option An option in which the underlying is an interest rate.

Interest rate parity A formula that expresses the equivalence or parity of spot and forward rates, after adjusting for differences in the interest rates.

Interest rate put An option in which the holder has the right to make an unknown interest payment and receive a known interest payment.

Interest rate swap A swap in which the underlying is an interest rate. Can be viewed as a currency swap in which both currencies are the same and can be created as a combination of currency swaps.

In-the-money Options that, if exercised, would result in the value received being worth more than the payment required to exercise.

Intrinsic value or exercise value The value obtained if an option is exercised based on current conditions.

Inverse floater A floating-rate note or bond in which the coupon is adjusted to move opposite to a benchmark interest rate.

Law of one price The condition in a financial market in which two financial instruments or combinations of financial instruments can sell for only one price. Equivalent to the principle that no arbitrage opportunities are possible.

Legal risk The risk that the legal system will not enforce a contract in case of dispute or fraud.

Leveraged floating-rate note or leveraged floater A floating-rate note or bond in which the coupon is adjusted at a multiple of a benchmark interest rate.

Limit down A limit move in the futures market in which the price at which a transaction would be made is at or below the lower limit.

Limit move A condition in the futures markets in which the price at which a transaction would be made is at or beyond the price limits.

Limit up A limit move in the futures market in which the price at which a transaction would be made is at or above the upper limit.

Liquidity The ability to trade a futures contract, either selling a previously purchased contract or purchasing a previously sold contract.

Liquidity risk The risk that a financial instrument cannot be purchased or sold without a significant concession in price due to the size of the market.

Locked limit A condition in the futures markets in which a transaction cannot take place because the price would be beyond the limits.

London Interbank Offer Rate (LIBOR) The Eurodollar rate at which London banks lend dollars to other London banks; considered to be the best representative rate on a dollar borrowed by a private, high-quality borrower.

Long The buyer of a derivative contract. Also refers to the position of owning a derivative.

Long-term equity anticipatory securities (LEAPS) Options originally created with expirations of several years.

Lower bound The lowest possible value of an option.

Macaulay duration The duration before dividing by $1 + y_B$. The term, named for one of the economists who first derived it, is used to distinguish the calculation from modified duration. See also *modified duration*.

Maintenance margin requirement The margin requirement on any day other than the first day of a transaction.

Margin The amount of money that a trader deposits in a margin account. The term is derived from the stock market practice in which an investor borrows a portion of the money required to purchase a certain amount of stock. In futures markets, there is no borrowing so the margin is more of a down payment or performance bond.

Market risk The risk associated with interest rates, exchange rates, and equity prices.

Marking to market A procedure used primarily in futures markets in which the parties to a contract settle the amount owed daily. Also known as the *daily settlement*.

Model risk The use of an inaccurate pricing model for a particular investment, or the improper use of the right model.

Modified duration An adjustment of the duration for the level of the yield. Contrast with *Macaulay duration*.

Moneyness The relationship between the price of the underlying and an option's exercise price.

Monte Carlo simulation method An approach to estimating VAR that produces random outcomes to examine what might happen if a particular risk is faced. This method is widely used in the sciences as well as in business to study a variety of problems.

Netting When parties agree to exchange only the net amount owed from one party to the other.

Nondeliverable forwards (NDFs) Cash-settled forward contracts, used predominately with respect to foreign exchange forwards.

Normal backwardation The condition in futures markets in which futures prices are lower than expected spot prices.

Normal contango The condition in futures markets in which futures prices are higher than expected spot prices.

Off-market FRA A contract in which the initial value is intentionally set at a value other than zero and therefore requires a cash payment at the start from one party to the other.

Offsetting A transaction in exchange-listed derivative markets in which a party re-enters the market to close out a position.

Operations risk or operational risk The risk of loss from failures in a company's systems and procedures (for example, due to computer failures or human failures) or events completely outside of the control of organizations (which would include "acts of God" and terrorist actions).

Option A financial instrument that gives one party the right, but not the obligation, to buy or sell an underlying asset from or to another party at a fixed price over a specific period of time. Also referred to as contingent claims.

Option price, option premium, or premium The amount of money a buyer pays and seller receives to engage in an option transaction.

Out-of-the-money Options that, if exercised, would require the payment of more money than the value received and therefore would not be currently exercised.

Overnight index swap (OIS) A swap in which the floating rate is the cumulative value of a single unit of currency invested at an overnight rate during the settlement period.

Payer swaption A swaption that allows the holder to enter into a swap as the fixed-rate payer and floating-rate receiver.

Payment netting A means of settling payments in which the amount owed by the first party to the second is netted with the amount owed by the second party to the first; only the net difference is paid.

Payoff The value of an option at expiration.

Performance guarantee A guarantee from the clearinghouse that if one party makes money on a transaction, the clearinghouse ensures it will be paid.

Plain vanilla swap An interest rate swap in which one party pays a fixed rate and the other pays a floating rate, with both sets of payments in the same currency.

Position trader A trader who typically holds positions open overnight.

Potential credit risk The risk associated with the possibility that a payment due at a later date will not be made.

Pre-investing The strategy of using futures contracts to enter the market without an immediate outlay of cash.

Present (price) value of a basis point (PVBP) The change in the bond price for a 1 basis point change in yield. Also called *basis point value* (BPV).

Price discovery A feature of futures markets in which futures prices provide valuable information about the price of the underlying asset.

Price limits Limits imposed by a futures exchange on the price change that can occur from one day to the next.

Protective put An option strategy in which a long position in an asset is combined with a long position in a put.

Put An option that gives the holder the right to sell an underlying asset to another party at a fixed price over a specific period of time.

Put–call parity An equation expressing the equivalence (parity) of a portfolio of a call and a bond with a portfolio of a put and the underlying, which leads to the relationship between put and call prices.

Put–call–forward parity The relationship among puts, calls, and forward contracts.

Ratio spread An option strategy in which a long position in a certain number of options is offset by a short position in a certain number of other options on the same underlying, resulting in a risk-free position.

Receiver swaption A swaption that allows the holder to enter into a swap as the fixed-rate receiver and floating-rate payer.

Regulatory risk The risk associated with the uncertainty of how derivative transactions will be regulated or with changes in regulations.

Replacement value The market value of a swap.

Rho The sensitivity of the option price to the risk-free rate.

Risk budgeting The establishment of objectives for individuals, groups, or divisions of an organization that takes into account the allocation of an acceptable level of risk.

Risk governance The setting of overall policies and standards in risk management.

Risk management The process of identifying the level of risk an entity wants, measuring the level of risk the entity currently has, taking actions that bring the actual level of risk to the desired level of risk, and monitoring the new actual level of risk so that it continues to be aligned with the desired level of risk.

Risk-neutral probabilities Weights that are used to compute a binomial option price. They are the probabilities that would apply if a risk-neutral investor valued an option.

Risk-neutral valuation The process by which options and other derivatives are priced by treating investors as though they were risk neutral.

Sandwich spread An option strategy that is equivalent to a short butterfly spread.

Scalper A trader who offers to buy or sell futures contracts, holding the position for only a brief period of time. Scalpers attempt to profit by buying at the bid price and selling at the higher ask price.

Scenario analysis A risk management technique involving the examination of the performance of a portfolio under specified situations. Closely related to *stress testing*.

Seats Memberships in a derivatives exchange.

Settlement date or payment date The date on which the parties to a swap make payments.

Settlement period The time between settlement dates.

Settlement price The official price, designated by the clearinghouse, from which daily gains and losses will be determined and marked to market.

Settlement risk When settling a contract, the risk that one party could be in the process of paying the counterparty while the counterparty is declaring bankruptcy.

Short The seller of a derivative contract. Also refers to the position of being short a derivative.

Single-payment loan A loan in which the borrower receives a sum of money at the start and pays back the entire amount with interest in a single payment at maturity.

Spread An option strategy involving the purchase of one option and sale of another option that is identical to the first in all respects except either exercise price or expiration.

Storage costs or carrying costs The costs of holding an asset, generally a function of the physical characteristics of the underlying asset.

Straddle An option strategy involving the purchase of a put and a call with the same exercise price. A straddle is based on the expectation of high volatility of the underlying.

Strangle A variation of a straddle in which the put and call have different exercise prices.

Strap An option strategy involving the purchase of two calls and one put.

Stress testing A risk management technique in which the risk manager examines the performance of the portfolio under market conditions involving high risk and usually high correlations across markets. Closely related to *scenario analysis*.

Strip An option strategy involving the purchase of two puts and one call.

Structured note A variation of a floating-rate note that has some type of unusual characteristic such as a leverage factor or in which the rate moves opposite to interest rates.

Swap An agreement between two parties to exchange a series of future cash flows.

Swap spread The difference between the fixed rate on an interest rate swap and the rate on a Treasury note with equivalent maturity; it reflects the general level of credit risk in the market.

Swaption An option to enter into a swap.

Synthetic call The combination of puts, the underlying, and risk-free bonds that replicates a call option.

Synthetic forward contract The combination of the underlying, puts, calls, and risk-free bonds that replicates a forward contract.

Synthetic index fund An index fund position created by combining risk-free bonds and futures on the desired index.

Synthetic put The combination of calls, the underlying, and risk-free bonds that replicates a put option.

Tax risk The uncertainty associated with tax laws.

Tenor The original time to maturity on a swap.

Termination date The date of the final payment on a swap; also, the swap's expiration date.

Theta The rate at which an option's time value decays.

Time to expiration The time remaining in the life of a derivative, typically expressed in years.

Time value decay The loss in the value of an option resulting from movement of the option price toward its payoff value as the expiration day approaches.

Time value or speculative value The difference between the market price of the option and its intrinsic value, determined by the uncertainty of the underlying over the remaining life of the option.

Total return swap A swap in which one party agrees to pay the total return on a security. Often used as a credit derivative, in which the underlying is a bond.

Tracking error The condition in which the performance of a portfolio does not match the performance of an index that serves as the portfolio's benchmark.

Transaction exposure The risk associated with a foreign exchange rate on a specific business transaction such as a purchase or sale.

Translation exposure The risk associated with the conversion of foreign financial statements into domestic currency.

Underlying An asset that trades in a market in which buyers and sellers meet, decide on a price, and the seller then delivers the asset to the buyer and receives payment. The underlying is the asset or other derivative on which a particular derivative is based. The market for the underlying is also referred to as the spot market.

Valuation The process of determining the value of an asset or service.

Value The amount for which one can sell something, or the amount one must pay to acquire something.

Value at risk (VAR) A probability-based measure of loss potential for a company, a fund, a portfolio, a transaction, or a strategy over a specified period of time.

Variation margin Additional margin that must be deposited in an amount sufficient to bring the balance up to the initial margin requirement.

Vega The relationship between option price and volatility.

Yield beta A measure of the sensitivity of a bond's yield to a general measure of bond yields in the market that is used to refine the hedge ratio.

Yield spread The difference between the yield on a bond and the yield on a default-free security, usually a government note, of the same maturity. The yield spread is primarily determined by the market's perception of the credit risk on the bond.

Zero-cost collar A transaction in which a position in the underlying is protected by buying a put and selling a call with the premium from the sale of the call offsetting the premium from the purchase of the put. It can also be used to protect a floating-rate borrower against interest rate increases with the premium on a long cap offsetting the premium on a short floor.

INDEX

ANALYSIS OF DERIVATIVES FOR THE CFA® PROGRAM: EQUATIONS

CHAPTER 2: Forward Markets and Contracts

2-1. Value of Forward Contract at Expiration

$$V_T(0,T) = S_T - F(0,T)$$

2-2. Forward Price

$$F(0,T) = S_0(1 + r)^T$$

2-3. Value of Forward Contract During Its Life

$$V_t(0,T) = S_t - F(0,T)/(1 + r)^{(T-t)}$$

2-4. Forward Price for Stock Paying Dividends Based on Present Value of Dividends

$$F(0,T) = [S_0 - PV(D,0,T)](1 + r)^T$$

2-5. Forward Price for Stock Paying Dividends Based on Future Value of Dividends

$$F(0,T) = S_0(1 + r)^T - FV(D,0,T)$$

2-6. Forward Price for Stock Paying Continuous Dividends

$$F(0, T) = (S_0 e^{-\delta^c T}) e^{r^c T}$$

2-7. Value of Forward Contract for Stock Paying Discrete Dividends

$$V_t(0,T) = S_t - PV(D,t,T) - F(0,T)/(1 + r)^{(T-t)}$$

2-8. Value of Forward Contract for Stock Paying Continuous Dividends

$$V_t(0,T) = S_t e^{-\delta^c(T-t)} - F(0,T)e^{-r^c(T-t)}$$

2-9. Forward Price for Bond Paying Interest Based on Present Value of Coupons

$$F(0,T) = [B_0^c(T + Y) - PV(CI,0,T)](1 + r)^T$$

2-10. Forward Price for Bond Paying Interest Based on Future Value of Coupons

$$F(0,T) = [B_0^c(T + Y)](1 + r)^T - FV(CI,0,T)$$

2-11. Value of Forward Contract for Bond Paying Interest

$$V_t(0,T) = B_t^c(T + Y) - PV(CI,t,T) - F(0,T)/(1 + r)^{(T-t)}$$

2-12. Payoff of FRA

$$\frac{[L_h(m) - FRA(0,h,m)]\left(\dfrac{m}{360}\right)}{1 + L_h(m)\left(\dfrac{m}{360}\right)}$$

2-13. FRA Rate

$$FRA(0,h,m) = \left[\frac{1 + L_0(h+m)\left(\dfrac{h+m}{360}\right)}{1 + L_0(h)\left(\dfrac{h}{360}\right)} - 1 \right]\left(\frac{360}{m}\right)$$

2-14. Value of FRA During Its Life

$$V_g(0,h,m) = \frac{1}{1 + L_g(h-g)\left(\dfrac{h-g}{360}\right)} - \frac{1 + FRA(0,h,m)\left(\dfrac{m}{360}\right)}{1 + L_g(h+m-g)\left(\dfrac{h+m-g}{360}\right)}$$

2-15. Forward Price for Currency Based on Discrete Interest

$$F(0,T) = \left[\frac{S_0}{(1+r^f)^T}\right](1+r)^T$$

2-16. Forward Price for Currency Based on Continuous Interest

$$F(0,T) = (S_0 e^{-r^{fc}T})e^{r^c T}$$

2-17. Value of Forward Contract on Currency Based on Discrete Interest

$$V_t(0,T) = \frac{S_t}{(1+r^f)^{(T-t)}} - \frac{F(0,T)}{(1+r)^{(T-t)}}$$

2-18. Value of Forward Contract on Currency Based on Continuous Interest

$$V_t(0,T) = (S_t e^{-r^{fc}(T-t)}) - F(0,T)e^{-r^c(T-t)}$$

CHAPTER 3:   Futures Markets and Contracts

3-1. Futures Price at Expiration

$$f_T(T) = S_T$$

3-2. Value of Futures Contract at Initiation Date

$$v_0(T) = 0$$

3-3. Value of Futures Contract During Its Life

$$v_{t+}(T) = f_t(T) - f_{t-1}(T) \text{ \textit{an instant before the account is marked to market}}$$
$$v_{t-}(T) = 0 \text{ \textit{as soon as the account is marked to market}}$$

3-4. Futures Price When Underlying Has No Costs, Benefits, or Cash Flows

$$f_0(T) = S_0(1+r)^T$$

3-5. Futures Price When Underlying Has Storage Costs

$$f_0(T) = S_0(1+r)^T + FV(SC,0,T)$$

3-6. Futures Price When Underlying Generates Positive Cash Flows

$$f_0(T) = S_0(1+r)^T - FV(CF,0,T)$$

3-7. Futures Price When Underlying Generates Costs Minus Benefits

$$f_0(T) = S_0(1+r)^T + FV(CB,0,T)$$

3-8. Treasury Bill Futures Price

$$f_0(h) = B_0(h+m)[1+r_0(h)]^{h/365}$$

3-9. Implied Repo Rate for Treasury Bill Futures

$$r_0(h)* = \left[\frac{f_0(h)*}{B_0(h + m)}\right]^{365/h} - 1$$

3-10. Discount Rate Implied by Treasury Bill Futures Price

$$r_0^{df}(h) = [1 - f_0(h)]\left(\frac{360}{m}\right)$$

3-11. Treasury Note and Bond Futures Price

$$f_0(T) = B_0^c(T + Y)[1 + r_0(T)]^T - FV(CI,0,T)$$

3-12. Treasury Note and Bond Futures Price Based on Conversion Factor

$$f_0(T) = \frac{B_0^c(T + Y)[1 + r_0(T)]^T - FV(CI,0,T)}{CF(T)}$$

3-13. Stock Index Futures Price Based on Compound Value of Dividends

$$f_0(T) = S_0(1 + r)^T - FV(D,0,T)$$

3-14. Stock Index Futures Price Based on Present Value of Dividends

$$f_0(T) = [S_0 - PV(D,0,T)](1 + r)^T$$

3-15. Stock Index Futures Price Based on Discrete Dividend Yield: Variation 1

$$f_0(T) = \left(\frac{S_0}{(1 + \delta)^T}\right)(1 + r)^T$$

3-16. Stock Index Futures Price Based on Discrete Dividend Yield: Variation 2

$$f_0(T) = S_0(1 - \delta*)(1 + r)^T$$

3-17. Stock Index Futures Price Based on Continuous Dividends

$$f_0(T) = (S_0e^{-\delta^c T})e^{r^c T}$$

3-18. Currency Futures Price Based on Discrete Interest

$$f_0(T) = \left(\frac{S_0}{(1 + r^f)^T}\right)(1 + r)^T$$

3-19. Currency Futures Price Based on Continuous Interest

$$f_0(T) = (S_0e^{-r^{fc}T})e^{r^c T}$$

CHAPTER 4: Option Markets and Contracts

4-1. Payoff of Interest Rate Call

$$\text{(Notional Principal)Max(0,Underlying rate at expiration} - \text{Exercise rate)}\left(\frac{\text{Days in underlying rate}}{360}\right)$$

4-2. Payoff of Interest Rate Put

$$\text{(Notional Principal)Max(0,Exercise rate} - \text{Underlying rate at expiration)}\left(\frac{\text{Days in underlying rate}}{360}\right)$$

4-3. Value at Expiration (Payoff) of European and American Calls

$$c_T = Max(0,S_T - X)$$
$$C_T = Max(0,S_T - X)$$

4-4. Value at Expiration (Payoff) of European and American Puts

$p_T = Max(0, X - S_T)$

$P_T = Max(0, X - S_T)$

4-5. Minimum Values of European and American Calls and Puts

$c_0 \geq 0, C_0 \geq 0$

$p_0 \geq 0, P_0 \geq 0$

4-6. Maximum Values of European and American Calls

$c_0 \leq S_0, C_0 \leq S_0$

4-7. Maximum Values of European and American Puts

$p_0 \leq X/(1 + r)^T, P_0 \leq X$

4-8. Lower Bounds (Intrinsic Values) of American Calls and Puts

$C_0 \geq Max(0, S_0 - X)$

$P_0 \geq Max(0, X - S_0)$

4-9. Lower Bounds of European and American Calls

$c_0 \geq Max[0, S_0 - X/(1 + r)^T]$

$C_0 \geq Max[0, S_0 - X/(1 + r)^T]$

4-10. Lower Bounds of European and American Puts

$p_0 \geq Max[0, X/(1 + r)^T - S_0]$

$P_0 \geq Max(0, X - S_0)$

4-11. Relationship Between Prices of Calls of Different Expirations

$c_0(T_2) \geq c_0(T_1)$

$C_0(T_2) \geq C_0(T_1)$

4-12. Relationship Between Prices of Puts of Different Expirations

$p_0(T_2)$ can be either greater or less than $p_0(T_1)$

$P_0(T_2) \geq P_0(T_1)$

4-13. Put–Call Parity for European Options

$c_0 + X/(1 + r)^T = p_0 + S_0$

4-14. Relationship Between American and European Call and Put Prices

$C_0 \geq c_0$

$P_0 \geq p_0$

4-15. Hedge Ratio for Binomial Model

$$n = \frac{c^+ - c^-}{S^+ - S^-}$$

4-16. European Call Prices in One-Period Binomial Model

$$c = \frac{\pi c^+ + (1 - \pi)c^-}{1 + r}$$

4-17. Risk-Neutral (Binomial) Probability

$$\pi = \frac{1 + r - d}{u - d}$$

4-18. European Call Prices at Time 1 in Two-Period Binomial Model

$$c^+ = \frac{\pi c^{++} + (1 - \pi)c^{+-}}{1 + r}$$

4-19. European Call Prices at Time 2 in Two-Period Binomial Model

$$c^- = \frac{\pi c^{-+} + (1 - \pi)c^{--}}{1 + r}$$

4-20. Hedge Ratios for Two-Period Binomial Model

$$n = \frac{c^+ - c^-}{S^+ - S^-}$$

$$n^+ = \frac{c^{++} - c^{+-}}{S^{++} - S^{+-}}$$

$$n^- = \frac{c^{-+} - c^{--}}{S^{-+} - S^{--}}$$

4-21. Black–Scholes–Merton Model for Calls and Puts

$$c = S_0 N(d_1) - X e^{-r^c T} N(d_2)$$
$$p = X e^{-r^c T}[1 - N(d_2)] - S_0[1 - N(d_1)]$$

4-22. d_1 and d_2 in Black–Scholes–Merton Model

$$d_1 = \frac{\ln(S_0/X) + [r^c + (\sigma^2/2)]T}{\sigma\sqrt{T}}$$
$$d_2 = d_1 - \sigma\sqrt{T}$$

4-23. Option Delta

$$\text{Delta} = \frac{\text{Change in option price}}{\text{Change in underlying price}}$$

4-24. Payoffs of Options on Futures

$$c_T = \text{Max}[0, f_T(T) - X]$$
$$p_T = \text{Max}[0, X - f_T(T)]$$

4-25. Minimum and Maximum Prices of European and American Options on Futures

$$0 \le c_0 \le f_0(T)$$
$$0 \le C_0 \le f_0(T)$$
$$0 \le p_0 \le X/(1 + r)^T$$
$$0 \le P_0 \le X$$

4-26. Lower Bounds of European Options on Futures

$$c_0 \ge \text{Max}\{0, [f_0(T) - X]/(1 + r)^T\}$$
$$p_0 \ge \text{Max}\{0, [X - f_0(T)]/(1 + r)^T\}$$

4-27. Lower Bounds (Intrinsic Values) of American Options on Futures

$$C_0 \ge \text{Max}[0, f_0(T) - X]$$
$$P_0 \ge \text{Max}[0, X - f_0(T)]$$

4-28. Put–Call Parity for Options on Forward Contracts

$$c_0 + [X - F(0,T)]/(1 + r)^T = p_0$$

CHAPTER 5:   Swap Markets and Contracts

5-1. Fixed Rate on Interest Rate Swap

$$FS(0, n, m) = \frac{1.0 - B_0(h_n)}{\sum\limits_{j=1}^{n} B_0(h_j)}$$

5-2. Market Value of Equity Swap During Its Life

$$\left(\frac{S_t}{S_0}\right) - B_t(h_n) - FS(0,n,m) \sum\limits_{j=1}^{n} B_t(h_j)$$

5-3. Payoff of Payer Swaption

$$Max[0, FS(0, n, m) - x] \sum\limits_{j=1}^{n} B_0(h_j)$$

5-4. Payoff of Receiver Swaption

$$Max[0, x - FS(0, n, m)] \sum\limits_{j=1}^{n} B_0(h_j)$$

CHAPTER 6:   Risk Management Applications of Forward and Futures Strategies

6-1. Sensitivity of Futures Price to Yield Change

$$\Delta f \approx -MDUR_f f \, \Delta y_f$$

6-2. Sensitivity of Bond Yield to Implied Yield on Bond Futures

$$\Delta y_B = \beta_y \Delta y_f$$

6-3. Hedge Ratio for Bond Futures

$$N_f = -(MDUR_B/MDUR_f)(B/f)\beta_y$$

6-4. Number of Bond Futures to Adjust Duration

$$N_f = \left(\frac{MDUR_T - MDUR_B}{MDUR_f}\right)\left(\frac{B}{f}\right)\beta_y$$

6-5. Number of Stock Index Futures to Adjust Beta

$$N_f = \left(\frac{\beta_T - \beta_S}{\beta_f}\right)\left(\frac{S}{f}\right)$$

6-6. Number of Stock Index Futures to Create Synthetic Index Fund

$$N_f{}^* = \frac{V(1 + r)^T}{qf} \qquad \text{(rounded to an integer)}$$

6-7. Effective Amount Invested in Synthetic Index Fund Using Futures

$$V^* = \frac{N_f{}^* qf}{(1 + r)^T}$$

6-8. Effective Amount of Stock Converted to Cash Using Futures

$$V^* = \frac{-N_f{}^* qf}{(1 + r)^T}$$